Autism

Autism

TEACHING MAKES A DIFFERENCE

Second Edition

Brenda Scheuermann
Texas State University

Jo Webber
Texas State University

Russell Lang
Texas State University

CENGAGE

Australia • Brazil • Mexico • Singapore • United Kingdom • United States

Autism: Teaching Makes a Difference,
Second Edition

Brenda Scheuermann
Jo Webber
Russell Lang

Product Director: Marta Lee-Perriard

Product Manager: Steve Scoble

Content Developer: Julia White

Product Assistant: Megan Nauer

Marketing Manager: Andrew Miller

Digital Content Specialist: Justin Hein

Content Project Manager: Samen Iqbal

Production Service Project Manager:
Kayci Wyatt, MPS Limited

Intellectual Property Analyst: Jennifer Bowes

Intellectual Property Project Manager: Carly
Belcher

Photo Researcher: Anjali Kambil, Lumina
Datamatics

Text Researcher: Aruna Sekar, Lumina Datamatics

Copy Editor: Steven Summerlight

Art Director: Helen Bruno

Cover and Text Designer: Lisa Buckley

Cover Image: Maria Berrios/Creativity Explored

Compositor: MPS Limited

For product information and technology assistance, contact us at
Cengage Customer & Sales Support, 1-800-354-9706.

For permission to use material from this text or product,
submit all requests online at **www.cengage.com/permissions.**
Further permissions questions can be e-mailed to
permissionrequest@cengage.com.

Library of Congress Control Number: 2017937043

Student Edition:
ISBN: 978-1-337-56490-8

Loose-leaf Edition:
ISBN: 978-1-337-56496-0

Cengage
20 Channel Center Street
Boston, MA 02210
USA

Cengage is a leading provider of customized learning solutions with employees residing in nearly 40 different countries and sales in more than 125 countries around the world. Find your local representative at **www.cengage.com**.

Cengage products are represented in Canada by Nelson Education, Ltd.

To learn more about Cengage platforms and services, visit **www.cengage.com**. To register or access your online learning solution or purchase materials for your course, visit **www.cengagebrain.com**.

Brief Contents

Contents

CHAPTER 6   Teaching Communication Skills   167

CHAPTER 7   Remediating Deficits in Socialization   200

Preface

This is a book for anyone who is now or will be working with children and youth with low-functioning autism and related disorders, a difficult job under the best of circumstances. Low-functioning autism, a component of autism spectrum disorder (ASD), is characterized by relatively severe deficits in social interaction and social communication skills, and displays of restricted, repetitive behaviors, interests and activities, and, often, challenging behavior. The condition generates intense emotions in educators, parents, family members, and caregivers. Perhaps more than any other disability area, the field of ASD is characterized by a continual search for "what works." What methods will produce a shift from social isolation to social interest and engagement? What are the most effective strategies for increasing meaningful communication? And perhaps the most common concern: What can we do about the challenging behaviors?

Our experiences with teachers of students with low-functioning autism lead us to conclude that too often educators are charged with developing and implementing educational programs for these students without having the background, training, or resources necessary to guide their efforts effectively. This book is part of our effort to provide critical information that empowers educators to identify and implement evidence-based practices for educating children and youth with low-functioning autism and related disorders. Throughout the book, we describe state-of-the-art, scientifically supported practices in a clear, user-friendly format. We explain theoretical underpinnings of recommended practices and provide instructions and examples for implementation of the techniques presented.

The field of autism is inundated with an incredible range of treatments, philosophical approaches, and intervention recommendations. It seems we are constantly learning about "new, highly effective" programs that provide "the answer" for the challenges associated with ASD. Television, magazines, social media, websites, books, and even word-of-mouth are all sources for spreading the word about new programs. Unfortunately, many of these programs lack any scientific evidence of effectiveness, only to be adopted on the basis of testimonials, convincing advertising slogans, or their fleeting popularity. We believe that pursuing interventions without first demanding rigorous evidence of effectiveness is a waste of valuable time at best; at its worst, it may thwart any chance of positive outcomes for these students who need only the best teaching and most focused curriculum.

The good news is that although questionable and unproven approaches continue to proliferate, a well-established and rapidly growing body of evidence-based practices (EBPs) offers clear guidance to educators who must plan, implement, monitor, and evaluate educational programs for students with autism. These techniques are part of a field known as *applied behavior analysis* (ABA), a robust set of principles and procedures for generating behavioral change. ABA techniques are strongly grounded in extensive scientific support that has demonstrated efficacy under a variety of conditions with positive and encouraging outcomes. In short, ABA techniques offer a broad collection of scientifically driven techniques for achieving desired outcomes in behavior, socialization, communication, daily living, and other areas of concern.

Although there is no cure for low-functioning autism, problematic symptoms can be alleviated, necessary skills can be taught, and quality of life can be assured. The "answer," we believe, lies in the approaches described in this book—that is, the careful, systematic application of ABA techniques. Correct use of these techniques will improve the prognosis for most of these students. ASD is a lifelong disorder, meaning that aspects of the condition will probably always be present. However, well-planned and accurately implemented applied behavior analytical interventions will increase the potential for independent adult functioning in integrated settings.

Throughout this book, we describe the evidence supporting the techniques presented, plus we have attempted to show why these techniques are effective with individuals with autism. In addition, we have tried to explain how to use the techniques in clear, step-by-step fashion, with many examples illustrating application under a variety of conditions. Because these techniques are seldom applied in isolation, we have made an effort to show how ABA techniques are used to address needs across areas of functioning and the interconnectedness among components of educational programming. For example, we discuss socialization interventions with reference to communication and managing challenging behavior, and we discuss challenging behavior by explaining how to assess communicative functions of that behavior.

Text Features

This book includes several unique features.

- Each chapter begins with a **chapter outline**, **learning objectives**, and **"Did You Know"** feature to pique readers' interest.
- Throughout each chapter, new **vocabulary terms** are highlighted; those terms are defined in the **end-of-book glossary**.
- **Colorful headings** organize content in each chapter.
- **Tables and figures** illustrate and expand upon chapter content. Many of these practical resources are also available as **Professional Resource Downloads** in this book's companion MindTap. The student can download these tools and keep them forever, enabling preservice teachers to build their library of professional resources. Look for the Professional Resource Download label that identifies these items.
- Several of the chapters have **boxed features** that provide more detailed discussion of a particular topic or **vignettes** to illustrate application of techniques.
- At the end of each chapter, **key points** summarize the chapter.

Overall, the text is designed to present evidence-based content in an easy-to-read format that provides an interesting and engaging reading experience.

Text Organization

Chapter 1 presents an overview of autism, including a history of the condition, etiology, characteristics, and definition and diagnosis of autism. Chapter 2 describes the basic principles of applied behavior analysis. ABA concepts and techniques are organized around the three-term contingency: antecedents–behavior–consequences. Strategies for assessing challenging behavior are described in Chapter 3 and are followed by brief discussions of challenging behaviors often exhibited by children with low-functioning autism. Next we discuss how to develop interventions that reflect probable functions of challenging behaviors and specific techniques for reducing challenging behaviors. Chapter 4 describes a step-by-step process for developing curriculum (e.g., determining what to teach) for these students. Chapter 5 presents a wide array of ABA instructional strategies, including direct instruction, discrete trial teaching, milieu teaching, prompting, task analysis, and chaining. We explain how to apply ABA instructional techniques in both one-on-one and group teaching situations We also present strategies for providing structure through classroom organization, materials, schedules and routines. Finally, in this chapter we cover techniques for progress monitoring and analyzing progress data. Chapter 6 presents in-depth discussion of language and communication, including definitions of language components, language development, and language/communication problems characteristically present in children with low-functioning autism. We also explain informal strategies for language/communication assessment, and ABA techniques for language training. While this chapter presents ideas from multiple disciplines, we mostly adhere to a behavioral (ABA) approach to language assessment and intervention. The majority of the chapter reflects concepts described in Skinner's classic, *Verbal Behavior* (1957), which emphasizes communicative function over form. In Chapter 7, we discuss techniques for assessing and teaching social skills for students with low-functioning autism. In this chapter, we also address inclusion issues for these students, particularly with respect to socialization. Chapter 8 presents techniques for assessing and remediating deficits in life skills, including play and leisure skills, self-help skills, and vocational skills. In Chapter 9, we provide readers with an overview of the development of EBPs in the field of autism and guide readers to reputable sources for learning more about EBPs.

Chapter-by-Chapter Revisions

Autism research has expanded appreciably since the first edition of this book. This edition has been extensively revised to include the most current and relevant content and research throughout, including more than 440 new citations. This edition has also been enriched by the presence of artwork by several young artists. Chapter-specific revisions are listed in the rest of this section.

Chapter 1

New

- 66 new citations
- Chapter introduction
- Box: The Biology of Autism
- Table: DSM-5 Criteria for Autism Spectrum Disorder (ASD)

Revised

- Extensive revision of chapter content and research throughout
- Sections
  - Nature of Autism
  - Characteristics
  - Behavioral Deficits
  - Diagnoses and Definitions
  - Family Issues
- Tables
  - Parent and Professional Organizations Serving Individuals with Autism
  - Sample Diagnostic Instruments

Chapter 2

New

- 28 new citations
- Chapter introduction
- Sections
  - Applied Behavior Analysis
  - Tenets of Applied Behavior Analysis
  - The Three-Term Contingency
  - Implementing ABA Techniques
  - Concepts and Techniques Related to Antecedents
- Tables
  - Examples and Nonexamples of Operationally Defined Behaviors
  - How to Establish Stimulus Control
  - Steps in Measuring Behavior
- Box: Tenets of Applied Behavior Analysis

Revised

- Extensive revision of chapter content and research throughout
- Sections
  - Focus on Antecedents
  - Focus on Behavior
  - Concepts and Techniques Related to Behavior
  - Concepts and Techniques Related to Consequences
- Tables
  - Measurement Systems for Specific Target Behaviors
  - How to Graph and Interpret Data
  - How to Select Reinforcers

Chapter 3

New

- 43 new citations
- Chapter introduction
- Sections
  - Assessing Challenging Behavior
  - Challenging Behavior Interventions
  - Self-Injurious Behavior
  - Aggression
  - Stereotypy
  - Function-Matched Interventions
  - Differential Reinforcement
  - Punishment Procedures
  - Case Study Examples in Reducing Challenging Behavior

Revised

- Extensive revision of chapter content and research throughout
- Sections
  - Conducting a Functional Behavioral Assessment
  - Noncompliance

Chapter 4

New

- 40 new citations
- Chapter introduction
- Sections
  - A Curriculum Should Be Developed by a Team
  - A Curriculum Should Relate to Postschool and Adult Goals
- Figure: Potential Risks and Benefits of Curriculum Choices
- Table: Postschool Options for Students with Autism
- Box: Transition from School to Postschool Activities

Revised

- Extensive revision of chapter content and research throughout
- Sections
  - Curricular Areas
  - Curricular Considerations
  - Develop a Curricular Inventory for Reaching the Goals
  - Prioritize Activities and Skills
  - Develop the Individualized Education Program

- Figures
  - Sample Task Analysis Checklist
  - Curriculum Arranged by Domain, Goals, and Objectives
- Table: Sample Published Curricula for Use with Students with Autism

Chapter 5

New

- 88 new citations
- Chapter introduction
- Sections
  - Direct Instruction: di and DI
  - Discrete Trial Training (DTT)
  - Milieu Teaching (MT)
  - Grouping
  - Embedded ABA Teaching Strategies
- New tables
  - Direct instruction (di) Steps
  - A Sample of Direct Instruction (DI) Academic Curriculum from McGraw-Hill Direct Instruction Series
  - Comparison of ABA Instructional Formats

Revised

- Extensive revision of chapter content and research throughout
- Sections
  - Structuring Through Lesson Presentation
  - Structuring with Physical Organization
  - Plans and Reports
- Figures
  - Sample Classroom Schedule Organized by (a) Teaching Adults and (b) Child
  - Teacher Self-Monitoring Checklist
- Table
  - Discrete Trial Training (DTT) Components
  - Prompt Fading Procedures
  - Sample Skills Taught through Chaining Techniques
  - Suggestions for Providing Structure in Learning Situations

Chapter 6

New

- 42 new citations
- Chapter introduction
- Sections
  - Defining Language and Communication
  - Communication and Language Components

Revised

- Extensive revision of chapter content and research throughout
- Sections
  - Language-Development Sequence
  - Language Difficulties in Autism
  - Receptive Language Problems
  - Expressive Language Problems
  - Language and Communication Assessment Instruments

- ○ Informal Language Assessment
- ○ Strategies for Teaching Language and Communication
- Table: Milieu Teaching Procedures for Language Development

Chapter 7

New

- 40 new citations
- Chapter introduction
- Sections
  - ○ Socialization Characteristics and Implications
  - ○ Interventions for Increasing Social Skills and Social Competence
- Tables
  - ○ Steps in Determining the Demands of Target Environments
  - ○ Potential Problems with Inclusion

Revised

- Extensive revision of chapter content and research throughout
- Sections
  - ○ Implications of Socialization Deficits
  - ○ Social Competence Versus Social Skills
  - ○ Assessment of Contexts and Determining Socially Valid Skills
  - ○ Assessment of Student Skill Levels
  - ○ General Considerations for Socialization Interventions
  - ○ Intervention Approaches
- Table: Rating Scales for Assessing Social Skills
- Vignettes
  - ○ Ms. Jacobs Teaches Social Skills
  - ○ Ms. Jacobs Uses Antecedent Prompting

Chapter 8

New

- 70 new citations
- Sections
  - ○ Play, Leisure, and Recreation Skills
  - ○ Vocational Skills

Revised

- Extensive revision of chapter content and research throughout
- Chapter introduction
- Sections
  - ○ Ecological Assessment
  - ○ Inventories, Interviews, and Checklists
  - ○ General Considerations for Teaching Self-Help Skills
  - ○ Toileting Skills
  - ○ Eating Skills
  - ○ Dressing Skills
  - ○ Personal Grooming and Hygiene Skills
  - ○ General Considerations for Teaching Play, Leisure, and Recreation Skills
  - ○ General Considerations for Teaching Vocational Skills
- Tables
  - ○ Commercial Instruments for Career and Vocational Assessment
  - ○ Ideas for Independent Play and Leisure Materials
  - ○ Toileting and Toileting-Related Skills

Chapter 9

New

- 26 new citations
- Chapter introduction
- Sections
  - Definition of Evidence-Based Practices
  - How to Determine EBPs
  - Effective Practices as Identified by the NAC and NPDC
  - Developing and Evaluating Effective Educational Programs
- Table: Reliable Sources for Identifying EBPs

Revised

- Extensive revision of chapter content and research throughout
- Sections
  - Intervention Outcomes
  - Evidence
  - Program Evaluation
  - Lack of a Clearly Articulated Program
  - Choosing Popular Rather Than Appropriate Options
  - Teaching Dependency
  - One-Size-Fits-All Mentality
- Table: Established Evidence-Based Practices Identified by NAC and NPDC

Accompanying Teaching and Learning Resources

This second edition of *Autism: Teaching Makes a Difference* is accompanied by an extensive package of instructor and student resources.

MindTap™: The Personal Learning Experience

MindTap for Scheuermann/Webber/Lang, *Autism: Teaching Makes a Difference*, 2nd edition, represents a new approach to teaching and learning. A highly personalized, fully customizable learning platform with an integrated eportfolio, MindTap helps students to elevate thinking by guiding them to:

- Know, remember, and understand concepts critical to becoming a great teacher;
- Apply concepts, create curriculum and tools, and demonstrate performance and competency in key areas in the course, including national and state education standards;
- Prepare artifacts for the portfolio and eventual state licensure, to launch a successful teaching career; and
- Develop the habits to become a reflective practitioner.

As students move through each chapter's Learning Path, they engage in a scaffolded learning experience, designed to move them up Bloom's Taxonomy, from lower- to higher-order thinking skills. The Learning Path enables preservice students to develop these skills and gain confidence by:

- Engaging them with chapter topics and activating their prior knowledge by watching and answering questions about authentic videos of teachers teaching and children learning in real classrooms;
- Checking their comprehension and understanding through Did You Get It? assessments, with varied question types that are autograded for instant feedback;

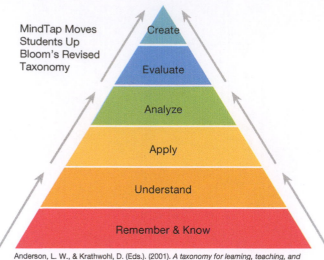

MindTap Moves
Students Up
Bloom's Revised
Taxonomy

Create
Evaluate
Analyze
Apply
Understand
Remember & Know

Anderson, L. W., & Krathwohl, D. (Eds.). (2001). *A taxonomy for learning, teaching, and assessing: A revision of Bloom's taxonomy of educational objectives.* New York: Longman.

- Applying concepts through mini-case scenarios—students analyze typical teaching and learning situations, and then create a reasoned response to the issue(s) presented in the scenario; and
- Reflecting about and justifying the choices they made within the teaching scenario problem.

MindTap helps instructors facilitate better outcomes by evaluating how future teachers plan and teach lessons in ways that make content clear and help diverse students learn, assessing the effectiveness of their teaching practice, and adjusting teaching as needed. MindTap enables instructors to facilitate better outcomes by making grades visible in real time through the Student Progress App so students and instructors always have access to current standings in the class.

MindTap for Scheuermann/Webber/Lang, *Autism: Teaching Makes a Difference*, 2nd edition, helps instructors easily set their course since it integrates into the existing Learning Management System and saves instructors time by allowing them to fully customize any aspect of the learning path. Instructors can change the order of the student learning activities, hide activities they don't want for the course, and—most importantly—create custom assessments and add any standards, outcomes, or content they do want (e.g., YouTube videos, Google docs). Learn more at **www.cengage .com/mindtap**.

Instructor's Manual

An online Instructor's Manual accompanies this book. It contains information to assist you in designing the course, including sample syllabi, discussion questions, teaching and learning activities, field experiences, learning objectives, recommended readings, and additional online resources.

Test Bank

For assessment support, the Test Bank includes true–false, multiple-choice, short-answer, and essay questions for each chapter.

PowerPoint Lecture Slides

These vibrant Microsoft PowerPoint lecture slides for each chapter assist you with your lecture by providing concept coverage using images, figures, and tables directly from the textbook.

Cognero

Cengage Learning Testing Powered by Cognero is a flexible online system that allows you to author, edit, and manage Test Bank content from multiple Cengage Learning solutions; create multiple test versions in an instant; and deliver tests from your LMS, your classroom, or wherever you want.

Conclusion

We hope this book helps teachers as well as other professionals and practitioners, caregivers, and parents more effectively support, educate, and enrich the lives of children and youth with low-functioning autism. Behavioral science has built on decades of theory to produce viable, practical, efficient techniques that educators and family members can apply to effectively expand the horizons for these unique individuals. This book provides clear explanations of those techniques and how they are applied in everyday settings in school and community. Without high-quality, long-term, behaviorally based educational programs, students with low-functioning autism will likely make little progress toward normalized and independent functioning. As the title of this book suggests, good teaching does indeed make a difference. Never forget: All children can learn.

Acknowledgments

As with most books, this book has been enhanced by the efforts of many people: our students at Texas State University, the clients and staff of our Clinic for Autism Research, Evaluation, and Support (CARES), and our always supportive colleagues in the field. We are grateful to our editor, Julia White, for her guidance, feedback, and patience. She was quick to answer questions or provide needed information, offered very helpful suggestions, and graciously tolerated our deadline-challenging approach to this revision. Samen Iqbal provided efficient communication throughout production, which made the process fairly easy and painless.

We would be extremely remiss if we did not thank our spouses, Billy, Tom, and Erin, and other family members, friends, and colleagues who were forced to the "back burner" as the book progressed. Any major writing project is a team effort, and our team understood our distraction and were untiring in their encouragement. Without their support, this project would not have been possible.

We would like to thank the reviewers of this text: Marissa Congdon, Ph.D., BCBA-D, California State University, San Bernardino; Elisa Cruz-Torres, Ph.D., BCBA-D, Florida Atlantic University; Eric G. Kurtz, Ph.D., University of South Dakota; Amanda L. Mazin, Ph.D., BCBA, St. Thomas Aquinas College; Jennifer McFarland-Whisman, Ph.D., BCBA, Marshall University; Dianna L. Meade, Ph.D., Bethel University; and Shannon Stuart, Ph.D., University of Wisconsin Whitewater.

Finally, we would like to thank the students with ASD with whom we worked and their families. This book is a direct result of their teaching and sharing. We hope our work reflects positively on them.

Dedication

The most basic guiding principle for us (our prime directive) is simple: we strive to educate, support, and empower every child in the manner we want our own children and grandchildren to be treated by their teachers.

I am indebted to my husband, Billy, and children, Colin, Leah, and Ben, each of whom has taught me more than they could possibly know.

—*Brenda Scheuermann*

This book is for Tom, who has provided me with much more than support of my writing, and for my daughter, Mary Jo, one of the best teachers I've ever known.

—*Jo Webber*

This book is dedicated to my daughter, Emerson Lang, who makes me happy when skies are gray.

—*Russell Lang*

Overview
of Autism

1

© Arnio

LEARNING OBJECTIVES

After reading this chapter, you should be able to:

1-1 Relate historical descriptions of individuals with autism to current diagnoses, definitions, and treatment of the disorder.

1-2 Discuss reasons for the efficacy of ABA as the theoretical basis of educational programming for students with autism.

1-3 Describe the nature of autism and related characteristics, including typical behavioral excesses and behavioral deficits.

1-4 Discuss the role of biology in explaining autism and related disorders.

1-5 Identify diagnostic criteria of ASD according to the DSM-5 and eligibility criteria for autism in IDEA 2004.

1-6 Identify key educational program considerations based in ABA and discuss the teacher's role in ensuring student progress.

1-7 Identify challenges families experience in parenting children with autism and discuss the teacher's role in supporting these families.

Autism is an intriguing disorder that has generated public and professional interest for decades. Mirroring reported increases in prevalence, it is also reflected in more and more coverage of the disorder in popular media. Beginning with Dustin Hoffman's 1988 portrayal of a young adult with autism in *Rain Man,* various documentary, movie, and television characters have exhibited the disorder or its common characteristics. For example, in early 2017, *Life Animated,* a documentary about the coming-of-age of a young man with autism was nominated for an Academy Award, and the Public Broadcasting Service announced that *Sesame Street* will soon add a new character, Julia, a 4-year-old girl with red hair, green eyes, and autism. Similarly, researchers have consistently intensified their efforts to identify the causes of and effective treatment for the disorder.

Although the heightened interest in autism should be applauded, the rise in autism prevalence has been cause for concern. In 1992, the Centers for Disease Control and Prevention (CDC) reported the prevalence of autism, including those with high-functioning autism, at 1 in 150 children; in 2012, it reported a prevalence of 1 in 68 children (CDC, 2016), an astounding increase in reported occurrence. Furthermore, the 38th annual report of the Individuals with Disabilities Education Act (IDEA) from the U.S. Office of Special Education Programs reported a 124-percent increase in school-age students (ages 6 to 11 years) served under the label of autism from 2005 to 2014, even though the percentage of special education students in general dropped during that period (U.S. Department of Education, 2016a).

This increase in the number of children served under the special education category of autism might be the result of several factors: (a) the broadened definition of autism (we discuss this later in this chapter), (b) better diagnostic procedures, (c) a wider awareness of the disorder as previously mentioned, and (d) a parental preference for the autism label over other disability labels. However, it is widely thought that we simply have more children with autism than we had in the 1970s and 1980s.

In this book, we have chosen to specifically target school-age students who meet the criteria for *autism spectrum disorder* (ASD) as defined by the American Psychiatric Association (APA) (2013) and who also have *intellectual disabilities* (IDs) with more severe symptoms. These individuals require added supports for learning and adaptive functioning. For simplicity's sake, we will use the term *autism* to describe this target population, although **low-functioning autism** is also a common term. For information pertaining to individuals at the less severe end of the autism spectrum (sometimes described as **high-functioning autism**) and who require different curricula and instructional considerations, we refer the reader to McConnell and Ryser (2014) and Simpson and McGinnis (2016).

In any case, autism is not new. Since the 1975 inception of the Education for All Handicapped Children Act (Public Law [PL] 94-142) and the more recent Individuals with Disabilities Education Act (IDEA) of 2004, public school personnel have been developing educational programs for these students. Various approaches have been and continue to be recommended and used with varying degrees of success. In this text, we intend to share what we consider to be the most effective of these approaches based on the best available research. In other words, this book will focus on evidenced-based practices (EBPs), specifically teaching and behavior management procedures that enjoy the most well established body of scientific research.

This book's content will follow a logical progression from describing educational needs to delineating methods for addressing those needs. The chapters will thus cover techniques for preventing and managing challenging behavior, curriculum development, instructional strategies, and special issues. After reading this book, practitioners should be able to develop an appropriate educational program for individual students with autism.

1-1 History of Autism

Researchers believe that individuals with autistic characteristics were living long before the 20th century. One of the most interesting accounts of such a child is described by French physician Jean-Marc-Gaspard Itard in 1803 (Itard, 1972), and depicted in Francois Truffaut's *The Wild Child*, a French film, in 1970. Itard wrote of a boy found living in the wilds of France who appeared to be about 11 years old. At the time he was found, the boy could not speak, did not try to communicate, preferred objects to human contact, displayed few adaptive behaviors, appeared to have perceptual difficulties, and often engaged in bizarre and inappropriate behaviors. Itard and his colleagues set out to socialize the boy they named Victor. The account of that process could be a lesson for special educators today. Victor was taught communication, social, self-help, attending, discrimination, and imitation skills, and he was often integrated into the community for dining and other functional activities. Certainly, Itard's careful account of Victor's progress in highly specific skill areas and his constant questioning of his own expectations challenge us all to evaluate our intentions and teaching techniques and to document progress toward students' long-term goals.

Despite Itard's early account of Victor, the syndrome of autism was not named and described as such until 1943 when psychiatrist Leo Kanner published his landmark descriptive study (Kanner, 1985). Kanner described 11 children "whose condition differs so markedly and uniquely from anything reported so far, that each case merits . . . a detailed consideration of its fascinating peculiarities" (p. 11). The common characteristics that set these children apart from others included the following:

1. An inability to relate to others in an ordinary manner
2. An extreme autistic aloneness that seemingly isolated the child from the outside world. Interestingly, the term *autism* was taken from the Greek word *auto*, meaning self, because the children described by Kanner were thought to be intensely self-absorbed.
3. An apparent resistance to being picked up or held by the parents
4. Deficits in language including mutism (complete lack of speech) and echolalia (repeating the speech of other people)
5. More restrictive food preferences than is expected in typical development
6. Extreme fear reactions to loud noises
7. Obsessive desire for repetition and maintenance of sameness; strict adherence to rituals and routines
8. Few spontaneous activities such as typical play behavior
9. Bizarre and repetitive physical movement such as spinning or perpetual rocking
10. Normal physical appearance

Children who display these characteristics are often described as having *classic Kanner syndrome*. Despite the fact that Kanner (1985) surmised that these children came into the world *biologically* unable to form "affective contact" (p. 50), which means the disorder probably has a biological basis, the comments that most define his work have to do with his observation that within this "autistic" group "were very few really warmhearted fathers and mothers" (p. 50). These observations set the stage for speculation that the condition was actually caused by cold, nonresponsive parents. A preponderance of subsequent research has refuted that assumption, instead pointing directly toward organic causes such as genetic predisposition, abnormal brain structure, and abnormal brain chemistry (Anderson, 2016; Zürcher & Hooker, 2016).

Currently, several organizations serve parents and families of individuals with autism, their teachers, and other practitioners. Table 1.1 lists major organizations that provide resources, general information, research findings, advocacy services, and training. We recommend that parents and practitioners join appropriate organizations so they may keep abreast of current trends and issues in the field.

1-2 Nature of Autism

Current research supports the assumptions that autism is a neurodevelopmental disorder characterized by impairment in brain development with differences in brain chemistry, brain structure, and brain function (Anderson, 2016; Zürcher & Hooker, 2016). The exact cause of the neurological impairment is not yet known, although researchers have found strong evidence for genetic links (Anderson, 2016). Box 1.1 provides a review of current research in regard to biology and autism. Even though the exact etiology of the disorder is unknown, the symptoms are well defined, thus providing essential information for educational treatment. Remember that a biological abnormality (e.g., genetic mutation) does not preclude a child, in this case one with autism, from learning. Teachers should never think, "This student can't learn because he has autism"! We believe that all people can learn, and these children deserve to be taught by good teachers using the most effective techniques.

Understanding how best to educate students with autism should be based on an understanding of the symptomology of autism. Traditionally, treatment approaches have been

TABLE 1.1 ● Parent and Professional Organizations Serving Individuals with Autism

ORGANIZATION	FUNCTION
American Speech-Language-Hearing Association (ASHA) www.asha.org	Speech and communication resources
The ARC of the United States Facebook: facebook.com/thearcus Twitter: twitter.com/thearcus YouTube: youtube.com/user/thearcoftheus http://www.thearc.org/who-we-are	Advocacy and resources for individuals with intellectual and developmental disabilities
Association for Behavior Analysis International (ABA) www.abainternational.org	Behavior management, teaching strategies, research and resources
Autism Centers of Excellence www.nichd.nih.gov/research/supported/Pages/ace.aspx	Provides funding and support for large-scale autism studies
Autism Speaks www.autismspeaks.org Autism Speaks Websites for Families www.autismspeaks.org/family-services/resource-library /websites-families	Treatment research, advocacy, blogs, resources
Autism Society of America www.autism-society.org	Parent and family resources, advocacy, training
Cambridge Center for Behavioral Studies www.behavior.org/interest.php?id=2	Provides training and training materials for parents and professionals on the use of ABA treatments for individuals with ASD
Center for Autism and Related Disorders (CARD) www.centerforautism.com	Provides ABA interventions for individuals with ASD and consultation to others using ABA interventions
The Center for Parent Information and Resources (CPIR) www.parentcenterhub.org	Funded by the Department of Education, Office of Special Education Programs, to house and provide resources for various parent support centers around the country
Council for Exceptional Children (CEC) www.cec.sped.org	Special education resources, advocacy, training
Council for Exceptional Children (CEC) Division of Autism and Developmental Disabilities (DADD) www.daddcec.org	Subdivision of the CEC, professional organization for special educators Provides resources and training for special education professionals
Families for Early Autism Treatment (FEAT) www.feat.org	Parent support, information, newsletter and publications
Ohio Center for Autism and Low Incidence (OCALI) www.ocali.org/center/autism	Information clearinghouse, conferences
Wrights Law www.wrightslaw.com	Special education law and advocacy resources

based on three main theories that explain the presence of common symptoms, although subsequent research has not supported all three theories in terms of related treatment approaches. Nevertheless, knowledge of these theories will help readers better understand autism-related terminology and treatment approaches that may be discussed by parents or professionals from other disciplines.

The first theory, a **perceptual and cognitive theory**, posits that brain malfunction can lead these children to have (a) specific differences in their thinking ability (Birtwell, Willoughby, & Nowiski, 2016) and (b) differences in the way they receive external input (Ben-Sasson et al., 2009; Schuler, 1995). For example, researchers have found that individuals with autism display deficits in empathic functioning (Baron-Cohen & Wheelwright, 2004), cognitive flexibility, and executive functioning (Russo et al., 2007). In addition, individuals with autism seem to over- or underrespond to visual, auditory, and tactile stimuli (Schaaf et al., 2014) and thus need to withdraw as well as have a difficult time making sense of or processing physical phenomena.

BOX 1.1 ● The Biology of Autism

As early as 1943, Leo Kanner wrote of inborn traits in his description of infantile autism. However, the search for the biological basis of autism only began in earnest in the early 1990s. The general thinking is that genetic and environmental factors result in functional and structural brain differences in individuals with autism; these in turn lead to cognitive differences that are responsible for the symptoms and impairments related to the disorder (Coghill, Nigg, Rothenberger, Sonuga-Barke, & Tannock, 2005). Although other causal models are being discussed (Coghill, 2015), this original model may serve as a framework for this review.

Genes and Autism. To investigate whether human traits are inherited, researchers often conduct studies using twins and families. Studying autism at the family level (particularly in twins) allows researchers to determine the number of family members with similar traits and to consider both genetic and environmental factors in a controlled way. Researchers can also directly investigate the genetic makeup of individuals showing particular traits or symptoms (e.g., ASD) and compare them to a group without those traits. In the case of ASD, early twin and family studies show that the disorder is present in identical twins that share identical genes (i.e., both twins have ASD) more often than in fraternal twins who share only some of the same genes. This implies that the gene similarity to someone with ASD increases the chances of acquiring the disorder and provides strong evidence of the heritability of autism (Baily et al., 1995). In fact, the chance of having a child with ASD increases with family history of the disorder. Some researchers estimate the heritability factor to be between 37 percent and 70 percent (Constantino et al., 2013). To further strengthen the heritability notion, family studies have shown clusters of autism or autistic traits (e.g., anxiety) among siblings and parents or extended family members of individuals with autism (Murphy et al., 2000; Trottier, Srivastava, & Walker, 1999). For example, some families have multiple children with the disorder, and in some cases, parents exhibit milder symptoms of the disorder.

Although autism is commonly assumed to be heritable, research to locate single genes or gene variants related to the disorder has been difficult. There is much

variation in the symptoms shown by individuals who fall on the autism spectrum, which is reflected in genetic heterogeneity, resulting in a high number of genetic variants being identified and more than 1,000 risk genes being estimated (Sanders et al., 2012). Some researchers are now focusing on shared biological pathways of these genes, rather than the genes themselves, as better information for treatment (Vorstman et al., 2014). At this time, the assumption that a single gene causes ASD has been dismissed. Rather, ASD is called a *multigenetic disorder*, and a search for gene mutations, variants, and pathways continues. Some researchers are assuming that ASD may not be a distinct disorder but might be on a continuum with other neurodevelopmental disorders such as *attention-deficit hyperactivity disorder* (ADHD) and *intellectual disabilities* (IDs) that show similar genetic complexity (Coghill, 2015). Interesting research is also being conducted to identify biomarkers at the molecular or cellular level to assist with diagnosis and prediction of behavior in autism (Levin & Nelson, 2015).

Brain Impairment. ASD is a neurodevelopmental disorder, which means that individuals with this disorder have impaired brain development. Perhaps inherited genetic makeup causes this impaired development, but environmental contributors may also be involved. Nevertheless, a great deal of research has outlined structural and functional brain differences of individuals with and without ASD. This research is examining brain size, the amount of gray and white matter in various brain areas, and differences in actual brain components (e.g., the cerebellum). For example, younger individuals with ASD have been found to have larger than average head circumferences. This may show that the brain is also larger than average at this time (Piven, Arndt, Bailey, & Andreasen, 1996). However, the enlarged head circumference is reduced over time and is average or sometimes below average by adulthood (Sivapalan & Aitchison, 2014).

Studies have shown that gray and white brain matter, related to brain size in individuals with ASD, show variation by brain region. There are deficits of gray matter in some portions of the brain and of white matter in others (Palmen & van Engeland, 2004). Finally, studies that have targeted certain sections

(continued)

BOX 1.1 ● The Biology of Autism (continued)

of the brain have found variations in the structure of these areas (e.g., size and number of cells) as compared to control populations. The targeted brain areas relate to the core symptoms of autism—communication, social interaction, and repetitive behaviors. For example, the frontal lobe seems to be related to social interaction. However, the findings of this type of research have been inconsistent (Sivapalan & Aitchison, 2014), prompting more attention to dysfunctions in the neural networks of individuals with ASD (Zielinski et al., 2012). Knowledge about brain differences can lead to better medical treatment, particularly psychopharmacological treatments.

Environmental Contributors. Although there is strong evidence of a genetic basis for autism, many researchers think that environmental variables may contribute to the disorder during gestation, birth, or after birth in interaction with the genes. These factors may include familial autoimmune disorders, maternal drug use, smoking, difficult births, and congenital malformations (Beversdorf et al., 2005; McDougle et al., 2015). However, direct causal factors are difficult to ascertain because it is not yet possible to separate the environmental stressors from a disorder that might already exist in the fetus. Unfortunately, many people have heard of the false assumption that vaccines cause autism because thimerosal, a preservative containing mercury, was included in vaccines for decades. Thimerosal was found to be safe for humans when included in vaccines in trace amounts. However, faulty research and faulty logic have fueled public suspicion about the relationship between vaccines and autism (Offit, 2008). Subsequently, many parents now refuse to have their children vaccinated against highly contagious diseases such as diphtheria, tetanus, and whooping cough. Many large-scale studies over more than a decade have found no link between vaccines and autism; to enhance prevention, diagnosis, and treatment, efforts are now needed to focus on those biological and environmental indicators that have been shown to have a relationship to autism.

Given this perceptual and cognitive view, treatment of the disorder may include teaching students to attend to and communicate with people in socially appropriate ways, to monitor their own performance, to plan their future goals, and to more easily react to environmental changes. This theory implies that a classroom needs to be highly structured and predictable (e.g., follow the same schedule and routines every day), that methods should include primarily visual materials, and that external stimuli be kept to a minimum (e.g., no mobiles hanging from the ceiling, no wall decorations). In addition, given the cognitive processing problems, it is recommended that information should be presented in ways that take those cognitive deficits into account, such as giving instructions one step at a time with no extraneous verbalizations (Grandin, 1995).

A second theory from a **developmental** explanation holds that brain malfunctions have caused individuals with autism to fail to meet typical developmental milestones in language, cognition, socialization, and motor ability. Because they are developmentally delayed, it is assumed that these students need to progress through developmentally sequenced experiences in order to master necessary skills just as children without disabilities might progress (Tager-Flusberg, 2014). Techniques derived from this theory might include environmental arrangements that encourage communication. For example, the teacher might have favorite items or foods present so that the student is motivated to interact with his or her environment. This model might also include: (a) facilitating children's presumably natural desire to communicate by, for example, repeating the sounds or words they might emit and expanding their verbalizations; (b) allowing them to lead during play (following the child's lead); (c) acknowledging the child's gestures and expressions as attempts to communicate; and (d) encouraging language and cognitive development by teaching play skills (Lang, Hancock, & Singh, 2016).

A third theory, the **behavioral** explanation, holds that the neurological impairment has prevented normal learning and resulted in **behavioral deficits** (i.e., most social, communicative, and imitative behaviors are not present) and some **behavioral excesses** (i.e., bizarre, aggressive, and noncompliant behaviors occur too frequently). Intervention within this view is based in **applied behavioral analysis (ABA)** and assumes that learning (defined as a relatively permanent change in behavior) can be achieved through an analysis of behavioral deficits and excesses, the manner in which people respond to those behaviors (reinforcing or punishing), and direct training focused on observable and measurable skills (Baer, Wolf, & Risely, 1968).

Appropriate behavior can be taught through the use of behavioral techniques such as direct instruction, antecedent control, and reinforcement strategies, whereas inappropriate behavior can be reduced with reductive techniques such as time-out and response cost. Instead of waiting for development to occur, researchers have shown that the direct training of desired behavior is the best way to educate individuals with autism (Granpeesheh, Tarbox, & Dixon, 2009; Green, 1996; Howard, Sparkman, Cohen, Green, & Stanislaw, 2005; Smith, 1999). To better illustrate these theories with regard to educational programs, Table 1.2 provides a list of educational techniques matched to each of the three theories. Note that there is a great deal of overlap in the treatment approaches relative to these theories. Each approach may not be mutually exclusive, although terminology for the same approach may vary. For example, a predictable environment acts as a cognitive organizer under the cognitive theory and as an antecedent intervention under the behavioral model.

The techniques presented in this book come primarily from the last theory previously described—behavioral theory—for several reasons. First, the vast majority of current research regarding the effectiveness of instruction with students with autism has been

TABLE 1.2 ● Instructional Components by Theory

Perceptual and Cognitive Theory	▪ Use visual cues such as pictures and color. ▪ Teach left–right and up–down orientation. ▪ Prevent loud noises and avoid excessive verbalizations. ▪ Establish and follow routines. ▪ Prepare child for pending environmental changes. ▪ Rehearse for new situations. ▪ Teach attending and imitating. ▪ Arrange the classroom using visual cues (e.g., carpet = leisure time activities) and avoid changing arrangement.
Developmental Theory	▪ Provide many stimulating toys, objects, and people. ▪ Follow the child's interests. ▪ Take advantage of the teachable moment. When a child appears interested, interact only as much as necessary for the child to achieve independence. ▪ Refrain from direct guidance, commands, or punishment. ▪ Repeat sounds or words as the child spontaneously makes them. ▪ Encourage play and exploration. ▪ Provide gross motor opportunities and sensory stimulation.
Behavioral Theory	▪ Teach compliance, attending, and imitating. ▪ Use one-to-one, trial-by-trial, and milieu training. ▪ Reinforce correct responding. ▪ Use prompting techniques. ▪ Provide intensive teacher-directed instruction. ▪ Train functional skills. ▪ Train to generalization. ▪ Use data-based progress monitoring.

conducted within a behavioral framework (Granpeesheh, Tarbox, & Dixon, 2009). Second, behavioral techniques have been used successfully with this population for more than 45 years, not including Itard's case analysis (e.g., Keenen & Dillenburger, 2011). Third, special education preservice teachers are typically taught behavioral principles for instruction and managing behavior. Thus, these techniques are compatible with most teacher-training programs. Fourth, the behavioral approach provides for the best accountability system in terms of student progress because it relies on data-based decision making and student responses to intervention. Finally, ABA includes ethical requirements for interventions; ethical requirements include correct application of treatments and choosing treatments that are in the best interest of the student.

Once again, choosing this particular theory of treatment does not preclude using strategies from the other two theories. For example, the provision of color-coded materials, visual presentations such as picture-guided activities, and high-interest functional tasks such as learning how to prepare a preferred meal not only reflects the cognitive model but also would motivate desired student responses, which is a key component of ABA (the behavioral model). An important point is that ABA assumes a direct approach to teaching as opposed to an indirect, developmental one. This means, for example, that to teach a student to ask for a desired object (e.g., a favorite stuffed animal), the teacher would show the student how to request the object, prompt the student to ask for the object, and reinforce the student for asking appropriately rather than waiting for that skill to simply emerge without systematic deliberate support.

1-3 Characteristics

Despite the various ways of explaining autism and related disorders, for a child to be given a diagnosis of autism, certain similar characteristics (discussed shortly) must be present to some degree. Autism is believed to be present at birth in most cases and should be evident in the child's behavior and development before 3 years of age. Although in rare cases some children may acquire enough skills to be nearly indistinguishable from same-age children without autism (e.g., Lovaas, 1987), autism remains recognizable across the individual's life span in most cases (APA, 2013). The incidence of ASD is four to five times higher in boys (CDC, 2016). Those who use language to communicate as young children and those with higher cognitive functioning (e.g., higher IQ scores) have the best prognosis (Fernel, Eriksson, & Gillberg, 2013). A high percentage (approximately 20 percent to 30 percent) of these young people will develop seizure disorders in adolescence, and many will suffer from a comorbid mental illness such as anxiety, depression, hyperactivity disorder, or obsessive–compulsive disorder (National Institute of Neurological Disorders and Stroke [NINDS], 2016).

As we mentioned previously, the characteristics of autism can be categorized as either behavioral excesses or behavioral deficits. For example, these children show many behaviors that are disturbing to those around them and sometimes dangerous to the child and others (e.g., aggression, self-injurious behavior, and tantrums). We call these behaviors that happen too often *behavioral excesses*. These behaviors may get in the way of learning, result in punishment, and make it extremely difficult for the child to be socially successful in normalized situations such as in the community or general education classrooms. For this reason, it is critical to reduce or eliminate behavioral excesses. Chapters 2 and 3 will provide effective techniques for reducing these challenging behaviors.

Directly related to behavioral excesses are what we call *behavioral deficits*—that is, children with autism who do not display adequate essential behaviors such as talking, dressing, reading, and playing. Without adequate life skills (sometimes referred to as "daily living skills" or "functional behaviors") such as dressing, hygiene, and toileting, an individual is more likely to be excluded from the types of activities associated with happiness and good quality of life. For example, he may be unable to ask for what he wants. In this case, the communication deficit may lead to excessive tantruming as a method for getting a favorite food. A student who is not toilet trained must continue to wear diapers even when it is age

TABLE 1.3 ● Common Behavioral Deficits and Excesses

DEFICITS	EXCESSES
■ Receptive language	■ Tantrums
■ Expressive language	■ Screaming
■ Communicative intent	■ Self-stimulation
■ Social skills	■ Self-abuse
■ Self-care skills	■ Aggression
■ Compliance	■ Bizarre behaviors
■ Attending	■ Echolalia
■ Imitating	■ Perseveration
■ Auditory and visual discrimination	■ Refusing to follow directions
■ Vocational skills	
■ Self-advocacy skills	
■ Leisure and play skills	
■ Academic skills	
■ Eye contact	

inappropriate and socially stigmatizing and makes forming friendships difficult. As an adult, the individual may not be able to live and work independently in the absence of essential life skills. It is believed that the more skills and abilities an individual lacks, the more that particular individual is forced to rely on inappropriate behavioral excesses for communicative and functional purposes. For example, a child who cannot ask someone to leave him alone may have to curl up in the corner and engage in repetitive motor behavior (rocking back and forth) to get the person to go away. A child who cannot ask to leave the cafeteria may resort to hitting another student, which usually results in the teacher removing him. In Chapter 3, we will discuss ways to determine how a student's challenging behavior can be related to skill deficits, particularly communication deficits.

If behavioral excesses are linked to behavioral deficits, then it follows that teaching appropriate communicative, social, and functional behavior is a primary goal. Chapters 4, 6, 7, and 8 will give information about assessing deficits in such a way that the assessment results facilitate instruction aimed at ameliorating those deficits. Teaching appropriate behavior is almost always an essential part of intervention packages focused on reducing behavioral excesses. Educating individuals with autism and related disorders requires a balance of reductive techniques (sometimes referred to as *punishment*) and good skill-training strategies, covered in Chapter 5. As the individual acquires mastery of communicative and functional skills, problem behavior that arose as a means to compensate for those deficits should diminish. Table 1.3 provides a list of common behavioral deficits and excesses observed in individuals with ASD.

1-3a Behavioral Deficits

An Inability to Relate

A cardinal symptom of autism is the inability to relate to others, which may be demonstrated in many ways. Specifically, individuals with autism may:

- exhibit a total absence of smiling in response to social situations or may smile and laugh for little or no apparent reason;
- avoid direct eye contact, preferring instead to turn their heads and look out of the corner of their eyes;
- spend hours alone manipulating favorite objects, although usually not in the way the object was meant to be used; for example, a child may twirl a piece of string with one hand or flap objects against his palm;
- have an aversion to physical contact; for example, they may show distress, or no response whatsoever, when a family member attempts to show physical affection;

- lack appropriate play skills; for example, a child with autism may repeatedly stack blocks in the same configuration and knock them down or may turn a toy car over and spin the wheels rather than push it along the floor with accompanying "car noises";
- be unwilling to share toys or display cooperative play behaviors even when in close physical proximity to other children playing (APA, 2013; NINDS, 2016);
- have highly restricted patterns of behavior, interests, and activities (APA, 2013; McCoy, 2011); or
- show no special recognition of parents, family members, or familiar people such as teachers; for example, a child with autism may show no response when a parent enters or leaves the room.

Lack of Functional Language

Many individuals with autism have no language at all, and those who do have language may not integrate their language abilities into social interaction or emotional attachment (APA, 2013). Following are some specific language characteristics related to autism:

- Some children with autism appear to lack **communicative intent**. In other words, they do not seem to want to communicate for social purposes, to get others to behave certain ways, or to get others' attention.
- It is thought that some 40 percent of these children are **mute**—possessing few or no verbal skills. They simply do not talk (CDC, 2016).
- Even when oral language is present, frequent **echolalia** and **perseveration** may be observed. With echolalia, the individual immediately repeats words and phrases that have been uttered by someone else, sometimes with the exact same intonation, with no appreciation of the conventional meaning. In other words, their utterances seem to be from rote memory rather than reflecting spontaneous speech. Similarly, **palilalia** (or delayed echolalia) refers to the same oral imitation, but the original speech being imitated ("echoed") may be from hours or even weeks before the imitation (repeating lines from a movie a week later). Nevertheless, such speech may, in some cases, actually be communicative, serving to indicate turn taking, yes answers, requests, declarations, or perspective taking (Prizant, 1983; Sterponi & Kirby, 2016). For example, a child may repeat a TV advertisement for a particular store when he wants to go for a ride in the car. In perseveration, the individual repeats the same words or phrases over and over or insists on discussing only one specific topic. Often the perseveration increases in times of high demand, anxiety, or increased demands.
- Those children with autism who have speech may show abnormal use of **prosody**, or use of voice tone and inflection. Individuals with autism typically speak in a monotone voice with little inflection. For example, a child requesting help when he is hurt may use the same tone and inflection as he does when requesting a cookie after dinner.
- Difficulty with pronoun usage, specifically **pronoun reversals**, is also not uncommon in children with autism. The child may use his name or the pronoun "you" when referring to "I." For example, "*You* want to go to the store" may be intended to mean "*I* want to go to the store."
- Individuals with autism appear to show little variety in their language, using one phrase to communicate several functions. For example, they will use the phrase "You want out" to communicate wanting to have free time, go to the store, go for a ride, and other desired activities.
- Individuals with autism tend to be extremely *literal* in both expressive and receptive language. For example, in *Rain Man*, Raymond waited at the crosswalk for the sign to flash "Walk." He then began to cross the street. The sign then changed to "Don't walk" before he reached the other side. Raymond stopped in the middle of the street even though cars were honking and people were yelling because he literally interpreted the crosswalk sign and refused to walk until it said so.
- Individuals with autism may use only simple grammar and sentence structure. For example, they may use only short sentences in a simple noun–verb format or often talk only in phrases (e.g., "Want car?").

- Language *comprehension* (sometimes referred to as **receptive language**) is generally limited in individuals with intellectual disabilities (Rapin, Dunn, Allen, Stevens, & Fein, 2009; Skwerer, Jordan, Brukilaccio, & Tager-Flusberg, 2015).

Cognitive Deficits

Considerable speculation surrounds the cognitive abilities and disabilities of individuals with autism. Closely tied to language ability and social communication abilities, cognitive functioning is best assessed with intelligence tests and reported in the form of developmental and intelligence quotients (DQ and IQ). Although the percentage of children with ASD who show intellectual disabilities ($<$ 70 IQ) ranges from 24 to 66 percent, depending on age and type of study, most researchers agree that (a) cognitive development in this population appears uneven in childhood showing differences in both verbal and nonverbal abilities, (b) most children with autism show more deficits in verbal than nonverbal ability such as assembling puzzles, and (c) cognitive ability as measured by the IQ can improve with early diagnosis and intervention (Clark, Barbaro, & Dissanayake, 2016).

Another area of cognitive delay that is characteristic of individuals with autism exists in cognitive control processes known as **executive functions (EFs)**, which are demonstrated by the ability to monitor and adapt one's performance in a changing environment (Geurts, Sinzig, Booth, & Happe, 2014). EFs are thought to include distinct skills such as planning, goal setting, problem solving, cognitive flexibility (the ability to adjust to unexpected information), and response inhibition (self-control) (Gökçen, Frederickson, & Petrides, 2016). Executive functioning ability is closely tied to IQ (children with higher IQ show better executive functioning) and age (older children, adolescents, and adults show better executive functioning), so young children with intellectual disabilities will likely show distinct delays in various EFs. It is interesting that deficits in EFs are present in other disorders such as attention-deficit hyperactivity disorder (ADHD), so it is not a core characteristic of autism, just one that might indicate attention to certain educational goals.

Related to executive functioning is the notion of cognitive perspective-taking, which is the ability to understand and make inferences about how another person is thinking or feeling. This inability to take another's perspective does appear to be a core feature of autism (APA, 2013). Referred to as **theory of mind (ToM)**, this cognitive process is believed to play a foundational role in successful social interaction and expression of empathy (Baron-Cohen & Wheelwright, 2004). Children with autism tend to appear uninterested in another's view of the world or feelings. They often just assign their own feelings and thinking to others. In this way, their interactions may appear overly demanding, "arrogant," or in most cases inappropriate and ill-timed.

Although many children with autism have cognitive deficits and suffer from limited ability to function without support, some show what is known as islands of precocity or **splinter skills**—that is, a child may be quite gifted in math computation but not be able to tell time or determine whether he has enough money to make a purchase. Although highly advanced or refined splinter skills comparable to savant syndrome are more common in autism than in the typical population, such skills remain rare. The most common include (a) calendar abilities, such as being able to give the day of the week for any date provided to them (e.g., May 12, 1896); (b) the ability to count visual things quickly, such as telling how many toothpicks are on the floor when a box is dropped; (c) artistic ability, such as the ability to paint or draw; and (d) musical ability, such as playing the piano. These splinter skills have falsely led many to believe that individuals with autism have "hidden" cognitive abilities that just need to be released through as yet unproven interventions (Offit, 2008).

1-3b Behavioral Excesses

Individuals with autism not only show many behavioral deficits but also many possess a repertoire of behavioral excesses. In other words, when individuals cannot make their needs and wants known through functional communication, they must resort to a nonverbal means of communication such as tantrums or other forms of challenging behavior. Over time, if excesses result in desired outcomes for the child (e.g., she gets what she wants when she hits her head), the behavioral excess is strengthened. We say that the undesired behavior is reinforced and will occur often in the future.

Self-Stimulation

Self-stimulation is behavior that is repetitive and stereotypical in nature (NINDS, 2016). For example, children with autism might engage in these activities:

- spinning themselves and objects;
- repetitive hand movements;
- rocking;
- humming in a monotone;
- arranging and rearranging objects;
- twirling strings or ribbon;
- moving their hand between their eyes and a light to achieve a strobe effect;
- hand gazing;
- jumping up and down;
- gazing up at the ceiling or lights;
- smiling or laughing, not in response to social cues; and
- compulsive eating.

Self-stimulatory behaviors, also called *stereotypy, stereotypic behavior*, or *restrictive and repetitive patterns of behavior*, seem to occur for the purpose of obtaining sensory input or avoiding unpleasant sensory input. When the source of reinforcement is internal to the individual engaging in the behavior (such as relief from itchy sensation followed by scratching), the behavior is said to be the result of automatic reinforcement (Ahrens, Lerman, Kodak, Worsdell, & Keegan, 2011). The high frequency of these automatically reinforced stereotypical behaviors is a classic feature of autism. Many of us engage in some self-sensory input such as leg bouncing or nail biting. However, for people with autism, self-stimulation is more likely to be a highly preferred activity. Given the opportunity, a child with autism may engage in self-stimulation for especially long periods of time and become upset if interrupted.

There is good news and bad news concerning this propensity to engage in self-stimulation. The bad news is that, given the motivation to engage in self-stimulation, motivation to engage in more productive behaviors is diminished. The good news is that allowing students to earn self-stimulation time (free time) by completing learning tasks may provide the necessary motivation for the student to respond appropriately to instruction. Note, however, that using self-stimulation as a reinforcer is controversial because it may be difficult to control its administration. It also may encourage nonfunctional and inappropriate behavior, and some forms of self-stimulation may be unhealthy (e.g., compulsive eating).

Resistance to Change and Insistence on Sameness

Because children with autism have a tightly narrow activity focus, they may show an extreme resistance to relatively benign changes to their environment, food, room arrangements, familiar routes, and other established routines (APA, 2013). This insistence on sameness has been hypothesized to be related to anxiety and to be used as a self-calming strategy (Gotham et al., 2013). For anyone with cognitive processing and perceptual problems, a clear, predictable environment is often indicated.

When change occurs, resistance can be abated through prior cognitive preparation. For example, begin talking about any planned family trip a week or more before it is to occur. Describe exactly what will happen in regard to eating, sleeping, and so on, preferably in visual terms (e.g., what the motel room will look like). Also, it might be good to have a calendar hanging in the child's room with pictures of the car or the destination (e.g., grandmother's house) pasted on the days of the trip. Then have the child mark each day of the month with an "X" so that the impending trip will not be a surprise. At school, if there is to be an assembly on Friday, the teacher could tell the student on Monday and each following day about the assembly, where it is to be, what time it will be, how long it will last, what the behavioral expectations might be (e.g., sit on the floor with quiet hands), and what will happen after it is over. Again, a calendar might be used to indicate each day's activity, and a destination card with a picture of the gym or auditorium given to the child on Friday morning with another verbal rehearsal before departing for the assembly.

Severe Challenging Behaviors

Finally, individuals with autism often engage in severe challenging behaviors. In some instances, they may display extreme fear reactions as did Raymond did when a fire alarm went off in *Rain Man*. He screamed, held his hands over his ears, and slammed his head against the wall. Others may display problem behaviors such as hyperactivity, short attention span, impulsivity, tantrums, aggression, and self-injurious behavior (APA, 2013).

Self-injurious behavior (SIB) may also be displayed by students with autism. For example, individuals with autism may smash their heads on the ground or on a wall, pull their hair or bite their hands, gouge their eyes, hit themselves repeatedly, or hold their breath until they faint. Research has repeatedly demonstrated that SIB and other challenging behaviors may have a communicative function (Durand & Berotti, 1991). This means that the individual may be asking for something desirable or asking to get out of something undesirable with these behaviors. One of the teacher's major instructional tasks is to teach these students an appropriate way to ask for what they want; providing other avenues for getting needs met usually reduces challenging behavior. This strategy and other reductive techniques will be discussed further in Chapter 3.

1-4 Diagnoses and Definitions

Using the current fifth edition of the *Diagnostic and Statistical Manual of Mental Disorders* (DSM-5), children with autistic characteristics are classified as having **autism spectrum disorder (ASD)**, an umbrella term for a wide range of symptoms that include "persistent deficits in social communication and social interaction across multiple contexts" and restricted, repetitive patterns of behavior such as the presence of stereotyped behavior, interests, and activities (APA, 2013). This is a change from the previous edition of the DSM, which included these individuals under the diagnostic umbrella of pervasive developmental disorders (PDDs) with five subtypes: autistic disorder, Asperger's syndrome, Rett syndrome, childhood disintegrative disorder, and pervasive developmental disorder not otherwise specified (PDD-NOS).

The change in the diagnostic criteria has been controversial because many experts believe that some individuals, particularly those at the high-functioning end of the spectrum and previously included under the PDD diagnosis, will be excluded from the current ASD diagnosis and thus not receive certain services and funding (Bent, Barbaro, & Dissanayake, 2016). It is also thought that the current diagnostic criteria may present barriers to early diagnosis because PDDs are diagnosed in early childhood and early diagnosis has been found to be crucial for positive outcomes for this population. The exact impact of the new criteria on the prevalence of autism will take some time to ascertain; however, there is evidence that the number of autism diagnoses have leveled off in 2015 after many years of continual increase (Bent, Barbaro, & Dissanayake, 2016). A portion of the DSM-5 diagnostic criteria is presented in Table 1.4.

At the less severe end of the autism spectrum, students with high-functioning autism (referred to as Asperger's syndrome in the DSM-IV) may have an average or above average IQ and highly developed verbal skills. Nevertheless, they may communicate poorly, display poor social skills, have few friends, become upset if routines or expectations are violated, have learning difficulties, show deficits in motor skills including handwriting, and may show stereotypical behaviors (McPortland, Klin, & Volkmar, 2014). These children need interventions not unlike students with ADHD and learning disabilities. These interventions include structured routines, tutoring, speech and occupational therapy (for motor skill deficits), specific social skills training, cognitive behavioral interventions, contingency management, and individualized educational programs (IEPs). In some cases, medication may be prescribed to

TABLE 1.4 ● DSM-5 Criteria for Autism Spectrum Disorder (ASD)

A. Persistent deficits in social communication and social interaction across multiple contexts, as manifested by the following, currently or by history:
   1. deficits in social–emotional reciprocity, including abnormal social approach, conversational deficits, reduced sharing of interests, and so on, and failure to initiate or respond to social interactions;
   2. deficits in nonverbal communicative behaviors used for social interaction, including poor verbal and nonverbal communication; little eye contact and body language; and
   3. deficits in developing, maintaining, and understanding relationships such as difficulties matching behavior to social contexts, difficulties with imaginative play and making friends, and possibly no interest in peers.

B. Restricted, repetitive patterns of behavior, interests, or activities as manifested by at least two of the following, currently or by history:
   1. stereotyped or repetitive motor movements, use of objects, or speech (e.g., frequently twirling string);
   2. insistence on sameness, inflexible adherence to routines, or ritualized patterns or verbal nonverbal behavior (e.g., difficult transitioning);
   3. highly restricted, fixated interests that are abnormal in intensity or focus (strong attachment to certain objects such as trains); and
   4. hyper- or hyporeactivity to sensory input or unusual interests in sensory aspects of the environment.

Adapted from *Autism Speaks: DSM-5 Diagnostic Criteria*. Retrieved December 9, 2016, from https://www.autismspeaks.org/what-autism/diagnosis/dsm-5-diagnostic-criteria.

relieve anxiety, psychotic responses, attention deficits, and obsessive–compulsive behaviors (Westphal, Kober, Voos, & Volkmar, 2014). Some have a good chance of functioning independently as adults. However, children with more severe forms of ASD, particularly with intellectual disabilities, need the instructional strategies described in this book.

For special education purposes, school assessment personnel must determine that a student meets the definition of a disability as outlined in the special education law, the IDEA 2004. The category of autism was added to the special education law in 1990 during the reauthorization of PL 94-142. Subsequently, the number of students served in special education under the label of autism has continued to rise ever since that time. The definition of autism under the IDEA parallels the DSM-5 diagnostic criteria, although it is less specific. Definitions are developed for the purpose of identifying a distinctive group. If someone falls within a defined group, then it is assumed that services and treatment provided to others in that group might benefit this individual and that things that have failed to help others in the group will not help this individual. More important, funding, services, and advocacy are dispersed to populations who meet a particular definition. The definition of autism according to the IDEA 2004 at this writing is provided as follows:

Autism . . .

means a developmental disability significantly affecting verbal and nonverbal communication and social interaction, generally evident before age 3, that *adversely affects* a child's educational performance. Other characteristics often associated with autism are engagement in repetitive activities and stereotyped movements, resistance to environmental change or change in daily routines, and unusual responses to sensory experiences.

Autism does not apply if the child's educational performance is adversely affected primarily because the child has an emotional disturbance.

A child who manifests the characteristics of autism after age [3] could be diagnosed as having autism if the criteria above are satisfied. (U.S. Department of Education, 2016b)

The important thing to remember is that school personnel should develop instructional programs based on individual assessments rather than simply matching educational plans to diagnoses or definitions.

1-5 Diagnostic Instruments

The diagnosis of autism can be conducted by psychologists, psychological associates, school psychologists, or psychiatrists who are trained to use the DSM-5 for that purpose (APA, 2013). However, special education assessment personnel may use other assessment instruments to determine eligibility for special education services. Some of these instruments are checklists with subsections that address communication and interaction behaviors that are completed by parents and teachers. Some instruments are interviews with those who know the student best, and some are direct observation assessments. The special education comprehensive evaluation may also include intelligence tests and behavioral assessments.

Table 1.5 presents a description of a few formal assessment instruments other than the DSM that are used to diagnose autism and obtain information to plan educational programs. More than one instrument should be used for these purposes to ensure reliability and a well-rounded view of the child. Keep in mind that a diagnosis or label gives only

TABLE 1.5 ● Sample Diagnostic Instruments

- *Autism Diagnostic Observation Schedule*, 2nd ed. (ADOS®-2) (Lord et al., 2012)

  This instrument is a semistructured observational assessment of ASD targeting communication, social interaction, play, and restricted and repetitive behaviors. Sets of activities in each area are presented to the child, and the child's reactions and behaviors are coded and analyzed relative to the diagnosis of autism. This assessment takes as long as an hour to complete and is administered and coded by trained personnel. It can be used with all school-age children and adolescents as well as adults and includes a toddler module for children 12 to 48 months old.

- *Autism Diagnostic Interview, Revised* (ADI®-R) (Rutter, Le Couteur, & Lord, 2003)

  The ADI-R is a semistructured interview conducted by a trained individual with a parent or caretaker who knows the individual well. It can be used for individuals of all ages with a mental age of 2 or more years. The interview can take as long as 3 hours and includes items related to communication, social interaction, and restricted and repetitive behaviors. The ADI-R is often used in conjunction with the ADOS-2 to support diagnostic decisions and differentiate autism from other disorders.

- *Autism Screening Instrument for Educational Planning*, 3rd ed. (ASIEP-3) (Krug, Arick, & Almond, 2008)

  The ASIEP-3 is a combination of checklists and direct observations. It can be used with preschool and school-age children suspected of having autism. Its five subtests include a behavior checklist, a sample of vocal behavior, an interaction assessment, educational or functional skills, and a prognosis of learning rate. The instrument can be used to differentially diagnose those with autism from those with other severe disabilities while giving useful information for placement, planning educational programs, and analyzing progress. The ASIEP-3 requires some training but can be administered by special education personnel, including teachers.

- *Gilliam Autism Rating Scale*, 3rd ed. (GARS-3) (Gilliam, 2013)

  The GARS-3 is a rating scale that consists of four subtests listing typical characteristics of children and youth with autism. The subtests include stereotypical behaviors, communication, social interaction, and developmental disturbances manifested in the first 36 months of life. The rated characteristics closely match those described in the DSM-5. The GARS can be completed by family members and special education personnel, including teachers.

some of the necessary information needed for educational planning. Teachers will need to more fully assess specific educational needs using the assessment methods described throughout this book.

1-6 Program Considerations

The presenting symptomology of individuals with autism can lead to impressive obstacles to learning. These students not only have language and behavioral disorders but also display perceptual deficits, limited comprehension abilities, social limitations, and interfering self-stimulatory responses. As a result, they tend to develop few academic and functional skills when left to their own devices. In addition, these students may be less motivated to explore new environments, communicate their wants and needs, or participate in learning activities.

Another challenge is that students with autism may only attend to unimportant environmental cues (referred to as **stimulus overselectivity**) and will thus struggle to learn discrimination tasks, the foundation for subsequent cognitive development. For example, a teacher may use two or three shirts to teach a student to sort white clothes from colored clothes for washing purposes. The student may notice that the shirt the teacher calls white has a tear on the sleeve and may separate that shirt each time from the other two—not on the basis of color, but on the basis of the sleeve tear. In this case, color discrimination was not learned, so that given different clothes, he probably will not be able to sort whites from colors (unless all of the white clothes happen to have tears).

In addition, individuals with autism tend to display highly individualized responses to typical reinforcers and punishers—that is, they do not prefer things that most other children enjoy such as group activities, but they may enjoy things others do not like such as social isolation. This challenging picture sounds discouraging in terms of educational potential. However, by using techniques that result in direct skills training, that bring clarity to a student's environment, and that accommodate the child's multifaceted needs, much can be done to alleviate the barriers common to this condition (Webber & Scheuermann, 2008). The critical task is to develop and implement a practical and comprehensive educational program.

1-6a A Practical Program

The first consideration for programming for this population is to establish a practical approach to education well founded in ABA. This approach should include clearly sequenced goals and objectives derived from direct observation and behavioral assessment in the areas of communication, social competence, and functional life skills. It should also include direct (explicit) instruction such as discrete trial training in an organized, predictable environment. Behavior management, including functional assessment, positive reductive techniques, and aversive consequences when necessary, should be an integral part of the program. Finally, an effective program will include ongoing data collection and evaluation to ensure that progress toward the goals continues in a consistent manner.

Clearly Sequenced Goals

Establishing educational goals depends not only on targets for current functioning but also on consideration of the level at which students will need to function in the next few years and what skills they may need as adults. Assessment for educational programming calls for school personnel and parents to collaborate in pinpointing specific functional tasks that will serve the student well at home, in the community, and at school each year. It also requires speculation about and analysis of future placements. For example, if a student is to be transferred to a middle school in the next few years, it would be best to teach those skills that will be necessary for a successful transition. In addition, goals should include consideration of the ultimate objective of preparation for independent adult functioning in normalized settings (Brown, Nietupski, & Hamre-Nietupski, 1976). Later chapters explain how to conduct assessments to determine educational goals in all areas of functioning.

Explicit Instruction of Skills

Functional goals are one aspect of a practical program; explicit instruction is another. Explicit instruction implies that the teacher purposefully uses systematic, direct, engaging, and success-oriented instruction to move a student toward designated goals (Archer & Hughes, 2017). Explicit instruction strategies use a stimulus–response format.

Explicit instruction usually includes a multistep approach. First, the teacher gains the student's attention, sometimes indicating what is to be learned (e.g., "Dana, look at me. It's time to work on your words."). Second, the teacher presents a stimulus, usually in the form of a command, although it could also be a visual stimulus such as written directions. For example, the teacher may say, "Point to the word 'stop.'" Third, the teacher may prompt the correct response by guiding the student's hand or offering visual or verbal cues. Fourth, the teacher waits for the clearly defined student response (e.g., the student will point to the correct word card with the index finger within 10 seconds). Depending on the student's response, the teacher will now give a consequence or feedback as step 5. If the response is correct, then the teacher may reinforce the student by saying "Good." If the response is incorrect, the teacher may not say anything, repeat the stimulus command, and provide more effective prompting.

This drill-and-practice format has been found to be an effective instructional strategy for students with autism who need to learn new skills or become fluent in skills already learned (Granpeesheh, Tarbox, & Dixon, 2009). Explicit instruction allows for training skills in incremental steps (e.g., teaching each step for brushing teeth) or for teaching skills as whole tasks (e.g., teaching how to go through the cafeteria line as an entire process). In both cases, the teacher presents a cue, assists the student to respond correctly, identifies a correct response, and gives feedback to the student.

Explicit instruction can be used one on one or with groups of students. Such strategies can be used to teach someone to talk, read, or compose a research paper. The point is that explicit instruction provides clear expectations, assistance, and feedback, making the student's environment predictable and success more likely. Chapter 5 will provide more specific information about explicit instruction strategies.

Explicit instruction models also include ongoing assessment. Teachers will need to keep a record of correct and incorrect student responses. This type of assessment provides information as to whether the student is learning what the teacher intends to teach. Often these data are transferred to graphs, providing a visual presentation of the student's progress. This type of assessment forms the basis for revising goals, moving to new goals, or adapting instructional strategies. Without systematic program evaluation, the teacher may waste valuable instructional time either teaching things the student has already mastered or failing to teach things that the student needs to learn. Chapters 2 and 5 will provide more information on this type of assessment and evaluation.

Behavior Management

A third important component of a practical program involves behavior management. Because many students with autism display behavioral excesses that could interfere with learning appropriate skills, teachers may find it necessary to apply strategies for reducing these excesses. An **instructional approach** to behavior management is generally recommended (Alberto & Troutman, 2017).

An instructional approach to behavior management includes a **functional assessment** that will determine the relationship of the excessive behavior to environmental variables such as time of day or certain people. A functional assessment also provides information regarding the purpose of the student's excessive behavior (e.g., he gets out of the task when he tantrums).

After determining what might be cueing and maintaining an excessive behavior, an intervention plan is developed. This plan should include ways to change or eliminate environmental contributors to inappropriate behavior and ways to change things that might be happening apart from the school that might exacerbate inappropriate behavior (e.g., a new bus driver who yells). In addition, the plan should include alternate appropriate or replacement behavior that the student needs to learn that will be functional for the student. In most cases, these replacement behaviors will be communicative—that is, act as **functional communication**. For example, if a student is thought to tantrum in order to get out of work, it would be best to teach him to say "Out please" for that purpose. The plan should include strategies for teaching these replacement behaviors and for reinforcing their use. **Differential reinforcement** is an important component of this instructional approach. Sometimes additional reductive techniques such as time-outs or response cost are needed so that the student can learn to respond in ways that will enhance learning. Chapters 2 and 3 provide specific information about reductive strategies and behavior management in general.

Ecological Assessment

One program component that almost guarantees an individualized and thus effective educational plan is **ecological assessment**. Such an assessment results in a list of skills that a particular student needs to function in settings in which she currently participates and those in which she will participate in the future (Browder & Spooner, 2011).

First, an inventory of skills is constructed using checklists or direct observation or both. The subsequent inventory of necessary skills then becomes an assessment tool for determining the student's current functioning. Through further observations and interviews, the teacher can determine which skills on the inventory the student has already mastered, partially mastered, or still needs to learn. After delineating which specific skills remain to be learned, school personnel can work with parents to prioritize exactly what needs to be taught that will best meet the student's needs now and in the future. Chapter 4 will offer more specific information regarding ecological assessment.

Curriculum Related to Postschool Adult Goals

The ecological assessment process results in an emphasis on *skills*, usually **functional skills** (i.e., those that an individual must perform to avoid dependence on others), and on *age-appropriate* activities and settings. Sometimes this curriculum includes content from the standard academic curriculum.

Educators must constantly evaluate curriculum for the purpose of weeding out that content and those skills that are not directly relevant to a particular individual in light of current and future performance. It also means choosing learning activities that meet a student's developmental and educational needs while reflecting activities in which other children of the same age participate. For example, a 17-year-old student who wants to listen to music would best be taught to access the music on a smartphone rather than on a CD player. Chapter 4 will offer more information about developing appropriate, individualized curriculum.

Attention to Generalization

Functional and maybe academic age-appropriate skills not only should be taught but also taught in a way that will allow the student to perform those skills in natural settings (e.g., where those skills are actually used). Thus, educators must plan and teach these students to use their language, social, and functional skills with different people, using different materials, and in different settings. This will increase the likelihood that the student will eventually be able to use those skills independently in all settings. We call this transfer of skills **generalization**. Students with autism typically do not generalize their skills because of their dependence on rote memorization and their tendency to attend to unimportant environmental cues. If a student can only perform tasks with specific materials, then the task loses some of its functional qualities. For example, if a student can only sort whites from colors using the shirt with the torn sleeve, then he will not be able to appropriately wash any clothes except those three shirts. Or if a student can only read from one textbook, then she will not be able to read labels in the grocery store, signs on doors, or the newspaper. Or if a student learns to use a specific toaster in the classroom, he may not be able to use the toaster in his home simply because it is a different type of toaster.

Students not only may need to learn to use various types of materials but also may need to learn to perform in various settings even with the same materials. Because students with autism overattend to environmental cues, they often become dependent on those specific cues to respond. Thus, a student may read his book only when sitting in his bedroom because a specific chair by the window cues him. This is one reason why change typically bothers individuals with autism—because the external cues they come to rely on may no longer be available. It is therefore imperative that students with autism be taught to perform in a variety of settings and under various conditions.

One way to ensure generalization across settings is to teach skills in the environment in which they will be used. Referred to as **community-based instruction**, students are taken to various places—such as their home, a laundromat, a recreational center, restaurants, or a shopping mall—and taught skills required to operate in those specific environments. For example, a student is taught to order hamburgers during lunchtime at the local hamburger restaurant instead of during a drill-and-practice session in the special education classroom. Other methods of ensuring generalization across people, materials, and settings will be discussed further in Chapter 5.

Integration and Placement

Attention to generalization across settings also means that teachers, in keeping with the least restrictive environment clause of IDEA 2004, may teach students to perform successfully in general education classrooms if the student's IEP committee determines such a placement is appropriate. Integration and independent functioning in normalized settings are always long-term goals. Thus, we encourage consideration of placement into specific integrated settings based on individual needs. General education classrooms do not typically simulate out-of-school environments, so teaching particular students in settings outside of school altogether may be more effective than concentrating on inclusion in general education, particularly at the secondary level. Placement, which should be age appropriate, is determined by deciding where particular targeted goals can best be taught. A practical program emphasizes that curricular, strategy, and placement decisions are dictated by individualized assessment. This is not only practical but also required by law.

1-6b Teacher Characteristics

A final point regarding educational programming for students with autism concerns teacher competency. Given that the best program will require individualized assessment, an organized classroom, specific and detailed curriculum development, collaboration skills, and the relentless application of behavioral principles, successful teachers are those with certain attributes. Table 1.6 lists those attributes thought to enhance successful instruction for students with autism. These attributes probably do not predict success nor does their absence prohibit success, but given the requirements for personnel who will be teaching these challenging students, discussion of facilitating characteristics seems helpful.

TABLE 1.6 ● **Characteristics of Successful Teachers**

- Consistency
- Persistence
- Flexibility
- Creativity
- Organization
- Intuitive sensitivity
- Energy
- Likes children
- Well-developed sense of humor
- Mastery of applied behavioral analysis and developmental theories
- Mastery of data-based instruction
- Commitment to the right to the most effective treatment

Consistency

Because individuals with autism have difficulty with discrimination and social interactions, they respond best within consistent environments. In fact, they often insist on routine and sameness. Teachers who are consistent in terms of their commands, prompts, routines, body language, and consequences will elicit the best responses from students with autism.

Persistence

Teachers need to be persistent in their effort to teach in the sense that they should continually try to find effective instructional strategies.

Flexibility

A teacher of these students must be flexible and be willing to try new things when others do not work. They need to refrain from insisting on "the way they've always done it." In this book, we will provide a toolbox of options from which teachers can choose. The important thing is to work with an expansive toolbox.

Creativity

Creativity is called for because of this population's idiosyncratic responses to common stimuli and their often bizarre behavior. For example, an adolescent who insists on carrying bags of trash might be taught to put his trash in a briefcase and limit himself to only 10 trash items. A teacher's creative idea to redefine the way trash is carried rather than eliminating the behavior altogether would probably result in socially appropriate behavior without causing undo anxiety or aggression.

Organization

Teachers also need to be extremely organized in several ways. First, the classroom and the instructional process need to be predictable. Second, goals and objectives must be specified, sequenced, and clearly communicated to anyone who works with the student. Third, the teacher needs to monitor interventions conducted by related service personnel (i.e., speech therapists, occupational therapists, teacher assistants) and ensure that consistency is established. Finally, the teacher needs to document progress in a fashion that is understandable to everyone. The primary emphasis of the educational program is on an organized classroom.

Intuitive Sensitivity

Because students with autism do not communicate well, it is important for teachers to be intuitively sensitive. By this, we mean that teachers need to be able to understand what a child is trying to communicate even though he cannot say it. This sensitivity depends on astute observations of body language and contextual variables. Chapter 3 provides instruction on functional assessment that will facilitate this skill. Low communication ability also dictates that teachers be able to view the world from the student's point of view or "walk in his shoes."

Energy

Teachers who are tired and lethargic are not likely to be able to elicit responses from these unique and often challenging students who typically cannot easily decipher subtle social cues or ask clarifying questions. Monotone voices and apathetic facial expressions do little to facilitate responses from these children.

Likes Children

A teacher needs to *like children*. Teaching is a strenuous profession that requires long hours of planning and coordination. Students with autism need teachers who genuinely care for them and enjoy spending time with young people. Although these students may need assistance attending to social cues, they seldom have trouble determining who likes or dislikes them.

Well-Developed Sense of Humor

A sense of humor is one attribute that will do much to prevent burnout among professionals working with challenging students. Humor provides a successful outlet for stress and prevents teachers from taking failures or themselves too seriously. A good sense of humor also facilitates the flexibility factor previously mentioned.

Belief in Efficacious Programs

Effective teachers of students with autism also hold certain beliefs. These essential beliefs for teachers of students with autism have to do with program efficacy. We have found that the most effective professionals believe in the efficacy of ABA and *data-based instruction*. This mindset results in their mastery and implementation of behavioral programming and formative assessment. Clearly, these effective instructional techniques will be adequately applied if personnel believe they will work. If they do not believe these techniques will work, then there is a good chance they will not.

Commitment

Finally, a key attribute for school personnel is the *commitment to the right to the most effective treatment* (Van Houten et al., 1988). Programs should be chosen based on what we know through research will work rather than what is easy to apply; based on what the student needs to learn rather than what the teacher wants to teach; and based on the student's best interest rather than the teacher's disposition.

Scrutinizing fad cures and refusing to apply techniques that have no efficacy basis in research is critical. It is also important to be willing to apply techniques that are known to be effective with this population, even though they may require a great deal of work. Chapter 9 will offer further discussion of efficacious programs. Furthermore, these techniques must be applied correctly—what we call *treatment fidelity*. Time-out, for example, is a widely used—but often misused—technique.

Teacher competence can be one of the deciding prognostic influences for students with autism, especially for young children (Lang et al., 2010). It is extremely important that teachers be well trained, possess essential attributes, and implement the most effective program possible. Without this, most students with autism will not only fail to progress in their learning but, unfortunately, may regress.

1-7 Family Issues

Given the characteristic behavioral excesses and deficits associated with autism, it should come as no surprise that parenting these children is a difficult task—one for which most parents are ill prepared. The trials associated with raising a child with autism can negatively affect their ability to provide basic care and nurturing as well as hurt their family relationships (Soresi, Nota, & Ferrari, 2007).

Educators must understand the continuous and pervasive challenges faced by these parents. In this way, teacher will be better able to establish a collaborative relationship with parents and family members and provide necessary support. It is also important to confront the tendency of some educators to blame parents for their children's disability, for not taking highly active roles in the child's education, for not accepting "reality" when it comes to their child's needs, for not being willing to look ahead and plan for the future, and so forth. As the saying goes, "walking a mile in their shoes" will build empathy and should make for a better parent–teacher relationship. Perhaps most important, good collaborative relationships with parents can benefit all parties. Our experiences have been that parents are invaluable information sources and are often especially well informed about current research, legislation, and issues.

Although it is widely accepted that parents cannot cause autism and that evidence strongly points to a biological basis for the disorder, parents of children with autism still have to deal with many practical and emotional problems. Emotionally, many parents experience shame and guilt with the birth of a child with a disability. Despite evidence to the contrary, they may believe they are somehow responsible for their child's disorder. As the child grows older, thwarted expectations continually arise as parents see normal children reach the milestones of childhood and adolescence while their own child lags behind. The child's lifelong dependency on his or her parents causes anxiety about what will happen after the parents die. Will their child with autism be able to live and work independently? Will siblings have to assume responsibility for their brother or sister with autism?

If the child has an intellectual disability, he may linger in infant and toddler stages. This creates the practical problems of teaching self-help skills that other children seem to learn effortlessly, dealing with general health factors and managing difficult behavior. In addition, few services (e.g., child care, respite services, health care, supported living, leisure and recreational options, job placement) might be available to the family because of the child's communication and social deficits and behavioral problems. Social activities for the family might be severely curtailed, and financial burdens may increase as additional services such as ABA therapy are purchased.

Because individuals with autism usually appear physically normal, the general public may not realize the child or adolescent has a disability when he displays aggressive or bizarre behavior in public places. Onlookers may blame parents for inadequate parenting. Furthermore, the parents, seeing some precocity in memory, artistic tendencies, or mathematical skills, may have unrealistic expectations for the child and continue to be disappointed or blame themselves or the school if the child does not meet perhaps unrealistic expectations. Children with autism may show little affection and appear aloof, so overwhelmed and disappointed parents will likely receive little reinforcement from their children themselves.

Parents living in rural areas often must deal with difficult children virtually alone because support groups made up of people who understand the disorder may not be readily available. Naturally, under these conditions a family will likely experience stress and strain. This means that educators must attempt to understand the extreme emotional turmoil and practical challenges experienced by families with children with special needs and assist in supporting them while including them in their individualized planning process.

Supporting parents might be in the form of *support* that includes sharing resources and referrals to community agencies, and providing information about autism, effective teaching strategies, and the process for developing appropriate curriculum. *Training* parents might be required for skills such as parent-mediated interventions for social and communication skills and for reducing problem behaviors (Bearss, Burrell, Stewart, & Scahill, 2015). Positive outcomes for students with ASD have been found to increase when parents acquire appropriate knowledge about ASD (e.g., prognosis, characteristics, etiology, the nature of the disorder), ABA (e.g., reinforcement, prompting, functional behavioral assessment, reductive techniques), and communication and social skills training (e.g., spontaneous speech, milieu teaching, functional communication) (Kaminski, Valle, Filene, & Boyle, 2008; Schultz, Schmidt, & Stichter, 2011).

Like students, parents have unique abilities, needs, and limitations, so their involvement needs to be individualized. Some parents may need someone to listen to them and provide basic information and support, and others may be ready to be involved in advocacy activities, as classroom volunteers, or as equal partners with teachers to provide and evaluate educational programs. Some may want regular communication with the teacher, whereas others may ask for assistance with problem solving for their many challenges (e.g., behavior at home). In working with families, it is also important to consider mental health status, socioeconomic status, family composition (e.g., multiple children with disabilities), parental stress, and parental abuse of alcohol or drugs (Machalicek, Lang, & Raulston, 2015; Matthews & Hudson, 2001). For teachers, the important thing to remember is to be prepared to involve and support parents as individuals and to avoid drawing false generalizations about them. Advocacy organizations such as the Autism Society of America, Families for Early Autism Treatment (FEAT), and Autism Speaks (see Table 1.1) also provide parent and family programs and resources.

Parents who receive adequate support and good training in the techniques outlined in this book not only enhance their child's functioning but also feel more in control of their own lives (Schultz, Schmidt, & Stichter, 2011). Meaningful parental involvement plus good teachers are essential ingredients for effective education.

Summary

Although we can read about historical characters who appear to have autism, the disorder has only been described and its etiology researched in recent years. Currently, the social, language, and cognitive characteristics are believed to be functions of neurological impairment. Unfortunately, the exact nature of this impairment and its possible causes remain elusive. Despite this, we have learned much since the early 1970s about how to educate children and youth with autism.

The most convincing findings regarding effective education pertain to behavioral interventions based in ABA. This means that curriculum is clearly and specifically delineated, that the teacher directs instruction, often in a one-to-one format, and that the teacher collects data to ensure that learning is occurring. Furthermore, it means that behavior management of excessive behavior includes an analysis of contextual contributors, manipulation of environmental predictors, and the application of positive reductive techniques whenever possible.

The best curriculum for a student with autism is one that is developmentally appropriate, matched to targeted adult goals, and taught in suitable environments. The curriculum should also be determined based on individual needs and assessment information. Best practices dictate that parents and family members be included as much as possible in their child's program. Keeping in mind the notable emotional, physical, and economic toll a child with autism can place on a family, parents should be encouraged to participate at their own pace. Because students with autism have such multifaceted needs, their education and treatment require teachers to be committed to evidence-based practices, individualized curriculum development, and, most important of all, to believe that this type of programming will work.

Key Points

1. The syndrome of *autism* was first named and described by Leo Kanner in 1943.

2. Current research supports the hypothesis that autism is a neurological disorder characterized by impairment in communication and social ability and a display of restrictive interests and repetitive behaviors. Exactly what causes the neurological impairment has not yet been determined, although it is thought there may be many causes.

3. The symptoms associated with the autism spectrum range from mild (requiring only some support) to severe (requiring substantial support) (APA, 2013).

4. Behaviors associated with autism can be divided into behavioral deficits and behavioral excesses.

5. Techniques based in ABA are recommended, including explicit instruction, reinforcement, environmental arrangement, and data-based instruction.

6. Families with children with autism have valuable perspectives and insight. Teachers should include family members as integral participants in educational program planning and be prepared to provide support and training when needed.

References

Ahrens, E. N., Lerman, D. C., Kodak, T., Worsdell, A. S., & Keegan, C. (2011). Further evaluation of response interruption and redirection as treatment for stereotypy. *Journal of Applied Behavior Analysis, 44,* 95–108.

Alberto, P. A., & Troutman, A. C. (2017). *Applied behavior analysis for teachers* (9th ed.). Columbus, OH: Pearson.

American Psychiatric Association (APA). (2013). *Diagnostic and statistical manual of mental disorders: DSM-5* (5th ed.). Washington, DC: American Psychiatric Association.

Anderson, M. P. (2016). Neuropathology of autism spectrum disorder. In C. J. McDougle (Ed.), *Autism spectrum disorder* (pp. 205–223). New York: Oxford University Press.

Archer, A. L., & Hughes, C. A. (2017). Explicit instruction: Effective and efficient teaching. Retrieved February 22, 2017, http://explicitinstruction.org/

Baer, D. M., Wolfe, M. M., & Risley, T. R. (1968). Some current dimensions of applied behavior analysis. *Journal of Applied Behavior Analysis, 1,* 91–97.

Baily, A. M., Le Couteur, A., Gottesman, I., Bolton, P., Simonoff, E., Yuzda, E., & Rutter, M. (1995). Autism as a strongly genetic disorder: Evidence from a British twin study. *Psychological Medicine, 25,* 63–77.

Baron-Cohen, S., & Wheelwright, S. (2004). The empathy quotient: An investigation of adults with Asperger syndrome or high functioning autism, and normal sex differences. *Journal of Autism and Developmental Disorders, 34,* 163–175.

Bearss, K., Burrell, T. L., Stewart, L. M., & Scahill, L. (2015). Parent training in autism spectrum disorder: What's in a name? *Clinical Child and Family Psychology Review, 18,* 170–182.

Ben-Sasson, A., Hen, L., Fluss, R., Cermak, S. A., Engel-Yeger, B., & Gal, E. (2009). A meta-analysis of sensory modulation symptoms in individuals with autism spectrum disorders. *Journal of Autism and Developmental Disorders, 39,* 1–11.

Bent, C. A., Barbaro, J., & Dissanayke, C. (2016). Change in autism diagnoses prior to and following the introduction of DSM-5. *Journal of Autism and Developmental Disorders, 47,* 163–171.

Beversdorf, D. Q., Manning, S. E., Hillier, A., Anderson, S. L., Nordgren, R. E., Walters, S. E., et al. (2005). Timing of prenatal stressors and autism. *Journal of Autism and Developmental Disorders, 35,* 471–478.

Birtwell, K. B., Willoughby, B., & Nowinski, L. (2016). Social, cognitive, and behavioral development of children and adolescents with autism spectrum disorder. In C. J. McDougle (Ed.), *Autism spectrum disorder* (pp. 19–30). New York: Oxford University Press.

Browder, D. M., & Spooner, F. (2011). *Teaching students with moderate and severe disabilities.* New York: Guilford Press.

Brown, L., Nietupski, J., & Hamre-Nietupski, S. (1976). The criterion of ultimate functioning and public school services for severely handicapped students. In M. A. Thomas (Ed.), *Hey, don't forget about me! Education's investment in the severely, profoundly and multiply handicapped* (pp. 2–15). Reston, VA: Council for Exceptional Children.

Centers for Disease Control and Prevention (CDC). Autism spectrum disorder (ASD). Retrieved November 29, 2016, from https://www.cdc.gov/ncbddd/autism/data.html.

Clark, M. L. E., Barbaro, J. & Dissanayake, C. J. (2016). Continuity and change in cognition and autism severity from toddlerhood to school age. *Journal of Autism Developmental Disorders*, 1–12.

Coghill, D. (2015). Commentary: We've only just begun: Unraveling the underlying genetics of neurodevelopmental disorders—a commentary on Kiser et al. (2015). *The Journal of Child Psychology and Psychiatry*, 56(3), 296–298.

Coghill, D., Nigg, J., Rothenberger, A., Sonuga-Barke, E., & Tannock, R. (2005). Whither causal models in the neuroscience of ADHD? *Developmental Science*, 8, 105–114.

Constantino, J. N., Todorov, A., Hilton, C., Law, P., Zhang, Y., Molloy, E., et al. (2013). Autism recurrence in half siblings: Strong support for genetic mechanisms of transmission in ASD. *Molecular Psychiatry*, 18, 137–138.

Durand, V. M., & Berotti, D. (1991). Treating behavior problems with communication. *American Speech and Hearing Association*, 11, 37–39.

Fernell, E., Eriksson, M.A., & Gillberg, C. (2013). Early diagnosis of autism and impact on prognosis: A narrative review. *Clinical Epidemiology*, 5, 33–43.

Geurts, H. M., Sinzig, J., Booth, R., & Happe, F. (2014). Neuropsychological heterogeneity in executive functioning in autism spectrum disorders. *International Journal of Developmental Disabilities*, 60, 155–162.

Gilliam, J. E. (2013). *Gilliam Autism Rating Scale*, 3rd ed. (GARS-3). Austin: Pro-Ed.

Gökçen, E., Frederickson, N., & Petrides, K. V. (2016). Theory of mind and executive control deficits in typically developing adults and adolescents with high levels of autism traits. *Journal of Autism and Developmental Disorders*, 46, 2072–2087.

Gotham, K., Bishop, S. L., Hus, V., Huerta, M., Lund, S., Buja, A., et al. (2013). Exploring the relationship between anxiety and insistence on sameness in autism spectrum disorders. *Autism Research*, 6, 33–41.

Grandin, T. (1995). The learning style of people with autism: An autobiography. In K. A. Quill (Ed.), *Teaching children with autism: Strategies to enhance communication and socialization.* New York: Delmar.

Granpeesheh, D., Tarbox, J., & Dixon, D. R. (2009). Applied behavior analytic interventions for children with autism: A description and review of treatment research. *Annals of Clinical Psychiatry*, 21, 162–173.

Green, G. (1996). Early behavioral intervention for autism: What does research tell us? In C. Maurice (Ed.), G. Green, & S. C. Luce (Co-Eds.), *Behavioral intervention for young children with autism: A manual for parents and professionals* (pp. 29–44). Austin: Pro-Ed.

Howard, J. S., Sparkman, C. R, Cohen, H. G., Green, G., & Stanislaw, H. (2005). A comparison of intensive behavior analytic and eclectic treatments for young children with autism. *Research in Developmental Disabilities*, 26, 359–383.

Itard, J. (1972). *The wild boy of Aveyron* (E. Fawcett, P. Ayrton, & J. White, Trans.). London: NLB Publishers. (Original work published 1801.)

Kaminski, J. W., Valle, L. A., Filene, J. H., & Boyle, C. L. (2008). A meta-analytic review of components associated with parent training program effectiveness. *Journal of Abnormal Child Psychology*, 36, 567–589.

Kanner, L. (1985). Autistic disturbances of affective contact. In A. M. Donnellan (Ed.), *Classic readings in autism* (pp. 11–53). New York: Teachers College Press.

Keenen, M., & Dillenburger, K. (2011). When all you have is a hammer . . . : RCTs and hegemony in science. *Research in Autism Spectrum Disorders*, 5, 1–13.

Krug, D. A., Arick, J. R., & Almond, P. J. (2008). *Autism screening instrument for educational planning*, 3rd ed. (ASIEP-3). Austin: Pro-Ed.

Lang, R., Hancock, T. B., & Singh, N. N. (2016). Overview of early intensive behavioral intervention for children with autism. In R. Lang, T. Hancock, & N. N. Singh (Eds.), *Evidenced-based practices in behavioral health.* New York: Springer.

Lang, R., O'Reilly, M. F., Sigafoos, J., Machalicek, W., Rispoli, M., Shogren, K., Chan, J. M., Davis, T., Lancioni, G., & Hopkins, S. (2010). Review of teacher involvement in the applied intervention research for children with autism spectrum disorders. *Education and Training in Autism and Developmental Disabilities*, 45, 268–283.

Levin, A. R., & Nelson, C. A. (2015). Inhibition-based biomarkers for autism spectrum disorder. *Neurotherapeutics*, 12, 546–552.

Lord, C., Rutter, M., Dilavore, P. C., Risi, S., Gotham, K., & Bishop, S. L. (2012). *Autism diagnostic observation schedule*, 2nd ed. (ADOS®-2). Torrance, CA: WPS.

Lovaas, O. I. (1987). Behavioral treatment and normal educational and intellectual functioning in young autistic children. *Journal of Consulting and Clinical Psychology*, 55, 3–9.

Machalicek, W., Lang, R., & Raulston, T. J. (2015). Training parents of children with intellectual disabilities: Trends, issues, and future directions. *Current Developmental Disorders Reports*, 2, 110–118.

Matthews, J. M., & Hudson, A. M. (2001). Guidelines for evaluating parent training programs. *Family Relations*, 50, 77–86.

McConnell, K., & Ryser, G. R. (2014). *Practical ideas that really work for students with autism spectrum disorder: High functioning autism.* Austin: Pro-Ed.

McCoy, K. M. (2011). *Autism from the teacher's perspective: Strategies for classroom instruction.* Denver: Love Publishing.

McDougle, C. J., Landino, S. M., Vahabzadeh, A., O'Rourke, J., Zürcher, N. R., Finger, B. C., Palumbo, M. L., Helt, J., Mullett, J. E., Hooker, J. M., & Carlezon, W. A. (2015). Toward an immune-mediated subtype of autism spectrum disorder. *Brain Research*, 1617, 72–92.

Murphy, M., Bolton, P. F., Pickles, A., Fombonne, E., Piven, J., & Rutter, M. (2000). Personality traits of the relatives of autistic probands. *Psychological Medicine*, 30(6), 1411–1424.

National Institute of Neurological Disorders and Stroke (NINDS). (2016). Autism Spectrum Disorder Fact Sheet. Retrieved December 3, 2016, from http://www.ninds.nih.gov/disorders/autism/detail_autism.htm.

Offit, P. A. (2008). *Autism's false prophets: Bad science, risky medicine, and the search for a cure.* New York: Columbia University Press.

Palmen, S., & van Engeland, H. (2004). Review on structural neuroimaging findings in autism. *Journal of Neural Transmission*, 111(7), 903–929.

Piven, J., Arndt, S., Bailey, J., & Andreasen, N. (1996). Regional brain enlargement in autism: A magnetic resonance imaging study. *Journal of the American Academy of Child and Adolescent Psychiatry, 35*(4), 530–536.

Prizant, B. M. (1983). Language acquisition and communicative behavior in autism: Toward an understanding of the "whole" of it. *Journal of Speech and Hearing Disorders, 48*, 296–307.

Rapin, I., Dunn, M. A., Allen, D. A., Stevens, M. C., & Fein, D. (2009). Subtypes of language disorders in school-age children with autism. *Developmental Neuropsychology, 34*, 66–84.

Russo, N., Flanagan, T., Iarocci, G., Berringer, D., Zelazo, P. D., & Burack, J. A. (2007). Deconstructing executive deficits among persons with autism: Implications for cognitive neuroscience. *Brain and Cognition, 65*, 77–86.

Rutter, M., Le Couteur, A., & Lord, C. (2003). *Autism Diagnostic Interview, revised* (ADI®-R). Torrance, CA: WPS.

Sanders, S. J., et al. (2012). De novo mutations revealed by whole-exome sequencing are strongly associated with autism. *Nature, 485*, 237–241.

Schaaf, R. C., Benevides, T., Mailloux, Z., Faller, P., Hunt, J., van Hooydonk, E., Freeman, R., Leiby, B., Sendecki, J., & Kelly, D. (2014). An intervention for sensory difficulties in children with autism: A randomized trial. *Journal of Autism and Developmental Disorders, 44*, 1493–1506.

Schultz, T. R., Schmidt, C. T., & Stichter, J. P. (2011). A review of parent education programs for parents of children with autism spectrum disorders. *Focus on Autism and Other Developmental Disabilities, 26*(2), 96–104.

Simpson, R. L., & McGinnis, E. (2016). *Skillstreaming children and youth with high-functioning autism*. Champaign, IL: Research Press.

Sivapalan, S., & Aitchison, K. J. (2014). Neurological structure variations in individuals with autism spectrum disorder: A review. *Bulletin of Clinical Psychopharmacology, 24*(3), 268–275.

Skwerer, D. P., Jordan, S. E., Brukilaccio, B. H., & Tager-Flusberg, H. (2015). Comparing methods for assessing receptive language skills in minimally verbal children and adolescents with autism spectrum disorders. *Autism, 20*(5), 591–604.

Smith, T. (1999). Outcome of early intervention for children with autism. *Clinical Psychology: Science and Practice, 6*, 33–49.

Soresi, S., Nota, L., & Ferrari, L. (2007). Considerations on supports that can increase the quality of life of parents of children with disabilities. *Journal of Policy and Practice in Intellectual Disabilities, 4*, 248–251.

Sterponi, L., & de Kirby, K. (2016). A multidimensional reappraisal of language in autism: Insights from a discourse analytic study. *Journal of Autism and Developmental Disorders, 46*(2), 394–405.

Tager-Flusberg, H. (2014). Autism spectrum disorder: Developmental approaches from infancy through early childhood. In M. Lewis & K. D. Rudolph (Eds.), *Handbook of developmental psychopathology* (3rd ed., pp. 651–664). New York: Springer.

Trottier, G., Srivastava, L., & Walker, C. D. (1999). Etiology of infantile autism: A review of recent advances in genetic and neurobiological research. *Journal of Psychiatry and Neuroscience, 24*, 103–115.

U. S. Department of Education (2016a). *Thirty-Eighth Annual Report to Congress on the Implementation of the Individuals with Disabilities Education Act, 2016*. Washington, DC: Office of Special Education and Rehabilitative Services, Office of Special Education Programs.

U. S. Department of Education. (2016b). Center for Parent Information and Resources: Subpart A of the Part B Regulations: General Provisions, Part 300.8. Retrieved April 17, 2017, from http://www .parentcenterhub.org/repository/partb-subparta/

Van Houten, R. Axelrod, S., Bailey, J. S., Favell, J. E., Foxx, R. M., Iwata, B. A., & Lovaas, O. I. (1988). The right to effective behavioral treatment. *Journal of Applied Behavior Analysis, 21*, 381–384.

Vorstman, J. A. S., Spooren W., Persico, A. M., Collier, D. A., Aigner, S., Jagasia, R., Glennon, J. C., & Buitelaar, J. K. (2014). Using genetic findings in autism for the development of new pharmaceutical compounds. *Psychopharmacology, 231*, 1063–1078.

Webber, J., & Scheuermann, B. S. (2008). *Educating students with autism: A quick start manual*. Austin: Pro-Ed.

Westphal, A., Kober, D., Voos, A., & Volkmar, F. R. (2014). Psychopharmacological treatment of Asperger syndrome. In J. C. McPartland, A. Klin, & F. R. Volkmar (Eds.), *Asperger syndrome: Assessing and treating high-functioning autism spectrum disorders* (2nd ed.). New York: Guilford Press.

Zielinski, B. A., Anderson, J. S., Froehlich, A. L., Prigge, M. B. D., Nielsen, J. A., Cooperrider, J. R., et al. (2012). scMRI reveals large-scale brain network abnormalities in autism. *PLoS ONE, 7*(11), e49172.

Zürcher, N. R., & Hooker, J. M. (2016). Neuroimaging of autism spectrum disorder. In C. J. McDougle (Ed.), *Autism spectrum disorder* (pp. 149–159). New York: Oxford University Press.

2

Basic Behavioral Principles and Strategies

LEARNING OBJECTIVES

After reading this chapter, you will be able to:

2-1 Define and describe applied behavior analysis (ABA).

2-2 Define the *three-term contingency* and related ABA terminology.

2-3 Explain how to implement basic ABA techniques.

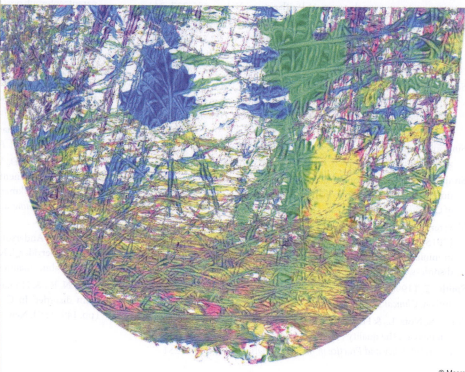

© Moore

As you learned in Chapter 1, children and youth with autism exhibit behavioral characteristics that make this population challenging to teach. An effective educational program for students with autism must be designed to address both behavioral excesses (e.g., challenging behavior) and behavioral deficits (e.g., social skills). Instructional approaches that work well with students with other types of disabilities may not always produce desired outcomes for students with autism. However, research in autism and related fields has produced an abundance of techniques that have been found effective for most students with autism, even for those students who face the most severe challenges. These evidenced-based practices are grounded in behavioral science and involve basic principles that can be used across settings, professionals, and caregivers.

The field of study that has generated a majority of these techniques is **applied behavior analysis (ABA)**. Currently, many agencies and institutions recommend ABA to educate and treat people with autism, including the American Academy of Pediatrics as well as the Centers for Disease Control and Prevention (CDC). In addition, well-designed ABA-based interventions include all of the characteristics of effective intervention as described by the National Research Council (e.g., CDC, 2015; Keenan & Dillenburger, 2011).

Although many people tend to associate ABA procedures only with behavior management aimed at reducing challenging problem behaviors, ABA-based approaches are also powerful tools for teaching. ABA procedures can be used to increase a child's social, communicative, academic, vocational, and functional behaviors; decrease or eliminate challenging behaviors; and teach new behaviors to individuals with or without disabilities, of all levels of functioning and ages (e.g., Palmen, Didden, & Lang, 2012; Virues-Ortega, 2010). Based on the available research, ABA-based procedures are clearly essential components of effective programs for students with autism (Walsh, 2011).

This chapter describes some of the basic behavioral principles and several common ABA-based practices suitable for students with autism. The primary aim of this chapter is to provide an overview of these fundamental elements of high-quality behavioral programs and to introduce many of the terms and concepts that will be explored in greater detail in subsequent chapters. Diligent students may find themselves referencing this chapter repeatedly as they work through the remainder of the text.

> **Did you know that:**
>
> - Education and intervention programs based on a field of study called *applied behavior analysis* (ABA) have been shown to be effective in teaching many important skills to students with autism?
> - ABA views behavior as predominantly influenced by environmental (nurture) rather than by internal (nature) factors?
> - Reinforcement is an important tool for *reducing* challenging behaviors by increasing appropriate behaviors and teaching new skills?
> - If you want a student's behavior to change, you must change something that *you* are doing or change something about the student's environment?

2-1 Applied Behavior Analysis

ABA can be defined as the application of findings from the scientific study of behavior to issues of importance to society, families, and individuals in which data are collected as part of an ongoing effort to confirm or refine targeted behavioral outcomes (Baer, Wolf, & Risley, 1968). The central tenets are: (a) ABA is an applied science that relies on empirical methods to identify the factors that produce behavior change; (b) tactics (sometimes referred to as *technologies*) are then applied systematically through defined steps for implementation; and (c) the focus is on socially significant behavior; in this case, that leads to improved quality of life and educational outcomes for students with autism (Cooper, Heron, & Heward, 2007).

ABA is the *applied* branch of the larger field of behavior analysis and is ideally carried out in natural settings such as schools, homes, and workplaces (e.g., Koegel, Matos-Freden, Lang, & Koegel, 2012). Discussion of the history of ABA is beyond the scope of this text, but even a cursory discussion of ABA would be remiss by not referencing the foundational work of B. F. Skinner, whose research changed the way we discuss, measure, and influence human behavior of all forms (e.g., Skinner, 1938, 1945, 1953, 1981, 1989).

2-1a Tenets of Applied Behavior Analysis

ABA interventions are based on several basic underlying tenets that are founded in behavioral theory and supported by extensive research. These assumptions are explained in Box 2.1. All of the techniques described in the remainder of this text reflect these assumptions. When training others to implement behavioral techniques, we often start by discussing these foundational concepts. This chapter will describe the most essential concepts necessary in effective ABA-based educational programs for students with autism. In the following sections, we explain ABA concepts and principles and provide examples of application in programs for children and youth with autism.

BOX 2.1 • Tenets of Applied Behavior Analysis

Learning history, biological makeup, and current environment all influence an individual's behavior in any given instant (Skinner, 1953). Nature (genetics and physiology) and nurture (learning history) both contribute to human behavior, and that behavior occurs in the context of an interaction between a person and his or her current environment. In terms of a student with autism, this means that even the challenging or unusual behaviors associated with autism have been learned by the child as a result of past experiences in life (i.e., the individual's nurture and learning history). However, in terms of nature, the physiological and genetic differences that may be found in children with autism account to some extent for the differences in the types of behavior they might learn and the elements of the environment that might function as reinforcement or punishment. For example, all children have needs and wants and, although children of typical development will learn to communicate their wants, needs, and emotions through spoken language, many children with autism—who may not as easily develop typical communication skills as a result of autism—may learn to communicate by screaming, crying, or hitting. The learning process is the same (i.e., a result of interaction with environment), but the behaviors acquired may differ.

Here the critical element is that, even when a biological explanation exists for the unusual deficits and excesses associated with autism, research indicates that ABA procedures can help change the behavior by first considering the way children interact with their current environment and then making plans to change future environments in a way that is conducive to skill development. Even when factors related to nature account for the origin of a disorder, behavioral procedures can be successfully applied to help ameliorate the associated symptoms. This is also true for conditions other than autism. For example, behavioral programs can help treat depression (Kanter et al., 2006), seizures (Zlutnick, Mayville, & Moffat, 1975), and attention deficit hyperactivity disorder (Cox & Virues-Ortega, 2016; Gulley et al., 2003).

All operant behavior (i.e., voluntary, nonreflex behavior that is learned), whether appropriate and inappropriate, is governed by the same principles. Generally, a student's behavior can be explained in terms of a combination of basic behavioral principles described in this chapter. Knowing that all operant behavior is governed by the same principles, teachers can attempt to identify the behavioral principles that may explain a student's challenging behavior or skill deficits and then use those principles to teach or increase desired behaviors and reduce challenging behaviors. Even unusual or challenging behaviors serve a purpose—or a function—for the child. For example, a child's challenging behaviors may function to get the child something she wants (positive reinforcement function) or help the child avoid something she does not like (negative reinforcement function). Unless the function of an inappropriate behavior is correctly identified and an intervention is designed based on that function, the intervention is likely to be ineffective. For this reason, functional assessment is a critical step in designing behavioral interventions (Hurl, Wightman, Haynes, & Virues-Ortega, 2016). In Chapter 3, we explain how to conduct a functional assessment.

Behavior is contextual (Foster-Johnson & Dunlap, 1993). Behavior is related to the environment in which it occurs. Attempts to change a behavior without first identifying contextual elements that may be contributing to the problem behavior are often nonproductive. Contextual elements may be external—such as the way instructions are given, a difficult or disliked task, or a distracting environment (e.g., excessive noise in the classroom, a crowded cafeteria, large open spaces in the gym). However, contextual elements may also be internal factors that influence a child's desire for specific reinforcers or aversion to specific punishers. For example, when children are hungry, sleepy, or comfortable because of illness or injury, they often find it more difficult to concentrate and follow directions. In such cases, behaviors that have resulted in negative reinforcement in the form of escape and avoidance of academic tasks will become more likely at the same time behaviors that have been previously reinforced with food, sleep, or comfort also become more likely. An important part of behavioral assessment is the identification of relevant contextual elements and addressing those issues (treating illness, alleviating hunger, etc.).

When the factors influencing behavior are not as easily remediated, intervention might involve changing how instructions are given, reducing the time the student is required to work on certain tasks, offering more choices, or teaching the student a better way to interact with the environment. For example, careful analysis of noncompliance may reveal that the noncompliance is a result of vague, ambiguous directions or directions that are given without having the student's full attention. Rather than punishing the student for noncompliance, a more effective intervention would be to change the manner in which directions are given.

2-2 The Three-Term Contingency

Behavior does not occur in isolation and does not originate solely from within an individual student. Instead, most behaviors exhibited by students with autism—both appropriate and challenging behaviors—are related to events in the environment that occur either before the behavior is exhibited (called **antecedents**) or immediately after a given behavior occurs (**consequences**). Because behavior occurs in response to the antecedent context (e.g., current situation in the classroom), we say the behavior is *contingent* on the antecedent, meaning the behavior (whether it is appropriate or inappropriate) would not have occurred in the same way in the absence of that antecedent. Further, the consequence (whether it be punishing or reinforcing) is contingent on the behavior because the consequence would not have occurred if the behavior had not occurred. For this reason, these three interrelated concepts (antecedent–behavior–consequence) are jointly referred to as the **three-term contingency**. Note that the term *consequence*, which is sometimes taken to be equivalent with the word *punishment* in the vernacular, may refer to reinforcement or punishment in ABA. The three-term contingency is an essential concept in developing effective intervention strategies for students with autism.

Table 2.1 provides several examples of how student behavior can be conceptualized using the three-term contingency. In the first example, a common life skill (dressing) is being taught, and the interaction between the teacher and the student is summarized using the

TABLE 2.1 ● The Three-Term Contingency

Example 1: The three-term contingency during instruction of a self-help skill in a life skills classroom

ANTECEDENT	BEHAVIOR	CONSEQUENCE
Teacher asks a student to button his shirt as part of a program to teach the student to independently dress himself.	The student grasps shirt and pulls at fabric while screaming.	Teacher calmly redirects the student's hand to the button and prompts the correct fine motor skill. (*Note*: Pulling and screaming may have been an attempt to ask for help.)
The teacher prompts the student to button the first button and then says, "Let's try the next button together." Instead of waiting to see if the student does it independently, this time the teacher provides assistance from the start. (*Note*: The previous consequence is often the antecedent for the next behavior.)	The student attempts to button with teacher's assistance (no pulling at clothes and screaming).	The teacher praises the student: "Great job pushing the button through the hole!" (*Note*: Progress on the skill was positively reinforced with praise that specifically acknowledged the aspect of the skill that improved.)

Example 2: The three-term contingency involving a teacher's unintentional reinforcement of challenging behavior

ANTECEDENT	BEHAVIOR	CONSEQUENCE
Teacher tells her preschool class for children with disabilities that it is time for activity centers and then directs a child with autism to the art center where paint and a blank canvas are available.	The child runs from the center and hits a nearby peer.	The teacher says "We do not hit" and then sends the child to time-out.
The child is in time-out, no other students are nearby, and the teacher ignores him.	The child rocks back and forth while humming.	The child has escaped the art center (he may not like the texture of paint) and is now free to engage in stereotypy (which may be a more preferred activity).
The next day the teacher is preparing the room for center time and is about to tell the class to go to centers.	The child hits a peer.	The teacher sends the child to time-out. [*Note*: Even though the teacher's intent was to decrease the child's aggression, she actually has been teaching that hitting is a way to request escape from a nonpreferred activity (centers) or a way to request access to a preferred activity (free time for stereotypy)!]

(continued)

TABLE 2.1 ● **The Three-Term Contingency** (*continued*)

Example 3: The three-term contingency involving a teacher appropriately using extinction and reinforcement to teach a child to remain on-task

ANTECEDENT	BEHAVIOR	CONSEQUENCE
The teacher gives a child several coins (pennies and nickels) and asks the child to sort the coins.	The child begins sorting the coins.	The teacher gives the child a small sticker of a train (a known reinforcer) and pairs it with behavior-specific praise ("Thank you for following directions!").
Child receives a sticker and praise, and the teacher moves away to help another student.	The child continues to stay on task for 2 minutes.	The teacher returns and delivers another sticker and more praise. (*Note:* The teacher knows this child typically stays on task for 2 to 3 minutes before getting up and wandering around the room. She intentionally reinforced his on-task behavior before he stopped working.)
Again, the child a receives sticker and praise, and the teacher moves away to help another student. The other student needs to use the restroom and requires teacher assistance. The teacher is gone for 5 minutes.	The child gets up from desk and begins walking around the room.	The teacher returns and, while providing as little attention as possible, redirects the child back to his seat. As soon as the child sits down and touches the coins, the teacher delivers praise but not a sticker.
Teacher moves away a short distance but monitors the child closely.	The child sorts coins for 30 seconds but does so slowly.	The teacher returns and delivers praise, and another sticker is placed on the child's chart.
Teacher moves away a greater distance and helps another child.	The child begins sorting coins more quickly and finishes the task.	The teacher immediately returns and delivers praise and another sticker. She then tells the student that he has enough stickers to go use the computer, which is the child's highest preferred activity. (*Note:* This example involves extinction, reinforcement, redirection, and a token economy system!)

Example 4: The three-term contingency involving an interaction with a peer on the playground

ANTECEDENT	BEHAVIOR	CONSEQUENCE
A student with autism on the school playground is wiggling the chain that holds the swing and is staring as the chain reflects sunlight. A peer approaches and asks the student to play.	Student with autism continues wiggling the chain and does not look at or respond to the peer.	The peer walks away. The student with autism continues wiggling the chain in the sunlight.

three-term contingency model. In that example, the teacher recognizes that the challenging behavior may be a request for assistance with a difficult task. To avoid reinforcing the child's challenging behavior (grabbing shirt and screaming), the teacher does not allow the child to escape the task. Instead, she changes her approach to prompting and increases her use of praise as the child begins to do some small part of the task.

In the next example presented in Table 2.1, the teacher is unaware of how his actions will influence the student's behavior and unintentionally increases the child's challenging behavior through a combination of positive and negative reinforcement. (Reinforcement is discussed in more detail later in this chapter.) In the third example, the teacher is expertly using a combination of extinction and reinforcement to assist a student learning an early skill related to counting money. An important point illustrated in Table 2.1 is that children are always learning—but it may not always be the lesson we intend to teach.

Finally, in the fourth example, the teacher is not involved, but the three-term contingency model is applied to help identify a potential skill to teach (i.e., social skills on the playground) and a potential obstacle to acquiring that skill (i.e., preference for stereotypic behavior). Remember, children learn from a variety of sources (including other children) and across a variety of settings (e.g., recess on the playground). This example underscores the importance of observing children with autism in multiple environments as part of an effort to identify target skills for instruction.

2-2a Focus on Antecedents

As revealed in Table 2.1, **antecedents** are events that occur immediately before a behavior is exhibited, and antecedents play an important role in the occurrence of subsequent behaviors. Antecedents serve as cues for both appropriate *and* inappropriate or challenging behavior. It is important to identify the antecedents that consistently precede challenging behaviors and examine whether those antecedents should be changed. In addition, when teaching new behaviors, you should identify the specific antecedent components that should cue those behaviors. For example, if you are teaching a student to request a desired food (perhaps by verbally asking or maybe using a picture card exchange), you might teach the student to exhibit that behavior in response to the antecedent cue "What do you want to eat?" Similarly, you might teach a student to shake hands in response to an antecedent context that includes someone extending their hand in greeting.

Specific aspects of the antecedent condition that evoke a specific behavior are referred to as **discriminative stimuli**, which is often abbreviated S^D. S^Ds are elements of the antecedent environment that signal when a specific reinforcing consequence is available for a specific behavior (e.g., the availability of social attention is signaled when someone offers his or hand during a greeting). The S^D concept is presented in additional detail later in the chapter.

Antecedents usually occur in proximity to the behavior in question (see Table 2.1). For example, if you give a student a task that will involve a loud mechanical noise (e.g., vacuuming) and he dislikes that type of noise, the task may serve as S^D for escape or avoidance of noise and evoke aggression that has previously (and unintentionally) been negatively reinforced when the child is sent out of the room away from the noise. On the other hand, music time is likely to be an antecedent for paying attention and following directions for a student who loves music.

Teachers should understand the contingent relationship between antecedents, S^Ds, and behavior and use this information when planning instruction or behavior management programs. If a specific antecedent is known to likely result in challenging behavior, then you may be able to either eliminate or modify the antecedent to reduce the challenging behavior. The following examples illustrate how modifying antecedents can produce desirable changes in behavior.

- For the student who dislikes mechanical noises, you could modify the task to make it more agreeable by teaching the student to vacuum while listening to music on headphones.
- Consider a student who tantrums in the hallway each time the class goes to lunch. You speculate that the tantrums are the result of the chaotic and crowded conditions in the hallway. You might arrange to go to lunch at another time when the hallways are not filled with students or to take an alternative and less crowded route.
- Perhaps a student has severe tantrums unless allowed to have a favorite object. You might allow the student to keep the object on his desk during work times if it does not decrease his on-task behavior.
- For a student who is noncompliant to verbal instructions, you may need to simplify instructions (e.g., giving only one direction at a time).

Additional exciting and effective antecedent intervention techniques are discussed throughout this chapter and the remainder of the book.

2-2b Focus on Behavior

Behavior refers to specific voluntary (e.g., not reflexive), observable actions (sometimes referred to as *responses*) exhibited by students. These might be academic behaviors (reading, solving math problems, writing their names), language behaviors (answering yes–no questions, initiating social greetings, using sign language to make requests), motor behaviors (throwing a ball, climbing stairs, riding a bike), play or leisure behaviors (stacking blocks, playing a video game, reading a comic book), work or daily living behaviors (folding towels, stocking shelves), or self-help behaviors (combing hair, tying shoes, toileting). In terms of teaching students with autism, some behaviors must be increased or strengthened, some must be decreased or eliminated, and some must be newly taught.

We have said that data-based teaching is an important element of programs for students with autism. To accurately measure progress, target behaviors must be described precisely using observable, measurable terms. We refer to this as **operationalizing** a behavior or creating an **operational definition**. A good strategy for determining if a behavior is adequately operationalized is to consider whether two people would be able to observe the student and agree on whether the defined behavior is or is not occurring. Operational definitions of target behaviors should enable you and others working with the student to be consistent when measuring and providing contingent consequences for a behavior. Vague descriptions of behavior will often result in ineffective interventions and inaccurate measures of progress. Table 2.2 lists examples and nonexamples of operationally defined behaviors and notes why each nonexample is unsuitable.

Different terms are often used to refer to different types of behavior. When a teacher identifies a behavior that needs to change (either increase or decrease), it is often referred to as a **target behavior**. The behaviors that tend to cause teachers the most distress are **challenging behaviors**. Challenging behaviors are those that are harmful or dangerous (e.g., hitting or biting self or others, running away from caregivers), interfere with the child's learning (e.g., knocking work tasks off the table, tearing materials), or interfere with desired

TABLE 2.2 ● Examples and Nonexamples of Operationally Defined Behaviors

Examples

- *Finger flicking:* holding or wiggling fingers in front of or to the sides of the eyes
- *Self-injury:* hitting head with fist or open hand with sufficient force to make a sound or that appears likely to produce tissue damage or bruising
- *Rocking: moving the torso* back and forth or side to side for more than 5 consecutive seconds while sitting in chair
- *Toy play:* using a toy or other play material (e.g., clay, puzzle) in the manner in which it is intended to be used without spinning, smelling, or tasting the object
- *On task:* actively engaging with the materials associated with a task demand in a manner consistent with the materials' intended use or looking at the teacher while instructions are being delivered

Nonexamples and Why Each Is Not a Good Operational Definition

- *Silly:* acting in a way that is inappropriate
  - It is not clear what the child is actually doing or what is considered inappropriate.
- *On task:* being compliant
  - *Compliance* is just another word for being on task and does not provide any additional information.
- *Aggression:* intending to hurt someone
  - We can never know someone's intent with certainty. In addition, a child's intention may be to escape or avoid something (as in Example 2 in Table 2.1) or to obtain attention or some tangible. Hitting, for example, is aggression regardless of intent.
- *Self-esteem:* how children feel about themselves or their performance
  - It is not possible to directly observe self-esteem or to know how a child feels. We can only guess based on the child's observable behavior, and that behavior is not described.

social and developmental goals (Didden et al., 2012). Teachers often target challenging behaviors to be reduced or eliminated. We discuss approaches to the functional assessment and treatment of challenging behaviors in Chapter 3.

Attempting to simply reduce or eliminate a challenging behavior is seldom productive without simultaneously teaching the child an appropriate alternative behavior that serves the same function or purpose—that is, a **replacement behavior**. Sometimes, replacement behaviors are already in the child's repertoire (i.e., something they can already do), and we simply need to teach the child to use those behaviors more consistently or produce those behaviors in response to different and more appropriate discriminative stimuli. Finally, some desired replacement behaviors are *not* part of a child's repertoire and must be taught. (e.g., these may become the **target skills**).

2-2c Focus on Consequences

The last part of the three-term contingency is the **consequence**. The type of consequence that follows a behavior determines whether or not the behavior will be more or less likely to occur again the next time the same discriminative stimulus occurs in the antecedent environment. If the consequence is reinforcing (i.e., desired by the student), the behavior will probably be repeated when similar circumstances arise again. If the consequence is undesirable, chances are that the behavior will occur less often in the future.

In general, consequences are divided into two main categories: *reinforcement*, which increases the likelihood that a behavior will be repeated, and *punishment*, which reduces the likelihood that a behavior will be repeated. Reinforcement is the most important ABA concept for teachers, and there are two types of reinforcement contingencies: positive and negative reinforcement. Understanding the concepts of positive and negative reinforcement in some preliminary detail is important before proceeding through the remainder of the chapter.

Positive Reinforcement

Positive reinforcement is a process in which something (praise, tangible item, etc.) is given to the student or added to the student's environment following a behavior. Remember, "positive" in positive reinforcement means to add or give and does not necessarily mean "good." If, as a result of that consequence, a behavior occurs more often in the future, positive reinforcement has occurred. Positive reinforcement has occurred *only* if there is an increase in the behavior. Thus, you cannot be sure positive reinforcement has occurred unless you observe an increase in the behavior it follows. The actual item—praise or activity—that is delivered is called a **positive reinforcer** or **reinforcer**. For example, each time a student responds correctly during individual teaching time, you praise her. If she responds correctly more often in the future, you could assume that you have positively reinforced correct responding using praise as a reinforcer.

Negative Reinforcement

The second type of reinforcement is **negative reinforcement**. In the same way that "positive" does not mean "good" in positive reinforcement, the word *negative* in negative reinforcement does not mean "bad." Instead, "negative" denotes the fact that something was taken away or avoided. Specifically, negative reinforcement has occurred when an aversive condition is avoided or ends contingent on a particular behavior. When something the student finds aversive or simply does not like is removed or avoided contingent on a behavior, then that behavior is reinforced and becomes more likely to occur again when circumstances are similar.

Negative reinforcement is *not* a type of punishment and does not decrease behavior. Instead, it is used to increase desired behaviors. For example, a teacher may tell a student "if you stay on task for this class period, I will allow you to skip today's homework." Because homework (likely an aversive unwanted task) is avoided contingent on a behavior, this is an example of negative reinforcement if, of course, the target on-task behavior increases.

For children with autism, other potential forms of negative reinforcement include breaks from in-class work, removal of an unwanted item, or stopping some form of aversive stimulation. For example, some children with autism may find certain types of light, sounds, or textures to be aversive; using negative reinforcement, these students can be taught to request that the lights be dimmed, music be turned down, or clothes be changed.

Negative reinforcement may also be the reason some challenging behavior occurs. For example, if children hit peers they want to go away and the peers leave as a result of the aggression, the children's aggression has been negatively reinforced. Similarly, if a student with autism is having a tantrum because he does not want to go to circle time and the teacher sends the child to time-out (i.e., child is allowed to avoid circle time), then the child is more likely to tantrum next circle time because of negative reinforcement (see Table 2.1).

Chapter 3 discusses negative reinforcement and challenging behavior in more detail. Additional detail on how to implement reinforcement effectively is discussed later in this chapter.

2-3 Implementing ABA Techniques

This section is an introduction to ABA techniques and provides brief descriptions of how a teacher might implement basic ABA techniques. To cover these issues, it is necessary to use several scientific terms related to ABA. These terms (presented in bold throughout this book) are useful because they facilitate precise communication and empower teachers to consider new research that may be helpful to improving their practice. However, because this terminology is not often in the vernacular, many parents, professionals, and others will not know these scientific definitions. Therefore, teachers and other practitioners of ABA should avoid using jargon that alienates or precludes meaningful input from stakeholders (Bailey & Burch, 2016).

2-3a Concepts and Techniques Related to Antecedents

As you can see in Table 2.1, the term *antecedent* refers to a broad category of environmental events that may lead to certain behaviors. Teachers should be able to identify antecedents that consistently proceed challenging behaviors and create antecedent environments that facilitate desired behaviors for individual students.

Motivating Operations

Even when antecedents are carefully considered and arranged appropriately, certain factors change the likelihood that a particular behavior will occur. For example, when you have a bad cold and cough, you may not smile or talk to your colleagues as much as you normally do, or you may avoid going to work that day altogether. Your discomfort from the cold reduces the reinforcing value of social interaction with your colleagues and increases the reinforcing value of avoiding some activities. Conditions that indirectly affect behavior by increasing or decreasing the power of a specific contingent consequence are known as **motivating operations (MOs)** (Langthorne & McGill, 2009; Laraway, Snycerski, Michael, & Poling, 2003). If you feel badly enough when you are ill, the potential social reinforcement of interacting with your friends may not be enough to motivate you to stop and talk. However, if you have not seen a particular friend in a long time, you may go out of your way to stop and talk to her because of an increase in the reinforcing value of the interaction. Similarly, a student with autism and attention-deficit hyperactivity disorder (ADHD) (the conditions can co-occur) who did not take his ADHD medication may be less likely to complete certain tasks, even though he usually likes the activity that is contingent on task completion (e.g., finishing desk work is reinforced by being allowed to read a comic book). The appeal of the reinforcer (referred to as **reinforcer power** or **reinforcer value**) may be insufficient to motivate him under this condition. A teacher who understands the concept of MOs might offer this student more powerful reinforcers, reinforce more frequently during work tasks, or may reduce the number or difficulty of work tasks on the day the student forgets his medication.

Stimulus Control

When a specific element of the antecedent environment (an S^D) reliably cues a specific behavior (or class of behaviors), the behavior is said to be under **stimulus control**. For example, when the fire alarm sounds in a school, students predictably stop what they are doing and exit the building according to the route on the school's fire-safety plan. They do not engage in this behavior unless they hear the fire alarm, so stopping what they are doing and moving to the exit in that specific way means they are under stimulus control of the fire alarm. As noted earlier, antecedents that predictably cue certain behaviors are called *discriminative stimuli* (S^D). S^Ds cue specific behaviors by signaling the availability of a reinforcer. For example, a teacher asking a question to her class should be an S^D that signals the availability of attention and praise from the teacher contingent on providing an answer.

There are many examples of stimulus control in everyone's life across every environment. For example, when your phone vibrates, you probably check the screen to see who is calling or texting. The vibration (the S^D) serves as a cue for you to check the screen (behavior). What you see on the screen then serves as an S^D for you to answer the call (if you want to talk to the caller) or screen and avoid the call if you do not want to talk to the person calling. The ring or vibration is an S^D because you typically do not pick up the phone and say "What's up?" unless you hear the ring and check the screen. Comparably, when a new acquaintance extends his hand and says, "Hi, my name is Rajeev" (S^D), you grasp his hand and reply, "Hi, Rajeev. I'm glad to meet you" (behavior). When you are driving and see a stop sign next to the intersection, you predictably apply the brakes. The stop sign serves as an S^D to cue the behavior of stopping the vehicle. Therefore, stopping the vehicle is under the stimulus control of the stop sign.

Stimulus control is a valuable concept in teaching and has the potential to facilitate an increase in desired behaviors and reduction in challenging behavior. In fact, it is a primary component of a teaching method known as *discrete trial teaching*, which we will present in Chapter 5. S^Ds can come in many different forms: verbal signals, nonverbal signals, mechanical signals, printed text, visual schedules, environments, and situations. Table 2.3 lists examples of S^Ds that might be useful for working with students with autism and potential target behaviors that could be taught in response to those S^Ds.

Stimulus control is learned. Although some students will learn to respond to some S^Ds without special instruction (e.g., students typically learn that the end of one activity within the daily schedule signals the beginning of the next activity in a familiar schedule), other stimulus control relationships must be directly taught using the steps described in Table 2.4.

Antecedents play an important role in teaching students with autism. Modifying antecedents and teaching stimulus control are usually simpler and often more effective approaches to behavior management than relying on consequences alone. Sometimes, however, antecedent modification alone is insufficient, and consequences (reinforcement) are necessary for behavior change. In addition, consequences are always necessary for learning new skills. We discuss consequences later in this section, but first we describe the second element in the three-term contingency, *behavior*, which refers to responses or skills targeted for change.

2-3b Concepts and Techniques Related to Behavior

Previously, we discussed the importance of using operational definitions for behaviors that are targeted for intervention. In this section, we explain how to measure those behaviors. Behavior measurement is an essential part of ABA-based programs.

TABLE 2.3 ● Examples of Discriminative Stimuli and Possible Responses

VERBAL S^Ds	
DISCRIMINATIVE STIMULUS	**RESPONSE**
"Quiet hands."	Student stops stereotyped behavior and puts hands in lap.
"Time to work."	Student sits in assigned seat and waits for task.
"Stop, please."	Student who is running from teacher stops immediately.
"Playtime!"	Student goes to toy shelf, selects a toy, and sits on play rug.

NONVERBAL S^Ds	
DISCRIMINATIVE STIMULUS	**RESPONSE**
Teacher turns off the classroom lights for a few seconds.	Students stop talking and look at the teacher.

MECHANICAL S^Ds	
DISCRIMINATIVE STIMULUS	**RESPONSE**
Timer runs during independent work time.	Student remains on task.
Bell rings following recess.	Students line up in front of teacher.

SCHEDULE AS AN S^D	
DISCRIMINATIVE STIMULUS	**RESPONSE**
A regularly scheduled activity ends.	Student stands up and places the picture card for that activity in the "finished" pocket and then selects the picture card for the next activity.
Student finishes toileting.	Student approaches sink and washes hands.

ROUTINE AS AN S^D	
DISCRIMINATIVE STIMULUS	**RESPONSE**
Student approaches the lunchroom worker waiting at the end of the lunch line.	Student enters her lunch number on the keypad.
Youth gets in car.	Youth fastens seat belt.
A peer approaches student on playground and asks if he wants to play ball.	Student responds verbally and joins the game.
Young man approaches fast-food counter.	Young man places order.
Girl enters checkout lane at grocery store.	Girl unloads cart.
Bus pulls up to bus stop and door opens.	Student enters bus.

Measuring Behaviors

Michael is a student with autism who exhibits high rates of off-task behavior (e.g., he repeatedly places his hands over his face in a way that blocks his vision) during individual work sessions with the teacher. Before intervention, Michael was touching his face this way an average of 139 times per 20-minute work session. In the first phase of intervention, Michael's face touching dropped to 130 face touches per work session and then 120 touches in the second phase. Without counting those face touches, it would have been especially difficult for Michael's teacher to determine that intervention appeared to be reducing face touches. In fact, if she had not counted face touches, she may have abandoned her intervention, incorrectly assuming that it was not working. By measuring the

TABLE 2.4 ● **How to Establish Stimulus Control**

1. *Determine the desired target behavior.* What is it you want the student to do in the presence of the S^D? Examples of target behaviors include begin work, continue working (remain on task), respond to a greeting, look at the teacher, stop stereotyped behavior or self-injurious behavior, or stop running away from the teacher.

2. *Determine what the S^D will be.* Virtually any word, phrase, sound, sign, picture, gesture, and so on can be established as an S^D. However, the S^D that you select should be easy to use; ideally, it will be an S^D for the same behavior in other environments outside of the classroom. It should also be something that the student sees or hears only when the target behavior is called for; something that will get the student's attention—that is, it must be noticeable by the student—even when accompanied by many distractions.

3. *Present the S^D and prompt the desired response.* (Chapter 5 discusses prompting in detail.) Remember, the student does not yet know what he is supposed to do, so immediately after you present the S^D, help the student perform the desired response. For example, one approach to teaching a child to stop walking or running when he hears a teacher say "Stop, please" is to hold hands and walk with the student (e.g., down the hall) and say "Stop, please" (the S^D) after a few steps as you gently hold the student's hand to prompt him to stop. When he stops, reinforce the stopping by saying, "You stopped walking when I said stop. Wonderful!" while you also present a tangible reinforcer at the same time if necessary. Then "Let's walk again" and repeat the steps. This practice could be embedded into the student's daily schedule by presenting the S^D a couple times during each transition with the student.

4. *Teach the student to discriminate between the S^D and other stimuli.* Because you want the student to respond predictably to specific stimuli, the next step is to introduce other stimuli. After the behavior occurs predictably and without prompting in the presence of the S^D, use other stimuli as part of the instructional process. Of course, the target response is reinforced only when it occurs in the presence of the S^D. For example, the student should not stop when he hears nearby children talking to each other saying the word *stop* in a different context.

5. After the desired stimulus control is established (i.e., the student consistently exhibits the correct response with no prompts when the S^D is presented), **fade** (gradually reduce) the reinforcement beginning with any tangible reinforcer that might have been necessary when the skill was first being taught. After the response is established, reinforce intermittently (that is, reinforce regularly but not for every response) using only praise.

target behavior, the teacher was empowered to detect the subtle changes in the frequency of face touching and thus made a correct instructional decision to continue her approach. Sometimes, such as in Michael's case, target behaviors change in such small increments that it would be difficult to determine whether the intervention is working without data and a corresponding graph.

Behavior measurement allows you to determine pretreatment levels of behavior, called a baseline. After intervention is initiated, continued measurement of target behaviors enables you to carefully oversee the effects of instructional and behavioral interventions so that adjustments can be made in a timely fashion if the intervention is not producing desired effects. The following sections explain the most common behavior measurement techniques.

Behavior Measurement Techniques

Behavior measurement systems are used to monitor many types of behavior, including both behavioral excesses (a behavior decrease is desired) and deficits (an increase is desired). Data collected using these systems are usually displayed in line graphs for easy interpretation. Visual analysis of graphed data allows teachers or parents to determine objectively whether target behaviors are changing in the desired direction and to check progress of target behaviors over time. Behavior measurement does not have to be difficult. The steps for measuring behavior are explained in Table 2.5.

There are many ways to measure behavior, and a creative teacher—or a teacher who has studied data collection, analysis, and graphing in more detail—will be prepared to track student progress on a wider range of skills. Although many behavior measurement techniques exist, the two presented in this chapter will provide teachers with sufficient information to make informed instructional decisions in most cases. The following sections describe two behavior measurement systems, give general examples for application, and explain how to graph data.

TABLE 2.5 ● Steps in Measuring Behavior

1. *Operationally define the target behavior.*

2. *Determine which measurement system you will use.* In this chapter, we describe two commonly used measurement systems. The system you use is determined by the characteristics of the target behavior to be measured.

3. *Determine a specific place and time when data collection will occur.* Depending on the target behavior and other logistics, you may want to collect data on a target behavior during the student's entire day every day. That would certainly provide the most comprehensive data to consider. However, it may be impractical unless the target behavior occurs only a few times per day. For more frequent target behaviors or those that occur only in one specific setting (e.g., wiggling the chain on the swing set on the playground), your data-collection sessions may be limited to when the child is in a specific location or conducted during briefer periods of time. When data collection occurs only during a subset of the student's day or on some days but not others, then we refer to it as a **data probe**. Probes may be as brief as a few minutes in some cases. If possible, try and collect data in the same way consistently over time. If you change the way you collect data, it may be difficult to determine if changes in the behavior you are measuring are the result of changes in the child's behavior or changes in the way you collect data. If necessary, convert your data to a rate or percentage of time for easier comparison. Note any change to the way you collect data on the graph of your data in such a way that you can tell when the change occurred.

4. *If possible, measure behavior for three to five observation periods before you begin intervention.* Data from these observations are called **baseline data** and will allow you to examine the effects of the intervention on the level of the target behavior compared to the level of the behavior before intervention began (**baseline**). For example, in Michael's case, his teacher counted how many times Michael touched his face during three work sessions before implementing the intervention. These baseline data were graphed (see Figure 2.2) before the intervention was implemented. The teacher continued collecting data during work sessions and charting those data on the graph. These data, compared to baseline data, indicated improvement in the target behavior. In some cases, you may need to implement intervention quickly for safety reasons. For example, if the child is engaging in severe self-injury or aggression, it may not be ethical to allow him to continue to do so in the absence of an intervention. You can still determine if a behavior is decreasing, but you will not be able to know for sure if the decrease is caused by your intervention unless you can compare to a baseline.

5. *Regularly graph the data so you can monitor your student's progress closely and adjust your approach as needed.* Generally, data are graphed using a simple line graph. This gives you a picture of how the behavior is changing—if it is increasing or decreasing as desired. Graphs are helpful for making instructional decisions and for communicating with parents and other professionals about a student's progress. Sometimes it is appropriate to have students participate in graphing data collected on their target behaviors. For example, using data collected by the teacher, a student who is able to do so might graph how many times he initiated social interactions with peers during the day, how many math problems he completed correctly, or how long it took her to vacuum the carpet. Participating in graphing such data or observing daily improvements in target behaviors depicted on the graph may be reinforcing to some students.

Event Recording The method of **event recording** (also called **frequency recording**) is used when the goal is to increase or decrease the *number of times* a student exhibits a target behavior that:

- has a clearly observable beginning and end (e.g., reading a sight word, using the restroom);
- does not occur over long periods of time (sleeping, staring out the window, vacuuming, playing with a toy, or staying in a seat would probably not be appropriate for event recording); or
- does not occur at extremely high frequencies (hand flapping or finger flicking may not be appropriate for event recording if the motions occur too quickly to count).

Event recording involves simply marking a tally each time the target behavior occurs during the measurement period. Golf stroke counters or handheld mechanical counters are easy to obtain and may be useful for situations in which it is inconvenient to carry a pencil and recording sheet (e.g., on the playground or on field trips).

Some behaviors should only occur in response to a specific stimulus (e.g., number of times a student follows a verbal direction or number of social responses). These types of behaviors should be under tight stimulus control; specifically, they should not occur unless a specific stimulus is present. For example, the skill of responding appropriately to a social initiation can only occur after another person has initiated the social interaction.

In measuring behaviors that are restricted by the occurrence of an opportunity (e.g., presentation of a particular S^D), you should record the number of opportunities to respond as well as the number of times the desired behavior occurred (see sample form

TARGET BEHAVIOR: Compliance with verbal directions

OBSERVATION PERIOD: 9:15–9:30 (morning group)

DATE	DIRECTIONS GIVEN	DIRECTIONS FOLLOWED	CALCULATION	PERCENTAGE
10/21	卌 卌 III	卌 III	8/13 x 100	62%
10/22	卌 卌 IIII	卌 II	7/14 x 100	50%
10/23	卌 卌 II	卌	5/12 x 100	42%

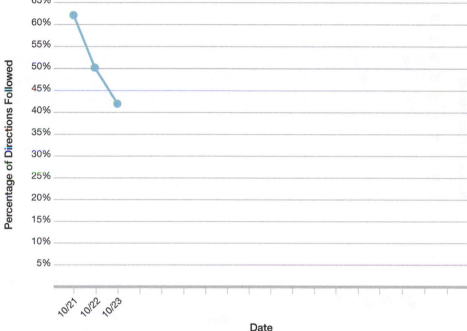

FIGURE 2.1 Sample data form for recording event data per opportunity and corresponding graph

⌄ **Professional Resource Download**

in Figure 2.1). Data should then be converted to a percentage of opportunity for graphing purposes. Otherwise, a change in the frequency of the target that is merely the result of a change in the number of opportunities to engage in the target skill may be mistaken as a change a skill proficiency.

When collecting data using event recording, it is important to remember that the period of time during which data collection is occurring should either be held constant (e.g., collecting data for 20 minutes every day; see Figure 2.2) or be converted to a rate. For frequency data, the rate is an expression of how often the target behavior occurs within a given time frame. For example, if you witness 3 incidents of self-injury during a 30-minute observation on Monday and then observe 6 incidents during a 60-minute observation on Tuesday, you might be tempted to conclude that self-injury was increasing. However, because the observation period during which data were collected was twice as long on Tuesday, the rate (1 hit every 10 minutes on average—0.1 hits per minute) did not change.

Duration Recording The technique of **duration recording** is used to measure how much time is spent engaged in a behavior and is a better choice when the goal is to increase or decrease the amount of time a behavior is exhibited. It is used for behaviors that have a clear beginning and end such as how long it takes a student to wash his hands, how long

TARGET BEHAVIOR: Number of face touches (face touching any surface for any length of time)

OBSERVATION PERIOD: 2:00–2:20 (working 1:1 with teacher or assistant)

DATE	OCCURRENCES	TOTAL FOR DAY
9/02	卌 卌 卌 卌 卌 卌 卌 卌 卌 卌 卌	55
9/03	卌 卌 卌 卌 卌 卌 卌 卌 卌 卌 卌 卌	61
9/04	卌 卌 卌 卌 卌 卌 卌 卌 卌 卌	50
9/05	卌 卌 卌 卌 卌 卌 卌 卌 卌 卌 卌 卌 卌 IIII	64

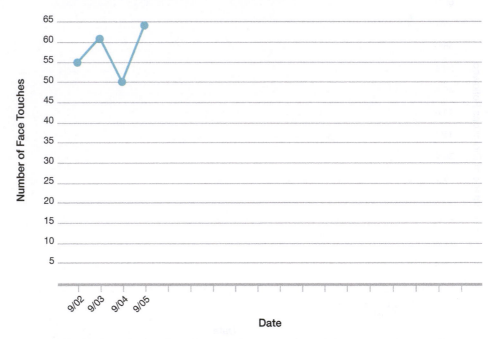

FIGURE 2.2 Sample data form for recording event data and corresponding graph

it takes a student to complete an assigned task, or how long a student sits next to a peer. A stopwatch is a convenient way to measure the duration of behaviors, or you may simply record the start and stop times of the target behavior. Duration data should be graphed as units of time (e.g., minutes and seconds). (See Figure 2.3.)

As with a frequency count, data-collection sessions involving a duration measure must either be the same amount of time every session or the data will need to be adjusted to allow for accurate comparison across sessions. When duration data collection occurs for differing periods of time across sessions, it is necessary to convert the data to a percentage of time spent engaged in the target behavior.

To do this, divide the amount of time spent engaging in the target behavior by the total amount of observation time for that session and then convert to a percentage. For example, if Aubree spent 15 minutes of a 45-minute observation session pacing around the room on Monday (33 percent of the time) and 15 minutes pacing out of a 30-minute observation on Tuesday (50 percent of time), then Aubree's pacing may have increased even though the total amount of time was 15 minutes on both days.

For many behaviors, more than one measurement system may be appropriate. You should select the measurement system (or systems) that best matches the nature of the behavior you are measuring but is also practical in the context of your teaching situation. It may be

TARGET BEHAVIOR: Amount of time student keeps headphones correctly placed on his head

OBSERVATION PERIOD: Free time (in classroom), 3:00–3:20

DATE	START	STOP	DURATION
1/07	3:04	3:05	1 minute
1/08	3:05	3:05:30	30 seconds
1/12	3:07	3:07:30	30 seconds
1/13	3:00	3:03	3 minutes
1/14	3:06	3:08:30	2 min., 30 sec.
1/15	3:05	3:10	5 minutes
1/16	3:08	3:14	6 minutes

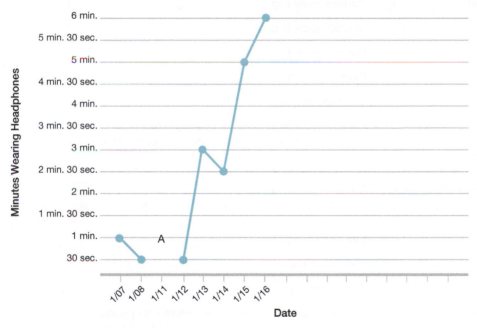

FIGURE 2.3 Sample data form for recording duration data

⌄⌄ **Professional Resource Download**

impossible to count every single occurrence of a target behavior for all students every day. Only accurate data are valuable, and data are only accurate when data-collection systems are manageable. Therefore, you may need to define daily or weekly data-collection periods for each target behavior. For example, frequency of refusals for each student may be counted each morning, between 9 and 11. Stereotypical behaviors might be counted during daily structured play periods.

We provide examples of behaviors and potentially appropriate measurement systems in Table 2.6. However, you may find it necessary to be creative in your approach to data collection. For example, some teachers may be able to record video of their students and collect data from the recording after the students leave.

Without precise monitoring of these behaviors, you will probably not know in a timely manner whether an intervention is working because you may not be able to detect subtle changes in target behaviors. In Chapter 5, you will learn how to apply event and duration recording for tracking behaviors targeted for increase, including how to use these measurement systems as part of a structured teaching format known as *discrete trial teaching*.

TABLE 2.6 ● Measurement Systems for Specific Target Behaviors

The following measurement systems can be used to monitor each of the target behaviors listed. More than one measurement system can be used.

DESIRED BEHAVIORS	POTENTIAL MEASUREMENT SYSTEM
Responding to a greeting	Event recording calculated as percentage of opportunities
Number of words read correctly from a passage	Event recording calculated as percentage of opportunities
Number of math problems solved	Event recording calculated as percentage of opportunities
Following directions	Event recording calculated as percentage of opportunities
Number of dishes washed before refusing	Event recording calculated as percentage of opportunities
Making a request	Event recording
Number of envelopes stuffed	Event recording
Amount of time spent vacuuming before refusing	Duration recording
How long it takes student to put on jacket	Duration recording
Amount of time spent listening to music	Duration recording
Sitting next to peers without hitting	Duration recording
Time spent playing with a peer	Duration recording
Keeping glasses on face	Duration recording
Participating in group game	Duration recording (length of time until student walks away) or event recording (number of turns student takes before leaving game)
How long student spends brushing teeth	Duration recording
Amount of time spent climbing on playground equipment	Duration recording
CHALLENGING BEHAVIORS	POTENTIAL MEASUREMENT SYSTEM
Biting self or others	Event recording
Grabbing materials	Event recording
Screaming	Event recording
Hitting teacher in response to a direction	Event recording calculated as percentage of opportunities
Finger flicking	Event recording or duration recording
Rocking	Event recording or duration recording
Posturing (holding body in unusual positions)	Event recording or duration recording

Graphing Data

After you have gathered data on target behaviors, the next step is to graph the data. A graph allows for visual inspection of data and empowers teachers to make more informed decisions about how to proceed with a student's educational program.

Table 2.7 explains the steps in graphing data. Figures 2.1, 2.2, and 2.3 each show graphs of the raw data depicted in each figure. For the sake of simplicity, these instructions are for drawing your own graph without the need of a computer or software. However, many teachers are comfortable with software programs that produce lovely professional graphs (e.g., Excel®), and we encourage that when possible.

TABLE 2.7 ● How to Graph and Interpret Data

Graphing Data

1. *Convert the data to rate or percentage of time if necessary.* This ensures consistency within data for each target behavior. Guidelines for deciding if you need to convert follow.

    a. If the target behavior can only occur when an opportunity arises, convert the data to a percentage:

    $$\text{number of correct responses} \div \text{number of opportunities to respond} \times 100$$

    b. If you collect data for different amounts of time each day using event recording, convert your data to a rate:

    $$\text{number of times behavior occurred} \div \text{the amount of time,}$$
    expressed as X behaviors per unit of time (e.g., 0.5 behaviors per minute)

    c. If you collect data for different amounts of time each day using event duration recording, convert your data to a percentage of time:

    $$\text{minutes or seconds the behavior occurred} \div \text{total amount of time data were collected}$$

2. *Set up a graph for each target behavior.* To set up a graph, use commercially available graph paper or draw precisely using a ruler.

    a. Draw the vertical line (*y*-axis) and label it to reflect the target behavior that was measured. For example, "number of head hits during play group," "number of responses to social questions," "time spent brushing teeth," or "time between being told to put on jacket and when task actually began."

    b. Draw the horizontal line (*x*-axis) and label it to reflect each observation period. For example, your label might be "daily language sessions" or "daily play periods."

    c. Divide the vertical line into *equal* increments (using squares on graph paper or tick marks on a ruler) and number each increment to show number or percentage or minutes or seconds. The intersection of the vertical and horizontal lines is always zero (0), and numbering begins from there. For example, to set up a graph for event data, you might number the increments "10%, 20%, 30%, 40%," and so on. For a graph to depict duration data, the increments may be numbered "15 sec.; 30 sec.; 45 sec.; 1 min.; 1 min. 15 sec.; 1 min. 30 sec.;" and so on.

    d. Divide the horizontal line into equal increments to reflect the observation periods when data were collected. For example, "2/19, 2/20, 2/21," or "10/4, a.m.; 10/4, p.m.; 10/5, a.m.; 10/5, p.m."

3. *Plot baseline data.*

    a. Data from each observation session are plotted on a consecutive vertical line. These points are called **data points**.

    b. Connect data points using straight lines.

4. *After you are finished gathering baseline data, draw a vertical dotted line next to the last baseline data point.* This **phase line** separates the baseline phase data from the intervention phase data.

5. *Begin intervention and continue the same methods of collecting and graphing data.*

6. *Do not connect the last baseline data point and the first intervention data point*—that is, do not draw a line across the dotted vertical line to connect data points.

7. *If a student is absent for a day or if data are not collected during an observation session, skip that vertical line. Do not connect data points across this space.* Figure 2.3 shows an example of a student's absence and how this is handled on the graph.

8. *If you change anything about the intervention, again draw a dotted vertical phase line next to the last data point of the last intervention. Begin plotting data from the new intervention on the other side of the dotted line.*

Interpreting Data

1. *If a data line shows steady progress in the desired direction (up for behaviors you are trying to increase, down for behaviors you wish to decrease), continue the intervention or instruction until the student's behavior reaches criterion.* It is good practice to measure the behavior occasionally (weekly, monthly) even after the goal has been meet to be sure behavior is maintained at desired levels.

2. *If the data line is flat (suggesting no change) or erratic or inconsistent (too chaotic to determine any change), you should do one or more of the following:*

    a. Examine the intervention to be sure it is being done consistently and correctly.

    b. Modify the intervention slightly. For example, you may wish to reinforce more frequently, use a different reinforcer, or break a target skill down into smaller steps for instruction.

    c. If the target behavior is a challenging behavior, you may need to develop a new hypothesis regarding the contributing factors or function of the behavior (see Chapter 3).

    d. Change interventions entirely. This may mean using a different instructional technique. For a challenging behavior, the new intervention should reflect your new hypothesis.

2-3c Concepts and Techniques Related to Consequences

The term *consequence* refers to environmental events that immediately follow certain behaviors. Consequences are critical because they determine whether or not a behavior will be repeated. Effective teachers need to be aware of consequences that influence behaviors, and must become adept at managing those consequences to facilitate desired changes in behaviors.

Reinforcement

The behavioral deficits of children with autism include both behaviors and skills that are nonexistent and those that do exist but occur too infrequently to be genuinely useful to the student. As discussed previously in this chapter, the frequency of behaviors can be increased using the behavioral principles of positive reinforcement and negative reinforcement. In addition, challenging behaviors exhibited by students with autism are inadvertently strengthened and maintained over time by these same principles. This section will explain these principles and provide tips on how to use them effectively.

Positive and negative reinforcement are important tools in ABA-based classrooms and programs. Reinforcement has the power to increase students' repertoires of appropriate behaviors and is necessary to establish stimulus control. However, like any tool, reinforcement must be used correctly to be effective. In fact, incorrectly used reinforcement can create problems.

The correct use of reinforcement requires systematic and contingent application. *Systematic* application means that reinforcement is planned. Specifically, the behavior(s) targeted for reinforcement, the timing and rate of reinforcement (referred to as the **reinforcement schedule**), and the specific reinforcers to be used must all be predetermined. *Contingent* means that the reinforcer is *only* accessed when the student exhibits the target appropriate behavior.

Reinforcers can take many forms. The following section will introduce you to the different categories of reinforcers and offers suggestions for which type of reinforcer to use under certain conditions.

Categories of Reinforcers When teaching students with autism, teachers sometimes face a challenge when trying to identify effective reinforcers they can control. Many things that are powerful reinforcers for other children and adolescents are either disliked by some students with autism or not useful because the students have not learned to value the specific stimuli intended to function as a reinforcer. For example, students with autism may not be reinforced by receiving a good grade on an assignment or even by teacher praise. This does not mean that teacher-controlled reinforcement cannot be used with these students, only that teachers must carefully identify potential reinforcers. And in some cases they may also have to *teach* students to value certain stimuli so they can create new reinforcers.

There are two basic categories of reinforcers: **primary reinforcers** and **secondary reinforcers**. Examples of each type of reinforcer are listed in Table 2.8.

Primary Reinforcers Primary reinforcers are biological necessities such as food, drink, and items that meet physical needs (e.g., escape from discomfort or pain). Most children do not have to learn to value these reinforcers because these are naturally reinforcing from the beginning of life. Because some children with autism, especially young children, have not learned to like other types of reinforcers, primary reinforcers are valuable teaching tools. For example, you may teach students with autism to begin communicating with other people by teaching them to request a favorite food during snack time. In the context of this instruction, you might also begin teaching a child to make eye contact by requiring her to make eye contact in addition to requesting before positively reinforcing the communication with the requested food. You should also begin **pairing** the primary reinforcer (food) with praise in an effort to establish praise as a more powerful reinforcer.

TABLE 2.8 ● **Examples of Reinforcers**

PRIMARY REINFORCERS

- Sips of juice or water
- Small bites of apples, crackers, carrots, cheese, pretzels, chips, etc.
- Pieces of cereal
- Popcorn

SECONDARY REINFORCERS	
SOCIAL REINFORCERS	**ACTIVITY REINFORCERS**
<ul><li>Praise statements—be sure to be enthusiastic, specific, and use lots of variety when giving praise statements!<ul><li>"Way to go!"</li><li>"Excellent job . . . !"</li><li>"What a great job you did on . . . .!"</li><li>"You're such a hard worker! You finished all of your work before the timer rang."</li><li>"Good job sitting quietly, with hands on desk!"</li><li>"All right! Good following directions!"</li></ul></li><li>High five</li><li>Thumbs-up</li><li>Clap hands</li><li>Shake hands</li><li>A quick tickle</li><li>Hug</li></ul>	<ul><li>Play a game</li><li>Listen to music with headphones</li><li>Play a computer game</li><li>Use a special toy or material</li><li>Do classroom jobs: water plants, feed animals, erase board, take attendance form to office, empty pencil sharpener, pass out snack items, and so on</li><li>Take a walk with a teacher</li><li>Make toast or sandwich, popcorn, lemonade, pudding, and so forth</li><li>Jump on trampoline</li><li>Play in water or sand</li><li>Watch a video</li><li>Choose a favorite chair or place to sit (e.g., beanbag chair)</li><li>Use roller skates or inline skates</li><li>Assemble models</li><li>Do arts and crafts activities</li><li>Watch or feed fish in the class aquarium</li><li>Use visual entertainment activities (e.g., lava lamp, perpetual motion balls, wave machine)</li></ul>
MATERIAL REINFORCERS	**TOKEN REINFORCERS**
<ul><li>Stickers: regular or scratch-and-sniff</li><li>Pictures of favorite objects or people</li><li>Small trinkets</li><li>Posters</li><li>Personalized pencil</li><li>"Good Work" certificate</li><li>Cologne</li><li>Hand cream</li><li>Bubbles</li><li>Silly Putty, Slime, or other toys with interesting texture</li><li>Balloons</li><li>Nail polish</li><li>Bracelets, necklaces, or other inexpensive jewelry</li><li>Noisemakers</li><li>Slinky toy</li><li>Kaleidoscope</li></ul>	<ul><li>Points</li><li>Play money</li><li>Stickers</li><li>Self-inking stamps</li><li>Plastic counting chips</li><li>Legos</li></ul>

Secondary Reinforcers Secondary reinforcers are items or events that we learn to like. The following are four examples of secondary reinforcers.

- **Social reinforcers** include praise, smiles, gestures (e.g., a high five or fist bump), attention, hugs or pats, and even close physical proximity. Social reinforcers are important because they are available in any environment containing other people and can usually be delivered in many different school settings. For these reasons, it is important to teach children with autism to value social interactions to the point they can function as reinforcers. As already noted, this can be done through pairing.

- **Tangible reinforcers** are objects such as stickers, toys, posters, pictures, magazines, pencils, and any other stimulus that has mass (i.e., can be held or touched). Children with autism may prefer specific objects, and they sometimes prefer items not likely to be of interest to other children. In some cases, a child with autism may prefer the same tangible object but for different reasons than most other children. This pattern of interest is evident when the child plays with an age-appropriate toy but not in the way the toy was intended and not in a way typically recognized as play by other children (Lang et al., 2014). For example, Jason, a young boy with autism, loved little toy cars. However, his interest was not in rolling the car around a racetrack or in any other recognizable play behavior that might involve a toy car. Instead, he preferred turning the car upside down on a flat surface and repeatedly spinning it. He used delicate, graceful actions to spin the car and found it fascinating to watch. Similarly, Travis loved stickers, but only if he was allowed to repeatedly touch the sticky surface with his finger. He had no interest in the picture on the sticker or in adhering it to a surface. In some cases, the object may not be a toy at all. For example, Erica had a favorite spoon that she carried with her everywhere and tapped lightly on herself or on surfaces, but she did not use it to eat or to pretend to feed a doll (e.g., Kang et al., 2013).
- **Activity reinforcers** include doing things such as playing a game, singing a song, doing a special job, drawing a picture, or listening to music. Although both tangible and activity reinforcers may be appealing for students with autism, and those reinforcers are used in other environments (e.g., children in general education classrooms often get to do special activities when they finish their work, and they earn stickers for good work), teachers should not rely on them exclusively. Rather, teachers should rely on tangible reinforcers largely as part of intervention plans for the most challenging instructional needs and as part of the process of teaching students to more highly valued social reinforcers.
- **Token reinforcers** (or tokens) are small items (poker chips, stickers placed on a behavior chart, and even fake money) that can be exchanged for reinforcers in a school store as part of a token economy system. Because it is often impractical to deliver activity or material reinforcers in some educational settings or in the context of some instructional tasks, tokens may be more practical in some settings. The student accumulates tokens and then exchanges them for a **backup reinforcer** such as an item in a school store, a get-out-of-homework pass, extra recess time, and so on. Because token reinforcers are more abstract and indirect than other forms of reinforcers, they should be introduced gradually, with backup reinforcers earned quickly in the beginning of the token economy program. As the student learns the connection between the token reinforcer and the backup reinforcer, he or she may be able to work for longer periods of time before earning the backup reinforcer. If the student has a particular fascination with a specific character or item, then incorporating that item into the token may increase the power of the token as a reinforcer (Carnett et al., 2014). For example, a student who loves trains might respond more favorably to a token economy system in which the token has a sticker of a train on it.

Identifying Potential Reinforcers

How do you determine what will be an effective reinforcer? Several approaches are described in Table 2.9. You should consider potential reinforcers that are similar to what might be found in the natural environment or used with other children of the same age. The more you can teach your students to respond to **naturally occurring reinforcers**, the more likely the student is to generalize skills to natural environments (Stokes & Baer, 1977).

However, you may need to first use primary reinforcers (i.e., preferred foods) for the youngest children and older students with more severe delays even when that type of reinforcement is not typically contingent on the target behavior in the natural environment. When this is the case, you should pair the contrived reinforcer (that which is not available

TABLE 2.9 ● **How to Select Reinforcers**

1. *Observe the child.*
   - What activities, objects, foods, and so on does the child choose when allowed free choice?
   - Are there certain phrases, gestures, and so on that seem to produce a pleasant response from the child?
   - Try to identify possible reinforcers based on the child's stereotypic behaviors. For example, a child who engages in rocking might earn rocking in a rocking chair or using a swing. A child who bounces on tiptoes might earn jumping on a small trampoline.

2. *Use a reinforcer menu to let the child choose reinforcers.*
   - Create a menu of possible reinforcers listed by name (if the child can read), by picture (photographs of the actual item), or by lining up the potential items in front of the child. The item selected by the child from this menu of options may be an effective reinforcer. You may have to repeat this process multiple times until the child's selection from the menu is consistent. You may have to teach the child how to make choices. This might involve allowing the child time to sample each option on the menu in some way (e.g., taste each snack item, play briefly with each toy). Further, you may need to prompt the child to make a selection initially. If the child refuses to make a selection or appears disinterested in all of the items, consider selecting new potential reinforcers to consider.

3. *Ask others.*
   - Ask the child's parents what the child likes to do, play with, or eat at home.
   - Ask other teachers who have worked with the child.

4. *Conduct a preference assessment.*
   - Arrange several possible reinforcers on a table.
   - Allow the child to choose what she likes from the various objects, foods, and so on.
   - Note that just because a child prefers one object over another, that does not mean that item will function as an effective reinforcer for all skills. A child might prefer a small piece of candy over a small piece of cracker, but that does not mean that a small piece of candy will effectively reinforce math skills, for example. Preference can help identify a reinforcer, but only behavior change can confirm a stimulus's actual reinforcing power.

5. *Use an autism reinforcer checklist.*
   - Consider using a formal checklist that has been specifically designed to identify potential reinforcers. An autism reinforcer checklist is one potential option and has been provided in Table 2.10.

in the natural environment) with the naturally occurring reinforcer. For example, you might use small edibles to teach a child to provide a social greeting when friends enter the room. However, until the child is able to maintain the skill even when food is not used as a positive reinforcer, the skill should not be considered mastered. This is because it is highly unlikely that greeting friends outside of class will ever result in them giving you candy (at least in this author's experience). A forward-thinking teacher will pair social praise with the candy early on and, when the graphed data suggests skill acquisition is underway, will begin gradually fading the candy to rely increasingly on praise in an effort to best prepare the student for the natural contingencies involved in most social interactions outside the classroom.

Guidelines for Using Reinforcement

Like any procedure, there are correct and incorrect ways to apply positive reinforcement. The following sections describe steps for using reinforcement correctly that should increase the likelihood that reinforcement-based interventions will produce the desired effects.

Deliver Reinforcement Immediately After the Desired Behavior The more closely in time the reinforcer follows the behavior, the more effective the reinforcer will be. Immediacy of reinforcement is often essential during acquisition of new skills. The longer the delay between the behavior and reinforcement, the less likely the student is to associate the behavior with the reinforcing consequence. Also, the longer the delay, the more likely it is that you will inadvertently reinforce unacceptable behaviors that occur before the reinforcer is delivered.

TABLE 2.10 ● Autism Reinforcer Checklist

Name: _____   Rater: _____

Age: _____   Date: _____

Edible Reinforcers

		Yes	No				Yes	No
Candy:	1. M&Ms	_____	_____	Frozen:	26. Popsicle		_____	_____
	2. Jelly Beans	_____	_____		27. Ice Cream		_____	_____
	3. Licorice	_____	_____		28. _____		_____	_____
	4. Candy Canes	_____	_____	Soft:	29. Pudding		_____	_____
	5. Gum	_____	_____		30. Jell-O		_____	_____
	6. Smarties	_____	_____		31. Yogurt		_____	_____
	7. Lollipops	_____	_____		32. Marshmallows		_____	_____
	8. Candy Kisses	_____	_____		33. Cheese		_____	_____
	9. Chocolate	_____	_____		34. Cottage Cheese		_____	_____
	10. _____	_____	_____		35. Peanut Butter		_____	_____
Cereals:	11. Cheerios	_____	_____		36. Jam/Jelly		_____	_____
	12. Fruit Loops	_____	_____		37. _____		_____	_____
	13. Trix	_____	_____	Other:	38. Cake		_____	_____
	14. _____	_____	_____		39. Animal Crackers		_____	_____
Fruits:	15. Raisins	_____	_____		40. Applesauce		_____	_____
	16. Apples	_____	_____		41. Crackers		_____	_____
	17. Oranges	_____	_____		42. Frosting		_____	_____
	18. Bananas	_____	_____		43. Pretzels		_____	_____
	19. _____	_____	_____		44. Corn Chips		_____	_____
Liquids:	20. Milk	_____	_____		45. Cheez Balls		_____	_____
	21. Chocolate Milk	_____	_____		46. Doritos		_____	_____
	22. Juice	_____	_____		47. Cookies		_____	_____
	23. Sparkling Water	_____	_____		48. Popcorn		_____	_____
	24. Lemonade	_____	_____		49. Vegetables		_____	_____
	25. _____	_____	_____		50. _____		_____	_____

Material Reinforcers

	Yes	No			Yes	No
1. Stopwatch	_____	_____	14. Fans		_____	_____
2. Hand Cream	_____	_____	15. Balloons		_____	_____
3. Bubbles	_____	_____	16. Bean Bags		_____	_____
4. Combs	_____	_____	17. Hats		_____	_____
5. Stickers	_____	_____	18. Mirrors		_____	_____
6. Play Dough	_____	_____	19. Books		_____	_____
7. Perfume	_____	_____	20. Coloring Books		_____	_____
8. Toy Instruments	_____	_____	21. Whistles		_____	_____
9. Puzzles	_____	_____	22. Blocks		_____	_____
10. Beads	_____	_____	23. Paints		_____	_____
11. Stamps	_____	_____	24. Colored Chalk		_____	_____
12. Masks	_____	_____	25. _____		_____	_____
13. Crayons	_____	_____				

(continued)

TABLE 2.10 ● **Autism Reinforcer Checklist (*continued*)**

Activity Reinforcers

	Yes	No			Yes	No
1. Rocking	___	___	39. Playing in Boxes		___	___
2. Brushing Hair	___	___	40. Dressing Up		___	___
3. Clapping Hands	___	___	41. Climbing		___	___
4. Swinging	___	___	42. Time to Engage in Preferred Stereotypy		___	___
5. Drawing Pictures	___	___	43. Rocking in Boat		___	___
6. Run Outside	___	___	44. Cutting Pictures		___	___
7. Hide and Seek	___	___	45. Playing with Glue		___	___
8. Stack and Knock Down Blocks	___	___	46. Treasure Hunt		___	___
9. Chase	___	___	47. Looking at Pictures		___	___
10. Peek-A-Boo	___	___	48. Basketball		___	___
11. Sing Songs	___	___	49. Finger Paint		___	___
12. Sprinkle Glitter	___	___	with Pudding		___	___
13. Tickles	___	___	with Whipped Cream		___	___
14. Water Play	___	___	with Soap		___	___
15. Puppets	___	___	with Paint		___	___
16. Sand Play	___	___	50. Racing		___	___
17. Trampoline	___	___	51. Wagon Rides		___	___
18. Dancing	___	___	52. Play Game with Preferred Adult		___	___
19. Bring Toy from Home	___	___	53. Make Copies		___	___
20. Turn Lights On/Off	___	___	54. Water Plants		___	___
21. Pour Liquids Back & Forth	___	___	55. Going for Walks		___	___
22. Watch YouTube Videos	___	___	56. Making Treats		___	___
23. Stories	___	___	57. Icing Cupcakes		___	___
24. Being the Teacher	___	___	58. Making Popcorn		___	___
25. Talking on Phone	___	___	59. Playing Ball		___	___
26. Go to Office for Treat	___	___	60. Playing with Tools		___	___
27. Drawing	___	___	61. Play Parachute Activity with Peers		___	___
28. Draw on Whiteboard	___	___	62. Playing with Zippers		___	___
29. Lunch/Snack Helper	___	___	63. Blowing Bubbles		___	___
30. Field Trips	___	___	64. Swimming		___	___
31. Twirling	___	___	65. Listen to Music		___	___
32. Blankets over Head	___	___	66. Play Games on Computer		___	___
33. Taking Pictures	___	___	67. Stringing Beads		___	___
34. Going to Trash	___	___	68. Turning Water On/Off		___	___
35. Roll Down Hill	___	___	69. Smelling Spices		___	___
36. Teacher's Helper	___	___	70. Fishing Game		___	___
37. Making Pictures:	___	___	71. Dart Board		___	___
with Popcorn	___	___	72. Grab Bag		___	___
with Noodles	___	___	73. Surprise Box		___	___
with String	___	___	74. Spinner		___	___
38. Running Errands	___	___	75. _____		___	___

Social Reinforcers

	Yes	No			Yes	No
1. Hugs	___	___	8. Smiling		___	___
2. Shaking Hands	___	___	9. Whistling		___	___
3. Kisses	___	___	10. Patting		___	___
4. Tickling	___	___	11. Praising		___	___
5. Winking	___	___	12. Back Scratch/Rub		___	___
6. Give Me Five	___	___	13. Praise		___	___
7. Rubbing Noses	___	___	14. _____		___	___

Source: Adapted from Atkinson, R. P., Jenson, W. R., Rovner, L., Cameron, S., Van Wagenen, L., & Petersen, B. P. (1984). Brief report: Validation of the Autism Reinforcer Checklist for Children. *Journal of Autism and Developmental Disorders, 14,* 429–433.

Use Social Reinforcers When Possible, Even When Using Other Types of Reinforcers Some students with autism have not learned to value social reinforcers. However, you can teach students to like praise, smiles, and so on by using social reinforcers each time you give the student another type of reinforcer. As noted previously, this procedure is called **pairing** and may also be referred to as **conditioning**. Eventually, you should be able depend more on social reinforcement contingencies to maintain behavior. This is important for generalization (using target behaviors in new situations or in the presence of new adults). Of course, primary reinforcers such as food should still be used when the natural consequence for a target behavior in the real world is a primary reinforcer (learning to request a snack).

Be Sure Reinforcers Are Contingent on Appropriate Behavior The term **contingent** means that the student does not get the reinforcer until the behavior occurs. This helps students learn to associate the behavior with the reinforcer. If students have access to reinforcers without exhibiting desired target behaviors, they have less motivation to engage in the target behaviors and the contingency between the target behavior and the programmed reinforcer is less clear.

Be Aware that Reinforcers Change Often A student may find something reinforcing one day but then not desire the same thing at all the very next day, which is why it is important to frequently assess reinforcers. Some teachers will ask students what they want to earn at the beginning of every school day or even at the start of every lesson to ensure that effective reinforcers are in place during instruction.

A reinforcer can also lose its power if it is overused. Children can become tired of (or satiated by) a particular snack food, game, or other stimuli if they have a lot of it or have free access to the same thing in other settings. To avoid satiation, try to limit the quantity of reinforcement or restrict access to the reinforcer outside of class. For example, if the same toy that is freely available on the playground is used as a reinforcer after recess, the child may not be as interested in working hard to obtain it (Rispoli et al., 2011).

Tell Students Specifically Why They Are Being Reinforced You want to be sure that a student knows *why* she is being reinforced. For example, providing **behavior-specific praise** such as "Good job picking up your pencil" is better than merely saying "Good job!" because it helps the student learn contingency between the behavior and the consequence.

Be Concise When Delivering Praise Although specificity is important, praise should never be drowned by details. For example, "I saw you pick up your red pencil and put it back in your desk when I told everyone to clean up. That was great! Your dad will be proud. Be sure to tell him this afternoon" is less likely to be effective with students with receptive language delays than simply "Good job picking up your pencil!" However, we do encourage telling this student's dad!

Move to Natural Reinforcers as Soon as Possible Gradually stop using the reinforcers that are only available in the classroom and are not related to the target behavior in the real world and replace them with natural reinforcers. A student who learns to do his own laundry in an intervention that uses candy as a reinforcer is not nearly as likely to maintain that skill when he leaves the classroom setting and clean laundry is almost never reinforced with anything except a clean smelling shirt and the avoidance of negative social interactions caused by soiled clothes. Fading the contrived reinforcer (candy) while also complimenting the student on his fresh clean clothes (pairing candy with social praise) will more likely result in the maintenance of the skill in real life.

Fade the Frequency (or Schedule) of Reinforcement Until It Matches the Natural Environment When teaching a new behavior, you may initially reinforce the student each time that behavior is exhibited (**continuous reinforcement**). However, after the behavior is established (e.g., the student exhibits the behavior regularly and consistently), you should gradually reinforce less frequently—only after several behaviors or several minutes of the behavior (**intermittent reinforcement**). This process is known as **fading**, or fading reinforcement. Be careful, though, not to move too abruptly from continuous reinforcement to intermittent reinforcement— the student may not maintain the skill through the transition. Ongoing data collection and analysis of your graphed data will help you determine how gradually you need to fade the reinforcement schedule.

You are not done teaching (i.e., the skill is not truly mastered) until the schedule of reinforcement is the same as would be expected in the natural environment. For example, when teaching a child to ask other children to play (i.e., to initiate a social interaction), you will likely instruct the other child to always say "yes" as you practice with the student. This will help the child with autism acquire the skill by ensuring reinforcement consistently follows the target behavior. However, on the community playground outside of instruction, other children will not always say "yes." Your student must learn what to do when her appropriate social initiation is not reinforced (e.g., ask someone else or play alone). If she expects every request to play to be met with a happy willing play partner, she may not maintain the skill in the real world when this does not happen. Therefore, your instruction should fade from a continuous to an intermittent reinforcement schedule gradually to better prepare your student for the thinner reinforcement schedules found outside of the supportive classroom environment.

> **The Golden Rule of Reinforcement**: you are not done teaching until the target behavior is maintained by the same type of reinforcer on the same reinforcement schedule that is found in the real world.

In Vignette 2.1, "Colin Learns to Sit Next to His Friends," you will see how Colin's teacher applies many of these rules for using reinforcement.

● VIGNETTE 2.1
Colin Learns to Sit Next to His Friends

Ms. Preston had a new student in her room, Colin, who hit or pinched any student who sat next to him. To teach Colin to sit next to other students without hurting them, Ms. Preston determined that one replacement behavior for Colin would be for him to sit next to another student during morning group with his hands folded in his lap. She gave Colin a piece of cookie and praised him every 30 seconds that he remained seated with folded hands. Realizing that she needed to teach Colin to respond to other types of reinforcers for appropriate sitting, Ms. Preston followed this sequence:

- When Colin could sit correctly for 30 seconds with no hitting or pinching attempts, Ms. Preston began giving him the cookie after sitting appropriately for 1 minute.
- When Colin was successful at this level, Ms. Preston began giving him a happy face stamp on a card at the same time she gave him the piece of cookie. At the end of the group, Ms. Preston helped Colin count the stamps. If he had 10 stamps, he earned a small cup of juice. He was still getting pieces of cookie for each minute of appropriate sitting.
- Next, Ms. Preston gave Colin the happy face stamp at the end of each minute of sitting appropriately, but she gradually eliminated the cookie by giving him the cookie only every few times he earned a stamp. Of course, she continued to praise him each time he earned a happy face stamp, and he still earned juice if he had 10 happy faces at the end of group.
- When Ms. Preston had eliminated the cookie reinforcer and was using only the happy face stamps, she began increasing the length of time Colin was required to sit appropriately before earning a happy face stamp.
- Eventually, Colin learned to sit next to other students with folded hands, without hitting or pinching, and with only verbal praise as his reinforcer.

Both positive reinforcement and negative reinforcement produce increases in behaviors. You must understand these principles, learn to apply them correctly, and be able to evaluate their effects. You must also be aware that both positive and negative reinforcement can affect challenging behaviors as well as desired behaviors. If a challenging behavior is present, it must be maintained by some form of reinforcement. Likewise, when a student fails to exhibit desired behavior, you may assume that the response has not been sufficiently taught or reinforced or that competing behaviors have been more strongly reinforced.

Extinction: Disrupting the Contingency Between Challenging Behavior and Reinforcement

In some cases, a challenging behavior may need to be decreased but simply reinforcing an alternative behavior may not be enough. It may also be necessary to ensure that no reinforcement is provided following the challenging behavior. **Extinction** means to withhold the reinforcement previously contingent on a target behavior. For example, if it is determined that a child screams to obtain attention from a teacher, extinction would involve ignoring that screaming. Similarly, if a child screams to obtain a preferred toy, extinction involves not providing that item. Finally, extinction can be applied to challenging behaviors maintained by negative reinforcement also. For example, a child who screams to avoid work should not have the requirement to do work removed. Note that reinforcement is withheld for a specific target *behavior*. As soon as the target behavior ceases or the appropriate behavior occurs, you should provide the reinforcement in most cases.

A few cautions should be noted if you plan to use extinction. First, *never* use extinction by itself. Always have a plan for reinforcing a replacement behavior or even just a plan to reinforce the absence of the target challenging behavior any time you plan to include extinction in your intervention. If you do not also include reinforcement in your plan, the challenging behavior will likely worsen before it begins to diminish (Lerman & Iwata, 1995). This effect is known as **extinction burst**. For example, if a brief scream no longer produces attention, the child may scream louder and longer. If that still does not produce the desired consequence, he may leave his seat to stand directly in front of the teacher to scream. In a more dangerous example, if a child is engaging in self-injury or aggression, the use of extinction alone and the resulting extinction burst may cause physical injury. Unless there are clear reinforcement contingencies in place, extinction may not be an appropriate intervention for students who engage in these more dangerous behaviors.

Sometimes a behavior that has been eliminated using extinction spontaneously reappears later, even weeks later, in a phenomenon known as **spontaneous recovery**. You must be ready to withhold attention for the behavior anytime it is exhibited. Inconsistent application of extinction may inadvertently teach the child that he must persist in his challenging behavior because eventually it will result in the desired reinforcer. This means you must be prepared to apply the intervention for an extended period of time, even on days when the behavior does not particularly annoy you, when you have visitors in the room, or when you are in other parts of the school or on field trips.

For these and other reasons beyond the scope of this text, we urge caution in using extinction with children and youth with autism. Consult with your school district behavior specialist or board-certified behavior analyst (BCBA) to be sure that other potentially effective techniques have not been overlooked or to proactively plan for extinction-produced side effects. However, if extinction is applied alongside reinforcement, many of these side effects become unlikely (Lerman, Iwata, & Wallace, 1999). **Differential reinforcement** combines extinction and reinforcement within an intervention package intended to reduce challenging behavior; it increases an appropriate behavior with reinforcement while simultaneously decreasing a challenging behavior. The process is discussed in detail in Chapter 3.

Punishment: Direct Efforts to Decrease Challenging Behavior

The more children's repertoires of appropriate behaviors can be expanded and strengthened, the less likely they will need to rely on challenging behaviors. Thus, the emphasis in any educational program for children and youth with autism should be on teaching and reinforcing functional, prosocial behaviors. However, despite your best efforts and reliance on positive, preventative approaches, some children may continue to exhibit challenging behaviors. To maximize your students' opportunities for success in natural environments—such as playing with typical age peers, participating in activities general education settings, working in mainstream employment settings, and living in typical, age-appropriate settings—you must minimize those challenging behaviors. To accomplish this, you may need to use behavior reductive procedures for certain behaviors. These types of consequences are referred to as *punishment.*

In many cases, challenging behavior can be decreased by combining extinction and reinforcement without the need for punishment. However, in other cases, punishment may be an important component of a comprehensive intervention package alongside reinforcement and extinction. Like reinforcement, punishment can be negative or positive, which again does not refer to "good" or "bad" but to whether or not something was taken away or given. However, unlike reinforcement, **positive punishment** means giving or adding something that the student does *not* like, and **negative punishment** involves taking away something the student values. These are delicate intervention components that require an extensive amount of planning and care. The primary focus of Chapter 3 is on strategies to reduce challenging behavior, and these concepts will be discussed more fully in that chapter.

Summary

As we have seen in this chapter, ABA procedures are effective and efficient ways of achieving desirable outcomes for students with autism. Of course, a specific process must be followed, and procedures for changing behavior must be designed and implemented correctly to attain desired outcomes. In particular, you must consider information gathered through functional assessment, which we explain in Chapter 3, and interventions should reflect your students' unique characteristics, likes, and dislikes, as well as the skills of the adults who will be implementing the interventions. Chapter 3 will also provide specific uses of ABA to reduce challenging behavior, and Chapter 5 will describe specific ABA strategies for teaching new behaviors. However, if you adhere to the guidelines we described throughout this chapter and you pay careful attention to other important aspects of the educational program such as curriculum (as described in several later chapters), we predict you will see positive results.

Key Points

1. ABA is a comprehensive approach that offers empirically based strategies for measuring behavior, increasing behavior, and reducing behavior.

2. The three-term contingency is a framework for (a) understanding how behavior is connected to and influenced by the settings in which it occurs and (b) planning interventions.

3. Stimulus control is a powerful teaching tool in which students learn to respond in a predetermined way to specific antecedents.

4. Target behaviors must be defined in operational terms to better ensure consistency in measurement and interventions.

5. Target behaviors should be measured using one or more behavior measurement systems. The nature of the target behavior determines the most appropriate measurement system for obtaining valid data. Data are collected, graphed, and used to guide intervention decisions.

6. Graphing data provides an easy-to-interpret visual representation of progress.

7. Reinforcement may be positive or negative; both are valuable to the student and can increase behavior.

8. Secondary reinforcers include social reinforcers, material reinforcers, activity reinforcers, and token reinforcers. Children may need to be taught to appreciate secondary reinforcers using a technique called *pairing*.

9. Extinction involves the intentional withholding of a reinforcer in an effort to decrease challenging behavior. In some cases, it is associated with adverse side effects such as extinction burst and spontaneous recovery. Therefore, extinction should only be used as part of an intervention approach that also includes reinforcement.

10. Punishment may be needed to reduce some challenging behaviors. Like reinforcement, it can be classified as positive or negative. Punishment is not often desirable for a variety of reasons and should be pursued with notable caution.

References

Atkinson, R. P., Jenson, W. R., Rovner, L., Cameron, S., Van Wagenen, L., & Petersen, B. P. (1984). Brief report: Validation of the Autism Reinforcer Checklist for Children. *Journal of Autism and Developmental Disorders, 14*, 429–433.

Baer, D. M., Wolf, M. M., & Risley, T. R. (1968). Some current dimensions of applied behavior analysis. *Journal of Applied Behavior Analysis, 1*, 91–97.

Bailey, J. S., & Burch, M. R. (2016). *Ethics for behavior analysts* (3rd ed.). New York: Routledge.

Carnett, A., Raulston, T., Lang, R., Tostanoski, A., Lee, A., Sigafoos, J., & Machalicek, W. (2014). Effects of a perseverative interest-based token economy on challenging and on-task behavior in a child with autism. *Journal of Behavioral Education, 23*, 368–377.

Centers for Disease Control and Prevention (CDC). (2015). *Autism Spectrum Disorder (ASD): Treatment.* Retrieved February 21, 2017, from https://www.cdc.gov/ncbddd/autism/treatment.html

Cooper, J. O., Heron, T. E., & Heward, W. L. (2007). *Applied behavior analysis* (2nd ed.). Upper Saddle River, NJ: Pearson/Merrill/Prentice Hall.

Cox, A. D., & Virues-Ortega, J. (2016). Interactions between behavior function and psychotropic medication. *Journal of Applied Behavior Analysis, 49*, 85–104.

Didden, R., Sturmey, P., Sigafoos, J., Lang, R., O'Reilly, M. F., & Lancioni, G. E. (2012). Nature, prevalence, and characteristics of challenging behavior. In J. L. Matson (Ed.), *Functional Assessment for Challenging Behaviors* (pp. 25–44). New York: Springer.

Foster-Johnson, L., & Dunlap, G. (1993). Using functional assessment to develop effective, individualized interventions for challenging behaviors. *Teaching Exceptional Children, 25*, 44–50.

Gulley, V., Northup, J., Hupp, S., Spera, S., LeVelle, J., & Ridgway, A. (2003). Sequential evaluation of behavioral treatments and methylphenidate dosage for children with attention deficit hyperactivity disorder. *Journal of Applied Behavior Analysis, 36*, 375–378.

Hurl, K., Wightman, J., Haynes, S. N., & Virues-Ortega, J. (2016). Does a pre-intervention functional assessment increase intervention effectiveness? A meta-analysis of within-subject interrupted time-series studies. *Clinical Psychology Review, 47*, 71–84.

Kang, S., O'Reilly, M., Rojeski, L., Blenden, K., Xu, Z., Davis, T., Sigafoos, J., & Lancioni, G. (2013). Effects of tangible and social reinforcers on skill acquisition, stereotyped behavior, and task engagement in three children with autism spectrum disorders. *Research in Developmental Disabilities, 34*, 739–744.

Kanter, J. W., Landes, S. J., Busch, A. M., Rusch, L. C., Brown, K. R., Baruch, D. E., & Holman, G. I. (2006). The effect of contingent reinforcement on target variables in outpatient psychotherapy for depression: A successful and unsuccessful case using functional analytic psychotherapy. *Journal of Applied Behavior Analysis, 39*, 463–467.

Keenan, M., & Dillenburger, K. (2011). When all you have is a hammer . . . : RCTs and hegemony in science. *Research in Autism Spectrum Disorders, 5*, 1–13.

Koegel, L. K., Matos-Freden, R., Lang, R., & Koegel, R. (2012). Interventions for children with autism spectrum disorders in inclusive school settings. *Cognitive and Behavioral Practice, 19*, 401–412.

Lang, R., Machalicek, W., Rispoli, M., O'Reilly, M., Sigafoos, J., Lancioni, G., Peters-Scheffer, N., & Didden, R. (2014). Play skills taught via behavioral intervention generalize, maintain, and persist in the absence of socially mediated reinforcement in children with autism. *Research in Autism Spectrum Disorders, 8*, 860–872.

Langthorne, P. & McGill, P. (2009). A tutorial on the concept of the motivating operation and its importance to application. *Behavior Analysis in Practice, 2*, 22–31.

Laraway, S., Snycerski, S., Michael, J., & Poling, A. (2003). Motivating operations and terms to describe them: Some further refinements. *Journal of Applied Behavior Analysis, 36*, 407–414.

Lerman, D. C., & Iwata, B. A. (1995). Prevalence of the extinction burst and its attenuation during treatment. *Journal of Applied Behavior Analysis, 28*, 93–94.

Lerman, D. C., Iwata, B. A., & Wallace, M. D. (1999). Side effects of extinction: Prevalence of bursting and aggression during the treatment of self-injurious behavior. *Journal of Applied Behavior Analysis, 32*, 1–8.

Palmen, A., Didden, R., & Lang, R. (2012). A systematic review of behavioral intervention research on adaptive skill building in high-functioning young adults with autism spectrum disorder. *Research in Autism Spectrum Disorders, 6*, 602–617.

Rispoli, M. J., O'Reilly, M. F., Sigafoos, J., Lang, R., Kang, S., Lancioni, G., & Parker, R. (2011). Effects of presession satiation on challenging behavior and academic engagement for children with autism during classroom instruction. *Education and Training in Autism and Developmental Disabilities, 46*, 607–618.

Skinner, B. F. (1938). *The behavior of organisms: An experimental analysis.* New York: Appleton-Century.

Skinner, B. F. (1945). The operational analysis of psychological terms. *Psychological Review, 52*, 270–277, 291–294.

Skinner, B. F. (1953). *Science and human behavior.* New York: Macmillan.

Skinner, B. F. (1981). Selection by consequences. *Science, 213*, 501–504.

Skinner, B. F. (1989). The origins of cognitive thought. *American Psychologist, 44*, 13–18.

Stokes, T. F., & Baer, D. M. (1977). An implicit technology of generalization. *Journal of Applied Behavior Analysis, 10*, 349–367.

Virues-Ortega, J. (2010). Applied behavior analytic intervention for autism in early childhood: Meta-analysis, meta-regression and dose-response meta-analysis of multiple outcomes. *Clinical Psychology Review, 30*, 387–399.

Walsh, M. B. (2011). The top 10 reasons children with autism deserve ABA. *Behavior Analysis in Practice, 4*, 72–79.

Zlutnick, S., Mayville, W. J., & Moffat, S. (1975). Modification of seizure disorders: The interruption of behavioral chains. *Journal of Applied Behavior Analysis, 83*, 1–12.

Reducing Challenging Behavior

3

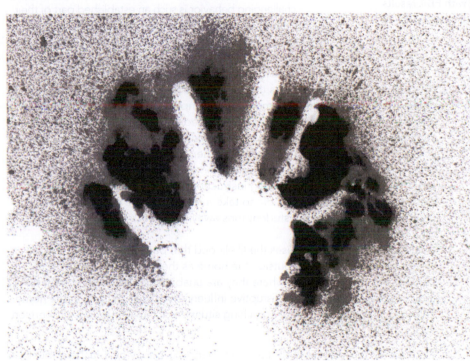

© Lang

LEARNING OBJECTIVES

After reading this chapter, you will be able to:

3-1 Describe how challenging behavior is related to environmental conditions or events.

3-2 Describe how to determine a behavior's function using a functional behavior assessment (FBA) and how to select appropriate function-matched interventions for challenging behaviors maintained by positive and negative reinforcement.

3-3 Conceptualize the treatment process beginning with the FBA and moving to function-matched intervention through consideration of case study examples.

Unfortunately, students with autism, particularly those with severe language deficits and intellectual disability (ID), are more likely to engage in challenging behavior than other students (Didden et al., 2012; Lowe et al., 2007). Challenging behavior can range from mild noncompliance, such as appearing to ignore directions, to severe potentially life-threatening behaviors, such as aggression and self-injury (Luiselli, 2012).

In milder cases, a behavior may be appropriate in some settings but inappropriate and challenging in other settings. For example, some students engage in self-stimulatory behaviors such as rocking their torsos back and forth, hand flapping, finger flicking, or spinning objects (Rapp & Vollmer, 2005). These behaviors may be less concerning when a child is at home but might cause problems in school if these stereotypic behaviors distract from learning or result in the person becoming stigmatized in such a way that makes it harder to make friends.

In terms of more severe forms of challenging behavior, some students with autism bite, pull hair, pinch, or exhibit other aggressive acts directed toward classmates, school personnel, and parents. When aggression is self-directed, the term **self-injurious behavior (SIB)** is used. SIB includes self-abusive behaviors such as a student biting his own hand(s) and banging his head against stationary objects such as the corner of a desk.

Challenging behaviors may negatively affect individuals' current and future options in terms of living, learning, and working. The following list shows possible negative effects of persistent challenging behavior for students with autism.

- Challenging behavior interferes with learning (Powell, Fixsen, Dunlap, Smith, & Fox, 2007). For many students, challenging behavior is such an established part of their behavioral repertoire that attempts to teach them new behaviors and skills are ineffective. In fact, for some students with autism, merely asking them to perform simple tasks may lead to an episode of challenging behavior.
- Challenging behavior increases the likelihood that a student will need a more restrictive instructional arrangement. For example, students who exhibit high levels of challenging behavior may be assigned to one-on-one instruction in a separate classroom and given fewer opportunities for interactions with other students (Lauderdale-Littin, Howell, & Blacher, 2013).
- Challenging behavior decreases the likelihood that a student will be able to participate in community-based instructional activities and field trips. For example, it may not be advisable to take a student to the grocery store to teach shopping skills if the student runs away from teachers or attempts to bite others.
- Challenging behavior increases the likelihood that parents may be forced to seek residential placement outside the home as their child with autism ages. Parents may reach the point where they are unable to keep the child safe, or the child may be too great a disruptive influence on other children in the home. This is among the most heart-wrenching situations a family may face (Robertson et al., 2004).

Because of the negative effects of challenging behavior, teachers must be able and willing to use effective, evidence-based strategies to reduce or eliminate these behaviors. Teachers report that managing the challenging behavior of their students with autism is one of their most pressing concerns (e.g., Quesenberry, Hemmeter, Ostrosky, & Hamann, 2014). Furthermore, many in-service teachers report feeling unprepared and undertrained to manage challenging behavior in students with autism (e.g., Scheuermann, Webber, Boutot, & Goodwin, 2003; Shyman, 2012). Teachers may find many common classroom and behavior management solutions to be of little use for these students. Instead, teachers need to become knowledgeable about the principles of ABA (see Chapter 2) and evidence-based strategies for reducing or eliminating challenging behaviors for students with autism.

Reducing challenging behavior begins with conducting specialized assessments and analyses to determine why a student is engaging in the behavior (e.g., the potential **function** of a student's challenging behavior). This assessment and analysis process provides essential information for creating a behavior intervention plan (BIP) (Hurl, Wightman, Haynes, & Virues-Ortega, 2016). When used in this way, the term *function* refers to the contingency reinforcing the behavior. A student with autism might engage in certain behaviors to obtain something (praise, toy, etc.) or avoid something (certain person, task demand, etc.). Intervention would be quite different for behaviors that function to obtain something (positive reinforcement) than for behaviors that function to avoid something (negative reinforcement). For example, if a student screams when you ask her to vacuum, and she screams because she does not like vacuuming, then simply having her sit in time-out as a consequence for screaming may not work. Instead, time-out might actually negatively reinforce the screaming. In such a case, going to time-out where vacuuming is not required would actually *increase* the likelihood the student will scream again the next time vacuuming is required because she received the consequence she wanted by screaming (avoiding vacuuming). Similarly, sending a student to the assistant principal's office to talk about his behavior as a form of punishment for aggression may be counterproductive if the function of aggression (i.e., the reason why the student hit) was to obtain attention. In this case, aggression resulted in receiving attention from everyone in the office.

These counterintuitive increases in challenging behavior are caused by the interaction between challenging behavior and the student's environment (Matson, 2012). Over time, some students will learn how to obtain or avoid certain people, things, or activities via challenging behavior as a result of how the teacher responds to those challenging behaviors in the classroom. Of course, this is not the lesson teachers intend to teach! For example, a student who wants attention from a teacher may engage in challenging behavior in an effort to initiate an interaction with the teacher. If the teacher reprimands the student in response to the challenging behavior and then talks to the student about making different choices, the challenging behavior may become more likely in the future. Although the teacher's intent was to teach the student not to engage in challenging behavior, the teacher's one-to-one attention, even though scolding, was what was desired by the student. The unintentional lesson was that challenging behavior is a way to request attention. In that example, we would say the challenging behavior's function is to obtain attention and that the intervention (i.e., reprimand plus discussion of choices) was ineffective because it was not properly matched to this function. Similarly, a student with autism who does not want to help clean the classroom may engage in challenging behavior in an effort to avoid the work or to request a break. If the teacher sends that student to time-out where no work is required, then the teacher may unintentionally teach that challenging behavior is a way to request a break. In this case we would say the challenging behavior functions to escape cleaning and would again note the mismatch between the challenging behavior's function and the programmed contingency in the intervention.

These well-intentioned teachers may be successful in temporarily stopping challenging behavior in the moment (perhaps the tantrumming stops when the child is sent to time-out or during the discussion of choices), but ultimately these teachers are increasing challenging behavior by making it more likely the same behaviors will occur next time attention or a break from work is desired (Lancioni, Singh, O'Reilly, Sigafoos, & Didden, 2012). Unless the function of the behavior is addressed as part of the BIP, the intervention will not likely produce the desired results (Hurl et al., 2016).

This chapter further describes how challenging behavior is related to environmental conditions or events and how to determine a behavior's function. The procedure used to assess for function is known as a **functional behavioral assessment (FBA)**. We also describe how FBA results can be used to develop an effective BIP (Machalicek, O'Reilly, Beretvas, Sigafoos, & Lancioni, 2007). The chapter delineates potential strategies using a function-matched approach for reducing common challenging behaviors exhibited by students with autism. Finally, the chapter concludes with two case studies that illustrate the procedures and concepts described in the chapter.

3-1 Assessing Challenging Behavior

Functional behavioral assessment is a process used to answer the question "*Why* does the student engage in that challenging behavior?" This is not the same question as "*How* does the student misbehave?" or "*What* does the challenging behavior look like?" The answers to "how" and "what" would emphasize appearance or form of the challenging behavior (sometimes referred to as a behavior's **topography**). It is not uncommon to encounter a teacher who has spent a great deal of time and effort documenting exactly what the student's challenging behavior looked like (e.g., a blow-by-blow account of an aggressive incident) but who has neglected to provide the type of information necessary to answer *why* those behaviors occurred (the function). The answer to the "why" question cannot be found by considering only the topography of a challenging behavior.

Imagine two students who both kick classmates. In other words, both students engage in the same topography of challenging behavior—kicking. It is possible that the students kick for entirely different reasons. Perhaps one student kicks when he wants people to leave him alone (i.e., the function of kicking is to escape from others and avoid attention) and the other student kicks when he wants someone to interact with him. These two students engage in the same topography of challenging behavior but will require decidedly different interventions because behavioral functions are different. In short, teachers must learn these two fundamental facts: (a) the appearance or topography of a behavior does not reliably indicate the function of the behavior, and (b) the most effective interventions are based on a challenging behavior's function, not topography.

Teachers and other professionals often suggest deep-seated psychological or physiological explanations for challenging behavior. For example, it might be suggested that a student who throws his instructional materials around the classroom has a problem with "impulse control." Similarly, a student might be judged to have "limited ability to manage anger" or a "low tolerance for frustration." These types of explanations are not particularly helpful in selecting or designing an effective intervention, in part because they place the cause of a challenging behavior completely inside the student without considering classroom factors, people's interaction styles, and other contextual variables that are likely contributors. For example, if the assumption is that a student's poor impulse control is the cause of his challenging behavior, what intervention options does the teacher have? The teacher cannot prescribe medication to address impulse control, and teaching impulse control to an individual with autism is an ambiguous and difficult pursuit. Considering behavioral function, however, results in multiple strategies available to teachers that will likely reduce the challenging behavior.

Determining why challenging behavior occurs (identifying the function) is accomplished through systematic consideration of how the student's challenging behavior affects his immediate surroundings. In other words, what in the student's most immediate environment changes as a direct result of the challenging behavior? It could be that something is added to the environment contingent on that behavior. For example, a student might be given attention or access to a special toy immediately after he engages in challenging behavior such as whining (i.e., positive reinforcement). Or perhaps something in the environment is removed or avoided contingent on challenging behavior. For example, a student might escape or avoid a specific task, person, or item when he pinches (i.e., negative reinforcement). Remember, negative reinforcement is not punishment: Negative reinforcement increases behavior because something that is aversive or undesirable (e.g., an undesired task) is taken away. Please refer to Chapter 2 as needed for additional discussion of positive and negative reinforcement.

Specifically, functional behavioral assessment helps determine why a student is behaving a certain way by analyzing the environmental variables in place before (antecedents) and after (consequences) that target behavior occurs (see three-term contingency in Chapter 2). A typical FBA is based on five fundamental points: (a) like all operant behavior, challenging behavior occurs in the context of antecedents and consequences; (b) motivating operations influence the reinforcing power of consequences that maintain challenging behavior; (c) some challenging behaviors are influenced by medical conditions or other physiological and biological factors; (d) all operant challenging behavior serves a function; and (e) challenging behavior is often directly related to a skill deficit (Foster-Johnson & Dunlap, 1993; O'Neill, Albin, Storey, Horner, & Sprague, 2015). Each fundamental point is discussed briefly as follows.

First, behavior is related to specific antecedents and consequences in the immediate environment. This means that challenging behavior is often occasioned or cued by certain antecedent stimuli (e.g., nature of the task the student is asked to do, sitting close to another student, being asked to stop a preferred activity) and is maintained by reinforcing consequent stimuli (e.g., getting a desired object, escaping a disliked task or situation). For example, a student who dislikes writing may force herself to vomit when asked to work on writing tasks because this means the student has avoided the task when the teacher sends the student to the nurse. A student who tantrums because she wants a snack probably does so because tantrumming has resulted in someone giving her a snack in the past. Identifying contributing antecedent and consequent stimuli provides important information necessary for selecting an effective intervention.

Second, events or conditions outside of immediate antecedent conditions and consequence contingencies may increase or decrease the likelihood of challenging behavior. These conditions, known as **motivating operations (MOs)** (Chapter 2), do not directly cause problem behavior per se. Rather, MOs influence the likelihood of a specific behavior by altering the reinforcing power of the contingent consequence (Langthorne & McGill, 2009). For example, a student who has learned that screaming often results in someone bringing him a snack will scream more if he did not have breakfast that morning because the consequence of receiving food is more reinforcing when hungry. Comparably, a student who engages in SIB to avoid academic tasks may pull his own hair more often when sick because avoiding academic work is often more desirable when a person is not feeling well (O'Reilly, 1995).

MOs may be events or conditions internal to the student (e.g., pain, hunger, fatigue, illness, or boredom) or external to the student (e.g., a long bus ride or a noisy cafeteria). The important feature is that an MO changes the reinforcing value of a specific consequence by making it more or less desirable. MOs may occur temporally and contextually distant from the behavior (e.g., loss of sleep the night before increases a student's desire to avoid exercise during gym class) (Langthorne, McGill, & Oliver, 2014). Being able to identify factors that affect a student's motivation to behave for specific consequences may lead to more effective interventions. For example, providing a snack earlier in the day before the occurrence of a challenging behavior (e.g., head hitting) that functions to obtain food may prevent behavior spikes on days the student misses breakfast.

Third, challenging behavior may be related to a medical condition. For example, some SIB may be related to insufficient levels of the neurotransmitter serotonin in the brain or to a genetic condition (e.g., Kolevzon et al., 2014). In both cases, a medical solution such as medication may appear necessary, and the involvement of a medical professional may be warranted. Although some behaviors may improve as a result of medication, currently few medication options are available to treat challenging behavior in people with autism (Dove et al., 2012; Earle, 2016). Even in cases where a clear medical or biological explanation exists, medication may still not be an option for many reasons (undesirable side effects, parental choice, etc.). In addition, establishing a definitive medical explanation for most challenging behaviors is difficult, if not impossible. Even if a challenging behavior has clear biological (nature) underpinnings, environmental (nurture) factors (e.g., history of reinforcement for the challenging behavior) are often also involved and need to be assessed (Lang et al., 2013). Being aware of biological conditions and medications that may influence a student's challenging behavior is important, but behavioral interventions may still be necessary. Regardless, it is imperative, particularly in cases of SIB and behaviors that potentially have a medical cause (e.g., ruminative vomiting, failure to appropriately toilet) to seek screening for potential medical issues.

Fourth, like all operant behavior, challenging behavior serves a function. As repeatedly noted, in most cases challenging behavior functions as a way for the student to obtain or avoid certain people, places, items, activities, and so forth. For example, a student who dislikes running for exercise may hit his gym teacher or bite his own arm to communicate his dislike for the activity when his gym teacher tells him to run around the track. If, as a result, the student is allowed to watch the running activity from the bleachers instead, thus avoiding an undesirable activity, he may continue arm biting in similar future circumstances. Before planning interventions for challenging behavior, you should first identify the possible function(s) that behavior serves for the student.

Fifth, challenging behavior may be the result of a skill deficit. Often, a student's challenging behavior reflects the fact that the student does not know a more appropriate way to meet needs or communicate. For students with autism, this is especially important, because language and social deficits are common. A student unable to use socially acceptable forms of communication will likely come to depend on challenging behavior as a way to communicate. Therefore, when a student lacks appropriate functional communication skills, part of the intervention must be to teach the student more suitable and effective ways of communicating (e.g., Boesch, Taber-Doughty, Wendt, & Smalts, 2015).

A comprehensive FBA will address all five of these areas by (a) noting the antecedents and consequences surrounding occurrences of challenging behavior, (b) considering possible factors that may influence the value of reinforcers related to those antecedents and consequences (i.e., MOs), (c) consideration of possible medical or biological issues (e.g., lack of sleep, medication side effects, illness) that may be related to the challenging behavior, (d) identifying the type of reinforcement (i.e., positive or negative reinforcement) and any specific reinforcers that may be maintaining the challenging behavior (e.g., access to a specific toy or attention from a particular person), and (e) identifying target skills that serve the same function as the challenging behavior (e.g., requesting a break verbally for a child who engages in aggression maintained by escape from work).

3-1a Conducting a Functional Behavioral Assessment

The FBA process typically involves several different components and steps. The first is to gather information about the student's behavior and related contextual and environmental variables. In other words, you should identify MOs that may set the stage for challenging behavior, antecedents that immediately precede the challenging behavior, and consequences regularly associated with the target behavior. The information (data) you collect will provide clues to the challenging behavior's function. Ideally, the information you gather should also identify how regularly the challenging behavior results in the student obtaining something he wants or avoiding something he dislikes.

It is also important to determine the power of the reinforcing consequences delivered for challenging behavior compared to the reinforcers delivered for appropriate behavior. For example, challenging behavior often produces a much larger reaction from others (more powerful reinforcer) than appropriate behavior. Imagine a student who politely asks her teacher to come talk and another student who kicks a nearby peer. Who will receive the biggest and most immediate reaction (attention) from the teacher? The teacher must consider how efficiently the challenging behavior receives reinforcement so that equally or more efficient appropriate behaviors can be taught. For example, imagine a student capable of requesting a break from work by either screaming or by handing a card with a picture of the break area on it to the teacher. When the student screams, the teacher believes the student is "overstimulated" and always sends her to the break area for five minutes to calm down. However, when the student uses the picture card to request a break, the teacher tells her she can rest at her desk for one minute. In this example, picture card exchange and screaming are in the same response class because they both function to escape work (request a break). Even though picture card use is reinforced, it is less efficient than screaming, which results in a longer break farther from the work area. Therefore, the child is likely to use the picture card infrequently and to continue to scream for breaks. The important point here is that, if the challenging behavior produces a better reinforcer or is easier to do than alternative responses with the same function, then it will continue to occur even if a more appropriate replacement behavior has been acquired (Fuhrman, Fisher, & Greer, 2016).

Conduct Indirect Assessment

Information regarding relevant contextual variables and possible functions may be obtained using both indirect and direct assessment methods. **Indirect assessment** involves interviewing people familiar with the student to determine, in their opinion (a) when appropriate and challenging behaviors are most likely to occur and not occur, (b) what happens after challenging behavior occurs, and (c) how regularly these consequences occur. The forms shown in Tables 3.1, 3.2, and 3.3 address these questions. This approach is considered *indirect* because the person assessing the behavior is not directly observing the student but merely asking others about what they have observed. It is recommended that people familiar with the student's behavior—teachers, paraprofessionals, support personnel, parents—complete the functional assessment report (FAR) shown in Table 3.1.

TABLE 3.1 ● Functional Assessment Report (FAR)

PART I	
INAPPROPRIATE BEHAVIOR	**APPROPRIATE BEHAVIOR**
Describe inappropriate behavior(s). Be specific.	Describe appropriate behavior(s). Be specific.
When are these most likely to occur? Describe specific situations.	When are these most likely to occur? Describe specific situations.
When are these least likely to occur? Describe specific situations.	When are these least likely to occur? Describe specific situations.
Are there conditions under which the behavior is more likely to occur (student is ill, problems at home, etc.)?	Are there conditions under which the behavior is more likely to occur (certain days or times of day, etc.)?
A.	A.
B.	B.
C.	C.
D.	D.
What happens when the student exhibits this behavior (e.g., what do other students do? What does teacher do? What is obtained or avoided?)?	What happens when the student exhibits this behavior (e.g., what do other students do? What does teacher do? What is obtained or avoided?)?
A.	A.
B.	B.
C.	C.
D.	D.

(continued)

TABLE 3.1 ● **Functional Assessment Report (FAR)** (*continued*)

WHY DO YOU THINK THE STUDENT EXHIBITS EACH INAPPROPRIATE BEHAVIOR?	A	B	C	D
PART II				
Attention from teacher				
Attention from peers				
Attention from other adults				
Self-stimulation				
Avoid work or other tasks				
Avoid situations				
Avoid peers, teachers, or other people				
Lack of social skills for situation				

TABLE 3.2 ● **Motivation Assessment Scale**

NAME: _____ RATER: _____ DATE: _____

DESCRIPTION OF BEHAVIOR (BE SPECIFIC): _____

SETTING DESCRIPTION: _____

Instructors: The MAS is a questionnaire designed to identify those situations where an individual is likely to behave in specific ways. From this information, more informed decisions can be made about the selections of appropriate replacement behaviors. To complete the MAS, select one behavior of specific interest. Be specific about the behavior. For example, "is aggressive" is not as good a description as "hits other people." Once you have specified the behavior to be rated, read each question carefully and circle the one number that best describes your observations of this behavior.

QUESTIONS	ANSWERS						
1. Would the behavior occur continuously if this person was left alone for long periods of time?	Never 0	Almost Never 1	Seldom 2	Half the Time 3	Usually 4	Almost Always 5	Always 6
2. Does the behavior occur following a request to perform a difficult task?	Never 0	Almost Never 1	Seldom 2	Half the Time 3	Usually 4	Almost Always 5	Always 6
3. Does the behavior seem to occur in response to your talking to other persons in the room/area?	Never 0	Almost Never 1	Seldom 2	Half the Time 3	Usually 4	Almost Always 5	Always 6
4. Does the behavior ever occur to get a toy, food, or an activity that this person has been told he/she can't have?	Never 0	Almost Never 1	Seldom 2	Half the Time 3	Usually 4	Almost Always 5	Always 6
5. Would the behavior occur repeatedly, in the same way, for long periods of time if the person was alone (e.g., rocking back and forth for over an hour)?	Never 0	Almost Never 1	Seldom 2	Half the Time 3	Usually 4	Almost Always 5	Always 6
6. Does the behavior occur when any request is made of this person?	Never 0	Almost Never 1	Seldom 2	Half the Time 3	Usually 4	Almost Always 5	Always 6
7. Does the behavior occur whenever you stop attending to this person?	Never 0	Almost Never 1	Seldom 2	Half the Time 3	Usually 4	Almost Always 5	Always 6

(continued)

TABLE 3.2 ● **Motivation Assessment Scale** (*continued*)

QUESTIONS	ANSWERS						
8. Does the behavior occur when you take away a favorite food, toy, or activity?	Never 0	Almost Never 1	Seldom 2	Half the Time 3	Usually 4	Almost Always 5	Always 6
9. Does it appear to you that the person enjoys doing the behavior (it feels, tastes, looks, smells, sounds pleasing)?	Never 0	Almost Never 1	Seldom 2	Half the Time 3	Usually 4	Almost Always 5	Always 6
10. Does this person seem to do the behavior to upset or annoy you when you are trying to get him/her to do what you ask?	Never 0	Almost Never 1	Seldom 2	Half the Time 3	Usually 4	Almost Always 5	Always 6
11. Does this person seem to do the behavior to upset or annoy you when you are not paying attention to him/her (e.g., you are in another room, interacting with another person)?	Never 0	Almost Never 1	Seldom 2	Half the Time 3	Usually 4	Almost Always 5	Always 6
12. Does the behavior stop occurring shortly after you give the person a food, toy, or requested activity?	Never 0	Almost Never 1	Seldom 2	Half the Time 3	Usually 4	Almost Always 5	Always 6
13. When the behavior is occurring does this person seem calm and unaware of anything else going on around her/him?	Never 0	Almost Never 1	Seldom 2	Half the Time 3	Usually 4	Almost Always 5	Always 6
14. Does the behavior stop occurring shortly after (1 to 5 minutes) you stop working with or making demands of this person?	Never 0	Almost Never 1	Seldom 2	Half the Time 3	Usually 4	Almost Always 5	Always 6
15. Does this person seem to do the behavior to get you to spend some time with her/him?	Never 0	Almost Never 1	Seldom 2	Half the Time 3	Usually 4	Almost Always 5	Always 6
16. Does the behavior seem to occur when this person has been told that he/she can't do something he/she had wanted to do?	Never 0	Almost Never 1	Seldom 2	Half the Time 3	Usually 4	Almost Always 5	Always 6

	SENSORY	ESCAPE	ATTENTION	TANGIBLE
	1.	2.	3.	4.
	5.	6.	7.	8.
	9.	10.	11.	12.
	13.	14.	15.	16.
Total Score =				
Mean Score =				
Relative Ranking =				

Motivation Assessment Scale: Functions for usage

Caveat: Person(s) filling out the form must be familiar with the individual who has the behavior challenge.

■ To direct our understanding of the behavior challenge to the intent of the challenge versus the way it appears or makes us feel.
■ To understand the correlation between the frequency of the challenging behavior and its potential for multiple intents.
■ To identify those situations in which an individual is likely to behave in certain ways (e.g., requests for change in routine or environment lead to biting).

Outcomes:

■ To assist in the identification of the motivation(s) of a specified behavior.
■ To make more informed decisions concerning the selection of appropriate reinforcers and supports for a specified behavior.

Note well: Like any assessment tool, the MAS should be used in an ongoing continually developing mode.

The Motivation Assessment Scale, copyright Monaco & Associates Incorporated, may be obtained from Monaco & Associates Incorporated, 4125 Gage Center Drive, Topeka, KS 66604. 1-785-272-5501, 1-800-798-1309, http://www.monacoassociates.com.

TABLE 3.3 ● **Completed Motivation Assessment Scale**

NAME: *Eddie*   RATER: *Scheuermann*   DATE: *3/10*

DESCRIPTION OF BEHAVIOR (BE SPECIFIC): *Hits self, grabs teacher*

SETTING DESCRIPTION: *Work time*

Instructors: The MAS is a questionnaire designed to identify those situations where an individual is likely to behave in specific ways. From this information, more informed decisions can be made about the selections of appropriate replacement behaviors. To complete the MAS, select one behavior of specific interest. Be specific about the behavior. For example, "is aggressive" is not as good a description as "hits other people." Once you have specified the behavior to be rated, read each question carefully and circle the one number that best describes your observations of this behavior.

QUESTIONS	ANSWERS						
1. Would the behavior occur continuously if this person was left alone for long periods of time?	Never 0	Almost Never ①	Seldom 2	Half the Time 3	Usually 4	Almost Always 5	Always 6
2. Does the behavior occur following a request to perform a difficult task?	Never 0	Almost Never 1	Seldom 2	Half the Time 3	Usually 4	Almost Always ⑤	Always 6
3. Does the behavior seem to occur in response to your talking to other persons in the room/area?	Never 0	Almost Never ①	Seldom 2	Half the Time 3	Usually 4	Almost Always 5	Always 6
4. Does the behavior ever occur to get a toy, food, or an activity that this person has been told he/she can't have?	Never 0	Almost Never 1	Seldom ②	Half the Time 3	Usually 4	Almost Always 5	Always 6
5. Would the behavior occur repeatedly, in the same way, for long periods of time if the person was alone (e.g., rocking back and forth for over an hour)?	Never 0	Almost Never ①	Seldom 2	Half the Time 3	Usually 4	Almost Always 5	Always 6
6. Does the behavior occur when any request is made of this person?	Never 0	Almost Never 1	Seldom 2	Half the Time 3	Usually 4	Almost Always 5	Always ⑥
7. Does the behavior occur whenever you stop attending to this person?	Never 0	Almost Never 1	Seldom ②	Half the Time 3	Usually 4	Almost Always 5	Always 6
8. Does the behavior occur when you take away a favorite food, toy, or activity?	Never 0	Almost Never 1	Seldom ②	Half the Time 3	Usually 4	Almost Always 5	Always 6
9. Does it appear to you that the person enjoys doing the behavior (it feels, tastes, looks, smells, sounds pleasing)?	Never 0	Almost Never ①	Seldom 2	Half the Time 3	Usually 4	Almost Always 5	Always 6
10. Does this person seem to do the behavior to upset or annoy you when you are trying to get him/her to do what you ask?	Never 0	Almost Never 1	Seldom 2	Half the Time ③	Usually 4	Almost Always 5	Always 6
11. Does this person seem to do the behavior to upset or annoy you when you are not paying attention to him/her (e.g., you are in another room, interacting with another person)?	Never ⓪	Almost Never 1	Seldom 2	Half the Time 3	Usually 4	Almost Always 5	Always 6
12. Does the behavior stop occurring shortly after you give the person a food, toy, or requested activity?	Never 0	Almost Never 1	Seldom ②	Half the Time 3	Usually 4	Almost Always 5	Always 6
13. When the behavior is occurring does this person seem calm and unaware of anything else going on around her/him?	Never 0	Almost Never ①	Seldom 2	Half the Time 3	Usually 4	Almost Always 5	Always 6
14. Does the behavior stop occurring shortly after (1 to 5 minutes) you stop working with or making demands of this person?	Never 0	Almost Never 1	Seldom 2	Half the Time 3	Usually 4	Almost Always ⑤	Always 6
15. Does this person seem to do the behavior to get you to spend some time with her/him?	Never 0	Almost Never ①	Seldom 2	Half the Time 3	Usually 4	Almost Always 5	Always 6
16. Does the behavior seem to occur when this person has been told that he/she can't do something he/she had wanted to do?	Never 0	Almost Never 1	Seldom ②	Half the Time 3	Usually 4	Almost Always 5	Always 6

(continued)

TABLE 3.3 ● Completed Motivation Assessment Scale (*continued*)

	SENSORY		ESCAPE		ATTENTION		TANGIBLE
1.	*1*	2.	*5*	3.	*1*	4.	*2*
5.	*1*	6.	*6*	7.	*2*	8.	*2*
9.	*1*	10.	*3*	11.	*0*	12.	*2*
13.	*1*	14.	*5*	15.	*1*	16.	*2*
Total Score =	*4*		*19*		*4*		*8*
Mean Score =	*1*		*4.75*		*1*		*2*
Relative Ranking =	*1*		*4.75*		*1*		*2*

Motivation Assessment Scale: Functions for usage

Caveat: Person(s) filling out the form must be familiar with the individual who has the behavior challenge.
- To direct our understanding of the behavior challenge to the intent of the challenge versus the way it appears or makes us feel.
- To understand the correlation between the frequency of the challenging behavior and its potential for multiple intents.
- To identify those situations in which an individual is likely to behave in certain ways (e.g., requests for change in routine or environment lead to biting).

Outcomes:
- To assist in the identification of the motivation(s) of a specified behavior.
- To make more informed decisions concerning the selection of appropriate reinforcers and supports for a specified behavior.

Note well: Like any assessment tool, the MAS should be used in an ongoing continually developing mode.

The Motivation Assessment Scale, copyright Monaco & Associates Incorporated, may be obtained from Monaco & Associates Incorporated, 4125 Gage Center Drive, Topeka, KS 66604. 1-785-272-5501, 1-800-798-1309, http://www.monacoassociates.com.

To complete the FAR form, list specific challenging behaviors and appropriate behaviors. Then, for each behavior, answer the remaining questions. The response recorded next to "A" refers to the first behavior described in the first question. "B" responses refer to the second behavior from question 1 and so forth. Part II pertains only to the inappropriate behaviors "A," "B," "C," and "D" as described in the first question. The responses to the questions should help identify contextual events and possible functions associated with the challenging behaviors.

The Motivation Assessment Scale (MAS) (Delaney & Durand, 1986) shown in Table 3.2 is designed to help identify possible functions of challenging behaviors and the efficiency of those behaviors in attaining those functions. Again, the people most familiar with the student should complete the form by circling the number that best describes the frequency of the situation described in each item. After the form is completed, record the number associated with each answer in the box on the second page that corresponds with the item number. For example, if "5" was circled for item 1, you would record "5" in box number 1 on the second page. The total for each column can then be calculated. Finally, find the mean (average) score for each column by dividing the total score for the column by 4. The column with the highest score suggests what the person who completed that form believes it to be the function of the behavior.

As you can see from Eddie's MAS (Table 3.3), escape appears to be the function of his challenging behavior. If more than one person is willing to complete the MAS, it is sometimes wise to have each person complete the form independently. Giving the MAS to multiple people one at a time will allow you to compare results across people and may provide important clues regarding effective intervention. For example, perhaps the student's mother's MAS suggests that the behavior functions to obtain attention, but the teacher assistant's suggests that the behavior functions to escape work. It is possible that the behavior serves both functions but that undesirable task demands are more common in school and therefore the teacher assistant is more aware of the escape function than the parents. By considering and discussing areas of disagreement across stakeholders (teachers and parents) or environments (home and school), a more accurate and comprehensive description of the behavior's function may be obtained (e.g., Lang et al., 2010).

Conduct Direct Assessment

Indirect assessment is helpful, but **direct assessment** (i.e., actually observing the student in various contexts) is an indispensable step in a comprehensive FBA (Matson, 2012). In addition, legal cases have established the expectation that FBAs include in-depth indirect *and* direct data (e.g., Etscheidt, 2006). The two techniques discussed next are methods of direct assessment.

Scatterplots As shown in Figure 3.1, scatterplots come in the form of a matrix relating behavior to one or more external variables (e.g., time of day) in order to determine the occurrence of behavior under the specified conditions. Although a scatterplot may not always help identify specific antecedents and consequences associated with the challenging behavior, it may provide a general picture of the patterns of the behavior over time.

In the sample shown in Figure 3.1, you can see that Erica seems to pinch and scratch other students mostly during snack and play times or during gym class. The next step would be to examine these times more closely using an antecedent-behavior-consequence (A-B-C) report,

STUDENT: Erica   OBSERVATION DATES: 9/11 thru 9/18

DESCRIPTION OF PROBLEM: pinches and scratches other students

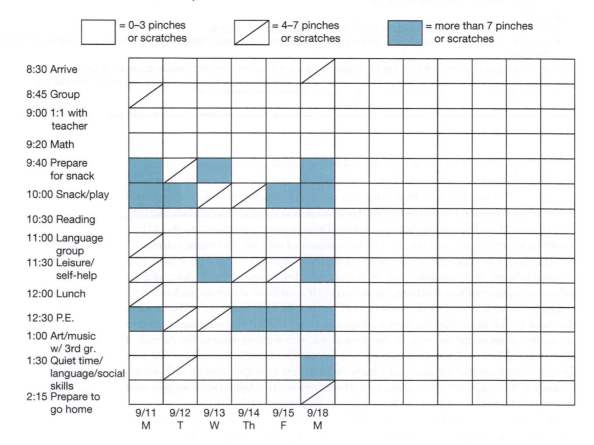

FIGURE 3.1 Scatterplot. Reprinted by permission of *Journal of Applied Behavior Analysis*.

which is described in the next section. Also, these data suggest that Mondays are especially problematic for Erica. At this point we do not know why this is, and we would need to more closely examine Mondays to see if something unique occurs on Monday that might be contributing to the challenging behavior. For example, maybe there are people present on that day who are not present other days, or perhaps she gets less sleep on Sunday nights. We may need to change something about her schedule to make it less likely that pinching and scratching will occur on Monday.

A-B-C Recording After you have determined the locations, times, and days when challenging behavior is most likely to occur, you should do an antecedent-behavior-consequence (A-B-C) report during those times. An A-B-C report is a written description of everything that happens during a specific observation period (Alberto & Troutman, 2017). The A-B-C report is arranged in a three-column format as antecedents, behaviors, and consequences. An A-B-C report can help you determine antecedents that may trigger the behavior (e.g., specific types of tasks, certain directions, being asked to end an enjoyable activity) and consequences that may be maintaining the behavior (e.g., getting out of a disliked task, gaining teacher attention, gaining access to desired objects). This information will help you formulate hypotheses about why the student exhibits the challenging behavior.

Figure 3.2 shows an example of an A-B-C report. To conduct this anecdotal report, observe the student during the time when the challenging behavior is most likely to occur.

Note: Observation during vocational activity in classroom; 4 students and teacher present.

	ANTECEDENT	BEHAVIOR	CONSEQUENCE
9:03	1. T: "Work time, Eddie. Come to the work area."	2. E. begins rocking and moaning, stays in seat.	3. T. busy preparing materials in work area.
9:05	4. T: "Eddie, time to work. Come now or you won't earn your money for today."	5. E. screams and hits his head with his fist.	6. T: "Eddie, no hitting. It's time to work and earn your money so you can go the store."
9:06		7. E. screams and hits his head repeatedly with both fists.	8. T. waits.
9:07	9. T: "Eddie, come now or I'll have to help you." 11. T. approaches Eddie and says, "I said it is time for work." T. places hands under Eddie's arms and lifts him to a standing position. 14. T. guides E. to time-out area.	10. E. continues screaming and hitting his head with both fists. 12. E. screams and grabs teacher's hair with both hands. 15. E. sits in time-out chair and rocks.	13. T. says loudly: "NO PULLING HAIR! Go to time-out."
9:11	16. T: "Time-out is over, Eddie. Go to the work area." 19. T. points to time-out chair.	17. E. screams and grabs teacher's hair. 20. E. sits.	18. T: "NO PULLING HAIR! BACK TO TIME-OUT!"
9:15	21. T: "Time-out is over, Eddie. I'm sorry. You've lost your work time for today. No work. Go back to your seat."	22. E. returns to seat quietly and sits down.	23. T. gathers materials.
9:16	24. T: "OK, Eddie. You need to practice writing your name in cursive. Here is your paper and pen."	25. E. writes quietly.	26. T. works with another student.

Summary: Eddie's inappropriate behavior escalates each time he is asked to go to the work area. However, he is compliant with requests that do not involve going to the work area (e.g., sitting in time-out, working on writing at his desk). This report suggests four possible conclusions:
  1. Eddie does not like working in the work area.
  2. Eddie prefers time-out to going to the work area.
  3. The money earned at the work area is not a strong enough reinforcer for Eddie.
  4. Eddie may not know an appropriate way to communicate his desire not to go to the work area.

FIGURE 3.2 A–B–C report

If you know that the behavior usually occurs just before lunch, for example, you might begin observation an hour before lunchtime. If you are not sure about when the behavior occurs, it may be helpful to do several A-B-C reports during different times of the day or different days of the week or both. Use a form that allows you to record time along the left side of the page and has three additional columns for antecedent, behavior, and consequence. Figure 3.3 shows a sample anecdotal recording form set up in this way.

Make a note of environmental conditions that might alter the reinforcing value of some consequences (MOs) on the A-B-C report. For example, make a note of who (e.g., teachers and students) is present, a brief description of the physical arrangement of the room, and any unusual circumstances that might help explain the behavior in question (e.g., the room is next to the band hall and the band can be heard playing). In particular, make note of MOs that might be related to the functions suggested by the indirect assessments. For example, if the MAS suggests that the behavior may function to obtain preferred tangibles and the student's favorite toy is in sight but out of the student's reach, that would be particularly important to note. Then, as you observe, write down what happens related to the student in question in the appropriate column (antecedent, behavior, or consequence). You should record everything the teacher says to the student, which tasks are given to the student, the student's behaviors, teacher and other students' responses, and so forth. Record fact only, not opinion. For example, although you might be tempted

NAME: _____ DATE: _____

SETTING: _____

ACTIVITY: _____

TIME	ANTECEDENT	BEHAVIOR	CONSEQUENCE

FIGURE 3.3 A–B–C form

▼ Professional Resource Download

to say "Emmy is angry and throws her food," you should simply record "Emmy throws her French fries."

After you are finished with the observation, review the report. According to Alberto and Troutman (2017) you should look for:

- what the student is doing that is inappropriate;
- how frequently this challenging behavior occurs;
- consistent patterns of obtaining or avoiding specific tasks, people, or tangibles following the challenging behavior;
- potential antecedents to the challenging behavior;
- patterns to the antecedents;
- recurring chains of specific antecedents, behaviors, and consequences; and
- possibilities for intervention (e.g., change antecedents, change consequences, teach the student a more appropriate response).

Note how the summary of the report shown in Figure 3.2 addresses these areas.

Formulate Hypotheses

After indirect and direct data have been gathered, the next step in the FBA process is to develop one or more hypotheses about why the student is exhibiting the challenging behavior. Your hypotheses should address one or more of the following areas.

- **The function of the behavior.** Based on the information you have gathered, consider what the student might obtain or avoid contingent on the challenging behavior. For example, do you think the student's challenging behavior functions to obtain teacher attention? Is the student avoiding certain tasks or situations after the behavior occurs? Does the student appear to be communicating something through the behavior? Try to be specific when possible. It may be possible to identify a specific item, task demand, or form of attention as a powerful reinforcer. For example, do not limit your consideration of teacher attention to only praising or positive feedback; recognize that reprimands, physical touch, closer proximity, and gestures are all forms of attention and may be acting as reinforcers. It is possible that not all forms of attention are equally reinforcing (Lang et al., 2014a). Reviewing the anecdotal report shown in Figure 3.2, we might conclude that Eddie's behavior is functioning as a form of communication that says he does not want to go to the work area. His hitting often results in his avoiding vocational work.
- **Possible skill deficits.** It can be difficult to identify skill deficits with certainty. We recommend this rule of thumb: If you seldom see the student exhibit the desired behavior under similar circumstances, assume they do not know how to do the behavior (i.e., assume a skill deficit). Students with autism frequently exhibit challenging behaviors that reflect skill deficits in language (both expressing wants or needs and understanding what others say) and interpersonal social skills (e.g., responding to conversational initiations, sharing, taking turns). For example, in Figure 3.2 we might assume Eddie lacks the skill to appropriately communicate his dislike for vocational work, and he may also lack the skills necessary to complete the work.
- **The behavior's relation to antecedents and consequences.** Do you see a pattern in terms of when or where appropriate and inappropriate behavior occurs? Does it typically occur in the presence of certain people, in response to particular demands, or around the same time each day? Also, do you see a pattern in the consequences for the behavior—positive or negative reinforcement? From the data shown in the scatterplot in Figure 3.1, we might assume that Erica is more likely to pinch or scratch during less structured times (snack or play and gym class). In Eddie's case (Figure 3.2), it appears that hitting himself or acting aggressively toward the teacher occurs most often when he is told to go to the work area. We might also conclude that this behavior is reinforced and thus will increase by Eddie avoiding going to the work area. During this observation period, Eddie avoided going to the work area every time he was asked to do so. Therefore, his hitting behavior appears to be very efficient because it consistently produces desired results.

PLANNING FORM

NAME: _____ DATE: _____

PROBLEM BEHAVIOR: _____

Motivating Operation/Antecedents	Skill Deficit	Function

REPLACEMENT BEHAVIOR: _____

Motivating Operation/Antecedents	Skills to Teach	Consequences

DESIRED BEHAVIOR: _____

Motivating Operation/Antecedents	Skills to Teach	Consequences

FIGURE 3.4 Functional assessment intervention planning form

⌄ **Professional Resource Download**

Figure 3.4 provides a format for organizing the information you have gathered and planning interventions based on your hypotheses about function and the contributing roles of MOs, antecedents, skill deficits, and consequences. The top portion of this form provides space for you to describe (in pinpoint terms) the challenging behavior, MOs, skill deficits that may be contributing to the behavior, and hypothesized function(s) of the target behavior.

The second section allows you to identify **replacement behavior(s)**—one or more appropriate way(s) for the student to attain the same or similar outcomes as the original challenging behavior. Sometimes, moving from the challenging behavior to the ultimate desired replacement behavior may be too great a change to attempt all at once. Identifying an interim replacement behavior enables the student to continue receiving desired consequences without necessitating the challenging behavior while you teach the student the more appropriate desired behavior. On the form, you should list antecedents that will typically precede the replacement behavior, what replacement behavior needs to be taught, and consequences contingent on the replacement behavior.

For example, in Eddie's case, our hypothesis is that he dislikes the work area or work task but lacks an appropriate way to communicate the need for a break or access to an alternative activity. Currently, Eddie's challenging behavior often results in his avoiding work. Our ultimate goal is for Eddie to go quietly to the work area when told to do so. However, given the effectiveness of his challenging behavior in avoiding work, this replacement behavior probably will not be easily acquired. Therefore, in the meantime, we recommend teaching an interim replacement behavior that produces the same results (avoiding work) for some period of time. In Eddie's case, his teacher could teach him to say or sign "no" when told to go to work.

At first, each time Eddie signs "no," the teacher should respond, "Eddie, that's a good way to tell me you don't want to work," then allow him to escape from the demand to work for a short time. After Eddie is signing or saying "no" consistently, the teacher should begin requiring a small amount of time in the work area before allowing him to leave (e.g., he must complete one brief task). Gradually, he should be required to work for longer periods of time before leaving the work area. However, occasionally, he should still be allowed to avoid work entirely when he signs "no." This type of intermittent reinforcement involving multiple reinforcement schedules will help avoid the recurrence of challenging behavior (Fuhrman et al., 2016).

The third section of the form helps you identify target desired behaviors, MOs and antecedents that may cue those behaviors, skills that need to be taught, and consequences that should follow the desired behaviors. Figure 3.5 shows a sample planning form that was completed for Eddie. When using the planning form, a separate form should be used for each behavioral **response class** (a group of behaviors with the same function). In Eddie's case, we would use one planning form for hitting, screaming, or any other behaviors associated with escape from a task. However, for behaviors associated with getting something he desires, we would use a separate form because behaviors that function to escape or avoid (negative reinforcement) are in a different response class than behaviors that function as a means to obtain something (positive reinforcement).

Table 3.4 presents some sample hypotheses (categorized in terms of MOs, antecedents, skill deficits, and consequences) and possible interventions for each hypothesis. Note how closely each intervention matches the perceived function of the behavior or the assumed relationship between the behavior and contextual circumstances. The intervention examples described in Table 3.4 are *not* meant to be definitive recommendations for interventions for

PLANNING FORM

NAME: _Eddie_   DATE: _3/15_

PROBLEM BEHAVIOR: _Noncompliance: screaming, hitting head, grabbing teacher_

Motivating Operation/Antecedents	Skill Deficit	Function
– Work time, being asked to go to work area	– Communicating that he doesn't like work or that he doesn't want to go to work	– Escape "work"/avoid

REPLACEMENT BEHAVIOR: _Sign "no" when asked to go to work_

Motivating Operation/Antecedents	Skills to Teach	Consequences
– Being asked to go to work	– Sign "no"	– Avoid work

DESIRED BEHAVIOR: _Going to work and working on assigned tasks_

Motivating Operation/Antecedents	Skills to Teach	Consequences
– Being asked to go to work, given work tasks	N/A	– Money earned may be used to buy "break passes," to be used during work time

FIGURE 3.5 Completed planning form

the specific problem behaviors listed but are intended only to illustrate the relationship between the nature of the hypothesis and the type of function-matched intervention that might be indicated. Interventions for your students should be individualized—in other words, designed based on the unique variables associated with each student, behavior, and context.

TABLE 3.4 ● **Sample Hypothesis Statements and Related Interventions**

POTENTIAL MOTIVATING OPERATIONS	
HYPOTHESES	**POSSIBLE STRATEGIES**
1. Tim is more likely to hit himself when he has a cold or allergies.	1a. Talk to Tim's parents about considering ways to relieve symptoms of colds or allergies.
2. Jonathan's noncompliance increases toward lunchtime when he is getting hungry.	2a. Provide a midmorning snack for Jonathan.
3. Thomas is noncompliant in the mornings when his morning bus arrives late.	3a. Talk to the transportation company about a new route or new schedule for Thomas. 3b. Talk to Thomas' parents about sending activities for him to do on the bus.

ANTECEDENTS	
HYPOTHESES	**ANTECEDENT STRATEGIES**
1. Erica is more likely to pinch or scratch during unstructured times (e.g., free play at recess).	1a. Provide more structure: clear expectations and instructions, frequent feedback, clearly defined activities, and so on.
2. Colin is likely to hit or pinch other students when he sits next to them during group time.	2a. Allow Colin to hold a favorite object in his hands during group time (as long as this does not interfere with his participation in the group). 2b. Teach Colin to sit with his hands tucked under his legs. Reinforce him for increasingly longer periods of time in which his hands are tucked under his legs.

SKILL DEFICITS	
HYPOTHESES	**STRATEGIES FOR TEACHING NEW SKILLS**
1. Eddie hits because he does not know how to express his dislike for a specific vocational task.	1a. Teach Eddie to shake his head "no" rather than hitting. 1b. Give Eddie choices of vocational tasks.
2. Aviv screams when required to use his spoon or fork for eating, as opposed to his hands.	2a. Provide modified utensils Aviv will use (assistive technology) or serve food that can be eaten with hands. 2b. Use DRI to teach utensil use.

(continued)

TABLE 3.4 ● **Sample Hypothesis Statements and Related Interventions (*continued*)**

CONSEQUENCES	
HYPOTHESES	**CONSEQUENCE STRATEGIES**
1. Eddie avoids going to the work area by hitting.	1a. Allow Eddie to earn breaks as a reinforcer, at first for saying "no" (or some other appropriate communicative behavior) in response to the direction to go to the work area, or for moving in the direction of the work area without hitting. Later, he will be required to complete a portion of his assigned task before being allowed to leave the work area. Eventually, he must complete all of the task.
2. Ben runs away to get attention.	2a. Provide Ben with high levels of attention for walking within arms' length of teacher. In addition, if he runs, retrieve him but provide as little attention as possible in doing so.
3. Travis engages in auditory self-stimulatory behaviors (e.g., cups his hand between his mouth and ear and makes noises) because he likes the echolike sound.	3a. Use DRA: Reinforce Travis for listening to seashells or for using headphones.

Develop the Behavior Intervention Plan

The last step is to develop a behavior intervention plan based on the data you collected and the hypotheses you developed. Your BIP will include, as appropriate, MOs, antecedents, changing consequences, targeted replacement behaviors, and strategies for teaching these new behaviors. Once intervention has started, be sure to monitor the effects of the intervention program on the challenging behaviors using one of the measurement techniques described in Chapter 2. If intervention fails, first check to ensure that the intervention was being consistently implemented as planned. If the intervention was not implemented properly, steps to better train the people assisting with the implementation are necessary (Rispoli, Neely, Lang, & Ganz, 2011). If implementation was consistently accurate but the intervention did not reduce the challenging behavior, then you may need to collect additional information and consider revising your FBA function hypothesis before creating a new function-matched intervention package for the student (Lang et al., 2010).

The FBA process is a critical step in designing effective interventions for the challenging behaviors of students with autism. Because students with autism may have limited repertoires of appropriate behaviors (significant skill deficits), their challenging behaviors may be among the only ways they have of getting needs met. Failure to recognize this may result in BIPs that do little to reduce challenging behaviors (Hurl et al., 2016).

3-2 Challenging Behavior Interventions

Students with autism may exhibit a wide range of challenging behaviors that do not need to be described in detail here. Instead, we discuss a few common types of challenging behavior topographies that illustrate the concepts we have discussed.

3-2a Noncompliance

Noncompliance can take many forms ranging from passive noncompliance (e.g., the student simply does not do as told) to overt aggression in response to a demand. At the least, noncompliance can interfere with instruction. At worst, it can result in placement in more restrictive settings, limit opportunities for meaningful interaction with peers and adults, and even cause physical injury (e.g., refusal to get out of the road). Furthermore, noncompliance in young children can escalate into more serious challenging behaviors that are unlikely to dissipate with age (Didden et al., 2012). Although *noncompliance* is a term that often appears in the research literature and is commonly used in practice, it is not particularly descriptive because it is not clear exactly what the student is doing, only that whatever the student is doing is not what was asked or expected. In most cases, it is better to specifically identify what the student does when defining the challenging behavior. For example, does he yell "No!" and turn his back to the person giving a direction or attempt to run away? This level of specificity in the description of the challenging behavior's topography is preferable because it helps facilitate more accurate data collection.

3-2b Self-Injurious Behavior

Many people with autism engage in self-directed aggressive behaviors that may cause physical injury such as hitting themselves in the head, biting their own arms or hands, and skin picking. An SIB sometimes occurs with such intensity or frequency that it results in physical damage: bruising, bleeding, tissue damage, vision loss, and so on (Richman et al., 2013; Dunlap, Ferro, & dePerczel, 1994). Because of the potential for causing serious injury and because of the highly stigmatizing nature of SIB, it is critical to develop effective intervention plans to treat such behavior. However, in some cases, it may be essential for teachers to seek additional support from specialists, the child's educational team, and other appropriate sources to ensure the child's safety during the treatment of serious SIB.

3-2c Aggression

Aggression is defined by the potential to cause injury to other people or property. Aggression can take many forms, including hitting, kicking, pinching, throwing objects, property destruction, pulling hair, spitting, biting, and grabbing clothing (Brosnan & Healy, 2011). Because aggression places the safety of other people at risk, it is one of the most common reasons for referral for professional treatment and a great deal of research literature has focused on identifying effective interventions. Further, because aggressive acts are illegal, older students are at risk of a variety of legal consequences that can dramatically impede their ongoing education and treatment efforts. Like SIB, aggression may be serious and risky enough to warrant additional support and guidance, particularly when the student is formidable or medically fragile.

3-2d Stereotypy

These behaviors are sometimes referred to as **self-stimulatory** or **stereotypic behaviors** and are among the core defining features of autism (see Chapter 1). Stereotypic behaviors include spinning objects, body rocking, repetitive vocalizations, flapping hands, and a host of other similar behaviors. Stereotypy poses unique challenges for educators because it is often self-reinforcing for the child (Reed, Hirst, & Hyman, 2012). For example, staring at her hands while waving them in front of her face may function only to provide the child with a form of visual stimulation. In other words, the reinforcing consequence maintaining stereotypic behavior often involves a sensation experienced by the student as a direct result of the behavior. Unlike other forms of challenging behavior with a function that requires another person's behavior (e.g., obtaining attention or provision of an out-of-reach item), it is difficult and sometimes impossible for teachers or parents to control that same or similar reinforcer following the stereotypic behavior. Although self-reinforcing behaviors (sometimes referred to as self-stimulating because they are maintained by **automatic**

reinforcement) are common in children with autism, remember that topography does not reliably predict function, and the FBA process is still warranted when addressing stereotypic behaviors.

Interestingly, addressing stereotypic behavior is often beneficial for other domains of functioning. For example, research has demonstrated an inverse relationship between stereotypic behaviors and nontargeted functional behaviors. For example, many researchers have reported collateral improvements in academic performance, language, and play when self-stimulatory behaviors are reduced. Research has also found spontaneous decreases in self-stimulatory behaviors as a result of students mastering skills in play and physical exercise (e.g., Kern, Koegel, & Dunlap, 1984; Lang et al., 2014b; Lang, Koegel, Ashbaugh, Regester, Ence, & Smith, 2010; Kern, Koegel, Dyer, Blew, & Fenton, 1982; Koegel, Firestone, Kramme, & Dunlap, 1974). Table 3.5 provides examples of the various forms of stimulation that may be obtained via stereotypy and suggests more appropriate activities that may compete with each of them.

3-2e Function-Matched Interventions

Because the topography of challenging behavior does not reliably predict what type of intervention will be effective, there is little need to focus discussion on the various forms (topography) of challenging behavior. A "one-size-fits-all" approach to selecting an intervention based solely on topography is nearly always unsuitable. As noted extensively in this chapter, the first step in dealing with challenging behavior is to use the FBA results to create an intervention that is aligned with the function of the challenging behavior. Interventions properly derived from FBA results can be referred to as **function-matched interventions**.

In this section, we will describe several function-matched interventions that are commonly used to reduce the challenging behavior of students with autism. Specifically, we first describe interventions that are typically used to address challenging behaviors with a **positive reinforcement function**—for example, challenging behaviors are maintained because the student receives attention, delivery of a toy, access to a preferred activity, or other contingent consequences in which something is obtained or access is granted. Second, we describe interventions that can be used to address challenging behaviors with

TABLE 3.5 ● Alternatives for Self-Stimulatory Behaviors

SENSORY SYSTEM	REPLACEMENT BEHAVIORS
Visual	Prism, pinwheel, kaleidoscope, toys that make flashing lights, View-Master, Lite-Brite, Slinky, lava lamp, windup toys, perpetual motion balls, string puppets, or yo-yos
Auditory	Talking toys, music boxes, music through headphones, noisemakers, clickers, seashells, talking through a microphone (amplification), using headphones to listen to recordings of the child's own voice, animal noises (whales, dolphins), or white noise
Tactile	Pieces of cloth with a variety of textures (velvet, burlap, chenille, suede, satin, fur), Silly Putty, Slime, Koosh balls, vibrator, finger paints, bean bags, Beanie Babies, plastic bubble wrap, hand exercise balls, "worry" beads, or rocks
Vestibular	Rocking horse, rocking chair, hammock, swing, tire swing, trampoline, pogo stick, Sit 'n Spin, ring-around-the-rosy, rolling on large therapy balls or in barrels, or somersaults
Proprioceptive*	Wave handheld fan, wrist or ankle weights, isometric exercises, hanging on monkey bars or chin-up bars, hand weights, weight machines, gymnastic exercises (headstands, handstands, cartwheels, somersaults, etc.), or grip-strengthening exercise tool
Olfactory	Cologne or aftershave either worn on the student's body or offered in small vials; or other fragrances offered in vials (e.g., scents used in making potpourri or dropped on lightbulbs)
Gustatory	Gum, mints, or hard candies

*Most of the activities listed as substitutes for proprioceptive self-stimulatory behaviors should be used with parent permission, with guidance from a physical therapist, or physical education teacher.

a **negative reinforcement function** that are maintained because the student is allowed to avoid some person, place, task, object, or other similar stimuli. Third, interventions designed to address skill deficits, particularly language deficits that can contribute to challenging behavior, are discussed. Fourth, we discuss **differential reinforcement** interventions, which have been found to be effective for challenging behaviors with a positive or negative reinforcement contingency (e.g., Falcomata & Gainey, 2014). Differential reinforcement may also be valuable when addressing behaviors with an unclear function (often the case with stereotypy). A variety of differential reinforcement procedures (e.g., functional communication training) will be discussed. Finally, in some cases, **punishment** procedures may be necessary. We discuss some basic punishment procedures while offering several precautions that should be observed when punishment is used. Although these different interventions are discussed separately, note that many of these approaches can be used together as part of a larger intervention package involving multiple components.

Remember that our purpose in describing these interventions is not to provide a "cookbook" approach to responding to challenging behavior. In fact, such a cookbook would never work if it failed to acknowledge the tremendous variability found across behaviors, settings, functions, and individual students! This section is simply meant to illustrate the process of selecting interventions based on FBA data. The extent to which teachers will be able to apply this model to their own students with autism will depend in large part on their ongoing and careful study in this area.

Challenging Behavior Maintained by Positive Reinforcement

Sometimes students have access to better reinforcement via challenging behavior than through appropriate behavior. For example, a student may work appropriately for several minutes with no teacher feedback, but as soon as the student stops working, the teacher approaches, talks to the student, examines work done so far, and encourages the student to continue working. Thus, the student gets more attention for noncompliance than compliance. If FBA data indicate that a student's challenging behavior is for the purpose of obtaining attention, for example, one potential intervention option is differential reinforcement using a preferred form of attention as the reinforcer (Lang et al., 2014a). In this case, compliance would be immediately, consistently, and strongly reinforced (differential reinforcement) while noncompliance would not receive reinforcement.

Intentionally withholding reinforcement for a targeted challenging behavior is referred to as **extinction**. In the previous example, the student could be given frequent attention for on-task behavior, and no (or minimal) attention when he stops working before the task is finished. Likewise, a student could be given strong reinforcement for following directions quickly and no reinforcement for not following directions. The same logic would be used if the positive reinforcement were in the form of a desired object or access to some activity. The student receives access to the object for following directions but does not receive the object for not following directions. Several variations of differential reinforcement are discussed later in this chapter.

Noncontingent reinforcement (NCR) involves providing the reinforcer that maintains challenging behavior (what the FBA identified as the function such as obtaining attention) for any appropriate behavior the student displays. By providing the reinforcer independent (or noncontingent) of the challenging behavior, the need to engage in that behavior is removed (Falcomata & Gainey, 2014). It simply is not necessary to engage in challenging behavior to obtain a preferred item, for example, if the preferred item is already in hand. To illustrate noncontingent reinforcement consider Anthony.

After an extensive FBA, Anthony's teacher determines that Anthony is most likely to hit himself when he is required to play independently with little or no attention. One way to decrease Anthony's SIB is to simply increase the amount of attention Anthony receives while he is playing using NCR. NCR involves delivering the reinforcer that is maintaining challenging behavior independently of behavior or before challenging behavior occurs. Specifically, the teacher could (a) play with Anthony during the period of time when independent play had previously been expected, (b) make a plan to provide attention to Anthony at least every *x* number of minutes while he is playing (e.g., every 2 minutes consistently), or (c) provide attention to Anthony after a variable amount of time playing independently (e.g., approximately every 1 to 3 minutes on average). Regardless of which approach is used, NCR works by reducing Anthony's motivation to engage in the challenging behavior: There should be little to no motivation to request attention via SIB if you are already receiving attention. Over time, NCR can be faded such that Anthony must go for longer durations before receiving attention. A drawback of NCR is that it does not actually teach Anthony to request attention appropriately (Luczynski & Hanley, 2013).

Challenging Behavior Maintained by Negative Reinforcement

If assessment data suggest challenging behavior functions to avoid a disliked task, situation, or person (negative reinforcement), then it may be helpful to try to reduce the student's motivation to escape by making the situation, task, or environment more appealing. In other words, decrease a student's motivation to escape or avoid a situation by considering MOs that may reduce the reinforcing value of escape. Doing so will make challenging behaviors that result in escape or avoidance less likely. Depending on the situation, this might be done in several ways.

First, consider changing *how a task is done*. For example, perhaps a student who dislikes writing could be given the choice to write with a colored marker instead of a pencil (Rispoli et al., 2013). A student who dislikes washing dishes because she does not like putting her hands in water could be allowed to wear rubber gloves. Or a student who dislikes using the vacuum cleaner because of the noise could be allowed to listen to music through headphones while vacuuming. In all of these examples, the antecedent condition and discriminative stimulus (S^D) may still be the same (e.g., teacher says, "It is time for us to do the dishes."), but challenging behavior that functions as a way to escape is less likely because the reinforcing value of escape has been abated.

Second, it is also important to consider the *functionality of the tasks* the student is asked to complete. Tasks should be meaningful for the student, which is to say that tasks should lead to independence in some aspect of daily living or in some other way improve the student's quality of life. Tasks that are not functional are not only a waste of time but also may be boring for students. For example, rather than have students sort colored blocks, a more functional task would be to sort clothes and towels by color to be washed. A nonfunctional approach to addressing the goal of strengthening pincher grasp would be to have the student place spring clothespins on a piece of cardboard. A functional way to develop pincher grasp is to have the student package items in plastic bags with zipper seals as part of packing food for a class picnic.

Third, in some cases you may need to *increase reinforcement* during the disliked situation. Sometimes a task cannot be sufficiently altered to make it more appealing or less aversive. If this is the case, then stronger positive reinforcement provided throughout the task can be provided. For example, M'Kayla disliked sitting next to peers and resisted when requested to do so during group work and games. Her teacher designed an intervention to frequently reinforce M'Kayla (e.g., praise and primary reinforcers) for sitting appropriately next to peers. Or if a student does not like shaving, the student could earn a token for each stroke of the electric razor. When he is finished, tokens could be exchanged for a desired item or activity (Carnett et al., 2014). Or the student could simply be allowed to choose a favorite cologne or aftershave to apply once he is finished.

Fourth, when appropriate, consider *decreasing the time* the student is required to participate in the disliked situation. In the early stages of intervention, the student would be required to engage in the activity for brief periods of time but then gradually be required to participate for longer durations of time. For M'Kayla, who disliked sitting next to her peers, an alternate intervention would be for her to sit next to peers for 1 minute. At the end of 1 minute of appropriate sitting, her sitting would be reinforced by being allowed to move away. After several days of successful 1-minute periods, she would next be required to sit appropriately for 2 minutes before being allowed to move away. The required time is gradually increased until M'Kayla is able to sit next to peers for an entire group activity. Likewise, if a student dislikes loading the dishwasher, the first step of intervention might be to have her place one dish in the dishwasher, then stop the activity. After several days of loading one dish without challenging behavior, the student would be required to put two dishes in the dishwasher before stopping the activity each day. The number of dishes required to be loaded before the activity ends would gradually be increased until the student is loading all the dishes at one time.

Finally, be sure the student *has the skills necessary* to complete the task. Noncompliance often occurs when students lack the ability to perform the target task (skill deficit) (Cipani, 1998). Therefore, it is critical that teachers have definitive evidence the student can do a task before presenting instructions and tasks to the student. The teacher should rely on recent educational assessment information to determine a student's readiness for tasks rather than assume a student has the necessary skills. For example, Walter is noncompliant when he is asked to sort coins. His teacher, Ms. Page, incorrectly assumes that Walter should be able to do this task because he can use the vending machine without assistance—even though coin discrimination has not been taught. What Ms. Page failed to realize is Walter's apparent ability to use the vending machine is because he continues inserting coins until the machine lights up to allow him to make a selection. He was not really counting money! In fact, he lacked the ability to distinguish between subtle elements of coins (e.g., size). Or consider Emmy, a 14-year-old new to Mrs. Garrett's class. Emmy resists when asked to put on and tie her shoes. Mrs. Garrett has been treating this as a form of disrespect and has been putting Emmy in time-out for refusing to tie her shoes. However, during their first conference, Mrs. Garrett learns from Emmy's mother that Emmy has never learned to tie her shoes; her mother does it for her every day. Emmy needs to be taught, not punished!

A practice referred to as **behavioral momentum** may also be useful in reducing challenging behavior maintained by escape or avoidance (negative reinforcement), particularly noncompliance (Pritchard, Hoerger, & Mace, 2014; Mace et al., 1988). This technique can increase the likelihood that a student will comply with a command for a disliked task by preceding it with several commands the student is likely to complete. In other words, a student is given two or three high-probability directions (directions to which the student is usually compliant and thus can be reinforced) before giving the low-probability direction (the command to which the student is typically noncompliant) (Knowles, Meng, & Machalicek, 2015). Immediately after the student finishes complying with those directions, the low-probability direction is given. For example, if Rusty is predictably noncompliant to the request "Rusty, you need to line up for lunch," you would first give two or three commands to do tasks that Rusty likes. So, you might instruct him as follows: "Rusty, turn off the radio" (and praise him when he complies), "Rusty, turn off the light" (followed by praise), "Rusty, give me 'five'" (followed by enthusiastic praise), and then ask him to line up.

Challenging Behavior Because of Skill Deficits

Sometimes students will display challenging behavior to obtain or avoid something because they do not know any other way to get what they want. They have not been taught as many socially appropriate ways to interact with the world as most people have. The following are descriptions of two primary skill deficits associated with challenging behavior.

Receptive Language Deficits Receptive language deficits can cause challenging behavior simply because the student does not understand the teacher's instructions. Receptive language is the ability to comprehend language; an inability to recognize such language is something most of us experience in a foreign country. Imagine attending school in which all instructions and social interactions were in a different language (e.g., Greek). Many of us would likely be labeled noncompliant in such a situation, particularly if the teacher did not know we could not understand. Remember from Chapter 1 that people with autism often have difficulty acquiring language, which may include speaking or understanding the speech of others. This characteristic has implications for how verbal directions are given.

Research suggests that, for some students, challenging behavior is related to the clarity of instructions (Walker & Walker, 1991). Therefore, you may want to consider poor understanding of verbal directions as an explanation for the challenging behavior, particularly when language assessment suggests the presence of deficits. Intervention would consist of modifying how verbal commands are given (Forehand & McMahon, 1981). Verbal instructions should have the following characteristics.

- **One or two steps only.** Do not give long, multistep directions. For example, instead of "Aubree, take off your coat, hang it up, then go choose a center—don't forget to hang your name tag on the center you choose," say "Aubree, take off your coat." When Aubree finishes that task, give her the next instruction.
- **Brief.** Do not make instructions confusing by adding explanations, cajoling, repeated reminders or warnings, or other discussion. Do not, for example, give an instruction such as "Kelly, I want you to set the table. Don't forget the placemats—yesterday you left them out. And remember where the napkins go. Are you going to fold the napkins? Remember—if you finish quickly you may watch TV until dinner, but if I have to keep reminding you, no TV."
- **Clear and specific.** For example, if you want a student to clean his desk area, say, "Johnny, please put your books away and throw away the trash on the floor around your desk." This type of specificity is important; a clear direction such as this is more likely to be followed to the expected standard than a vague direction such as "Please clean up now."
- **Use a command, not a question.** If you want students to do something, politely tell them; do not ask them. Do not ask a student, "Do you want to go to Ms. Ochoa's room now?" Tell him, "You are going to go to Ms. Ochoa's room now." Likewise, "Are you ready to work on writing?" has a lower probability of compliance than "Get out your pencil for writing time, please."
- **Given in such a way that they are prominent and distinct.** You should first get the student's attention before giving an instruction. Prefacing the instruction with the student's name is one possibility. Be sure the student is not engaged in a distracting activity when you give instructions. And it may be necessary to bend down to eye level with the student before giving an instruction. For example, Angelo's teacher Mr. Christen reported that he was noncompliant. During the FBA it was noted that Angelo was very compliant during class time when most students were quietly engaged in task-related behavior. However, during transition times, which were noisy and somewhat chaotic, Angelo's noncompliance increased substantially. It was hypothesized that noncompliance was the result of the loud chaotic environment. In such situations, Angelo was not attending to instructions and seemed disturbed by the noise and activity level. The recommendation was to give this student individual instructions before entering noisy environments and, when in noisy chaotic environments, remain in close proximity to Angelo so that reminders or additional instructions could be given with improved clarity. This should help increase the prominence of the directions. Instructions that are given from across the room are less pronounced than instructions given in immediate proximity to the student.

Compliance Skill Deficits Some students with autism, particularly young children or students who have not been in highly structured, instructionally focused educational programs, simply may not have learned to comply with the instructions and directives from a teacher yet. In such cases, direct instruction that targets compliance may be helpful. This situation is analogous to the fact that parents of toddlers must teach their children to follow directions. They do this by giving their children many opportunities to practice, using reminders, giving feedback, and applying consequences for both compliance and noncompliance. As a result, in most cases, young children eventually learn to follow instructions. However, students with autism may need more than the typical instruction received at home. One intervention option is a procedure known as *compliance training* (Durcharme & Ng, 2012; Simpson & Regan, 1986).

Compliance Training Compliance training is designed for students who have compliance skill deficits. In compliance training, the student is taught to comply using a highly structured teaching format that presents simple commands and prompts and reinforces compliance. This instructional procedure is presented several times per day until the student is compliant during the instructional sessions at a predetermined target level (e.g., 90% of the time). A form such as the one shown in Figure 3.6 is used to record compliant and noncompliant responses. After attaining compliance in the initial setting, the same structured teaching sessions are presented in a different environment such as the playground or workshop or with a different person (e.g., the teaching assistant) for generalization purposes. The steps and teaching strategies for compliance training are described in the following section. The recommended teaching strategy, discrete trial training, is described further in Chapter 5.

Conduct compliance training several times throughout the day. The length of these sessions should reflect the student's age, functioning level, and attention span. For some students, 3-minute sessions would be appropriate; other students could work for 10 or 15 minutes per session. During the compliance training sessions, the student should be seated in an appropriately sized chair with the teacher in a chair immediately in front of the student. If you are working with a student who may try to leave the training area, the

NAME: _____

+ = correct response − = incorrect response	DATE		
Phase I			
Sit down			
Touch your nose			
Clap hands			
Stand up			
Do this (imitate movement)			
Phase II			
Go get the ball			
Go touch the door			
Put this on the table (give object)			
Go touch your desk			
Come here (when child is a few feet away from teacher)			
Phase III			
Take off your coat			
Stack the blocks			
Throw the ball			
Go to group			
Get your lunch			

FIGURE 3.6 Compliance training form

⌄ Professional Resource Download

training area should be configured in a way that prevents this from happening. For example, the student's chair might be placed in a corner (facing the room) with the teacher's chair blocking the child's exit path.

Phase I: Beginning Training Commands are given using three steps:

1. *Give the child simple commands* such as those listed in Figure 3.6. Commands should be simple tasks that the child can perform and should not involve the student leaving the immediate training area. The command should be stated succinctly with no unnecessary verbiage.
2. *If the child does not comply within approximately 5 seconds, repeat the command while gently physically guiding the child to perform the task.*
3. *Deliver praise immediately after you have helped the child perform the task.* Praise should be descriptive and enthusiastic: "Dorothy, good job standing up!" or "Carl, I like the way you sat down!" No other reinforcement should be provided if you had to prompt the child to perform the task. If the child performs the task independently, give praise and a small amount of another reinforcer. Primary reinforcers are often appropriate for compliance training: small bites of cookie, a small sip of juice or milk, or a small bite of fruit. On the data-recording form, record the appropriate code next to the command that was just given.

Repeat steps 1 through 3, giving the various commands in random order. Once the student is consistently complying to these commands 80% of the time or more, move on to phase II.

Phase II: Advanced Training In phase II of training, the student is given commands that require movement away from the training area (see Figure 3.6). Follow steps 1 through 3 as described in phase I. In this phase of training, you may consider thinning the schedule of reinforcement. For example, rather than giving a reinforcer after every correct unprompted response, provide the reinforcer after three to five correct responses. Once the student is complying to these commands consistently 80% of the time or more, move on to phase III.

Phase III: Generalized Training In this phase of training, the student is given commands in natural contexts throughout the day. For example, the student might be told "Rolando, take off your jacket" or "Olivia, get out your book." These are commands that are given as part of the daily routine. However, all incorrect or incomplete responses are prompted and correct responses are reinforced. In addition, data should be recorded so that the child's rate of compliance in generalized settings can be monitored. Even after the student is complying with these commands consistently, you should still continue to reinforce compliance on an intermittent basis.

The goal of compliance training is to teach the student that compliance is expected and required when a command is given by a teacher, parent, or other adult familiar to the student. This highly structured, instructional approach to noncompliance reflects requirements for an effective program (e.g., clarity, practicality) as discussed in Chapter 1. Compliance training is especially important if you are working with primary- or intermediate-age children. It is critical that students with autism learn compliance, and compliance training is often an efficacious route to this goal. A potential limitation of the approach is that it involves contrived trials, and the compliance skills that are acquired in this way may not readily generalize to the student's natural routine. It is vital to prompt and reinforce compliance during the student's natural routine because doing so may preclude the need for this more intensive compliance training approach. Even when this more intensive approach is necessary, prompting and reinforcement during the natural routine in addition to during the structured trials will likely facilitate generalization. Finally, students with severe escape-maintained challenging behavior may not be good candidates for compliance training if it results in an unsafe escalation of challenging behavior during trials. As with any intervention, ongoing data collection, careful progress monitoring, and involvement of the student's family and school team are important.

In the remainder of this chapter, we describe two additional categories of behavior reductive techniques that can be implemented in conjunction with function-matched interventions: differential reinforcement techniques and punishment techniques.

3-2f Differential Reinforcement

In all of the various differential reinforcement interventions described in the following paragraphs, it is preferable to match the specific reinforcer used with the function of the challenging behavior identified in the FBA. However, differential reinforcement has been found to be effective even when not function matched, albeit with an increased chance of intervention failure. For example, a child who engages in challenging behavior to escape work (negative reinforcement) may still experience a reduction in challenging behavior when the reinforcer used in the differential reinforcement intervention involves the delivery of a preferred item or praise.

Differential reinforcement is a set of unique procedures used to reduce behaviors. In differential reinforcement, you determine what the student should do instead of the challenging behavior, and then you teach and systematically reinforce that desired behavior. The desired behavior (or replacement behavior) is reinforced, while the undesired or challenging behavior receives no reinforcement (extinction). As a result, the desired behavior increases and the undesired behavior diminishes over time. Differential reinforcement involves reinforcement and extinction but not punishment (in most cases). It is an effective procedure for reducing challenging behaviors without worrying about the detrimental side effects that sometimes occur with punishment. Four basic types of differential reinforcement are described in the following section. The differential reinforcement procedure you should use depends largely on the nature of the challenging behavior, as you will see.

Differential Reinforcement of Lower Levels of Behavior (DRL)

The strategy of differential reinforcement of lower levels of behavior (DRL) is used when the target challenging behavior does not need to be reduced immediately or completely. For example, it is acceptable and even desirable for a student to ask once or twice when it is time for a snack. It is unacceptable to ask the same question dozens of times in rapid succession. To use this strategy, you determine how many instances of the target challenging behavior the student is allowed to exhibit during a certain time period and still earn a reinforcer. This initial criterion is based on how many behaviors the student is currently exhibiting (baseline): You should choose a criterion that is achievable. Once the student meets that first criterion (perhaps for two or three consecutive days), you slightly reduce the number of target behaviors allowed. When the student is successful at this level, the number of behaviors allowed is reduced still further. This pattern continues until the behavior is reduced to acceptable levels.

DRL can also be used to reduce the duration of a challenging behavior: The student would be reinforced if challenging behavior stopped before the determined time, which should probably be marked by a timer. Gradually, as the student successfully stops the behavior within the determined period, the time allowed is shortened. This process continues until the behavior is reduced to desired levels.

DRL is not recommended for dangerous or hurtful behaviors or behaviors that cannot be tolerated at any level.

Differential Reinforcement of Alternative or Incompatible Behaviors (DRA or DRI)

This strategy involves the teacher selecting a specific replacement behavior to reinforce. The target replacement behavior is either directly incompatible with the challenging behavior (DRI) or a desirable alternative behavior (DRA). The student receives reinforcement for the replacement behavior while the target challenging behavior is on extinction. For example, a student could be reinforced for walking down the hall (as opposed to running):

This is DRI, because walking cannot occur at the same time as running. Or a child could be reinforced for sitting upright with her hands in her lap as an alternative to hand biting SIB. DRA and DRI are particularly effective when the replacement behavior is reinforced with the same reinforcer found in the FBA to be maintaining the challenging behavior.

Functional Communication Training (FCT) A subset of DRA, **functional communication training (FCT)**, consists of teaching students who may be communicating with their challenging behavior to use appropriate language responses instead. FCT involves reinforcing communicative behavior using the same reinforcer (or class of reinforcers) that was contingent on challenging behavior (Tiger, Hanley, & Bruzek, 2008).

As you have learned, sometimes challenging behavior may be a form of communication, particularly if the child does not have other effective ways of communicating. For example, a child may bite himself or attempt to pull your hair when he does not want to do the task you are presenting. When FBA data identify a communicative function for challenging behavior, the alternative behavior that you select should be an appropriate form of communication that sends the same message. For example, if a student pulls your hair to communicate "I don't want to do this," you may wish teach the student to say or touch a picture card that represents "No, thank you" instead.

But you might wonder if it is appropriate to teach the student refusal skills. In our opinion, the student is already refusing—you are simply teaching a more acceptable way to do it. Appropriate refusal is a valuable life skill that we all use. Also, although you might withdraw tasks at first, eventually you will require the student to complete more of the disliked tasks. You should still sometimes reinforce the appropriate use of "No, thank you" to avoid a resurgence of the challenging behavior. You will learn more about communication and language intervention options in Chapter 6.

Differential Reinforcement of Other Behavior (DRO)

This differential reinforcement procedure is especially helpful when the target behavior such as aggression or an SIB must be eliminated quickly. DRO (sometimes called *differential reinforcement of zero rates of behavior*) means that the student is reinforced at the end of a period of time during which the target challenging behavior was *not* exhibited. The reinforcement periods are brief at first and then gradually increase as the student learns to control the behavior. For example, a student receives a reinforcer at the end of each 30-second interval during which he does not hit his head. When he has been successful at controlling head hitting for 80% of the 30-second intervals over several days, the reinforcement period is increased to 45 seconds, then later to 1 minute, then 1.5 minutes, and so on. The actual duration of sessions and time intervals you select should be based on baseline data, typical behavior of the student's peers, the student's ability, and ongoing data collection.

To implement DRO, you must decide how long the initial reinforcement interval should be. To do this, gather baseline data to determine how frequently the behavior occurs. The initial reinforcement interval should be slightly less than the baseline average. For example, if baseline data indicate that Erin pokes her eyes approximately every 25 minutes, you might set 15 minutes as the initial reinforcement interval: If she does not poke her eyes for 15 minutes, she earns a reinforcer. The initial reinforcement interval must be short enough for the student to have a high probability of success. In addition, the duration of the intervals should not be increased too rapidly.

One potential drawback of DRO is that the student receives reinforcement if the target challenging behavior is not exhibited, no matter what else the student does or does not do during the interval. Obviously, under these circumstances you run the risk of reinforcing behaviors that are not desirable. However, this is a trade-off that sometimes must be made to get a more serious behavior under control. After the more serious behavior is eliminated, you can address other behaviors.

Another drawback is that a DRO may reduce a behavior that served an important function for the student. Unless the teacher eventually targets and reinforces an appropriate replacement behavior, the original or some other form of challenging behavior may return.

3-2g Punishment Procedures

Punishment is a consequence that reduces the likelihood that the preceding behavior will be repeated (Azrin & Holz, 1966). Thus, you can only determine whether a consequence is a punisher by monitoring the effect on the target behavior. If the behavior decreases as a result of the consequence, we may assume the consequence is punishing to the individual.

Perhaps more so than any other procedure, ethical concerns are associated with the misuse of punishment. Therefore, if you determine that it is necessary to use a punishment procedure, you must take care to ensure that the procedure is applied correctly, its effects are monitored, and it is used in conjunction with reinforcement of desired behaviors. Two mild punishment approaches that can be used to reduce challenging behavior are presented in this chapter: response cost and time-out.

Response Cost

Response cost is a procedure in which reinforcers are removed as a consequence for challenging behavior. Society commonly uses response cost to punish undesired behaviors. For example, if you are caught speeding, you may have to give up some of your reinforcers (money). If you fail to make your car payments, you may lose your car.

In the classroom, response cost involves removing tokens, material reinforcers, or activity reinforcers. If removing the reinforcer can be done quickly with little to no interruption in instruction and without retaliation from the student, then response cost can be considered. However, it is not an appropriate consequence for all behaviors, and you must be sure that removing the stimulus is not actually negatively reinforcing an unacceptable behavior. For example, taking away a disliked task as a consequence for stereotyped behavior during the task may actually be reinforcing to the student. Rely on data to inform you of the effectiveness of the procedure.

You also need to make sure not to remove all of a student's reinforcers. If the student has nothing left (lost entire field trip, party, all of his tokens, access to the computer for a month), it is quite possible the student is now outside the reinforcement system and will feel free to act as he, rather than the teacher, wants (he has nothing to lose at this point). Rather it is recommended that teachers remove portions of activities, for example (lost 5 minutes of free time) as punishment so the student still has something to work for.

Time-Out

Time-out is the procedure in which an individual is denied access to reinforcement for a specific period of time. If time-out is to be effective, the difference between the "time-in" situation and the time-out situation must be obvious. In other words, the time-in environment must be reinforcing to the child; the child must *want* to avoid time-out. It would make no sense to have them withdraw as a form of punishment if the function of the challenging behavior is to escape or avoid. In fact, such a procedure might well increase the challenging behavior over time. If students appear to like being in the classroom, around other peers and adults, then typical time-out procedures might work as punishers. If this is the case, then time-out offers several potential advantages over other types of punishment. When applied correctly, time-out usually reduces behavior quicker than other reductive procedures sometimes after only a few applications.

The two basic approaches to time-out are **nonexclusionary** and **exclusionary**. There are several forms of time-out within each of these two approaches. We do not recommend or endorse exclusionary time-out (also called **seclusion**) for students with autism. Several significant legal and ethical concerns have been associated with the use of exclusionary forms of time-out (Scheuermann, Peterson, Ryan, & Billingsley, 2015). For these reasons, we strongly advise against any use of exclusionary or seclusionary time-out procedure.

The following are a few simple guidelines that will help ensure that nonexclusionary time-out is used correctly.

- **Be sure that time-in is more reinforcing than time-out.** Time-out will not work if students *like* the time-out situation.

- **Determine the specific target behavior(s) that will be consequated with time-out.** Do not decide in the moment to use time-out. As with any other intervention, time-out should be carefully planned beforehand and not used on the spot without proper preparation.
- **Establish a consistent time-out area and procedure.** For the student to understand that the inappropriate behavior results in time-out, the same time-out procedure must be followed.
- **Determine the length of time-out.** Use brief time-outs. Time-out does not need to be long to be effective. The longer a student is in time-out, the more likely he is to forget why he is there, and the more likely he is to engage in challenging behaviors during time-out. We argue that the old adage "1 minute per year of age" is too long for most students. Five minutes feels like a long time even for an adult who has a well-developed sense of time. To a 5-year-old, it may seem endless. For many students, a 30-second time-out may be sufficient.
- **Determine the criterion for ending time-out.** The three basic approaches to ending time-out are as follows: (a) Time-out is for a predetermined period of time. When that time is up, the student again regains access to reinforcers. (b) Time-out is for a predetermined period of time. However, if the student is misbehaving at the end of that time, the student remains in time-out until she is behaving appropriately. (c) The student must exhibit appropriate behavior throughout the predetermined length of time-out for the time-out to end. If he misbehaves, the timer is reset.

For students with autism, we urge the first approach only. Furthermore, do not tell the student to "Come back when you're ready to behave!" Time-out is a teacher-managed procedure, and the teacher should decide when time-out is over.

- **Do not threaten the student with time-out.** If time-out is the predetermined consequence, use it each time the target misbehavior occurs.
- **When the target inappropriate behavior occurs, simply describe the behavior and tell the student to take a time-out.** Do not explain, remind, or argue. Simply say, "You hit Samantha. Time-out," or "No screaming. Put your head down."
- **Ignore mildly inappropriate behavior while the student is in time-out.** Students may scream, cry, engage in stereotyped behaviors, or exhibit other mildly challenging behaviors in time-out situations. It is important, however, to not give any reinforcement, especially attention, to a student in time-out.
- **As soon as possible after the time-out is over, reinforce the student for an appropriate behavior.** Remember, you are trying to help the student differentiate appropriate from inappropriate behavior and learn the desirability of the time-in environment compared to the time-out situation.
- **Monitor the effects of time-out.** If the target behavior does not begin to diminish within a few applications of time-out, reevaluate the form of time-out or time-out as an intervention for that particular target behavior.

When an FBA is properly conducted, it is likely to identify the challenging behavior's function. When reinforcement-based interventions involving careful changes to antecedent conditions and target replacement behaviors are matched to that function, punishment is not often necessary. The relationship between a teacher and student is critically important. Teachers want students to find their praise reinforcing and to enjoy being around them because that facilitates the educational process and makes students happier at school. Punishment, particularly when done carelessly, has the potential to undermine that relationship. Although the preceding procedures are relatively mild, we strongly encourage teachers to use them with caution and only when other interventions have failed or the behavior is severe enough to necessitate the more intense approach.

In the following section we offer two vignettes that focus on the challenging behavior interventions that do not involve punishment but do involve many of the other concepts and procedures we have discussed.

3-3 Case Study Examples in Reducing Challenging Behavior

In this section we present the cases of two students with autism who engage in challenging behavior. You should be able to identify the connection between the FBA results (function of challenging behavior) and the interventions used.

● VIGNETTE 3.1

Reducing Melissa's Screaming with Functional Communication Training

Melissa is in an early childhood classroom. Her teacher is concerned because she will often begin screaming loudly for extended periods of time, causing havoc in the classroom and disrupting her educational progress. FBA results suggest that Melissa screams when she does not have access to a toy or other item she desires. Simply giving Melissa the item before she screams and allowing her to keep it all day or access it at regular or variable intervals (i.e., noncontingent reinforcement) might be effective, but the teacher decides it would be best to teach Melissa to request tangibles appropriately.

After detailed consultation with Melissa's family, the teacher decides that Melissa should be taught to request items by exchanging pictures of desired objects. The teacher first takes a picture of several of Melissa's favorite toys in the classroom. Next she positions these items in places where Melissa can see them but cannot access them without assistance. When Melissa appears interested in an item, the teacher prompts her to select the appropriate picture and hand it to her. Screams are put on extinction and only picture exchanges are reinforced by giving the desired item to Melissa. This process of selecting a specific communication replacement behavior (e.g., picture exchange) to be taught through prompting and reinforcement while placing the challenging behavior on extinction is an example of functional communication training. FCT can be embedded in situations that arise naturally throughout Melissa's day or by setting aside specific times of day to practice the communicative replacement behavior. Over time, the prompts are faded gradually until Melissa is able to independently request desired items without relying on challenging behavior.

● VIGNETTE 3.2

Leah Learns and Mr. Feldman Stops Being Frustrated!

Mr. Feldman was frustrated! For the most part, his elementary class of students with autism was doing well. However, 11-year-old Leah was still exhibiting high levels of challenging behavior. Mr. Feldman consulted with another, more experienced teacher, who reminded him not to forget what he knows: step-by-step FBA of the challenging behavior followed by interventions designed to address the functions of the behavior. Mr. Feldman sheepishly admitted that, although he had tried various reinforcement programs, he had not sufficiently considered the behavior's function.

Realizing he had skipped an important step in designing behavioral interventions, Mr. Feldman, his paraprofessional, and the adaptive physical education teacher each completed the functional assessment report form. Mr. Feldman then compared the information on these forms. All three teachers agreed that noncompliance was a problem: at times, Leah refused to work, giggled loudly and repetitively, and sometimes threw materials. Everyone indicated that Leah typically started an activity with few problems but became increasingly noncompliant about 20 minutes into an activity. Noncompliant behaviors were worse when Leah was asked to do repetitive tasks (e.g., sort shape blocks, collate papers, do calisthenics). All three teachers also agreed that Leah did some activities with no problems: preparing for lunch, many self-care tasks, and playing kickball.

Next, Mr. Feldman had a fellow teacher conduct an A-B-C observation during prevocational class. The assigned task was folding papers, inserting the papers in an envelope, and sealing the envelope. The A-B-C report indicated that Leah worked for about 15 minutes without incident but, after 15 minutes, began giggling and looking at the ceiling. Mr. Feldman redirected her. Leah did two more envelopes very slowly and then began spinning around in her chair giggling. Attempts to redirect her back to task resulted in her grabbing the stack of envelopes and throwing them. Mr. Feldman then placed Leah in time-out.

Based on the indirect and direct assessment results, Mr. Feldman formulated the following hypotheses:

- Leah goes off task after approximately 15 minutes when doing some types of work.
- The repetitive nature of tasks like stuffing envelopes may be what increases Leah's motivation to spin, giggle, and throw materials as a way to escape.
- Leah has no trouble with compliance when she understands the purpose of the task (i.e., the task is functional for Leah).

With these hypotheses in mind, Mr. Feldman made a few changes in Leah's daily schedule. First, he made sure that Leah worked on tasks that had a clear purpose for her. The following are some of the tasks Leah had been working on (with the task objective in parentheses) and how Mr. Feldman changed them to make them more meaningful to Leah.

Old Task (Objective)	New Task
Sort coins (recognize like coins)	Pick out like coins to spend in the school store
Collate papers (engage in a vocational activity)	Collate letters in the school office 10 minutes at a time
Name pictures (articulation, increasing vocabulary)	Name the same objects as part of playing the game "I Spy" with the teacher
Cut on quarter-inch lines (improve fine motor skills)	Cut out coupons to use on class shopping trip

In addition, Mr. Feldman developed a reinforcement system for use during low-probability tasks. During these activities, Leah earned stars for compliance (on-task behavior). When she accumulated 10 stars, she could "take a break." At first stars were given frequently; gradually, the amount of time or completed work required to earn each star was increased.

Although these changes did not completely eliminate Leah's challenging behavior, Mr. Feldman believed these interventions were responsible for challenging behavior occurring less often and with less severity. The result was that Leah began making measurable progress on other target skills. And Mr. Feldman learned an important lesson: remember basic rules for assessing challenging behavior and using assessment data to design interventions any time you are dealing with challenging behavior. Oh, and yes, he also learned to never send a student who wants to escape to time-out!

Summary

Challenging behaviors may pose one of the most difficult aspects of teaching students with autism. These behaviors are often well-established components of students' behavioral repertoires and, without diligent application of the best practices for managing such behaviors, may be highly resistant to change. Challenging behaviors, perhaps more than any other characteristic of students with autism, pose significant threats to learning and functioning in normalized environments. It is critical that these behaviors be reduced or eliminated.

This chapter has described how to conduct functional behavior assessment to determine purposes (functions) of challenging behavior and to match intervention to that function when possible. In addition, we described evidenced-based strategies for dealing with specific challenging behaviors and functions that are commonly present in children and youth with autism. These strategies are not recipes for "fixing" these behaviors, but must be selected based on the behavior's function, the student's individual skills and needs, as well as other classroom and contextual considerations.

Key Points

1. FBA is a process of identifying contextual variables that may be contributing to challenging behavior and determining potential functions for that specific challenging behavior.

2. The FBA should include both indirect (interviews and checklists) and direct (scatterplots and A–B–C recording) assessment methods.

3. Possible functions for challenging behavior include obtaining some item, attention, stimulation, or activity access (positive reinforcement) as well as avoiding or escaping a social interaction, task demand, sensory stimulation, or activity (negative reinforcement).

4. BIP should be function matched: Specifically, they should be developed based on hypotheses resulting from the FBA.

5. Sometimes, challenging behavior reflects a failure to learn other, more appropriate behavior, thus prosocial and functional replacement behaviors should be taught to students with autism.

6. In some cases, punishment (e.g., time-out or response cost) may be necessary. However, these interventions should be used carefully and involve input from parents and other stakeholders.

References

Alberto, P. A., & Troutman, A. C. (2017). *Applied behavior analysis for teachers* (9th ed.). Columbus, OH: Pearson.

Azrin, N. H., & Holz, W. C. (1966). Punishment. In W. K. Honig (Ed.), *Operant behavior: Areas of research and application.* New York: Appleton-Century-Crofts.

Boesch, M. C., Taber-Doughty, T., Wendt, O., & Smalts, S. S. (2015). Using a behavioral approach to decrease self-injurious behavior in an adolescent with severe autism: A data-based case study. *Education and Treatment of Children, 38,* 305–328.

Brosnan, J., & Healy, O. (2011). A review of behavioral interventions for the treatment of aggression in individuals with developmental disabilities. *Research in Developmental Disabilities, 32,* 437–446.

Carnett, A., Raulston, T., Lang, R., Tostanoski, A., Lee, A., Sigafoos, J., & Machalicek, W. (2014). Effects of a perseverative interest-based token economy on challenging and on-task behavior in a child with autism. *Journal of Behavioral Education, 23,* 368–377.

Cipani, E. (1998). Three behavioral functions of classroom noncompliance: Diagnostic and treatment implications. *Focus on Autism and Other Developmental Disabilities, 13*(2), 66–72.

Delaney, M. J., & Durand, M. V. (1986). *Motivation Assessment Scale.* Topeka, KS: Monaco & Associates.

Didden, R., Sturmey, P., Sigafoos, J., Lang, R., O'Reilly, M. F., & Lancioni, G. E. (2012). Nature, prevalence, and characteristics of challenging behavior. In J. L. Matson (Ed.), *Functional assessment for challenging behaviors* (pp. 25–44). New York: Springer.

Dove, D., Warren, Z., McPheeters, M. L., Taylor, J. L., Sathe, N. A., & Veenstra-VanderWeele, J. (2012). Medications for adolescents and young adults with autism spectrum disorders: A systematic review. *Pediatrics, 130,* 717–726.

Dunlap, G., Ferro, J., & dePerczel, M. (1994). Nonaversive behavioral intervention in the community. In E. C. Cipani & F. Spooner (Eds.), *Curricular and instructional approaches for persons with severe disabilities* (pp. 117–146). Needham Heights, MA: Allyn & Bacon.

Durcharme, J. M., & Ng, O. (2012). Errorless academic compliance training: A school-based application for young students with autism. *Behavior Modification, 36,* 650–669.

Earle, J. F. (2016). An introduction to the psychopharmacology of children and adolescents with autism spectrum disorder. *Journal of Child and Adolescent Psychiatric Nursing, 29,* 62–71.

Etscheidt, S. (2006). Behavioral intervention plans: Pedagogical and legal analysis of issues. *Behavioral Disorders, 31,* 223–243.

Falcomata, T. S., & Gainey, S. (2014). An evaluation of noncontingent reinforcement for the treatment of challenging behavior with multiple functions. *Journal of Developmental and Physical Disabilities, 26,* 317–324.

Forehand, R., & McMahon, R. (1981). *Helping the noncompliant child.* New York: Guilford Press.

Foster-Johnson, L., & Dunlap, G. (1993). Using functional assessment to develop effective, individualized interventions for challenging behaviors. *Teaching Exceptional Children, 25,* 44–50.

Fuhrman, A. M., Fisher, W. W., & Greer, B. D. (2016). A preliminary investigation on improving functional communication training by mitigating resurgence of destructive behavior. *Journal of Applied Behavior Analysis, 49,* 884–899.

Hurl, K., Wightman, J., Haynes, S. N., & Virues-Ortega, J. (2016). Does a pre-intervention functional assessment increase intervention effectiveness? A meta-analysis of within-subject interrupted time-series studies. *Clinical Psychology Review, 47,* 71–84.

Kern, L., Koegel, R. L., & Dunlap, G. (1984). The influence of vigorous versus mild exercise on autistic stereotyped behaviors. *Journal of Autism and Developmental Disorders, 14,* 57–67.

Kern, L., Koegel, R. L., Dyer, K., Blew, P. A., & Fenton, L. R. (1982). The effects of physical exercise on self-stimulation and appropriate responding in autistic children. *Journal of Autism and Developmental Disorders, 4,* 399–419.

Knowles, C., Meng, P., & Machalicek, W. (2015). Task sequencing for students with emotional and behavioral disorders: A systematic review. *Behavior Modification, 39,* 136–166.

Koegel, R. L., Firestone, P. B., Kramme, K. W., & Dunlap, G. (1974). Increasing spontaneous play by suppressing self-stimulation in autistic children. *Journal of Applied Behavior Analysis, 7,* 521–528.

Kolevzon, A., Lim, T., Schmeidler, J., Martello, T., Cook, E. H., & Silverman, J. M. (2014). Self-injury in autism spectrum disorder: An effect of serotonin transporter gene promoter variants. *Psychiatry Research, 220,* 987–990.

Lancioni, G. E., Singh, N. N., O'Reilly, M. F., Sigafoos, J., & Didden, R. (2012). Function of challenging behaviors. In J. Matson (Ed.), *Functional assessment for challenging behaviors* (pp. 45–64). New York: Springer.

Lang, R., Davis, T., O'Reilly, M., Machalicek, W., Rispoli, M., Sigafoos, J., Lancioni, G., & Regester, A. (2010). Functional analysis and treatment of elopement across two school settings. *Journal of Applied Behavior Analysis, 43*, 113–118.

Lang, R., Koegel, L. K., Ashbaugh, K., Regester, A., Ence, W., & Smith, W. (2010). Physical exercise and individuals with autism spectrum disorders: A systematic review. *Research in Autism Spectrum Disorders, 4*, 565–576.

Lang, R., Machalicek, W., Rispoli, M., O'Reilly, M., Sigafoos, J., Lancioni, G., Peters-Scheffer, N., & Didden, R. (2014b). Play skills taught via behavioral intervention generalize, maintain, and persist in the absence of socially mediated reinforcement in children with autism. *Research in Autism Spectrum Disorders, 8*, 860–872.

Lang, R., Sigafoos, J., Lancioni, G., Didden, R., & Rispoli, M. (2010). Influence of assessment setting on the results of functional analyses of problem behavior. *Journal of Applied Behavior Analysis, 43*, 565–567.

Lang, R., Sigafoos, J., van der Meer, L., O'Reilly, M. F., Lancioni, G. E., & Didden, R. (2013). Early signs and early behavioral intervention of challenging behavior. In R. P. Hastings & J. Rojahn (Eds.), *Challenging behavior: International review of research in developmental disabilities* (pp. 1–35). London: Elsevier Inc. Academic Press.

Lang, R., van der Werff, M., Verbeek, K., Didden, R., Davenport, K., Moore, M., Lee, A., Rispoli, M., Machalicek, W., O'Reilly, M., Sigafoos, J., & Lancioni, G. (2014a). Comparison of high and low preferred topographies of contingent attention during discrete trial training. *Research in Autism Spectrum Disorders, 8*, 1279–1286.

Langthorne, P., & McGill, P. (2009). A tutorial on the concept of the motivating operation and its importance to application. *Behavior Analysis in Practice, 2*, 22–31.

Langthorne, P., McGill, P., & Oliver, C. (2014). The motivating operation and negatively reinforced problem behavior: A systematic review. *Behavior Modification, 38*, 107–159.

Lauderdale-Littin, S., Howell, E., & Blacher, J. (2013). Educational placement for children with autism spectrum disorders in public and non-public school settings: The impact of social skills and behavior problems. *Education and Training in Autism and Developmental Disabilities, 48*, 469–478.

Lowe, K., Allen, D., Jones, E., Brophy, S., Moore, K., & James, W. (2007). Challenging behaviours: Prevalence and topographies. *Journal of Intellectual Disability Research, 51*, 625–636.

Luczynski, K. C., & Hanley, G. P. (2013). Prevention of problem behavior by teaching functional communication and self-control skills to preschoolers. *Journal of Applied Behavior Analysis, 46*, 355–368.

Luiselli, J. K. (2012). *The handbook of high-risk challenging behaviors in people with intellectual and developmental disabilities.* Baltimore: Paul H. Brookes Publishing.

Mace, F. C., Hock, M. L., Lalli, J. S., West, B. J., Belfiore, P., Pinter, E., & Brown, D. K. (1988). Behavioral momentum in the treatment of non-compliance. *Journal of Applied Behavior Analysis, 21*, 123–141.

Machalicek, W., O'Reilly, M. F., Beretvas, N., Sigafoos, J., & Lancioni, G. E. (2007). A review of interventions to reduce challenging behavior in school settings for students with autism spectrum disorders. *Research in Autism Spectrum Disorders, 1*, 229–246.

Matson, J. L. (2012). *Functional assessment for challenging behaviors.* New York: Springer.

O'Neill, R. E., Albin, R.W., Storey, K., Horner, R. H., & Sprague, J. R. (2015). *Functional assessment and program development for problem behavior: A practical handbook* (3rd ed.). Stamford, CT: Cengage Learning.

O'Reilly, M. F. (1995). Functional analysis and treatment of escape-maintained aggression correlated with sleep deprivation. *Journal of Applied Behavior Analysis, 28*, 225–226.

Powell, D., Fixsen, D., Dunlap, G., Smith, B., & Fox, L. (2007). A synthesis of knowledge relevant to pathways of service delivery for young children with or at risk of challenging behavior. *Journal of Early Intervention, 29*, 81–106.

Pritchard, D., Hoerger, M., & Mace, C. F. (2014). Treatment relapse and behavioral momentum theory. *Journal of Applied Behavior Analysis, 47*, 814–833.

Quesenberry, A. C., Hemmeter, M. L., Ostrosky, M. M., & Hamann, K. (2014). Child care teachers' perspectives on including children with challenging behavior in child care settings. *Infants and Young Children, 27*, 241–258.

Rapp, J. T., & Vollmer, T R. (2005). Stereotypy I: A review of behavioral assessment and treatment. *Research in Developmental Disabilities, 26*, 527–547.

Reed, F. D. D., Hirst, J. M., & Hyman, S. R. (2012). Assessment and treatment of stereotypic behavior in children with autism and other developmental disabilities: A thirty-year review. *Research in Autism Spectrum Disorders, 6*, 422–430.

Richman, D. M., Barnard-Brak, L., Bosch, A., Thompson, S., Grubb, L., & Abby, L. (2013). Predictors of self-injurious behaviour exhibited by individuals with autism spectrum disorder. *Journal of Intellectual Disability Research, 57*, 429–439.

Rispoli, M., Neely, L., Lang, R., & Ganz, J. (2011). Training paraprofessionals to implement interventions for people autism spectrum disorders: A systematic review. *Developmental Neurorehabilitation, 14*, 378–388.

Rispoli, M., Lang, R., Neely, L., Camargo, S., Hutchins, N., Davenport, K., & Goodwyn, F. (2013). A comparison of within- and across-activity choices for reducing challenging behavior in children with autism spectrum disorders. *Journal of Behavioral Education, 22*, 66–83.

Robertson, J., Emerson, E., Pinkney, L., Caesar, E., Felce, D., Meek, A., Carr, D., Lowe, K., Knapp, M., & Hallam, A. (2004). Quality and costs of community-based residential supports for people with mental retardation and challenging behavior. *American Journal on Mental Retardation, 109*, 332–344.

Scheuermann, B., Peterson, R., Ryan, J. B., & Billingsley, G. (2015). Professional practice and ethical issues related to physical restraint and seclusion in schools. *Journal of Disability Policy Studies, 27*, 86–95.

Scheuermann, B., Webber, J., Boutot, E. A., & Goodwin, M. (2003). Problems with personnel preparation in Autism Spectrum Disorders. *Focus on Autism and Other Developmental Disabilities, 18*, 197–206.

Shyman, E. (2012). Teacher education in Autism Spectrum Disorders: A potential blueprint. *Education and Training in Autism and Developmental Disabilities, 47*, 187–197.

Simpson, R. L., & Regan, M. (1986). *Management of autistic behavior.* Rockville, MD: Aspen Publishers.

Tiger, J. H., Hanley, G. P., & Bruzek, J. (2008). Functional communication training: A review and practical guide. *Behavior Analysis in Practice, 1*, 16–23.

Walker, H. M., & Walker, J. E. (1991). *Coping with noncompliance in the classroom: A positive approach for teachers.* Austin, TX: Pro-Ed.

4

Deciding What to Teach: Curriculum Development

LEARNING OBJECTIVES

After reading this chapter, you should be able to:

4-1 List various curricular areas (academic, vocational, functional skills), and discuss legal and practical constraints on choosing student targets.

4-2 List benefits and challenges of standard academic curricula and functional, life skills curricula for students with autism.

4-3 State each step of the recommended curriculum-development process and briefly describe each one.

4-4 Define each level of competency, and identify behavioral objectives written at each level.

4-5 Discuss the benefits of various curricular formats.

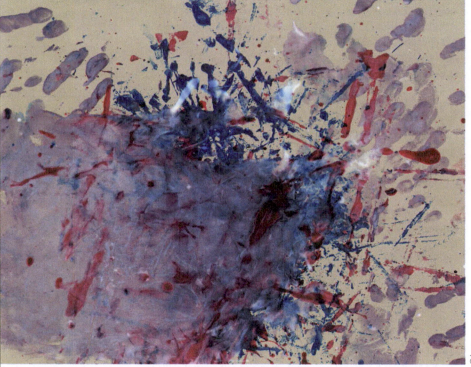

© Lang

I n Chapters 2 and 3, you learned various techniques for reducing unwanted excessive behavior that interferes with learning, social interactions, and community integration. Now Chapters 4 to 8 will present various methodologies for teaching new behavior—that is, teaching to alleviate deficits. In regard to students with autism, it is sometimes difficult to decide which should come first: reducing challenging behavior or remediating deficits. In some cases, if teachers do a good job teaching students what they need to learn (remediating deficits), challenging behavior will decrease or never occur in the first place. Conversely, if students are already displaying excessive challenging behavior, it will be difficult to teach anything new until that behavior is under control. The best course of action lies in a balance between effective instruction and behavior management. Establishing such a balance begins with curriculum development.

For our purposes, we define curriculum as *what* you teach (i.e., skills, activities, strategies, concepts, content). Ideally, what a teacher targets to teach will be what the student will learn. What the student learns directly affects not only current functioning but also postschool outcomes, which affects the choices that will ultimately be available for that individual in terms of independent living, community integration, employment, further educational opportunities, and interpersonal relationships. More important, what the teacher does *not* target for instruction (what the student will most likely *not* learn) will also greatly affect postschool outcomes, perhaps in a negative way. The time students spend in school is finite, and students with autism have much to learn. It is impractical to assume a teacher can teach everything a student with autism needs to learn in the time they are eligible for public school instruction, underscoring the significance of decisions regarding what will be taught each school year. Teachers must carefully choose to teach those things that will have the most beneficial impact on each student based on that student's needs, abilities, and long-term goals.

Did you know that:

- Curriculum development is among the most impactful of teacher responsibilities?
- The best curriculum is individualized for each student?
- Curriculum decisions must precede decisions about strategies and placement?
- A team approach is often the best way to determine what is important to teach?
- Curriculum must "fit" the student and his or her context?
- Postschool outcomes for students with autism lag behind other student groups?

Choosing what to teach individuals with autism spectrum disorder (ASD) and intellectual disability (ID) has been subject to controversy and differing opinions over the past decades. During the 1970s and 1980s, functional, life skills curricula were developed for this population based on the premise that it was most important for students to acquire skills necessary to live and work independently instead of mastering academic content such as science and social studies (Brown et al., 1979). This type of curriculum usually includes skills necessary for functional academics, vocational opportunities, community access, daily self-care, personal finance, independent living, transportation, social relationship development, and self-determination (Patton, Cronin, & Jairrels, 1997).

A functional life skills curriculum is not traditionally well aligned with the typical public school academic curriculum, which is designed to prepare students for postschool education options (e.g., college) (Balfanz, 2009). Thus, choosing a functional curriculum as the primary curriculum usually precluded inclusion in age-appropriate academic instruction. This also meant that students in the alternate functional life skills curriculum were primarily taught in self-contained classrooms with community-based instruction, often to the exclusion of social interaction with students without disabilities in general education classrooms (Haring, 1991).

During the 1990s, an effort emerged to socially integrate students with ID into nonacademic classes (e.g., music, art, physical education) and leisure time activities for the purpose of teaching social and leisure skills with same-age peers and encouraging friendships while still primarily targeting functional life skills (Patton, Polloway, & Smith, 2000). Emphasis was placed on allowing students' input into their own curriculum (self-determination), which was thought to enhance self-efficacy and motivation and lead to positive postschool outcomes (Chambers et al., 2007).

However, a foundational shift in special education curriculum policy occurred with the passage of the No Child Left Behind Act (NCLB) of 2001 and now the Every Student Succeeds Act (ESSA) of 2015, emphasizing that *all* students should reach grade level in the standard academic curriculum adopted by the specific state where the student attends school. Subsequently, the Individuals with Disabilities Act (IDEA) of 2004, which was coordinated with the NCLB, mandated that students with disabilities be given access to the general education curriculum to the maximum extent possible. It was assumed that, through this access, these students would "(i) meet developmental goals and, to the maximum extent possible, the challenging expectations that have been established for all children; and (ii) be prepared to lead productive and independent adult lives, to the maximum extent possible" (118, Stat. 2651). Although this mandate seemed to combine the targets of grade-level academic proficiency while also preparing for a productive adulthood, the placement of students primarily into a life skills curriculum was now seen as counter to legal mandates (Bouck & Satsangi, 2014).

This shift in educational policy has resulted in a corresponding shift in targeted long-term goals for students with autism and ID. Previous long-term goals of independent living and working are now often more focused on enrollment in postsecondary educational institutions (which is the goal of standard academic curriculum for all students). The ESSA continues to require that *all* school students, except those with significant ID, be tested on mastery of standard grade-level academic curriculum, with schools graded on the degree to which students with disabilities reach academic proficiency (Council of Chief State School Officers, 2016). School districts can allow up to 1% of the school population to be assessed with alternate assessments on alternate standards (i.e., curricula) and up to 2% of the population to be assessed with alternate assessments on modified academic standards, but the individualized education programs (IEPs) and assessments must be aligned with the standard academic curricula.

These mandates for academic mastery for *all* students appear to directly contradict the IDEA 2004's basic tenet that curriculum (goals and objectives) for students with disabilities be individualized based on comprehensive assessment of a student's needs toward individually determined postschool targets with parent and team input. This contradiction presents a dilemma for special educators in terms of curriculum development: should teachers establish truly individualized educational programs per the IDEA 2004 or should they simply include all their students in standard academic curriculum, whether they need to learn that content or not, per the ESSA?

The danger of the ESSA mandates is that precious instructional time might likely be spent teaching what many see as useless content for students with severe ID and autism (e.g., names of planets) instead of more meaningful targets aimed at independent functioning (e.g., self-help skills, vocational skills) (Ayres, Lowrey, Douglas, & Sievers, 2011, 2012). Nevertheless, IEP teams for students with ASD are frequently targeting standard academic curriculum, often modified or ungraded, along with communication and social behavior curricula, even though many teachers do not predict attendance in college as viable (Witmer & Ferreri, 2014). Bouck and Joshi (2014) found that only 25% of secondary students with ASD were receiving a functional life skills curriculum compared to 35% of the general secondary disability population.

Many in the field of special education have voiced agreement with the NCLB and ESSA mandates, arguing that it is best to include students with severe disabilities and those with autism and ID in standardized academic curriculum and assessments (Courtade, Spooner, Browder, & Jimenez, 2012). This contingent of special education leaders maintain that students with severe disabilities:

1. have a right to a full educational opportunity and that we do not know yet their potential to learn it,
2. can learn skills relevant to adult functioning (e.g., math skills for technology-related jobs) when placed in a standards-based curriculum,
3. do not need functional skills as a prerequisite to academic skills, and
4. may have an advantage with combined academic and functional curriculum in terms of self-efficacy, enjoyment, and possible adult outcomes.

They also make a case against irrelevant functional skills curriculum when it is not individualized according to a student's needs and context.

Unfortunately, students with ASD, regardless of curriculum type, show poor postschool outcomes. Compared to other groups of students with disabilities, students with autism have lower rates of college enrollment and employment, more restrictive living arrangements, and fewer options for recreational and leisure activities (Bouck & Joshi, 2014; Fleury et al., 2014; Wehman et al., 2014). Reasons other than curriculum choices for these poor outcomes might include inadequate provisions of transition planning, inadequate career counseling, and subsequent poor employment supports

(Bouck & Joshi, 2014). Poor social skills may also predict poor employment outcomes. Some people speculate that the nature of autism itself plays a factor in adult outcomes, such as anxiety, challenging behavior, lack of interpersonal skills, and communication deficits (Bouck & Joshi, 2014; Witmer & Ferreri, 2014).

Nevertheless, many leaders in special education assert that, unless immersion into academic curriculum shows definitive links to positive postschool outcomes for students with autism and ID, it is best to focus on individually determined and meaningful curriculum for each student that matches that student's targeted long-term goals (Alwell & Cobb, 2009; Ayres et al., 2011, 2012). This latter perspective is the vantage from which this text is written. If a student's long-term goals include attendance at college, then a curriculum with a strong academic focus is appropriate. However, if the long-term goals include independent living and meaningful community involvement (e.g., employment), then more functional life skills, social and communication skills, and vocational preparation curriculum would be better aligned with the student's goals.

Teachers and IEP teams make very important decisions about what students will be taught and not taught throughout their educational progression. There are hundreds of these choices over the course of the student's school career. The following challenges may illustrate how important and how difficult it is to develop an individualized, appropriate curriculum for your student. The potential benefits and associated risks of focusing curriculum at various points along a continuum of choices are also illustrated in Figure 4.1.

- Exclusively teaching standard academic curriculum, while not teaching functional life skills, may not prepare students to independently live and work in their community.
- Exclusively teaching a functional life skills curriculum and not teaching the standard academic curriculum may prevent students from performing successfully in general education classrooms and most likely removes the choice of postschool education options.
- Combining functional life skills curriculum and standard academic curriculum will most likely result in less learning in each. The student will remain behind age-appropriate peers in academic mastery and may not learn important vocational and independent living skills because there is no time to teach them.
- A curriculum that includes neither functional life skills nor standard academic curriculum may relegate the student to lifelong supervision and possible residential placement.

Exclusively teaching standard academic curriculum	Combining functional life skills curriculum and standard academic curriculum	Exclusively teaching a functional life and vocational skills curriculum	Teaching neither academic or functional, life skills curriculum
• Improved access to general education settings and post-secondary education • May be unprepared to live and work independently as adults	• Insufficient time to master either academic or functional goals • May continue to lag behind peers academically • May not be adequately prepared for independent functioning as adult	• Improved likelihood of independent living and working in adult integrated settings • Less access to general education settings and postschool educational options	• Relegate to lifelong dependency and supervision

FIGURE 4.1 Potential risks and benefits of curriculum choices

Despite these challenges, teachers must participate in a thoughtful, efficient curriculum-development process. Students cannot afford to have teachers squander precious instructional time teaching content or skills that will not benefit the student or that take so long to acquire that other important skills go unaddressed. This chapter will provide information regarding general procedures for choosing and organizing curriculum for students with autism and ID of various ages with an emphasis on the logical construction of meaningful and individualized curriculum. Chapters 6 through 8 will present specific curricula in the areas of language and communication, socialization, and life skills, as well as preferred methods for teaching those goals. Standard academic curricular sequences should be readily available at state departments of education websites. This chapter also provides information about published academic curricula for special education populations.

4-1 Curricular Areas

Public schools were established to create a literate, well-informed, self-sufficient citizenry (Balfanz, 2009). To meet that goal they were designated to provide basic academic curricula. These curricula may vary by state and consist of academic subjects (e.g., reading, writing, mathematics, history, geography, literature, foreign languages, computer literacy), personal care subjects (e.g., health, physical education, home economics), and fine arts (e.g., music, art, drama). It is commonly presumed that students enter school ready to learn the prescribed curriculum by having mastered basic social, behavioral, and oral language skills. These general education curricula currently aim to prepare students for college, where they typically consolidate and expand this education into a marketable profession.

Historically, students who preferred to pursue a trade rather than attend college were placed into a vocational curriculum (e.g., industrial arts, distributive education, home economics, business classes, auto mechanics), although such options have been greatly reduced in our high schools given the emphasis of the NCLB and the ESSA on standard academic mastery. Note that general education academic and vocational curricula are standardized, not individualized—that is, they are developed and organized by grade level or content area and based on students' ages rather than on individual needs and goals. For example, students are placed into fourth-grade social studies curriculum when entering fourth grade, whether or not they need to learn that curriculum or have the prerequisites to learn it.

As previously mentioned, for students with disabilities—particularly those with ID, as is the case with many students with autism—the standard academic curriculum may be irrelevant for their targeted postschool outcomes. Further, the standard curriculum may be too difficult for many students with ID because they have not mastered prerequisites and learn at a much slower rate than their peers without disabilities. This discrepancy becomes more pronounced at the secondary level, with students with autism and ID falling further and further behind (Schall, Wehman, & Carr, 2014). For secondary students with autism, appropriate curricular content may be quite different from that presented in general education classrooms.

In fact, the IDEA 2004 mandates that special educators develop a **transition curriculum** and **transition plan** for secondary students receiving special education services no later than age 16 (34 *Code of Federal Regulations* 300.320[b]). Although students in special education move through several transitions during their time in school (e.g., transition from early childhood programs to public schools, transitions from elementary schools to middle schools and then to high school), the term **transition** or **transition service** typically refers to the transition phase from high school to postschool activities, specifically educational, employment, and living options.

Table 4.1 lists some of these postschool options for secondary students with ASD so that teachers can refer to this list during transition planning and use it to establish long-term placement goals for younger children with autism. Planning a curriculum for secondary

TABLE 4.1 ● **Postschool Options for Students with Autism**

Community College. Community colleges offer 2-year academic and technical preparation programs for students who may not want to attend or are not prepared for 4-year colleges. Community colleges conveniently offer many full programs online, which may be attractive to individuals with ASD. Developmental education courses are also readily available for basic academic preparation, and state vocational rehabilitation commission support is typically readily available.

Four-Year Colleges and Universities. Four-year colleges and universities offer degree programs in liberal arts, business, education, health fields, the sciences, math, and other career areas. Students are expected to immerse themselves in their classes and campus life. Admission requirements focus on academic test scores, although exceptions are made. Vocational rehabilitation, disability, and counseling services are usually available and, in some cases, so are special programs for students with ASD.

Vocational Training Institutes. Training institutes may be appropriate for individuals who are not interested in an academic degree but want to achieve certification or licensure in areas such as cosmetology, film technology, and computer design. Vocational rehabilitation, disability, and counseling services may not be readily available at these institutions.

EMPLOYMENT

Competitive Integrated Employment. Various employment opportunities may be available for individuals with ASD *if* these individuals have been directly trained for the particular job, the employer is trained to support the individual, and other supports are readily available. Vocational rehabilitation counselors or school-based job coaches should be available to assist.

Day-Treatment Programs. Daily programs (4 to 6 hours) for individuals requiring additional supervision and support provide prevocational training, independent living skills, and leisure time activities. The typical goal is to transition individuals to supported employment.

Supported Employment. Referred to as *sheltered workshops, vocational training centers,* or *vocational training academies,* supported employment usually provides a hierarchy of supervised work situations and corresponding wages. Individuals are placed in settings that match their skill level and are helped in moving to more difficult vocational tasks when they are able. The goals are movement from supported employment to semi-independent employment (working alongside someone in competitive employment) and finally to competitive employment.

Military. Careers in the military may be available for some individuals with ASD if they are not dependent on medications, are able to pass entrance examinations, and can qualify for admission. These individuals must understand the circumstances surrounding such a career (possible combat, noise, crowds, many demands, no alone time, etc.) before proceeding with an application.

LIVING OPTIONS

With Parents or Other Family Members. Certainly, continuing to live with family members offers safety and parental control over decisions and activities that might be best for individuals with ASD. Family members can teach independent living skills and continue to support their child who may be working or attending a day-treatment program. Unfortunately, such an arrangement may cause stress for aging parents who may have relatively little community assistance.

Respite Services. If available, parents may rely on respite services from community agencies that provide supervised time, weekend housing, or other assistance to help family members find time for themselves.

Group Homes. Usually run by agencies, group homes can house as many as six individuals with similar functioning levels in a neighborhood house with live-in paid supervision. Leisure time and work activities are closely supervised. Individuals are placed by their required level of support and ability to get along with others in the home. Some group homes cater to individuals attending higher education institutions so that the residents would not have to live in a dormitory.

Assisted Living Facilities. Individuals who require less support than a group home may be able to live in an assisted living facility with some but not complete supervision. Individuals in this living option would need to be able to independently care for and feed themselves, unless the facility also has a cafeteria available.

Supervised Apartment. An alternative to assisted living may be to have two individuals with ASD live in an apartment with agency-provided supervision. Alternatively, an individual with ASD may choose to live with a roommate without disabilities who can provide necessary support.

Self-Contained Village. Some facilities provide dormitory or cottage living, leisure time activities, training programs, and supported employment in a self-contained setting. Residents are placed according their support level and typically remain in these settings as they age. Unfortunately, these types of settings are relatively rare and are costly, so they are not accessible to all individuals who may benefit from such a placement. Generally speaking, adult services are scarce, and many parents and families struggle to find satisfactory work and living situations for their adult children with ASD.

BOX 4.1 ● Transition from School to Postschool Activities

The IDEA 2004 describes transition planning as a results-oriented process leading to improved academic and functional achievement for the purpose of facilitating a student's movement to postschool activities (U.S. Department of Education, 2017). The planning process must consider the child's needs, strengths, preferences, and interests. The final plan, part of the IEP, should include instruction, related services (e.g., occupational therapy), and community experiences that target (a) employment, (b) adult living objectives, and (c) daily living skills. By the time students are 16 years old, the IEP must include transition components, although it is recommended that parents begin transition planning earlier if possible (e.g., when the child is 14 years old) to allow time for a quality plan and implementation before the student no longer receives IDEA services (Test et al., 2009).

Transition planning is required under the IDEA 2004 as a component of the Free Appropriate Public Education (FAPE) mandate and is initiated and led by special education personnel during IEP meetings—usually teachers, assessment personnel, and other school personnel as appropriate. However, planning should also involve state vocational rehabilitation (VR) personnel, usually a local VR counselor, because the student will be transitioning to support services offered by this agency under the Rehabilitation Act of 1973. This act provides for a continuum of services that includes pre-employment transition, transition, job placement,

and supported employment for youth with disabilities for the purpose of obtaining meaningful careers (U.S. Department of Education, 2017).

Teachers and parents must understand that when a student with ASD graduates from high school with either a regular high school diploma or an alternate high school diploma by age 22, she is no longer eligible for FAPE or related special education services. The laws that govern services for adults with disabilities include the Rehabilitation Act, especially Section 504, and the American with Disabilities Act (ADA). Under these laws, individuals with disabilities cannot be denied services that are available to nondisabled individuals, but there is no requirement for specific support services or appropriateness of services. In addition, at age 18, parents are no longer the primary advocates for their child's services; the adult individual himself becomes the advocate and must obtain services. Parents can only legally continue making service decisions for their adult child if they obtain guardianship of him at or after age 18. For individuals with ID, parents are encouraged to obtain such guardianship.

Transition services are typically evaluated by assessing postschool outcomes for students with disabilities. If these outcomes are positive, then it might be assumed that special education in general and transition services specifically were successful. The National Longitudinal Transition Study-2 (NLTS2) (IES National Center for Special Education Research, 2017) is a database of

students with autism must include transition, which in many instances will emphasize functional living skills, social skills, and direct vocational training. Box 4.1 provides more information about requirements and research pertaining to transition planning and resources to assist with that planning.

Deciding *what* to teach a student should be the first decision—before deciding *how* to teach it (e.g., instructional methods) or *where* to teach it (e.g., instructional placement). Unfortunately, placement decisions too often precede any other decision. For example, if a student needs to learn to purchase something at a store, it may be more appropriate to teach that skill in a store rather than the classroom, especially for students with ID who have difficulty applying newly learned skills in new settings. However, if that student's educational placement is a general education classroom, the curriculum must now more closely match what students are doing in that classroom such as adding and subtracting decimals using dollar amounts or solving math problems related to purchasing (e.g., "Terrell has $6.50. How many songs can he download if each song costs $1.25?"). This instructional activity is unlikely to prepare the student to make purchases in a store. In this case, the placement decision drove the curriculum decision to the detriment of the student. Thus, it is imperative information about students with disabilities after they leave high school. This study was funded by the U.S. Department of Education to survey a national sample of students 13 to 16 years of age in 2000 as they transitioned from high school to adult services. These students were 21 to 25 years old at final data collection in 2009 (IES National Center for Special Education Research, 2017). Researchers are invited to use the database to determine postschool success, typically in three dimensions: employment, independent living, and postsecondary education (Blackorby & Wagner, 1996; Henninger & Taylor, 2013).

Although researchers found that students with disabilities in general lag behind their peers in these three dimensions, students with ASD showed particularly dismal results (Hendricks & Wehman, 2009; Newman et al., 2011; Wehman et al., 2014). A majority of surveyed students with ASD were neither working nor attending postsecondary education 2 years out of high school, although the employment rate rose over time; less than one-sixth of these graduates were living independently (Bouck & Joshi, 2014). Howlin and colleagues (2004) found low rates of independent living and few meaningful friendships for adults with ASD.

Some researchers used the database to identify predictors of successful postschool outcomes for students with ASD. Foster and Pearson (2012) found no relationship between time in inclusive settings and postsecondary education enrollment for students with ASD, whereas Wehman et al. (2014) did find a relationship between transition goals directly aimed at postsecondary education and enrollment in these activities after high school.

Chiang et al. (2012) found that income, parental expectations, type of school (typical or special), and academic performance predicted enrollment in postsecondary education. Chiang et al. (2013) found that demographic variables such as comorbid ID, gender, and parental income and educational attainment predicted postschool employment for students with ASD. In addition, these researchers found that transition services such as social skills training, career counseling, coordination with employers, and high school graduation predicted postschool employment. Finally, Bouck and Joshi (2014) found no relationship between type of curriculum provided (academic or functional) and postschool outcomes. However, these authors cautioned that teachers should continue to provide curriculum matched to targeted postschool outcomes and to view curricula on a continuum (both academic and functional) to prepare students with ASD for successful adulthood.

Teachers and parents who want to know more about transition requirements and recommended transition strategies and services may refer to the following:

- *A Transition Guide to Postsecondary Education and Employment for Students and Youth with Disabilities* (U.S. Department of Education, 2017),
- Division of Vocational Rehabilitation (U.S. Department of Education, OSERS),
- Administration on Intellectual and Developmental Disabilities (AIDD),
- IES National Center for Special Education Research (NLTS2), or
- National Secondary Transition Technical Assistance Center.

that all decision makers have a clear idea of what each student needs to learn and let that knowledge direct other educational decisions.

For students who need a functional curriculum, instructional areas usually consist of functional academics (e.g., counting out money for making purchases, reading cooking instructions), communication, social skills, domestic skills, community living skills, leisure and recreational skills, motor skills, vocational skills, and self-determination skills (e.g., making decisions for oneself). In addition, for many individuals with autism, basic prerequisite learning behaviors may need to be taught, including skills such as compliance, attending, imitating, and discrimination skills. Many students with autism might need to learn these skills as their primary curriculum (Ayres et al., 2011; Falvey, Grenot-Scheyer, & Luddy, 1987).

Table 4.2 lists various curricular areas typically available in public schools. As the list shows, there is much to choose from in terms of setting target skills and content. Unfortunately, many important targets may not be chosen because of time limitations and other parameters. Therefore, several considerations must go into developing an educational program, regardless of the specific curriculum-development procedure utilized.

TABLE 4.2 ● Academic and Functional Curricular Areas

TOOL SUBJECTS	ACADEMIC SUBJECTS	FINE ARTS
▪ Reading ▪ Handwriting ▪ Spelling ▪ Written expression ▪ Computer literacy	▪ Social studies ▪ Math ▪ Science ▪ Foreign language ▪ Literature	▪ Art ▪ Drama ▪ Music
VOCATIONAL	**FUNCTIONAL DOMAINS**	**PERSONAL CARE**
▪ Industrial arts ▪ Cosmetology ▪ Auto mechanics ▪ Agriculture ▪ Horticulture ▪ Distributive education ▪ Building trades	▪ Communication ▪ Social competence ▪ Community living (domestic skills, self-care skills, community skills) ▪ Prevocational and vocational ▪ Leisure and recreational ▪ Learning strategies ▪ Motor ▪ Functional academics ▪ Self-determination	▪ Physical education ▪ Health ▪ Family and consumer sciences

4-2 Curricular Considerations

Curriculum development not only requires choosing what a student needs to learn but also engaging a process to organize the skills, activities, or content in ways that facilitate mastery. Choosing and organizing curriculum to produce a quality individualized education program is a complex process. Whatever we decide to teach students should facilitate that student's ability to live a productive, fulfilling life. When we are dealing with students who learn at a slower rate, pinpointing an appropriate curriculum is even more important because we do not want to waste instructional time on superfluous content. School personnel and families should consider the following guidelines when choosing and organizing what to teach to ensure the most effective and efficient educational program. Essentially, a curriculum for students with autism should be developed by a team, relate to individual postschool goals, be age appropriate, align over time, integrate various content areas, help students function in their communities, and enhance student communication and socialization.

4-2a A Curriculum Should Be Developed by a Team

The daunting task of developing an appropriate curriculum for a student should not be the responsibility of only one person. The IDEA 2004 mandates that IEPs be developed by a team consisting of various educational experts, the student's parents, and the student himself when appropriate. A team approach to curriculum development is thought to augment curriculum validity or effectiveness (Ayres et al., 2011). When parents and school personnel agree on *what* needs to be taught, there should be little disagreement about *how* it should be taught and *where* it should be taught. Parents can often best discuss what functional skills might need to be targeted by describing the student's current activities at home and in the community and by participating in setting long-term adult goals. Furthermore, if both teachers and parents reinforce targeted skills, with parents helping to choose the reinforcers to be used at home, students will likely learn those skills faster and continue to perform them over time. It is imperative for parents to be involved in curriculum development and to be knowledgeable of long-term goals because the parents, not a particular teacher, participate in IEP meetings year after year.

4-2b A Curriculum Should Relate to Postschool and Adult Goals

The curriculum-development process should begin with delineating long-term placement goals—where the student is to live, work, and play as an adult. After those goals are set, current curricular targets should be chosen that relate to those long-term goals. If it is decided that a student with autism should learn the standard grade-level academic curriculum, then it should be clear how the content proficiency is intended to enhance independent adult functioning. For example, if students who are functioning years behind their peers academically could learn to converse at some level about climate change with a peer after a lesson on the subject, then that instructional target might correlate well with the long-term goal of making friends. Choose the academic targets with consideration for how the subsequent knowledge will benefit the student both now and in the future.

As mentioned previously for students with ID, a functional life skills curriculum is frequently the best choice if adult goals are independent living and working in their community. A curriculum is **functional** if it results in the student being able to perform essential tasks independently (Brown et al., 1979). For example, everyone needs to be able to dress and toilet themselves. If an individual cannot perform these tasks, then someone must assist the individual in doing so, making those skills functional and a high priority for instructional targets. It would be extremely difficult to live and work independently without those skills. Everything taught to students with autism should align with targeted adult goals.

4-2c A Curriculum Should Be Chronologically Age Appropriate

Not only should curriculum align with adult goals, but it should also be age appropriate (Courtade et al., 2012). Consider what activities, materials, and places same-age peers perform, use, frequent, and desire, and provide similar content and conditions for the student with autism. In many cases, environments are age appropriate, but the activities to be performed may be different. For example, children of various ages participate in grocery shopping. However, young children are usually accompanied by their parents and assisted in the various skills. So, teaching a young child with autism to grocery shop would require teaching him to participate with parent assistance, or maybe not teaching this skill to elementary students at all. Conversely, adolescents often shop independently, so for a 16-year-old student with autism the curriculum would target skills necessary to accomplish this task. Or, rather than have an 18-year-old student with autism listen to music on CDs in a classroom, he might be taught to access music via internet streaming on a computer or a smartphone, just as his peers do. Delineating age-appropriate skills, materials, and activities may present a challenge for students with autism, but the benefits of applying the chronological age-appropriate criterion are worth the effort.

4-2d A Curriculum Should Be Aligned Over Time

Curriculum should be coordinated from one year to the next. This means that skills, activities, and content taught at one point in time should facilitate mastery of skills and activities that will be taught later (Brown et al., 1979). The way to this coordination is to establish long-term, intermediate, and short-term goals toward which all instruction leads. Too often, curriculum is established on an annual basis with no view at long-term implications. For example, knowing that a student should walk through middle school hallways without assistance, the elementary school teacher may set the instructional goal of teaching an 8-year-old student with autism to transition independently from room to room rather than walk holding the teacher's hand.

4-2e A Curriculum Should Be Integrated Across Content Areas

Skills, activities, or content in one curricular area or domain should connect to skills or content taught in another area. For example, a history teacher delivering a unit on the Revolutionary War would coordinate (integrate) her content with the literature unit being taught in the English class so that European literature from the late 1700s would be discussed relative to the politics of the time and vice versa. For individuals who need a functional curriculum, communication, social, and motor skills should be integrated with various curricular activities. For example, a student who is learning to ride a bus to work will need to learn communication skills (to ask what time a bus arrives, what the fare will be, and to ask to be let off) as well as the appropriate social skills for those interactions. He will need the fine motor skills to handle coins or payment cards and manage the pay machine on the bus and the gross motor skills to walk up the bus steps, ride a bus standing up if necessary, and climb down off the bus. In this case, the student may learn these skills most efficiently if the physical education teacher addresses the gross motor skills of balance and stair climbing, the speech and language pathologist (SLP) teaches the skills of asking bus-related questions and speaking loudly enough to be heard, and the special education teacher teaches money and time skills. This curricular integration toward each activity will result in stronger, more efficient learning experiences for the student.

4-2f A Curriculum Should Be Community Referenced

A community-referenced curriculum refers to the notion that all curricula are developed for the purpose of teaching a student to function independently as an adult in his or her community (Branham, Collins, Schuster, & Kleinert, 1999). Skills and activities are chosen with consideration for what is culturally appropriate, the types of environmental demands, the accessibility of the community environments, and those environments in which the individual will most likely function. Furthermore, researchers recommend that skills and activities be taught in those environments in which they will be used and at the times they would be used. For example, if a student lives in a small town, riding a bus would not be a relevant activity to teach; walking safely to and from school might be more important. If a student lives in an apartment building, then operating an elevator may be a useful thing to learn. This may be less important for someone living in a neighborhood where the use of appropriate social skills with neighbors is more essential to daily functioning.

4-2g A Curriculum Should Emphasize Communication and Socialization

Because individuals with autism often have communication and socialization difficulties, choosing and organizing curriculum to enhance these areas is an important consideration (Wehman et al., 2014). Appropriate communication and social skills should be interwoven into all skills and activities. Planning communication skills to be taught only in the presence of the SLP would be less effective than preparing everyone involved with a student with autism to implement a coordinated communication and social skills curriculum. For example, on the way to the cafeteria, the teacher asks the student to say or sign "lunch" or "eat" or "I would like to eat a sandwich, please." During lunch, the **paraprofessional** prompts the student to ask for "more" or "I would like more pizza" using "please" and "thank you." At home, when the student desires a favorite toy, his parents and siblings require him to communicate in order to obtain it, and he is reminded at dinner to look at others and take turns commenting. Specific strategies for teaching communication and social skills will be discussed in Chapters 6 and 7. The point is that skills, particularly in communication, should be incorporated into all curricular areas.

Developing an individualized curriculum is a dynamic process involving several decision points. Most of the decisions should be based on accurate and relevant assessment data.

Some decisions may be based on the student's or his family's personal preference, but *all* decisions should be based on what serves the particular student's best interest. By applying the above guidelines to any curriculum-development procedure, an individualized, appropriate educational program is most likely to emerge.

4-3 A Curriculum-Development Procedure

In addition to general curriculum guidelines, a curriculum-development process requires six principal steps: (a) delineate long- and short-term goals, (b) create an inventory of what needs to be learned to reach those goals, (c) assess what the student has already mastered, (d) prioritize what to teach, (e) organize it to achieve mastery, and (f) develop an IEP. Table 4.3 lists these steps. This process mirrors a discrepancy analysis: first decide where you want to go and then decide what steps it will take to get there. Next determine at which step you currently stand. The discrepancy (in the form of steps) between where you are and where you want to go becomes your plan of action. In this case, it becomes an individualized curriculum.

4-3a Establish Placement Goals

As previously mentioned, targeting *where* we want students to be functioning in the future is the first step of curriculum development. This look at the future includes setting long-term, intermediate, and short-term goals. This goal-setting process should include as many people as possible who are interested in the student's educational plan. The process should also allow review and revision as progress and priorities are appraised.

Long-Term Goals

Ideally, parents and professionals should engage in discussion about their vision for the student as an adult. This would involve discussing possible living situations, work situations, relationships, and recreational situations for the student. It might be best to begin this discussion when the child is very young, but parents often find it difficult to look that far down the road. First, they may not be aware of the various living and working options from which they can choose (see Table 4.1). Second, they may not be able to consider factors too far into the future, especially if their child is displaying frequent challenging behavior. Third, they may not be willing to engage in a long-term goal discussion because it means accepting the difficult conclusion that their child may differ significantly from other children. Fourth, parents and teachers may be reluctant to set goals early, fearing those decisions might affect the quality of intervention. For example, if a goal for preparing a student to function in a certain type of job (e.g., busing tables in a restaurant, sacking groceries) is set when the student is young, then he might not be taught the academic or employment skills needed for more competitive jobs that he may have been able to master.

TABLE 4.3 ● **Curriculum-Development Process Steps**

1. Establish placement goals.
   - Long-term adult goals
   - Intermediate goals (within the next 5 years)
   - Short-term goals (current environments)
2. Develop an activity or skill list in multiple domains to reach goals.
3. Assess for current level of functioning within each skill list.
4. Obtain social validity and prioritize targets for the current year.
5. Write annual goals and short-term objectives.
6. Develop an IEP.

⌄ Professional Resource Download

This notion of establishing long-term goals to guide current curriculum decisions is referred to as the **criterion of ultimate functioning** (Brown, Nietupski, & Hamre-Nietupski, 1976). Brown and his colleagues defined this criterion as "an ever-changing, expanding, localized, and personalized cluster of factors that each person must possess in order to function as productively and independently as possible in socially, vocationally, and domestically integrated adult community environments" (p. 8). This criterion ensures that special education students would have IEPs that (a) are continuous rather than short term, (b) recommend "real" rather than artificial materials, (c) specify education in integrated settings, and (d) target age-appropriate and culturally appropriate skills (Browder & Spooner, 2011).

Teachers also need to realize that the goal-setting process is dynamic—that is, goals can be adapted and altered as the student progresses. However, providing some long-term vision of the student as an adult will assist in keeping school personnel and parents on track in what they choose to teach him. Generally, for students with autism, long-term goals target independent living and competitive employment. For students with higher cognitive functioning, long-term goals may include postsecondary education at universities, community colleges, or trade schools as well as apartment living. For some, it might be reasonable to assume they will marry and have a family. However, many adults with autism and ID need regular supervision and assistance to work and live in the community. It might be wise for those involved in establishing individual long-term goals to visit supervised apartments, residential facilities, and group homes. In addition, it might be helpful to visit retail or manufacturing businesses in the community, speak with school- or agency-based job coaches, and visit employment options that offer highly structured jobs so that the parents and educators of young children have a realistic view of future possibilities and environmental demands. This view will be what drives the curriculum-development process.

Intermediate Goals

After long-term goals have been articulated, intermediate goals can be discussed. These goals should reflect the student's school placements or living placements or both within the next 3 to 5 years. This concept is known as the **criterion of the next environment** (Vincent et al., 1980). For example, the long-term decision may be that a student will remain at home as an adult and work in his father's hardware store, assisting with various tasks. This student is now 7 years old. In 3 or 4 years, regardless of functioning level, the student will be moved to the middle school because that is the age-appropriate placement. Thus, intermediate goals will also need to be established to plan for the student to function in the middle school; there he will need to be able to negotiate chaotic hallways, a crowded cafeteria, and bell-cued periods while continuing to learn skills that will contribute to the ultimate vocational goal of working with his father. Transitions from early childhood programs to elementary schools, from elementary schools to middle schools, and middle schools to high schools are difficult for all students. Students with autism and ID do not deal with change easily, so these transitions can be more traumatic. We need to target intermediate-range placements and prepare students for success in the next environment. Doing so will better facilitate progress toward long-term goals.

Short-Term Goals

Short-term goals are those goals that address the student's immediate learning needs (for the current year or less). Known collectively as the **criterion of the immediate environment** (Peterson, Trecker, Egan, Fredericks, & Bunse, 1983), these goals focus on skills necessary to function under current conditions. For example, the 7-year-old student previously mentioned may be placed in a general education classroom for academic instruction and opportunities to practice social skills, a special education classroom for communication and social skills, and an after-school program in the afternoons. In the general education class, the student will need to learn to interact with his general education peers, find his seat, take turns, participate in small-group instruction, and complete academic activities. In the special education classroom, he will need to learn skills required for one-to-one or small-group instruction in communication and social skills. He will need to learn how to choose free-time activities and how to communicate his wants and needs. At the after-school program, he is expected to "play" with other children (e.g., use toys appropriately, take turns).

In addition to curriculum that addresses these immediate goals, the student will need to be gradually exposed to large groups of peers, and he will need to learn how to negotiate hallways and cafeterias and to express his needs, skills that will serve him well in middle school. Essentially, the individualized curriculum should address skills and activities necessary to function in the immediate placements, those that will lead to a successful experience in the near future, and those that will facilitate success as an adult.

4-3b Develop a Curricular Inventory for Reaching the Goals

After short-term, intermediate, and long-term goals have been established, the curriculum team should examine published curricula and/or develop new curricula. From whatever curriculum is chosen, target skills and instructional activities that lead to the established goals can be identified or developed. Many commercial curricula are available and provide specific instructions and tools for assessing learning needs, organizing curriculum, and presenting instruction. Each state has an adopted standard academic curriculum that is readily available for teachers. Additional published academic curricula are also available through school district resource systems or commercial publishers. Table 4.4 lists sample published curricula for students with autism and ID. We recommend that teachers review published curricula online, through publishers' representatives, or by contacting the publisher for sample materials before selecting or recommending a specific curriculum.

Published functional skills curricula come in several forms (Bouck, 2009). Some curricula only consist of a teacher's manual, so teachers are expected to create teaching materials. Some may have teacher and student materials. Most are organized into functional domains or a series of activities. Some may have a series of books, each addressing one domain or skill area. Some curricula may include CDs, and others may be accessed entirely online. Some include many types of student materials as a separate cost. Once again, teachers must become critical consumers of published curricula and use these materials only if they match current and long-term goals of their student(s) and seem worth the price.

Ecological Inventory

Even the best commercial curriculum may need to be modified to address the needs of individual students and their short-, intermediate-, and long-term goals. An **ecological inventory** is one particularly useful tool to guide educators in identifying student needs relative to the demands of the environments in which students must function now and in the future (Ayres et al., 2011; Brown et al., 1979; Falvey, 1989). The inventory is produced from an ecological assessment. An "ecological inventory is the process of systematic identification of all of the functions critical for success in the collection of settings that one individual currently encounters and can be expected to encounter in the future" (Sobsey, 1987, p. 1).

Identify Environments, Subenvironments, and Activities The first component of the ecological inventory process requires identification of future and current environments as mentioned above, and subenvironments for each student. For example, a student may currently need to participate in her home, school, place of worship, shopping mall, grandmother's house, and the park (environments). Within her home, she must function in the kitchen, dining room, den, bedroom, and bathroom (called *subenvironments*). Note that students with ID might have access to a restricted set of environments and subenvironments.

After the student's subenvironments are delineated, the team should list the *activities* that a particular student would be expected to perform in each of those subenvironments. It might be best to obtain information about various environmental expectations from those persons who know the student best. For example, in the kitchen our student may be expected to make her breakfast, wash dishes, and obtain snacks; and toilet, take a shower, brush her teeth, and wash her face in the bathroom. The more comprehensive the list, the more useful a particular inventory will be. However, even conducting only a partial ecological inventory would likely positively influence the curriculum-development process.

TABLE 4.4 ● Sample Published Curricula for Use with Students with Autism

FUNCTIONAL CURRICULA

- Life Centered Education (LCE) Transition Curriculum and Assessment Portal, Council for Exceptional Children (CEC)
- Adaptive Living Skills Curriculum (ALSC), Houghton Mifflin Harcourt
- A Functional Assessment and Curriculum for Teaching Students with Disabilities—Volumes I–IV, PRO-ED
- Functional Curriculum for Elementary and Secondary Students with Special Needs—3rd edition, PRO-ED
- Living on your Own, Attainment Company
- Aligning Life Skills to Academic Program, Attainment Company

- DEAL: Daily Experiences and Activities for Living, PRO-ED
- Functional Routines for Adolescents & Adults, PRO-ED
- FISH: Functional Independence Skills Handbook: Assessment and Curriculum for Individuals with Developmental Disabilities, PRO-ED
- STAR Program, PRO-ED
- Enhance Series: Functional Life Skills; Transition, Attainment Company
- LINKS®: Linking Assessment and Instruction for Independence, STAR Autism Support

ACADEMIC CURRICULA

- Co:Writer Universal, Don Johnston Publishers
- Snap&Read Universal, Don Johnston Publishers
- Equals Mathematics, AbleNet
- Pathways to Literacy, Attainment Company
- Explore Math; American History, Attainment Company
- Edmark Reading Program, PRO-ED
- Early Reading Skills Builder, Attainment Company
- Early Literacy Skills Builder, Attainment Company
- Reading Mastery, McGraw-Hill

- Start-to-Finish CORE and Literacy Curriculum, Don Johnston Publishers
- Early Numeracy Curriculum, Attainment Company
- Early Science Curriculum, Attainment Company
- Teaching to Standards: English Language Arts; Math; Science, Attainment Company
- Read to Learn, Attainment Company
- Jamestown Readers, McGraw-Hill
- Corrective Reading, McGraw-Hill
- Corrective Mathematics, McGraw-Hill

SOCIAL SKILLS CURRICULA

- ACCEPTS Program, PRO-ED
- ASSET: A Social Skills Program for Adolescents, Research Press
- Spotlight on Social Skills series, PRO-ED

- Skillstreaming series, Research Press
- Getting to Know You! series, Research Press

COMMUNICATION CURRICULA

- Accessible Literacy Learning (ALL) Reading Program, Mayer-Johnson
- Boardmaker® Software, Mayer-Johnson
- Teaching Communication Skills: Autism, Attainment Company
- The Verbal Behavior Milestones Assessment and Placement Program (VB-MAPP), AVB Press
- Teaching Language to Children with Autism or Other Developmental Disabilities, AVB Press

- Autism Language Learning, ALL
- Picture Exchange Communication System (PECS), Pyramid Educational Consultants
- Enhancing Communication for Individuals with Autism, Brookes Publishing
- Social Language Training, PRO-ED
- Assessment of Basic Language and Learning Skills, Revised (ABLLS-R), Partington Behavior Analysis

This comprehensive list of activities now provides a working document for curriculum development or refinement. Each activity can be further analyzed to identify specific skills required for performing it. For example, taking a shower requires undressing, preparing the water, washing body and hair, drying, combing hair, dressing, and cleaning up. The skills can be further broken down into small units of instruction. For example, washing with soap requires several different steps (e.g., wet rag and soap, rub to create lather, apply to body, rinse). Remember to keep in mind long- and short-term goals throughout the process (e.g., will the student have access to a tub or just a shower in future residences?).

Table 4.5 provides the steps for developing an ecological inventory, and Table 4.6 contains sample ecological inventory questions that might facilitate the planning process. This process provides a structure for team planning of individualized curricular sequences by obtaining the necessary information about specific environments such that the activities and skills for a particular student can be easily identified.

Obviously, developing an ecological inventory involves much more work than simply purchasing a commercial curriculum and using it without adaptation. However, the advantage of the ecological inventory is that it directly matches each individual student's needs and meets the curriculum guidelines delineated early in this chapter. A commercial curriculum will need to be adapted to particular student goals and school, home, and community options for the student. Whether a curricular sequence of skills or activities is developed individually or obtained from another source, the next step for curriculum development involves determining which of those skills and activities the student has already mastered.

TABLE 4.5 ● Ecological Inventory Steps

1. List all environments in which the individual must function now and in the future.

   For example, home, school, church, child care, grandma's house

2. List the subenvironments for each environment.

   For example,

ENVIRONMENT	SUBENVIRONMENTS
Home	Den, bathroom, kitchen, bedroom, backyard
School	Special education class, music class, bathroom, cafeteria, playground

3. List the activities for each subenvironment that the individual must conduct.

   For example,

SUBENVIRONMENT	ACTIVITIES
Cafeteria	Go through food line. Eat lunch. Clean up self and area.

4. For each activity, list the requisite skills and the communication necessary for the student to participate in the activity.

   For example,

ACTIVITY	SKILLS
Go through food line.	Locate and obtain tray. Locate and obtain plate and utensils. Push tray through line. Obtain desired foods. Pay for lunch. *Communication*: Indicate desired foods; ask for tray, utensils, napkin if not available; ask how much it costs.

5. Organize the activities and skills into areas or domains.

   For example,

   Domain: self-help
   Environment: school
   Subenvironment: cafeteria
   Activity: go through food line
   Skills: locate and obtain tray, etc.

TABLE 4.6 ● Informal Ecological Assessment Sample Questions

Questions to Ask to Determine Requirements of a General Education Class

Physical arrangement of class	■ How are desks arranged? ■ Where will your student's desk be located? ■ Where is the bathroom? ■ Where are his materials kept?
Teacher's instructional style	■ What type of instructional activities does the teacher use (e.g., large-group instruction, small-group instruction, independent work, lots of pencil-paper activities, group work)? ■ What type of instructional materials are used (e.g., texts, workbooks, manipulatives, computers, tablets, digital activities, clickers)?
Teacher's management style	■ What types of student behaviors are and are not tolerated by the teacher? (For example: Is raising hand for permission to talk a requirement? Does teacher allow quiet talk among students? Are students allowed to leave seats without permission?)

Questions to Ask to Determine Requirements of a Work Situation

Physical aspects of job site	■ Is the job performed primarily indoors or outdoors? ■ Is the job site crowded or noisy? ■ Is the job performed in a place that is accessible to the public?
Work requirements	■ Are there aspects of the job that require specific physical skills (e.g., strength, fine-motor dexterity, standing for long periods of time, sitting for long periods of time)? ■ Does the job require specific communication skills (e.g., greeting customers, answering the telephone)? ■ Does the job require specific cognitive skills (e.g., handling money, telling time, reading or writing)? ■ Does the job require knowledge of specific tools (e.g., copier, dishwasher, machinery, hand tools)? ■ Does the job require independent decision-making or judgment? ■ Are there time constraints on the work to be completed? ■ How will the individual be supervised?
Social aspects of the job	■ Does the job require contact or interaction with the public? ■ Does the job require interaction with coworkers? ■ How and where are breaks taken, and what behaviors are permitted on break? (e.g., Is there a designated break room? Are there usually several people on break at once? Are there snack machines? Is smoking allowed on break? If so, where?)

Questions to Ask to Determine Home Needs

Leisure/recreational activities	■ What activities does the family enjoy doing together? ■ What skills would enable your child to participate more fully in these activities? ■ What activities would you like your child to do with his or her siblings (e.g., play board games, play outdoor games, play video games, text each other)? ■ What activities would you like your child to do independently (e.g., play video games, look at/read books, play with toys)?
Home jobs	■ What jobs would parents like their child to do independently (e.g., make his/her bed, carry dishes to the sink, clean room)? ■ What jobs would parents like their child to do with his/her siblings (e.g., wash dishes, wash the car, rake leaves)?
Home routines	■ What part of the child's daily routines needs to be done independently (e.g., dress self, comb hair, fix a snack)?
Language/communication	■ How does the child let you know when he/she needs or wants something (e.g., tugs on your clothes, makes noises, whines, points)? ■ How should the child let you know when he/she needs or wants something (e.g., use words, use communication book, use sign language)? ■ Does the child express affection to parents or siblings? If so, how? ■ Should the child learn how to express affection to parents or siblings (e.g., give/receive hugs, kisses)?

Assess for Current Level of Functioning The next step in an ecological inventory is to determine which skills required for the identified activities each student will need to learn. If a purchased curriculum is used for assessment purposes, then we call this assessment technique **curriculum-based assessment (CBA)**. A curriculum-based assessment can be conducted in several different ways, singly or in combination:

1. use sample indicators from the curriculum,
2. select assessment matched to the curriculum,
3. employ observational recording techniques to measure performance on given objectives, or
4. devise a checklist whereby each behavior is coded as to whether the student can do it, do it with help, or cannot do it at all.

All curriculum-based assessments must include a few critical features:

1. ongoing assessment to determine progress in the curriculum,
2. use of valid assessment instruments or strategies, and
3. use of quantitative and qualitative data (Fuchs & Deno, 1994; Fuchs & Fuchs, 2000; McMaster & Espin, 2007).

The advantage of curriculum-based assessment is that the assessment results tie directly to the instructional objectives and materials.

An example of a published curriculum-based assessment from Curriculum Associates is the *BRIGANCE® Comprehensive Inventory of Basic Skills II* (BRIGANCE CIBS II), which is also often used as a curriculum. The BRIGANCE CIBS II includes three separate components that measure reading, writing. and math achievement from kindergarten through ninth grade. The *BRIGANCE Inventory of Early Development* (IED) and the *BRIGANCE Transition Skills Inventory* (with a corresponding *BRIGANCE Transition Skills Activities*) provide assessments of developmental skills for young children and of postsecondary skills targeting functional rather than academic skills, respectively. Each test lists target objectives in different designated areas that are assessed through graduated-difficulty skill sequences. The tests are sequenced according to grade level and age level in some cases. These tests are widely used for pretesting and posttesting and for developing and evaluating IEP objectives. In general, they are easy and quick to use and score and provide helpful information for identifying current level of functioning, planning, and monitoring progress in specific instructional areas. Composing tests directly from an academic textbook is another example of CBA.

One of the most useful CBA techniques is to develop a checklist of target content or skills and determine whether the child can perform the behavior or skill, perform some of them, or not perform them at all. This type of assessment lends itself nicely to use with an ecological inventory. Given clear goals and steps in the form of sequenced skills or activities leading to those goals, the teacher and other team members can then ask the child to perform each identified skill and note those that have already been learned and those that need to be taught. Identifying which skills a student needs to learn to enable him or her to progress toward predetermined goals is like developing a road map for a long journey. The next step is to determine exactly where to begin teaching.

4-3c Ensure Social Validity

Determining what to teach a student with autism should be based not only on long-term goals and current level of functioning but also on what is viewed as appropriate and desirable by the child's family members and other significant people in that child's life. The concept of acceptability of a program by its consumer is known as **social validity** (Harris, Belchic, Blum, & Celiberti, 1994; Wolf, 1978). Social validity is an important component of curriculum development. This is one reason we recommend that the planning process be conducted by a team. School personnel and parents often differ in their perceptions of what a child needs to learn. It is important to obtain consensus about what is necessary and acceptable to teach. This type of consensus can be reached through mutual goal setting and assessment and frequent discussion. If teachers do not think it is important to teach something, then they may not put much energy into teaching it. If parents do not see importance or relevance in a particular skill, then they may not prompt it or reinforce it at home. In either case, the instructional program should be created through genuine discussion and careful compromise. Thus, parents, advocates, and various school personnel should tackle the curriculum-development process together with agreed-on priorities.

4-3d Prioritize Activities and Skills

Part of the work of developing an appropriate curriculum is to decide what to teach first—that is, what are the most important targets to teach in the current year? For students placed in the standard academic curriculum, the sequence of content objectives by age and grade level is already determined, and teachers are expected to follow this sequence in order. Even if a student cannot master all of the curricular objectives, the student is typically included in those objectives that general education students are learning at a given time with different teaching strategies and different progress monitoring techniques (e.g., watching content in a video and indicating answers to a few questions by choosing one of two answers).

For students who are placed into a functional life skills curriculum, sequencing content and skills objectives is left to teachers and parents. Several considerations go into deciding in what order things should be taught. Certainly, the social validity process mentioned previously will guide decisions regarding priority. Also, it might be wise to target those skills and activities that currently require more extensive supervision and that will have the largest impact on independent functioning. For example, if a child requires someone to help him get ready for bed each night, teaching those particular skills would give the parents time to do other household or family tasks. In addition, teaching independent bedtime skills prepares the child for self-sufficiency in the future.

Determining the complexity of the skill or activity is another useful consideration for designating priorities. Usually, simple, basic prerequisite skills are taught before more complex ones. For example, in learning to prepare food, children are taught simple meals (e.g., how to make a peanut butter and jelly sandwich) before they are expected to follow complex recipes. Developmental sequences that delineate simple to complex skills can be found in published developmental and adaptive behavior inventories and in published curricula. Some examples of published developmental inventories include:

- *Vineland Adaptive Behavior Scales*, 3rd edition (Vineland-3) (Pearson Education—Psychology). The Vineland-3 Scales can be used with individuals from birth to age 90. Subscales include communication, daily living skills, socialization, motor skills, and maladaptive behavior. The package includes teacher interview forms and parent and caregiver interview forms (also available in Spanish), and it allows for computerized or hand scoring.
- *Adaptive Behavior Assessment System*, 3rd edition (ABAS-3) (Pearson Education—Psychology). ABAS-3 also includes parent, caregiver, and teacher interviews and is organized into three major domains: conceptual, social, and practical with 11 skill areas. It can be used with individuals from birth to age 90 and is available in Spanish. It can be used for assessment, intervention planning, and progress monitoring.
- *Early Learning Accomplishment Profile System* (Chapel Hill Training-Outreach Project, Inc.). This system assesses young children's (birth to age five) development across a variety of developmental areas (e.g., gross motor, fine motor, cognitive, language, self-help). Items that the child does not pass become instructional targets. The system includes screening, assessment, and curriculum components with software and teaching materials. Parent involvement is also a major element of the system.
- *BRIGANCE Inventory of Early Development III* (IED-III) (Curriculum Associates). This is a criterion-referenced assessment of areas such as preambulatory motor skills, gross motor skills, and fine motor skills; self-help skills; and prespeech, speech, and language skills. The IED-III is easy to use and includes instructional objectives for each skill tested.

- *Behavioral Characteristics Progression* (BCP) (VORT Corporation). The BCP is a curriculum-based assessment with instructional activities for developmental ages 1 to 14 years used to assess, set objectives, track progress, and provide instruction.
- *Adaptive Behavior Evaluation Scale*—Revised 2nd edition (ABES-R2) (Hawthorne Educational Services). ABES-R2 is available in a home and school version and includes several subscales in the areas of communication, self-care, home living, social skills, community use, self-direction, health and safety, functional academics, and leisure and work skills organized in developmental order. This instrument can be used with students ages 4 to 18 and can assist teachers in determining educational goals and objectives for individual students.

Those skills and activities that the child or adolescent performs frequently are also good first things to teach. For example, because every individual needs to eat several times a day, eating activities are good ones to teach if they have not been mastered. Furthermore, you should choose skills that are necessary to guarantee one's safety in current and future environments. For example, teaching the proper use of electrical appliances (e.g., how to operate a toaster) if the child is old enough to use them may take priority over teaching him to set the table.

Another consideration for selecting priorities for students with autism involves behavior management. By choosing to teach a student to obtain what he wants or needs in socially appropriate ways, considerable inappropriate behavior can be prevented. This means that teaching functional communication and social skills is quite likely to be a high priority (Pituch et al., 2011). For example, if a child with autism perseverates on flashlights, then it would be appropriate to teach the word *light* or the phrase "I want the flashlight." It is also important to teach skills that will result in natural reinforcement (i.e., the reinforcement that would be expected when the skill is used in real life outside of educational context). What things does the child need to do to get people around her to like her and want to work with her? It could be a priority to teach essential social skills to elicit positive reactions from people (smiling, eye contact, appropriate body language). Finally, it is important to initially teach students with autism and related disorders basic learning behaviors such as compliance, attending, and imitating (motor and language imitation). Because these skills empower future learning (e.g., improved attending and compliance facilitates faster skill acquisition in other areas), it is difficult to progress far within any curricula until sufficient skills in these areas are acquired.

4-3e Write Annual Goals and Objectives

After the team has determined exactly what the student needs to learn, this information should be organized as goals and objectives. The ultimate goal for students with autism and related disorders is to achieve the ability to participate in their school, home, work, and community as independently as possible. Annual goals and objectives should lead toward that end. Goal statements communicate annual program intent, and **behavioral objectives** communicate the actual intent of instruction (Alberto & Troutman, 2017), or what the student is expected to achieve. Both goals and objectives should be written such that mastery will be recognized when it is achieved and skill development short of mastery will not be considered mastered. Specifically, teachers should be able to measure incremental progress toward attaining goals and objectives. We therefore recommend that both goals and objectives be written in behavioral terms (see Chapter 2).

Usually, at least one annual goal is written for each domain or curricular area that has been targeted for teaching. The goals are then broken into smaller instructional components. These components are written as behavioral objectives. Several objectives are usually written for each goal. Table 4.7 provides sample goals and objectives for students of various ages in various domains.

Note that behavioral objectives contain four pieces of information: (a) who is doing the learning, (b) what the student must do to show learning, (c) under what conditions this behavior must be performed, and (d) the quality or quantity of behavior that signifies mastery. Identifying the learner, the target behavior, the conditions of the instruction, and the criteria for acceptable performance may take some practice. For more information about the

TABLE 4.7 ● **Sample Goals and Objectives**

EARLY CHILDHOOD		
COMMUNICATION	**MOTOR**	**SELF-HELP**
Goal: Henry will label common objects.	*Goal:* Henry will demonstrate the correct use of scissors.	*Goal:* Henry will demonstrate the ability to dress himself independently.
Objective: Given the command "What is this?" and the presentation of a (shoe, sock, toy, spoon), Henry will say the correct label 10 of 10 trials for 3 days.	*Objective:* Given a drawn square, Henry will cut out the square along the lines using single-handle scissors with no more than two errors.	*Objective:* Given a shoelace tied in a bow, Henry will untie the shoelace by pulling with one hand until the loops disappear each time over 3 days.

ELEMENTARY		
COGNITIVE	**WRITING**	**SOCIAL**
Goal: Mary will demonstrate the ability to identify colors.	*Goal:* Mary will reproduce written models.	*Goal:* Mary will participate in group activities.
Objective: Given randomly placed construction paper circles (green, yellow, red), one additional red circle, and the command "Match this," Mary will match the color red 9 of 10 trials.	*Objective:* Given a lightly drawn cross, Mary will use a pencil to trace the cross with no more than one error for each of 15 trials.	*Objective:* During recess, Mary will remain with her group during the Red Rover game for 10 consecutive minutes each day this week.

SECONDARY		
VOCATIONAL	**MONETARY CONCEPTS**	**PERSONAL MANAGEMENT**
Goal: Tad will complete laundry tasks.	*Goal:* Tad will demonstrate knowledge of money values.	*Goal:* Tad will demonstrate the ability to use the telephone correctly.
Objective: When the dryer buzzer sounds, Tad will remove all clothes from the dryer, fold them, and place them in the laundry basket 10 consecutive times.	*Objective:* Given a quarter, nickel, dime, and penny and the request "Find the _____," Tad will pick up the correct coin with 90% accuracy.	*Objective:* Given several scenarios and an unplugged phone, Tad will dial the correct number for assistance each time.

mechanics of writing goals and objectives, the reader is referred to Alberto and Troutman (2017) and to Robert Mager's classic booklet *Preparing Instructional Objectives* (1997).

Remember that goals and objectives should be integrated across content areas into a total curricular approach rather than treated in isolation. This means, for example, that if a goal in the self-help domain addresses toileting, there should be a corresponding goal in the communication domain of labeling things that pertain to toileting such as the words *toilet*, *toilet paper*, *pants*, *up–down*, *button*, and *snap*. Also, remember that the development of goals and objectives is an ongoing process in which the goals and objectives are modified as the student's progress is assessed and long-term goals are reevaluated. This dynamic longitudinal planning process should guarantee that the student is being taught essential skills at every opportunity. In addition, parents can rest assured that delineating a long-term curriculum at one point in time will not preclude optimal outcomes because a student capable of faster goal acquisition can be assigned more challenging goals or altered long-term goals as a result of this iterative process.

4-3f Develop the Individualized Education Program

The IDEA 2004 specifies that for each student who receives special education services a document (the IEP) must be developed that prescribes and records appropriate educational services (IDEA Partnership, 2006). Each IEP should address the student's current level of academic and social functioning, student needs, assessment issues, and prescribed educational and related services. The IEP, however, should not just be viewed as a legal document but as an "ongoing, flexible, and useful procedure from which a framework emerges to guide an ongoing educational program" (Smith, Slattery, & Knopp, 1993, p. 3). Smith and colleagues point out that viewing the IEP as a process rather than a product (a) allows for participation and program ownership by many "players" in the child's life, (b) can result in a broader, more comprehensive plan, and (c) can facilitate integrated placement decisions.

If the IEP is generated based on individualized assessment rather than a published curriculum and assuming the IEP guides what happens in the classroom, then the document is being used as intended. Teachers and other school personnel would do well to develop a document that is a functional plan for instruction and the provision of related services. Daily lesson plans and class schedules should be derived directly from this document.

In most school districts, IEPs are generated using computer software. Several different software options exist for this purpose, so new teachers must learn to use the IEP computer program adopted by their particular schools. Goals and objectives in these programs are typically prewritten and teachers simply designate which might pertain to an individual student, although most IEP programs also provide space for additional individualized goals and objectives to be written. Allowing a published curriculum, whether computer generated or not, to dictate the IEP may preclude the individualized process mandated by law and recommended in this chapter. Software programs that are used to generate the IEP document based on a long-term vision, individualized assessment, and a social validity process should be useful. However, teachers should also rely on individualized assessment, which might include an ecological inventory, to determine the appropriateness of objectives contained in the IEP software. Consider writing your own objectives for students with autism who are eligible for alternate standards and assessments and who have targeted long-term adult goals.

By no later than age 16, a student's IEP must contain an **individual transition plan (ITP)**. Box 4.1 provides information about transition planning. The purpose of the ITP is to provide a "structure for preparing an individual to live, work, and play in the community as fully and independently as possible" (U.S. Department of Education, 2017, p. 1). Remember that school district personnel and vocational rehabilitation (VR) agency personnel participate in the planning process with the family and student when appropriate. Long-term goals are to be based, at least in part, on the student's self-determined desires and abilities. Transition services that might be included on an ITP include assistive technology, travel training (e.g., riding the bus or light rail), vocational assessment, work experiences with coaching, direct instruction of work skills, self-advocacy, management of home and personal finances, and self-help and social skills training. Table 4.1 lists possible postschool placements for additional education, employment, and living to help guide ITP development. According to the IDEA 2004, the ITP must be updated annually with the IEP and include:

1. appropriate measurable postsecondary goals based on age-appropriate transition assessments related to training, education, employment, and, where appropriate, independent living skills; and
2. the transition services (including courses of study) needed to assist the student with a disability in reaching those goals) (U.S. Department of Education, 2017, p. 1).

An IEP might also include a **behavior intervention plan (BIP)** (covered in Chapter 3) if the student shows excessive challenging behavior that interferes with learning. This plan should be based on a functional behavior assessment, which is discussed in Chapter 3, and should contain target behaviors (in the form of behavioral objectives), replacement behaviors, antecedent manipulations, reinforcement strategies, and strategies for managing dangerous and aggressive behaviors.

The IEP, in fact, includes the student's curriculum for a given year. The IEP can drive meaningful instruction if:

1. it is developed through participation of professionals, parents, advocates, and students in a planning process that includes longitudinal goal determination;

2. it is a sequenced and organized list of functional community-referenced skills and activities; and

3. it includes personalized comprehensive assessment and well-written goals and objectives.

For more specific information about developing IEPs, new teachers should refer to the special education procedural guide usually available in each school district. Each state department of education's website should also provide guidance in all matters pertaining to the requirements of the IDEA, including IEP development. The U.S. Department of Education (2011) also published A *Guide to the Individualized Education Program* to assist school personnel and parents in implementing the IDEA 2004. Falvey, Grenot-Scheyer, and Luddy (1987) recommended several questions that remain pertinent for parents and professionals to consider when developing and prioritizing curricular content. Table 4.8 lists those questions. The answers will help to guarantee that an IEP is the most appropriate one for a particular student.

TABLE 4.8 ● **Questions for Determining Curricular Content and Priorities**

I.   What skills need to be taught?
   A. Are the skills functional for the student?
      1. Are the skills being considered chronologically age appropriate?
      2. Are these skills required across a variety of environments?
      3. Can these skills be used often?
      4. Does someone have to do it for the student if he cannot?
      5. How do students without disabilities perform the skill?
      6. What skills would the student desire?
      7. What is the student's current level of performance on these skills?
      8. What family needs have been considered in choosing these skills?
   B. Will the skills result in more integration and independence?
      1. What skills does the society value?
      2. What are peers without disabilities being taught?
      3. What activities are peers without disabilities doing?
      4. What skills would reduce the discrepancy between student and peers?
      5. What skills would result in increased opportunities for interaction?
      6. What skills would lead to less restrictive placements?
      7. What skills would promote independence?
   C. What are the skill and task characteristics?
      1. What are the skills involved in this task or activity?
      2. What skills can be integrated across tasks?
      3. What skills can be recombined into other more complex skills?
      4. What skills will meet the largest variety of the student's needs?
      5. What family needs have been considered when determining skills?
II. Where should the skills be taught?
   A. Are the environments chronologically age appropriate?
   B. Are the environments accessible for teaching during school hours?
   C. Are the environments preferred by the student?
   D. Are the environments frequented by the student, peers, and family members?
   E. Are there opportunities to teach many skills in these environments?
   F. Are the environments appropriate for the student now and in the future?

Source: Adapted from "Developing and implementing integrated community referenced curricula" by M. A. Falvey, M. Grenot-Sheyer, & E. Luddy (1987). In D. J. Cohen, A. M. Donnellan, & R. Paul (Eds.), *Handbook of autism and pervasive developmental disorders* (pp. 241–242). New York: John Wiley & Sons. Copyright © 1987 by John Wiley and Sons.

4-4 Curricular Refinement

Developing a curriculum requires further refinement than just creating a list of prioritized skills and activities. Once this list has been created, the teacher needs to decide the level of competency necessary to master a designated goal and needs to break down each skill and activity into instructional units that are small enough for the student to grasp. In this section, we will discuss levels of competency and task analysis—two concepts that facilitate pinpointing highly specific curricular bits for each student.

4-4a Levels of Competency

The initial phase of curriculum development results in an individualized sequence of skills and activities in the form of goals and behavioral objectives. The second phase is to ensure that mastery of the objective will be useful to a particular student. Ensuring functional use requires an expansion of the curriculum such that each objective is taught to mastery at each of four hierarchical stages. These stages are acquisition, fluency, maintenance, and generalization (Alberto & Troutman, 2017).

Acquisition

Teaching a skill to mastery at the acquisition stage means that a student can reliably identify a target behavior when someone else performs it correctly, and can perform it correctly himself with some degree of accuracy. This is the lowest level of response competency. For example, a student able to provide exact correct bus fare out of several coins 8 times out of 10 during three consecutive sessions could be considered to have "acquired" the skill of choosing correct bus fare. However, if it still takes him a long time to pick the correct coins, then the student's ability to actually ride the bus to work remains uncertain. Teaching only to the acquisition level seldom results in functional, generalized learning.

Fluency

Fluency refers to the rate of performance of a behavior. If it currently takes the student 5 minutes to find the correct change, then he still is not able to ride the bus because the bus driver cannot wait that long for him to insert his fare into the machine. As a matter of fact, adults who see him trying to find change may assist with the task to expedite the process or attempt to take advantage of the student in some nefarious way. Regardless, the long-term goal of improved independence via the ability to use public transportation has not yet been met. To teach the student to pick out the correct amount faster, the objective is changed to incorporate a time limit on the behavior as part of the criteria for mastery. Now we want to teach "choosing correct bus fare within 20 seconds." Teaching a behavior at the fluency level demands different strategies such as massed practice and reinforcing more timely responses.

Maintenance

Maintenance of a behavior implies that the student can perform the response at an acceptable rate over weeks or months without having to reteach it. For example, if our student can "pick the correct bus fare out of a group of coins within 20 seconds," we now want to make sure that he can display that same proficiency next month and the month after that. Teaching to maintenance does not necessarily require that the objective be written differently, but it does require some adjusted teaching strategies such as distributed practice and intermittent reinforcement. Again, teaching the bus fare skill is not finished if the student can only perform the skill for 2 weeks and then never again.

Generalization

If our curriculum goals target independent functioning in the community as they should, then we must teach all functional skills to the level of generalization. *Generalization* means that the student can perform a behavior under different conditions and that the student can adapt or change the behavior regardless of the conditions.

The first type of generalization is known as **stimulus generalization**. Stimulus generalization means that even if things such as instructional cues, materials, people, time of day, and settings change, the student will still perform the behavior at the same acceptable rate. For example, if the student mentioned previously must find bus fare while he stands at the bus stop rather than when simply sitting in the classroom, we want to ensure that he can do that. Or if he must find fare when the bus driver says "Good morning" one day and "$2.25, please" the next day, then we need to teach the student to respond accordingly. It does little good to assume that he can apply his new skill in a functional way without directly instructing him to do so. Several methods are available for teaching stimulus generalization, including **community-based instruction**. Community-based instruction means teaching students target skills in settings in the home and community where those skills are needed.

The second type of generalization is known as **response generalization**. Response generalization means that as one behavior is mastered, other related, similar behaviors may emerge. For example, after our student is choosing correct bus fare, he may also begin choosing correct change for doing his laundry. Similarly, after he has learned to provide the correct fare amount, he may still be able provide the correct fare when bus driver informs him that the price of the ride has increased (i.e., different coins are now required).

Behavioral objectives will need to be altered to focus instruction on generalization. Usually the conditions statement of the behavioral objective is changed to indicate a new setting or person or cue. For example, the objective "Given the command 'What is this?' and the presentation of a (shoe or sock or toy or spoon), Henry will say the correct label 10 of 10 trials for 3 days" is changed to read "Given any of the following commands: 'What is this?' 'Say this,' or 'Label these,' Henry will say the correct label 10 of 10 trials for 3 days."

Note that students with autism and ID typically have difficulty generalizing skills. Because of a tendency to overselect contextual cues (e.g., rely on potentially irrelevant cues for the correct response), overreliance on rote memory, preference for routine and aversion to change, and inattention to social cues and others' behavior, many students with autism and ID will need well-planned instruction to generalize their responses.

4-4b Task Analysis

An additional way to refine curriculum is to break skills down into subskills or break content down into subcontent so that the steps of learning are more accessible to the learner. This process is known as **task analysis**. The number of steps in a task analysis is related to a student's ability to grasp them. For one student, going through the cafeteria line may be broken into four steps: get tray, pick out food, pay the cashier, walk to table. However, for another student, going through the cafeteria line may require 20 steps (e.g., locate cafeteria, walk to line, wait in line, pick up tray, get fork and spoon, get napkin, place all on tray, pick out salad, point to meat and vegetable, take plate that is offered by the server, place plate on tray, obtain drink, push tray to cashier, pay cashier, wait for change, put change on tray, carry tray, find table, place tray on table, sit down). Wehman and Kregel (1997) recommended the following guidelines for developing a task analysis:

1. Each step should be listed in specific behavioral terms so that mastery can be easily determined.
2. Write each step so that it can become a prompt for the next step.
3. If the step has the word *and* in it, determine whether the learner can achieve it or whether it needs to be broken down further.
4. Pilot test the task analysis with the student before finalizing it for instruction.

Many published curricula contain task analyses; however, they should be adapted for individual students. When developing a task analysis from scratch, the adult should try the task and write down each step performed, watch another student perform the task, or interview someone who knows how to perform the task so the necessary steps can be delineated. The interview technique is best used for vocationally related tasks for which the teacher or parent has little information (e.g., stocking grocery shelves; replacing library books on shelves). Also remember that task analyses assume certain conditions (e.g., a specific library) and will need to be adapted if conditions might change.

After the task analysis has been written, it can become a curriculum-based assessment whereby the student is asked to perform each step to determine which ones need to be taught at the acquisition level, which at the fluency level, and which at the maintenance and generalization level. In a curriculum-development process, we need to know not only what general skills need to be taught but also what specific subskills are yet to be mastered. A sample task analysis assessment checklist is provided in Figure 4.2.

Other ways to conduct task analyses are available. One way is to list steps, with each one specifying a change in the duration of a behavior (e.g., student will work independently for 2 minutes, 5 minutes, 15 minutes, 25 minutes, 40 minutes). Another task analysis is such that each step signifies a decrease in the amount of assistance needed (e.g., the student will ask to leave the cafeteria with three prompts, two prompts, one prompt, no prompt). Finally, a task analysis could be such that each step indicates more complex conditions (e.g., student will attend to task for 10 minutes while alone with the teacher in a room, while three other students are in the room, while 10 other students are in the room).

Behavioral objectives do not necessarily need to be written for each step of a task analysis. Rather, task analysis steps could simply be listed under a behavioral objective, assuming that mastery of all the steps leads to mastery of the behavioral objective.

ACTIVITY: Setting table for dinner

NAME: _____   DATE: _____

TASK ANALYSIS	NEEDS ASSISTANCE	VERBAL ASSISTANCE ONLY	PHYSICAL ASSISTANCE ONLY	INDEPENDENT
Ask how many will be eating. Repeat number back				
Obtain that many placemats				
Set placemats in front of each chair				
Count the number of placemats				
Move chairs without placemats back from table				
Obtain the same number of napkins as the placemat number				
Place one napkin on left side of each placemat				
Obtain the same number of forks as the napkin number				
Place one fork on top of each napkin				
Obtain the number of knives and spoons to match number of forks				
Place one knife and one spoon on right side of each placemat				
Obtain the number of plates to match placemat number				
Set one plate in center of each placemat				
Obtain the number of glasses to match placemat number				
Set one glass on right side of each placemat above knife and spoon				
Obtain salt and pepper				
Set salt and pepper in middle of table				

FIGURE 4.2 Sample task analysis checklist

(From *Functional Curriculum for Elementary and Secondary Students with Special Needs* (3rd ed.), by P. Wehman and J. Kregel (Ed.), 2012, p. 193. Austin: Pro-Ed Publishing. Copyright 2012, by Pro-Ed, Inc. Adapted by permission.)

✔ **Professional Resource Download**

4-5 Curricular Format

Curricula can be compiled and presented in several different ways. A curriculum can be lists of activities or skills or both, sometimes organized by domain. It can be presented as goals with accompanying objectives, also in lists, as is required on an IEP. It can be formatted in a matrix configuration so that additional information can be added. Additional information in the curricular document may include any of the following:

1. specified environments in which a particular skill or objective will be taught,
2. the teaching activity description,
3. the person responsible for teaching the skill,
4. methods for evaluating the specific curricular item,
5. materials necessary for instruction, and
6. the current level of functioning.

Sometimes the skill or activity is displayed as a task analysis. A matrix design could also allow for the skills to be delineated at various learning levels (e.g., acquisition, fluency, maintenance, and generalization). Figures 4.3 through 4.9 provide examples of several curricular formats.

Remember that a curriculum is the guide for all other instructional decisions, so it should be developed in a format that illustrates its vertical and horizontal coordination. It should be obvious to all those who plan to use it how long-term goals will be reached through mastery of short-term objectives (i.e., activities and skills). The format should also depict the relationship among various domains or curricular areas (e.g., communication, self-help, vocational). In most instances, there will be more than one curricular document. One curriculum format option is to prepare a comprehensive multiyear curriculum, either a commercial version or individualized version, that delineates goals, activities, or objectives for all domains until long-term goals are mastered. In this case, the IEP for each student should also designate some of these goals and objectives targeted for that particular year. Another option might be a document listing each student's goals and objectives that are paired with formative assessment data (e.g., a checklist format as in Figure 4.2, with graphs and work samples). Because curricula appear in so many formats, they may be confusing to parents and others not familiar with school forms and procedures. We recommend that curricula be presented in a clear and coherent manner so they will be useful now and in the future. We also recommend that curricula be accessible to all interested parties so that they can understand the long-term ramifications of the annual IEP.

DOMAIN	GOAL	OBJECTIVES
Interpersonal relationships	Will be able to initiate a conversation.	• Will maintain appropriate distance from another for conversational purposes. • Will face another, make eye contact, and smile. • Will verbalize a greeting (i.e., Hi, how are you?; Nice day, isn't it?).
Grooming	Will improve grooming skills.	• Will conduct all steps of a toileting routine. • Will comb hair each morning. • Will wash face and hands each morning, noon, and evening.
Receptive language skills	Will improve receptive language skills.	• Will follow two- and three-step commands. • Will identify alike objects. • Will identify objects that are different.

FIGURE 4.3 Curriculum arranged by domain, goals, and objectives

MOTOR SKILLS	SELF-HELP SKILLS
• Sit down from standing position	• Discriminate between being dry and wet
• Roll ball when seated on floor	• Indicate need to go to the toilet
• Roll objects while on feet	• Walk to the bathroom
• Open and shut a door	• Unbutton/unsnap pants
• Walk forward	• Unzip pants
• Walk backward	• Pull down pants
• Walk sideways	• Etc.
• Roll on sides	
• Walk up and down stairs	
• Run	
• Toss and catch objects with both hands	
• Etc.	

FIGURE 4.4 Curriculum arranged by domain and skills

OBJECTIVES	ACTIVITIES	MATERIALS
The child will locate tissue.	• Take child to tissue box. • Label tissue box. • Provide many tissue boxes around room.	Facial tissues (colored) Markers/papers/tape Facial tissues (colored)
The child will wipe nose.	• Model procedure. • Provide full physical prompt. • Provide practice opportunities. • Reinforce approximations.	Tissues
The child will dispose of tissue.	• Label trash can and provide picture of throwing away tissue. • Prompt to locate trash can. • Model disposing of tissue.	Trash can, paper, tape, marker, Mayer-Johnson picture Colored trash can

FIGURE 4.5 Curriculum arranged by objectives, activities, and materials

DOMAIN	OBJECTIVE	ACTIVITY	ENVIRONMENT
Domestic	Making cereal	Using supplies purchased in the community, makes cereal each morning	Classroom kitchen
Communication	Making picture choices	Providing a list of picture choices for breakfast	Classroom kitchen
Social	Greeting others	Greeting the bus driver, the teacher, fellow students	Bus, hallway, classroom

FIGURE 4.6 Curriculum arranged by domain, objective, activity, and environment

GOAL	OBJECTIVE(S)	PERSON	EVALUATION TECHNIQUE
Will indicate needs and desires nonverbally.	Will point to desired object.	Teacher, teaching assistant, parent	Nonrestricted event recording (pointing behaviors)
Will improve understanding of verbal commands.	Will sit in response to verbal command.	Teacher, teaching assistant	Restricted event recording
	Will stop in response to verbal command.	Teacher, parent	Restricted event recording
	Will come in response to verbal command.	Teacher, teaching assistant, parents	Restricted event recording
Will improve matching skills.	Will match pictures of objects to actual objects.	Teacher	Restricted event recording
	Find match for object among many objects.	Teacher	Restricted event recording

FIGURE 4.7 Curriculum arranged by goal, objective, person, and evaluation technique

CURRICULAR AREA: WRITING	REQUIRED: SCHOOL/HOME	HAS SKILL DATE	NEEDS TRAINING
Will grasp pencil.	X/X	10/20	

Will trace lines:
    Horizontal
    Vertical
    Diagonal
    Curved
    Letters
    Numbers
	X		X

Will copy model.	X		X

STEPS	DURATION	DATE: 4/6	DATE: 4/9	DATE: 4/11
Exits bus.	30 secs	FP	FP	FP
Walks directly to front door.	5 secs	FP	FP	FP
Opens door.	3 secs	V	V	V
Walks through door.	3 secs	I	I	I
Proceeds down the hall.	60 secs	PA	PA	V
Walks directly into classroom.	4 secs	V	V	I

Key: FP, full physical prompt; V, verbal prompt; PA, partial physical; I, independent.

FIGURE 4.8 Curriculum arranged for formative assessment

CONTENT	BEHAVIOR				
	Identification	Production			
	A. Acquisition	B. Acquisition	C. Fluency	D. Application	E. Generalization
1. Conversation skills					
(1) with employer	1(1)A	1(1)B	1(1)C	1(1)D	1(1)E
(2) with coworker	1(2)A	1(2)B	1(2)C	1(2)D	1(2)E
(3) with customers	1(3)A	1(3)B	1(3)C	1(3)D	1(3)E
2. Task-related skills					
(1) asking for clarification	2(1)A	2(1)B	2(1)C	2(1)D	2(1)E
(2) asking for assistance	2(2)A	2(2)B	2(2)C	2(2)D	2(2)E
(3) volunteering to assist	2(3)A	2(3)B	2(3)C	2(3)D	2(3)E
3. Personal appearance					
(1) appropriate grooming	3(1)A	3(1)B	3(1)C	3(1)D	3(1)E
(2) appropriate dress	3(2)A	3(2)B	3(2)C	3(2)D	3(2)E

Sample Objectives:

1(1)A   Students will identify the scenarios that exhibit an employee having appropriate conversation skills with an employer 10 out of 10 times.

2(2)C   Students will ask for assistance in completing job-related tasks as often as appropriate during all of the roleplay scenarios.

3(1)E   Students will come to work after they have showered and neatly combed their hair.

FIGURE 4.9 Curriculum arranged by level of learning

From *Effective Instruction for Special Education* (3rd ed.) by M. A. Mastropieri and T. E. Scruggs, 1994, p. 328. Upper Saddle River, NJ: Pearson.

Summary

This chapter has presented various considerations and procedures for developing an appropriate curriculum for students with autism. Given the large number of deficits typically displayed by these students, developing the most effective curriculum is imperative. Teachers and IEP teams will need to choose goals and objectives from standard academic and vocational content and skills, functional life skills, social and communication skills, and transition skills. What we do *not* choose to teach may affect postschool outcomes more than what we choose to teach. Everything we teach should be designed to address postschool goals and be chronologically age appropriate, community referenced, and refined to such an extent that the student progresses at an acceptable rate. All other educational decisions pale in comparison to the importance of curricular decisions. If we do not choose to teach what the learner needs to learn and organize it in a way to ensure mastery, then decisions about instructional methods and placement become dubious. In Chapters 6 through 8, we will discuss specific curricular areas in terms of recommended sequences, instructional strategies, and specific assessment techniques. Preparing students with autism and related disorders to function independently in integrated adult environments is a difficult task only made easier by the knowledge that every step achieved is one step closer to that ultimate goal.

Key Points

1. Curricular decisions should precede all other educational decisions, including placement.
2. What a student is taught affects many life choices and may prevent the development of inappropriate behavior.
3. A team of people who know the student best should develop the individualized curriculum.
4. Many students with autism and related disorders may not benefit from a standard academic curriculum, particularly at the secondary level.
5. Curriculum should be matched to postschool goals, be chronologically age appropriate, longitudinally aligned, integrated across content areas, and community referenced.

6. Communication and socialization goals are often priorities for this population.
7. It is important to establish placement goals for the long-term, intermediate term, and the current year, allowing those goals to guide curricular decisions.
8. Individualized procedures best guarantee the most functional goals and objectives.
9. Curriculum-based assessment and ecological assessment provide a starting point when deciding what to teach next.
10. Refining a curriculum includes teaching to acquisition, fluency, maintenance, and generalization, and task analyzing content and skills when necessary.
11. A curriculum can be organized into several different formats. It is important to pick the format that works best for the team involved.

References

Alberto, P. A., & Troutman, A. C. (2017). *Applied behavior analysis for teachers* (9th ed.). Columbus, OH: Pearson.

Alwell, M., & Cobb, B. (2009). Functional life skills curricular interventions for youth with disabilities: A systematic review. *Career Development and Transition for Exceptional Individuals, 32,* 82–93.

Ayres, K. M., Lowrey, K. A., Douglas, K. H., & Sievers, C. (2011). I can identify Saturn but I can't brush my teeth: What happens when the curricular focus for students with severe disabilities shifts. *Education and Training in Autism and Developmental Disabilities, 46,* 11–21.

Ayres, K. M., Lowrey, K. A., Douglas, K. H., & Sievers, C. (2012). The question still remains: What happens when the curricular focus for students with severe disabilities shifts? A reply to Courtade, Spooner, Browder, and Jimenez (2012). *Education and Training in Autism and Developmental Disabilities, 47,* 14–22.

Balfanz, R. (2009). Can the American high school become an avenue of advancement for all? *The Future of Children, 19*(1), 17–36.

Blackorby, J., & Wagner, M. (1996). Longitudinal postschool outcomes of youth with disabilities: Findings from the National Longitudinal Transition Study. *Exceptional Children, 62*(5), 399–413.

Bouck, E. C. (2009). Functional curriculum models for secondary students with mild mental impairment. *Education and Training in Developmental Disabilities, 44*(4), 435–443.

Bouck, E. C., & Joshi, G. S. (2014). Does curriculum matter for secondary students with Autism Spectrum Disorders: Analyzing the NLTS2. *Journal of Autism and Developmental Disorders, 45,* 1204–1212.

Bouck, E. C., & Satsangi, R. (2014). Evidence base of a functional curriculum for secondary students with mild intellectual disability: A historical perspective. *Education and Training in Autism and Developmental Disabilities, 49*(3), 478–486.

Branham, R. S., Collins, B. C., Schuster, J. W., & Kleinert, H. (1999). Teaching community skills to students with moderate disabilities: Comparing combined techniques of classroom simulation, videotape modeling, and community-based instruction. *Education and Training in Mental Retardation and Developmental Disabilities, 34,* 170–181.

Browder, D. M., & Spooner, F. (2011). *Teaching students with moderate and severe disabilities.* New York: Guilford Press.

Brown, L., Branston, M. B., Hamre-Nietupski, S., Pumpian, I., Certo, N., & Gruenewald, L. (1979). A strategy for developing chronological-age-appropriate and functional curricular content for severely handicapped adolescents and young adults. *The Journal of Special Education, 13*(1), 81–90.

Brown, L., Nietupski, J., & Hamre-Nietupski, S. (1976). Criterion of ultimate functioning. In M. A. Thomas (Ed.), *Hey, don't forget about me!* Reston, VA: Council for Exceptional Children.

Chambers, C. R., Wehmeyer, M. L., Saito, Y., Lida, K. M., Lee, Y., & Singh, V. (2007). Self-determination: What do we know? Where do we go? *Exceptionality, 15*(1), 3–15.

Chiang, H.-M., Cheung, Y. K., Hickson, L., Xiang, R., & Tsai, L. Y. (2012). Predictive factors of participation in postsecondary education for high school leavers with autism. *Journal of Autism and Developmental Disorders, 42,* 685–696.

Chiang, H.-M., Cheung, Y. K., Li, H., & Tsai, L. Y. (2013). Factors associated with participation in employment for high school leavers with autism. *Journal of Autism and Developmental Disorders, 43,* 1832–1842.

Cohen, D. J., Donnellan, A. M., & Paul, R. (Eds.). (1987). *Handbook of autism and pervasive developmental disorders.* New York: John Wiley & Sons.

Council of Chief State School Officers. (2016). *ESSA: Key provisions and implications for students with disabilities.* Retrieved February 5, 2017, from http://www.ccsso.org/Documents/2016/ESSA/ESSA_Key_Provisions_Implications_for_SWD.pdf.

Courtade, G., Spooner, F., Browder, D. M., & Jimenez, B. (2012). Seven reasons to promote standards-based instruction for students with severe disabilities: A reply to Ayres, Lowrey, Douglas, & Sievers (2011). *Education and Training in Autism and Developmental Disabilities, 47,* 3–13.

Falvey, M. A. (1989). *Community-based curriculum: Instructional strategies for students with severe handicaps* (2nd ed.). Baltimore: Paul H. Brookes.

Falvey, M. A., Grenot-Scheyer, M., & Luddy, E. (1987). Developing and implementing integrated community referenced curricula. In D. J. Cohen, A. M. Donnellan, & R. Paul (Eds.), *Handbook of autism and pervasive developmental disorders* (pp. 238–250). New York: John Wiley & Sons.

Fleury, V. P., Hedges, S., Hume, K., Browder, D. M., Thompson, J. L., Fallin, K., El Zein, F., Reutebuch, C. K., & Vaughn, S. (2014). Addressing the academic needs of adolescents with autism spectrum disorder in secondary education. *Remedial and Special Education, 35*(2), 68–79.

Foster, E. M., & Pearson, E. (2012). Is inclusivity an indicator of quality of care for children with autism in special education? *Pediatrics, 130* (Supplement 2), S179–S185.

Fuchs, L. S., & Deno, S. L. (1994). Must instructionally useful performance assessment be based in the curriculum? *Exceptional Children, 61*(1), 15–24.

Fuchs, L. S., & Fuchs, D. (2000). Analogue assessment of academic skills: Curriculum-based measurement and performance assessment. In E. S. Shapiro & T. R. Kratochwill (Eds.), *Behavioral assessment in schools: Theory, research, and clinical foundations* (2nd ed., pp. 168–201). New York: Guilford Press.

Haring, T. G. (1991). Social relationships. In L. H. Meyer, C. A. Peck, & L. Brown (Eds.), *Critical issues in the lives of people with severe disabilities*. Baltimore, MD: Paul H. Brookes.

Harris, S. L., Belchic, J., Blum, L., & Celiberti, D. (1994). Behavioral assessment of autistic disorder. In J. L. Matson (Ed.), *Autism in children and adults: Etiology, assessment, and intervention* (pp. 127–146). Pacific Grove, CA: Brooks/Cole.

Hendricks, D. R., & Wehman, P. (2009). Transition from school to adulthood for youth with autism spectrum disorders: Review and recommendations. *Focus on Autism and Other Developmental Disabilities, 24,* 77–88.

Henninger, N. A., & Taylor, J. L. (2013). Outcomes in adults with autism spectrum disorders: A historical perspective. *Autism, 17,* 103–116.

Howlin, P., Goode, S., Hutton, J., & Rutter, M. (2004). Adult outcome for children with autism. *The Journal of Child Psychology and Psychiatry, 45,* 212–229.

IDEA Partnership. (2006). Dialogue guides: *IDEA regulations, IEP*. Retrieved February 4, 2017, from http://www.ideapartnership.org/index.php?option=com_content&view=article&id=846&oseppage=1.

IES National Center for Special Education Research. (2017). National Longitudinal Transition Study-2 (NLTS2). Retrieved February 6, 2017, from http://www.nlts2.org/.

Mager, R. F. (1997). *Preparing instructional objectives: A critical tool in the development of effective instruction*. Atlanta: Center for Effective Performance.

Mastropieri, M. A., & Scruggs, T. E. (1994). *Effective Instruction for Special Education* (3rd ed.). Upper Saddle River, NJ: Pearson.

McMaster, K., & Espin, C. (2007). Technical features of curriculum-based measurement in writing: A literature review. *The Journal of Special Education, 41*(2), 68–84.

Newman, L., Wagner, M., Knokey, A.-M., Marder, C., Nagle, K., Shaver, D., & Wei, X. with Cameto, R., Contreras, E., Ferguson, K., Greene, S., & Schwarting, M. (2011). *The post-high school outcomes of young adults with disabilities up to 8 years after high school: A report from the National Longitudinal Transition Study-2 (NLTS2)* (NCSER 2011-3005). Menlo Park, CA: SRI International.

Patton, J. R., Cronin, M. E., & Jairrels, V. (1997). Curricular implications of transition: Life skills instruction as an integral part of transition education. *Remedial and Special Education, 18,* 294–306.

Patton, J. R., Polloway, E. A., & Smith, T. E. C. (2000). Educating students with mild mental retardation. *Focus on Autism and Other Developmental Disabilities, 15,* 80–89.

Peterson, J., Trecker, N., Egan, I., Fredericks, H. D., & Bunse, C. (1983). *The teaching research curriculum for handicapped adolescents and adults: Assessment procedures*. Monmouth, OR: Teaching Research Publications.

Pituch, K. A., Green, V. A., Didden, R., Lang, R., O'Reilly, M. F., Lancioni, G. E., & Sigafoos, J. (2011). Parent reported treatment priorities for children with autism spectrum disorders. *Research in Autism Spectrum Disorders, 5,* 135–143.

Schall, C., Wehman, P., & Carr, S. (2014). Transition from high school to adulthood for adolescents and young adults with autism spectrum disorders. In F. R. Volkmar, B. Reichow, & J. McPartland (Eds.), *Adolescents and adults with Autism Spectrum Disorders* (pp. 41–60). New York: Springer.

Smith, S. W., Slattery, W. J., & Knopp, T. Y. (1993). Beyond the mandate: Developing individualized education programs that work for students with autism. *Focus on Autistic Behavior, 8*(3), 1–15.

Sobsey, D. (Ed.). (1987). *Ecological inventory exemplars*. Edmonton: University of Alberta.

Test, D. W., Fowler, C. H., Richter, S. M., White, J., Mazzotti, V., Walker, A. R., Kohler, P., & Kortering, L. (2009). Evidence-based practices in secondary transition. *Career Development for Exceptional Individuals, 32,* 155–128.

U.S. Department of Education. (2011). A guide to the individualized education program. Retrieved February 7, 2017, from https://www2.ed.gov/parents/needs/speced/iepguide/index.html?exp=0

U.S. Department of Education. (2017). *A transition guide to postsecondary education and employment for students and youth with disabilities*. Office of Special Education and Rehabilitative Services.

Vincent, L. J., Salisbury, C., Walter, G., Brown, P. Gruenewald, L. J., & Powers, M. (1980). Program evaluation and curriculum development in early childhood special education: Criteria of the next environment. In W. Sailor, B. Wilcox, & L. Brown (Eds.), *Methods of instruction for severely handicapped students* (pp. 303–328). Baltimore: Paul H. Brookes.

Wehman, P., & Kregel, J. (Ed.). (1997). *Functional curriculum for elementary, middle, and secondary age students with special needs*. Austin: Pro-Ed.

Wehman, P., Schall, C., Carr, S., Targett, P., West, M., & Cifu, G. (2014). Transition from school to adulthood for youth with autism spectrum disorder: What we know and what we need to know. *Journal of Disability Policy Studies, 25*(1), 30–40.

Witmer, S. E., & Ferreri, S. J. (2014). Alignment of instruction, expectations, and accountability testing for students with autism spectrum disorder. *Focus on Autism and Other Developmental Disabilities, 29*(3), 131–144.

Wolf, M. M. (1978). Social validity: The case for subjective measurement or how applied behavior analysis is finding its heart. *Journal of Applied Behavior Analysis, 11,* 203–214.

5

Teaching: General Strategies

LEARNING OBJECTIVES

After reading this chapter, you will be able to:

5-1 Relate common characteristics of students with autism to recommended environmental structure, order, and clarity.

5-2 Compare and contrast the recommended instructional formats: direct instruction, discrete trial teaching, and milieu teaching.

5-3 List several strategies for organizing a classroom to communicate student expectations.

5-4 Explain the benefits of both whole-class and individual schedules and give several examples of ways to use visual supports in the classroom.

5-5 Define a workstation and list its essential components.

5-6 Identify the essential portions of an appropriate ABA-based lesson plan for instruction and discuss the benefits of organizing and archiving essential instructional information for each student.

© Lang

Chapter 4 presented a decision process regarding *what* to teach a specific student. This chapter will provide recommendations for *how* to teach the designated curriculum. Because of their social, cognitive, and communicative characteristics, students with autism have been found to learn best with clear, structured, predictable instructional formats based in applied behavior analysis (ABA) (Granpeesheh, Tarbox, & Dixon, 2009; Lovaas & Smith, 1989; Maurice, Green, & Luce, 1996; Peters-Scheffer, Didden, Korzilius, & Sturmey, 2011). These formats provide motivation and explicit delivery and expectations. More specifically, they involve teacher-directed procedures in carefully sequenced curricula that include (a) clear and repetitive presentations of small increments of information, (b) multiple practice opportunities designed to foster correct responding, (c) feedback, and (d) progress monitoring.

Students with autism also learn best in highly structured environments that include materials, consistent routines and procedures, and various visual aids that serve as prompts, or cues (discriminative stimuli, S^Ds), for desired behaviors (Webber & Scheuermann, 2008). Structure and clarity help students avoid confusion and misinterpretations about learning expectations (e.g., National Institute for Direct Instruction [NIFDI], 2015a). In the case of autism, structured teaching strategies also take advantage of the student's preference for routine, sameness, and predictability. As progress is documented, teachers are encouraged to gradually decrease structure to facilitate maintenance and generalization in natural environments (e.g., inclusive classrooms, home, and community settings).

5-1 Structure and Teaching

When we talk about **teaching strategies** we refer to everything a teacher does to facilitate learning. This includes instructional formats, student–teacher ratios, pace of instruction, type of activity, assessment strategies, physical arrangement of the classroom, classroom procedures and routines, and the types of materials used.

A highly structured approach to instruction would imply that the teacher develops the classroom, materials, schedule, and lesson such that desired student responses are cued and prompted, frequent performance feedback is provided, and student progress is regularly monitored. With this type of structure, students make fewer mistakes, which means they have frequent opportunities to practice correct responding.

The goal of highly structured teaching is often **errorless learning**. In other words, students do not have to make mistakes to master learning objectives. We do not want students to learn incorrect responses. First, it is more difficult for students to learn a correct response if they have already acquired an incorrect response. Second, motivation to participate in learning activities is diminished with each failure. This could be true for any student but is particularly so for students with autism who may initially find participation in learning activities aversive. Thus, it is imperative that these students engage daily in multiple successful learning interactions.

5-2 Structuring through Lesson Presentation

Lesson presentations based in ABA come in several formats, but the most common is **explicit instruction**, meaning the lessons are systematic, direct, engaging, and success oriented (Archer & Hughes, 2011). Teachers will need to choose appropriate lesson presentation formats based on curricular goals and student abilities. Some students with autism need higher structure and repetition (e.g., young students and students with lower cognitive ability), whereas others may need to be able to benefit from formats better designed for academic mastery in general education classes (less structure and repetition). Teachers of students with autism need to be aware of all of these instructional formats and should master those that are appropriate for the educational needs of the students they teach.

5-2a Direct Instruction: di and DI

Direct-instruction formats are best for students who receive the majority of their instruction in general education classrooms, especially those students who are working on academic goals similar to those of their peers without disabilities. Direct instruction comes in two models: (a) direct instruction (lowercase "di"), which was promoted by Rosenshine (1986), and (b) Direct Instruction (capital "DI"), authored by Siegfried Engelmann and his colleagues in the mid-1960s (NIFDI, 2015a).

Both models have common components such as highly structured lessons, consistent types of instructional activities and instructional delivery methods, and reviews of previously taught content included as part of each lesson (Watkins, Slocum, & Spencers, 2011). However, di is described as a sequenced set of teaching steps and procedures, and DI is described as a "research-based integrated system of curriculum design and effective instructional delivery based on over 30 years of development" (Watkins, 2008, p. 25).

Direct Instruction (di)

Rosenshine's (1986) description of direct instruction (di) generally recommended that teachers present lessons systematically in seven sequential steps:

1. getting the students ready to learn;
2. reviewing prior learning that is related to new concepts in the day's lesson;
3. presenting new content in task-analyzed format, with models and nonexemplars that highlight salient elements of the concept being taught;
4. checking for understanding of the new content;
5. providing teacher-guided practice with corrections and feedback;
6. providing independent practice; and
7. weekly and monthly reviews.

In the first step, the teacher obtains the attention of the students, perhaps with an interesting stimulus or a set signal (e.g., teacher says, "Get ready to begin in one minute"). Also during this step, the teacher states the behavioral objective and why it is important. In the second step, the teacher should review the previous lesson, check that students remember the major components, and correct any learning errors.

The third step requires the teacher to present the new content in small steps using examples and nonexamples to illustrate essential concepts. During the lesson presentation, the teacher checks for understanding typically through large group questioning using choral responding (e.g., students all respond together either verbally or with response cards), signaled responding (e.g., students respond to true–false, yes–no, or other simple questions with a hand gesture), or calling on individual students.

If students demonstrate skill acquisition, the teacher moves to the fifth step and provides in-class guided practice in which the teacher prompts correct responses in a practice format. Often this includes worksheets, work on the whiteboard, response cards, computer work, or responses to other teacher-generated stimuli. The teacher corrects errors, reteaches as necessary, and gives feedback about responses. The sixth step may include the teacher giving an assignment incorporating the lesson content as independent practice (e.g., a task done without teacher assistance) to see if students have mastered the new content. The independent practice may be in the form of in-class or homework assignments.

Finally, teachers incorporate weekly and monthly reviews of the content to make sure students retain (maintain) their mastery of the content. **Progress monitoring** could include worksheet and homework grades, teacher-made quizzes and tests, and formal achievement tests. Table 5.1 summarizes these di steps.

Many general educators have been taught to use a di approach and use it frequently in their classes, especially for large-group instruction. This type of instruction may be beneficial for some students with autism, but they may need to first learn certain behaviors required of students in this instructional format, such as attending to the teacher, who may be standing far away; waiting their turn; and responding during choral responses. If a student with autism is expected to participate in a direct instruction lesson, then we encourage teachers to use ecological assessment procedures to identify the demands of those lessons and the student's current skill level with respect to those demands. Teaching these behaviors before including the student in the direct-instruction lesson is preferable to simply placing the student in the group with an accompanying paraprofessional to prompt each response. (See Chapter 7 for a more complete discussion of overreliance on paraprofessionals.)

Although this explicit instructional approach (di) and modified versions of it have been recommended over decades for both general and special education students (e.g., Çelik & Vuran, 2014; Hecht, 2016; Mertes, 2014; Rosenshine & Stevens, 1986), current research has more often focused on the use of Direct Instruction (DI) for academic instruction

TABLE 5.1 ● Direct Instruction (di) Steps

1. *Focus students' attention.* Teachers can use interesting or stimulating materials to get student attention. Tell students what they are expected to learn and why it is important.

2. *Review prior lesson content and correct learning errors.* Check for understanding of prior content with group and individual questions.

3. *Present the lesson content in small increments in a sequenced order.* Use models (demonstrations) to illustrate critical concepts and give nonexemplars (examples of what it is not) to help students discriminate between correct and incorrect examples of the concept.

4. *Check for understanding of the new material.* The teacher can use choral responding where the entire class answers a question; signaled responding in which the students are required to indicate true or false or answer choices with hands, clickers, and so forth; or calling on individual students.

5. *Provide guided practice.* The teacher provides practice items in the form of worksheets, board work, or computer work, while moving around to provide correction and feedback on their responses. This is a time to correct misunderstandings and reteach if necessary.

6. *Provide independent practice.* This is usually an assignment assessing mastery of the new content that each student is to complete alone (or maybe in groups). Often this is in the form of homework.

7. *Provide weekly or monthly reviews of the content* to ensure retention and maintenance of responding.

---

of students with autism and other disabilities (Plavnick, Marchand-Martella, Martella, Thompson, & Wood, 2015).

Direct Instruction (DI)

Direct Instruction (DI) programs are considered those developed by Siegfried Engelmann and his colleagues and others that keep to a set of basic tenets (e.g., Adams & Engelmann, 1996; Engelmann & Carnine, 2003; Engelmann & Hanner, 2008; Engelmann & Osborn, 1998; Watkins, 2008). Direct Instruction "is a model for teaching that emphasizes well-developed and carefully planned lessons designed around small learning increments and clearly defined and prescribed teaching tasks. It is based on the theory that clear instruction eliminating mis-interpretations can greatly improve and accelerate learning" (NIFDI, 2015a, p. 1). Unlike di, which is used with any curricula, DI includes prescribed and carefully sequenced curricula in the areas of reading, mathematics, language, language arts (writing, spelling), science, and social studies formatted in scripted lesson presentations. The lessons are delivered either one to one or in small groups. Table 5.2 lists some of the best known and studied DI curricula.

Direct Instruction also has a set of prescribed components that includes (a) presentation of information, (b) tasks, (c) task chains, (d) exercises, (e) sequences of exercises or tracks, (f) lessons, and (g) organization of content (Engelmann & Colvin, 2006). Importantly, DI requires frequent responses from students, uses errorless learning, and requires frequent reinforcement for correct responding. For example, teachers are urged to practice DI by demonstrating behaviors from the following list:

- Hold the presentation book so students can see it.
- Present the examples at a quick pace.
- Follow the scripted lessons.
- Know which words to emphasize.
- Signal at the right time after giving students enough "think time."
- Observe whether all students respond in unison.
- Detect any errors in students' responses.
- Correct errors immediately.
- Reinforce students for working hard.
- Record points for the "Teacher–Student Game" (NIFDI, 2015c, p. 1).

TABLE 5.2 ● A Sample of Direct Instruction (DI) Academic Curriculum from McGraw-Hill Direct Instruction Series

READING

- **Reading Mastery:** has reading, language arts, and literacy modules with data-driven placements and continuous curriculum-based progress assessments.
- **Corrective Reading:** includes modules to teach decoding and reading comprehension with placement tests, a scope and sequence, and online progress monitoring.
- **Horizons (grades K–4):** teaches young students word attack skills, story reading, spelling, reading comprehension, and independent working.
- **Read to Achieve:** increases reading comprehension skills in content areas for secondary students. Includes modules for comprehending content, narratives, and ongoing assessments.

LANGUAGE ARTS

- **Language for Learning, Thinking, and Writing:** contains kits to teach students words, concepts, and statements to prepare them for oral instruction and written language. Includes sequences, multiple practice opportunities, and program resources.
- **Spelling Mastery:** combines phonemic, morphemic, and whole-word instruction for mastery of spelling skills.

MATH

- **Corrective Mathematics (grades 3–adult):** includes materials for students who need to learn basic math concepts and word problems. Includes seven modules, placement tests, and mastery tests.
- **Connecting Math Concepts (grades K–5):** includes Common Core aligned content and digital resources and activities so students can meet state standards.
- **Essentials for Algebra:** contains materials for middle and high school students who need to obtain readiness skills for algebra instruction. Includes multiple practice opportunities, uniform procedures, problem-solving strategies, and a designated curriculum sequence.

PROGRESS MONITORING

- **SRA2inform Online Progress Monitoring System:** includes Common Core alignment tracking and administrator reporting for student, class, and school progress monitoring.

New teachers are referred to the National Institute for Direct Instruction website for video tutorials, information about various lesson components, and related research. Teachers can locate DI curricula on the McGraw-Hill Publishers Direct Instruction website.

Over four decades, DI has been found to improve academic functioning for students with disabilities of all ages (Gersten, 1985; NIFDI, 2015b; White, 1988). Fortunately, some current research has specifically targeted the effects of DI on the academic performance of students with autism spectrum disorder (ASD), including those with intellectual disabilities (ID). DI was found to have positive effects on letter recognition, beginning literacy skills and early reading, general literacy, simple concepts, reading comprehension, reading in content areas (e.g., science), language development, early math concepts, and math problem solving (Bechtolt, McLaughlin, Derby, & Blecher, 2014; Çelik & Vuran, 2014; Finnegan & Mazin, 2016; Flores & Ganz, 2007; Flores et al., 2013; Ganz & Flores, 2009; Grindle, Hughes, Saville, Huxley, & Hastings, 2013; Kamps, Heitzman-Powell, Rosenberg, Mason, Schwartz, & Romine, 2016; Knight, Smith, Spooner, & Browder, 2012; Thompson, Wood, Test, & Cease-Cook, 2012; Whitby, 2013; Whitcomb, Bass, & Luiselli, 2011).

In the previously referenced studies, students with ASD of varying cognitive abilities responded positively to modified and whole DI modules in one-to-one instruction and in small-group instruction. Teachers can keep **progress monitoring** data on samples of student performance or choose to use the SRA 2Inform Online Progress Monitoring System from McGraw-Hill. This system is available for DI reading, language arts, and math programs and allows for the collection and interpretation of data by both teachers and administrators. In addition, this system has a component for Common Core alignment tracking to ensure movement toward target goals.

Plavnick and colleagues (2015) recommended small-group explicit instruction and DI as preferred methods of preparing students with ASD for success in general education academic instruction, including at the secondary level to remediate skill deficits in reading, math, or writing. Further, Ledford and colleagues (2012) specifically recommended small-group direct instruction (di or DI or both) as a less restrictive approach than one-to-one formats. Small group instruction is more time efficient for the teacher and is better for social learning.

Both di and DI are instructional delivery formats that can be used with large or small groups, and both of these instructional formats are built on ABA principles. However, one of the best-known ABA approaches for teaching students with autism, known as discrete trial training, is usually delivered in intensive one-to-one instruction.

5-2b Discrete Trial Training (DTT)

Probably the most widely used and best-documented ABA-based teaching strategy for individuals with autism was developed by Ivar Lovaas at the University of California, Los Angeles in the 1960s and 1970s (e.g., Lovaas, Koegel, Simmons, & Long, 1973). This explicit instructional technique is known as **discrete trial training (DTT)** (Lerman, Valentino, & LeBlanc, 2016; Lovaas, 1987; Maurice et al., 1996; Sallows & Graupner, 2005). DTT is a highly structured teaching method based on the three-term contingency (A-B-C) you learned about in Chapter 2. Skills are taught through repeated, structured presentations that consist of (a) teacher directions, input, and prompting (antecedent stimuli); (b) student responding; (c) teacher feedback (consequence stimuli); and (d) some method of tracking student progress toward predesignated goals and objectives. By using these simple steps, teachers can bring clarity to the way information is presented for those students who need intensive instruction. By regularly collecting data on student responding, teachers can make decisions about future teaching situations.

The theory governing DTT is that we want students to respond with certain behaviors to certain external stimuli and *not* to respond other ways—that is, we want certain stimuli to function predictably as S^Ds for specific responses. For instance, given the word card "cat," we want a student to say (or read) "cat," *not* say or read "car," "pat," or "dog." Or if we give the command "Sit down," we want the child to sit down, *not* run around, stand up, or lay down. This is called **discrimination training**, and it occurs by bringing responses under **stimulus control**. As you remember from Chapter 2, stimulus control occurs when certain antecedent stimuli cue particular behaviors (e.g., a stop sign cues coming to a halt). By providing a clear, discrete stimulus and reinforcing correct responses to that stimulus while *not* reinforcing incorrect responses, students learn to perform certain responses under specified conditions (e.g., only reading "cat" when presented with the printed word, "cat"). This type of training sets the stage for teaching a myriad of skills.

The five steps to a DTT lesson presentation are:

1. presentation of a discriminative stimulus (S^D),
2. **prompt** if necessary,
3. student response,
4. presentation of consequences, and
5. an **intertrial interval** or pause before the next trial.

The steps always proceed in this set order, and each presentation of these five steps is called a **trial**. A trial has a clear beginning and a clear ending. If one skill is being taught, several trials may be presented that require that skill. In this way, a student is able to practice a new response several times in a row. For example, if the student is learning to point to a pizza card to indicate that he wants pizza, the teacher may give 5 to 10 trials in a row requiring this behavior and receiving a bite of pizza after each correct response.

On the other hand, it might be more motivating to present alternating trials on different tasks. For example, a student may be given a trial requiring naming objects, then a trial for saying his name, followed by a gross motor imitation trial. In this way, neither the child nor the teacher becomes bored; however, throughout the course of a day the student receives enough practice on each skill to acquire it.

In addition, it may be beneficial to intersperse opportunities to perform mastered skills alongside opportunities to practice new target skills that have not yet been mastered as a way to maintain students' motivation. Specifically, because the student is more likely to be correct on mastered tasks, he will receive reinforcement more often during the lesson when mastered tasks are interspersed (e.g., Benavides & Poulson, 2009). Further, this process facilitates probing for maintenance of mastered tasks and may reduce escape-maintained behaviors by using **behavioral momentum** (see Chapter 3).

Remember to ensure that new learning or difficult tasks are repeated sufficiently. Teachers must find the proper balance for an individual student through ongoing progress monitoring. Table 5.3 provides a brief description of DTT's components.

TABLE 5.3 ● Discrete Trial Training (DTT) Components

1. *Instruction* (S^D—discriminative stimulus): The instruction given to the child.
2. *Prompt (optional):* Extra assistance to bring about a correct response.
3. *Response:* Observable and measurable behavior the child engages in after the instruction.
4. *Consequence:* A stimulus presented after a response to increase or decrease that response in the future—in this case, reinforcement for correct responses and no reinforcement for incorrect responses.
5. *Intertrial interval:* A brief period that provides for (a) a clear onset and end of each trial, (b) recording the outcome of each trial, and (c) allowing the student to use the reinforcer that was provided for a correct response.

Things to Remember:

1. Instruction (S^D)
   a. Child must be attending.
   b. The instruction must be easily discriminable—clear and brief.
   c. The instruction must be appropriate and relevant.
   d. Be consistent in the instructions at first. Give a complete instruction.
   e. Do not give unintended prompts (e.g., looking at correct item).
2. Prompt (extra help)
   a. Must be effective (it actually increases the probability of the desired response).
   b. Must eventually be faded. Within-stimulus prompts may be the easiest to fade.
3. Consequence
   a. For correct response: Praise alone or with small amount of food or tangible reinforcer.
   b. For incorrect response: Say "no." Determine (in advance of trial) whether to prompt the correct response before starting another trial.
   c. Ensure that the consequence is:
      i. contingent and immediate.
      ii. consistent and clear.
      iii. salient (prominent in the environment).
      iv. effective.
   d. Reinforcers should increase correct responding; if they do not, change the reinforcer or motivating operation, or add a prompt.

Discriminative Stimulus

The discriminative stimulus (S^D) is the teacher's instruction to the child. This stimulus is anything that naturally cues a response, such as a picture, a command, a bell, or a red circle cueing where to sit on the floor. A discriminative stimulus is a cue that indicates that a correct response will be reinforced and an incorrect response will *not* be reinforced. Before presenting an S^D, the teacher must ensure that the child is attending. This usually means that the child is sitting, facing the teacher, feet on floor, hands quiet, and looking at the teacher. These behaviors are typically cued with some verbal signal (S^D) such as "do good sitting," "ready," or "look." Once a student has learned to be attentive, these commands can be faded such that the behavior comes under the stimulus control of the intended S^D (e.g., the teacher delivering the first task demand).

When the student is attending, the teacher presents the S^D, usually a verbal direction or command. The verbal direction should *consist of only a few words, be clear, be given only once*, and *be followed by a short pause*. For example, typical S^Ds may include "Touch the circle," "Do this (with a model of touching nose)," "Point to *my* shoes," "Say, 'I want a cookie,'" "Show which one is salty," or "Tell me what are you doing." Notice that most S^Ds are *statements* that pertain directly to the desired response. Rather than ask a student "Do you know which one is the circle?" when differentiating a circle from a square, the teacher might say "Point to the circle," which is the behavior that is required for reinforcement.

In addition, an S^D should be *complete*. If there is an interruption while giving an S^D, stop the trial, obtain attention, and deliver the S^D again. When teaching new behaviors, particularly to young children and those with ID, it is recommended that at first the S^D stay consistent across trials in the acquisition and fluency phases (see Chapter 4 for levels of learning). The teacher would say, "Point to my shoes" for every trial rather than "Where are my shoes?" or "Can you find my shoes?" After the student is performing consistently to one S^D, then the teacher can vary the S^D to promote generalization to various naturally occurring S^Ds.

Prompts

Prompts are added stimuli that are helpful in getting targeted responses to occur. A prompt can be instructions, gestures, demonstrations, touches, or other stimuli that the teacher arranges or does to assist the student to respond correctly. In other words, a prompt is an artificial bridge between the S^D and the target response. When we follow the S^D with a prompt, the target behavior may initially come under the stimulus control of the prompt and not the intended S^D. As such, prompts should be faded (the bridge slowly taken down) until the response comes under control of the original S^D. If prompts are not properly faded, then prompt dependence may arise. Remember that prompts should only be used when independent responding is not forthcoming.

There are many different types of prompts. Verbal or **auditory prompts** are typically additional spoken directions or examples giving more information about responding. For example, a student may be given the S^D "What's your name?" and the auditory prompt "Sam." However, auditory prompts could also be just producing the "S" sound as in Sam, which is less helpful but may still be effective with some children.

Visual prompts include gestures such as touching, tapping, or pointing to the correct response and **modeling** or demonstrating the correct response. For example, the S^D "Touch your nose" might be followed by the teacher touching her own nose. Visual prompts also include picture prompts. Many examples of visual prompts will be discussed later in this chapter.

Tactile or **physical prompts** are the most intrusive prompts. This type of prompting involves physically guiding a correct movement. For example, a student who is to "sign candy" may need the teacher to physically maneuver his hand into the correct position. Or if a student is to imitate gross motor behavior (e.g., hands up), the teacher, after giving the S^D "Do this," might need to physically guide the student's hands above her head. Physical prompts are the most difficult to fade and should be used only when necessary.

Prompts can also be differentiated based on the amount of assistance provided. **Full prompts** provide enough assistance that students do not have to complete any of the behavior alone. **Partial prompts** provide some assistance by requiring the student to do some of the behavior alone.

Prompts are often faded by moving from full to partial assistance. For example, a teacher may initially use a full physical prompt to teach a student to comply with instructions to "stand up" and "sit down." This means that after the teacher gives the cue, she holds the student's arms or shoulders and guides him to stand up or sit down. After several trials using full physical prompts, the teacher begins using partial physical prompts if needed to cue the correct response. For example, if the student does not respond following the cue, the teacher might simply touch the student's elbow to prompt "stand up" or shoulder for "sit down." Eventually, partial prompts should no longer be necessary.

A fourth type of prompt is referred to as stimulus modification or **within-stimulus prompt** (Schoen, 1986; Schreibman, 1975). Within-stimulus prompting means that the S^D, usually a material, is altered in certain ways (size, color, position, texture, or some other dimension) to make it more likely that the child will respond correctly. For example, while teaching a student to discriminate a circle from a square, the student may at first be presented a very large circle and a tiny square, making it more likely that he will point to the circle.

The type of prompting necessary for a particular student is determined through initial assessment. Give the student instructions or natural S^{D}s and observe to see how much of the response the student performs independently. As a general rule, prompts that effectively prevent errors have been found to be most effective and more motivating (Lerman, Valentino, & LeBlanc, 2016), although avoiding prompt dependence is a concern (McClannahan & Krantz, 1997).

For example, physical and verbal prompts may be necessary for learning a new task, but less intrusive prompts (e.g., gestural) can be used as trials are repeated. Remember that independent functioning is a goal, so any procedure (even one-to-one instruction) that promotes student dependence on a person, procedure, or material will need to be eliminated, if possible, to allow natural cues and consequences to maintain appropriate skills.

Before initiating a prompt, you should develop a system for fading the prompt. In this way, prompts will only be used when necessary and eliminated as soon as possible, thus facilitating independent responding. Various **prompt fading techniques** have been described (Leaf & McEachin, 1999; Webber & Scheuermann, 2008) and found to be effective for increasing correct responding in students with autism (MacDuff, Krantz, & McClannahan, 2001). Table 5.4 lists common prompt fading procedures.

Because prompts must be faded, it is important to use the least intrusive prompt that successfully occasions the target behavior. If a prompt provides more help than necessary (e.g., using a full physical prompt when a simple gesture prompt would have sufficed), it may be more difficult to fade prompts when the time comes. In most instructional systems, prompted responses will be recorded as incorrect or prompted responses, meaning not yet mastered. Remember this important axiom: a skill has *not* been truly acquired if a prompt that is not normally found in the natural environment is still required or if the S^D that should occasion the target behavior fails to do so in the natural environment!

Responses

Once the S^D (and the optional prompt) has been delivered, the student is then expected to respond, usually beginning the response within 1 to 5 seconds. He may either respond correctly, incorrectly, or not at all. If the response is correct, he should be reinforced. In the case of incorrect responding, no reinforcement should be given.

Thus, both the teacher and student must be able to distinguish when a response is correct or not correct. For example, if a student is told to "Sit in chair" and he sits sideways with his feet tucked under him, then we do not want to reinforce that behavior if it is not what we expect. More likely what we want and what we must operationally define is "good sitting." Good sitting usually means sitting in a chair, facing forward, feet on floor, head up,

TABLE 5.4 ● **Prompt Fading Procedures**

1. *Graduated Guidance.* The graduated guidance technique is used with physical prompts. Initially, use as much prompting as necessary to obtain a correct response (e.g., in response to "Point to ____," teacher takes student's hand and moves it to the correct item). Gradually, use less guidance by moving the location of the prompt (e.g., move student hand above item—student must touch it; move student arm toward item—student must use hand to touch it; touch student's arm—student must move hand to correct item; touch student's upper arm—student does response; shadow student's response; use no physical prompt). Prompted correct responses should be reinforced until acquisition is obtained.

2. *Increasing Assistance or Least to Most Prompting (LTM).* Increasing assistance begins with allowing the student to respond independently. If she does not, then give a verbal cue. If this does not get the correct response, then add a gestural cue. Add physical prompt if these do not work. For example, given the S^D "Sit down," student does not comply. Teacher says "Come to your seat," but student does not comply; teacher says "Sit down" and points to the chair but no compliance; teacher says "Sit down" and moves the student to the chair. This type of prompting should not be used in dangerous situations. With increasing assistance, there is a high probability of incorrect responding at first. Prompted correct responses should be reinforced.

3. *Decreasing Assistance or Most to Least Prompting (MTL).* Decreasing assistance, similar to graduated guidance, is a process of systematically using weaker prompts, regardless of whether or not they are physical ones. Begin by providing the amount of prompt necessary to obtain the correct response. Gradually (usually after three successful trials) use less prompting as long as the student is still responding correctly. If an error occurs, back up to the stronger prompt. Prompts are usually presented before the response occurs, but they can also be used as a corrective strategy after an incorrect response (provide a prompt, then repeat the trial). Let's say you are teaching shape discrimination. With an MTL fading procedure, you would initially use a larger version of the target shape (e.g., circle) than the distracter shapes (e.g., square, triangle). Gradually reduce the size of the circle until size is no longer a prompt for correct responding. At this point, the student must discriminate by shape alone. Prompted correct responses should be reinforced.

4. *Probing.* Probing is an assessment strategy for determining if the student is able to respond independently and thus needs no further prompting. At regular intervals, give the S^D and observe the student's responses. Use this information to plan further prompting strategies. For example, if a teacher has been using gestures to prompt the student to put his tray up before leaving the cafeteria, then try giving the S^D only ("Line up") and see if the student takes his tray back with no gestural prompt. If so, eliminate the gestural prompt thereafter.

5. *Flexible Prompting.* With flexible prompting, the teacher is not bound by a prompting strategy but just provides prompts as she thinks necessary and always after several incorrect trials. The goal is to reach a high level of success. This strategy has been found to be effective in teaching new skills (Leaf, Leaf, Taubman, McEachin, & Delmolino, 2014).

6. *Simultaneous Prompting.* With simultaneous prompting, the teacher presents a prompt at the same time as the S^D and does not systematically fade the prompt, instead allowing the student to demonstrate correct responses during frequent probe sessions.

7. *No No Prompt (NNP).* In the NNP procedure, a prompt is given only after two trials of incorrect responding. If the student responds incorrectly, the teacher says "no" and initiates a second trial. If the student responds incorrectly again, the teacher says "no" and initiates a third trial. During this third trial, the teacher will use a prompt to elicit a correct response.

---

eyes open, and hands in lap. If we do not operationally define the behavior in such a way that everyone working with the student knows when it is correct, then incorrect responding may be reinforced and maintained. Conversely, correct responding may not be reinforced consistently. In addition, operationally defining responses will allow precise data collection regarding student progress.

Consequences

Consequences in DTT are teacher behaviors that follow student responses. For correct student responses, the teacher should reinforce enthusiastically with praise ("good") and other designated reinforcers (e.g., small bite of food or sip of juice, hugs, pats, preferred toy).

Obtaining effective reinforcers to motivate students to attend and respond correctly is critical. In some cases, teachers should give more powerful reinforcers for unprompted correct responses; in some instances, they should withhold reinforcement altogether if the response is prompted, correct or incorrect, so the student is more motivated to respond independently (Karsten & Carr, 2009). See Chapter 2 for a discussion about reinforcers and ways to ensure effectiveness.

For incorrect responding, the consequence should be withheld reinforcement (e.g., attention, touch, eye contact). Simply say "No," keep a straight face and be monotone, and perhaps briefly turn your head away. Usually, it would be best to quickly prompt a correct response on the next trial. Sometimes teachers correct the incorrect response before moving on to the remaining steps in the trial. However, in this instance, there is a danger of reinforcing an undesirable behavior chain (i.e., incorrect response—teacher corrected response—reinforcement in the form of teacher attention). The teacher should make a judgment about whether to correct a response in a new trial (e.g., by prompting the correct response in the next trial) or immediately after a mistake.

If the child does not respond at all, then begin another trial immediately, physically guiding the desired response following the S^D. If the teacher is reinforcing correct prompted trials, prompt a few more trials and then try fading the prompt. If correct responding does not increase, check to see if the reinforcers are effective and if the prompting is occurring in a way that ensures errorless learning.

Because individuals with autism have difficulty distinguishing social cues, the teacher should be highly demonstrative in delivering social reinforcers and bland after incorrect responses. Furthermore, consequences should be immediate and contingent. Only give reinforcers for correct responses (contingent) and give feedback immediately after the student responds so that he learns that his behavior determines teacher behavior. If the consequence is presented too slowly, because the teacher is thinking about the next step, removing materials, or so forth, intervening student behavior may occur (e.g., whining). In this case, if a reinforcer is given, the student may learn, for example, to respond and then whine to obtain reinforcement. Timing in DTT is crucial for avoiding inappropriate learning and ensuring successful responding.

Consequences should be applied consistently. Determine what schedule of reinforcement might be appropriate (see Chapter 2 for a discussion of reinforcement schedules) and systematically thin the schedule. In general, it is best to reinforce every correct response, prompted or not, when targeting new skills during the acquisition phase, particularly with young children and for those with the most significant ID.

As fluency and maintenance are obtained, space the reinforced trials to approximate the reinforcement schedule most likely in place in the natural reinforcement. For generalization training, use frequent reinforcement during initial use of the skill under new generalization conditions but eventually thin to naturally occurring schedules. Ensuring that the first few occurrences of the target responses in the generalized setting are reinforced may facilitate more efficient generalization while continuing to schedule the fading procedure (Stokes & Baer, 1977).

If prompting and reinforcement procedures are effective, there should be little problem in obtaining stimulus control in DTT. If students frequently display interfering challenging behaviors, refer to Chapter 3 for recommended reduction procedures.

Intertrial Interval

The intertrial interval is a 3- to 5-second period during which no instructions are given. This brief interval provides a distinct ending to the trial and sets the stage for a clear onset of the next trial. During the intertrial interval, the teacher should record data regarding the student's response for that trial and perhaps reinforce the student for good attending or good waiting. During the intertrial interval, the student may be enjoying his reinforcer (e.g., food, preferred toy), which was previously delivered immediately after a correct response.

Assessing Student Progress within DTT

To determine whether students are learning what has been targeted, teachers need to gather data regarding their responding. Usually, teachers use event recording to count correct, unprompted responses. This is similar to counting the number of correctly spelled words on the weekly spelling quiz. When the number of opportunities to perform a target skill is not the same across sessions, it is important to remember to calculate a percentage of correct responses out of the opportunities presented (see Chapter 2).

In the case of DTT, the count (or percent correct) reflects the number of correct verbalizations, imitations, or correct responses. An accurate count of correct responding lets the teacher determine whether the student is progressing toward the designated mastery criteria (as stated in the instructional objective). If the student is not progressing satisfactorily, then the teacher will need to adjust the instructional strategies (e.g., break the task into smaller steps, adjust the prompting system, assess to see if the student has the necessary prerequisites, provide more practice, or select more powerful reinforcers).

Because mastery is defined as independent correct responding, data collection also needs to reflect whether the correct response was a prompted or unprompted one. Progress is evident when unprompted correct responding increases. If data reflect several prompted incorrect responses, then a more helpful prompt may be necessary.

Figure 5.1 provides a data collection sheet for DTT. Each of the six sections represents 10 trials of a skill acquisition (i.e., "do this"—clap; "do this"—touch head; "do this"—arms

Hector		TASK 1: "Do this": clap DATE: 4/19				TASK 2: "Do this": touch head DATE: 4/19				TASK 3: "Do this": arms in air DATE: 4/19			
1		XP	OP	(X)	O	XP	OP	(X)	O	(XP)	OP	X	O
2		XP	OP	(X)	O	XP	OP	(X)	O	XP	OP	(X)	O
3		XP	OP	(X)	O	XP	OP	(X)	O	XP	OP	(X)	O
4		XP	OP	(X)	O	XP	OP	(X)	O	XP	OP	(X)	O
5		XP	OP	(X)	O	XP	OP	(X)	O	XP	OP	(X)	O
6		XP	OP	(X)	O	XP	OP	(X)	O	XP	OP	(X)	O
7		XP	OP	(X)	O	XP	OP	(X)	O	XP	OP	(X)	O
8		XP	OP	(X)	O	XP	OP	(X)	O	XP	OP	(X)	O
9		XP	OP	(X)	O	XP	OP	(X)	O	XP	OP	(X)	O
10		XP	OP	(X)	O	XP	OP	(X)	O	XP	OP	(X)	O
Total				10				10		1	9		
Comments:		*Excellent attending* —————————————→											

		TASK 1: "Give me": elephant DATE: 4/19				TASK 2: "Point to": (bus) (baseline) DATE: 4/19				TASK 3: "Point to": bus DATE: 4/19			
1		XP	OP	(X)	O	XP	OP	X	(O)	(XP)	OP	X	O
2		XP	OP	(X)	O	XP	OP	X	(O)	(XP)	OP	X	O
3		XP	OP	(X)	O	XP	OP	X	(O)	(XP)	OP	X	O
4		XP	OP	(X)	O	XP	OP	X	O	(XP)	OP	X	O
5		XP	OP	(X)	O	XP	OP	X	O	XP	OP	(X)	O
6		XP	OP	(X)	O	XP	OP	X	O	XP	OP	(X)	O
7		XP	OP	(X)	O	XP	OP	X	O	XP	OP	(X)	O
8		XP	OP	(X)	O	XP	OP	X	O	(XP)	OP	X	O
9		XP	OP	(X)	O	XP	OP	X	O	XP	OP	(X)	O
10		XP	OP	(X)	O	XP	OP	X	O	XP	OP	(X)	O
Total				10				0	5	5			
Comments:													

FIGURE 5.1 Discrete trial data sheet

⌄ Professional Resource Download

Student: _Mason_

Staff: _Ms. Cohen_

Date: _2/25_

Time start/stop: _11:30–11:45_

Task/step: _4_

Criterion: _8/10 Trials_

Cue(s): _"Hand me" array_ = Cup
Spoon
Dish
Fork

Trials

Cue (S^D) only	1 2 3 4 5 6 7 8 9 10	1 2 3 4 5 6 7 8 9 10	1 2 3 4 5 6 7 8 9 10	1 2 3 4 5 6 7 8 9 10	1 2 3 4 5 6 7 8 9 10
Verbal	1 2 3 4 5 6 7 8 9 10	1 2 3 4 5 6 7 8 9 10	1 2 3 4 5 6 7 8 9 10	1 2 3 4 5 6 7 8 9 10	1 2 3 4 5 6 7 8 9 10
Gesture	1 2 3 4 5 6 7 8 9 10	1 2 3 4 5 6 7 8 9 10	1 2 3 4 5 6 7 8 9 10	1 2 3 4 5 6 7 8 9 10	1 2 3 4 5 6 7 8 9 10
Partial physical	1 2 3 4 5 6 7 8 9 10	1 2 3 4 5 6 7 8 9 10	1 2 3 4 5 6 7 8 9 10	1 2 3 4 5 6 7 8 9 10	1 2 3 4 5 6 7 8 9 10
Full physical	1 2 3 4 5 6 7 8 9 10	1 2 3 4 5 6 7 8 9 10	1 2 3 4 5 6 7 8 9 10	1 2 3 4 5 6 7 8 9 10	1 2 3 4 5 6 7 8 9 10

Observation _____

Comments _____

_____

_____

_____

FIGURE 5.2 Data collection form for controlled presentations
(From *Applied behavior analysis for teachers*, by P. A. Alberto and A. C. Troutman, 1999, p. 115. Columbus, OH: Merrill, an imprint of Prentice-Hall. Copyright 1999, 1995 by Prentice-Hall, Inc.)

❯❯ Professional Resource Download

in air; "give me"—elephant; "point to"—bus). An "X" signifies an unprompted correct response, an "O" indicates an unprompted incorrect response, and "P" indicates prompted responses (either correct, "XP," or incorrect, "OP"). The teacher simply circles the appropriate indicator during intertrial intervals. Because the number of opportunities is held constant (10 trials), the percent correct does not need to be calculated.

Progress is also evident when the teacher uses less intrusive prompts to elicit correct responding. Thus, it is often useful to gather data not only about correct–incorrect responding but also about the type of prompt required to get correct responses. In this way, teachers can detect progress as prompts are faded even when independent correct responding has not been mastered.

Figure 5.2 illustrates a form that indicates the use of full and partial physical prompts, gestural and verbal prompts, and unprompted responses. Note that a visual graph can be drawn right on this dual-purpose data sheet. In some cases, what is helpful to one student may not be a helpful prompt for a different student. For example, a visual prompt may not be appropriate for a student with poor visual acuity or a physical prompt for a student who dislikes touch. This form can be adjusted to meet the individualized needs of a given student.

We recommend graphing all recorded data to support communication about student progress to parents and other personnel who are working with students. A graph is much easier to decipher than a stack of data-collection forms. There are many ways to graph data.

Figure 5.3 is a simple graph constructed from Hector's data sheet in Figure 5.1 for April 19 for the response, point to bus, and subsequent training sessions. Note that the teacher initially gave three trials without prompting to gather a baseline (an indication of correct responding before trial training began). In this case, Hector gave no correct responses, so the baseline was graphed as "0." Subsequent DTT sessions resulted in an increasing

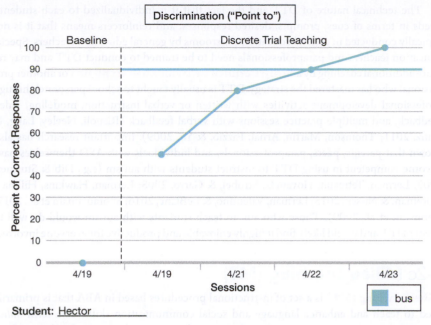

Student: Hector

Target Behavior: Within 5 seconds of the S^D "Point to," Hector will point to the picture indicated by the teacher (bus).

Criterion: Nine out of 10 trials correct for three consecutive sessions.

FIGURE 5.3 Graph of student progress

number of correct, unprompted responses. This graph indicates four days of training; however, graphs should be continued until skill mastery has been attained (usually more than three to five days) and also to show maintenance (distributed trials conducted as **probes** one or more times per week over several weeks). Construct data-collection forms and graphs such that they will be easy to use, give useful information, and clearly depict the student's progress.

Remember that this five-step DTT procedure can be repeated as necessary until the student meets the criterion on a step in a task analysis, the entire task, or a specific response (e.g., pointing to the picture of a bus). DTT is best used for focused skill training at the initial stages of learning (i.e., acquisition and fluency). It can also be used for more complex content and skills (e.g., addition computation, ordering objects by size, complex motor skills such as skipping, complex self-help skills such as tying shoes, verbal behaviors). However, it may not be an appropriate way of teaching to generalization in a naturalized setting.

Imagine learning to play tennis. For basic skills such as holding the racket, forehand and backhand swings, and serving, repetitive trials and practice (one-to-one) may be required. Once the skills are acquired, however, it is time to apply them in real game situations. For this, a coach uses a different type of instruction (naturalistic teaching, delayed feedback, corrective prompts or models). This is also true for teaching skills to students with autism. Apply DTT for those skills needing an intensive, highly structured approach, but avoid using DTT as the only instructional technique because other techniques will often better facilitate students' fluency and generalization in target skills.

DTT alone or as part of a comprehensive behavioral program has been used with individuals with autism for more than 50 years and has been found to result in significant gains in intellectual functioning, adaptive skills, communication skills, academic skills, and social and play skills (e.g., Granpeesheh et al., 2009; Howard, Sparkman, Cohen, Green, & Stanislaw, 2005; Lerman, Valentino, & LeBlanc, 2016; Lovaas, 1987; Sallows & Graupner, 2005). In some cases, DTT has even led to reduced problem behaviors and the amelioration of autism symptomology. Although DTT is essentially a simple instructional format, the nuance lies in prompting, pacing, reinforcement, and error-correction procedures.

The technical nature of DTT and the fact that it is individualized to each student's needs in terms of cues, prompts, desired responses, and reinforcers means that it is not typically conducted in general education classrooms by general education teachers. Special education teachers and paraprofessionals need to be trained to conduct DTT and may require additional coaching by a **Board Certified Behavior Analyst (BCBA)** or another professional who has mastered the strategy. DTT is usually taught to school personnel through professional development activities with written or verbal instruction, modeling, video feedback, and multiple practice sessions with verbal feedback (Rispoli, Neeley, Lang, & Ganz, 2011; Thomson, Martin, Arnal, Fazzio, & Yu, 2009). Important research has also shown that parents, peers, paraprofessionals, and individuals with ASD themselves have become competent in using DTT to instruct students with autism (e.g., Dib & Sturmey, 2007; Lerman, Tetreault, Hovanetz, Strobel, & Garro, 2008; Lerman, Hawkins, Hillman, Shireman, & Nissen, 2015; Lerman, Valentino, & LeBlanc, 2016; Subramaniam et al., 2017; Thomson et al., 2009). Those who aim to teach students with autism would do well to master DTT and would likely find it highly enjoyable and productive for everyone involved.

5-2c Milieu Teaching (MT)

Milieu teaching (MT) is a set of instructional procedures based in ABA that is primarily used to teach and enhance language and social communication skills. The term *milieu* means environment or setting in French. It was chosen as a descriptor for this teaching strategy because it depends on naturally occurring situations as the impetus for a teaching cycle. The underlying assumption of MT is that teachers purposefully take advantage of "teachable moments" to obtain social interaction followed by prompts and reinforcement for appropriate responses. According to Kaiser (1993), MT procedures are (a) short positive interactions, (b) administered in the setting in which the behavior naturally occurs, (c) used to teach a functional skill, and (d) guided by the student's interest in the task.

Like DTT, milieu teaching is based on the three-term contingency (A-B-C) but differs in several ways. First, although MT is firmly rooted in ABA, it also includes some developmental social-pragmatic components such as obtaining joint attention, confirming the desire to interact, following the child's lead, responding to any language attempt, and expansion of language utterances (Ingersoll, 2010). These components were gleaned from observing parent–child interactions during early language development. Second, DTT is used to teach multiple skills, including academic skills, while MT primarily aims to increase the frequency and quality of language and social communication responses (Kaiser & Roberts, 2013). Third, MT more strongly emphasizes naturally occurring S^Ds (although it can also occur in situations contrived by the teacher) rather than teacher-developed S^Ds used in DTT. Fourth, MT uses specified prompts in a least-to-most order and aligns programmed reinforcing consequences more directly with the anticipated naturally occurring reinforcer signaled by the S^D. For example, behaviors that would be reinforced with social consequences in the natural environment are reinforced with the same social consequences during intervention as opposed to more arbitrary or contrived reinforcement contingencies that are sometimes necessary in DTT. Fifth, MT avoids a drill and practice format, using only brief quick trials or naturally occurring opportunities for target skill practice. MT is considered a useful strategy for supporting maintenance and generalization of skills whereas DTT may be better suited for initial skill acquisition and, in some cases, reaching the fluency level of proficiency.

Kaiser and Roberts (2013) list the following main teacher actions of MT:

- Arrange the environment to increase the likelihood that a child will communicate.
- Select and teach developmentally appropriate language targets.
- Respond to the child's language initiations with joint attention and prompts for elaborated language matched to target skills.
- Reinforce communication attempts with access to requested objects, continued adult interaction, and expansions and confirmations of the child's utterances (p. 297).

As previously mentioned, MT emphasizes naturally occurring S^Ds that motivate a student to interact or communicate at some level to begin a trial. For example, a student may see a computer (S^D) and want it turned on, a student may see a favorite object (S^D) on a top shelf and want to hold it, or a student may see an apple (S^D) on the desk and want to eat it.

Sometimes the S^D occurs naturally, and sometimes the teacher can contrive the S^D. For example, a teacher may contrive a learning opportunity by arranging the environment such that a preferred item (e.g., favorite toy) is in sight but out of the child's reach in order to create an opportunity for the child to request the toy. The teacher then waits for the child's behavior to suggest that he wants the toy (e.g., child points to the object or attempts to reach for it). The teacher then prompts the target behavior (an appropriate request of some sort) and provides the natural reinforcer for such a request (i.e., the provision of the desired item). Teaching a student to appropriately request things he wants and protest things he does not want are often targeted skills of MT.

For MT to work, teachers must create environments that motivate students to communicate, and they must frequently and carefully observe those occasions when a student may show interest in a naturally occurring S^D. Teachers also should know what is reinforcing to the child (i.e., what the child wants to obtain or to avoid). Teachers should also refrain from preempting requesting behavior by anticipating student needs and providing desired items or activities without requiring the student to request them (Westling & Fox, 2009).

When natural S^Ds (e.g., opportunities to request) are infrequent, teachers can create them. The teacher could *disrupt a routine* such as hanging up a coat by having another coat hanging on the student's hanger. Or, as in the preceding example, a teacher could place desired objects just *out of reach* or hand a student his yogurt but no spoon (*insufficient tools*). The teacher could *leave the student unfulfilled* by giving the student a puzzle that is missing one or two pieces or only giving the student a few raisins out of the box. The teacher could *construct a barrier* such as standing in front of the toy shelf (Webber & Scheuermann, 2008). In any of these cases, the student might well be motivated to make a request to obtain the desired item or to have the obstacle removed. The purpose is certainly not to frustrate the student but to motivate communication. The careful use of prompts may help avoid the child becoming upset. When done correctly, MT appears similar to a natural (albeit supported) interaction between the child and teacher.

At the point where the teacher notices an interest in a natural S^D (e.g., child is staring at the reinforcer), the teacher should establish **joint attention** with the student. Joint attention is a social interaction that involves two people being aware that they are both focused on the same stimuli (i.e., each individual looking at the item and then shifting their gaze to make eye contact). A teacher can achieve joint attention by also showing interest in the S^D by prompting (e.g., "Look there!"), standing in front of the S^D, holding the S^D in front of the student, or physically moving the student's head to face the teacher.

Once joint attention is obtained, the teacher can begin an instructional sequence using specified prompting procedures, language expansion and confirmation, and natural reinforcers for correct responding. A more detailed description of these components of MT will be provided in Chapter 6 in the discussion about communication and language interventions. MT has been effectively used for many years to increase linguistic complexity and the social communicative use of language by students with disabilities including those with autism (Hancock & Kaiser, 2002; Kaiser & Trent, 2007).

Assessing Student Progress with MT

MT requires data that reflect not only the various situations in which a student responded but also the specific teaching procedures used. It would also include a notation for spontaneous correct responses (the target goal) when no prompting techniques were used.

Kaiser (1993) recommended using the data-collection form in Figure 5.4 in addition to notes about specific situations and responses. This form provides a format to gather MT data about three students for three targeted behaviors each. In this example, the targeted behaviors are language responses. Data consist of an annotation of the situation, tallies of the target responses, and codes that indicate which MT prompting procedure was used. Those marked "S" for spontaneous (independent responding) could be graphed by day to visually indicate progress over time. Gathering data is critical when using MT to avoid perpetuating ineffective teaching strategies and the haphazard application of the procedures.

Student: Alex   **Student:** Justin   **Student:** Anna

Target 1: want + noun

SETTING	TIMES	PROMPTS/ CONSEQ.
breakfast	//	S,TD
group	/	MQ

Target 1: photo + label

SETTING	TIMES	PROMPTS/ CONSEQ.
breakfast	///	MQ,MQ,MQ
sm. grp.		MT

Target 1: two words

SETTING	TIMES	PROMPTS/ CONSEQ.
group	/	S/T
math	/	TD

Target 2: new noun labels

SETTING	TIMES	PROMPTS/ CONSEQ.
math	/	M
hall	/	M
transition		
bus	/	M/T (peer)

Target 2: request assistance

SETTING	TIMES	PROMPTS/ CONSEQ.
arrival	/	S/T
departure	/	S/T

Target 2: action verbs

SETTING	TIMES	PROMPTS/ CONSEQ.
group		M/T
self-help	/	M/T
transition	/	M/T

Target 3:

SETTING	TIMES	PROMPTS/ CONSEQ.

Target 3:

SETTING	TIMES	PROMPTS/ CONSEQ.

Target 3: req. assistance "help please"

SETTING	TIMES	PROMPTS/ CONSEQ.
breakfast	/	MQ/T
self-help	/	TD/T

Setting: Specify activity when response occurred

Times: Use slash for each occurrence

Prompts: (Record one symbol for each occurrence): M = Model, S = Spontaneous, T = Acknowledged by adult or peer, MQ = Mand or question, TD = Time delay

FIGURE 5.4 Milieu teaching data form
(From "Functional Language" by A. P. Kaiser, p. 354. In *Instruction of students with severe disabilities*, by M. E. Snell [Ed.], © 1993. Reprinted by permission of Prentice-Hall, Inc., Upper Saddle River, NJ.)

⌄ Professional Resource Download

There are a number of additional naturalistic teaching strategies similar to MT that can be recommended for students with autism. For example, enhanced milieu teaching (Hancock, Ledbetter-Cho, Howell, & Lang, 2016; Kaiser & Roberts, 2013), incidental teaching (Hart & Risley, 1975; McGee, Krantz, Mason, & McClannahan, 1983; McGee, Krantz, & McClannahan, 1985; Miranda-Linné & Melin, 1992), pivotal response treatment® (e.g., Koegel, O'Dell, & Koegel, 1987; Koegel, Openden, Fredeen, & Koegel, 2006), and natural environment training (Sundberg & Partington, 1998) have been found to be effective.

MT and these other naturalistic teaching strategies target developmentally appropriate behaviors. In other words, target behaviors are selected by considering the next step in a typical developmental trajectory. Research has demonstrated that intervention tends to be more effective (e.g., skills are acquired more efficiently and more easily generalized) when target behaviors are developmentally appropriate (Lifter, Ellis, Cannon, & Anderson, 2005). In addition, all of these intervention approaches typically involve implementation in natural settings, and many approaches recommend parent involvement so that these strategies can also be provided in the home. This means that parents and other family members need to be carefully trained (Kaiser, Hancock, & Nietfeld, 2000; Kaiser, Hancock, & Trent, 2007; Lang, Machalicek, Rispoli, & Regester, 2009). Finally, all of these naturalistic interventions attempt to motivate students by following their interests and attention and by using a variety of stimuli, prompting techniques, and natural reinforcers (Allen & Cowan, 2008; Delprato, 2001; Koegel, Koegel, & Carter, 1999).

5-2d Grouping

One-to-one instruction has traditionally been recommended when using DTT, MT, and sometimes DI instructional formats with students with autism because it provides undivided teacher attention, more intensive instruction, and fewer distracting stimuli (Maurice et al., 1996; Rotholz, 1990). However, students can also learn new skills in small-group situations (Leaf et al., 2013; Taubman, Brierley, Wishner, Baker, McEachin, & Leaf, 2001). Grouping procedures allow for the teacher to decrease prompt dependency, loosen stimulus control, and promote generalization.

Few if any adult work or living situations will afford one-to-one instructional situations. For this reason, if long-term goals for individual students include independent living and working, then students must be taught to work and function with others present. Furthermore, group arrangements are common to general education classrooms if inclusion is of concern.

In addition, grouping students with autism with peers often creates opportunities for peer-to-peer interaction and modeling (Leaf et al., 2013). In some cases, peers without disabilities or with less severe delays may be trained to provide some form of intervention or instruction to students with autism. In fact, peer-mediated interventions have been found to be effective in a variety of settings with many different target behaviors (Chan, Lang, Rispoli, O'Reilly, Sigafoos, & Cole, 2009; Watkins et al., 2015). Group instruction is also more efficient than one-to-one instruction, allowing teachers to provide more response opportunities and teacher-directed interactions rather than having students work by themselves as the teacher engages in one-to-one instruction with others.

Reid and Favell (1984) described three general models of group instruction: (a) **sequential**, (b) **concurrent**, and (c) **tandem**. *Sequential* group instruction involves the teacher briefly teaching each student individually while sitting in a group with others who are either watching or engaging in their own independent tasks. The students may be working on the same or similar objectives or different ones. For example, three students may be sitting on one side of a curved table. Using DTT, the teacher instructs one to "Point to nose." The student does it and receives an edible reinforcer. The next student is asked to say "I want cereal," whereupon he receives a bit of cereal. The third student is given a puzzle to complete. The teacher then moves back to the first student and so on. Students learn to wait their turn, work independently for short periods of time, and attend to teacher cues with more distracters present. Leaf et al. (2013) demonstrated that the sequential group approach has the potential to work as a one-to-one DTT format in some cases. Of course, creating such a group may take time and require participating students to master some prerequisite sitting, waiting, and attending skills.

The *concurrent* group model involves the teacher providing instruction to the entire group and all children responding simultaneously to the S^D. In this model, one-to-one instruction can be interspersed if necessary. For example, the teacher may use DTT to have the entire group imitate motor skills (e.g., hands up, hands out, tongue out) or social skills (e.g., shake hands, smile at me). If one student does not smile, then the teacher can engage in one-to-one instruction with that student while the others continue to practice smiling at each other or shaking hands. Or using DI a teacher can deliver instruction to the entire group then ask all of them to "point to their left." Taubman et al. (2001) showed that the concurrent model was effective for multiple preschool children with autism.

The *tandem* model begins with one-to-one instruction and systematically expands to include more students. As more students are added, each needs to learn to work on a thinner reinforcement schedule, remain seated, and attend with more distracting stimuli. Koegel and Rincover (1974) demonstrated that effective DTT instruction could occur with as many as eight children with autism in a group using the tandem model.

Teachers should continue to record student responses during group instruction by recording each student's responses when giving individual cues or group cues. Data sheets might include the number of students in the group so that correct responding within groups can be evaluated. Figure 5.5 is a sample data-collection sheet for sequential group organization. This data sheet could be adapted for concurrent and tandem group structures.

We recommend beginning instruction with a one-to-one procedure until attending and compliance skills are mastered. At that point, students should be able to wait longer between trials, work for intermittent reinforcement, and emit multiple behaviors in response to one cue. Any of the aforementioned group formats may be introduced. Remember that students

DATE	4/5	4/7	4/10	4/11					
Aiden									
Give 1–5 pennies	3/5								
Identify penny	2/3								
Identify nickel	0/2								
Vivian									
Give 5–10 pennies	1/5								
Identify nickel	2/3								
Identify dime	3/3								
Sage									
Counts one object	3/4								
Counts two objects	0/4								
Counts three objects	0/4								
Justin									
Counts one object	3/5								
Counts two objects	1/4								
Counts three objects	0/4								

Record number of unprompted correct responses per number of opportunities (trials) to respond.

FIGURE 5.5 Group lesson data sheet
(© Cengage. Source: *Educational strategies for autistic children/youth: Autism teacher training program,* 1982, p. 333. Kansas City, KS: Department of Special Education, University of Kansas Press.)

⌄⌄ Professional Resource Download

who can only work one to one with an adult and who never learn to work in groups are not likely to be successful in integrated school or community settings. Group formats may be appropriate for MT if several students are interested in a naturally occurring S^D at the same time. For example, if a teacher is serving ice cream on a field trip, she could obtain all students' joint attention and apply the sequential group model by prompting each student to request ice cream before receiving a portion. Typically, however, MT is applied in one-to-one situations.

5-2e Embedded ABA Teaching Strategies

Within the four instructional formats previously described, teachers need to know how to use three additional ABA strategies: shaping, chaining, and generalization training. **Shaping** is essentially a reinforcement strategy for gradually achieving a desired response by strengthening approximations of that response. **Chaining** is a method for combining several response steps into a complex behavior. **Generalization training** methods are used when students need to learn to apply skills under a variety of conditions and to maintain skills over time.

Shaping is a procedure whereby the teacher systematically reinforces successive approximations toward a specific behavioral response until the full behavior response is achieved (Alberto & Troutman, 2017). Beginning with behaviors that the student already performs, the teacher would reinforce slight changes in those behaviors as long as they more closely resemble a targeted response. At the same time, no reinforcement would be given for behaviors that do not move the student closer to the designated target.

Shaping can be used for teaching various behaviors such as handwriting, sitting in a chair, dressing, and reading. For example, in teaching a student to write letters, she is reinforced for tracing the letter, then tracing only part of the letter while completing the rest independently, then copying the letter on her own, and then producing the letter on her own. Similarly, a student is reinforced for reading the word *dog* by sounding out the initial letter sound ("d"), then the "d" plus the next sound ("o"), then for the whole word "dog." Teachers should establish different success criteria as each is mastered so it is clear what behavior is to receive reinforcement. Always reinforce a behavior that more closely approximates the target behavior (reading entire word *dog*) and do not reinforce a previous approximation once a more accurate one has been produced.

To implement a shaping procedure, the final target behavior, the initial behavior, and successive steps toward that behavior must be operationally defined (Malott, Whaley, & Malott, 1997). Observe the student to determine which approximations are already being produced. In this way, the teacher will know where to begin reinforcing. Shaping may be used to teach the topography of a behavior (what it looks like), its duration (length of time), latency (time lapse before the behavior occurs), or rate (frequency of behavior relative to time) (Alberto & Troutman, 2017). For example, the teacher shapes a student's number writing to achieve all numbers written correctly instead of being written backward (topography). Or a teacher shapes the amount of time a student stays in his seat (duration) or shapes a reduced time after the bell rings of getting into her seat (latency). A teacher could shape the number of words a student reads in a minute (fluency). During a shaping procedure, the teacher would continue to use prompting and effective reinforcement techniques.

In terms of data collection, simply tally how many appropriate (unprompted and prompted) approximations occur per session or per day. Transfer these responses onto a graph either as the total number of correct responses (e.g., the number of times the student produced a correct letter or a designated approximation) or as a percentage of opportunities (the total number of letters she was asked to produce).

Shaping involves teaching one target behavior (e.g., printing an "A") through progressive approximations, but *chaining* is a procedure for combining several distinct behaviors that are usually determined through a task analysis (see Chapter 4) into a complex "chain" of behaviors. Most often the combined behaviors result in an activity or task (e.g., washing dishes, donning a jacket, proceeding through a cafeteria line, following a map to the bus stop, writing a paragraph) (Alberto & Troutman, 2017).

The first step in a chaining procedure is to conduct a task analysis of the target activity or task. The task analysis provides a list of essential sub-behaviors required to complete the task or activity. Task analysis and chaining can be used for a variety of school-related tasks and activities (e.g., computing long division) as well as self-help and functional activities (e.g., dressing, bathing, cooking). The teacher should ensure that the task analysis has resulted in sub-behaviors that can be attained by the target student; otherwise, it might be necessary to develop more steps with easier behaviors. Second, using the task analysis, assess whether a student can already perform any of the sub-behaviors. The third step, after assessment is completed, is to begin directly teaching each step not currently mastered in the task analysis sequence.

The sub-behaviors can be taught beginning with step 1 and progressing to the last step (**forward chaining**) or from the last step backwards to the first (**backward chaining**). For example, in teaching a student, Javier, how to write his name, the teacher could prompt and reinforce printing a "J" (step 1) and then physically guide the student through the other steps (letters). Step 2 (printing "a") would be taught when step 1 has been mastered while continuing to prompt the remaining letters until the entire name is written independently (forward chaining). Alternately, the teacher could physically guide the student through all the letters until the last one (printing "r"). This last step would be prompted and reinforced and, when mastered (i.e., prompts are faded and the student is responding independently), the second to the last step would be taught (backward chaining).

Many self-help tasks are commonly taught using backward chaining (e.g., tooth-brushing, dressing, tying shoes, opening and closing fasteners), as are certain basic academic skills (e.g., learning telephone number and address, writing letters and numbers). The repetition of steps and successful completion of the task provided by backward chaining seem to make this an effective strategy for such tasks.

On the other hand, vocational and leisure skills may be best taught using forward chaining. For example, a student may learn to stuff envelopes by first collating papers and then collating and stapling; then collating, stapling, and folding; then collating, stapling, folding, and inserting into an envelope; and so forth. Or a student may learn to swim by blowing bubbles underwater, then floating on stomach, then floating and kicking legs, and so on. Choose either forward or backward chaining based on which sequence might be easiest for a given student to learn and which is the most logical given the nature of the task.

Other tasks are best taught in entirety rather than in steps. For example, it would be difficult to teach skills such as reading a story, drawing a map, or eating breakfast only one step at a time, with full prompts on the remaining steps. The chaining format used for these tasks is called **total task presentation**. Like other forms of chaining, it includes S^Ds, prompts (if necessary), and consequences.

Total task presentation differs from forward and backward chaining in two ways. First, all steps in the sequence are performed by the student every time the task is presented. Second, partial prompts, verbal prompts, and stimulus prompts (e.g., list of steps or pictures displaying each step) are typically the prompts used because the nature of the tasks may preclude full physical prompts.

Total task presentation is recommended if the student can already perform many of the task steps but not in sequence. Thus, a student might perform each step in diving off the side of the pool (i.e., stand with feet together and arms together overhead, bend knees, lower chin, hold breath, push off in an outward and downward motion, keep form intact throughout dive) given only verbal prompts after the initial cue.

For total task presentation, a data sheet should include notations for each step. Although mastery is indicated when all the steps are performed independently and correctly, progress can be noted as more steps are mastered or require less assistance. Again, it is wise to include some indicator of prompted steps and the types of prompts needed to ensure correct responses.

Figure 5.6 shows a data-collection form for a total task presentation. This data sheet also shows the type of prompt: gestural, verbal, or physical. A plus sign (+) indicates correct re-

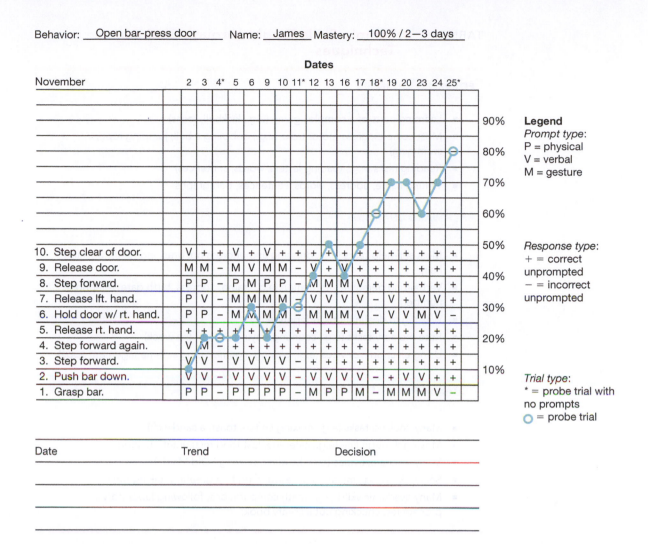

FIGURE 5.6 Total task presentation data form
(© Cengage. Source: *Assessment of individuals with severe disabilities: An applied behavior approach to life skills assessment* (2nd ed.), by D. M. Browder, 1991, p. 115. Baltimore, MD: Paul H. Brookes Publishing Co. Copyright 1991 by Paul H. Brookes Publishing Co.)

⌄ Professional Resource Download

sponding (unprompted), whereas a minus sign (−) indicates incorrect responding. This form also allows graphing—what an awesome form! Percentages are provided on the far right axis. Divide the number of unprompted correct responses (pluses) by the total number of steps to be performed and multiply by 100 to find the percent of correct responses per day. Plot a point to indicate the correct percent for each day and connect the points to form a graph.

Eventually, each step in the behavior chain becomes an S^D for the next step, and the student's behaviors are brought under control of the routine itself without requiring teacher or parent directives. For example, when putting on pants, you first insert your legs. The completion of this step is reinforced naturally by moving closer to the end goal (wearing pants) while also functioning as an S^D for the next step (pulling pants up to waist). The pants at the waistline functions as an S^D for the next step (zipping up), which in turn brings the button closer to the buttonhole (an S^D to button the pants), and so on until the pants are completely on. Table 5.5 provides sample complex tasks and activities that might best be taught with one of the techniques of forward chaining, backward chaining, or total task presentation.

The concept of *generalization* (defined and discussed in Chapter 4) refers to the ability of an individual to apply skills and knowledge under various conditions and to adapt

TABLE 5.5 ● Sample Skills Taught through Chaining Techniques

FORWARD CHAINING

- Learning parts of a complex game (e.g., kickball, races)
- Most complex gross motor tasks (e.g., dribbling a ball, jumping rope, swimming)
- Reading tasks (e.g., reading letters, words, sentences)
- Writing name, address, words, sentences, paragraphs

BACKWARD CHAINING

- Most self-help tasks (e.g., dressing and undressing, brushing teeth, washing hair)
- Verbalizing personal information (e.g., name, address, birth date, telephone number)
- Walking to destinations independently
- Rote memory tasks (e.g., counting, saying days of the week)
- Using electronic devices (e.g., playing a game, using self-management apps)

TOTAL TASK PRESENTATION

- Many cooking tasks (e.g., making coffee, toast, a sandwich)
- Moving through line (e.g., cafeteria, fast food restaurant, theater)
- Many leisure activities (e.g., bowling, playing "Old Maid")
- Social skills (e.g., initiating or responding to a greeting, taking turns)
- Many academic skills (e.g., math computations, following laboratory procedures, checking out a library book)

one's behavior accordingly. Generalization is often difficult for students with autism. For most children, generalization occurs without specific instruction as a function of their ability to attend to various types of models and distinguish similarities among social cues and situations. However, students with autism who have complex attending difficulties usually need deliberate instruction for generalization to occur. Stokes and Baer (1977) presented several specific techniques for programming for the generalization of behavior. Table 5.6 summarizes those techniques. We recommend that teachers use these techniques to ensure that functional skills reach maintenance and generalization.

To address generalization, consider altering the antecedents, required student responses, and consequences. For example, vary the conditions under which a student is expected to engage in the behavior. Vary the people giving instructions, number of students in the classroom or group, tone of voice, and the programmed S^D itself. Use different materials (three types of shoes, socks, coffeepots, toasters, etc.).

Also prompt the student to give similar but different responses, especially language responses, and then reinforce variation in appropriate responses when they occur. Rather than reinforce rote production of a phrase or sentence (e.g., "How are you today?"), require the student to say it differently (e.g., "How are you doing?").

Finally, vary the reinforcement schedule and fade to natural consequences. To do this, the student may need to be taught to recognize various types of reinforcers (head nods, smiles, winks) as positive feedback. For planning purposes, we recommend (a) identifying goals and objectives at the maintenance and generalization levels, (b) monitoring student behavior under natural conditions, and (c) using graphs to communicate progress.

TABLE 5.6 ● Generalization Training Strategies

1. *Sequential modification.* Implement a program that was successful in one setting in a different setting. For example, have parents reinforce communication responses at home (Lovaas, Koegel, Simmons, & Long, 1973). This is the most time-consuming technique. May need to provide multiple cues (S^{D}s) in the second environment (e.g., picture schedules, routines, recorded messages).

2. *Introduce natural reinforcers.* Teach students functional skills that will entrap natural reinforcers (e.g., asking for a preferred toy or something to eat, smiling, making eye contact, compliance). Also teach students to recognize natural reinforcers (a hug) as something positive. Need to determine age-appropriate skills that receive reinforcers in a particular setting and attempt to get others in that environment to provide high-frequency reinforcement at first.

3. *General case programming.* Known as "loosening stimulus control," teach using many relevant examples (S^{D}s). Once a response is learned to one S^D, begin to vary them so that the same response can be practiced in response to many S^{D}s. For example, change the commands, the people giving the commands, the materials used, the setting, and so forth. In this way, the students do not remain stimulus bound. Vary the reinforcers. Also teach different versions of the same behavior. Milieu teaching is a procedure for varying S^{D}s, responses expectations, and reinforcers and providing less structure.

4. *Use indiscriminable contingencies.* Thin reinforcement to intermittent schedules. This technique promotes the maintenance of behavior by providing unpredictable schedules of reinforcement (the slot machine schedule; see Chapter 2). Provide reinforcement for classes of behavior rather than specific behaviors (e.g., "You did a nice job at lunch").

5. *Program common stimuli.* Make settings more alike. Make the training classroom more like the general education classroom by adding more students, changing the classroom arrangement, and so forth. Or make the classroom more like the kitchen at home. Also introduce into the second setting something familiar from the first setting (e.g., the student's favorite chair) (Koegel & Rincover, 1974).

6. *Mediate generalization.* Teach students to monitor their own generalized behavior through self-recording or self-evaluation. Students can be taught to record each time they finish a certain task, no matter where the task is to be performed. The recorded responses are then reinforced.

7. *Train to generalize.* Provide reinforcers for generalized behavior. A student can receive reinforcers for displaying a learned behavior in a different environment or under different conditions. This would be true for prompted or unprompted behavior.

Source: From Stokes and Baer, 1977

Teachers should choose specific generalization-training techniques based on particular student characteristics. For example, if a student does not emit a response in the general education setting (e.g., remain in seat), then teachers might try providing familiar S^{D}s in the new environment (e.g., the teacher saying, "It's time to work."). Teachers should also provide prompts and cues in the general education classroom. For example, peers might be taught to prompt correct responses in the classroom, on the playground, or in the cafeteria. Sometimes, the student might be taught to use picture prompts kept in a wallet to cue correct behaviors in generalized settings.

Sometimes a behavior is **overgeneralized** and creates a problem. In other words, the behavior is performed under conditions where it should not be performed (e.g., reaching for food in the cafeteria line because he was taught to self-serve at the salad bar). In this case, the teacher may need to spend time teaching when *not* to give that particular response. This is another example of *discrimination training* because the teacher focuses on teaching the student to recognize the meaningful differences between the S^{D}s and environments where the behavior should occur and the S^{D}s and environments where the behavior should not occur.

Remember, in discrimination training, the teacher will identify a stimulus that signals when a particular behavior will not be reinforced. The signal that a behavior will not be reinforced is referred to as an **S-delta**. For example, in the situation above, the S-delta is being at school, and discrimination training would involve calling the child's attention to the S-delta and stating the absence of the contingency ("At school you cannot have food you reach for in line"). Differential reinforcement (see Chapter 3) is then used to reinforce the target behavior in the presence of the S^D, and extinction (no reinforcement) is used in the presence of the S-delta.

If a student demonstrates a generalized behavior once but not again, then the problem may be one of maintenance. In this case, more frequent reinforcement should initially be delivered in the generalized setting before moving to a thinner unpredictable delivery schedule. In some instances, the student can be taught to give himself reinforcement through self-monitoring or to elicit reinforcement by asking questions such as "Didn't I do a good job on this?" (i.e., training natural contingencies of reinforcement).

Progress monitoring for generalization differs from monitoring skill acquisition and fluency. For generalization, we are interested in noting whether a student responds appropriately (or inappropriately) under a variety of conditions. Thus, the student must have opportunities to respond in many situations. Each situation should be described on the data sheet. We are also interested only in unprompted first-time (spontaneous) responses. Once someone emits a response, natural prompts and consequences may occur. In this case, subsequent responding is not a true measure of generalization. Thus, generalization data should only reflect one entry per situation.

Students with autism may need much support to learn to generalize or transfer their learning to new situations, so it is important for teachers not to forget to teach to generalization. Failing to teach to generalization can have dire effects. Students may never attain independent living or working skills; the same goals and objectives may appear year after year on an individualized educational program (IEP) because skills learned in the classroom do not transfer to other school environments or home; or students may be compelled to remain in segregated settings because they cannot display appropriate behavior in natural settings. School personnel who do not aim for the generalization and maintenance of educational gains for all their students are doing them a disservice. Remember, unless the student is going to spend her whole life in your classroom, skills that do not occur outside of your classroom are going to eventually be worthless!

In summary, we have presented four recommended lesson-presentation formats for instructing students with ASD, three of which have been found to be effective with students who also have ID (i.e., DI, DTT, MT). Table 5.7 provides a side-by-side comparison of the

TABLE 5.7 ● Comparison of ABA Instructional Formats

LESSON COMPONENTS	DIRECT INSTRUCTION (di)	DIRECT INSTRUCTION (DI)	DISCRETE TRIAL TEACHING (DTT)	MILIEU TEACHING (MT)
Attention S^D	Teacher gains attention with signal or interesting material.	Teacher reads lesson script (e.g., "Put finger on . . .").	Teacher provides command to attend (e.g., "Look").	Natural occurrence gains attention. Teacher must observe this.
S^D	Teacher states learning objective, presents lesson content, asks questions, and presents visual, written, verbal cues.	Teacher reads scripted cues (e.g., "Read the word 'collide'") and gives new information ("This word is branch"). Written cues are presented in text.	Teacher preplans and presents S^D, usually a verbal cue but can be visual (written math problems).	Naturally occurring stimulus or one contrived by teacher is used to motivate communication.
Prompt	Include models in lesson. Teacher plans guided practice activities in which students practice lesson components (e.g., math computation) and receive immediate correction or feedback and reteaching as necessary.	Teacher reads scripted information and uses text (Look at picture, the sign says "Slow down," pointing to sign) and questions and cues ("Which way is north?" while pointing north herself).	Teacher plans prompts (verbal, physical, gestural) (e.g., moves hand to point correctly), and fading procedures (e.g., most to least).	Teacher spontaneously prompts with model, mand-model, or time-delay procedures (see Chapter 6), usually least-to-most fading procedure.
Responses	Used primarily in general education classrooms, elementary to secondary. Students' responses are physical (use clicker to answer question), verbal, or written, during lesson and independently later.	Used to teach basic and some advanced academic content. Student responses are physical (point to), verbal, or written as requested by teaching script during lesson.	Used to teach various skills, typically at acquisition and fluency levels. Students respond physically (put on), verbally, or written, immediately after teacher-provided S^D.	Used primarily to teach language and social communication responses at maintenance and generalization levels. Students respond verbally or physically (sign communication) immediately after teacher or naturally occurring S^D.

(continued)

TABLE 5.7 ● **Comparison of ABA Instructional Formats** (*continued*)

LESSON COMPONENTS	DIRECT INSTRUCTION (di)	DIRECT INSTRUCTION (DI)	DISCRETE TRIAL TEACHING (DTT)	MILIEU TEACHING (MT)
Reinforcement	Praise for some number of correct responses. Classwide or individual token systems can be used for correct responding, task completion, and appropriate behavior.	Praise for correct responding or movement to next item; accompanying point system can be paired with curriculum.	Teacher preplans reinforcement strategy for correct responding. Reinforcer not always related to expected behavior (e.g., bubbles blown for correct counting).	Natural reinforcer that initially engaged student attention (e.g., obtaining desired object). Given after three trials at most.
Lessons or Trials	Teacher plans lessons to coordinate with designated schedule (1-hour history class; 3-hour math class; 20-minute reading time).	Lessons are planned by publisher and scripted. Some are short for younger students, and some are longer for older students.	Teacher plans trials that are conducted in a series. Session may last as long as an hour.	As many as three trials embedded in naturally occurring situation. Sessions are short and successful.
Progress Monitoring	Grades on practice activities, homework, weekly quizzes, and tests.	Data collected on each lesson. SRA online data tracker used for progress reports.	Data collected after each trial or some predesignated number of trials is graphed to show progress.	Data collected after each session or at a later time if needed and graphed to show progress.
Learner Motivation	Teacher uses high-interest materials, quick pacing, high opportunity to respond rate, prompts for success, grades, praise, notes home, and so forth.	Teacher uses quick pace, small chunks of learning, frequent opportunities to respond, and point system.	Teacher manipulates pacing, prompts, reinforcement to keep student motivated to respond.	Student is naturally motivated to respond to the natural S^D.
Curriculum	Academic tool subjects and content, elementary and secondary	Reading, math, language arts, language, science, social studies for elementary students and secondary students needing high structure	Basic academics, communication, social, vocational, adaptive, and functional skills	Language and social communication skills
Group format	Large group	Either one to one or small group	Primarily one to one; can be used in small group	Usually one to one

four formats arranged by multiple lesson components. We have also provided descriptions of general ABA teaching strategies (shaping, chaining, generalization training) to be used within any of the four formats. We recommend that teachers, paraprofessionals, and others working with this population become proficient in these lesson-presentation formats and the other instructional strategies presented in this book. Students with autism need evidence-based educational programs. Maurice, Green, and Foxx (2001) listed a set of core features common to effective ABA instructional program models for students with autism:

- Instruction should begin as early as possible for the child (e.g., before school age).
- Instruction should be intensive (the more hours spent in instruction, the more and faster the learning).
- Instruction such as milieu teaching should occur most of the student's waking hours. Parents are trained and become coteachers to differing extents.
- Instruction should be individualized and comprehensive targeting a wide range of skills.
- Multiple ABA procedures should be used to develop adaptive behaviors.
- Instruction is generally initially delivered in a one-to-one format with gradual transition to group formats and natural contexts.

5-3 Structuring with Physical Organization

Providing structure through lesson presentation goes a long way toward effective instruction of students with autism. A second area of structure that can positively affect students with autism involves physical aspects of the classroom, essentially arranging the classroom to communicate expectations (McAllister & Maguire, 2012; Mostafa, 2008). By arranging a classroom to be predictable with defined expectations for each space, students with autism will more likely display appropriate behavior and engage in learning activities (Gaines, Curry, Shroyer, Amor, & Lock, 2014).

Arranging such an environment is easiest if the special education teacher has control over the classroom space (i.e., in a self-contained or resource classroom). General education classrooms do not typically include many of the structures we discuss, but collaboration between special education teachers and their general education counterparts may produce physical organizational structures that benefit not only students with autism in those general education classes but also other students. We specifically recommend constructing a visually organized room to communicate learning and behavioral expectations (Dalrymple, 1995; Quill, 1995; Schopler, Mesibov, & Hearsey, 1995).

Desks, chairs, dividers, shelves, rugs, and materials can be arranged in ways that readily communicate time demands, procedures, curriculum, and location. For example, if students are expected to function independently for academic, prevocational, and vocational skills; receive instruction in self-help skills and communication skills; and perform appropriate leisure time skills, then the classroom should be arranged to communicate these functions. Organize areas according to the activity and curriculum to be delivered. Clearly delineate physical boundaries and expected behaviors. To accomplish this, the teacher might do the following.

- Design an independent work area containing a long table and chairs with various **workstations** (independent self-explanatory tasks) that require the use of matching, assembly, job, and discrimination skills.
- Create a leisure time area to support appropriate leisure activities. This area might contain computers and games, tablets, a card table and chairs, beanbag chairs, and age-appropriate toys, books, and music.
- Indicate direct instruction in communication and academics with desks, chairs and small tables, mats, rugs, boxes for completed work, pencils, paper, and so forth.
- For adolescents and young adults, arrange a separate area with a stove, microwave, refrigerator, kitchen supplies, ironing board and iron, and washing machine to indicate that self-help lessons will occur.
- Younger students with autism may have areas of the room designated for snack time, play, direct instruction or DTT, and self-help skills (particularly toileting, grooming, and dressing skills).
- Designate one easily accessible area of each classroom as a transition area. This area should contain places for each student's belongings and picture or written activity schedule (described later in this chapter).

The point is that the room arrangement itself should function as an S^D for specific desirable behaviors and as an S-delta for challenging or off-task behaviors. For example, if the student is expected to work independently, then the area should be free of distracters such as noise and flickering lights. Furthermore, designated tasks (e.g., workstations) need to be at least somewhat self-explanatory for the student. For example, Schopler et al. (1995) recommend that independent tasks indicate to the student (usually with pictures) how much work must be completed, what work must be completed, when the work is finished, and what happens when the work is finished.

When students are expected to work one to one with the teacher, it might be best to place two chairs by a small table with instructional materials in proximity to the teacher's chair. If possible, this one-to-one instruction should be in a place somewhat visually isolated from everything else in the classroom. Of course, room arrangement is contingent on available resources, but access to a small, quiet work space for one-to-one instruction will be necessary for initial skill acquisition, for students with notable challenging behaviors, and for those who are more easily distracted. Once instructional control has been established, students will most likely be able to perform either one to one or within groups with fewer environmental supports.

Group work is usually performed with students surrounding a table, with students in a horseshoe-shaped sitting arrangement, or with students sitting on one side of a table and the teacher working from the opposite side. For older students, working in rows or groups of desks might be encouraged, particularly if inclusion in general education classrooms is a targeted placement. In any of these cases, student–teacher ratios are small. As more students are added to a group (student–teacher ratio becomes larger), structure correspondingly decreases, and it is assumed that students can operate for longer periods of time without teacher support.

Additional visual support for behavioral expectations can be provided with dividers such as filing cabinets, partitions, bookshelves, carpet sections, brightly colored duct tape on the floor, and pictures delineating areas and expectations within each area. More visual cues are needed (higher structure) for students with lower cognitive functioning, young students, and those engaged in new learning.

Materials pertaining to curriculum taught in a designated area of the room should be stored in that area, perhaps color coded or picture coded for that area. Color coding of storage boxes, labeling everything with pictures or words, and keeping things in the same place over time will help students learn procedures and understand expectations. For example, storage boxes in the prevocational area may be green, as is the carpet and the duct tape to indicate where chairs are placed. Green paper lines the walls in that area.

Another visual strategy might be to store each student's materials in color-coded boxes so that each student's daily tasks are in a different color box; each student's chair is marked with duct tape in his assigned color; and each student's place in line is marked with his initials in his unique color. Student photos may also be used to help each child to recognize his own possessions and places to sit, stand, and work. In other words, use physical cues as S^Ds to help students with autism learn to respond to those stimuli in the classroom and other areas of the school, which will facilitate higher levels of independent functioning.

Avoid rearranging the classroom unless absolutely necessary (Gaines et al., 2014). Once students with autism learn visual cues, they can become extremely confused and anxious if those cues are altered or removed without warning and without teaching other ways to predict what should happen next. Table 5.8 provides suggestions for visually organizing a classroom.

5-3a Organizing to Prevent Inappropriate Behavior

Because students with autism are easily distracted, masking irrelevant noises or visual distracters can be helpful. Teachers may want to close doors, use carrels, use headphones for tablets and computers, place rugs to absorb noise, or add white noise if other methods do not work.

Lighting might also need to be modified as needed. Some students with autism are distracted by the soft buzz of fluorescent lights, and lights that flicker are sure to be a distraction. In these cases, lamps might work better. However, some students may also be distracted by shadows, so light placement is important.

Observe individual students in order to target potential distracters. If self-stimulation or agitation increases under certain conditions, take the time to analyze what physical variables might need to be altered. Then, once the student is able to work calmly in carefully controlled environments, the teacher should begin gradually introducing more natural environmental stimuli to the situation. For example, perhaps you use the classroom fluorescent lights rather than lamps for increasingly longer periods each day. Remember that the world in general is full of auditory and visual distracters, so students must learn to function effectively in environments with significant noise, movement, and visual stimulation.

TABLE 5.8 ● Suggestions for Visual Organization

Use color coding to:
- organize materials by area,
- organize materials for each child (e.g., Javier's chair always has a red tape stripe, his cubby is marked with red tape, he sits on the red tape), and
- designate areas of the room (e.g., self-help is yellow, leisure is purple).

Use pictures to:
- designate each child's place, destinations, and daily schedules,
- delineate activities to perform in each area of the classroom,
- remind students of desired behaviors,
- designate personal belongings,
- designate where things belong, and
- designate tasks and activities.

Use lists for reminding:
- what things to take home or bring to school,
- what to buy at the store or in the cafeteria,
- what things to take on community outings,
- what jobs to do, and
- what tasks need to be done.

Use duct tape or paint to:
- designate transition paths (e.g., painted footsteps),
- designate a lineup area, and
- create a "personal space" area for each student (e.g., taped square around desk, taped square around area where students are to sit).

Use dividers to:
- designate transition paths,
- visually mask seductive stimuli (e.g., children playing outside), and
- provide obstacles to running out of the classroom.

The fact that students with autism are participating more than ever in general education activities and general education environments with high levels of stimulation might actually help students become more skilled at generalized responding. These general education environments and activities typically present high levels of visual, noise, movement, and other stimuli. However, simply moving a child with autism from the relatively quiet and stimuli-controlled special education class to the bright, noisy cafeteria without any planning or preparation probably will not produce desired results for the student with autism. Rather, that transition may need to occur gradually, and the natural stimuli of the cafeteria may need to be muted, at least at first (e.g., perhaps with headphones to reduce noise levels for the child, by first sitting at a table in the calmest corner of the cafeteria).

The teacher can be creative in arranging the classroom to help prevent inappropriate behavior. For example, students who elope should be placed far from doors, or teachers could place obstacles such as a cabinet some 3 to 5 feet in front of the door to serve as a deterrent. Arrange aisles or walkways such that an adult can reach any student in the room within 3 seconds. If students are destructive, keep valuable items such as electronics out of reach unless the student is supervised or until he learns alternate prosocial behavior. If students grab food, keep food reinforcers in an inaccessible place such as the pockets of a carpenter's apron worn around the teacher's waist. If a student likes to lie on the floor or grab the teacher's shirt, then situate the worktable so that it takes longer for the student to get out of his seat or reach the teacher. Keep favorite toys (those things that students prefer during free time) or any other seductive object out of sight unless students have earned them. Basically, teachers should monitor students and arrange the environment to ensure maximum time on task and prevent inappropriate behavior.

5-3b Organizing for Comfort and Safety

Everyone should be comfortable in the classroom. Small, cramped dark spaces or undefined spaces are usually not conducive to learning (Gaines et al., 2014). Messy rooms will fail to communicate learning expectations. Avoid excessive temperatures. Allow easy access to bathrooms. Everyone should be able to move easily around the classroom and obtain and return materials without major obstacles such as furniture or stacks of materials. Teach students and adults to return materials to their designated place (indicating "finished"). Use and teach safety precautions and closely supervise students when working with stoves, knives, or any material or item that has inherent risk. In sum, visually organizing the classroom to communicate expectations and provide a comfortable, safe place for each student will likely provide S^Ds for appropriate learning behaviors (e.g., on-task, attending, compliance) and result in more successful learning.

5-4 Structuring through Routines and Schedules

Students with autism appear to prefer routine and often become distressed if a routine is disrupted (American Psychiatric Association [APA], 2013). In fact, if routine activities are not imposed externally, some individuals with autism may impose their own. For example, a student may touch all the pieces of a puzzle before putting it together or arrange a desk and chair in a certain fashion before sitting down to work. Because routine is so easily learned and often preferred, we recommend that teachers take great care in deciding what routines, often called *procedures*, to establish in their classrooms so they help students comply and learn (Harris, 2016).

5-4a Teaching Routines and Procedures

Generally, we recommend that teachers establish routines or procedures for entering and leaving the classroom, having students check their individual schedules and choose activities, transitions, working, playing, toileting, and eating. For example, entering the classroom may entail walking to the central transition area, putting away coats, lunch boxes, and backpacks, and moving to an appropriate instructional area. This movement procedure will be facilitated if there are painted arrows or footsteps from the door to the transition area or other visual cues such as dividers guiding students through the procedure. In any case, the teacher should prompt a student to use established routines or procedures every time until the student can do them independently.

Students with autism may have difficulty with new routines or procedures, particularly transitioning between activities or from one step of an activity to another. Because of an inability to easily shift their attention and read social cues (APA, 2013), these students will require instruction and support to master routines or procedures. First, teachers should establish procedures for each transition and activity required during a day. For example, how will students determine where they should be and on what they should be working? How will they know when to change activities? What should they do if they finish their task and have free time? What are the procedures for going to lunch, the bathroom, and recess?

Schopler et al. (1995) recommend teaching students top-down and left-to-right routines so that they can "read" visual activity cues (regardless of where they may be posted) from top to bottom and approach all task and activity steps in the classroom from left to right. For example, a student may be taught to work from a picture activity schedule, picking the top picture to indicate what activity he should complete first and working down the list until all activities are completed (McClannahan & Krantz, 2010). A student may also be taught to sit down at an assigned workstation, which is arranged such that step 1 (pick up the first sheet of paper in a collating task) is positioned to the far left while the last step (stacking the stapled packets) is positioned to the far right.

It is also recommended that teachers establish routines or procedures for "waiting" (Dalrymple, 1995). For example, teach students to move to waiting chairs as part of the

Finished box for concrete objects (e.g., soda can)

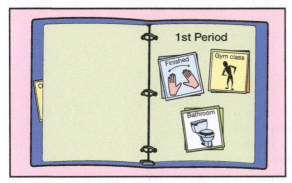

Picture activity schedule in notebook with finished pictures to Velcro over pictures of completed tasks

Picture activity schedule and finished box

FIGURE 5.7 Sample "finished" indicators

transition to new activities. This procedure will give the teacher a chance to set up workstations and ensure that all students are in the correct place. It will teach students an appropriate behavior routine to display at other times when waiting might be required (e.g., waiting for a bus, waiting for dinner, waiting to go to the bathroom). Eventually, the student should be taught to respond to a verbal cue—"Please wait"—by sitting nearby and possibly playing a handheld computer game or listening to music on a smartphone or iPod.

Another useful procedure or routine to teach is that of "finishing" activities and tasks. The concept of "finished" may be difficult to teach. Is one finished when a bell sounds, when the plate is empty, or when one has placed all completed tasks in the "finished" box? Depending on the activity, completion standards will vary.

Dalrymple (1995) and Schopler et al. (1995) recommended several cues to help students determine completion. These cues include:

1. using timers to indicate a time standard;
2. specifying the amount to be completed by using a counter, a card with a certain number of circles to be filled (e.g., one circle is filled in after each task or step is completed), a checkoff strategy to check off steps in a task, or completing the exact number of tasks set out;
3. setting cues for completion such as the end of a song means put materials away, a teacher signal to indicate time to put away lunch items, or a teacher putting materials away as a signal for lesson completion;
4. using finished boxes that indicate completion of an activity or an activity step; and
5. using peer models (e.g., when a certain student puts his tray away, then lunch is finished).

Figure 5.7 shows some sample "finished" indicators.

Finishing tasks can become a cue for changing tasks or transitioning. If actual task completion does not initially cue students to transition, auditory cues (e.g., bells, music) might help signal the time to change activities. For students who are first learning transition routines or procedures, teachers might provide them with an object related to the next task (e.g., a pencil indicating it is time for academic instruction) to signal when it is time to move to the next activity. The student can carry the object to the appropriate place and in this way be able to transition with less prompting from the teacher.

It might also be useful to teach students the routine that work always precedes free time and attending always precedes work. By requiring task responses before awarding "play" time, the student not only learns to work for longer periods of time but also makes play contingent on work, thus enhancing the motivation to participate in instructional tasks because the routine dictates that free time will follow. Asking the student for attention (e.g., "Look at me," "Pay attention," "Time to work") signals that work is to follow (which then leads to play time). Thus, promoting routines and establishing procedures has the added benefit of activities cueing (e.g., acting as S^Ds for) subsequent activities. For example, toileting may always precede lunch and snack times. After each instance of toileting, the student will learn quickly to wash his hands and make preparations for either snack or lunch. By following this routine every time, the student is better able to predict what activity comes next and perform independently.

Students with autism will not typically do well if procedures or routines are suddenly changed because they have memorized what to do next. In cases where procedures or routines must change, students should be prepared well ahead of time, for example, with pictures of what will be happening, pictures with an "X" marked through the cancelled activity, or by role-playing behavioral expectations for the new routine. New routines or procedures demand much repetition, effective prompting, visual cueing, and advanced warning.

5-4b Establishing Schedules

To assist with consistent teaching routines (the adults will be less adept at this than the students), we recommend that teachers develop detailed schedules. The two types of schedules generally used are **whole-class schedules** and **individual activity schedules**. The first is for the benefit of teachers and others working with the students, whereas the latter is for student use.

Whole-Class Schedules

A *whole-class schedule* is developed with several things in mind:

1. length of teaching sessions (10–20 minutes for young children; longer for older students, eventually approximating actual competitive employment expectations);
2. assignment of personnel (including teaching assistants, speech therapists, peer tutors, other related service personnel);
3. recess, lunch, snack, and toileting breaks;
4. number of students scheduled with each staff member (one-to-one or grouping);
5. students' specific scheduling needs (e.g., functioning level, IEP goals, learning preferences); and
6. out-of-class activities (inclusion or community-based activities or both).

Preparing a class schedule is a complex and necessary task. Start by filling in the "givens" in various time slots such as lunch time and arrival and departure times. For young children, class schedules are usually developed around half-hour blocks. This allows for transition time and as much as 20–25 minutes of work time in each instructional session. Of course, students can be given breaks during these blocks if necessary, but one curriculum area is usually designated for each time block. For older students, the time blocks may last longer, even as long as 50–60 minutes.

Note that during a given time block (e.g., 9–9:30), one student could be working on communication, three could be receiving instruction in self-help skills, two could be working on motor skills, and the rest could be learning appropriate leisure time activities. A time block does not necessarily dictate that all students in the class work on the same curricular objective (remember instruction is individualized), but it does imply an established routine for each student.

The scheduling of snacks and toileting at specified times each day is important. For students who are not toilet trained, toileting should happen frequently as a designated curricular goal (see Chapter 8). When establishing a class schedule, consider whether students can work in a group or whether they need one-on-one instruction for some skills and whether those who can work in a group need to master similar tasks. This part is tricky and is also related to the number of adults available to work with students.

Group students when it is appropriate to do so. In some situations, the students may be grouped, but each given a different task and instruction while the others engage in guided practice. In other instances, students may be grouped and all taught the same thing (e.g., imitation or choral responding).

For those students needing one-to-one instruction, consider the classroom space while scheduling so that they are not competing with other activities taking place in the classroom. If self-help skills necessitate the use of the restroom or the kitchen, avoid scheduling too many individuals in a one area at the same time.

In addition, consider when individual students work best. If most students begin getting restless at 11 A.M. each day, schedule exercise or physical activities during that time. If some students respond best in the early morning, schedule communication training and socialization instruction for them during that time.

Finally, consider inclusion or community activities specified in students' IEPs. Inclusion in general education classrooms will also require consideration of supports to be provided for the student during that time (usually specified in the IEPs). Community-based instruction activities may require monitoring from a job coach or the teacher.

Figure 5.8 provides two sample classroom schedules, one arranged by teaching adult and one by student. Remember that schedules must be developed based on individual student needs and abilities and available resources. Each classroom schedule will differ.

Individual Activity Schedules

Providing students with visual activity schedules is a widely used technique for helping students with autism understand expectations and function more independently, predict ensuing events, make choices, anticipate changes, learn self-management, and reduce challenging behavior (Dalrymple, 1995; Heflin & Simpson, 1998; Machalicek et al., 2009; McClannahan & Krantz, 2010; Nelson, 2014; National Autism Center [NAC], 2009, 2015; Schopler et al., 1995; Spriggs, Gast, & Ayres, 2007). As with the "to do" list that most of us keep, a visual activity schedule provides a way for students to understand what they are expected to do during a designated time period, determine the order in which it should be done, and recognize when individual tasks are completed and how much is left to do.

Individual activity schedules can use concrete objects or parts of objects (actual size or miniature), pictures (photos, three-dimensional drawings, line drawings), written words, videos, or digital images. Each student's schedule can be kept in a cubby box, fastened to a strip on the wall, on a calendar, on cards filed in a box, in a folder, in a notebook, on a hand-held device, or some other variation. The important thing is that the student be taught to use the schedule to determine what she is to do next or *not* to do next.

Schopler et al. (1995) recommended several issues to consider when choosing a schedule system for each student, such as determining:

1. whether the student can match objects, pictures, or words;
2. whether the student can read for comprehension;
3. whether the student can follow a sequence of activities using visual cues;
4. the student's level of distractibility;
5. the best way to make the system portable; and
6. how the student can indicate that a task or activity has been completed.

Teacher: Kay   **Assistants:** Debbie, Jan, Gloria

TIME	KAY	DEBBIE	JAN	GLORIA	OTHER
8:00–8:30	Morning prep. Planning/charting	Morning prep.	Morning prep.	Morning prep.	
8:30–9:00	Child 3: Receptive lang.	Child 6, 7: Fine motor Socialization	Child 1, 4: Self-help	Child 2, 5: Imitation	Child 8: Speech therapy
9:00–9:30	Child 6, 7: Independent matching	Child 1, 3, 4: Self-help	Child 8: Receptive lang. Cognitive	Child 2: Fine motor	Child 5: Speech therapy
9:30–10:00	Child 1, 2, 5: Independent cognitive	Child 4, 8: Leisure time skills	Child 3: Imitation	Child 6, 7: Self-help	
10:00–10:30	Child 1, 2, 3, 5, 6, 7: Group language and socialization			Child 4, 8: Gen. ed. art.	
10:30–11:00	Conference w/ parents/staff	Child 1, 2, 3, 4, 5, 6, 7, 8: Outside break and toileting			
11:00–11:30	Child 1, 3: Expressive lang.	Child 8: Independent/ matching	Child 4: Fine motor	Child 2, 5: Self-help	Child: 6, 7: Speech therapy
11:30–12:00	Child 1, 2, 3, 4, 5, 6, 7: Leisure time activities				Child 8: Music
12:00–12:15	Lunch preparation, self-help: toilet, wash hands, comb hair				
12:15–1:45	Lunch supervision		Break	Break	
1:45–2:15	Child 1, 2, 3, 4: Kitchen		Child 5, 6, 7, 8: Laundry		
2:15–2:45	Child 4: Expressive lang.	Break	Child 1, 2, 3: Laundry	Child 5, 7: Kitchen	Child 6, 8: Games with peer tutors
2:45–3:00	Preparation for leaving: Toileting, wash hands, comb hair, put away materials				

(a) Organized by teaching adults

FIGURE 5.8 Sample classroom schedule organized by (a) teaching adults and (b) child

TIME	CHILD 1	CHILD 2	CHILD 3	CHILD 4	CHILD 5	CHILD 6	CHILD 7	CHILD 8
8:30–9:00	Self-help	Imitation	Receptive lang.	Self-help	Imitation	Fine motor Socialization	Fine motor Socialization	Speech therapy
9:00–9:30	Self-help	Fine motor	Self-help	Self-help	Speech therapy	Independent matching	Independent matching	Receptive lang. Cognitive
9:30–10:00	Independent cognitive	Independent cognitive	Imitation	Leisure time skills	Independent cognitive	Self-help	Self-help	Leisure time skills
10:00–10:30	Group language and socialization	Group language and socialization	Group language and socialization	Gen. ed. art.	Group language and socialization	Group language and socialization	Group language and socialization	Gen. ed. art.
10:30–11:00	Outside break and toileting							
11:00–11:30	Expressive lang.	Self-help	Expressive lang.	Fine motor	Self-help	Speech therapy	Speech therapy	Independent/ matching
11:30–12:00	Leisure time activities							Music
12:00–12:15	Self-help: toilet, wash hands, comb hair							
12:15–1:45	Lunch							
1:45–2:15	Kitchen				Laundry			
2:15–2:45	Laundry	Laundry	Laundry	Expressive lang.	Kitchen	Games with peer tutors	Kitchen	Games with peer tutors
2:45–3:00	Preparation for leaving: Toileting, wash hands, comb hair, put away materials							

☐ Kay		☐ Jan		☐ Group		
☐ Debbie		☐ Gloria		☐ Other		

(b) Organized by child

FIGURE 5.8 Sample classroom schedule organized by (a) teaching adults and (b) child (*continued*)

Generally, teachers should use concrete objects on the schedule for students with low cognitive ability (e.g., a soap bar to indicate time to wash hands), parts of objects (a piece of a milk carton to indicate lunch time), or miniature objects (e.g., a dollhouse toilet for restroom time) to signal an activity. For students who have matching skills, use photos, three-dimensional pictures, or line drawings for the schedules. Concrete objects are usually kept in single or multiple cubby boxes or attached to strips of Velcro. The student is prompted to pick the first object (one at the top, or in the top cubby) and carry it to the appropriate area or activity where objects indicating steps in that activity are arranged left to right. After the activity is completed, the activity object is placed in a finished box, and the next activity object is retrieved. Figure 5.9 shows concrete object schedules on Velcro backings.

The same process is taught for a picture schedule. Pictures, such as those provided by the Boardmaker tool from Mayer-Johnson, may be fastened to a ribbon or strip of paper on the wall. The student can take the picture (usually with the top-most picture indicating the

Concrete object activity schedule
on Velcro backed by cardboard
(Calendar time, PE, vocational:
crushing cans, lunch)

Plywood backed Velcro activity schedule
with pictures and concrete objects.
Collating (folded paper), toileting (toilet
paper), art (paintbrush), can crushing
(can), lunch (spoon), newspaper sorting
(news clipping), leisure time (audio tape),
cooking (spoon), transition (backpack),
bus

FIGURE 5.9 Sample concrete object schedules

first activity to be completed) to the designated area or activity and then place it in a finished box on completion. Eventually, the student can work from a laminated picture strip without Velcro, simply looking to see what the next activity will be, marking an X through the picture when the activity is finished, and moving to the next picture (either top–down for the next scheduled activity or left–right for steps within an activity). Mobile electronic devices may be particularly useful for providing visual guidance because they allow the student access to the guides in various settings (Nelson, 2014). Similarly, picture or printed schedules can be kept in binders or specialized wallets to allow for more portability and generalization.

Eventually, students can be taught to match written words to tasks or activities, people, and destinations. Start with single words to indicate the next task or activity (e.g., "toilet" to indicate restroom activities) and move to phrases if the student learns to read and comprehend. Again, the student will need to be taught to cross off, place "finished" indicators on the tasks, or close a screen as they are completed.

Visual schedules not only can assist students through classroom procedures but also can guide students through each step of an activity. For example, a recipe may be shown with pictures arranged left to right rather than written in its standard form. Alternatively, turning on an iPad, for example, clicking on the appropriate icon, completing a search or an activity, and returning the iPad to the shelf on completion can be communicated through left-to-right picture sequences.

In addition, pictures on a monthly calendar can indicate future events. For example, a picture of the zoo can be pasted onto the calendar on the day that the zoo trip is to occur. Students can mark off each day approaching the trip so that they can better understand when it is to occur. Similarly, if something is canceled, pictures can be used to communicate the cancellation. By marking an "X" through the picture of the zoo because the field trip was canceled because of weather and placing a picture of a movie screen (or some other alternative activity) above it, a teacher can visually indicate the change and better prepare her students for it.

Pictures or written lists can also be used if the student is to be given a choice about the schedule. For example, leisure time might be scheduled for the 2–2:30 P.M. time slot. At the start of that period, the student is given a "list" of five pictures indicating choices for a leisure time activity. The student can choose any one of the pictures and match it to the given activity.

The schedule may also include destination pictures or words. For example, the student takes the picture of the gym or the library with him to that destination. This may prevent the student from forgetting where he is to go and enable him to become independent in this task.

Figure 5.10 provides samples of visual activity schedules. Using visual strategies as a way to communicate for students who are nonverbal will be covered in Chapter 6.

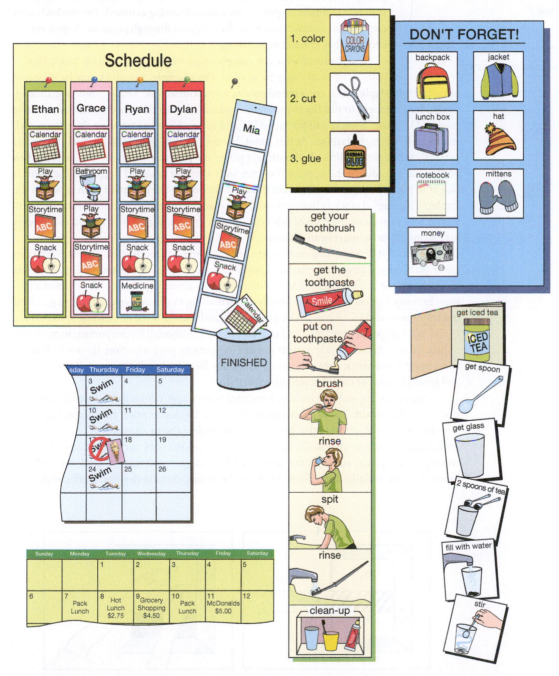

FIGURE 5.10 Sample visual schedules
(From *Visual strategies for improving communication*, by L. A. Hodgdon, 1995, pp. 32, 47, 80, 81, 83. Troy, MI: QuirkRoberts Publishing. Copyright 1995 by QuirkRoberts Publishing PO Box 71, Troy, MI 48099-0071. Reprinted with permission.)

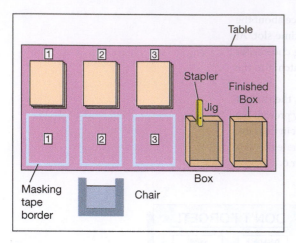

FIGURE 5.11 Sample structured workstation

5-5 Structuring through Materials

Related to physical organization, procedures, routines, and visual activity schedules is the notion of *learning* or *work systems* (e.g., Schopler et al., 1995). In this case, a self-contained system of activities or tasks is developed to provide guided or independent practice for particular skills (e.g., matching, fine motor skills, basic academics). The work system (e.g., set up at a desk or contained in a box) informs the student what he is to be doing (objective) and provides cues for what tasks are to be completed, how much work he is to do, when he is finished, and what happens after task completion. For students who can read, the system may be a box of materials with written instructions (similar to general education learning centers). For students who cannot read, instructions typically are given through pictures, shapes, colors, and alphabet or number matching.

For students who are completing complex and difficult tasks, **jigs** or **assistive devices** may be needed. For example, a student may be expected to collate and staple office correspondence as a vocational task. Using number matching, the student is taught to put the paper stack marked "1" onto the taped square of the table marked "1," stack "2" on top of the taped "2," and so on, as well as take one sheet from each stack in a left-to-right fashion. At this point, because straightening and holding the papers correctly for stapling is difficult, the student places the papers in an empty copier-paper box lid that has a cutout in the upper left corner with a stapler attached (a *jig*). The student is taught to place the papers as they were gathered, face up, in the jig and to push down on the stapler. The stapled stack is then removed and placed in the finished box to the far right. Figure 5.11 provides a diagram of this type of work system. Figure 5.12 shows a sample jig for folding paper to insert in an envelope.

The concept of organizing materials to prompt correct responses is not new. Most first-grade teachers use large multiple-lined paper to encourage correct handwriting. Teachers use highlighting and underlining to facilitate students attending to relevant points in a passage. In many aspects of our lives, we rely on formatting to get us through tasks (e.g., filling out tax returns and IEP forms). The purpose of establishing work or learning systems is to encourage independent practice and task completion. Although it is important to gradually reduce the number of visual prompts needed to promote generalization, do not hesitate to add physical and visual organization as necessary for errorless learning and maintenance and generalization of complex activities and tasks.

In the preceding sections we have presented several instructional strategies for use with students with autism. These strategies are based on the assumption that providing structure and order will enhance the likelihood that students with autism will respond to the environment and learn new skills. Table 5.9 summarizes many of our suggestions. Structure correspondingly increases with the number of these suggestions that are implemented. Use more structure initially, then move to natural classroom, community, and work conditions.

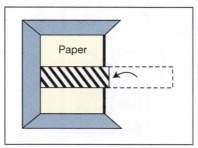

Flip over flap to hold paper while
folding a letter

Folding box

FIGURE 5.12 Sample jig

TABLE 5.9 ● Suggestions for Providing Structure in Learning Situations

PHYSICAL ARRANGEMENT

- Match the curriculum to the physical arrangement.
- Use visually clear boundaries.
- Make relevant stimuli salient (use color, shape, and so on, matching).
- Arrange for group or one-to-one instruction (or both).
- Mask interfering stimuli (auditory and visual).
- Arrange to prevent problem behaviors.
- Arrange convenient materials access and storage.
- Arrange to facilitate toileting.
- Include a transition area and "wait" chairs (e.g., a chair for each student to sit while waiting in a transition area such as at the door of the classroom).
- Maximize comfort (size, lighting, temperature, traffic flow).
- Avoid rearranging the classroom once students have learned the organizational systems.

ROUTINES OR PROCEDURES AND SCHEDULES

- Establish routines or procedures for entering and leaving the classroom.
- Establish routines for choosing activities.
- Establish routines for starting and completing activities.
- Establish routines for waiting.
- Establish routines for predicting times to work and play.
- Establish routines or procedures for toileting and eating.
- Establish routines or procedures for changing activities and other transitions.
- Establish a classroom schedule.
- Establish individual visual schedules and activity sequences.

STRUCTURED LESSONS

- Use direct instruction (di and DI) for teaching tool subjects, academic content, and social skills.
- Use discrete trial teaching (DTT) to instruct multiple skill acquisition and fluency.
- Use milieu teaching (MT) for instructing language and social communication skills in generalized settings.
- Use generalization training to promote maintenance and generalization of acquired skills.
- Provide prompts during instruction and systematically fade them to obtain stimulus control.
- Keep students engaged in learning activities at least 80 percent of the school day.
- Utilize group instruction as students are able to adequately progress in the curriculum as part of a group.
- Collect and graph student response data.
- Regularly evaluate learner progress.
- Construct detailed lesson plans.
- Store and maintain progress records and notebooks.
- Engage in self-evaluation.

5-6 Plans and Reports

Essential to ABA programming are planning and accountability. Once a teacher has made decisions about what to teach and how to teach it, the next step is to develop a written plan.

Typical lesson plans in general education classrooms consist of a few notes about which activities students are to perform that day. However, when teaching students with autism, extreme care should be taken to specify each piece of the instructional format (i.e., components of the ABA procedure).

Lesson plans should generally include:

1. the goal or objective (or both),
2. specific information about the conditions for responding (e.g., which S^D will be presented, which setting, which prompt system),
3. types of reinforcers and the reinforcement schedule,
4. mastery criteria (include baseline information), and
5. evaluation methods (e.g., probe technique, recording technique).

For example, Figure 5.13 illustrates a DTT lesson plan, which includes quite a bit of detail about each DTT step. The lesson plan indicates that Hector is to master pointing to a picture of a bus when the teacher gives the S^D "Point to bus." Included on this lesson plan form are the dates for skill introduction and mastery, the procedures for gathering a baseline count and for probing for mastery, the prompt system and steps for fading the prompts, the reinforcement schedule and the type of reinforcer, the mastery criteria (as well as the criteria for failure), and the data-recording strategy.

Detailed lesson plans enhance communication across trainers and better ensure **fidelity of implementation** (i.e., consistency and accuracy of teaching procedures). For students who master objectives at a quick pace, lesson plans can eliminate such detail, perhaps in-

Discrete trial training lesson plan

Student: Hector

Date Introduced: 4/19

Date Mastered:

Baseline Procedures: Present S^D "Point to" 3 times (bus). Calculate percentage of correct responses.

Probing Procedures: Present S^D "Point to" without prompt after every step of prompt fading procedure. Change position of target picture after every other trial.

Criterion	Data Recording Method
Mastery: 9 out of 10 trials correct for 3 consecutive sessions.	Trial-by-trial: X = correct O = incorrect
Fail: 3 consecutive incorrect responses.	XP = correct prompted OP= incorrect prompted

TARGET BEHAVIOR	STEP	S^D	CORRECT RESPONSE	CONSEQUENCES & SCHEDULES
Within 5 secs. of the presentation of S^D "Point to," Hector will point to the picture verbalized by the teacher (bus).	1.	Teacher places two pictures on table (train and bus) and says "point to bus."		
	a.	*Prompt:* Physically take Hector's hand and point to correct picture.	Hector points to the bus.	Correct: "Good job!" plus primary (popcorn, soda, pieces of cereal, etc.) 100%
	b.	*Prompt:* Wait to see if Hector makes move to point, then provide light taps to arm until he points to picture.	Same as above	Same as above
	c.	*Prompt:* Wait to see if Hector makes move to point, then teacher gestures toward pictures on table.	Same as above	Same as above
	d.	No prompt	Same as above	Same as above

FIGURE 5.13 Discrete trial training lesson plan
(Adapted from *Teaching makes a difference: A guide for developing successful classes for autistic and other severely handicapped children,* by A. Donnellan, L. D. Gossage, G. W. LaVigna, A. Schuler, & J. D. Traphagen, 1976, p. 56. Santa Barbara, CA: Santa Barbara Public Schools. Copyright 1976 Santa Barbara Public Schools. Adapted by permission.)

⌄ Professional Resource Download

cluding only the target goal and objective, related teaching activities, mastery criteria, special considerations, and progress-monitoring data. Regardless of the format used, providing specific information about antecedents, expected responses, and types of consequences will most likely enhance instruction and improve accountability.

Accountability (i.e., whether a student is learning what is being taught) is specifically provided through progress-monitoring procedures such as data collection and graphing. Unfortunately, many teachers gather data relative to student progress but never present those data in a way that others can understand and evaluate. Some teachers may not systematically assess progress at all. Progress monitoring is a key component of effective instruction and ABA and should be incorporated into the daily instructional routine.

We have recommended various methods for gathering data during instruction and for graphing the results. To facilitate this type of record keeping, we also recommend that assessment information, lesson plans, and graphs be maintained (archived) in a notebook for each student.

The first section of this notebook, entitled "Comprehensive Assessment," might contain all initial assessment information pertinent to what is to be taught (e.g., curriculum-based assessments, ecological inventories, adaptive behavior checklists). Designated sections for each curricular area can follow (e.g., language, basic academics, self-help, leisure, social skills, prevocational skills).

In each of these curricular sections are the lesson plan(s) for target skills, a graph depicting baseline performance and progress toward mastery, and any additional work samples, practice activities, or assessment information.

A final section might be labeled "Challenging Behavior." In this section, include a description of the targeted behaviors, the functional assessment results and analysis, a behavior intervention plan, and baseline and intervention graphs. This section might also include a list of effective reinforcers and notes about special considerations (e.g., medication side-effects).

Figure 5.14 provides a drawing of sample content in a notebook. Keeping such precise information about skill attainment promotes effective communication, collaboration, and accountability.

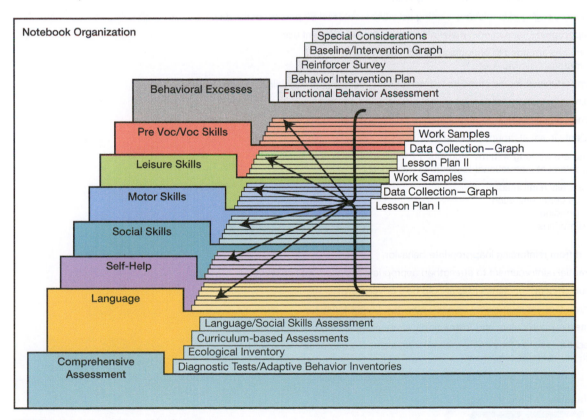

FIGURE 5.14 Sample notebook content

5-6a Evaluating Teaching Strategies

In Chapters 2 through 5, we have suggested various ways for teachers to develop curriculum and instruct students. Good teachers master a variety of techniques and strategies, formulating a "toolbox" from which to choose what is best for an individual student at any given instructional point. This toolbox includes curriculum decisions and pedagogical applications for managing student behavior, delivering instruction, and structuring the classroom environment. It also includes progress-monitoring methods so that teachers know whether to use different tools in the future.

We encourage teachers to regularly evaluate themselves in terms of their proficiency and consistency in using these best teaching practices. We have provided a teacher self-monitoring form (Figure 5.15) to facilitate this self-evaluation process. This form can be adapted to include additional instructional strategies and procedures. We recommend that teachers rate themselves and paraprofessionals working in their classroom for a few days each month to ensure that all aspects of effective instruction are regularly applied. If teacher behavior reflects best practices, then students are more likely to continue to learn and master necessary skills.

Place a check beside the behavior that was performed each day. Decide whether you are teaching what the students need to learn and whether you are using effective instructional strategies.

TEACHER BEHAVIOR	DAYS				
	M	T	W	TH	F
1. I/we taught my students only skills and content, which are relevant to each one's short-term, intermediate, and long-term objectives.					
2. I/we taught language skills at every possible opportunity with Milieu Teaching throughout the day.					
3. I/we targeted skills that will likely result in reinforcement for the students.					
4. I/we prompted effectively and only when necessary, encouraging independence whenever possible.					
5. I/we taught in generalized settings whenever possible.					
6. My students were engaged in relevant learning activities for at least 80 percent of the day.					
7. I used age-appropriate instructional materials adapted for independent use.					
8. My classroom was arranged to encourage independent functioning (schedules, materials available, etc.).					
9. I provided opportunities for my students to interact with peers without disabilities.					
10. I provided direct instruction for academic tool subjects and content when appropriate.					
11. I provided one-to-one Discrete Trial Training for skill acquisition and fluency.					
12. I taught students in small groups when appropriate.					
13. All adults who are working with my students are familiar with the objectives and administer implement instructional techniques with fidelity.					
14. I/we systematically reinforced: —spontaneous communication —correct responding —following directions —other:					
15. I/we refrained from reinforcing inappropriate behavior.					
16. I used differential reinforcement to strengthen appropriate replacement behaviors.					
17. I/we used punishment ____ times (this should be 0 or very low).					
18. I collected data (correct responses) on each objective taught today for ____ students.					
19. I have adjusted my curriculum and instructional strategies for tomorrow as necessary.					
20. I have shared the results of my day's evaluation/assessment with people who will be working with my students tomorrow. OTHER:					

FIGURE 5.15 Teacher self-monitoring checklist

Professional Resource Download

Summary

In this chapter, we have provided descriptions of a variety of strategies that might be used to teach students with autism. These students learn best under structured, predictable conditions promoted by highly structured lesson presentations, often in intensive one-to-one formats, with predictable physical arrangements used to cue learning behaviors and compliance. Teachers can develop S^Ds for appropriate learning and behaving with the use of visual supports, schedules and routines, and teaching materials. It is important that effective instruction include regular data collection and evaluation. High structure and intensive instruction will facilitate skill acquisition and fluency. Lower structure can be applied for skill maintenance. Generalization is enhanced by various structured applications that are "loosened" over time.

Chapters 6, 7, and 8 will provide information about curriculum and instructional strategies pertaining specifically to communication, social competence, and life skills. It is our opinion that teaching students with autism demands a great deal of technical knowledge and diligent attention. We encourage teachers to seek more specific instruction in ABA principles and instructional applications, as presented in this chapter, particular to students with autism and to evaluate their own practices and their students' progress on a regular basis. Self-evaluation and a willingness to alter one's own behavior to improve student learning can lead to master teaching. We hope all students with autism encounter master teachers throughout their school careers.

Key Points

1. Because of the nature of autism, students with this disorder are best taught with intensive instruction in highly structured, predictable environments.

2. Instructional formats based in ABA such as direct instruction, discrete trial training, and milieu teaching provide the necessary intensity and structure.

3. Direct instruction (di and DI) should be used for academic instruction, in small or large groups. DI is often also presented in one-to-one formats.

4. Discrete trial teaching (DTT) might be most effective for teaching various skills at the acquisition and fluency levels, usually in one-to-one formats.

5. Milieu teaching (MT) is a method of teaching that better promotes generalization and spontaneous responding in language and social communication.

6. Generalization is a problem for students with autism. Teachers need to plan and use specific strategies to facilitate generalization.

7. Progress monitoring is an important component of ABA and effective instruction. Data regarding student progress can be collected and graphed in various ways.

8. Careful physical arrangement of the classroom is one way to provide cues for expected student behavior. Arrangements should match the curriculum, prevent unwanted behavior, and provide for comfort and safety.

9. One of the most important ways to add structure to a classroom is through routines and schedules. Schedules can be for the entire class or for individuals. Individual activity schedules guide student behavior and results in self-management.

10. Visual cues can effectively prompt students who may not readily attend to auditory stimuli. Visual supports are used in various ways to enhance instruction.

11. Materials can be constructed to communicate expectations and assist students with independent practice and task completion.

12. Planning instruction and compiling instructional information for each student are important teaching functions.

13. Teacher self-evaluation is encouraged because instructing students with autism demands a wide variety of technical expertise.

References

Adams, G. L., & Engelmann, S. (1996). *Research on Direct Instruction: 25 years beyond DISTAR*. Seattle: Educational Achievement Systems.

Alberto, P. A., and Troutman, A. C. (1999). *Applied behavior analysis for teachers*. Columbus, OH: Merrill.

Alberto, P. A., & Troutman, A. C. (2017). *Applied behavior analysis for teachers* (9th ed.). Columbus, OH: Pearson.

Allen, K. D., & Cowan, R. J. (2008). Naturalistic teaching procedures. In J. K. Luiselli, D. C. Russo, W. P. Christian, & S. M. Wilcyznski (Eds.), *Effective practices for children with autism: Educational and behavior support interventions that work* (pp. 213–240). New York: Oxford University Press.

American Psychiatric Association (APA). (2013). *Diagnostic and statistical manual of mental disorders: DSM-5* (5th ed.). Washington, DC: American Psychiatric Association.

Archer, A. L., & Hughes, C. A. (2011). *Explicit instruction: Effective and efficient teaching*. New York: Guilford Press.

Bechtolt, S., McLaughlin, T. F., Derby, K. M., & Blecher, J. (2014). The effects of Direct Instruction flashcards and a model, lead, test procedure on letter recognition for three preschool students with developmental disabilities. *Journal on Developmental Disabilities, 20*(1), 5–15.

Benavides, C. A., & Poulson, C. L. (2009). Task interspersal and performance of matching tasks by preschoolers with autism. *Research in Autism Spectrum Disorders, 3*, 619–629.

Çelik, S., & Vuran, S. (2014). Comparison of direct instruction and simultaneous prompting procedure on teaching concepts to individuals with intellectual disability. *Education and Training in Autism and Developmental Disabilities, 49*(1), 127–144.

Chan, J. M., Lang, R., Rispoli, M., O'Reilly, M., Sigafoos, J., & Cole, H. (2009). Use of peer-mediated interventions in the treatment of autism spectrum disorders: A systematic review. *Research in Autism Spectrum Disorders, 3*, 876–889.

Dalrymple, N. J. (1995). Environmental supports to develop flexibility and independence. In K. A. Quill (Ed.), *Teaching children with autism: Strategies to enhance communication and socialization*. New York: Delmar/Cengage Learning.

Delprato, D. J. (2001). Comparisons of discrete-trial and normalized behavioral language intervention for young children with autism. *Journal of Autism and Developmental Disorders, 31*, 315–325.

Dib, M., & Sturmey, P. (2007). Reducing student stereotypy by improving teachers' implementation of discrete-trial teaching. *Journal of Applied Behavior Analysis, 40*, 339–343.

Donnellan, A., Gossage, L. D., LaVigna, G. W., Schuler, A., & Traphagen, J. D. (1976). *Teaching makes a difference: A guide for developing successful classes for autistic and other severely handicapped children*. Santa Barbara, CA: Santa Barbara Public Schools.

Engelmann, S., & Carnine, D. (2003). *Connecting math concepts, level A (teacher's presentation book, student material, and teacher's guide)*. Columbus, OH: SRA/McGraw-Hill.

Engelmann, S., & Colvin, G. (2006). Rubric for identifying authentic Direct Instruction programs. Retrieved February 23, 2017 from http://www.zigsite.com/PDFs/rubric.pdf

Engelmann, S., & Hanner, S. (2008). *Reading mastery® reading strand, level 1 (signature ed.) (teacher's presentation book, student material literature guide and teacher's guide)*. Columbus, OH: SRA/McGraw-Hill.

Engelmann, S., & Osborn, J. (1998). *Language for learning (teacher's presentation book, student material, and teacher's guide)*. Columbus, OH: SRA/McGraw-Hill.

Finnegan, E., & Mazin, A. L. (2016). Strategies for increasing reading comprehension skills in students with autism spectrum disorder: A review of the literature. *Education and Treatment of Children, 39*(2), 187–219.

Flores, M. M., & Ganz, J. B. (2007). Effectiveness of Direct Instruction for teaching statement inference, use of facts, and analogies to students with developmental disabilities and reading delays. *Focus on Autism and Other Developmental Disabilities, 22*, 244–251.

Flores, M. M., Nelson, C., Hinton, V., Franklin, T. M., Strozier, S. D., Terry, L., & Franklin, S. (2013). Teaching reading comprehension and language skills to students with autism spectrum disorders and developmental disabilities using Direct Instruction. *Education and Training in Autism and Developmental Disabilities, 48*(1), 41–48.

Gaines, K. S., Curry, Z., Shroyer, J., Amor, C., & Lock, R. H. (2014). The perceived effects of visual design and features on students with autism spectrum disorder. *Journal of Architectural and Planning Research, 31*(4), 282–298.

Ganz, J. B., & Flores, M. M. (2009). The effectiveness of Direct Instruction for teaching language to children with autism spectrum disorders: Identifying materials. *Journal of Autism and Developmental Disorders, 39*, 75–83.

Gersten, R. (1985). Direct instruction with special education students: A review of evaluation research. *Journal of Special Education, 19*, 41–58.

Granpeesheh, D., Tarbox, J., & Dixon, D. R. (2009). Applied behavior analytic interventions for children with autism: A description and review of treatment research. *Annals of Clinical Psychiatry, 21*, 162–173.

Grindle, C. F., Hughes, J. C., Saville, M., Huxley, K., & Hastings, R. P. (2013). Teaching early reading skills to children with autism using MimioSprout Early Reading. *Behavioral Interventions, 28*, 203–224.

Hancock, T. B., & Kaiser, A. P. (2002). The effects of trainer-implemented enhanced milieu teaching on the social communication of children with autism. *Topics in Early Childhood Special Education, 22*, 39–54.

Hancock, T. B., Ledbetter-Cho, K., Howell, A., & Lang, R. (2016). Enhanced Milieu Teaching. In R. Lang, T. B. Hancock, & N. N. Singh (Eds.), *Early intervention for young children with autism spectrum disorder* (pp. 177–218). New York: Springer.

Harris, A. (2016). Visual supports for students with autism. Johns-Hopkins School of Education. Retrieved March 10, 2017 from http://www.education.jhu.edu/pd/newhorizons/journals/specialedjournal/harris

Hart, B., & Risley, T. R. (1975). Incidental teaching of language in the preschool. *Journal of Applied Behavior Analysis, 8*, 411–420.

Hecht, J. Jr. (2016). Supporting special education teachers and increasing student achievement within the Valley School District. *Dissertation Abstracts International Section A: Humanities and Social Sciences, 77*, (4-A), (E).

Heflin, L. J., & Simpson, R. L. (1998). Interventions for children and youth with autism: Prudent choices in a world of exaggerated claims and empty promises. Part I: Intervention and treatment option review. *Focus on Autism and Other Developmental Disabilities, 13*(4), 194–211.

Howard, J. S., Sparkman, C. R., Cohen, H. G., Green, G., & Stanislaw, H. (2005). A comparison of intensive behavior analytic and eclectic treatments for young children with autism. *Research in Developmental Disabilities, 26*, 359–383.

Ingersoll, B. R. (2010). Teaching social communication: A comparison of naturalistic behavioral and development, social pragmatic approaches for children with autism spectrum disorders. *Journal of Positive Behavior Interventions, 12*, 33–43.

Kaiser, A. P. (1993). Functional language. In M. E. Snell (Ed.), *Instruction of students with severe disabilities*. Upper Saddle River, NJ: Prentice-Hall.

Kaiser, A. P., Hancock, T. B., & Nietfeld, J. P. (2000). The effects of parent-implemented enhanced milieu teaching on the social communication of children who have autism. *Early Education and Development, 11*, 423–446.

Kaiser, A. P., Hancock, T. B., & Trent, J. A. (2007). Teaching parents communication strategies. *Early Childhood Services: An Interdisciplinary Journal of Effectiveness, 1*, 107–136.

Kaiser, A. P., & Roberts, M. Y. (2013). Parent-implemented enhanced milieu teaching with preschool children who have intellectual disabilities. *Journal of Speech, Language, and Hearing Research, 56*, 295–309.

Kaiser, A. P., & Trent, J. A. (2007). Communication intervention for young children with disabilities: Naturalistic approaches to promoting development. In S. L. Odom, R. H. Horner, M. E. Snell, & J. Blacher (Eds.), *Handbook of developmental disabilities* (pp. 224–246). New York: Guilford Press.

Kamps, D., Heitzman-Powell, L., Rosenberg, N., Mason, R., Schwartz, I., & Romine, R. S. (2016). Effects of Reading Mastery as a small group intervention for young children with ASD. *Journal of Developmental and Physical Disabilities, 28,* 703–722.

Karsten, A. M., & Carr, J. E. (2009). The effects of differential reinforcement of unprompted responding on the skill acquisition of children with autism. *Journal of Applied Behavior Analysis, 42,* 327–334.

Knight, V. F., Smith, B. R., Spooner, F., & Browder, D. (2012). Using explicit instruction to teach science descriptors to students with autism spectrum disorder. *Journal of Autism and Developmental Disorders, 42,* 378–389.

Koegel, R. L., Koegel, L. K., & Carter, C. M. (1999). Pivotal teaching interactions for children with autism. *School Psychology Review, 28,* 576–594.

Koegel, R. L., O'Dell, M. C., & Koegel, L. K. (1987). A natural language teaching paradigm for nonverbal autistic children. *Journal of Autism and Developmental Disorders, 17,* 187–200.

Koegel, R. L., Openden, D., Fredeen, R. M., & Koegel, L. K. (2006). The basics of pivotal response treatment. In R. L. Koegel & L. K. Koegel (Eds.), *Pivotal response treatments for autism: Communication, social, & academic development* (pp. 3–30). Baltimore: Paul H. Brookes.

Koegel, R. L., & Rincover, A. (1974). Treatment of psychotic children in a classroom environment: Learning in a large group. *Journal of Applied Behavior Analysis, 7,* 45–49.

Lang, R., Machalicek, W., Rispoli, M., & Regester, A. (2009). Training parents to implement communication interventions for children with autism spectrum disorders (ASD): A systematic review. *Evidence-Based Communication Assessment and Intervention, 3,* 174–190.

Leaf, J. B., Leaf, R., Taubman, M., McEachin, J., & Delmolino, L. (2014). Comparison of flexible prompt fading to error correction for children with autism spectrum disorder. *Journal of Developmental and Physical Disabilities, 26,* 203–224.

Leaf, J. B., Tsuji, K. H., Lentell, A. E., Dale, S. E., Kassardjian, A., Taubman, M., . . . Oppenheim-Leaf, M. L. (2013). A comparison of discrete trial teaching in a one-to-one instructional format and in a group instructional format. *Behavioral Interventions, 28,* 82–106.

Leaf, R., & McEachin, J. (1999). *A work in progress: Behavior management strategies and a curriculum for intensive behavioral treatment of autism.* New York: DRL Books.

Ledford, J. R., Lane, J. D., Elam, K. L., & Wolery, M. (2012). Using response-prompting procedures during small-group direct instruction: Outcomes and procedural variations. *American Journal of Intellectual and Developmental Disabilities, 117*(5), 413–434.

Lerman, D. C., Hawkins, L., Hillman, C., Shireman, M., & Nissen, M. A. (2015). Adults with autism spectrum disorder as behavior technicians for young children with autism: Outcomes of a behavior skills training program. *Journal of Applied Behavior Analysis, 48,* 233–256.

Lerman, D. C., Tetreault, A., Hovanetz, A., Strobel, M., & Garro, J. (2008). Further evaluation of a brief, intensive teacher-training model. *Journal of Applied Behavior Analysis, 41,* 243–248.

Lerman, D. C., Valentino, A. L., & LeBlanc, L. A. (2016). Discrete trial training. In R. Lang, T. B. Hancock, & N. N. Singh (Eds.), *Early intervention for young children with autism spectrum disorder.* New York: Springer Publishing

Lifter, K., Ellis, J., Cannon, B., & Anderson, S. R. (2005). Developmental specificity in targeting and teaching play activities to children with pervasive developmental disorders. *Journal of Early Intervention, 27,* 247–267.

Lovaas, O. I. (1987). Behavioral treatment and normal educational and intellectual functioning in young autistic children. *Journal of Consulting and Clinical Psychology, 55,* 3–9.

Lovaas, O. I., Koegel, R., Simmons, J. Q., & Long, J. S. (1973). Some generalization and follow-up measures on autistic children in behavior therapy. *Journal of Applied Behavior Analysis, 6,* 131–166.

Lovaas, O. I., & Smith, T. (1989). A comprehensive behavioral theory of autistic children: Paradigm for research and treatment. *Journal of Behavior Therapy and Experimental Psychiatry, 20,* 17–29.

MacDuff, G. S., Krantz, P. J., & McClannahan, L. E. (2001). Prompts and prompt-fading strategies for people with autism. In C. Maurice, G. Green, & R. M. Foxx (Eds.), *Making a difference: Behavioral intervention for autism* (pp. 37–50). Austin: Pro-Ed.

Machalicek, W., Shrogen, K., Lang, R., Rispoli, M., O'Reily, M. F., Helinger Franco, J., & Sigafoos, J. (2009). Increasing play and decreasing the challenging behavior of children with autism during recess with activity schedules and task correspondence training. *Research in Autism Spectrum Disorders, 3,* 547–555.

Malott, R. W., Whaley, D. C., & Malott, M. E. (1997). *Elementary principles of behavior.* Upper Saddle River, NJ: Prentice-Hall.

Maurice, C., Green, G., & Luce, S. C. (Eds.). (1996). *Behavioral intervention for young children with autism: A manual for parents and professionals.* Austin: Pro-Ed.

Maurice, C., Green, G., & Foxx, R. M. (Eds.). (2001). *Making a difference: Behavioral intervention for autism.* Austin: Pro-Ed.

McAllister, K., & Maguire, B. (2012). Design considerations for the autism spectrum disorder-friendly Key Stage 1 classroom. *Support for Learning, 27*(3), 103–112.

McClannahan, L. E., & Krantz, P. J. (1997). In search of solutions to prompt dependence: Teaching children with autism to use photographic activity schedules. In D. M. Baer & E. M. Pinkston (Eds.), *Environment and behavior* (pp. 271–278). Boulder, CO: Westview.

McClannahan, L. E., & Krantz, P. J. (2010). *Activity schedules for children with autism: Teaching independent behavior* (2nd ed.). Bethesda, MD: Woodbine.

McGee, G. G., Krantz, P. J., Mason, D., & McClannahan, L. E. (1983). A modified incidental-teaching procedure for autistic youth: Acquisition and generalization of receptive object labels. *Journal of Applied Behavior Analysis, 16,* 329–338.

McGee, G. G., Krantz, P. J., & McClannahan, L. E. (1985). The facilitative effects of incidental teaching on preposition use by autistic children. *Journal of Applied Behavior Analysis, 18,* 17–31.

Mertes, E. S. (2014). A mathematics education comparative analysis of ALEKS technology and direct classroom instruction. *Dissertation Abstracts International Section A: Humanities and Social Science, 75,* (5-A), (E).

Miranda-Linné, F., & Melin, L. (1992). Acquisition, generalization, and spontaneous use of color adjectives: A comparison of incidental teaching and traditional discrete-trial procedures for children with autism. *Research in Developmental Disabilities, 13,* 191–210.

Mostafa, M. (2008). An architecture for autism: Concepts of design intervention for the autistic user. *International Journal of Architectural Research, 2*(1), 189–211.

National Autism Center (NAC). (2009). *Findings and conclusions: National standards project.* Randolph, MA: Author.

National Autism Center (NAC). (2015). *Findings and conclusions: National standards project, phase 2.* Randolph, MA: Author.

National Institute for Direct Instruction (NIFDI). (2015a). Basic philosophy of Direct Instruction (DI). Retrieved February 22, 2017 from http://www.nifdi.org/what-is-di/basic-philosophy

National Institute for Direct Instruction (NIFDI). (2015b). Literature reviews. Retrieved February 22, 2017 from http://www.nifdi.org/research/reviews-of-di/literature-reviews

National Institute for Direct Instruction (NIFDI). (2015c). Practicing. Retrieved February 22, 2017 from http://www.nifdi.org/how-to-be-successful/practicing

Nelson, L. L. (2014). Using a mobile device to deliver visual schedules to young children with autism. *Dissertation Abstracts International Section A: Humanities and Social Sciences, 75*(2-A)(E).

Peters-Scheffer, N., Didden, R., Korzilius, H., & Sturmey, P. (2011). A meta-analytic study on the effectiveness of comprehensive ABA-based early intervention programs for children with autism spectrum disorders. *Research in Autism Spectrum Disorders, 5*, 60–69.

Plavnick, J. B., Marchand-Martella, N. E., Martella, R. C., Thompson, J. L., & Wood, A. L. (2015). A review of explicit and systematic scripted instructional programs for students with autism spectrum disorder. *Review Journal of Autism and Developmental Disorders, 2*, 55–66.

Quill, K. A. (Ed.) (1995). *Teaching children with autism: Strategies to enhance communication and socialization.* New York: Delmar/Cengage Learning.

Reid, D. H., & Favell, J. E. (1984). Group instruction with persons who have severe disabilities: A critical review. *Journal of the Association for Persons with Severe Handicaps, 9*(3), 167–177.

Rispoli, M., Neely, L., Lang, R., & Ganz, J. (2011). Training paraprofessionals to implement interventions for people with autism spectrum disorders: A systematic review. *Developmental Neurorehabilitation, 14*(6), 378–388.

Rosenshine, B. V. (1986). Synthesis of research on explicit teaching. *Educational Leadership, 43*, 60–69.

Rosenshine, B., & Stevens, R. (1986). Teaching functions. In M. Wittrock (Ed.), *Handbook of research on teaching* (pp. 376–391). New York: Macmillan.

Rotholz, D. A. (1990). Current considerations on the use of one-to-one instruction with autistic students: Review and recommendations. *Focus on Autistic Behavior, 5*(3), 1–6.

Sallows, G. O., & Graupner, T. D. (2005). Intensive behavioral treatment for children with autism: Four-year outcome and predictors. *American Journal on Mental Retardation, 110*, 417–438.

Schoen, S. F. (1986). Assistance procedures to facilitate the transfer of stimulus control: Review and analysis. *Education and Training of the Mentally Retarded, 21*, 62–74.

Schopler, E., Mesibov, G. B., & Hearsey, K. (1995). Structured teaching in the TEACCH system. In E. Schopler & G. B. Mesibov (Eds.), *Learning and cognition in autism* (pp. 243–268). New York: Plenum Press.

Schreibman, L. (1975). Effects of within-stimulus and extra-stimulus prompting on discrimination learning in autistic children. *Journal of Applied Behavior Analysis, 8*, 91–112.

Spriggs, A. D., Gast, D. L., & Ayres, K. M. (2007). Using picture activity schedule books to increase on-schedule and on-task behaviors. *Education and Training in Developmental Disabilities, 42*, 209–223.

Stokes, T. F., & Baer, D. M. (1977). An implicit technology of generalization. *Journal of Applied Behavior Analysis, 10*, 349–367.

Subramaniam, S., Brunson, L. Y., Cook, J. E., Larson, N. A., Poe, S. G., & St. Peter, C. C. (2017). Maintenance of parent-implemented discrete-trial instruction during videoconferencing. *Journal of Behavioral Education, 26*, 1–26.

Sundberg, M. L., & Partington, J. W. (1998). *Teaching language to children with autism or other developmental disabilities.* Pleasant Hill, CA: Behavior Analysts.

Taubman, M., Brierley, S., Wishner, J., Baker, D., McEachin, J., & Leaf, R. B. (2001). The effectiveness of a group discrete trial instructional approach for preschoolers with developmental disabilities. *Research in Developmental Disabilities, 22*, 205–219.

Thomson, K., Martin, G. L., Arnal, L., Fazzio, D., & Yu, C. T. (2009). Instructing individuals to deliver discrete-trial teaching to children with autism spectrum disorders: A review. *Research in Autism Spectrum Disorders, 3*, 590–606.

Thompson, J. L., Wood, C. L., Test, D. W., & Cease-Cook, J. (2012). Effects of Direct Instruction on telling time by students with autism. *Journal of Direct Instruction, 12*, 1–12.

Watkins, C. L. (2008). From DT to DI: Using Direct Instruction to teach students with ASD. *The ABAI Newsletter, 31*(3), 25–29.

Watkins, C. L., Slocum, T. A., & Spencers, T. D. (2011). Direct Instruction: Relevance and applications to behavioral autism treatment. In E. A. Mayville & J. A. Mulick (Eds.), *Behavioral foundations of effective autism treatment* (pp. 297–319). Cornwall-on-Hudson, NY: Sloan.

Watkins, L., O'Reilly, M., Kuhn, M., Gevarter, C., Lancioni, G. E., Sigafoos, J., & Lang, R. (2015). A review of peer-mediated social interaction interventions for students with autism in inclusive settings. *Journal of Autism and Developmental Disorders, 45*, 1070–1083.

Webber, J., & Scheuermann, B. S. (2008). *Educating students with autism: A quick start manual.* Austin: Pro-Ed.

Westling, D. L., & Fox, L. (2009). *Teaching students with severe disabilities* (4th ed.). Upper Saddle River, NJ: Prentice Hall.

Whitby, P. J. S. (2013). The effects of *Solve It!* on the mathematical word problem solving ability of adolescents with autism spectrum disorders. *Focus on Autism and Other Developmental Disabilities, 28*, 78–88.

Whitcomb, S. A., Bass, J. D., & Luiselli, J. K. (2011). Effects of a computer-based early reading program (Headsprout®) on word list and text reading skills in a student with autism. *Journal of Developmental and Physical Disabilities, 23*, 491–499.

White, W. A. T. (1988). A meta-analysis of the effects of Direct Instruction in special education. *Education and Treatment of Children, 11*, 364–374.

Teaching Communication Skills

6

© Morgan

LEARNING OBJECTIVES

After reading this chapter, you will be able to:

6-1 Define language and communication and differentiate the two.

6-2 Identify the language and communication characteristics associated with autism.

6-3 Describe the components and importance of a comprehensive assessment of language and communication.

6-4 Identify specific approaches to teaching language and communication skills and compare and contrast the components of each.

anguage empowers us to form social relationships, obtain knowledge, and live and work independently. Those who struggle to communicate often experience difficulty making choices, requesting basic wants and needs, and establishing meaningful social relationships. It is not surprising (particularly if you have read Chapter 3) that limitations in the ability to communicate have been linked to challenging behaviors (Durand & Moskowitz, 2015). Although many children learn language through typical interactions in their natural environments (e.g., playing with parents and siblings at home), children with autism are more likely to need systematic and comprehensive language instruction within responsive and supportive natural environments (e.g., Hampton & Kaiser, 2016). Indeed, for teachers of students with autism, often the most valuable use of time and effort is teaching effective communication.

6-1 Defining Language and Communication

Language can be defined as the use of arbitrary symbols, with accepted referents, that can be arranged in different sequences to convey different meanings (Lefrançois, 2001). For the majority of children, language development occurs in a relatively predictable sequence and time frame. For example, most children first learn to babble, then produce single word approximations (e.g., "da" for daddy), and finally produce complete words and sentences. Most children will learn to make requests (e.g., ask for a snack) before they learn to comment, answer questions, or label objects.

Typical language-development sequences are important to teachers for several reasons. First, skill acquisition is often more efficient when targeted skills are developmentally appropriate for the child (e.g., Lifter, Ellis, Cannon, & Anderson, 2005; Vygotsky, 1962). In other words, selecting target language goals based on a child's current skills is often more efficient than attempting to teach a more advanced skill in the absence of prerequisites. For example, it is best to teach functional one-word requests before targeting skills related to maintaining a conversation.

Further, when language skills are taught in the context of another activity (e.g., embedding language instruction during play sessions), language acquisition may be more efficient if the other activity is also developmentally appropriate (Pierce-Jordan & Lifter, 2005). For example, teaching a 2-year-old child to make eye contact and request toys during play sessions (e.g., Ninci et al., 2013; Sigafoos et al., 2013) is likely more efficient than attempting to teach the same skills while seated at a table for a long period of time. Finally, by understanding the typical developmental progression of language skills, teachers can determine a sequence of skills that should be taught throughout the year and proactively plan appropriate supports and scaffolding (Bruner, 1977; Vygotsky, 1962). Understanding typical developmental language skill sequences is particularly important for teachers of students who have no (or minimal) spoken language.

Communication, on the other hand, can be defined more broadly as any behavior with a socially mediated function. In other words, any behavior that is intended to influence another person's behavior is a form of communication. As noted in Chapter 3, challenging behavior (e.g., aggression and tantrums) often functions as a form of communication. In many ways, communication is not that different from any other behavior discussed in this text. Specifically, children communicate in response to their environment (antecedent condition with a discriminative stimulus $[S^D]$) and when motivated (motivating operation) to obtain or avoid something (positive and negative reinforcement). Because communication is not fundamentally different from other behaviors, communication is often referred to as **verbal behavior**, even when the communicative behavior does not involve speech (Skinner, 1957). For example, a child who cries at night to call her daddy to her room after a nightmare is communicating, even if no speech is involved. The exchange of picture cards, use of technology to generate a recorded message (i.e., **speech-generating device [SGD]**), and manual sign language are all topographies of verbal behavior other than speech that have been taught to children with autism.

6-1a Communication and Language Components

In a general sense, communication involves someone sending a message and someone receiving a message (Plavnick & Normand, 2013). Typically, these messages are sent through a language system, most often speech. Thus, skill deficits in language can inhibit both the sending and receiving of a message. **Receptive language** refers to the ability to receive and comprehend the message. Deficits in receptive language may result in an individual not following instructions, being unable to answer questions, and failing to react appropriately to someone else's attempt to communicate. Because it is not possible to actually see inside a person's brain as he or she processes a message, it can be difficult to identify receptive language deficits. Traditional tests of receptive language may be unreliable with individuals with autism. What may appear to be receptive language deficits (e.g., failure to comply with instructions, errors in complying with instructions) may be the result of factors other than receptive language, such as insufficient motivation to respond or respond correctly or insufficient attention to the instructions.

Expressive language refers to the ability to produce a message that others understand. Deficits in expressive language may result in reliance on challenging behavior to communicate and a limited ability to function independently or to self-advocate. Expressive language involves rules (structure) and the ability to produce meaning for a wide variety of purposes. Table 6.1 lists and defines the main components of language. The interaction of **phonology**, **morphology**, **semantics**, **pragmatics**, **prosody**, and **syntax** typically develops in an established sequence as a child matures so that most children have mastered receptive and expressive oral language structure by 9 years of age (Eigsti, de Marchena, Schuh, & Kelley, 2011).

Language, as with any behavior, should also be considered in terms of its form and function. *Form* (or *topography*) refers to the appearance and body movements involved in a behavior (i.e., what can be directly observed and measured). All aspects of language structure presented in Table 6.1 can be considered dimensions of language topography because they can be directly observed and measured in some way.

All communicative behaviors (not just speech) have a topography. For example, pointing, nodding the head to indicate yes, exchanging pictures, and manual signing are all topographies because they describe the form of a communicative behavior. In many cases, it is helpful to teach a child multiple topographies. For example, a child with an SGD may benefit from knowing how to use a picture-exchange communication system in situations where the iPad running the speech-generating software runs out of power. Similarly, a child with some speech may benefit from learning common gestures and hands signs as an alternative to augment her overall communicative repertoire. Use of multiple topographies of communication (particularly when referring to the combination of manual sign and speech) is referred to as **total communication** and is a recommended practice for children with autism, one we discuss in more detail later in this chapter (Carbone, Lewis, Sweeney-Kerwin, Dixon, Louden, & Quinn, 2006).

As with any other operant behavior, *function* refers to the various possible consequences (i.e., positive and negative reinforcement) that maintain verbal behaviors. For example, is the individual trying to request something (positive reinforcement) or reject something (negative reinforcement)? The extent to which communicative form and function are each emphasized in language instruction vary across different disciplines. For example, the

TABLE 6.1 ● Language Components and Definitions

- **Phonemes:** Individual speech sounds used within a language (in English we have approximately 40 phonemes).
- **Morphemes:** The smallest units of meaning in a language resulting from a combination of phonemes (e.g., "base" "ball" "s"). Each morpheme must have a referent for which it clearly stands.
- **Syntax:** Grammar rules in a given language (e.g., sentence structure, use of articles).
- **Prosody:** Cadence, rhythm, and pitch in speech.
- **Semantics:** The general meaning of language, including discrete words and contextual connotations.
- **Pragmatics:** Situational context of language including speaker–listener interaction and determining who says what to whom, how they say it, why and when they say it.

speech language pathology field offers different categories and descriptions of language from the field of applied behavior analysis (ABA). Each professional discipline also puts a different instructional emphasis on form and function. (For a classic discussion of these differences, see MacCorquodale, 1970.)

In this chapter, we present (and to some extent integrate) ideas from multiple disciplines, some with a stronger emphasis on form as in the field of speech language pathology, and some from fields that have a stronger emphasis on function such as ABA. Although there are notable differences across paradigms (e.g., one is based more on developmental and social-cognitive research and the other more on behavioral research), we maintain that a blended conceptualization is best suited for teachers working with students with autism because the instructional team usually consists of professionals from different disciplines. Note that these differences in opinions about instructional methods for teaching students with autism to acquire language may never be resolved. These differences hinge on basic beliefs about the origins of language in humans: (a) the belief that language ability is inherited (nature argument) and just needs to be facilitated (e.g., Noam Chomsky, 1967), or the belief that language ability must be taught through social interaction and scaffolding (e.g., Jerome Bruner) or, as with any behavior, through reinforcement for verbal behavior (B. F. Skinner), which are the nurture-focused arguments (MacCorquodale, 1970).

In this book we are emphasizing the nurture explanation of language to include both behavioral and social-cognitive theories. These approaches posit that individuals can be directly taught language form and functions with prompting and reinforcement procedures within a language-rich environment. The notion that children can be taught what they need to learn regardless of their heredity is an important assumption of the nurture explanation and one that has decades of research to support it (Lang, Hancock, & Singh, 2016). Note that the behavioral model (ABA), which has been the primary educational approach recommended in this book, emphasizes communicative function rather than form, and it originates from B.F. Skinner's seminal book *Verbal Behavior* (1957), which classified *verbal behaviors* according to their eliciting and motivating stimuli and function. The most common types of verbal behaviors targeted for students with autism (mands, tacts, and intraverbals) are briefly described.

A **mand** is a verbal behavior that is motivated by the desire to obtain or avoid something: all mands are requests. For example, "May I have a snack?" (obtain a tangible), "What time is it?" (obtain information), and "Can I skip piano class?" (avoid an activity) are all mands. A person is motivated to mand when his desire requires another person and when the environment signals that the request might be honored (S^D is present). Mands are reinforced in the natural environment when a listener honors the request (e.g., giving a snack, telling the time, or allowing a break from playing piano scales).

A **tact** is a verbal behavior that involves labeling or identifying something in response to a S^D, and the S^D does not involve the verbal behavior of another person. For example, a child may see a cow through the window (S^D) and tact "Cow!" even though no one asked, "What do you see out your window?" Tacts often function to call someone's attention to something and are typically reinforced with some form of social interaction. For example, a child on the playground who sees a snake (S^D) points and calls out "Snake!" (tact). The teacher moves all the children away from the area (socially mediated negative reinforcement) and thanks the child for tacting the snake (socially mediated positive reinforcement).

An **intraverbal** is a verbal behavior that occurs in response to another person's verbal behavior. For example, if a teacher asks "What is 2 plus 2?" (teacher's verbal behavior is S^D) and the child responds "four," then the child's response was an intraverbal. In many cases, the most salient difference between an intraverbal and a tact is the S^D. Specifically, the S^Ds that elicit tacting are not another person's verbal behavior (e.g., seeing a cow out the window), while intraverbals are elicited by another person's verbal behavior (e.g., being asked a question).

The distinction between tacts, mands, and intraverbals may at first seem arbitrary, but the differences have important implications for teaching (Greer & Ross, 2007). Specifically, children with autism may not generalize across functions of verbal behavior. For example, a child who learns to say "cow" as a mand (e.g., to request a toy cow), may not be able to tact "cow" or answer a question by saying "cow" (i.e., use cow as an intraverbal). In short, being able to use a word in one context (in response to one type of S^D) does not necessarily mean the same person is able to use the same word in a different context (Greer & Ross, 2007; Stokes & Baer, 1977). Therefore, in some cases, it is necessary to teach the same word as a mand, tact, and intraverbal. Consider, for example, trying to teach a child to say "cow." If the teacher holds up a picture of a cow and asks the child "What is this?" then the intraverbal is being targeted because the child is answering a question (i.e., responding to another person's verbal behavior). If a teacher observes a child pointing to a toy cow on a high shelf (i.e., teacher knows the child wants the cow) and then delivers the verbal prompt "say cow," then cow is being taught as a mand. Of course, the teacher would then reinforce the mand by providing the toy cow that was requested. Finally, if a child says "cow" after seeing a picture of a cow on a poster (the S^D is not the verbal behavior of another person), then "cow" was a tact. Of course, the teacher should praise the child for using a target word in the natural environment and expand the utterance to model more language (e.g., "Right, that is a cow! Cows moo!"). Usually, children learn to make requests first, so manding is typically the first type of verbal behavior targeted. Although many children will generalize a word acquired during mand training by using the same word as a tact or intraverbal, others will require additional instruction specifically targeting generalization to tacts and intraverbals.

In addition to Skinner's classic 1957 description of verbal behavior, there are other ways to consider the functional properties of communication that may be helpful to teachers as they design language and communication lessons. For example, Neel and Billingsley (1989) delineate a conceptually compatible taxonomy of communicative functions that may help guide lesson planning for individuals with autism:

- **Requesting** (type of mand maintained by positive reinforcement)—to satisfy needs such as obtaining food, approval, affection, or help with a task.
- **Protesting** (type of mand maintained by negative reinforcement)—saying "No" to tasks, toys, food, activities (e.g., refusing to go to bed).
- **Responding to social initiatives** (type of intraverbal)—a range of behaviors such as following someone who says "Come on," agreeing to join a game after being invited, and answering the teacher's question "What did you do this summer?"
- **Initiating and maintaining social interaction** (a combination of mands, tacts, and intraverbals)—sustaining a conversation by staying on topic, appropriate conversational turn taking and appropriate use of communicative gestures and mannerisms (e.g., eye contact and head nods) that indicate listening.
- **Seeking comfort** (type of mand)—behaviors such as running to daddy when hurt or distressed and asking for a hug.
- **Expressing interest in the environment** (type of tact)—commenting on something new or unusual in the room or pointing to something interesting.

It is obvious that language, particularly speech, is composed of complex components and may be extremely difficult for children to learn, especially if they also have intellectual disabilities (ID) or other neurological disorders. Unfortunately, this is true for some individuals with autism who never master sufficient speech to communicate adequately. Even those who do acquire speech may use it inappropriately or ineffectively (Taylor & Whitehouse, 2016). The consequences of not acquiring adequate language and communication skills are dire and often negatively affect future outcomes. Thus, teaching and facilitating language and communication for students with autism should be a major priority for parents and teachers.

As stated previously, we recommend a combination of developmental, social-cognitive, and ABA approaches to language training. Specifically, we recommend that teachers (a) encourage imitation of correct language usage (also known as echoing); (b) directly instruct students to tact, mand, and respond to other people (intraverbal); (c) create a responsive environment that reinforces students for the use of language during their typical routines; and (d) increase opportunities for students to use language by contriving opportunities for language use and embedding opportunities in daily routines. This type of instruction and facilitation requires adults to frequently model correct language usage, reinforce communicative effort, and provide a rich social context for their students.

6-1b Language-Development Sequence

Language develops in a sequence of simple to complex skills beginning in early infancy with gestures, crying, and cooing. At first the crying may be purely physiological (reflexive) rather than a form of communication, but because crying often affects the behavior of other people in the environment, the infant soon learns to use various behaviors and vocalizations to influence the environment. Operant verbal behavior (referred to as *intentional communication* in some fields) develops well before 12 months of age (Berk & Meyers, 2016). The second critical ability that develops in infancy is the knowledge that language relates to the real world. This means that things are designated by an auditory or visual symbol. Soon these early expressive and receptive abilities progress to echoing usually through playful interaction with the parents. An interesting note is that many individuals with autism continue echolalic responses beyond this initial developmental period (Neely, Gerow, Rispoli, Lang, & Pullen, 2016; Saad & Goldfeld, 2009).

As the desire to communicate for the purpose of meeting his needs grows, the infant develops a one- or two-word expressive language repertoire. These few words are typically names of favorite objects or people and are known as **holophrases**. The holophrase serves multiple functions many functions such as socializing, requesting, and protesting. For example, the infant may say "Mama" with different intonations (subtle topography variations) to mean "Help me," "Give me . . . ," "Stop that," and so forth. Understanding the communicative intent of a holophrase requires a listener who can interpret what the child is intending to communicate based on subtle topography and contextual variations.

By age 2, most children begin using two-word phrases known as **telegraphic speech** (Berk & Meyers, 2016). Telegraphic speech leaves out unnecessary words. For example, it includes word combinations such as "Go play," "Come outside," "Sit, mama," and "Give juice?" but not "I'd really like to have some juice" and so on. Once a child uses combinations of these phrases (e.g., "Baby sleepy. Go bed."), he is demonstrating grammatical rules. Also during this period, children appear to understand most things an adult says; that is, they seem to have an expansive receptive vocabulary or, at least, they have learned to respond to adult behavior and expressions. For example, a mother may say "See the doggy" and then look over at the dog. Her child follows her gaze and gives the impression that she understands the sentence, or a child may imitate a routine and appear to follow directions (e.g., close the door).

Note that the ability to follow another's gaze and share attention (a skill referred to as **joint attention**) and the ability to imitate modeled behavior are foundationally important skills for language development. Unfortunately, joint attention and imitation are often not demonstrated by young children with autism and require systematic instruction. In fact, teaching joint attention to children with autism has been shown to occasion a collateral increase in other social behaviors (e.g. cooperative play) and even improve untargeted communication and language skills (White et al., 2011).

Between ages 2 and 5, most children move from telegraphic speech to multiple-word sentences to adultlike speech structures (Lefrançois, 2001). They learn to use articles, word endings, and correct inflection before finally mastering most of the exceptions to grammatical rules (e.g., using "went" instead of "goed"). Their sentences become more complex. Preschool-age children learn to express concepts and refer to events that are remote in time and space (Gleason, 1997) and use language for pretending and conversing. During middle childhood, oral language development continues in the form of vocabulary expansion and syntactic development. Usually, at this point, emphasis shifts from oral language development to written language development (i.e., reading, spelling, and written expression). Table 6.2 lists the language milestones of a normally developing child.

Related Factors

Language development is influenced by many factors, including genetics, environment (parenting, social class, familial factors), and maturation of neurological systems (Wallace, Cohen, & Polloway, 1987). If a child is born with an ID or physical impairments (e.g., vision, hearing impairments, cerebral palsy), then language development may be adversely

TABLE 6.2 ● Language-Development Milestones

YEAR	MILESTONES	BEHAVIORS	SAMPLE
First	Prespeech	Gestures, cooing, crying, babbling	Looking at bottle. "Dadadadada."
	Holophrase	Word plus gestures	"Dada" plus pulling stuck toy, meaning "Help me."
Second and third	Two-word sentences	Modifiers plus nouns	"No juice." "Where doggy?" "More cheese." "Baby sleep."
	Multiple-word sentences	Subject plus predicate	"Shark bites water." "I want juice please." "No play with kids." "Shoes are upstairs."
Third and fourth	Complex grammatical structures are added	Nouns, verbs, prepositions	"I can't find it."
		Combined clauses	"Give me some juice." "Where are my shoes?"
	Adultlike structures	Structural distinctions	"He promised to help me make it."

affected. Similarly, if the family fails to provide adequate sociolinguistic interaction and support, or if the child has neurological problems that prevent typical developmental maturation, then language may be delayed or absent. In the case of autism, neurological abnormalities appear to increase risk of language delays.

Some researchers believe that thought (cognition) precedes language development. For example, Piaget (1954) maintained that children must develop the ability to think symbolically before language can develop—in other words, thinking ability precedes language development. On the other hand, Vygotsky (1962) believed that intelligence develops as a function of language—in other words, thought cannot occur without language. In either case, thinking and language abilities are intricately connected, particularly after 2 years of age when language becomes the primary method for transmitting and acquiring knowledge. ID, therefore, may cause language disorders, and language disorders may exacerbate cognitive delays.

A cognitive ability that typically develops in infancy is the concept of cause and effect—specifically, that behavior causes things in the environment to be altered. Babies may discover that hitting the mobile makes it move or that pulling a string makes the toy doll talk. They learn that dropping food on the floor results in mother picking it up and interacting with them (a game this author's daughter called "momma fetch"). Without an understanding of cause and effect, the motivation to communicate is compromised (Layton & Watson, 1995). For example, if a child does not understand that sounds, words, and phrases affect the environment, she is not likely to use those things to meet her needs and desires. Learning about cause and effect typically happens through play. Perhaps because children with autism may not play in the typical manner, prelinguistic cognitive abilities are delayed. Furthermore, even if a child develops communicative intent, based on cause-and-effect awareness, he still may not understand that objects are represented by sounds and words.

In addition to cognitive abilities, social ability is also closely linked to language development. Social interactions with the infant (i.e., eye contact, smiling, laughing) are behaviors that result in reciprocal social interaction from nearby adults. For example, a baby smiles and his mother says, "Hi, little fellow, are you awake? Do you want to eat?" This type of verbal interaction then elicits early language responses such as cooing. In fact, Bruner (1977) claims that language will only develop from such interaction. He claims that children learn to make eye contact, take turns, direct others' attention through gestures and eventually words, and converse through interaction with others (Lefrançois, 2001). If the child is given little social contact and spends the majority of his time alone, then language development will be hampered. Furthermore, if children are given everything they want or need without having to communicate, there is little motivation or opportunity to acquire communication skills. Thus, we recommend that students with autism spend time around verbal children and adults and that sociocommunicative interaction be encouraged through antecedent manipulation, scaffolding and prompting, and reinforcement strategies. We also recommend that social language be taught so that social interactions are more likely to be successful.

Finally, for language to develop, an individual needs a topography of communication that they can master. The best language topography is often speech because it is widely understood and has the greatest productivity potential. However, if children cannot develop speech because of cognitive or physical disabilities, then other topographies of communication (visual systems, sign language, SGDs) should be made available (e.g., Lorah, Parnell, Whitby, & Hantula, 2015). The paramount goal is to teach functional communication while supporting cognitive and social skill development and preventing or reducing challenging behaviors.

6-2 Language Difficulties in Autism

Many individuals with autism experience difficulties in almost all aspects of language along with deficits in cognition and social interaction skills (e.g., American Psychiatric Association [APA], 2013; Hinerman, 1983; Paul, 1987). In addition to severe language impairment, many cognitive prerequisites to language may also be impaired. For example, many children with autism (a) have an ID (APA, 2013), (b) fail to develop the awareness of cause and effect, and (c) struggle to interpret symbols in their environment and to use symbols to transmit messages to others (Hinerman, 1983; Kamhi, 1981).

Evidence of cognitive impairment is apparent in toddlers who:

- do not imitate social behavior such as waving bye-bye, playing pat-a-cake, or other parental behaviors;
- avoid eye contact;
- show no preference for their parent's voice over a stranger's voice;
- do not point to things of interest;
- do not readily respond to their names;
- show little or no desire to explore the environment;
- have difficulty learning relational concepts (e.g., over, under, behind); or
- rarely refer to events that happened in the past or in various places.

6-2a Receptive Language Problems

Abnormal responses to auditory stimuli (i.e., how a person attends to auditory input, acts on it, imitates it) may also contribute directly to language problems, particularly to receptive language. Many individuals with autism perform poorly on tests of language comprehension and seem to have trouble understanding sentences (Pelios & Sucharzewski, 2004). Children with autism may also appear agitated in the presence of certain voice tones and pitches. Learning to attend to the spoken word and obtain meaning from it is difficult when the ability to attend to contextual cues in general is impaired or when the auditory stimuli involved in communication are found to be aversive to an individual.

In addition, some children with autism appear to emphasize syntactic structure (grammar) rather than semantic content (meaning) in their understanding of language (Paul, Fischer, & Cohen, 1988). For example, they may glean more meaning from word order than from word definition. In other words, children with autism have a tendency to interpret a message literally even when a nuanced or more abstract interpretation might be more appropriate. Thus, a child with autism may readily understand that "Come to dinner" means to come and eat but not understand that "Dinner's on" has the same meaning and may wonder what exactly the dinner has been placed on. Receptive language can be enhanced with direct cues and consistent wording. In one study, children with autism tended to misunderstand the speaker's intention when indirect sentences such as "How about getting ready for lunch?" were used and when sentences were uttered in nonstructured settings (Paul et al., 1988).

Unfortunately, language comprehension problems often result in increasingly restricted interactions and experiences that can contribute to delays. For example, if parents and teachers do not think a child understands what is said, they may find it hard to maintain a social interaction. Some may resort to only giving directions rather than engaging in imitative play, conversational speech, complex social interactions, and novel activities. Without the connection of various experiences to words and sentences, the child with autism may not develop appropriate language comprehension, functional expressive language, and social competence.

6-2b Expressive Language Problems

Expressive language problems are commonly associated with autism. Those who speak may display limited and idiosyncratic speech patterns (unusual prosody) that create a variety of problems and increase the likelihood of communication breakdowns (misunderstandings). Even those at the mild end of the autism spectrum may have an impaired ability to initiate and sustain conversation (Edmunds, Ibañez, Warren, Messinger, & Stone, 2017).

Word Use and Articulation

Some individuals with autism develop fairly large vocabularies because they can memorize what words mean; however, they may fail to use that vocabulary for a variety of functions or to organize their speech appropriately (Paul, 1987). Many individuals also have an obsessive interest in certain words resulting in perseveration (repeating words over and over). Articulation is typically not a problem for children with autism who acquire speech, although it may be somewhat delayed (Needleman, Ritvo, & Freeman, 1980).

Syntax and Morphology

Individuals with autism seem to be able to use the common grammatical morphemes (sounds) and many have at least some syntactic awareness (McGonigle-Chalmers, Alderson-Day, Fleming, & Monsen, 2013). However, it is not uncommon for children with autism to have trouble with verb tenses and articles, perhaps because referents change according to the point of view of the speaker (Bartolucci, Pierce, & Streiner, 1980). For example, present and past tenses may be altered as a result of which speaker is making the comment. Thus, children with autism may display some grammatical errors. Their syntactic ability (using rules to produce language) may be simplistic, but most speaking children with autism use correct word order. Delays most often occur in the use of questions, negatives, conjoined sentences, and passive sentences (Giddan & Ross, 2001). Some individuals with autism, in fact, rely on questioning as their primary mode of initiating and maintaining conversations (Hurtig, Ensrud, & Tomblin, 1982), whereas others must be directly taught how to ask questions (Raulston et al., 2013).

Pronoun Reversal

A somewhat unique characteristic of children with autism is the propensity to misuse personal pronouns. For example, they may use the pronoun "you" when they mean "I." "You want to eat now?" may mean "I want to eat now." As previously mentioned, pronouns are connected to changing referents. For example, "father" is always one person, but pronouns do not always refer to the same person. This shifting reference may be especially difficult for individuals with autism.

Echolalia

Echolalia, the inappropriate repetition of words, phrases, or sentences, is one of the most classic characteristics of autistic speech (Neely et al., 2016). Generally, echolalia comes in three types: immediate, delayed, and mitigated (Hinerman, 1983). **Immediate echolalia** entails all or part of an utterance that is repeated following its occurrence. The repetition duplicates the intonation, pitch, and articulation patterns of the speaker and quite often is repeated several times. For example, a teacher tells a student to "wash your hands and sit down." The student repeats "wash your hands." **Delayed echolalia** (also called *palilalia*) is the duplication of an utterance that occurred sometime but not immediately before the imitated response. This type of echolalia often comes in the form of repeated TV commercials, lines from jingles or songs, or radio announcements. **Mitigated echolalia** refers to repetitions that differ slightly from the original utterance. For example, a parent may tell a child to "stay away from the swimming pool," and the child repeats "no swimming pool" each time he goes outside.

As mentioned previously, most children typically display echolalia in their early language, usually repeating sounds slightly more advanced than their spontaneous language (Berk & Meyers, 2016). Children with autism, however, are more likely to repeat questions and commands when they lack an appropriate response. Echolalia does often serve socially mediated functions and may facilitate turn taking, assertions, affirmative answers, requests, and rehearsal (Sterponi & Shankey, 2014). Echolalia may also be maintained by nonsocially mediated reinforcers—for example, self-regulation and self-stimulation (i.e., automatic reinforcement). It is interesting that delayed echolalia seems to follow nondemand types of interactions while immediate echolalia seems to follow specific, complex demands (Rydell & Mirenda, 1991).

Prosody

Prosody refers to intonation, speech rhythm, inflection, voice volume, intensity, quality, and pitch. This aspect of language may also be impaired or abnormal for individuals with autism who may be described as having "robotic" speech and flat affect. Children with autism may speak in a monotone voice or a consistently high-pitched tone with muttering, and they may have loud outbursts or poor volume control.

Nonverbal Communication

Typical nonverbal communication includes bodily contact, proximity, physical orientation, appearance, posture, head nods, facial expressions, gestures, and eye contact. In conjunction with speech production, these features convey interpersonal attitudes and assist in establishing relationships and conveying information. Individuals with autism often struggle to use gestures, make eye contact, and display facial expressions to convey meaning. In fact, they may display facial grimaces and tics and actively avoid eye contact (Wing, 1996).

6-2c Problems with Pragmatics

For those individuals with autism who do master a language system, one of the most debilitating deficits involves pragmatics. Mastery of pragmatics involves following conversational rules such as turn taking, relevant responses, maintaining a conversation topic, being clear and unambiguous, and using cohesive sentences. Pragmatics also involves taking another's perspective and using language for greeting, predicting, referring to things, narrating, commenting, explaining, comparing, and joking (Eigsti et al., 2011). Individuals with autism typically show sparse verbal expression and lack of spontaneity. They have historically been characterized as individuals who struggle to:

* reciprocate in speech,
* attend and respond (listen) to the speech of others,
* move from an obsessive topic to a topic of interest to the listener,
* take turns in conversations, or
* avoid highly rigid and contextually inappropriate speech.

When responding to adult verbalizations, children with autism were less likely than age-matched peers to make relevant responses, expand the discussion, or add new information; more typically they spend their time imitating responses or do not respond at all

(Tager-Flusberg, 1996). They often provide one-word answers when two or three sentences would be socially appropriate. One of the overriding pragmatic struggles is the limited ability to use contextual cues. Individuals with autism often experience difficulty recognizing the speaker's intent, monitoring their listeners' needs, and using contextual stimuli to convey meaning—for example, looking, pointing, holding something up. Many have a propensity to interpret and produce language literally without attention to variations and connotations. Finally, some individuals with autism do not align the content of their speech to their meaning. For example, a child may say "The Ford is green?" which means "Let's go for a ride in the truck." This difference in pragmatics appears directly tied to the fundamental characteristic: limited social competence and difficulty relating to people.

6-2d Problems with Language Form

Because of problems in acquiring and using language, individuals with autism often resort to idiosyncratic topographies of communication. Instead of imitating adult speech and learning communicative forms through natural reinforcers, children with autism may display a wide range of behavior to convey meaning. These various language forms may include aggressive behavior, speech, pointing, pulling others to something, self-injury, tantrums, echolalic behavior, sign language, or changes in physical proximity (Prizant & Schuler, 1987). We discussed communicative functions of challenging behavior in Chapter 3.

Even for those who speak well, speech is not always used to convey meaning and may be used in noncommunicative ways (functions that are not socially mediated), as evidenced with some echolalia. Accepted nonverbal communication forms (e.g., facial expressions, intonation, body orientation) are less likely in children with autism, but challenging behavior is more common than in children without autism (Lang, Sigafoos, van der Meer, O'Reilly, Lancioni, & Didden, 2013). This propensity to use idiosyncratic forms of communication as opposed to conventional forms suggests that we should assume communicative intent in most behavior. The complex and varied language and communication, cognitive, and social difficulties experienced by individuals with autism clearly indicate assessment and intervention in all of these areas as early as possible. Table 6.3 summarizes the language characteristics associated with autism.

6-3 Assessing Language and Communication

Because students with autism tend to experience difficulties across many aspects of language and communication, extensive language and communication assessment is often indicated. Proper assessment should facilitate instruction in essential and functional communication skills. Given the complexity of language, assessment should occur in several areas:

1. The social domain, including ways in which the child initiates interaction, responds to others, and displays nonverbal social behaviors.
2. The communicative domain, including the degree of communicative intent and the types of verbal and nonverbal communicative functions displayed. The frequency of communicative behaviors and the types of communicative forms used should also be assessed.
3. The linguistic domain, including all receptive and expressive language components. Assessment might also include analysis of echolalic speech if present.
4. The cognitive domain, including the ability to understand symbolic representation.

Assessing language and communication can be a daunting task because so many components are involved and because language is so closely related to social and cognitive skills. Thus, we recommend that teachers and parents seek assistance from a speech and language pathologist (SLP) or school psychologist, particularly in the areas of linguistic and cognitive assessment, and a Board Certified Behavior Analyst (BCBA), particularly in the area

TABLE 6.3 ● Language and Communication Problems in Autism

RECEPTIVE LANGUAGE PROBLEMS

- Inability to attend to auditory stimuli
- Inability to act on auditory stimuli
- Inability to imitate auditory stimuli
- Inability to use contextual cues to obtain meaning

- May appear deaf
- Overly sensitive to sounds
- Obtain meaning from word order, not semantic content
- Failure to understand indirect or complex sentences

EXPRESSIVE LANGUAGE PROBLEMS

- Mutism
- Word use and articulation
- Imprecise articulation

- Obsessive use of vocabulary
- Incorrect use of vocabulary

SYNTAX AND MORPHOLOGY

- Trouble with verb tenses and articles
- Failure or delay in use of syntactic rules

- Perseverative use of questions
- Pronoun reversal

ECHOLALIA

- Immediate
- Delayed (palilalia)

- Mitigated
- Noncommunicative echolalia

PROSODY

- Wooden speech and flat affect
- Monotonal speech
- High-pitched tone

- Hoarseness, harshness, hypernasality
- Poor volume control
- Sing-song speech

NONVERBAL COMMUNICATION

- Fail to use nonverbal communication to enhance communicative intent

- No eye contact or appropriate body orientation
- Facial grimacing

PRAGMATIC PROBLEMS

- Limited language uses
- Lack of spontaneity
- Failure to reciprocate and take turns in conversation
- Respond with inappropriate amount of communication

- Failure to maintain a conversation
- Failure to recognize the speaker's intent
- Failure to match speech content to meaning
- Rigid and contextually inappropriate speech

FORM PROBLEMS

- Idiosyncratic communication forms
- Often use aggressive behavior or self-injurious behavior to communicate
- Failure to use appropriate nonverbal forms of communication

- Speech often not used to communicate
- May use crying, tantrums, echolalia, physical manipulation, gestures to communicate

RELATED PROBLEMS

- Intellectual disabilities
- No awareness of cause and effect
- Failure to understand symbolic representation
- Lack of toy and imitative or imaginative play
- Nonfunctional use of objects
- Failure to attend to environmental stimuli
- Failure to take turns or understand another's perspective

- Egocentric thinking
- Little interest in exploring the environment
- Little interest in people
- Little response to communicative models
- Overselection of stimuli
- Failure to transfer or adapt learned skills

of functional assessment. Professionals from different disciplines and parents should work together to conduct comprehensive language and communication assessment. The more comprehensive and accurate the assessment, the more likely it is that appropriate communication goals and objectives will be targeted and acquired. Because so many language and communication skills must be assessed, comprehensive skill-based assessments may be particularly helpful in producing results that directly inform the selection of target behaviors.

6-3a Language and Communication Assessment Instruments

Note that formal norm-referenced language tests for children with autism and related disorders may not provide useful information for selecting goals and target behaviors for a student with autism (Prizant & Schuler, 1987). Because of the developmental discontinuity of autism, comparing the development of a person with autism to what is expected in typical child development may not necessarily produce information useful for guiding intervention. We suggest assessments that have been specifically developed for individuals with autism such as the following.

Verbal Behavior Milestones Assessment and Placement Program (VB-MAPP) was specifically designed to determine skill levels across multiple domains for children with autism (Sundberg, 2008). Further, because VB-MAPP assessment results identify specific observable skill deficits relative to typical developmental sequences, the VB-MAPP is remarkably useful for identifying target skills for intervention (Barnes, Mellor, & Rehfeldt, 2014). Often results will reveal a missing skill that is considered a prerequisite for a more advanced skill that is not missing. Such skills make excellent target behaviors because not only are they developmentally appropriate and typically acquired quickly but also may have a collateral effect on other important behaviors.

The *Assessment of Basic Language and Learning Skills–Revised* (ABLLS-R) (Partington, 2008) is also a criterion-referenced assessment, curriculum guide, and skills tracking system created specifically for children with language delays. The purpose of this instrument is to determine what the child with language delays can already perform and what skills should be targeted. Both the VB-MAPP and ABLLS-R are based on B. F. Skinner's analysis of verbal behavior, which focuses on the different conditions in which language occurs and the maintaining contingencies. The ABLLS-R assesses a variety of language skills: the child's motivation to respond, ability to attend to verbal and nonverbal stimuli and to generalize language skills, and spontaneous language use.

Finally, the *PEAK Relational Training System* (PEAK) is another criterion-based assessment created specifically for children with language and cognitive delays that is directly tied to a curriculum guide (Malkin, Dixon, Speelman, & Luke, 2017). PEAK has three separate modules: direct training, generalization, and equivalence. Although the VB-MAPP and ABLLS-R appear to be more widely used and are cited more often in research, PEAK has accumulated the most supportive psychometric data (e.g., Dixon, 2014; 2015; 2017).

A BCBA is best qualified to conduct assessment with the VB-MAPP, ABLLS-R, and PEAK because most SLPs are typically not trained to use these ABA-based instruments. Teachers may be asked to assist with these assessment administrations. Detailed assessment instructions are beyond the scope of this chapter (e.g., Barnes et al., 2014).

6-3b Informal Language Assessment

Informal procedures such as ecological assessment, direct observations, and interviews are often necessary components of a comprehensive assessment battery for students with autism. Assessment of linguistic quality and related social and cognitive skills are also important, but we recommend assessing the communicative domain first. To assist teachers and parents in their understanding of language and communication assessment, use the sample assessment questions for the social, communicative, linguistic, and cognitive domains listed in Table 6.4.

TABLE 6.4 ● Sample Language Assessment Questions

SOCIAL DOMAIN

- How often and in what way does the child initiate interaction?
- How does the child respond to others' initiations?
- What types of nonverbal behaviors are used in social and conversational situations?
- How often does the child desire to interact?
- Under what conditions does the child interact the most?
- Under what conditions does the child interact the least?
- What does the child communicate about?
- Does the child maintain communicative exchanges? If so, how?
- Does the child terminate interaction? If so, how?
- Does the child play? If so, how interactive is the play?
- Who does the child typically interact with?

COMMUNICATIVE DOMAIN

- What communicative functions does the child display? (Consider whether the child makes various requests, protests, declares, makes choices, asks for help, expresses affection, communicates emotion, shares information.)
- How does the child communicate each of the functions? (Consider challenging behavior, gazing, pointing, reaching, vocalizations, nodding, signs, pictures.)
- How do different conditions affect the ways a child communicates?
- How often does the child communicate each function?

LINGUISTIC DOMAIN

LANGUAGE COMPREHENSION

- Does the child follow simple directions?
- Does the child look at objects that might be the topic of discussion (i.e., joint attention)?
- Does the child follow new or complex directions?
- Under what conditions does language comprehension seem best? (Consider focused attention, speed of speech, intonation, length of utterance, gestures, pictures.)

EXPRESSIVE LANGUAGE

- What are the primary forms of communication? (Consider echolalia, signs, challenging behavior, vocalizations.)
- Does the child use correct grammar?
- Does the child use correct meanings?
- Does the child carry on appropriate conversations?
- How much vocabulary is evident?
- Does the child use nouns, verbs, word combinations, "wh-" questions, articles, prepositions, adverbs, negating?
- Does the child articulate well? (Consider use of plurals and verb tenses.)
- Is appropriate prosody evident? (Consider accent, timing, and vocal intonation.)

ECHOLALIA

- What functions might the child communicate through echolalia?
- Is there flexibility in the echolalic responses (i.e., mitigated echolalia)?
- Does the echolalia seem to be self-stimulatory or unfocused?

COGNITIVE DOMAIN

- Does the child refer to or show awareness of objects and people that are out of sight?
- Does the child show interest in a variety of people and things?
- Does the child categorize objects based on various dimensions?
- Does the child discriminate color, shape, size, and so forth?
- Does the child move to get what he wants?
- How well does the child handle change? (Consider conditions such as interruptions, new people, type of activities, ending activities.)
- Does the child insist on routines and rituals?
- Does the child imitate adult behaviors? If so, are they novel actions or learned ones?

In Chapter 4, we discussed conducting ecological assessments to identify future curriculum targets for students with autism: what they will need to be able to do to be successful in future placements. We suggest that assessment of communication and social skills should typically accompany language assessment. For example, if a student is going to work at a toy store to demonstrate to customers how to use particular toys, he must be able to greet customers, label the parts of each toy, answer customer questions, and verbally conclude the demonstration. All of these interactions will require social and pragmatic skills (e.g., facing the customer, waiting for the customer to attend, standing at an appropriate distance, making eye contact). When developing an individualized skill inventory (life skills, leisure skills, vocational skills) for students, do not forget the related language and communication skills that should accompany those targets. The second step of ecological assessment is to determine the current level of functioning for a specific student, which language and communication skills the student has already mastered. This assessment step can be accomplished with the formal assessment instruments listed previously or with informal observations and interviews. Finally, a list of language targets (the difference between current mastered skills and needed skills) emerges to form the individualized curriculum.

To determine the current level of language mastery, an informal assessment must contain two primary components: (a) the range of communicative functions and forms exhibited by a student and (b) the conditions and contexts under which each type of communication occurs (Quill, 1995). Figure 6.1 provides a sample informal assessment checklist for determining what communicative forms the student currently uses for various functions. For each function listed on the left, teachers and parents can note the communication forms the child uses to achieve that function. For example, when requesting help, does the student whine or pull the teacher to the cabinet or both? Note that the checklist has a comment section for information about contextual conditions. This type of checklist can be modified for each student to include relevant functions and can also be adapted to include specific questions about the conditions under which various communicative behaviors occur (e.g., when the most and least communication occurs).

Observations in naturally occurring or simulated situations can also provide excellent information about language skills. For children with autism who may not attend well to their surroundings, naturally occurring situations may not stimulate language production or may be too infrequent to result in mastery. In these cases, the assessor might need to intentionally set up situations that motivate communication (establish a motivating operation—see Chapter 2) to assess quantity and quality (Greer & Ross, 2007). For example, a teacher may engage in an interaction whereby she repeatedly opens a container with a favorite toy. Once the student seems to be anticipating the opening, the teacher does not open it. At this point the student may gaze at the container, gesture toward it, pull the teacher's hand toward it, produce vocalizations, be echolalic, or perhaps produce challenging behavior (tantrum). In this way, the teacher is able to record the various communicative behaviors, the conditions under which they occurred, and make judgments about their social validity and potential functionality.

Familiar routines are also a good time to structure interactions to facilitate language assessment. For example, a student may be accustomed to having his milk handed to him once he sits down for lunch. In an assessment situation, the teacher could intentionally engage in something else and "forget" to give the student the milk. Often communicative behavior will result. However, teachers must be cautious because challenging behavior may also occur. Functional behavioral assessment, as described in Chapter 3, provides useful information about how communicative attempts relate to environmental conditions and about the relationship of communication to challenging behavior.

Likewise, interviews with parents and others who know the child well can provide information regarding those situations in which the target child is most likely to be socially interactive, whether they interact with peers or adults, the types of current communicative behaviors, and a list of activities that the child likes to do with others. Neel and Billingsley (1989) included questions about communication form and function on their environmental inventory questionnaire. They also ask about a target child's cognitive abilities such as how well he handles situations involving new people or activities,

NAME: _____   DATE: _____

EXAMINER: _____

Indicate ways the child communicates for the various purposes.

Functions   **Communicative Forms**

Functions	COMPLEX SPEECH	PHRASES	SINGLE WORDS	SIGNS	ECHOLALIA	GESTURES/POINTING	NODS YES OR NO	MOVES ANOTHER	CRYING OR WHINING	TANTRUMS/SIB	AGGRESSION	OTHER	COMMENT
Requests objects/food/event.													
Requests adult to act.													
Requests out of activity/task.													
Requests help.													
Requests to leave.													
Chooses person/activity/object.													
Protests change in routine.													
Protests adult action.													
Protests loss of something.													
Indicates pain.													
Indicates affection.													
Shares information.													
Initiates interaction.													
Other.													

FIGURE 6.1 Sample informal language and communication checklist

❯❯ Professional Resource Download

the termination of activities, and notification about impending changes. If target children display little interactive behavior, you might want to record them in comfortable surroundings with familiar people. Check the recordings for basic nonverbal communication such as head and mouth movements, intentional vocalizations, upper-extremity movements, and facial expressions.

Assessment across the various social, communication, linguistic, and cognitive domains will provide a profile of the likely conditions under which a given child will communicate and the quality and functionality of current verbal or nonverbal behaviors. After this type of assessment has been conducted, teachers, SLPs, BCBAs, and parents can begin to shape existing responses into more complex socially appropriate functional language to match future target placement demands. The assessment information provides a starting point for communication and language instruction. The VB-MAPP, ABLLS-R, or PEAK results are particularly helpful for language and communication skill selection. Finally, it might be wise to assess the characteristics of the people who frequently interact with each child because responsive communication partners and social contexts are necessary to stimulate spontaneous interactions (Hampton & Kaiser, 2016). In Chapter 7, we discuss using ecological assessment for this purpose.

6-4 Language and Communication Training

Comprehensive language and communication assessment is necessary to develop appropriate curriculum (what the student needs to learn) and inform decisions about effective instruction (how the student will learn best). Goals and objectives should be established before deciding the best way to teach, and they should be based on the interrelationship of communicative, social, cognitive and linguistic abilities, and the overriding purpose of fostering independence and competence.

6-4a Deciding What to Teach in a Language or Communication Program

After using assessment information and the ecological inventory to determine language and communication targets for each student, the resulting curriculum should include both structural and functional goals. Although teaching linguistically appropriate communication forms is important, teaching a means of achieving sociocommunicative functions for meeting one's own current and future needs should take an even higher priority. Without functional communication, students' motivation may wane, challenging behavior may escalate, and intellectual development may stagnate.

Structural Goals and Curriculum

Structural goals in language and communication training pertain primarily to the linguistic and cognitive domains and include abilities in the following areas: prelinguistic cognitive skills, receptive comprehension, expressive vocabulary development, correct grammar, articulation (with speech), and appropriate prosody (with speech). Most of these goals also apply when teaching students to use **alternate and augmentative forms of communication (AAC)** such as sign language, SGDs, and visual communication systems. Specific structural goals for early language development might include the following.

1. Create an association between objects or activities and symbols for those objects and activities (i.e., referentially). For example, pair the sign or word for cookie with pieces of cookie until the student associates the sign or word with the item.
2. Increase receptive language skills (e.g., following simple directions).
3. Teach relevant and simple vocabulary, beginning with meaningful concrete nouns, particularly those frequently desired by the student.
4. Teach protest words (e.g., "No").
5. Combine nouns and verbs or nouns and adjectives into phrases such as "Want juice."
6. Add pronouns and proper nouns to make simple sentences and phrases such as "I want to swing."
7. Systematically add grammatical categories (nouns, verbs, pronouns) and more vocabulary.
8. Work on articulation or correct sign formation while encouraging the motivation to communicate.

As part of language training, ensure that students have the ability to imitate motor responses ("Do this" and clap hands or touch nose). Once imitation is acquired, teaching language responses will likely be more efficient. Initially begin language training with teaching vocabulary words (tacts and mands) that the student is frequently motivated to use. For students with autism, these are typically favorite objects, places, or foods. Initial vocabulary from the categories of self-care, activities, animals, body parts, colors, and numbers may also be included. Vocabulary, particularly initial vocabulary, should be directly related to an individual's environment. For example, if the student's parents call a soft drink "pop," then teach the student to request or label it "pop," not "soda."

Early language training also includes receptive comprehension (following simple directions) and receptive labeling (e.g., point to the cookie). The training then moves to expressive labeling (tacting) (e.g., "What is this?"). As one-word responses are mastered, add two-word combinations often consisting of a simple subject and predicate (e.g., "Want juice," "Go play"). Initial vocabulary may also include a word to protest (i.e., say "No"). Teaching students an appropriate way to express refusal should reduce challenging behavior maintained by negative reinforcement (see Chapter 3).

At this point, the teacher must also decide whether general vocabulary (e.g., "food," "more," "want," "hey," "clothes") might serve the individual better or whether specific vocabulary (e.g., "cookie," "orange juice," "red sweater") should be emphasized (Reichle & Sigafoos, 1994). The advantage of general vocabulary is that, for those students who learn slowly, these words serve a variety of functions in a variety of settings. The advantage of specific vocabulary is that the individual can more precisely communicate, especially with unfamiliar listeners. Usually explicit vocabulary is taught after mastery of general vocabulary.

The formal assessment instruments listed in the previous section provide a recommended order for teaching skills. In addition, published language curricula provide lists of developmental goals and objectives that might be useful for individual students. Relate these skill lists to results of the ecological inventory for a particular student (what needs to be mastered for target adult outcomes relative to what is already mastered) and other assessment data to ensure that the resulting curriculum is individualized. As illustration, a sample structural curricular sequence is presented in Table 6.5.

New teachers or those conducting lengthy comprehensive assessments (for new students, for example) may temporarily rely on published curricular lists. However, overreliance on published curricula that do not allow for sufficient individualization should be avoided. By law, school personnel must develop individualized goals and objectives based on comprehensive assessment results. Furthermore, published curricula reflect typical language milestones, and students with autism may not master skills in a typical order given their related cognitive disorders. We recommend either using a skills list developed specifically for students with autism such as the VB-MAPP or ABLLS-R or a thoughtful ecological assessment to guarantee an appropriate individualized curriculum.

Functional Goals and Curriculum

The many structural aspects of language may be difficult to teach in the absence of motivation to communicate. Thus, functional language and communication goals may be even more important. Teaching students to spontaneously communicate for various purposes better serves the individual in everyday activities. Broad typical functional goals might include the following:

1. Use appropriate topography of communication to request favorite objects or access to activities.
2. Use appropriate topography of communication to request a break or refuse something being offered.
3. Use appropriate topography of communication to recruit the attention of adults and peers.
4. Expand the use of communicative functions and semantic (categories of meaning) categories.

TABLE 6.5 ● Sample Curricula for Structural Communication Goals

RECEPTIVE LANGUAGE

- Discriminates nonlanguage sounds (TV vs. lawn mower).
- Discriminates voices (goes to who is talking).
- Follows one-step instructions.
- Identifies body parts, objects, people.
- Identifies pictures.
- Identifies possessions.
- Identifies objects by function.
- Identifies environmental sounds.
- Identifies places.
- Identifies emotions.
- Follows two-step instructions.
- Retrieves objects out of view.

- Identifies attributes and categories.
- Follows directions with prepositions.
- Answers yes–no questions about objects and actions.
- Follows three-step instructions.
- Identifies item that is missing.
- Answers "wh-" questions about objects and pictures.
- Follows complex instructions from a distance.
- Identifies items as same or different.
- Identifies plural vs. singular.
- Answers "wh-" questions about short story or topic.
- Follows instructions: "ask" vs. "tell."

ARTICULATION

- Produces isolated sound.
- Produces sound in words (initial, medial, final positions).
- Produces sound in one of two words.

- Produces sound in sentence.
- Produces sound in sentence in response to questions.
- Produces sound in sentence in conversation.

EXPRESSIVE LANGUAGE

- Uses correct form of "to be."
- Answers general knowledge questions.
- Describes picture in a sentence.
- Recalls immediate past experience.
- Answers "where" and "when" questions.
- Describes sequence of pictures.
- Retells a story.
- Recalls past events.
- Describes topics and objects not in view.
- Tells own story.
- Uses correct verb tense.
- Uses appropriate passive forms.
- Asserts knowledge.
- Answers advanced general knowledge questions.

- Describes how to do something.
- Answers "which" questions.
- Uses appropriate contractions.
- Moves to abstract language skills.
- Uses elicited sentence to request items.
- Spontaneously uses sentence to request items.
- Calls parent from a distance.
- Labels body parts, places, emotions, categories.
- Uses present progressive verbs.
- Uses simple sentences ("It's a…").
- States "I don't know."
- Asks "wh-" questions.
- Uses prepositional forms.
- Uses appropriate plural forms.

SYNTAX

- Nouns (chair).
- Simple verbs (want).
- Uses noun phrases with intransitive verb.
- Indefinite pronouns (that).
- Personal pronouns (I, you).
- Main verbs (is).
- Uses noun phrase with transitive verb plus noun phrase.
- Uses noun phrase and form of "to be" and noun object.
- Secondary verbs (want to see).

- Uses irregular past forms of verb tenses.
- Negatives (no).
- Conjunctions (and).
- "Wh-" questions ("What is that?").
- Prepositions (in or on).
- Adjectives (red).
- Possessives (hers).
- Adverbs (fast).

5. Increase the frequency and variety of interactive experiences.
6. Increase spontaneous and self-initiated communication.
7. Use appropriate nonverbal communication.
8. Use appropriate social conventions (manners).

An important goal in teaching functional language is to move from elicited intraverbal responses (e.g., the teacher asks "What do you want?" and the child responds "Sandwich") to spontaneous tacts, mands, and intraverbals (e.g., the child comes to the teacher and says

TABLE 6.6 ● Sample Functional Communication Curricular Sequence

SEMANTICS (MOVE FROM ELICITED TO SPONTANEOUS)	
■ Uses nouns as agents and objects. ■ Uses action words appropriately. ■ Uses appropriate social words in greetings, farewells, apologies. ■ Describes attributes of people or things. ■ Uses agent–action–object constructions. ■ Indicates location of objects with three-word sentences. ■ Correctly uses common pronouns.	■ Responds verbally to questions. ■ Uses proper nouns appropriately. ■ Uses possessives appropriately. ■ Uses negatives appropriately. ■ Verbally affirms or agrees. ■ Coordinates two ideas into a sentence. ■ Identifies time or duration of an event.

PRAGMATIC FUNCTIONS (MOVE FROM ELICITED TO SPONTANEOUS)	
■ Requests food or object. ■ Requests attention, affection, assistance. ■ Requests information, permission, peer or adult interaction. ■ Refuses. ■ Protests. ■ Expresses cessation of an activity.	■ Affirms in answer to a question. ■ Comments about an object, action, mistake. ■ Expresses humor. ■ Expresses confusion or fear. ■ Expresses frustration or anger. ■ Expresses happiness or sadness.

FUNCTIONAL COMMUNICATION	
■ Asks appropriate questions. ■ Interrupts appropriately. ■ Initiates greetings and farewells. ■ Uses eye contact, gesture, or name to identify the next speaker. ■ Responds appropriately with smiling, frowning, and other facial expressions. ■ Modifies voice volume for various situations. ■ Clarifies a topic for discussion. ■ Asks for clarification of a topic. ■ Takes turns in a conversation.	■ Accepts momentary silence in a conversation. ■ Uses short responses ("Why?" "Really," "Oh") to keep a conversation going. ■ Closes conversations appropriately. ■ Is polite and tactful. ■ Adjusts the formality of language for various situations. ■ Resists topic change when more discussion is desired. ■ Facilitates a positive social interaction. ■ Communicates negative statements appropriately.

"I want a sandwich" or "What time do we need to make sandwiches?"). Functional language curricula such as the sample sequence in Table 6.6 typically list semantic and pragmatic skills that may first be elicited from the student but are ultimately produced spontaneously in appropriate contexts. Teaching language functions that match students' desires and their environmental demands is important. For example, if a student is currently most interactive when she is hungry, facilitate spontaneous requesting during snack and meal times where food can be requested (i.e. mands for food). The important thing to remember is that the skill being taught should be potentially useful to a particular student. Further, functional goals should be taught concurrently with structural goals so that the individual can receive natural reinforcement for using language.

Cognitive Goals and Curriculum

As previously mentioned, developmental theorists in the field of language development believe that language cannot be mastered without cognitive prerequisites, believing that essential cognitive skills precede language development. Prelinguistic cognitive skills that may indicate readiness for formal language and communication interventions include the following: (a) imitation (motor and speech), (b) attending to things in the environment and to what others attend to (joint attention), (c) guiding others' behavior (e.g., placing an adult's hand on the cabinet door), (d) using simple gestures for communicative purposes, (e) tool use and symbolic play, and (f) taking another's perspective. A more specific sample prelinguistic cognitive sequence appears in Table 6.7. Although these

TABLE 6.7 ● Sample Prelinguistic Curricular Sequence

ATTENDING	
■ Makes eye contact when prompted or called. ■ Sits in seat on command. ■ Responds to simple motor direction. ■ Sustains eye contact for up to 5 seconds in response to prompt.	■ Makes eye contact in response to name from a distance. ■ Responds verbally when name is called. ■ Makes eye contact during conversation. ■ Makes eye contact during group instruction.

IMITATION	
■ Imitates gross motor movements. ■ Imitates actions with objects. ■ Imitates fine motor movements. ■ Imitates oral motor movements. ■ Imitates sequenced gross motor movements. ■ Imitates sequenced actions with objects.	■ Imitates actions paired with sounds. ■ Imitates block patterns and drawings. ■ Imitates complex sequences. ■ Imitates peer play. ■ Imitates verbal responses of peers.

PLAY	
■ Explores toy operations. ■ Hands toy to adult if needing help. ■ Pretends (sleeping and eating). ■ Uses common objects and toys appropriately. ■ Plays with dolls. ■ Pretends with more than one person or object (brushes doll's and mother's hair). ■ Combines two toys in pretend play (pours from pitcher into cup). ■ Plays house.	■ Plays with sand and water (filling, pouring, dumping). ■ Pretends external events (store shopping, doctor, teacher). ■ Pretends in sequences (combs hair, gives bath, puts to bed). ■ Associative play. ■ Imaginative play. ■ Uses dolls and puppets to act out scenes. ■ Plans a sequence of pretend events. ■ Full cooperative play.

From Maurice, C., Green, G., & Luce, S. C. (Eds.). (1996). *Behavioral intervention for young children with autism: A manual for parents and professionals* (pp. 66–69, 306–309). Austin: Pro-Ed.

skills do not necessarily need to be mastered before language instruction is initiated, it is often helpful to teach these skills in tandem with behavioral interventions that target communication skills such as teaching a child to mand for preferred items and activities. Further, if language and communication target behaviors are not being acquired efficiently, increasing emphasis on these targets may be advisable (e.g., allocating more instruction time).

Although these skills do not necessarily need to be mastered before language acquisition can be expected, teaching these skills in tandem with target structural and functional language skills is often helpful (Maurice, Green, & Luce, 1996). Further, if language and communication target behaviors are not being acquired efficiently, increasing emphasis on these targets may be advisable, especially for young children with autism or those with more severe cognitive delays. Note that cognitive and language development will be enhanced by both specific skill training and by a context that is rich in interaction and instructional support. Language acquisition, as complex as it is, may necessitate instructional techniques emanating from both behavioral and social-cognitive language theories in some cases.

6-4b Strategies for Teaching Language and Communication

The best practices for teaching language and communication skills to students with autism continue to be debated by researchers. The reason for disagreement about effective instructional approaches, particularly regarding language and communication training, is directly related to differences in language-development theories. One's philosophy about how language develops dictates training methods. Those who believe it must unfold with age would advocate an indirect, facilitative approach. Those who believe language is acquired through interaction, reinforcement and imitation would advocate a more direct approach.

The methods for teaching language acquisition presented in this book are primarily based on two theoretical models—behavioral (ABA) and interactive (social-cognitive), sometimes called *naturalistic teaching* or *milieu teaching*. These two schools of thought have a long history of supportive research involving individuals with autism (Kaiser, 1993; Lovaas, 1977, 1987; Pindiprolu, 2012; Prizant & Wetherby, 1998). Thus, we recommend strategies based on a combination of these models. The interactive model is based on Bruner's (1977) view that language is learned through social interactions. The behavioral model is based on Skinner's (1957) view that language needs to be directly shaped and reinforced.

Behavioral Model

Discrete trial training (DTT), which was discussed in detail in Chapter 5, is the teaching strategy most commonly associated with the behavioral model (ABA). With DTT, students are taught predominantly discrete behaviors through massed repetitive trials. Reinforcement and data collection are integral parts of the program. In DTT, the student responds to teacher cues, receiving immediate feedback from the teacher as to whether the response was correct or not. We recommend teachers use DTT to directly teach language skills at the acquisition and fluency levels (initial learning) and to teach any skills that dictate drill and practice for mastery (e.g., receptive and expressive labeling). Although natural social interactions typically stimulate language development, many children with autism may not readily participate in natural interactive contexts. In these cases, a highly structured behavioral approach such as DTT may be necessary. After mastery of early structural and prelinguistic skills, teachers and parents should begin to apply interactive (naturalistic teaching) and generalization strategies toward complex structural and functional language goals.

Using DTT for language training has the advantages of (a) creating a predictable routine in which to learn, (b) providing consistency in terms of cues and feedback, and (c) usually more efficient initial skill acquisition. As a result, children with autism may find this type of training preferable to less structured indirect strategies, and teachers may prefer the scheduled teaching. For example, a teacher may want to teach a student to point to an object when she says "Point to (target vocabulary word)." Rather than awaiting a natural opportunity to label or contriving multiple opportunities throughout the day that appear natural, the teacher may structure a DTT session as follows:

> The teacher has a sock, a shoe, and a shirt on the table in front of the student.
> **Teacher**: Emerson, look at me. Point to shoe.
> **Emerson**: (*Looks away.*)
> **Teacher**: Emerson, look at me. (*Physically moves head to face her.*)
> **Teacher**: Point to shoe. (*Takes Emerson's hand and points to shoe.*)
> **Emerson**: (*Complies.*)
> **Teacher**: Good pointing. (*Gives Emerson a raisin and marks response on data form.*)

This teaching trial would probably be repeated several times in a row or interspersed with other teaching trials. At some point, the prompts would be faded and Emerson would learn to point to each named item, regardless of its position on the table. Similarly, teaching a student to make a request using a DTT session may go like this:

> The teacher has a lemon, a cookie, and some juice on the table in front of the student.
> **Teacher**: Page, look. (*Teacher sweeps hand over items.*) What do you want?
> **Page**: Juice.
> **Teacher**: Use a sentence. What do you want? I . . .
> **Page**: I want juice, please.
> **Teacher**: Good talking! (*Gives a sip of juice and marks response on data sheet.*)

The teacher may continue trials until no verbal prompting is necessary and should soon move to interactive and naturalistic procedures to maintain and generalize the responses.

Many language behaviors can be taught using massed trials of DTT, and adults can be taught to apply DTT effectively. However, being consistent in presenting antecedent stimuli, prompts, and consequences until generalization and spontaneity are targeted is important. For generalization and spontaneity, antecedent stimuli should be "loosened," prompts faded, and reinforcement thinned.

The more DTT is used, the more the child typically learns. But overly intensive training may actually have detrimental effects on the learner, the trainers, and the parents (Matson & Smith, 2008). The decision about how much time should be spent with DTT sessions should be based on a comprehensive needs assessment, environmental demands, and learner tolerance. For example, a student who has speech and occasionally interacts with others would probably not need hours of one-to-one drill and practice to improve language. However, a child who rarely interacts, shows little or no desire to communicate, and has no speech may well benefit from intensive training. DTT can also be effective for teaching AAC systems (i.e., visual communication systems, picture-exchange systems, sign language, SGDs).

Interactive or Naturalistic Model

Contrary to the rather clinical training approach, the interactive model of language development is based on the assumption that language develops through social interactions in natural contexts and therefore "language should always be presented to the child in a meaningful situation" (Snyder & Lindstedt, 1985, p. 31). In this approach, teachers and parents would engage children in functional activities that allow them to manipulate the environment, and training would occur in natural settings such as the cafeteria, bus, restroom, or kitchen. The interactive model also implies that language develops as a function of cognitive development and promotes cognitive development in turn. Thus, language acquisition is facilitated through play, exploring and manipulating the environment, motor imitation, and prelinguistic nonverbal interactions (e.g., Bruner, 1983; Harris & Vanderheiden, 1980).

Many aspects of the interactive model are important for language acquisition in children with autism (i.e., teaching in natural contexts, individual control of the environment, frequent social interactions, and teaching prelinguistic skills). However, using the interactive approach alone is not recommended. The problem with this methodology is that it assumes an internal motivation to communicate and natural acquisition of prelinguistic skills. Because these characteristics are difficult to measure and may be areas of difficulty for children with autism, a combination of interactive and behavioral methodology is usually indicated, especially as teachers and students work toward spontaneous and generalized language use (Pindiprolu, 2012).

Milieu teaching (MT), which was summarized in Chapter 5, illustrates this combination of behavioral and interactive models. (The reader is referred to Kaiser, 1993, for a detailed description of MT as a strategy for increasing functional language.) MT emphasizes finding a communication system that is easy to learn, teaching responses that are immediately useful to an individual, and training in natural contexts to ensure generalization and functionality.

Three things must happen before a MT trial can occur: (a) the student must show interest in an S^D, (b) the teacher must control access to the S^D, and (c) the teacher must establish joint attention with the student after noting her interest (Webber & Scheuermann, 2008). The natural S^Ds are usually something the student wants or wants to avoid. Once the student attends to the S^D, the teacher should obtain joint attention with the student and apply one or more of three specific prompting procedures: (a) the model procedure, (b) the mand model or instruction-model procedure, and (c) time delay. These prompting procedures can be used individually or in combination.

Model procedure refers to the process of the teacher (or some other model) engaging in the target behavior while the student observes. For example, while outside on the playground, a student tugs on the teacher's sleeve and looks at the swing. The teacher, noting the student's desire to swing, gains joint attention and provides the verbal prompt for what she wants the student to say ("Want swing"). The student may respond by pointing. In this case, the teacher provides a corrective model, "Want swing." The student says, "Want swing." (or some verbal approximation). The teacher then reinforces this response with praise, expanded language, and access to the swing ("Good talking! You want to swing. Go ahead!"). To keep the interaction natural, avoid excessive demands for correct responses before allowing the student to obtain the object or activity of his interest. The purpose of MT is to insert prompts and instructions into natural situations to promote responding without distracting from the natural context (i.e., during recess the students are typically allowed to swing).

The second type of MT prompting procedure, the *mand model*, involves giving a direct instruction (mand) within natural contexts when the student is interested in responding and is attending to the teacher, followed by a model if necessary. For example, a student reaches for a toy truck the teacher has near him. The teacher blocks the hand, gains the child's attention and mands ("Ask for it"). If the student appropriately mands ("Truck, please."), the teacher should expand the utterance ("Yes, a truck!") and deliver the truck (the natural reinforcer). If the student does not appropriately mand, the teacher should provide a model ("Truck, please"). The mand-model procedure provides more prompting than the model procedure alone, so it should only be used when modeling alone does not elicit correct responding (i.e., least-to-most prompting).

Time delay is a procedure whereby the teacher, after noticing student interest and obtaining joint attention, waits 5 to 15 seconds for a student-initiated response after a stimulus has occurred. If the student does not respond, the teacher provides a mand model. The purpose of a time delay is to decrease the student's dependence on teacher instructions and models and to encourage the student to act independently. For example, a student has donned his jacket but needs help with his zipper. The teacher, aware that the student will need assistance, waits for a request for help. If the student says, signs, or points to the zipper (depending on his communication abilities), the teacher gives immediate praise and a correct model ("Help me with my zipper") and provides assistance. If the student does not initiate a response within 15 seconds, the teacher can then provide a mand-model procedure. However, with a time-delay procedure, the teacher runs the risk of losing student interest. Thus, the teacher should wait only as long as a student will tolerate while remaining interested in the material or activity (Kaiser, 1993). Remember that request situations are extremely important opportunities for teaching new skills, promoting fluency, and expanding skills because students are naturally motivated to perform under these conditions. The teacher, after noticing that the student wants something, should obtain joint attention and then apply modeling, mand modeling, or time-delay procedures to teach the student appropriate functional communication.

Table 6.8 lists the prompting procedures for MT as it applies to language development. Particular MT procedures should be chosen based on the amount of assistance required. Avoid using too many prompts and be ready to fade them as soon as possible. Also, pick the procedure that matches the natural flow of the activity. For example, if a student wants a baby doll but does not know what it is called, the teacher should model: "Baby. Say, baby." On the other hand, if a student has requested the baby doll in the past but now only points, the teacher might use time delay, because the student knows how to correctly respond without prompts. Note that MT still requires direct instruction or the components of DTT (i.e., cueing, prompting, responding, reinforcing, data collection). The difference is that in MT the teacher arranges the environment so that the instruction occurs in natural situations and natural consequences provide reinforcement.

A sample milieu teaching session might go something like this:

The teacher places Tommy's stim toy out of reach and tells him it is time for work (contrived opportunity to motivate manding).

Tommy: (Goes to the shelf and reaches for the stim toy.)
Teacher: What do you want, Tommy? (mand or instruction)
Tommy: (Signs "Toy.")
Teacher: Good signing, Tommy. You can have the toy after we work for 15 minutes. Do you want to work with the puzzle or with the word cards? (Holds one in each hand.)
Tommy: (Turns to the teacher and reaches for the puzzle.)
Teacher: (Pauses.) (time delay)
Tommy: (Points to the puzzle.)
Teacher: (Signs "Want puzzle.") (model)
Tommy: (Imitates signs.)
Teacher: Good signing, Tommy! (Hands him the puzzle and tells him to sit down at the table.) (reinforcement)

TABLE 6.8 ● Milieu Teaching Procedures for Language Development

MODEL

1. Present a model related to child's interest (e.g., wants water) (e.g., Teacher says, "Drink water").
   a. If response is correct, then praise, expand, and give access to object.
   b. If response is incorrect, move to step 2.
2. Repeat model (say "Drink water").
   a. For correct response, praise, expand, and give access to object.
   b. For incorrect response, move to step 3.
3. Provide corrective feedback ("Drink water") and access to object.

MAND MODEL

1. Present instruction related to child's interest ("Tell me what you want").
   a. For correct response, praise, expand, and give access to object.
   b. For incorrect response, move to step 2.
2. Provide a second instruction or mand ("Tell me what you want").
   a. For correct response, praise, expand, and give access to object.
   b. For incorrect response, move to step 3.
3. Go back through the steps in the model procedure.

TIME DELAY

1. Wait for response for approximately 5 seconds.
   a. For correct response, praise, expand, and give access to object.
   b. For incorrect response, move to step 2.
2. Present second time delay (wait about 5 seconds).
   a. For correct response, praise, expand, and give access to object.
   b. For incorrect response, move to step 3.
3. Present steps in mand-model procedure.
   a. For correct response, praise, expand, and give access to object.
   b. For incorrect response, move to step 4.
4. Present steps in the model procedure.

An enhanced form of MT, **enhanced milieu teaching (EMT)**, focuses on three major components: (a) connecting, (b) supporting, and (c) teaching (Hancock, Ledbetter-Cho, Howell, & Lang, 2016). *Connecting* involves creating a language-rich environment, obtaining joint attention and engagement, and mirroring the child's behavior as is seen in natural parent–child interactions. *Supporting* is based on the adult responding to all child attempts to communicate by noting the desire to communicate and providing language models. It also involves expanding language utterances—for example, child says "Toy," adult says "I want the toy" (models pronoun from child's referent point) while allowing access to the toy. The teaching portion of EMT uses the MT teaching format with prompts and reinforcement. EMT has been successfully taught to parents of young children with autism, and these parents have been successful in enhancing their child's language skills (Hancock et al., 2016).

MT and EMT have been used to increase linguistic complexity and social communicative use of language by students with disabilities, including those with autism (Hancock et al., 2016). Further, these approaches have been found to be particularly useful when training parents to enhance their child's language acquisition at home (Kaiser & Roberts, 2013; Lang, Machalicek, Rispoli, & Regester, 2009). Paraprofessionals have also been trained using verbal instructions, modeling, video examples, role-play, and feedback to successfully use EMT and MT to instruct students with autism (Rispoli, Neely, Lang, & Ganz, 2011). Using MT or EMT and DTT together may be a particularly strong teaching methodology for young students with autism.

MT and EMT are logical instructional choices for students in inclusive settings. General education teachers and peers could be taught to use these techniques to support students with autism in general education activities, perhaps reducing the need for sole reliance on one-on-one paraprofessionals for support in these situations. MT and EMT may be particularly well suited for use as a universal instructional strategy for early childhood or primary grades. However, general education teachers and others would need sufficient training and support for implementation.

One of the primary components of MT and EMT requires school personnel to arrange environments in such a way as to stimulate requesting and commenting. Kaiser (1993) recommends several strategies for arranging the physical environment such that a student *wants* to communicate and so that many opportunities occur in which to prompt and reinforce language responses. Table 6.9 describes several ways for teachers to create situations that stimulate language use. In addition, a stimulating classroom should contain interesting, reinforcing activities and materials and be staffed with adults who are ready and able to respond appropriately to language attempts by their students. This means that the adult must immediately attend, give feedback, provide the requested material or assistance, and provide expanded language and appropriate affect (e.g., smiling, touching, warm tone of voice, positive interactive style). Note that adults should refrain from providing too much help in the absence of communicative responses. An interactive or naturalistic model will not work if adults do not attend to, cue, prompt, and reinforce students for communicating.

Additional Language Strategies

Additional teaching strategies appropriate for language training can be used in conjunction with DTT and MT or EMT. One such strategy involves the notion of observational learning (Charlop, Schreibman, & Tryon, 1983), a primary method for language development

TABLE 6.9 ● **Ways to Arrange the Environment to Elicit Language**

- *Interesting materials.* Entice students to attend to and want materials and activities that are known to interest them. For example, a teacher purposely activates a computer game that includes ringing bells when Delise is sitting on the couch self-stimulating. Delise stops and looks at the computer.
- *Out of reach.* Not being able to reach a desired object often results in communication attempts. For example, the teacher places a banana on the shelf above the sink when Tommy is washing his hands. Tommy finishes washing and reaches for the banana.
- *Inadequate portions.* Language can be elicited when students want to participate in an activity but lack the material(s) to do so. For example, everyone is handed headphones for music listening except Dylan. The teacher turns on the digital recorder and Dylan says "No."
- *Choice making.* Very likely students will communicate when given a choice. For example, Tomas is asked whether he wants a lemon or a cookie. Tomas says, "Cookie."
- *Assistance.* Often students will communicate when they want to do something and need assistance doing it. The teacher locks the door then announces that it is time to go outside. Sara reaches the door first and cannot open it. "Open door," she says.
- *Silly situations.* Often language can be stimulated by doing something unexpected and silly. For example, when folding towels with Phillip, the teacher wraps the towel around her head. Phillip looks at the teacher and says, "No, fold it."

in typically developing children. **Observational learning** is based on the premise that children learn by watching others (modeling). Because children with autism typically do not naturally attend to relevant models in their environment or learn to imitate easily, using language models has not been a primary intervention technique. Nevertheless, peer models can be used to increase receptive labeling and increase verbalizations in individuals with autism (Chan, Lang, Rispoli, O'Reilly, Sigafoos, & Cole, 2009). These authors reinforced a peer model for appropriate voice tone and for using different vocabulary. The target student with autism also improved voice tone and vocabulary usage after watching the other student receive reinforcement. In some instances, video modeling has been found to be effective in teaching conversation skills and question asking in students with autism (Charlop & Milstein, 1989; Wilson, 2013). If a student with autism has a propensity to echo, then modeling may be a useful strategy to try.

Expansion is another method of facilitating language development that is often also a part of EMT. Expanding the student's language means repeating a child's utterance or gesture and adding one word or sign. Next, have the student repeat the expanded sample. For example, a student may say "Airplane" while looking up at the sky. The teacher then says "Airplane flying." If the student does not repeat the utterance, the teacher uses a mand model by saying, "You say, 'Airplane flying.'"

To facilitate spontaneous communication, teachers should take a "listener's" role, observing and attending to students. Spontaneous communication posits that rather than the teacher initiating language learning, the child is instructed to initiate interactions that result in various learning opportunities. For example, Koegel (1995) recommends teaching individuals to make queries as a method for enhancing child-initiated and spontaneous interactions. Queries such as "What's that?" are common in typically developing children and usually result in interaction and labeling, both opportunities for learning. Queries can be used across settings, providing a learning tool and an opportunity for expanded language. A recent review of the research (Raulston et al., 2013) supports Koegel's recommendations for teaching queries.

- **Teach "What's that?"** Place favorite objects in a sack and prompt the child to say, "What's that?" If the response is given, the teacher removes the item, labels it, and gives it to the child. Gradually fade the prompt. Once the query is produced unprompted, prompt and require the child to label the item (tact) before receiving it. Fade the sack and place items on a table. Elicit the query and label for each while verbally praising for correct responses. Prompting can occur in generalized environments so that ultimately the child has acquired a method for learning vocabulary without adult initiation.
- **Teach "where" questions.** Place favorite items in various locations without the child's knowledge. The child is then prompted to ask, "Where is it?" Given that question, the adult, using prepositions, tells the child where an item is, and the child is allowed to retrieve it. The child is next prompted and required not only to ask where it is but also to state the appropriate preposition (e.g., "under," "on," "behind") before being allowed to retrieve it.
- **Teach "whose" questions.** Using attractive items, prompt the child to ask "Whose is it?" before being given the item. Next require the child to give the possessive before receiving the item ("Mama's," "Baby's," "Yours," "Mine"). The first-person possessives will be the most difficult to teach.
- **Teach "What happened?"** Using a pop-up book or other interactive toy, prompt the child to ask "What happened?" after the adult manipulates the toy. Reinforce for correct responding and next require the child to repeat the past tense of the verb (e.g., "The cow jumped"). In this way, students can learn verb tenses through a structured yet self-initiated procedure.

Language-training techniques should be embedded within nearly every activity throughout the day. Teachers and parents should take advantage of every opportunity to elicit, expand, motivate, and reinforce communication and language. However, it is also important to avoid frustrating children to the point of challenging behavior.

6-4c Augmentative and Alternative Communication (AAC) Systems

Because speech is so difficult to prompt and shape, some students who have not responded to intensive speech training may need to be taught alternative ways to use expressive language. These are typically individuals who require intensive drill and practice to master basic skills, who seem unmotivated to use speech for communicative purposes, or who never acquire speech at all. Typical augmentative and alternative communication (AAC) systems include (a) sign language; (b) visual communication systems using objects, pictures, or words; or (c) SGDs, which are portable devices that can produce computerized speech at the touch of a button, switch, or picture. For example, iPads with speech-generating software can be made available to express various language functions. Deciding when to use AAC systems and which particular system to use requires deliberate consideration. Speech is always the preferred expressive form because it requires no physical aids and is more widely understood. However, in some cases, another system may be considered. Above all, it is important to provide each student with some means of useful communication.

Decisions about the type of AAC system to teach must be based on individualized assessment. Consider such factors as developmental abilities, age, cognitive and motor skills, environmental demands, vocabulary needs, communication partners, and functional skills. Matching a particular AAC system to an individual who has no physical or sensory (visual or hearing) impairment means thinking through several issues. Consider the following.

1. Is the system portable?
2. Will the student be motivated to use it?
3. Is the system flexible and allow a wide variety of vocabulary and functions?
4. How easy it is to prompt responses?
5. Will others will understand communicative responses?
6. What is the potential for expanded language?
7. Will the system will be useful for a particular individual?

Frequently, the communication program will consist of a variety of language systems rather than a singular approach.

Sign Language

In the 1970s, probably out of frustration from trying to teach speech, several researchers attempted to teach individuals with autism to communicate using **sign language** (Carr, 1979; Schaeffer, Musil, & Kollinzas, 1980). Instead of using sign language as though the child were deaf, signs were paired with speech *as total communication*. In many instances, total communication resulted in better speech ability for children with autism (Carr, 1979; Miller & Miller, 1973; Mirenda, 2003). These positive results may result from the visual nature of this system. Many signs also directly illustrate the referent. This means that some signs look like what they symbolize (e.g., combing hair, crying, drinking) and thus are perhaps easier to pair with the referent than speech symbols.

From an instructional point of view, signs are much easier to prompt and shape than are speech responses. Thus, children may acquire functional language at a faster rate. Like speech, sign language is an **unaided language system**. This means that no physical aids are required for communication to take place. So, sign language is readily portable (the language system follows the child) and flexible (various concepts can be communicated because it is a full language system similar to speech). Signs can be delivered rapidly and constructed into sentences with complex meanings. However, mastering sign language, as with speech, presupposes that those with whom the child interacts model sign language and understand it. Because most people outside of the classroom do not comprehend sign language, the potential for naturally occurring expansion and reinforcement is usually limited. A language system that others do not understand may also inhibit integration efforts and most certainly will not be functional across contexts (Mirenda, 2003).

Nevertheless, communicating with even a few signs is superior to not communicating at all or communicating with challenging behavior. Sign language is generally recommended for use with older students who have failed to acquire speech rather than with very young students who may simply be language delayed. It is also important to determine if a student has the motoric capabilities to make discrete signs. If fine motor development is delayed and the child does not readily imitate motor responses, then sign language may not be a viable choice. Sign language can be taught through DTT and MT procedures using similar curricular sequences as those developed for speech acquisition. The most common manual communication systems are American Sign Language and Signing Exact English.

Visual Communication Systems

Speech and sign language rely on transient auditory and visual stimuli. This means that language components are speedily delivered, so the listener or viewer must be able to comprehend quickly and remember after only fleeting exposure. Many students with autism have difficulty processing (attending to, discriminating, comprehending, and remembering) transient stimuli and appear to respond better to static visual cues. **Visual communication systems** that rely on objects, pictures, symbols, or printed words for transmitting messages provide such cues. Visual systems allow students to scan options and take the necessary time to select appropriate responses. Visual communication systems also do not require eye contact or imitative skills (difficult skills for many individuals with autism). Furthermore, responses can be easily prompted. Students can be taught to point to or hand pictures to a person so they can acquire a desired object or activity, make choices, or cue themselves about tasks, destinations, or time. For initial language acquisition, visual systems have been shown to be effective (Bondy & Frost, 1994; Hart & Banda, 2010).

Visual communication systems are **aided systems** because they require the use of physical paraphernalia. Either the student must carry pictures in a wallet or notebook or be able to access a communication board. This means that visual systems may not be particularly portable. Communication boards in particular are not easily transported. The board or notebook will need to be durable and lightweight, and the student will need to remember to take it with him. Otherwise various boards will need to be constructed and remain in each appropriate environment. Certainly, generalization is hampered by the necessity of this physical aid. Although most people understand when a picture of an object is shown, pictures of actions or concepts may not be as readily discernible. Furthermore, communication partners (e.g., teachers, parents, siblings) do not use picture communication, so modeling and expansion may be limited. Visual communication cannot be quickly delivered, and it is difficult to form sentences or complex meanings with visual aids (Mirenda, 2001). For example, a student is climbing up a slide and wants to tell the teacher to catch him. Will he have his pictures with him? Will the teacher be able to see the pictures from the ground? Certainly, communication is limited with picture aids.

However, many children with little or no communicative ability have been taught to use pictures for various communicative functions. Visual systems usually consist of boards, paper, or cloth containing objects or object symbols (e.g., fork for "lunch"); photographs of people, places, and things; or line drawings arranged for communicative use such as the Mayer-Johnson symbols. Using Velcro to attach the symbols allows teachers to change or rearrange the symbols, use symbols in various environments, and require the student to remove or place symbols as a signal to do something or to show they are finished doing something.

Frost and Bondy (2002) have developed a picture communication system, the **picture-exchange communication system (PECS)**, which initially teaches children to request (mand) objects or activities by handing others pictures symbolizing the desired item. They reason that manding, rather than tacting, should be taught first because manding occurs before tacting in typical development and the reinforcer for a mand (provision of the request) is often a powerful natural reinforcer that can result in efficient kill acquisition. Manding is then gradually shaped into other language functions and, in some cases with young children, functional speech develops (Bondy, 2000). Bondy and Frost (1994) also claimed that children previously using sign language developed a larger vocabulary with pictures.

Speech-Generating Devices

Many types of devices including handheld tablets and smartphones support software that can be used to generate speech by pressing a button, switch, or icon. These devices are available in a range of sizes and weights and can display various combinations of letters, symbols, pictures, and words. Some SGDs have monitors displaying a few items at a time, whereas others may have a static display for visual scanning. Some allow for recording voices, whereas others are programmed with a computer voice. In some cases, students might need to be taught to select among many displays for specific occasions, thus making their use more complicated (Kagohara et al., 2013).

Nearly all AAC systems can be taught using DTT and MT or EMT techniques in natural contexts (Olive et al., 2007). AAC systems have been effective in reducing and preventing problem behavior and providing individuals with an appropriate means of interaction. Thoughtfully choosing which language form or forms to teach a particular student to use is extremely important. Acquiring the ability to communicate with others is an essential human endeavor and impacts all other areas of development and learning. A danger lies in insistence on one particular language form to the exclusion of others, thus possibly depriving individuals of any communicative ability. There is also a danger in choosing a language form that may not be functional (e.g., sign language when no one at home understands it), thus wasting precious instructional time. A third danger pertains to generalizability. This is a particular problem for sign language and the use of unrecognizable symbols. Fortunately, none of these language systems needs to be used exclusively. In most instances, using a combination of AAC systems and speech may be best, and in some cases speech production might actually improve with the use of AAC systems (e.g., Mirenda, 2001, 2003; Ostryn, Wolfe, & Rusch, 2008).

Summary

Language and communication skills may be the most important thing to teach. Without such skills, a student is often powerless to affect his environment and may resort to challenging and stigmatizing behavior. The individual's prognosis, not to mention immediate well-being, depends on functional communication ability. However, the complexity of language and its interaction with cognitive and social development make for an instructional challenge. With a myriad of skills across several domains, teachers will do well to read and learn as much about language and communication training as possible. This chapter has provided a brief overview of language development, problems specific to individuals with autism, ways to assess communication and language for instructional purposes, curricular sequences, best practices in terms of teaching strategies, and alternate and augmentative communication systems. As with all instructions, teachers must consider long-term, intermediate, and short-term goals and remember that independence across settings is the ultimate target.

Key Points

1. Teaching individuals to communicate in appropriate and functional ways is one of our most important tasks and should be addressed at every opportunity.
2. Speech is only one form of communication. It includes many receptive and expressive components.
3. The structure of language is important; however, for individuals with autism, appropriate communicative forms and functions may be better assessment and intervention targets.
4. There are many theories about how language develops. The theories directly relate to methods of assessment and intervention. Behavioral theory espoused by B. F. Skinner and social cognitive theory espoused by Jerome Bruner are recommended.
5. Language typically develops from prespeech in infants to complex language understanding and use in the first 4 to 5 years of life.
6. Language development is closely related to cognitive development. Debate exists about exactly how they are related. Students with autism typically show many problems in both areas.
7. Assessment and intervention for language and communication development needs to occur in four areas: social domain, linguistic domain, communicative domain, and cognitive domain. Both formal and informal assessment methods can provide useful information in these domains.
8. DTT is a behavioral technique useful for initial language skill training.

9. MT and EMT combine the interactive and behavioral model to provide opportunities for spontaneous language and generalization.

10. AAC systems include an unaided system (sign language), and aided systems (visual systems and SGDs). These systems may be used individually or in combination when speech does not adequately develop and may result in more speech production.

11. Each individual should be provided with a means to communicate his needs and desires. This may mean combining strategies and language systems.

References

American Psychiatric Association. (2013). *Diagnostic and statistical manual of mental disorders: DSM-5* (5th ed.). Washington, DC: American Psychiatric Association.

Barnes, C. S., Mellor, J. R., & Rehfeldt, R. A. (2014). Implementing the verbal behavior milestones assessment and placement program (VB-MAPP): Teaching assessment techniques. *The Analysis of Verbal Behavior, 30,* 36–47.

Bartolucci, G., Pierce, S. J., & Streiner, D. (1980). Cross-sectional studies of grammatical morphemes in autistic and mentally retarded children. *Journal of Autism and Developmental Disorders, 10,* 39–50.

Berk, L. E., & Meyers, A. B. (2016). *Infants, children, and adolescents* (8th ed.). Boston: Pearson.

Bondy, A. (2000). Picture exchange communication systems. In J. Scott, C. Clark, & M. Brady (Eds.), *Students with autism: Characteristics and instructional programming for special educators* (pp. 209–211). Belmont, CA: Wadsworth/Cengage Learning.

Bondy, A. S, & Frost, L. A. (1994, August). The picture exchange communication system. *Focus on Autistic Behavior, 9*(3), 1–19.

Bruner, J. S. (1977). Early social interaction and language acquisition. In H. R. Schaffer (Ed.), *Studies in mother–infant interaction.* New York: Academic Press.

Bruner, J. S. (1983). *Child's talk: Learning to use language.* Oxford, UK: Oxford University Press.

Carbone, V. J., Lewis, L., Sweeney-Kerwin, E. J., Dixon, J., Louden, R., & Quinn, S. (2006). A comparison of two approaches for teaching VB functions: Total communication vs. vocal-alone. *The Journal of Speech-Language Pathology and Applied Behavior Analysis, 1,* 181–192.

Carr, E. G. (1979). Teaching autistic children to use sign language: Some research issues. *Journal of Autism and Developmental Disorders, 9,* 345–359.

Chan, J. M., Lang, R., Rispoli, M., O'Reilly, M., Sigafoos, J., & Cole, H. (2009). Use of peer-mediated interventions in the treatment of autism spectrum disorders: A systematic review. *Research in Autism Spectrum Disorders, 3,* 876–889.

Charlop, M. H., & Milstein, J. P. (1989). Teaching autistic children conversational speech using video modeling. *Journal of Applied Behavior Analysis, 22,* 275–285.

Charlop, M. H., Schreibman, L., & Tryon, A. S. (1983). Learning through observation: The effects of peer modeling on acquisition and generalization in autistic children. *Journal of Abnormal Child Psychology, 11,* 355–366.

Chomsky, N. (1967). The formal nature of language. In E. H. Lenneberg (Ed.), *Biological foundations of language* (pp. 397–442). New York: John Wiley.

Dixon, M. R., Belisle, J., Stanley, C., Rowsey, K., Daar, J. H., & Szekely, S. (2015). Toward a behavior analysis of complex language for children with autism: Evaluating the relationship between PEAK and the VB-MAPP. *Journal of Developmental and Physical Disabilities, 27,* 223–233.

Dixon, M. R., Belisle, J., Whiting, S. W., & Rowsey, K. E. (2014). Normative sample of the PEAK relational training system: Direct training module and subsequent comparisons to individuals with autism. *Research in Autism Spectrum Disorders, 8,* 1597–1606.

Dixon, M. R., Rowsey, K. E., Gunnarsson, K. F., Delisle, J., Stanley, C. R., & Daar, J. H. (2017b). Normative sample of the PEAK relational training system: Generalization module with comparison to individuals with autism. *Journal of Behavioral Education, 26,* 101–122.

Durand, M. V., & Muskowitz, L. (2015). Functional communication training: Thirty years of treating challenging behavior. *Topics in Early Childhood Special Education, 35,* 116–126.

Edmunds, S. R., Ibañez, L. V., Warren, Z., Messinger, D. S., & Stone, W. L. (2017). Longitudinal prediction of language emergence in infants at high and low risk for autism spectrum disorder. *Development and Psychopathology, 29,* 319–329.

Eigsti, I.-M., de Marchena, A. B., Schuh, J. M., & Kelley, E. (2011). Language acquisition in autism spectrum disorders: a developmental review. *Research in Autism Spectrum Disorders, 5,* 681–691.

Frost, L. A., & Bondy, A. S. (2002). *PECS: The picture exchange communication system: Training manual* (2nd ed.). Newark, DE: Pyramid Educational Products.

Giddan, J. J., & Ross, G. J. (2001). *Childhood communication disorders in mental health settings.* Austin: Pro-Ed.

Gleason, J. B. (1997). *The development of language* (4th ed.). Needham Heights, MA: Allyn & Bacon.

Greer, R. D., & Ross, D. E. (2007). *Verbal behavior analysis: Inducing and expanding new verbal capabilities in children with language delays.* Boston: Allyn & Bacon.

Hampton, L. H., & Kaiser, A. P. (2016). Intervention effects on spoken-language outcomes for children with autism: A systematic review and meta-analysis. *Journal of Intellectual Disability Research, 60,* 444–463.

Hancock, T. B., Ledbetter-Cho, K., Howell, A., & Lang, R. (2016). Enhanced milieu teaching. In R. Lang, T. Hancock, & N. N. Singh (Eds.), *Early intervention for young children with autism spectrum disorder.* New York: Springer.

Harris, D., & Vanderheiden, G. (1980). Augmentative communication techniques. In R. L. Schiefelbusch (Ed.), *Nonspeech language and communication: Analysis and intervention* (pp. 259–302). Austin: Pro-Ed.

Hart, S. L., & Banda, D. R. (2010). Picture exchange communication system with individuals with developmental disabilities: A meta-analysis of single subject studies. *Remedial and Special Education, 31,* 476–488.

Hinerman, P. S. (1983). *Teaching autistic children to communicate.* Rockville, MD: Aspen.

Hurtig, R., Ensrud, S., & Tomblin, J. B. (1982). The communicative function of question production in autistic children. *Journal of Autism and Developmental Disorders, 12*, 57–69.

Kagohara, D. M., van der Meer, L., Ramdoss, S., O'Reilly, M. F., Lancioni, G. E., Davis, T. N., Rispoli, M., Lang, R., Marschik, P. B., Sutherland, D., Green, V. A., & Sigafoos, J. (2013). Using iPods® and iPads® in teaching programs for individuals with developmental disabilities: A systematic review. *Research in Developmental Disabilities, 34*, 147–156.

Kaiser, A. P. (1993). Functional language. In M. E. Snell (Ed.), *Instruction of students with severe disabilities*. Upper Saddle River, NJ: Prentice-Hall.

Kaiser, A. P., & Roberts, M. Y. (2013). Parent-implemented enhanced milieu teaching with preschool children who have intellectual disabilities. *Journal of Speech, Language, and Hearing Research, 56*, 295–309.

Kamhi, A. G. (1981). Nonlinguistic symbolic and conceptual abilities of language-impaired and normally developing children. *Journal of Speech and Hearing Research, 24*, 446–453.

Koegel, L. K. (1995). Communication and language intervention. In R. L. Koegel & L. K. Koegel (Eds.), *Teaching children with autism: Strategies for initiating positive interactions and improving learning opportunities* (pp. 17–32). Baltimore: Paul H. Brookes.

Lang, R., Hancock, T., & Singh, N. N. (2016). Overview of early intensive behavioral interventions for children with autism. In R. Lang, T. Hancock, & N. N. Singh (Eds.), *Evidenced-based practices in behavioral health*. New York: Springer.

Lang, R., Machalicek, W., Rispoli, M., & Regester, A. (2009). Training parents to implement communication interventions for children with autism spectrum disorders (ASD): A systematic review. *Evidence-based communication assessment and intervention, 3*, 174–190.

Lang, R., Sigafoos, J., van der Meer, L., O'Reilly, M. F., Lancioni, G. E., & Didden, R. (2013). Early signs and early behavioral intervention of challenging behavior. In R. Hastings & J. Rojahn (Eds.), *Challenging behavior: International review of research in developmental disabilities, 44* (pp. 1–35). London: Elsevier.

Layton, T. L., & Watson, L. R. (1995). Enhancing communication in nonverbal children with autism. In K. A. Quill (Ed.), *Teaching children with autism: Strategies to enhance communication and socialization*. Clifton Park, NY: Delmar/Cengage Learning.

Lefrançois, G. R. (2001). *Of children: An introduction to child and adolescent development* (9th ed.). Belmont, CA: Wadsworth/Thompson Learning.

Lifter, K., Ellis, J., Cannon, B., & Anderson, S. R. (2005). Developmental specificity in targeting and teaching play activities to children with pervasive developmental disorders. *Journal of Early Intervention, 27*, 247–267.

Lorah, E. R., Parnell, A., Whitby, P. S., & Hantula, D. (2015). A systematic review of tablet computers and portable media players as speech generating devices for individuals with autism spectrum disorder. *Journal of Autism and Developmental Disorders, 45*, 3792–3804.

Lovaas, O. I. (1977). *The autistic child: Language development through behavior modification*. New York: Irvington.

Lovaas, O. I. (1987). Behavioral treatment and normal educational and intellectual functioning in young autistic children. *Journal of Consulting and Clinical Psychology, 55*, 3–9.

MacCorquodale, K. (1970). On Chomsky's review of Skinner's *Verbal Behavior. Journal of the Experimental Analysis of Behavior, 13*, 83–99.

Malkin, A., Dixon, M., Speelman, R. C., & Luke, N. (2017). Evaluating the relationships between the PEAK Relational Training System-Direct Training Module, Assessment of Basic Language and Learning Skills–Revised, and the Vineland Adaptive Behavior Scales–II. *Journal of Developmental and Physical Disabilities, 29*, 341–351.

Matson, J. L., & Smith, K. R. M. (2008). Current status of intensive behavioral interventions for young children with autism and PDD-NOS. *Research in Autism Spectrum Disorders, 2*, 60–74.

Maurice, C., Green, G., & Luce, S. C. (Eds.). (1996). *Behavioral intervention for young children with autism: A manual for parents and professionals*. Austin: Pro-Ed.

McGonigle-Chalmers, M., Alderson-Day, B., Fleming, J., & Monsen, K. (2013). Profound expressive language impairment in low functioning children with autism: An investigation of syntactic awareness using a computerized learning task. *Journal of Autism and Developmental Disorders, 43*, 2062–2081.

Miller, A., & Miller, E. E. (1973). Cognitive-developmental training with elevated boards and sign language. *Journal of Autism and Childhood Schizophrenia, 3*, 65–85.

Mirenda, P. (2001). Autism, augmentative communication, and assistive technology: What do we really know? *Focus on Autism and Other Developmental Disabilities, 16*, 141–151.

Mirenda, P. (2003). Toward functional augmentative and alternative communication for students with autism: Manual signs, graphic symbols, and voice output communication aids. *Language, Speech, and Hearing Services in Schools, 34*, 203–216.

Needleman, R., Ritvo, E. R., & Freeman, B. J. (1980). Objectively defined linguistic parameters in children with autism and other developmental disabilities. *Journal of Autism and Developmental Disorders, 10*, 389–398.

Neel, R. S., & Billingsley, F. F. (1989). *IMPACT: A functional curriculum handbook for students with moderate to severe disabilities*. Baltimore: Paul H. Brookes.

Neely, L., Gerow, S., Rispoli, M., Lang, R., & Pullen, N. (2016). Treatment of echolalia in individuals with autism spectrum disorder: A systematic review. *Review Journal of Autism and Developmental Disorders, 3*(1), 82–91.

Ninci, J., Lang, R., Davenport, K., Lee, A., Garner, J., Moore, M., Boutot, E., Rispoli, M., & Lancioni, G. E. (2013). An analysis of the generalization and maintenance of eye contact taught during play. *Developmental Neurorehabilitation, 16*, 301–307.

Olive, M. L., de la Cruz, B., Davis, T. N., Chan, J. M., Lang, R. B., O'Reilly, M. F., & Dickson, S. M. (2007). The effects of enhanced milieu teaching and a voice output communication aid on the requesting of three children with autism. *Journal of Autism and Developmental Disorders, 37*, 1505–1513.

Ostryn, C., Wolfe, P. S., & Rusch, F. R. (2008). A review and analysis of the picture exchange communication system (PECS) for individuals with autism spectrum disorders using a paradigm of communication competence. *Research and Practice for Persons with Severe Disabilities, 33*, 13–24.

Partington, J. W. (2008). *The assessment of basic language and learning skills—Revised* (ABLLS-R). Pleasant Hill, CA: Behavior Analysts.

Paul, R. (1987). Communication. In D. J. Cohen & A. M. Donnellan (Eds.), *Handbook of autism and pervasive developmental disorders*. New York: John Wiley & Sons.

Paul, R., Fischer, M. L., & Cohen, D. J. (1988). Brief report: Sentence comprehension strategies in children with autism and specific language disorders. *Journal of Autism and Developmental Disorders, 18,* 669–679.

Pelios, L. V., & Sucharzewski, A. (2004). Teaching receptive language to children with autism: A selective overview. *The Behavior Analyst Today, 4,* 378–385.

Piaget, J. (1954). *The construction of reality in the child.* New York: Basic Books.

Pierce-Jordan, S., & Lifter, K. (2005). Interaction of social and play behaviors in preschoolers with and without pervasive developmental disorder. *Topics in Early Childhood Special Education, 25,* 34–47.

Pindiprolu, S. S. (2012). A review of naturalistic interventions with young children with autism. *Journal of the International Association of Special Education, 12,* 69–78.

Plavnick, J. B., & Normand, M. (2013). Functional analysis of verbal behavior: A brief review. *Journal of Applied Behavior Analysis, 46,* 349–353.

Prizant, B. M., & Schuler, A. L. (1987). Facilitating communication: Theoretical foundations. In D. J. Cohen, A. M. Donnellan, & R. Paul (Eds.), *Handbook of autism and pervasive developmental disorders.* New York: John Wiley & Sons.

Prizant, B. M., & Wetherby, A. M. (1998). Understanding the continuum of discrete-trial traditional behavioral to social-pragmatic developmental approaches in communication enhancement for young children with autism/PDD. *Seminars in Speech and Language, 19*(4), 329–353.

Quill, K. A. (1995). *Teaching children with autism: Strategies to enhance communication and socialization.* Clifton Park, NY: Delmar/Cengage Learning.

Raulston, T., Carnett, A., Lang, R., Tostanoski, A., Lee, A., Machalicek, W., Sigafoos, J., O'Reilly, M. F., Didden, R., & Lancioni, G. E. (2013). Teaching individuals with autism spectrum disorder to ask questions: A systematic review. *Research in Autism Spectrum Disorders, 7,* 866–878.

Reichle, J., & Sigafoos, J. (1994). Communication intervention for persons with developmental disabilities. In E. C. Cipani & F. Spooner (Eds.), *Curricular and instructional approaches for persons with severe disabilities* (pp. 241–262). Needham Heights, MA: Allyn & Bacon.

Rispoli, M., Neely, L., Lang, R., & Ganz, J. (2011). Training paraprofessionals to implement interventions for people with autism spectrum disorders: A systematic review. *Developmental Neurorehabilitation, 14,* 378–388.

Rydell, P. J., & Mirenda, P. (1991). The effects of two levels of linguistic constraint on echolalia and generative language production in children with autism. *Journal of Autism and Developmental Disorders, 21,* 131–157.

Saad, A. G., & Goldfeld, M. (2009). Echolalia in the language development of autistic individuals: A bibliographic review. *Pró-Fono Revista de Atualização Científica, 21,* 255–260.

Schaeffer, B., Musil, A., & Kollinzas, G. (1980). *Total communication: A signed speech program for nonverbal children.* Champaign, IL: Research Press.

Sigafoos, J., Lancioni, G. E., O'Reilly, M. F., Achmadi, D., Stevens, M., Roche, L., Kagohara, D. M., van der Meer, L., Sutherland, D., Lang, R., Marschik, P. B., McLay, L., Hodis, F., & Green, V. A. (2013). Teaching two boys with autism spectrum disorders to request the continuation of toy play using an iPad-based speech generating device. *Research in Autism Spectrum Disorders, 7,* 923–930.

Skinner, B. F. (1957). *Verbal behavior.* New York: Appleton-Century-Crofts.

Snyder, L. S., & Lindstedt, D. E. (1985). Models of child language development. In E. Schopler & G. B. Mesibov (Eds.), *Communication problems in autism.* New York: Plenum Press.

Sterponi, L., & Shankey, J. (2014). Rethinking echolalia: Repetition as interactional resource in the communication of a child with autism. *Journal of Child Language, 41,* 275–304.

Stokes, T. F., & Baer, D. M. (1977). An implicit technology of generalization. *Journal of Applied Behavior Analysis, 10,* 349–367.

Sundberg, M. L. (2008). *Verbal behavior milestones assessment and placement program* (VB-MAPP). Concord, CA: AVB Press.

Tager-Flusberg, H. (1996). Brief report: Current theory and research on language and communication in autism. *Journal of Autism and Developmental Disorders, 26,* 169–172.

Taylor, L. J., & Whitehouse, A. J. O. (2016). Autism spectrum disorder, language disorder, and social (pragmatic) communication disorder: Overlaps, distinguishing features, and clinical implications. *Australian Psychologist, 51,* 287–295.

Vygotsky, L. S. (1962). *Thought and language* (E. Hanfman & G. Vakar, Trans.). Cambridge: MIT Press.

Wallace, G., Cohen, S. B., & Polloway, E. A. (1987). *Language arts: Teaching exceptional students.* Austin: Pro-Ed.

Webber, J., & Scheuermann, B. S. (2008). *Educating students with autism: A quick start manual.* Austin: Pro-Ed.

White, P. J., O'Reilly, M. Streusand, W., Levine, A., Sigafoos, J., Lancioni, G., Fragale, C., Pierce, N., & Aguilar, J. (2011). Best practices for teaching joint attention: A systematic review. *Research in Autism Spectrum Disorders, 5,* 1283–1295.

Wilson, K. P. (2013). Incorporating video modeling into a school-based intervention for students with autism spectrum disorders. *Language, Speech, and Hearing in Schools, 44,* 105–117.

Wing, L. (1996). *The autistic syndromes.* London: Constable.

7

Remediating Deficits in Socialization

LEARNING OBJECTIVES

After reading this chapter, you will be able to:

7-1 Describe socialization characteristics present in many individuals with autism and implications of those characteristics for social functioning.
7-2 Differentiate between social competence and social skills.
7-3 Explain methods for determining social skills needed by students with autism.
7-4 Describe interventions for improving socialization in students with autism.
7-5 Describe strategies for facilitating the generalization of new social behaviors.

© Lang

Children and youth with autism characteristically display low levels of social engagement. In fact, Kanner chose the term *autism*, from the Greek *autos*, meaning "self," to reflect this cardinal symptom of the disorder. Attempts to interact by teachers or peers without disabilities may produce challenging behaviors such as self-injury, aggression, tantrums, or crying from a child with autism. Most typically developing children and youth initiate social interactions and respond to social initiations by others with little or no direct, formal instruction in socialization skills. Such informal social learning occurs, in part, because children imitate the behaviors of peers and social interactions are reinforcing for most children and adults. However, social learning is less likely to occur for children and youth with autism through traditional (e.g., informal) channels for reasons related to why autism develops in the first place (e.g., atypical neurocognitive development) and because of deficits in social awareness, imitation skills, and self-awareness (American Psychiatric Association [APA], 2013). In addition, naturally occurring social interactions may not be reinforcing enough to children with autism to motivate them to initiate and respond to those interactions, and children with autism may lack the skills to learn from socialization interactions that do occur.

It is important not to conflate a lack of social skills with disinterest in social interaction or relationships. Although people with autism may lack the skills necessary to establish or maintain social relationships, many desire meaningful social relationships and cherish their interactions with friends and family. Further, even though social deficits are emphasized in autism spectrum disorder's diagnostic criteria, social skills can be taught to people with autism. Having the skills necessary to engage in more meaningful and successful social interactions is important regardless of whether or not those skills are consistently used. Improving the social skills of children with autism empowers them to make more choices regarding their social lives. Teachers of children with autism will need planned socialization interventions designed to address targeted socialization goals.

In this chapter, we will explore socialization characteristics common in individuals with autism and how those characteristics affect social engagement. In addition, we will describe interventions for improving social competence in children and youth with autism, in part by assessing students' current socialization deficits with respect to the demands of social environments and the skills that are naturally reinforced in those environments. We will also describe intervention strategies to teach social behavior.

7-1 Socialization Characteristics and Implications

Social behavior is complex and varied, and it can also be subtle. It involves both verbal and nonverbal behaviors, and relies heavily on communication as a facilitator. Social behavior differs by age, but several types of general social behaviors are critical throughout the life span. For example, children and adults alike are expected to initiate and respond to interactions, take turns, understand subtle social cues, be aware of another's point of view, and engage in activities and conversations based on shared interests.

Unfortunately, these critical skill areas are characteristically absent or limited in individuals with autism (Koegel, Matos-Freden, Lang, & Koegel, 2012). A long line of research has demonstrated deficits in social functioning of such individuals and the effects of those deficits. For example, individuals with autism not only exhibit fewer or markedly underdeveloped discrete social behaviors (e.g., making eye contact, adhering to polite social conventions) but also have fewer friendships, smaller peer networks, and greater isolation in social settings (e.g., on the playground) (Chang & Locke, 2016).

As with any other person, social initiations by a student with autism may serve many different functions. For example, a child may take the teacher's hand and lead him to the refrigerator and then place his hand on the refrigerator door. This form of social interaction typically involves physical contact, communicative intent, and joint attention (e.g., both people are aware that they are both attending to the refrigerator) and is maintained by positive reinforcement (i.e., the function is to obtain something to eat or drink). Leading someone by the hand to help obtain a desired object (e.g., food from the refrigerator) is sometimes referred to as **autistic leading**, and this behavior can be shaped into more appropriate social communication with careful intervention (e.g., Carr & Kemp, 1989). Even though the behavior may function to obtain a nonsocial reinforcer (e.g., food), that does not mean the behavior is not a social skill. All of us use our social skills to help us obtain and avoid certain stimuli and contingencies. Teachers should be mindful of the various functions that the social skills in the student's existing repertoire serve and use that knowledge to build new social competencies. For example, building from the autistic leading that functions to obtain food may involve teaching the student to verbally request food (Carr & Kemp, 1989).

Children and youth with autism who exhibit more socially oriented behavior (e.g., they watch people in their environment, initiate limited conversations, or respond to greetings) may still experience many social obstacles and related issues. For example, a student who initiates conversations may use unusual syntax or may talk only about one or two preferred

Did you know that:

- To improve social performance for children with autism, you must teach critical skills and provide opportunities to socialize?
- Teaching social skills is important but may not lead to better social relationships with peers?
- Sometimes we need to teach children how to be friends and provide opportunities for children to practice those friendship skills?
- Direct instruction of social skills does not necessarily result in improved friendships, increased social engagement, or richer social networks?

topics. In some cases, socially oriented behavior does improve as individuals age (Scott, Clark, & Brady, 2000), but without intervention limited socialization opportunities and restricted social skills will continue to detract from the individual's quality of life (Hochman, Carter, Bottema-Beutel, Harvey, & Gustafson, 2015). Well-planned and comprehensive interventions will increase opportunities for integrated placements and likely increase options for independent functioning.

In addition, individuals with autism typically do not exhibit joint attention, an important behavior necessary for both social and language development (Mundy, 2000; White et al., 2011). **Joint attention**, or shared attention, is a social experience shared by two or more people and often initiated by one person. For example, a toddler who is enjoying a toy may look away from the toy to the parent in the room and back to the toy as if to share the experience with the parent. Young students watching a magic act may look at and direct expressions of amazement toward their teacher on the conclusion of a dramatic trick. When adults experience a powerful stimulus (e.g., a good joke, a beautiful painting, a disturbing sight, a surprise), they often look at other people who are sharing the same experience and smile, nod, shake their heads, or exhibit other appropriate, shared responses. Joint attention is an essential prerequisite skill for later social communication and social interaction development (Kaale, Smith, & Sponheim, 2012) and should be a target for socialization interventions, especially with young children.

Other characteristics that interfere with socialization include deficits in social imitation skills, which are important for learning new social behaviors and also help us determine appropriate behavior in specific contexts, especially new contexts. Individuals with autism may also have difficulty with acknowledging or responding to the emotions of others (i.e., displaying appropriate empathy), perseverating on topics, choosing suitable conversational topics, maintaining conversations and other social interactions, and adhering to social norms of nonverbal social interactions (Howlin, 1986; Koegel et al., 2012; Pickles et al., 2016).

One of the most challenging aspects of improving social skills in students with autism is generalization of newly learned skills (Kasari et al., 2016). As you know, students with autism often do not automatically generalize new skills to different environments, unfamiliar peers or adults, or any other change from the original learning conditions. Lack of generalization can be particularly problematic for improving social behavior and social interactions in children and youth with autism. Effective social behavior is almost entirely a process of generalizing skills to novel conditions. For example, young children learn to say "hello" in response to a greeting. They probably exhibit this skill predictably in the presence of familiar adults, but they may turn away shyly or simply not respond when greeted by an unfamiliar adult. Eventually, with practice, prompting, and reinforcement, children learn to respond not only to unfamiliar adults but also to novel greetings (e.g., "Hi there!" "Good morning" or "What's up?") and in new settings (e.g., school, home, synagogue). Children with autism will not generalize most skills without structured interventions to achieve that goal.

7-1a Implications of Socialization Deficits

Many people believe that socialization deficits are related to—even rooted in—cognitive and communication deficits. Kanner (1943) attributed the characteristic social isolation of children with autism specifically to insufficient language skills. Furthermore, development of joint attention skills in infancy is thought to be an important prerequisite to cognitive and communication development in preschoolers. Perhaps most important is that higher-level skills in joint attention in very young children appear to be predictive of better language development later (Mundy, 2000; White et al., 2011). Thus, social skill deficits negatively affect future development in other crucial areas.

Social skills are important for successful functioning in nearly all aspects of life at home, school, and work, and fluency in social behavior can affect success in school, home, community, employment, and overall quality of life (Lovaas, 1987; McEvoy & Odom, 1987; Watkins et al., 2015). Even many daily living tasks that are not directly social activities require some degree of socialization: riding the bus, shopping for groceries, walking in the halls at school, interacting with fellow employees and supervisors, leisure activities, and so forth. The degree to which a child with autism exhibits social skills and social interest is an important predictor of successful functioning later in life (Hochman et al., 2015; Matson & Swiezy, 1994; Schopler & Mesibov, 1983; Watkins et al., 2015). Indeed, individuals who exhibit better social skills are more likely to be accepted in and benefit from integrated settings in school and the community, to live with a greater degree of independence, and to work in integrated settings.

Socialization and LRE

As you have learned, the Individual with Disabilities Education Act (U.S. Department of Education, 2016a) requires students with disabilities be educated in the **least restrictive environment (LRE)**, and to the extent educational progress can be made in inclusive settings, the LRE means that education should occur with peers without disabilities. Decisions regarding the LRE should be determined individually for students with disabilities based on each student's unique skills, interests, and educational goals as well as the resources available to support the student in various settings. This mandate was predicated on three principles:

1. that children with disabilities have a civil right to participate in the same activities and environments as students without disabilities,
2. that integration would result in improved attitudes of children without disabilities and general education teachers toward children with disabilities, and
3. that children with disabilities would benefit from exposure to peers without disabilities who model appropriate social, academic, play or leisure, and language skills.

The interpretation and implementation of LRE has evolved over the years from simply sending a child with disabilities to lunch or recess with typical-age peers to full-time placement of a child with disabilities in an age-appropriate general education class with a variety of support services. In addition, our understanding of the instructional procedures that are essential for children with disabilities to gain maximum benefit from integrated placements has grown tremendously. We now know, for example, that improving socialization outcomes for students with autism requires structured interventions directed both toward the child with autism and typically developing peers, along with carefully designed opportunities to interact in authentic contexts with peers. When program philosophies and practices emphasize socialization interventions and provide a wide array of opportunities for socialization, and when these practices are supported by effective intervention procedures, children and youth with autism can be expected to achieve improved social performance (Camargo et al., 2014; Chang & Locke, 2016; Kasari et al., 2016).

7-2 Social Competence Versus Social Skills

Teaching social skills is an important but insufficient goal. The purpose for teaching social skills is to improve individuals social behavior and ultimately their social functioning. But social functioning does not occur in isolation. Social functioning requires interactions among individuals, and successful social functioning requires positive, healthy, and developmentally appropriate interactions. Successful social functioning for children and youth with autism requires not only that the child with autism exhibit skilled social behavior but also that social partners respond appropriately to that behavior and that others view the child favorably (or even neutrally). This describes the difference between **social competence** and **social skills**. Social competence refers to other people's perceptions of the social performance of an individual (Hops, 1983). Socially competent individuals are usually able to initiate and maintain friendships and interpersonal relationships, interact appropriately with authority figures, and effectively manage stressful situations. Social skills are those discrete social behaviors that are typically exhibited by socially competent individuals, such as maintaining eye contact, asking relevant questions, greeting others, taking turns in conversations and other interactions, joining peers in play, standing an appropriate distance from others, and so forth.

The distinction between social competence and social skills is important. Appropriate use of discrete social skills does not necessarily result in social competence. This means that efforts focused only on teaching discrete social behaviors to students with autism (teaching the child to make eye contact, respond to adults' greetings, etc.) may be inefficient; the child's skills must be considered with regard to contexts in which he or she must function, including social behaviors needed for success in those contexts and desired social outcomes within those contexts. For example, little is accomplished by teaching a child with autism to respond to peers' greetings if peers do not initiate greetings. Nor is it particularly useful to teach a child with autism how to participate in leisure activities if he is then excluded from those activities by typically developing peers. Contextual targets include both settings (e.g., cafeteria, general education classrooms, playground) and potential social partners within those contexts (e.g., classmates and teachers).

Finally, increasing a child with autism's repertoire of social behaviors probably will not result in that child being viewed as socially competent if he continues to engage in high levels of stigmatizing behaviors that may dissuade others from interaction (e.g., stereotypy and challenging behavior). The child's challenging stigmatizing behaviors would likely overshadow more appropriate social behaviors, with the result that peers would not wish to interact with the student regardless of the quantity or quality of her social skills.

7-3 Assessment Strategies for Determining Socialization Curriculum

The first step in intervention for any area of instruction is to determine what the child needs to learn. Determining socialization deficits means evaluating three areas: (1) contexts in which the child functions to determine the social demands in each, (2) the social culture of those contexts to determine **socially valid skills** (skills that are reinforced in the natural environment) to teach, and (3) the child's level of socialization in those contexts to determine skills the child needs to learn.

7-3a Assessment of Contexts and Determining Socially Valid Skills

Assessment of contexts means determining contexts in which the student will—or could—potentially function and the types of opportunities for social interaction within each of those contexts. However, identification of social contexts alone is insufficient. In addition, you must identify what skills are needed within those environments and the naturally occurring reinforcement and punishment contingencies found in these environments. For example, the socialization demands of using a library may involve initiating interaction with librarians for assistance. A student with autism who attempts to talk to other students about topics unrelated to the reasons for being in the library may be redirected by the librarian or even asked to leave if the off-task talking continues or is too loud. The rules for social interaction in the library are rather standard and consistent across time. By contrast, having lunch with same-age peers would require the far different social skills of responding to peer social initiations and possibly adult directives, initiating social interactions with peers, choosing appropriate topics of conversation, understanding slang and colloquialisms used by peers, and being familiar with popular cultural references. The "rules" for lunchtime conversations are more subtle, and social responses to "rule-breaking" behavior is far different. A student with autism who talks about characteristics of animal droppings may find that other students laugh at first, but if the discourse continues, other students may verbally disapprove or move away.

The demands of specific target environments should be identified using four steps (see Table 7.1). The first step is to determine the target environments where students with autism will have opportunities for social interactions: cafeteria, recess, group instruction or center time in general education classrooms, and so forth.

TABLE 7.1 ● **Steps in Determining the Demands of Target Environments**

1. Determine the target environments where students will have opportunities for social interaction.
2. Interview teachers and other adults who supervise students in those environments.
3. Conduct ecological assessments in those environments. As part of each ecological assessment, answer these questions:
   - What activities occur within this environment?
   - How are these activities structured?
   - What types of interactions are directed to students from teachers or other adults in the environment?
   - What is the nature of peer interactions?
4. Conduct direct observations of typically developing peers in those environments.
   - Conduct anecdotal reports.
   - Identify specific social behaviors exhibited by peers.
   - Measure the most critical behaviors using event recording or duration recording.

The second step is to interview teachers and other adults who supervise those environments. Interview questions posed to these adults should focus on the type of social activities that occur (large or small groups of students, structured or unstructured, etc.), the nature of social interactions during those activities (informal or following specific rules or procedures, fixed groups versus fluid groups in which students come and go, etc.), and the types of social skills needed for success in those activities. The interviews should elicit the adults' opinions about the social demands of those environments and activities.

The third step is to conduct an ecological assessment that is designed based on the information obtained from your interviews. This process will result in an inventory of socialization demands, as well as skills needed for communication, play, work, self-determination, and so forth. For this ecological question, we recommend answering the following four questions:

1. **What activities occur within this environment?** For example, activities in the cafeteria might include waiting in line, getting food, moving to a table, eating, disposing of trash, and then exiting the cafeteria.
2. **How are these activities structured?** Activities may be teacher directed (e.g., small-group instruction or a teacher-led game); structured, but not teacher directed (e.g., peer tutoring or cooperative learning activities, lunch, bus rides); or unstructured (e.g., free time, passing in hall between classes, recess, break time at work). Each type of structure may require social skills with a different nuance. For example, delivering an appropriate social greeting may be an important skill across many environments, but the form of that greeting (e.g., "Hello, how are you?" or "Hey, man! What's up?") will likely depend on whether or not the environment is, for example, a formal work setting or a meeting with friends.
3. **What types of interactions are directed to students from teachers or other adults in the environment?** For example, do adults mostly give directives that require no response or directives that require a response? Or do they initiate social conversation with children in the area (e.g., a cafeteria monitor asking a student what she did over the weekend)?
4. **What is the nature of peer interactions?** This question addresses the important issue of selecting socially valid skills to teach. For example, in the cafeteria, students with autism will probably not only need to learn to talk to peers but also may find it beneficial to be familiar with popular TV, YouTube, video game, and music references. Elementary students may talk about their latest Minecraft™ world or a ROBLOX™ game they played. Secondary students may talk about texts they have received or sent,

social media, or upcoming extracurricular activities. On the other hand, playground interactions may require a completely different set of skills, such as initiating a request to participate in an activity or share equipment, giving and following directions during a game, and talking to one another.

The last step in determining the social demands of target environments is to conduct direct observations of typically developing same-age peers in those environments as they engage in target activities. The behavior observation methods described in Chapters 2 and 3 can be used for this purpose. For example, if the target environment is center time in a general education kindergarten class, then you might first observe using A-B-C recording during center time. The A-B-C record will probably help you then generate informal ecological assessment questions to consider about the specific environment in which you collected that data (e.g., kindergarten class) and related subenvironments (dress-up center, sand table center, blocks center, etc.) and activities (stacking blocks, sharing sand tools, etc.). In addition, from information gathered in the A-B-C report, you could extrapolate specific social behaviors that are likely to be exhibited by the target group (joint attention to activities, asking for blocks, taking turns, laughing at silly dress-up combinations, etc.).

Next, you could use event recording (or duration recording as appropriate) to determine at what rate certain skills are demonstrated or for how long. For example, you might measure the average rate at which students initiate verbal interactions with one another or the average duration of a conversational exchange. This information will help teachers establish valid target skills and criteria.

Information gathered through informal ecological assessment will constitute the framework for skills needed by a given student to facilitate full participation in social contexts. This information will help in the curriculum-development process described in Chapter 4. For example, as you will recall from Chapter 4 (Table 4.3), the first step in the curriculum-development process is to establish goals. The following are sample goals for socialization.

- *Long-term goal*: The student will live with a roommate without the need for check-ins from support staff or family more than once per week.
- *Intermediate goals*:
  The student will engage in cooperative cooking and cleaning activities (e.g., making lunch, tidying the living room).
  The student will initiate conversations with others.

- *Short-term goals*:
  The student will initiate questions directed to peers and teachers.
  The student will share supplies during a cooperative activity.
  The student will ask for supplies as needed.
  The student will exhibit joint attention during an activity with an adult or peer (e.g., while playing a multiplayer video game).

Teachers will need to task analyze target skills to facilitate instruction. For example, one of the skills identified as important to success in the cafeteria might be "responding to and talking with a peer who initiates." This general skill could be task analyzed into the following steps:

- Look at the person who spoke.
- Think about what he or she said.
- Respond appropriately (e.g., answer question or make a comment on the same topic).
- Listen for peer to respond.
- Repeat as appropriate.

Understanding the discrete steps involved in a complex skill such as "talking to a peer" will help you better identify what needs to be taught, prompted, or reinforced (Ledbetter-Cho et al., 2015).

Once the requisite skills have been identified, the next step is determining the student's level of proficiency in those skills. Skills that the student lacks become targets for instruction. Skills that are present but weak need to be strengthened through either increased opportunities for practice or stronger reinforcement for exhibiting the skills.

7-3b Assessment of Student Skill Levels

Student proficiency in target skills may be evaluated directly using direct-observation techniques, indirectly using rating scales, or via a combination of the two approaches. Direct-observation techniques use event recording or duration recording to measure the number, rate, percent, or duration of discrete skills, as described in Chapters 2 and 3. Table 7.2 lists the steps used in direct observation to assess the use of social skills.

There may be circumstances in which you do not want to assess your students' social behavior in authentic contexts. For example, if you have concerns that a student may exhibit challenging behaviors, especially aggressive or self-injurious behaviors, in the new or unfamiliar social context, then it would not be wise to place the child in that context to assess his or her social skills. For times when it is unwise or impractical to assess students' social skills in real contexts, role-play assessment may be the preferred approach (Matson & Wilkins, 2007). Role-plays consist of adults playing the role of peers during target social activities (e.g., playing during recess, sharing a snack during a break between classes). The student's social skill responses (or lack thereof) are recorded by the participating adults or by an observer (e.g., Ledbetter-Cho et al., 2016).

Another way to evaluate students' use of social skills is with formal social and behavior scales. Table 7.3 lists commercially available scales in these areas. Note that some of these instruments have not been normed on students with autism and developmental delays but may provide helpful information, particularly about the student's level of socialization in environments outside of school or progress in skill acquisition over time.

We should also reiterate that functional behavioral assessments (explained in Chapter 3) should result in hypotheses that indicate social skill deficits that may become targets for instruction.

TABLE 7.2 ● Steps in Assessing Social Skills Using Direct Observation

1. Determine the skills you wish to assess as described operationally. The following are examples of operational definitions of social skills.
   - Conduct anecdotal reports.
   - *Taking turns:* Student waits while other students take their turns in an activity; student participates without prompting when it is his turn.
   - *Initiating interactions with peers:* Student stands 2 to 3 feet from peer; within 5 seconds of approach, student says peer's name and makes a comment appropriate to the situation: asks a question, asks peer to play a game, asks to join a game, gives a compliment, and so on, and then waits for peer's response.
   - *Responding to peers' initiations:* Given an initiation from a peer (question, invitation, etc.), student responds appropriately (answers question, says "yes" or "no" to the invitation, etc.) within 5 seconds.
   - *Playing with a friend:* Student participates appropriately in an activity that requires turn taking or sharing with one or more peers (e.g., playing four square, jumping rope, playing a video game, playing a board game, using the slide).
2. Determine the most appropriate measurement system for each skill. For the skills previously described, appropriate measurement systems would include the following.
   - *Taking turns:* Event recording
   - *Initiating interactions:* Event recording
   - *Responding to peers' initiations:* Event recording (measure the SD [peer initiation] as well as the student's response)
   - *Playing with a friend:* Duration recording
3. Select a time and place to observe. Remember that you should observe when and where the skill is needed. Therefore, if you wish to increase a student's participation in social interactions during recess, you should observe during recess.
4. As you observe your target student, collect data for the same skills on a typical peer selected at random. This will provide an indication of the level of socialization that may be required for successful participation (if this step has not been completed during the process of identifying target skills). Data on peers' skills may also help determine a target criterion for your student(s).
   - Once data have been gathered, the last step is to compare your student's data against that of peers and then develop objectives for intervention.

TABLE 7.3 ● Rating Scales for Assessing Social Skills

- *Social Skills Improvement System* (SSIS) Rating Scales, Gresham and Elliott (2008)

This classic social skills rating system intended for students from ages 3 to 18 measures social skills, competing problem behaviors, and academic skills across four subscales, including an "Autism Spectrum" subscale. Companion intervention guides are available from the publisher.

- *Social Responsiveness Scale™, 2nd ed. (SRS™-2)*, Constantino (2012)

The SRS-2 is designed to assess the severity of social impairment in children and adults (ages 2.5 years to adult) with autism through the use of parent or teacher rating scales (or both). The rating scales provide a total score, plus five subscale scores and two subscales compatible with the DSM-5. A bachelor's or master's degree in special education, education, psychology, school counseling, or related fields is required.

- *Matson Evaluation of Social Skills with Youngsters* (MESSY), Matson, Rotatori, and Helsel (1983)

Parents or teachers complete the MESSY (or the MESSY-II), which consists of Likert-style items. Resulting scores are reported in three subscales.

- *Behavioral Characteristics Progression* (BCP), VORT Corporation (1997)

This is one of the most comprehensive programs available, a distinction that also makes it a bit unwieldy. The BCP includes 2,300 behaviors arranged in 56 strands. Social–emotional skills are addressed throughout the BCP. A companion instructional activities guide is available from the publisher.

Discrepancies between social demands of target environments and a student's level of proficiency in those skills becomes the basis for determining the social skills curriculum for that child. Target skills need to be directly taught via prompting and reinforcement in all pertinent environments. We discuss methods for teaching social skills in the remainder of this chapter.

7-4 Interventions for Increasing Social Skills and Social Competence

As you learned in Chapter 1, the Individuals with Disabilities Education Act (U.S. Department of Education, 2016a) requires that students with disabilities be educated in the LRE and with general education peers to the greatest extent possible. Fortunately, general education settings and activities are valuable venues for interventions to improve social behavior in students with autism. Without opportunities to interact with typically developing peers, it would be difficult to teach socially valid social skills and achieve generalization of those skills to natural contexts. In the remainder of this chapter, we describe evidence-based interventions for improving social behavior in students with autism. We first discuss overarching considerations for improving social behaviors. Next, we describe specific strategies in two categories: teacher-mediated interventions and peer-mediated interventions. Finally, we discuss how to facilitate generalization of newly learned skills.

7-4a General Considerations for Socialization Interventions

Several approaches have shown promise for improving the social skills, and ultimately the social competence, of students with autism. However, no matter what techniques are chosen to increase social skills, educators are more likely to achieve desired outcomes if certain considerations are observed, many of which relate to contextual factors associated with socialization interventions. A good number of these recommendations revolve around the importance of providing opportunities for practicing social behaviors in actual social contexts that involve peers without disabilities.

Start Early

Children with autism often exhibit characteristics of social withdrawal at extremely young ages (Osterling & Dawson, 1994; Scott et al., 2000). Given the correlation between socialization, cognition, and communication and the predictive aspects of socialization, the earlier interventions are implemented, the better the outcomes (Chang & Locke, 2016; Dawson et al., 2012). Inclusion in general education environments at a young age helps children with autism better learn social and play behaviors, assuming formal interventions are provided to improve target skills (Camargo et al., 2014; Whalon, Conroy, Martinez, & Werch, 2015). Many early intervention programs (birth to age 3) and early childhood programs (ages 3–5) provide structured opportunities for interaction with peers—typically developing peers or peers who have disabilities but exhibit developmentally appropriate social skills.

Teach Social Skills in Context

Socialization interventions are far more effective when provided in socially rich contexts in which peers and naturally occurring social stimuli and reinforcers are present (Chang & Locke, 2016; Whalon et al., 2015). It is difficult, if not impossible, to accurately imitate the SDs and contingencies of natural social interactions outside of those contexts. For example, it is probably not feasible to duplicate those social stimuli present in a play group of typically developing children (e.g., requests to play, comments about ongoing play activities, peer-to-peer instructions regarding a play activity) in a group solely composed of children with autism. Teaching children with autism to recognize and respond to those stimuli requires that they are repeatedly exposed to natural social stimuli and naturally occurring social reinforcers.

Teach Activities Preferred by Peers without Disabilities

Students with autism should be taught to use the materials that are commonly part of the social repertoire of typically developing students. For example, Koegel, Werner, Vismara, and Koegel (2005) found that teaching students with autism to engage in activities preferred by peers without disabilities, such as playing board games, playing with dolls, and painting, resulted in improved reciprocal social interaction and child affect. Therefore, as part of the ecological assessment process, teachers should carefully observe the types of toys, games, activities, gestures, verbal expressions, popular culture references (e.g., Star Wars™), and perhaps even clothing that are preferred by peers without autism. Then children with autism should be taught typical use of these materials and activities as part of socialization interventions.

Reduce Challenging Behaviors

Before and even while placing students with autism in natural social contexts with typically developing peers, teachers and others must address challenging behaviors exhibited by the students with autism. Challenging behaviors should be assessed using functional assessment (see Chapter 3), and interventions should be implemented to reduce those behaviors and establish functional replacement behaviors. Behaviors such as self-stimulation, self-injury, and aggression will undoubtedly result in fewer social initiations from peers and may result in the student with autism being restricted from participating in those activities. Furthermore, children with autism who exhibit such behaviors may become targets of negative social interaction such as bullying (Didden et al., 2009). Children with autism probably do not need to be completely free of negative behaviors before socialization interventions (Simpson, Myles, Sasso, & Kamps, 1997), but they must be basically compliant and safe (e.g., pose no threat of harm to themselves or peers) and have ways to communicate their wants and needs.

Teach Pivotal Behaviors

Koegel and his colleagues recommend targeting **pivotal behaviors**, or behaviors that are central to many areas of functioning (Mohammadzaheri, Koegel, Rezaei, & Bakhshi, 2015). Pivotal behaviors serve a similar purpose in a variety of areas of functioning, including social functioning (Koegel & Koegel, 1995). As such, they can lead to higher-quality social interactions and can improve generalization across behaviors and environments. Comprehensive socialization planning should include interventions targeting pivotal social behaviors (Koegel et al., 2012). Potential pivotal behaviors for improving socialization include initiating interactions, communication, using appropriate affect, responding to initiations, engaging in joint attention, and terminating interactions.

Guard Against Potential Problems Related to Inclusion

In 2013, approximately 40 percent of students receiving special education services for autism were educated in general education classes for 80 percent of the day or more (U.S. Department of Education, 2016b). An additional 20 percent spent approximately half of their day or more in general education settings. Although inclusion in general education offers significant opportunities, especially for socialization interventions, educators must guard against "inclusion missteps" (Schwartz, 2006, p. 87). We describe potential problems of inclusion with respect to socialization goals in Table 7.4. Fortunately, these problems can be avoided with the careful assessments described in Chapters 3, 4, 6, and this chapter by ensuring that evidence-based interventions are applied in the general education settings where students are taught and by teaching general education teachers and peers to deliver these interventions (Giangreco, Halvorsen, Doyle, & Broer, 2004; Koegel et al., 2012).

Emphasize Generalization

Children can be taught to exhibit discrete social skills in structured situations relatively efficiently, in many cases. The challenge is teaching students to use those skills in new situations, where all of the familiar original learning conditions have changed. Generalization is among the most essential components of learning (Stokes & Baer, 1977). If skills do not generalize to real-life conditions, the student has gained little. A large body of research has delineated specific strategies for facilitating generalization, some of which were described in Chapter 5. Later in this chapter, we will present generalization strategies that are that are particularly well suited for social skills.

7-4b Intervention Approaches

Three general approaches to intervention delivery have been used successfully to improve social behavior in students with autism: **teacher-mediated interventions**, **self-mediated interventions**, and **peer-mediated interventions**. Although each of these intervention

---

TABLE 7.4 ● **Potential Problems with Inclusion**

1. **Placement without planning**. Improvements in social behavior will probably not simply happen regardless of placement. Simply exposing students with autism to typically developing peers will not lead to acquisition of targeted social behaviors. Socialization interventions must be formally planned for general education settings, and they must be based on relevant ecological and functional assessment data.

2. **Placement without objectives**. Sometimes, particularly for students with autism who are educated in separate classes for much of the day, access to the general education class is determined by existing activities (e.g., lunch, recess, story time, library, PE) that "would be good for" the students with autism. Certainly, special educators need to take advantage of those existing activities as opportunities for students with autism—but with careful planning of instructional goals for the student with autism during those activities. Thus, general education activities should be selected by the individualized educational program team, along with the instructional objectives that will be taught in those activities and the instructional methods that will be used.

3. **Placement with overreliance on adult support**. The push for students with disabilities to spend all or most of their day in general education has led to significant increases in the number of paraprofessionals being employed to support those students in general education classes (Giangreco et al., 2004). Unfortunately, reliance on paraprofessionals as the primary support for special education services may be ill advised for many reasons, including concerns about training and preparation of paraprofessionals for these roles (Giangreco, 2009). Research has demonstrated detrimental effects of one-to-one support for students with disabilities, including lower levels of teacher and peer interactions directed toward the student with a disability, isolation within the general education classroom, insular relationships between the students and the paraprofessional, and increased dependency on the paraprofessional (Giangreco, 2009; Giangreco et al., 2004).

---

delivery approaches has been shown to improve the social performance of students with autism, research supports the use of multicomponent interventions, in which two or more of these procedures within or across these categories are applied in combination (Camargo et al., 2014; Simpson et al., 1997; Whalon et al., 2015). For example, teacher-mediated direct instruction could occur in the classroom, and then peer-mediated intervention could be arranged during recess. In the following sections we describe specific interventions in each of the categories previously described.

Teacher-Mediated Techniques

Two types of teacher-mediated interventions have been used to increase social behavior in children and youth with autism and developmental disabilities. The first is direct instruction of target skills, which typically involves discussion, modeling, and role-playing target skills. The second is social stories.

Direct Instruction of Social Behaviors The first teacher-mediated approach to improving socialization is direct instruction of social skills. In a direct-instruction approach, specific social skills are taught using procedures much like those used to teach academic skills. Generally this means that specific skills are taught in a teacher-led small-group format using explanation, demonstration, practice, and feedback; and that other behavioral procedures (e.g., self-monitoring, prompting, reinforcement) are used to facilitate generalization of skills. In Vignette 7.1, we present a description of a direct-instruction approach for teaching social skills.

● **VIGNETTE 7.1**

Ms. Jacobs Teaches Social Skills

Ms. Jacobs teaches an intermediate class for students with autism, ages 9–11. Each of her students participates in several different general education activities such as lunch, music, science, and language arts. Despite having many opportunities to interact with general education peers, Ms. Jacobs' students typically interact little. They respond minimally to peer initiations and do not initiate interactions.

Ms. Jacobs believes that her students do not know many basic social interaction skills. To remedy the problem, she has implemented a social skills instruction program. First, she made careful assessments to determine skills to teach. She observed both her students and their peers in general education environments and interviewed peers and teachers. This assessment indicated approximately 15 skills that seemed critical for social success. Skills targeted for instruction included answering questions, asking questions, carrying on a conversation with peers of at least several sentences, using humor, sharing, and taking turns.

Next, Ms. Jacobs solicited four peers from general education classes to assist with social skills instruction. These peers were students familiar to her students and were selected because they had been observed attempting to interact with the students with autism. The general education peers simply participated in the group instruction, just as did the students with autism.

Finally, Ms. Jacobs began instruction. The social skills group met daily for 20 minutes per session. One or two of the four peers attended each group. The first skill taught was "answering questions." Ms. Jacobs first explained what "answering questions" meant, and she gave several examples from her students' daily lives. Next, Ms. Jacobs and her paraprofessional, Ms. Rogers, modeled the skill: the paraprofessional posed questions to Ms. Jacobs similar to the types of questions peers might ask. Ms. Jacobs would "think out loud" ("She asked me a question. I need to look at her and answer her.") and then reply to the question. Ms. Jacobs and Ms. Rogers demonstrated several examples of "answering questions." After each example, Ms. Jacobs asked for feedback from students ("Did I answer the question? Did I look at my friend?"). Next, one of the general education peers role-played the skill with either Ms. Jacobs or Ms. Rogers. Again, after each role-play, Ms. Jacobs asked other students for feedback about the peers' use of the skill. After that, the peer and the students with autism (one at a time) role-played the skill, with other students giving feedback. The peer was instructed to ask questions similar to those typically posed at lunch or other noninstructional situations. Ms. Jacobs provided examples. Each successful role-play was accompanied by praise from the teachers.

As she was teaching the skill, Ms. Jacobs used a chart with a picture representing the skill and listing the steps to serve as a reminder for her students to use the skill. This chart was used at the start of each group to review the steps in the skill.

Once every student had successfully demonstrated the skill in role-play situations, students were shown a form that had the picture representing the skill at the top of the page and five blank boxes at the bottom. Students were informed that Ms. Jacobs or Ms. Rogers would be watching them at various times, and when students used the skill of answering questions, they would earn a sticker. When all five boxes were filled, they could take the form to the principal for a special treat.

Each time a student left the classroom to attend a general education activity, he or she was reminded about using the skill of answering questions and the steps involved. Ms. Jacobs and Ms. Rogers observed students at random times throughout the day. After each observation (e.g., at lunch), the adult gave the student feedback about his or her use of the skill and, if appropriate, gave a sticker for the student to apply to the form. In addition, any time any student was observed using the skill in any situation, Ms. Jacobs or Ms. Rogers would place a star on a chart that had a picture depicting the skill in the middle. When all the empty boxes on the chart were filled with stickers, the class could select a special group activity to do that day (e.g., make popcorn, play a game, go for a walk).

The last component of the direct-instruction approach was that Ms. Jacobs informed the general education teachers and peers as skills were being addressed. She asked these individuals to praise her students any time they observed the students using the skill correctly.

Ms. Jacobs spent approximately one and one-half weeks on each skill. In addition, from time to time, she conducted review sessions for all previously learned skills. According to Ms. Jacobs' data, her students' use of the targeted skills increased dramatically after instruction. Although work remained to be done to improve her students' socialization skills, Ms. Jacobs knew her students were now far better prepared to interact with their general education peers.

The effectiveness of direct-instruction social skills lessons can be increased by including typically developing same-age peers who are skilled in the social behaviors being taught (e.g., Peters, Tullis, & Gallagher, 2016). Peers serve as models and help with the role-play practice. The advantages of using peers are the increased likelihood of students with autism modeling peers' use of the skills being taught (e.g., Bandura, 1977), more realistic practice scenarios, and more realistic responses to target students' use of skills during role-play practice.

Table 7.5 describes the steps in a direct-instruction approach to teaching social skills. One major disadvantage of a direct-instruction approach is that skills acquired and demonstrated in the instructional setting often fail to generalize—that is, students may demonstrate proficiency in a skill during the social skills lesson but never use the skill in a natural environment (e.g., the cafeteria, playground, hallways, inclusion classes). Teachers can increase the likelihood of generalization by incorporating the strategies for enhancing generalization described in the next section and by observing the general recommendations for socialization interventions noted earlier in this chapter.

Social Skills Curricula Several commercial social skills curricula use a direct-instruction approach and may be helpful in guiding social skills instruction (see Table 4.4 in Chapter 4 for a listing of social skills curricula). The *ACCEPTS* (A Curriculum for Children's Effective Peer and Teacher Skills) and *ACCESS* (Adolescent Curriculum for Communication and Effective Social Skills) curricula are highly structured, even providing a script for teachers to follow. These are easy to use, and teachers who have never taught social skills appreciate the guidance that the script offers. The *Skillstreaming* series [*Skillstreaming in Early Childhood, Skillstreaming the Elementary School Child,* and *Skillstreaming the Adolescent* (all McGinnis,

TABLE 7.5 ● Direct-Instruction Sequence for Teaching Social Skills

Direct instruction of social skills typically involves the following steps:

1. **Describe the skill and why it is important (rationale)**. The description should include the task-analyzed steps of the skill being taught.

   EXAMPLE: "Today we're going to learn how to ask a friend to play with you. When you know how to ask a friend to play, you can play games that you like during recess and after school. Toni, you like to jump rope. You might ask a friend to play jump rope with you. Blake, you like to run. You could ask a friend to play tag with you." (Teacher would continue giving an example of how this skill could benefit each student.)

   "Here's how you ask a friend to play" (pointing to a chart with written or pictorial steps of the skill):

   - Think about what game you would like to play.
   - Decide which friend you want to ask.
   - Walk over to your friend.
   - Look at your friend and say in a nice voice, "Would you like to play _____ with me?"
   - If your friend says "no," choose another friend to ask.

2. **Demonstrate the skill**. Usually the paraprofessional or another adult assists the teacher with this step. You should demonstrate the skill several times; the more examples, the more likely students are to understand how to perform the skill.

   EXAMPLE: "Let me show you how you ask a friend to play. Let's pretend we're on the playground. I'm standing here by myself but I want to play." (Now teacher begins to act the part of a student on the playground as the other adults or students without disabilities are engaged in "playground" activities away from her.)

   (Teacher talks aloud to herself): "I'd really like to play catch. I think I'll ask Alicia if she wants to play with me. . . ."

   (Teacher approaches "Alicia"): "Alicia, do you want to play catch with me?"

   (Other adult or peer): "Sure! I'll get the ball."

   (*NOTE:* If students without disabilities are participating, they can be called on to demonstrate the skill).

3. **Solicit student feedback on the skill**. The teacher asks individual students to identify whether she correctly performed each step.

   EXAMPLE: "Did I decide what game I wanted to play?" (get student responses); "Did I ask someone to play?" (have students name the friend); and so forth.

4. **Have students role-play the skill**. Each student should practice the skill at least once and more if needed. During the students' role-play, other participants are needed to play the roles of other students. These can be the adults in the class or, preferably, peers without disabilities. Each role-play situation should reflect individual student preferences, styles, and so forth. If peers without disabilities are participating, they should demonstrate the skills first.

   EXAMPLE: "Toni, it's your turn to practice asking a friend to play. Let's pretend we're on the playground after lunch. What game do you like to play?" and so forth. Teacher arranges the role-play to reflect the situation on the playground.

5. **Provide feedback on student performance of the skill**. After each role-play, the teacher should solicit feedback from other students in the group about the role-play. The teacher should also give feedback to the student doing the role-play.

   EXAMPLE (to other students): "Did you see Toni decide what game she wanted to play? What did she want to play? Did she ask her friend nicely?" and so forth.
   Role-play continues until each student has had the opportunity to practice the skill.

6. **Do generalization activities**. Generalization activities take place after each student has demonstrated proficiency in the skill during the role-play sessions. The purpose of generalization activities is to facilitate use of target skills in natural settings. Generalization activities might include games that require students to use target skills, self-monitoring procedures in which students keep track of their use of skills in generalized settings, and reinforcement contingencies for use of target skills in generalized settings. One important generalization strategy is to conduct social skills lessons in environments in which skills are to be used (Frea, 1995). For example, the skill of asking a student to play might be taught on the playground. The skill of responding to greetings might be taught in the hallway and at the bus area.

2011)] are less structured, presenting each lesson in a brief outline form. Helpful features include the fact that each skill is task analyzed, and several self-monitoring forms are included for use with each skill. *The Social Skills Improvement System (SSIS) Intervention Guide* is coordinated with the *Social Skills Improvement System (SSIS) Rating Scales* (Gresham & Elliott, 2008; see Table 7.3).

However, commercial curricula should be used with three caveats in mind. First, most commercial social skills curricula have been field tested with students with autism. Second, the skills included in each curriculum may not match the skills needed by your students, as indicated by your ecological assessment data. Finally, the instructional procedures recommended may need to be slightly modified, depending on your students' language levels.

Instructional Scripts One variation on the direct-instruction approach involves using social scripts as a part of social interaction training. Haring and Ryndak (1994) describe social scripts as "routine social interaction patterns that can be repeated many times in a variety of contexts" (p. 303). As you have learned, social skills deficits and communication deficits are strongly interrelated. Children and youth with autism may have difficulty generating situation-appropriate words and phrases because of their language and communication deficits. Social scripts are useful in prompting students to use appropriate words in social interaction situations. Students are able to focus on other variables of the social situation without the obstacle of not having the words to say. Social scripts have been shown to be an effective intervention component with both preschoolers and adolescents with autism (e.g., Camargo et al., 2014; Goldstein & Cisar, 1992; MacDuff, Ledo, McClannahan, & Krantz, 2007).

To use social scripts, first identify situations in which scripts may be beneficial to facilitating social interaction. For example, perhaps the teacher's assessment reveals that peers without disabilities often extend verbal greetings to one of his students in the halls as the student is walking to class in the morning, but the student does not respond. The teacher could develop a generic script that would enable the student to respond appropriately to any greeting, such as "Hi, how are you?" or "Hey, how's it going?" or "Hi, see you later!" The teacher could then use a direct-instruction approach to teach the student to say these words in response to greetings.

Social scripts may be written or pictorial and can provide specific instructions or general prompts. As students begin consistently exhibiting the target social behaviors, the social scripts should be altered or faded to reduce the likelihood of the student becoming dependent on the script (Ledbetter-Cho et al., 2016).

Story-Based Interventions In **story-based interventions**, a brief, individualized story is read to the student immediately before a situation where challenging behavior is expected to occur. The purpose of the story is to remind the student of expected behavior(s) to use in that situation. **Social Stories**™ are one version of story-based interventions. Social Stories™ consist of brief, structured stories that describe specific social situations a student will encounter and appropriate responses to the social stimuli that will be encountered in that situation (Gray & Garand, 1993).

Story-based interventions are individualized to each student's social needs and can be developed for virtually any social situation the student will encounter (initiating greeting, waiting turns, sharing, responding to social initiations, etc.). Story-based interventions have been demonstrated to improve social behavior (communication, interpersonal, and self-regulation skills) and decrease challenging behaviors for some students with autism (e.g., Chan & O'Reilly, 2008; National Autism Center, 2015; Whalon et al., 2015). This intervention is thought to be beneficial because the individualized stories combine information about needed social skills with visual cues (pictures or words or both). We recommend, however, that stories not be used in isolation but as one component of a comprehensive social intervention plan that includes direct instruction of target skills, antecedent prompting, or peer-mediated interventions.

To create a story-based intervention, a target social situation is identified, along with the social stimuli the student will encounter in that situation and desired student response(s) to those stimuli. Next, the stories are put in written format, using approximately two to five sentences, and written using language and print size appropriate for the student. For students who need visual cues, one or more pictures or icons should be used to represent each sentence.

FIGURE 7.1 Example of a social story

Gray and Garand (1993) recommend including three types of sentences in a social story: (1) **descriptive sentences**, which provide information about the social context (setting, people, activities, etc.); (2) **directive sentences**, which tell the student what to do; and (3) **perspective sentences**, which describe feelings of individuals involved in the situation. For example, say you need to teach a student how to transition from a preferred activity to a less preferred one without tantrums. Figure 7.1 shows an example of a story that might be used for that purpose.

The teacher reads the story to the student just before the target social situation several days in a row. In the example in Figure 7.1, the story should be read to the student just before center time. Once the story has been introduced, students should be allowed access to it throughout the day. In addition to these guidelines, Scott, Clark, and Brady (2000) recommend having the student practice the target behavior in conjunction with reading the story. For example, the story in Figure 7.1 might be read to Brent; then during or after the story he should practice the target behaviors (putting a toy back on the shelf, walking to group, sitting in his chair).

Antecedent-Prompting Procedures Antecedent prompting is a strategy in which the teacher uses one or more types of prompts to facilitate the student exhibiting an interactive behavior, which is then reinforced by peers and the teacher. **Antecedent prompting** requires placing the student in a natural context that involves social interaction with one or more socially competent peers (e.g., sharing a toy, sharing a video game, playing a game, sharing a snack). The teacher remains in proximity to the child with autism and provides prompts to the child to initiate or respond to a social interaction. Although verbal prompts are the most common, other prompts could be used as well (gestures, pictures, etc.; see Chapter 5). Typically, peers are instructed to respond positively to any initiations by the student with autism.

Ms. Jacobs, whom you met earlier in this chapter, uses antecedent prompting, in addition to direct instruction, as part of her socialization program. Vignette 7.2 describes how Ms. Jacobs uses antecedent prompting.

● **VIGNETTE 7.2**

Ms. Jacobs Uses Antecedent Prompting

Remember Ms. Jacobs from Vignette 7.1? In addition to directly teaching social skills, she also uses antecedent-prompting procedures with each of her students. To do this, she and her paraprofessional, Ms. Rogers, accompany their students to activities that involve social interaction with peers and adults without disabilities. In these situations, any time there is an opportunity for their students to initiate or respond to a social initiation, they first wait 5 to 10 seconds to give their students an opportunity to respond independently. If they do not, Ms. Jacobs or Ms. Rogers prompts the correct behavior. Some of the many instances in which they use antecedent prompting include the following:

- During game time, in which general education students join the class for a variety of games and leisure activities. Stations are set up around the room, and students choose their preferred activity. During the game or activity, students are expected to make appropriate social initiations ("Do you want to play checkers?"—asking questions pertinent to the game) and responses (answering questions pertinent to the game).
- While waiting for the bus, students are expected to interact with peers by making greetings, asking questions, and responding to greetings and questions.
- In the lunch line, students are expected to indicate their food choices either verbally or by pointing. At the end of the line, they are to say "Thank you" when given their food and "You're welcome" when the cashier says "Thank you."

Antecedent prompting has been found to effectively increase social interaction, particularly when the intervention includes multiple interaction opportunities with competent peers in natural contexts (Simpson et al., 1997; Whalon et al., 2015; White et al., 2011). However, potential negative aspects of the procedure have been noted. These include interruption of a naturally occurring social exchange (Strain & Fox, 1981), and children with autism becoming prompt dependent, exhibiting social behavior only when prompted to do so (Odom & Strain, 1986). We recommend the following guidelines for using prompts, as well as the guidelines described in Chapter 5:

1. **Use prompts only if needed**. Prompt only if the student has not initiated or responded within a reasonable period of time (e.g., 5 to 10 seconds). When using prompts for social behavior, be careful not to interrupt the natural flow of social interaction to provide a prompt. The prompt is used only if the student *fails* to respond.

2. **Use the least intrusive prompts needed to solicit target behaviors**. Use verbal prompts if possible; if those fail to produce desired responding, physical prompts may be needed. Use partial verbal prompts; if those do not produce the desired response, use full verbal prompts.

3. **Fade prompts as soon as possible**. Use prompts as needed at first and then gradually increase the time that elapses between the opportunity for a social behavior and the teacher prompt. Also fade the level of prompts used. For example, if you begin training using full verbal prompts ("Eric, say 'Yes, I'd like to have a turn.'"), move to partial verbal prompts as soon as possible ("Eric, what do you say?" or "Eric . . . ?").

4. **If you detect that students are becoming prompt dependent, switch to another intervention or add a contingency in which unprompted initiations or responses are reinforced, using reinforcers in addition to naturally occurring social reinforcers**. For example, a prompt-dependent student might earn tickets for each unprompted social initiation or response. Prompted social behaviors do not earn tickets. When he has accumulated 10 tickets, he may exchange them for use of a preferred material or activity for 10 minutes.

Self-Mediated Techniques

Self-mediated techniques use strategies that involve the student doing something to facilitate the use of target skills. For purposes of this discussion, the self-mediated techniques we present are self-monitoring and video self-modeling.

Self-Monitoring Self-monitoring involves targeting a specific behavior, then teaching the student to systematically record each time that behavior is performed. Self-monitoring should also be considered a generalization strategy. It would not be appropriate to have students self-monitor skills that have not yet been taught. Once students have attained the acquisition level in a given skill, self-monitoring of that skill can be introduced as one tactic for facilitating attainment of fluency, maintenance, and generalization levels of performance.

Examples follow of self-monitoring systems that would be easy for students to use to record each time a target social skill is exhibited:

- Record a tally mark on an index card. The card can be kept on the student's desk or carried in a pocket.

- Place a poker chip in a jar.
- Place a star on a chart.
- Drop a small block in an egg carton section.
- Use a handheld or wearable digital counter.

These items are easy to use in generalization settings such as the playground or cafeteria.

Once the student has learned to use the system, a target performance criterion can be set, with reinforcement delivered on attainment of the criterion. For example, the student could be encouraged to make 10 social greetings during the day. If the self-monitoring system indicates 10 or more greetings were exhibited by the end of the day, the student earns a special reinforcer.

Self-monitoring has been used to effectively increase social behavior in children and youth with autism and developmental disabilities (e.g., Camargo et al., 2014; Koegel & Koegel, 1990; Koegel, Koegel, Hurley, & Frea, 1992; Parker & Kamps, 2011). In addition, self-monitoring can produce collateral decreases in challenging behavior and facilitate generalization of newly learned skills (Koegel et al., 2012).

One major consideration in using self-monitoring as an intervention to improve social behavior is the probability that many students will be able to self-monitor only one response at a time rather than multiple, complex responses (Haring & Ryndak, 1994). Because of this, the nature of the behavior targeted for self-monitoring is especially important. Koegel and his colleagues recommend that students self-monitor pivotal behaviors. For example, students may be taught to self-monitor the number of social questions initiated during the day. Social questions are pivotal because they invite responses and may result in extended social interactions. Even self-monitoring is considered a pivotal behavior because it can be used to facilitate generalization of many different behaviors across a wide variety of natural contexts (Verschuur, Didden, Lang, Sigafoos, & Huskens, 2014). Other examples of pivotal behaviors that students might self-monitor include eye contact, appropriate facial and verbal affect, initiating interactions, functional communication skills, and awareness and responsivity to environmental stimuli (Haring & Ryndak, 1994; Moes, 1995).

Video Self-Modeling Video self-modeling (VSM) involves making a brief video of the student with autism engaging in a target social behavior. VSM is a variation of video modeling. In **video modeling (VM)**, a model (another child or an adult) demonstrates the target skill in the video. In both VM and VSM, the student with autism views the video and is instructed (and taught) to imitate the behavior of the model (either the other student or adult, or the student him- or herself). Both VM and VSM are widely used, evidence-based interventions for teaching a variety of skills, including social behaviors, for students with autism and other disabilities (Bellini & Akullian, 2007; Wong et al., 2015).

In addition to efficacy, VM and VSM as socialization interventions offer other benefits, including ease of use and versatility. The relatively simple steps to create a VM or VSM are:

1. **Identify the target skills to be modeled**. A single video should focus on only one skill, but that skill may have multiple steps that should be clearly identifiable in the video. Also, a single skill may be depicted in multiple videos that depict different scenarios in which the skill should be used.
2. **Task analyze the skill**. If some of the steps are not observable (e.g., student must think about his response), then the hidden steps should be demonstrated by talking aloud in a quiet voice.
3. **Write a script for the VM or VSM**. Be sure that the script includes a clear antecedent for using the skill, a salient demonstration of each step in the skill, and a positive outcome for the scenario. The scenario(s) depicted in the VM or VSM should reflect a situation that the student will encounter as closely as possible.
4. **Record the video**. If possible, record the video in the environment where the target skill will be used. Videos are easily recorded using a cell phone or tablet. If you are making a video for VSM, you may need to prompt the student for some or all of the steps in the skill.

5. **Edit the video, if needed**. You may need to edit out mistakes, interruptions, or other elements that detract from the core message of the video. Many cell phone and tablet recording apps include simple editing features.
6. **Plan for when, where, and how many times the student will view the video**. Typically, videos are viewed just prior to the activity in which the skill is expected to be used.

Peer-Mediated Interventions

Peer-mediated interventions (PMIs) involve using socially competent peer confederates to initiate and maintain social interactions with students with autism. The **peer confederates** receive training in effective methods for accomplishing these outcomes before intervention. PMIs have been used successfully to increase social behavior in a variety of age groups of students with autism from preschool through secondary (Chang & Locke, 2016).

A substantial research base provides strong support for engaging typically developing peers as social change agents for students with autism using a wide variety of PMI formats. No single PMI format stands out as producing superior results (Chan et al., 2009). In general, PMI formats reflect the following elements:

- Peers are taught behavioral skills for initiating, prompting, and reinforcing desired social behaviors before starting the PMI.
- A high-interest activity (e.g., lunch or snack time, interest-based clubs, playtime, center time) is used as the venue for the PMI.
- PMIs are one component of a socialization intervention package that includes other evidence-based socialization interventions (e.g., direct instruction of target skills, scripts, self-monitoring, visual supports, communication supports).
- Some PMIs incorporate the novel or perseverative interests of the participants with autism by designing social interaction activities based on those interests.
- PMIs (and other socialization interventions) can address the function(s) of challenging behaviors by providing reinforcement socially acceptable behaviors.

The number of socially competent peers paired with a student with autism seems to affect the level of social behaviors exhibited by the students with autism. Using dyads (one peer without a disability paired with one student with autism) seems to result in a greater level of social responding than do triads (two peers without disabilities with one student with autism) (Sasso, Mundschenk, Melloy, & Casey, 1998). This suggests that when more than one peer without disabilities is present, those students tend to interact more with one another than with the student with a disability (Sasso et al., 1998).

7-5 Facilitating Generalization of Social Skills

We next discuss strategies that should increase the likelihood of generalization of social skills. These include the Stokes and Baer (1977) generalization strategies (described in Chapter 5) as they relate to social skills as well as additional recommendations that were not presented in Chapter 5.

1. *Teach skills that are naturally reinforced in target environments*. In school, these might include smiling, responding to peers, greeting teachers, and extending invitations to play. Many pivotal behaviors are selected because they typically result in natural reinforcement.
2. *Teach peers (and teachers) to respond appropriately to students' correct social behaviors and to ignore or redirect inappropriate behaviors*. Many PMIs teach peers to do this as part of the PMI training. Differential reinforcement of correct responses is especially important as students begin to exhibit new skills. In our experience, peers often do not respond spontaneously to these new skills, perhaps because peers do not recognize them

as appropriate social behaviors that warrant a response or because the new behaviors are "out of character" for the student with autism.

3. *Use many examples in the teaching process* (Baer, 1999). We would never teach long division by using only one example. Each social skill taught should be demonstrated several times in several different contexts.

4. **Program common stimuli** or *make the training situation as much like real-life situations as possible* (Stokes & Baer, 1977). This might mean having role-players use similar language, topics, even mannerisms, as would be used in the actual situation.

5. *Once students demonstrate acquisition of target behaviors in the instructional setting, begin to vary the components of instructional lessons*, what Stokes and Baer (1977) refer to as **general case programming**. For example, different teachers could conduct the social skills group at a different time of day and in a different setting. New students could be introduced into the group, and the instructional session might be conducted in a slightly different format (different order for role-players, for example).

6. *Teach students to actively recruit their own reinforcement* (Morgan, Young, & Goldstein, 1983). General education teachers, secondary teachers especially, often do not provide the high levels of reinforcement familiar to students with autism. Students can be taught to ask teachers "How did I do today?" or "Did I do a good job playing today?" as a way of soliciting reinforcement in case it is not provided automatically.

7. *Teach students to recognize the types of reinforcers used by general educators* (Graubard, Rosenberg, & Miller, 1974). As part of the initial ecological assessment conducted before developing socialization interventions, teachers should assess the types of reinforcers used in general education environments and then apply those in the special education setting as well.

Incorporating well-planned generalization strategies as part of an overall socialization program will increase functional use of social skills, including a greater likelihood that social behaviors will be used in appropriate contexts, with reinforcing social consequences from peers and adults.

Summary

Perhaps one of the most critical areas of intervention for students with autism is socialization, and improvements in social behavior often produce **concomitant improvements** (i.e., collateral changes in nontargeted behaviors) in other areas of functioning such as communication and play. Although children and youth with autism characteristically do not exhibit functional social behaviors that lead to social competence, intervention efforts to remediate socialization deficits can result in significant improvements in social behavior, particularly when applied to preschool-aged children.

Socialization interventions have evolved from rather simplistic interventions designed to improve discrete social skills in students with autism to interventions that emphasize the importance of the contexts in which those students participate and the social actions of peers in relating to students with autism. A variety of socialization interventions have been shown to produce desired outcomes, including teacher-mediated techniques (direct instruction, antecedent prompting, social stories), self-mediated techniques (self-monitoring), and peer-mediated techniques. The most robust outcomes will occur when two or more of these techniques within or across these categories are used in combination and when these techniques are used in conjunction with well-planned generalization strategies. For example, a teacher might directly teach students how to initiate social questions (a pivotal behavior) and may provide scripts for the students to follow in specific situations. Next, students could be taught to self-monitor their initiations involving social questions during activities with peer confederates. In those activities, peers would be taught to prompt and reinforce social questions from the students with autism in a way that extends the social interaction.

The goal of socialization interventions is social competence. Students with autism may never be viewed as highly socially competent and may never like social interaction to an extent similar to that of typically developing peers. However, thoughtfully planned socialization interventions designed to target critical skills and generalization of those skills should result in improved social outcomes, including a greater likelihood of social relationships such as friendships between students with autism and peers.

Effective social behavior is necessary for successful functioning in all areas of life and has been shown to be an important prerequisite to mental health and happiness. As educators, we must begin addressing socialization deficits in children with autism and developmental disabilities at a young age and continue applying effective interventions to continually expand these students' repertoires of social behaviors. Anything less may increase the likelihood of more restrictive placements for students, especially in adulthood.

Key Points

1. Students with autism typically have one or more of four common types of socialization deficits: (a) lack of interest in others, (b) social behaviors that are absent or insufficiently developed, (c) difficulty with perspective taking and understanding emotions of others, and (d) lack of joint attention.

2. Social competence refers to other people's perceptions of the social performance of an individual. Socialization interventions must address social competence of students with autism as well as social skills.

3. Assessment of socialization needs of students with autism requires evaluation of three areas: (a) contexts in which the child functions, (b) social culture of those contexts, and (c) the child's skills with respect to the demands of those contexts.

4. Programmatic emphasis on socialization may be characterized by (a) a program philosophy that emphasizes the importance of socialization experiences, (b) including social skills objectives on IEPs, and (c) ensuring that those objectives drive socialization intervention planning.

5. Socialization interventions include teacher-mediated interventions, self-mediated interventions, and peer-mediated interventions. Interventions are most effective when used in combination.

6. Generalization of social skills can be enhanced through careful planning and inclusion of specific strategies.

References

American Psychiatric Association (APA). (2013). *Diagnostic and statistical manual of mental disorders: DSM-5* (5th ed.). Washington, DC: American Psychiatric Association.

Baer, D. M. (1999). *How to plan for generalization* (2nd ed.). Austin: Pro-Ed.

Bandura, A. (1977). *Social learning theory.* Upper Saddle River, NJ: Prentice Hall.

Bellini, S., & Akullian, J. (2007). A meta-analysis of video modeling and video self-modeling interventions for children and adolescents with Autism Spectrum Disorders. *Exceptional Children, 73,* 264–287.

Camargo, S. P. H., Rispoli, M., Ganz, J., Hong, E. R., Davis, H., & Mason, R. (2014). A review of the quality of behaviorally based intervention research to improve social interaction skills of children with ASD in inclusive settings. *Journal of Autism and Developmental Disorders, 44,* 2096–2116.

Carr, E. G., & Kemp, D. C. (1989). Functional equivalence of autistic leading and communicative pointing: Analysis and treatment. *Journal of Autism and Developmental Disorders, 19*(4), 461–578.

Chan, J. M., Lang, R., Rispoli, M., O'Reilly, M., Sigafoos, J., & Cole, H. (2009). Use of peer-mediated interventions in the treatment of autism spectrum disorders: A systematic review. *Research in Autism Spectrum Disorders, 3,* 876–889.

Chan, J. M., & O'Reilly, M. F. (2008). A Social Stories™ intervention package for students with autism in inclusive classroom settings. *Journal of Applied Behavior Analysis, 41,* 405–409.

Chang, Y-C., & Locke, J. (2016). A systematic review of peer-mediated interventions for children with autism spectrum disorder. *Research in Autism Spectrum Disorders, 27,* 1–10.

Constantino, J. N. (2012). *Social Responsiveness Scale™, Second Edition* (SRS™-2). Torrance, CA: WPS.

Dawson, G., Jones, E. J. H., Merkle, K., Venema, K., Lowy, R., Faja, S., . . . Webb, S. J. (2012). Early behavioral intervention is associated with normalized brain activity in young children with autism. *Journal of the American Academy of Child and Adolescent Psychiatry, 51,* 1150–1159.

Didden, R., Scholte, R. H. J., Korzilius, H., de Moor, J. M. H., Vermeulen, A., O'Reilly, M., Lang, R., & Lancioni, G. E. (2009). Cyberbullying among students with intellectual and developmental disability in special education settings. *Developmental Neurorehabilitation, 12,* 146–151.

Frea, W. D. (1995). Social-communicative skills in higher functioning children with autism. In R. L. Koegel & L. K. Koegel (Eds.), *Teaching children with autism* (pp. 53–66). Baltimore: Paul H. Brookes.

Giangreco, M. F. (2009). *Critical issues brief: Concerns about the proliferation of one-to-one paraprofessionals.* Arlington, VA: Council for Exceptional Children, Division on Autism and Developmental Disabilities.

Giangreco, M. F., Halvorsen, A. T., Doyle, M. B., & Broer, S. M. (2004). Alternatives to overreliance on paraprofessionals in inclusive schools. *Journal of Special Education Leadership, 17*(2), 82–90.

Goldstein, H., & Cisar, C. L. (1992). Promoting interaction during sociodramatic play: Teaching scripts to typical preschoolers and classmates with disabilities. *Journal of Applied Behavior Analysis, 25,* 265–280.

Graubard, P. S., Rosenberg, H., & Miller, M. B. (1974). Student applications of behavior modification to teachers and environments or ecological approaches to social deviancy. In E. A. Ramp & B. L. Hopkins (Eds.), *A new direction for education: Behavior analysis.* Lawrence, KS: Support for Development Center for Follow Through.

Gray, C. A., & Garand, J. D. (1993). Social stories: Improving responses of students with autism with accurate social information. *Focus on Autistic Behavior, 8*(1), 1–10.

Gresham, F. M., & Elliott, S. N. (2008). *Social Skills Improvement System (SSIS).* San Antonio, TX: Pearson.

Haring, T. G., & Ryndak, D. (1994). Strategies and instructional procedures to promote social interactions and relationships. In E. C. Cipani & F. Spooner (Eds.), *Curricular and instructional approaches for persons with severe disabilities* (pp. 289–321). Needham Heights, MA: Allyn & Bacon.

Hochman, J. M., Carter, E. W., Bottema-Beutel, K., Harvey, M. N., & Gustafson, J. R. (2015). Efficacy of peer networks to increase social connections among high school students with and without autism spectrum disorder. *Exceptional Children, 82,* 96–116.

Hops, H. (1983). Children's social competence and skill: Current research practices and future directions. *Behavior Therapy, 14,* 3–18.

Howlin, P. (1986). An overview of social behavior in autism. In E. Schopler & E. G. Mesibov (Eds.), *Social behavior in autism* (pp. 101–131). New York: Plenum.

Kaale, A., Smith, L., & Sponheim, E. (2012). A randomized controlled trial of preschool-based joint attention intervention for children with autism. *The Journal of Child Psychology and Psychiatry, 53,* 97–105.

Kanner, L. (1943). Autistic disturbances of affective contact. *Nervous Child, 2,* 217–250.

Kasari, C., Dean, M., Kretzmann, M., Shih, W., Orlich, F., Whitney, R., Landa, R., Lord, C., & King, B. (2016). Children with autism spectrum disorder and social skills groups at school: A randomized trial comparing intervention approach and peer composition. *The Journal of Child Psychology and Psychiatry, 57*(2), 171–179.

Koegel, R. L., & Koegel, L. K. (1990). Extended reductions in stereotypic behavior of students with autism through a self-management treatment package. *Journal of Applied Behavior Analysis, 23,* 119–127.

Koegel, R. L., & Koegel, L. K. (Eds.). (1995). *Teaching children with autism: Strategies for initiating positive interactions and improving learning opportunities.* Baltimore: Paul H. Brookes.

Koegel, L. K., Koegel, R. L., Hurley, C., & Frea, W. D. (1992). Improving social skills and disruptive behavior in children with autism through self-management. *Journal of Applied Behavior Analysis, 25,* 341–353.

Koegel, L., Matos-Freden, R., Lang, R., & Koegel, R. (2012). Interventions for children with autism spectrum disorders in inclusive school settings. *Cognitive and Behavioral Practice, 19,* 401–412.

Koegel, R. L., Werner, G. A., Vismara, L. A., & Koegel, L. K. (2005). The effectiveness of contextually supported play date interactions between children with autism and typically developing peers. *Research and Practice for Persons with Severe Disabilities, 30,* 93–102.

Ledbetter-Cho, K., Lang, R., Davenport, K., Moore, M., Lee, A., Howell, A., Drew, C., Dawson, D., Charlop, M. H., Falcomata, T., & O'Reilly, M. (2015). Effects of script training on the peer-to-peer communication of children with autism spectrum disorder. *Journal of Applied Behavior Analysis, 48,* 785–799.

Ledbetter-Cho, K., Lang, R., Davenport, K., Moore, M., Lee, A., O'Reilly, M., Watkins, L., & Falcomata, T. (2016). Behavioral skills training to improve the abduction-prevention skills of children with autism. *Behavior Analysis in Practice, 9,* 266–270.

Lovaas, O. I. (1987). Behavioral treatment and normal educational and intellectual functioning in young autistic children. *Journal of Consulting and Clinical Psychology, 55*(1), 3–9.

MacDuff, J. L., Ledo, R., McClannahan, L. E., & Krantz, P. J. (2007). Using scripts and script-fading procedures to promote bids for joint attention by young children with autism. *Research in Autism Spectrum Disorders, 1,* 281–290.

Matson, J. L., Rotatori, A. F., & Helsel, A. (1983). *Matson Evaluation of Social Skills with Youngsters* (MESSY). Baton Rouge, LA: Disability Consultants.

Matson, J. L., & Swiezy, N. (1994). Social skills training with autistic children. In J. L. Matson (Ed.), *Autism in children and adults* (pp. 241–260). Pacific Grove, CA: Brooks/Cole Publishing Co.

Matson, J. L., & Wilkins, J. (2007). A critical review of assessment targets and methods for social skills excesses and deficits for children with autism spectrum disorders. *Research in Autism Spectrum Disorders, 1,* 28–37.

McEvoy, M. A., & Odom, S. L. (1987). Social interaction training for preschool children with behavioral disorders. *Behavioral Disorders, 12*(4), 242–251.

McGinnis, E. (2011). *Skillstreaming the Adolescent* (3rd ed.). Champaign, IL: Research Press.

McGinnis, E. (2011). *Skillstreaming in Early Childhood* (3rd ed.). Champaign, IL: Research Press.

McGinnis, E. (2011). *Skillstreaming the Elementary School Child* (3rd ed.). Champaign, IL: Research Press.

Moes, D. (1995). Parent education and parenting stress. In R. L. Koegel & L. K. Koegel (Eds.), *Teaching children with autism: Strategies for initiating positive interactions and improving learning opportunities* (pp. 79–93). Baltimore: Paul H. Brookes.

Mohammadzaheri, F., Koegel, L. K., Rezaei, M., & Bakhshi, E. (2015). A randomized clinical trial comparison between pivotal response treatment (PRT) and adult-driven applied behavior analysis (ABA) intervention on disruptive behaviors in public school children with autism. *Journal of Autism and Developmental Disorders, 45,* 2899–2907.

Morgan, D., Young, K. R., & Goldstein, S. (1983). Teaching behaviorally disordered students to increase teacher attention and praise in mainstreamed classrooms. *Behavioral Disorders, 8,* 265–273.

Mundy, P. (2000). Understanding the core social deficits of autism. In J. Scott, C. Clarke, & M. Brady, *Students with autism: Characteristics and instruction programming* (pp. 18–20). Belmont, CA: Wadsworth/Cengage Learning.

National Autism Center (2015). *Findings and conclusions: National standards project, phase 2.* Randolph, MA: Author.

Odom, S. L., & Strain, P. S. (1986). A comparison of peer-initiation and teacher–antecedent interventions for promoting reciprocal social interaction of autistic preschoolers. *Journal of Applied Behavior Analysis, 19,* 59–71.

Osterling, J., & Dawson, G. (1994). Early recognition of children with autism: A study of first birthday home videotapes. *Journal of Autism and Developmental Disorders, 24,* 247–257.

Parker, D., & Kamps, D. (2011). Effects of task analysis and self-monitoring for children with autism in multiple social settings. *Focus on Autism and Other Developmental Disabilities, 26,* 131–142.

Peters, B., Tullis, C. A., & Gallagher, P. A. (2016). Effects of a group teaching interaction procedure on the social skills of students with autism spectrum disorders. *Education and Training in Autism and Developmental Disabilities, 51,* 421–433.

Pickles, A., Le Couteur, A., Leadbitter, K., Salomone, E., Cole-Fletcher, R., . . . Green, J. (2016). Parent-mediated social communication therapy for young children with autism (PACT): Long-term follow-up of a randomised controlled trial. *The Lancet, 388,* 2501–2509.

Sasso, G. M., Mundschenk, N. A., Melloy, K. J., & Casey, S. D. (1998). A comparison of the effects of organismic and setting variables on the social interaction behavior of children with developmental disabilities and autism. *Focus on Autism and Other Developmental Disabilities, 13*(1), 2–16.

Schopler, E., & Mesibov, G. B. (Eds.). (1983). *Autism in adolescents and adults.* New York: Plenum.

Schwartz, I. S. (2006). Inclusion missteps. In W. L. Heward, *Exceptional children: An introduction to special education* (8th ed., pp. 87–89). Upper Saddle River, NJ: Prentice Hall.

Scott, J., Clark, C., & Brady, M. (2000). *Students with autism: Characteristics and instruction programming.* Belmont, CA: Wadsworth/Cengage Learning.

Simpson, R. L., Myles, B. S., Sasso, G. M., & Kamps, D. M. (1997). *Social skills for students with autism* (2nd ed.). Reston, VA: Council for Exceptional Children.

Stokes, T. F., & Baer, D. M. (1977). An implicit technology of generalization. *Journal of Applied Behavior Analysis, 10,* 349–367.

Strain, P. S., & Fox, J. J. (1981). Peer social initiations and the modification of social withdrawal: A review and future perspectives. *Journal of Pediatric Psychology, 6,* 417–433.

U.S. Department of Education. (2016a). Building the legacy: IDEA 2004. Retrieved April 4, 2016, from http://idea-b.ed.gov/explore/home.html

U.S. Department of Education, National Center for Education Statistics. (2016b). *Digest of Education Statistics: 2015* (NCES 2016-014). Retrieved from https://nces.ed.gov/programs/digest/d15/ch_2.asp

Verschuur, R., Didden, R., Lang, R., Sigafoos, J., & Huskens, B. (2014). Pivotal response treatment for children with autism spectrum disorders: A systematic review. *Review Journal of Autism and Developmental Disorders, 1,* 34–61.

Watkins, L., O'Reilly, M., Kuhn, M., Gevarter, C., Lancioni, G. E., Sigafoos, J., & Lang, R. (2015). A review of peer-mediated social interaction interventions for students with autism in inclusive settings. *Journal of Autism and Developmental Disorders, 45,* 1070–1083.

Whalon, K. J., Conroy, M. A., Martinez, J. R., & Werch, B. L. (2015). School-based peer-related social competence interventions for children with autism spectrum disorder: A meta-analysis and descriptive review of single case research design studies. *Journal of Autism and Developmental Disorders, 45,* 1513–1531.

White, P. J., O'Reilly, M., Streusand, W., Levine, A., Sigafoos, J., Lancioni, G., Fragale, C., Pierce, N., & Aguilar, J. (2011). Best practices for teaching joint attention: A systematic review of the intervention literature. *Research in Autism Spectrum Disorders, 5,* 1283–1295.

Wong, C., Odom, S. L., Hume, K. A., Cox, A. W., Fettig, A., Kucharczyk, S., . . . Schultz, T. R. (2015). Evidence-based practices for children, youth, and young adults with autism spectrum disorder: A comprehensive review. *Journal of Autism Developmental Disorders, 45,* 1951–1966.

Remediating Deficits in Life Skills

© Perkins

LEARNING OBJECTIVES

After reading this chapter, you will be able to:

8-1 Describe assessment strategies designed to provide necessary information for determining a functional, individualized life skills curriculum.

8-2 List various prompting strategies recommended for teaching self-help skills to students with autism.

8-3 Discuss the benefits and challenges of teaching play, leisure, and recreational skills and activities to students with autism.

8-4 Describe various types of supports that might be necessary for students with autism to master vocational skills and obtain and maintain employment.

As discussed in Chapter 4, federal legal mandates have created tension between advocates promoting an academic focus and those supporting a functional life skills focus for students with autism spectrum disorders (ASD) and intellectual disabilities (ID). The arguments are that an academic focus allows students better access to same-age peers while in school, opportunities to attain intellectual potential, and possible access to postschool educational options after graduation (Courtade, Spooner, Browder, & Jimenez, 2012), whereas a functional life skills focus will afford a more meaningful curriculum directly aligned with the goals of independent adult functioning in integrated living, working, and leisure activities (Alwell & Cobb, 2009; Ayres, Lowery, Douglas, & Sievers, 2011, 2012). We have made the case in this book that students need to be instructed in an individually determined curriculum that matches their long-term target goals. If a student's goals include enrollment in higher education programs, then an academic focus is indicated. However, if the student's goals include independent or supervised living and working or both, functional life skills are more likely indicated. Combining both types of curricula may serve a student well but runs the risk of inadequate mastery in either area. For those who are interested in learning more about teaching academics to students with ASD and ID, we recommend Browder and Spooner (2006, 2014) and Spencer, Evmenova, Boon, and Hayes-Harris (2014). This chapter will exclusively delineate evidence-based strategies for teaching functional life skills (self-help, leisure and recreation, and vocational skills) to students with autism.

Independence in self-help tasks, engaging in appropriate leisure activities, and being able to perform meaningful work are all critical prerequisites to living full productive lives as a contributing part of society (Alwell & Cobb, 2009; Fleming, Fairweather, & Leahy, 2013; Ninci et al., 2015). Each self-help task a student cannot do alone raises his or her level of dependence on others and may restrict living and working options. Students who are allowed to engage in socially unacceptable self-stimulatory behaviors rather than being taught to participate in age-appropriate leisure activities are likely to be excluded and teased by peers and to receive undesirable attention in public places. Young adults who are unable to participate in productive work activities, particularly competitive employment, miss one of the most important aspects of adult living, putting them at a social and economic disadvantage (Roux et al., 2013).

Most children learn self-help tasks with little instruction and typically choose age-appropriate and socially acceptable leisure activities with minimal adult guidance. Most young people learn to work by having responsibility for chores at home, acquiring part-time jobs, participating in technical training, and, perhaps, pursuing formal postsecondary degree and certificate programs. Unfortunately, many individuals with autism do not learn these skills through typical developmental channels. In fact, individuals with ASD, regardless of intellectual ability, have lower rates of employment and technical training than other groups of students with disabilities, more restricted living arrangements as adults, and fewer options for recreation and leisure activities (Bouck & Joshi, 2014; Fleury et al., 2014; Shattuck, Wagner, Narendorf, Sterzing, & Hensley, 2011; Wehman, Schall, Carr, Targett, West, & Cifu, 2014). Thus, students with ASD, especially those with ID, need long-term, formal, comprehensive, and systematic instruction to gain any degree of independence in these areas (e.g., Palmen, Didden, & Lang, 2012). This chapter will address what and how to teach in these essential life skills areas. For each area, we will describe general considerations, guidelines for developing curricula, and instructional recommendations. First, though, we will address assessment considerations.

8-1 Assessment of Self-Help, Leisure, and Vocational Skills

As you know by now, the first step in teaching is to conduct assessment to determine what the student needs to learn. Some common approaches to assessing functional life skills, including vocational skills, are ecological assessment, inventories, interviews, checklists, and direct observation. Teachers may need to use a combination of these strategies to effectively delineate each student's functional curriculum.

8-1a Ecological Assessment

Remember from Chapter 4 that ecological assessment means evaluating target environments to determine the activities and skills needed for success in those environments so that a comprehensive, individualized curriculum can be developed. Ecological assessment works well to set life skill targets. Ecological inventory steps are listed in Table 4.5, and Table 4.6 provides questions that can assist with determining environmental needs at school, home, and work for individual students.

Teachers could also determine life skill targets by observing and interviewing other adults. For example, determine what self-help skills 8-year-old students should be able to perform independently by observing 8-year-olds without disabilities or talking to general education teachers who teach that age group. Can most 8-year-olds tie their shoes? If so, that may be an important goal for some of your 8-year-old students. More fundamentally, all 8-year-olds without disabilities are toilet trained. Students with autism who are about that age should be toilet trained as well. If not, then toilet training must be a priority unless there is a physical or health reason why the child cannot learn self-toileting skills. Most 8-year-olds can feed themselves using forks and spoons correctly. Likewise, students with autism should exhibit similar eating skills and should not be allowed to engage in unusual or compulsive eating habits (e.g., a student who will eat only mashed potatoes, bologna, and mustard).

Similar steps should be used to identify target leisure skills. As discussed in Chapter 7, leisure activities that involve social interaction should be selected with regard to the norms of the local peer group. Target solitary leisure activities should also be similar to those engaged in by same-age peers. Therefore, teachers of students with autism can observe peers without disabilities on the playground and during free time for a list of play and leisure activities that would be appropriate.

Special education teachers can also ask general education teachers about their students' leisure and recreation preferences. Remember that your students with autism may show little interest in typical age-group activities, especially those requiring interaction or physical exertion because of social and communicative differences and restricted interests (American Psychiatric Association [APA], 2013; Eversole et al., 2016). Therefore, it is essential to explicitly instruct students how to engage in play activities and, as they age, in appropriate leisure and recreational activities. As we discussed in Chapter 3 and will discuss further in this chapter, it is often possible, even desirable, to try to adapt students' restricted interests and behaviors into socially acceptable and peer-preferred leisure or social activities.

Preparing an ecological inventory in the area of vocational skills means identifying potential work environments and subenvironments for each student and then determining what activities and skills, including communication and social skills, are necessary for success in those environments. Target work environments may be in the school, home, or community. Teachers or job coaches will need to survey the student's neighborhood or community to locate possible work environments, establish relationships with employers, and assess each in order to develop a meaningful vocational curriculum.

8-1b Inventories, Interviews, and Checklists

To assess self-help and leisure skills, teachers can also use adaptive behavior or developmental inventories, interviews, and checklists like those described in Chapter 4. Using comprehensive lists of adaptive and developmental behaviors and skills in several areas (e.g., communication, life skills, social skills, fine and gross motor skills, work and leisure skills), teachers and parents indicate which ones have been mastered, partially mastered, or are in need of teaching. Because behaviors and skills are typically listed in developmental order, it is quite easy to determine which ones need to be taught next. Some common adaptive behavior and developmental assessments include:

- *Vineland Adaptive Behavior Scales*, 3rd ed. (Pearson Education—Psychology)
- *Adaptive Behavior Assessment System*, 3rd ed. (Pearson Education—Psychology)

- *Early Learning Accomplishment Profile System* (Chapel Hill Training-Outreach Project, Inc.)
- *BRIGANCE Inventory of Early Development III* (Curriculum Associates)
- *Behavioral Characteristics Progression* (VORT Corporation)
- *Adaptive Behavior Evaluation Scale—Revised 2nd ed.* (Hawthorne Educational Services)

Skill deficits identified through the use of one of these instruments should then be compared to information gathered from ecological assessments to specifically identify which of those assessed skills the student needs in his or her own target contexts.

In addition to adaptive behavior and developmental inventories, checklists, and interviews, commercial vocational assessments are designed to help educators determine vocational preferences and abilities. Table 8.1 provides a list of four vocational assessments used with students with disabilities. Most of these vocational assessments also include self-help tasks that are work related (e.g., appropriate grooming and dressing) and even leisure skills (e.g., appropriate behavior during breaks). Be sure to compare results of the published assessments to ecological assessment results to obtain an individualized functional curriculum.

8-1c Direct Observation

Direct formal and informal observation of students' strengths and weaknesses in life skills may also play a role in the curriculum-development process when determining normative standards for performance and initial instructional criteria. The behavior measurement methods described in Chapter 2 can be used to assess life and vocational skills for the purpose of creating an individualized curriculum; these data may also serve as baseline for target skills. Examples of direct-observation methods as applied to life skills might include the following.

- **Event recording:** how many bites a student takes before she spits one out, how many times a student begins brushing his teeth within 2 minutes of putting toothpaste on the toothbrush; the number of times a student begins work within 5 minutes of clocking in; number of bites of food eaten with a fork rather than by hand; number of different sand toys used appropriately; number of items placed correctly in the dishwasher; number of times a student asks for assistance during work time.

TABLE 8.1 ● **Commercial Instruments for Career and Vocational Assessment**

BRIGANCE® TRANSITION SKILLS INVENTORY

- Publisher: Curriculum Associates
- This inventory assesses independent living, employment, and additional postsecondary skills to support transition planning for middle and high school students.

READING-FREE VOCATIONAL INTEREST INVENTORY (2ND ED.)

- Publisher: PRO-ED
- This inventory uses pictures to assess students' vocational interests across employment areas such as automotive trades, building trades, food service, animal care, and housekeeping.

OCCUPATIONAL APTITUDE SURVEY AND INTEREST SCHEDULE (3RD ED.)

- Publisher: PRO-ED
- This tool assesses aptitude in six areas directly related to skills and abilities required in 20,000 different jobs.

BECKER WORK ADJUSTMENT PROFILE (2ND ED.)

- Publisher: PRO-ED
- This rating scale assesses work adjustment in four areas: work habits and attitudes, interpersonal relations, cognitive skills, and work-performance skills.

- **Duration recording:** time spent brushing teeth; time spent engaged in appropriate interactive play behavior; time spent working on assigned vocational activity; time on task while ironing; engaged time during assigned document-shredding task; how long it takes a student to finish eating his lunch, how long a student looks at a magazine, or how long a student tolerates sitting on the toilet.

Of course, direct-observation methods can be combined with ecological assessment and information obtained with published assessment instruments. For example, if stocking shelves in a grocery store is a target job for a student, then the teacher might count how long it takes a typical employee to place all items from a carton onto the shelf. The teacher then times the student doing the same task for baseline data. The approximate duration time for the employee without a disability then becomes the target criterion for the student.

Brockett (1998) described an interesting approach to determining individual preferences and skills for developing independent play activities in young children with autism or, with some adaptations, for leisure or vocational activities for older students. He recommended assessing the selection of leisure materials for independent use. This is a structured approach to evaluating the child's or adolescent's response to toys or other leisure materials in three categories: (a) skill, (b) interest, and (c) independence. *Skill* refers to the child's current ability to use the toy or material correctly. *Interest*, of course, refers to the child's level of curiosity toward the item or the appeal the item seems to have for the student. *Independence* is an evaluation of the child's potential for independent use of the toy or material. The steps in the assessment portion of this structured play approach are as follow.

1. Collect a box of toys or leisure materials that you believe will interest the student and may be able to use appropriately and independently to some degree. Select these materials in consultation with the family and based on knowledge about the individual child. Table 8.2 lists toys and materials that can be used for this purpose.
2. Prepare a checklist for evaluating the student's response to each item in terms of skill, interest, and independence (see Table 8.3 for an example). *Skill* should be evaluated as *failing* (the student did not use the material correctly), *emerging* (the student appeared to know what to do with the item and attempted to use it correctly), or *passing* (the student played appropriately with the toy). *Interest* and *independence* are evaluated as *high, medium,* or *low,* depending on the student's level of interest and how quickly he might be able to use the item independently.
3. To conduct the assessment, sit with the student and hand him one item at a time. Observe the student for about 1 minute per item, evaluating each of the three areas. If the student shows no signs of being able to use the item independently, model the correct use of the item several times. If the student then attempts the correct use of the item, skill should be scored as *emerging.*
4. Continue in this fashion until all items have been presented. Of course, if the student's attention wanes, the activity can be stopped and resumed at another time.
5. Finally, after all items have been evaluated, select one item to teach the student to use independently. Any toys or materials rated as passing (skill), high (interest), and high (potential for independence) should be the first ones targeted for independent use. While independent use of that item is being shaped, teach correct use of other toys or materials that were rated at an emerging skill level, high interest, and high potential.

Given the information shown in the evaluation results in Table 8.3, using Play-Doh™ with the Play-Doh Fun Factory would be the logical first choice to teach as an independent activity. Using sticker books might be the second choice. Given the student's high interest and emerging skills in the remote-control car and Etch A Sketch™, either of those toys could be targets for an independent play activity.

This approach could also be used for selecting leisure materials and activities for older students by simply choosing different age-appropriate stimulus items. An adaptation of the process might also work for a skill-interest vocational assessment; follow the same procedure with vocational materials and tasks.

TABLE 8.2 ● Ideas for Independent Play and Leisure Materials

EARLY CHILDHOOD

- Beads on a string
- Plastic dishes and baking utensils
- Nesting cups or rings on a dowel
- Pop beads
- Shape boxes (putting shape blocks into matching holes)
- Nuts and bolts
- Large-piece puzzles, puzzles with knobs on pieces for holding
- Duplo blocks
- Blocks for stacking
- Bristle blocks
- Sand or water play with toys (shovels, buckets, pitchers, cups, sieve, etc.)
- Shapes with Velcro to be matched to shape outlines on poster
- Large plastic vehicles (cars, trucks, dump trucks, cranes, etc.)
- Dolls to dress and feed
- Play-Doh with cookie-cutter shapes, Play-Doh Fun Factory, and so on
- Fisher-Price Little Schoolhouse, Farm, or Parking Garage
- Sorting activities
- Small cars
- Theme-based toys (Thomas the Tank Engine, Spiderman, Star Wars, Shopkins, etc.)

INTERMEDIATE

- Wooden or cardboard jigsaw puzzles
- Three-dimensional puzzles
- Lite-Brite
- Legos
- Remote-controlled cars
- Art activities (chalk, markers, paint, poster board, construction paper, etc.)
- Origami
- Dot-to-dot pictures
- File folder activities (matching pictures, letters, words, numbers, vocabulary words, math facts, etc.)
- Screen-based media (video games, computer games, television, electronic social media software)
- Karaoke machine
- Etch A Sketch
- Books, magazines, comic books
- Sports equipment

SECONDARY

- Jigsaw puzzles with smaller pieces
- Exercise equipment (stationary bicycle, treadmill, weight machine, rowing machine, small trampoline, etc.)
- Crossword puzzles, find-a-word puzzles, and so on
- Art activities
- Screen-based media (video games, computer games, television, social media)
- Karaoke machine
- Operating audiovisual equipment (TV, iPad with headphones)
- Magazines
- Sports equipment

As you know, assessing critical skills to identify a student's current level of functioning in that skill relative to desired functioning levels is an essential step in curriculum development. Once this information is obtained, attention turns to completing the curriculum, choosing instructional strategies, and monitoring progress in the curriculum. The following sections provide information in each of the three curricular areas (self-help, leisure, and vocational) pertaining to issues and considerations, what to teach, and strategies for teaching.

TABLE 8.3 ● Sample Assessment Form for Structured Independent Play

Student: Jackson   **Date:** 10/19

Test conducted by Ms. Lockhart

ITEM	SKILL	INTEREST	INDEPENDENCE
Lite-Brite	Fail	High	High
Play-Doh, with Factory	Pass	High	High
Art activities			
Chalk	Pass	Low	Low
Paint	Emerging	Low	Low
Markers	Pass	Medium	Medium
Handheld video game	Emerging	Medium	High
Remote-controlled car	Emerging	High	High
Puzzles	Fail	Low	Low
File folder activities (match words, addition facts)	Pass	Low	Low
Sticker book	Pass	Medium	High
Etch A Sketch	Emerging	High	High

From S. Brockett (1998). Developing successful play activities for individuals with autism. *Advocate, 31*(6), 15–17. Reprinted with permission.

8-2 Self-Help Skills

Self-help skills are critical to success in almost any area of functioning as well as overall adult independence (Ayres et al., 2011, 2012; Volkmar & Wiesner, 2009). Individuals are more likely to gain acceptance in integrated settings if they are adequately groomed, toilet trained, and can take care of basic personal hygiene needs in socially acceptable ways (Hendricks, 2010; McManus, Derby, & McLaughlin, 2003; Stokes, Cameron, Dorsey, & Fleming, 2004). According to Snell (1993), toileting, eating, and dressing are the most critical self-care areas because these activities must occur frequently every day. To this list, we would add personal grooming and hygiene as an essential self-care category based on research that indicates individuals who are unkempt in appearance are more likely to be rejected by their peers and coworkers (e.g., Coie, Rabiner, & Lochman, 1992; Hendricks, 2010). Students with autism should acquire a variety of self-help skills to ensure successful independent functioning in postschool environments; much of this instruction should be started with young students because acquiring the skills may be a challenge for them (Bennett & Dukes, 2014; Hendricks & Wehman, 2009; Ninci et al., 2015).

8-2a General Considerations for Teaching Self-Help Skills

Several general considerations should guide instruction in self-help skills (Westling & Fox, 2008). First, choosing appropriate self-help skills should be the result of close collaboration between school personnel and parents. The personal nature of many self-help tasks requires that parents be informed and involved in selecting target skills. Also, parents can provide information about family practices that may shape how skills are taught. For example, when family members brush their teeth, is it standard practice to use a glass for rinsing or not? Do the parents plan for their son to use a safety razor or electric shaver? The teacher should teach skills in the same way that the student will need to perform them at home. Use an ecological assessment (parent interview or direct observation in the home) to obtain this type of information.

Second, self-help skills should be taught in natural contexts and at natural times whenever possible. For example, eating skills are best taught at breakfast, snack, and lunchtimes. Toileting skills are taught during toileting breaks (more frequently during the toilet training process). However, some self-help tasks do not naturally occur at school (e.g., dressing, shaving, washing hair, filing fingernails). For these skills, the teacher should provide instruction at the most natural time possible. For example, dressing skills for older students could be taught before and after changing clothes for physical education (PE) class. If naturally occurring opportunities do not offer sufficient learning time, then the teacher might need to discuss training options in the home with parents and family members.

Third, teachers must remember that many self-help tasks are extremely personal (e.g., dressing and undressing, toileting, caring for menstrual needs) and should be taught with respect for the student's privacy, regardless of his or her age. This means that instruction in these tasks should be done individually, not with several students at a time. It also means that the student's privacy should be ensured by teaching target skills in a bathroom, separate room, or behind a screen at a minimum. In addition, the person doing the instruction should be of the same gender as the student. Whereas we believe this is true for students of any age, it is particularly critical for adolescents. Finally, it is vital for teachers to involve and obtain consent from parents and the individualized educational program (IEP) team before beginning instruction on such tasks.

Fourth, instructional strategies based in applied behavior analysis (ABA) have been found to be effective for teaching daily living skills to students with autism (Matson, Hattier, & Belva, 2012; Ninci et al., 2015). Prompting, modeling, reinforcement procedures, shaping, chaining, self-monitoring, visual cueing, and video instruction have been successfully used for this purpose (Alwell & Cobb, 2009; Bennett & Dukes, 2014; McLay, Carnett, van der Meer, & Lang, 2015). Further, discrete trial training (DTT) and milieu teaching (MT) are frequently recommended for teaching self-help skills in natural contexts (Ninci et al., 2015). Studies have also found that video modeling often has positive additive effects when used with the strategies previously listed in natural settings. The following are examples of using ABA strategies discussed in Chapter 5 to teach self-help skills.

- Making a sandwich might be taught using DTT as part of total task presentation. Each day at lunchtime, the student is directed through four trials (one trial for a sandwich for each student in the class); the teacher records whether the student performed each step or not (e.g., needed assistance or prompting). The task is taught in the kitchen (natural context) with data kept on a clipboard in the kitchen area.
- Everything the student uses for hygiene might be color coded. For example, a student's toothbrushing supplies (toothbrush, toothpaste, and cup) might have green dots and be stored in a green box, and shaving supplies for that student would have red dots and be stored in the red box. Each box would have the student's picture on it.
- Use a timer to let the student know how long she is to remain on the potty.
- Provide picture activity schedules to remind students of the steps in washing hands.
- Use a stimulus prompt for setting the table. For example, placemats that have utensils, napkins, plates, and drinking glasses drawn in their proper spots could be used to prompt correct table setting.
- Using backward chaining and DTT, a student is taught to put on her shoes and fasten the Velcro straps. The teacher begins by placing a shoe on the student's foot, tightening the strap, and positioning it close to the Velcro closure strip. The teacher gives the cue "Put on your shoe." If the student responds by pressing the strap down correctly, the teacher records a "+" on the data sheet and then begins another trial with the other shoe. Later in the day, the process is repeated. Once the student correctly presses the strap down in five consecutive trials, she is required to do the last two steps of the task—tighten the strap and press it down. This process continues until the student is able to put her shoe on and fasten it independently.

Finally, self-help skills might be more efficiently taught if the *task* is simplified. Tasks may be modified by (a) eliminating steps, (b) combining steps, (c) changing how steps are done, or (d) modifying the materials used in the task. For example, materials can be modified by (a) making them easier to use, (b) reducing the likelihood of errors, or

(c) highlighting salient aspects of the material (those aspects that students must attend to). Materials can also be modified by using larger or smaller versions of the material, changing the appearance or form, or using color coding to highlight important components. Occupational therapists (OTs), specialists who work to improve students' functional living skills and fine motor skills, might offer good suggestions for self-help task and material modifications. These modifications may be permanent (the student will always use the modified spoon to eat soup or peas) or temporary—that is, a modified form is used during acquisition, and modifications are gradually faded as the student becomes more proficient with the skill (drawings on the placemats are faded). The following are examples of task and material modification.

- To teach drinking from a straw, use short straws (a few inches long) to minimize the time and intensity of sucking that is required before reinforcement is obtained (the liquid). Gradually increase the length of the straw.
- Toothbrushes, hairbrushes, spoons, forks, and so on may be easier to hold if handles are fat and not slippery. Specially designed utensils can be purchased commercially, or regular utensils can be adapted by gluing foam padding around the handle.
- Tying shoes is easier when the laces are large and flat (such as the laces used in athletic shoes) and not too long or short. Using two different color laces may help the student distinguish right and left laces at each step. Of course this task may be eliminated entirely by replacing the laces with Velcro straps.
- Tube socks may be easier to learn to pull on at first. In addition, socks that are one size larger than the child's foot may be easier to put on.
- Color coding may help the student differentiate right from left shoes, and fronts from backs of clothing items. For example, make a green foot shape for the right foot and a red foot shape for the left foot. Then place a green stick-on dot on the right shoe, and a red dot on the left shoe. Placing dots on the rounded outer edge of the shoe will help draw the student's attention to that part of the shoe (for discriminating right and left). Gradually fade use of the dots by cutting them smaller and smaller.
- It is easier to teach beginning dressing skills by using clothing that is slightly larger than the child's normal size.

In the next few sections, we will discuss considerations and strategies for teaching specific categories of self-help skills (i.e., toileting, eating, dressing, and grooming) that can greatly impact living and working options for students with autism.

8-2b Toileting Skills

Most children are toilet trained between 2 and 3 years old. Typically, this is a developmental process during which children exhibit signs of readiness for toilet training, and parents teach their child toileting skills. With patience, perseverance, and perhaps a sense of humor, the child soon is using the toilet with little direction from parents.

Children with autism may not show the signs of readiness for toileting exhibited by children without disabilities (Szyndler, 1996). They may even exhibit challenging behavior in opposition to efforts to teach them toileting skills. However, it is critical that children learn toileting skills, and the closer this occurs to the developmentally appropriate window of time, the better (Ardiç & Cavkaytar, 2014). Regardless of how old a student is, if he or she is in school and not toilet trained, and if there is no physical reason why the student cannot use the toilet, then toilet training must be a priority. Children who are not toilet trained have a much poorer prognosis than those who are, particularly in terms of integrated placements (McManus, Derby, & McLaughlin, 2003).

Snell (1993) presented three criteria for determining whether a student is ready for toileting instruction:

1. The student eliminates on a regular, predictable, schedule.
2. The student can remain clean and dry for a minimum of 1 to 2 hours, thus indicating some degree of voluntary control.
3. The student is at least 30 months old.

TABLE 8.4 ● Toileting and Toileting-Related Skills

- Indicates discomfort when wet or soiled.
- Defecates when placed on potty.
- Urinates when placed on potty.
- Indicates a need to go to the bathroom.
- Goes to the bathroom with little or no assistance.
- Uses the urinal or raises toilet lid to urinate (boys).
- Returns toilet seat and lid to proper position.
- Uses toilet paper.
- Flushes toilet.
- Pulls pants down without assistance.
- Pulls pants up without assistance.
- Washes and dries hands after toileting.
- Uses public restrooms appropriately: waits in line for open stall, closes and locks stall door, uses appropriate amount of toilet paper, makes no eye contact with others at urinals (boys), throws paper towels in trash.
- Differentiates between the men's and women's restroom by looking at various signs on the doors.
- Obtains assistance or uses appropriate adaptive behaviors if there are problems in the bathroom (e.g., toilet is overflowing, a toilet is labeled "Out of Order," no paper towels are available, someone else in restroom is behaving inappropriately).

Whereas students without disabilities may learn many toileting-related skills without formal instruction, students with autism may not learn such skills without direct instruction. Table 8.4 provides a partial list of toileting and toileting-related skills arranged in approximate developmental order. These skills may need to be adapted, depending on environmental demands (e.g., potty seat on toilet versus a small child's potty chair; bathrooms that are shared by other students in the school).

Teaching Toileting Skills

Historically, ABA-based teaching strategies (reinforcement, prompts, motivating operations such as increased liquid consumption, and other operant techniques) were used to teach toileting skills to individuals with ID (Cicero & Pfadt, 2002). Some of these methods used scheduled toileting times and clothing that would cue children that they needed to toilet (e.g., Azrin & Foxx, 1971). Many current toilet training programs have adapted these programs to be less intensive and eliminate special clothing, the required extra liquids, and adverse consequences for accidents (Ardiç & Cavkaytar, 2014). The following steps describe such a toilet training program for use in school classrooms (Westling & Fox, 2008). This program generally focuses on (a) teaching toileting behavior under natural conditions, (b) regularly scheduling toileting times, (c) differentially reinforcing desired toileting behaviors, and (d) using extinction (little or no attention) and a mild aversive (expressing disappointment) for accidents.

1. Collect data to determine the student's patterns of elimination. A chart such as the one in Figure 8.1 can be useful in this regard. Continue data collection until elimination patterns are discerned.
2. Take the student to the toilet during the times when he or she is most likely to void. According to the data in the chart in Figure 8.1, the student regularly eliminates between 8:30 and 9:30 a.m. Therefore, this student should be taken to the bathroom when he arrives at school and allowed to sit on the toilet for approximately 5 minutes. He should be able to have access to a favorite toy or item during this time to increase motivation to stay seated (wash the toy along with the hands when done). If the student does not void during the five minutes, have him get up and try again in 10 or 15 minutes (or less, depending on his age).
3. If the student voids while on the toilet, praise enthusiastically and maybe allow continued access to the favorite item for a short time.

TOILETING/PANTS CHECK RECORD BASELINE: _9/6–9/17_   INTERVENTION: _9/20_

NAME: _Jacob_   LOCATIONS: _gym, classroom, north hall, cafeteria, bathrooms_

Time	9/6	9/7	9/8	9/9	9/10	9/13	9/14	9/15	9/16	9/17	9/20	9/21	9/22	9/23	9/24	9/27	9/28	9/30	10/1	10/2
8:30		(WB)					(W)	W+	W+	A		W+		W+		W+	(W)	W+	A	(W)
8:45		D		(W)	(W)	W+	D	D	D	B		D	W+	D	W+	D	D	D	B	D
9:00	(W)	D		D	D	D	D	D	D	S	W+	D+	D	D	D	W+	D	D+	S	D
9:15	D	D	(BW)	D	D	D	D	D	D	E	(B)	D	D	D	D	D	D	D	E	D
9:30	D	D	D	(W)	(W)	D	D	(W)	D	N	D	D+	D	D+	D	D+	D+	D+	N	D+
9:45	P.E.	P.E.	P.E.	P.E.	P.E.	P.E.	P.E.	P.E.	P.E.	T	P.E.	P.E.	P.E.	P.E.	P.E.	P.E.	P.E.	P.E.	T	P.E.
10:00	D+	D	(WB)	(W)	W+	D	D	D	(W?)		D	D+	(W)	D+	W+	W+	WB+	D+		WB+
10:15	D	(WB)	D	D	D	D	D	D			D	D	D	D	D	D	D			D
10:30	D	D	D	D	W–	D	D	D			D	D+	D+	D+	D+	D+	D+			D+
10:45	D	D	D	(W)	D	W+	W+	D			(W)	D	(W)	D	(W)	D	D			D
11:00	W–	D	D	D	D	D	D	(W)	D		D	D+	D	D+	D	W+	D+	D+		W+
11:15	D	D	(W)	(W)	D	D	D	D	D+		D	D	D	D	D	D	D			D
11:30	D	D	D	D	(W)	D	D	D	D		D	D+	D+	D	D+	D+	D	BW+		D
11:45	L	L	L	L	L	L	L	L	L		L	L	L	L	L	L	L	L		L
12:00	D	D	D	D	D+	D	D	D	D		D	B+	B+	D	D	D?	D			
12:15	(WB)	(W)	D	(WB)	W+	(W)	WB+	D	(WB)		D	D	D	B+	WB+	B+	WB+	D–		WB+
12:30	D	D	(WB)	D	D	D	D	B+	D		(WB)	(W)	D	D	D	D	D+			D
12:45	D	D	D	D	D	(BW)	D	D	D		D+	D	D	D+	D+	D	D			D
1:00	D	D	D	D	D	D	D	D	D		D	(WB)	D	D	D+	D+	A			D+
1:15	D	D	D	D	D	D	D	D	D		D	D	D	D	(W)	D	B			D
1:30	D	(W)	D	D	D	D	D	D	D		D	D+	D	D+	D	D+	D+	S		(W)
1:45	D	D	D	D	D	D	D	(W)	D+		D	D	D	D	W–	D	E			D
2:00	(BW)	(W)	D	(W)	D	D–	(W)	D	D+		D	D–	D+	W+	W+	W+	D+	N		D
2:15	D	D	(B)	(WB)	(W)		(W)						W–	D	W–	T				D
2:30				D																
# Self initiations / # Accidents	1/3	0/5	0/5	0/8	2/4	3/2	2/2	2/4	4/2		2/3	9/1	5/3	9/0	7/1	11/1	9/1	7/0		6/2

Key
D = Dry
L = Lunch

Student Initiated
W+ = Wet on toilet
B+ = BM on toilet
D+ = Self-initiated, no elim.

Teacher Assisted
W– = Wet on toilet
B– = BM on toilet
D– = Teacher-initiated, no elim.

Accidents
(W) = Wet
(B) = BM

FIGURE 8.1 Data collection form for toilet training (From Snell & Farlow, 1993. Reprinted by permission of Pearson Education, Inc., Upper Saddle River, NJ 07458).

Continue to check for dryness during periods when the child is not on the toilet. Praise dry pants ("Good for you—you are clean and dry! I'm proud of you!"). If the child has an accident during training, the teacher should make a brief comment of mild disapproval ("I'm disappointed that you are wet! Next time I hope you'll tell me when you need to go") and not allow access to the favorite toy. Change the student into dry clothes and do nothing more.

8-2c Eating Skills

Mealtimes not only offer rich opportunities for practicing a variety of skills but also are natural contexts for integration with peers without disabilities, and they have the advantage of being centered on food, which often functions as a strong primary reinforcer for students. Eating skills include everything from finger feeding to using knives to cut and spread. Furthermore, mealtimes are good times to teach many eating-related skills such as appropriate vocabulary and conversation skills, appropriate behavior in restaurants (ordering from a menu, ordering at a counter, etc.), money skills, home meal preparation and cleanup, grocery shopping, and nutrition. Table 8.5 provides a partial list of eating and eating-related

TABLE 8.5 ● Eating and Eating-Related Skills

Young children (preschool, primary) typically are able to:

- Self-feed appropriate finger foods.
- Drink from a cup.
- Drink with a straw.
- Use a spoon (fist grasp acceptable).
- Use a spoon to eat soup with some spilling.
- Spear food with a fork.
- Use a knife for spreading (incomplete spreading, may tear bread or break crackers).
- Use a napkin with reminders.
- Remain seated for duration of meal (with reminders).
- Ask for drinks and snacks and more of particular foods at mealtime.
- Eat independently, probably with food remaining on mouth and hands after eating and crumbs on table, chair, and floor.
- Wash and dry hands with reminders and possibly assistance.
- Clean hands and face after eating with reminders and assistance.
- Talk to others at table while eating.
- Ask for and use condiments (ketchup, steak sauce, salsa, etc.).
- Self-serve some foods (mashed potatoes, yogurt, applesauce, etc.).
- Pour from a pitcher with some spilling; may need reminders when to stop.

Primary to intermediate-age children typically are able to:

- Use fork and spoon with correct grasp.
- Drink without spilling from any type of cup, can, or bottle.
- Cut foods with a knife and fork with no assistance.
- Use a napkin.
- Eat soup with a spoon with little spilling.
- Use a knife for spreading with little difficulty.
- Ask for and use most condiments, including salt and pepper.
- Request foods to be passed.
- Pass food to others at the table on request.
- Self-serve from serving bowls.
- Pour liquids from a pitcher or carton with little spilling.
- Select desired items and place order at restaurants.
- Prepare snacks.
- Use kitchen utensils and appliances with supervision (mixer, blender, oven, etc.).
- Perform most cleanup tasks (clear table, wash dishes, load dishwasher).
- Adjust behavior to a variety of restaurant settings, with prompts (e.g., drive-in, cafeteria, formal restaurant).
- Assist parents with grocery shopping (help make list, retrieve items in store).
- List foods that are good for you and foods that have no nutritional value.
- Describe, at least in part, elements of a nutritionally sound diet.

Adolescents typically are able to:

- Fix snacks and some meals.
- Perform meal-preparation tasks, including chopping, measuring, cleaning, peeling, and so on.
- Do cooking and cleanup activities (e.g., load and empty dishwasher).
- Use kitchen appliances without supervision.
- Set table.
- Verify accuracy of restaurant tab and calculate tip.
- Adjust behavior to a variety of public eating settings.
- Work in eating-related jobs (wait tables, bus tables, cook, wash dishes, etc.).
- Use public transportation to get to eating establishments.
- Go to restaurants with friends without supervision.
- Do grocery shopping independently.
- Describe and plan nutritionally sound meals.

skills that students with autism may need to learn arranged in approximate developmental order. Please note that the skills listed in Table 8.5 are not meant to be a complete curriculum. They should serve simply as examples of the types of skills that may be targeted. As described in Chapter 4, all self-help curricular areas will depend on each student's individual needs.

Note that students with autism are likely to display eating difficulties in addition to a lack of eating skills. These students may have restricted dietary variety, select foods only with certain textures, be fussy eaters, have a fear of new foods, eat too slowly or too rapidly, and be under- or overweight (Marshall, Hill, Ziviani, & Dodrill, 2014). Students with restricted food variety may suffer from a lack of nutrition, low energy, weight loss, and other physical problems stemming from nutritional deficiencies (Keen, 2008). Students with eating difficulties may also display challenging behavior (e.g., tantrums) when faced with nonpreferred foods or food in general. ABA-based techniques such as shaping, chaining, physical prompting, noncontingent and contingent reinforcement, and escape extinction have been found to be effective in alleviating such eating problems (Marshall, Ware, Ziviani, Hill, & Dodrill 2014; Sharp, Jaquess, Morton, & Herzinger, 2010). Eating interventions and instruction in eating skills should be conducted with young children whenever possible to avoid related medical issues. Just be aware that teaching eating skills to students with autism may be more complex than teaching these skills to other students.

Teaching Eating Skills

Teaching eating skills as with other skill training, can be accomplished with task analysis, chaining, shaping, reinforcement, and physical and video prompting (e.g., Anglesea, Hoch, & Taylor, 2008; Bennett & Dukes, 2014). It is best to teach skills in sequence from the most basic, such as appropriate finger feeding, to more complex skills, such as cutting food with a knife and fork. In addition, target skills should be age appropriate such as drinking from a cup for young children to using straws and drinking from soda cans for older students. However, a 14-year-old who still has not learned basic eating skills may need to start by learning skills that are typical for much younger students.

The following list describes recommendations for teaching eating skills.

1. Educators should teach socially valid eating skills and determine socially valid criteria as standards for those skills (Alper, McMullen, McMullen, & Miller, 1996). Observing same-age peers without disabilities in a variety of meal and snack contexts will help teachers determine socially valid eating and eating-related skills. Furthermore, this type of ecological assessment will help teachers determine acceptable levels of performance. For example, do most children regularly use a napkin? Do most children eat pizza with their fingers or a fork? What are peers' conversational topics at lunch? These skills and standards may become targets for students with autism.

2. Teach skills during meals and snacks consisting of foods that are highly motivating for the student. It would be a mistake to try to teach a new skill (e.g., using a spoon) with a food the student dislikes (e.g., tomato soup).

3. In the early stages of learning new skills, use food that makes the skill easier. The following are examples of foods that work well for students who are not yet skilled in the stated tasks.
   - **Finger feeding:** cheese cubes, raw vegetables, peanuts, grapes (foods that are not slippery and are chunky enough to be easily picked up).
   - **Using a spoon:** mashed potatoes, pudding, soft ice cream, oatmeal (foods that cling to the spoon).
   - **Using a fork:** meat cubes, oven-roasted potato cubes, cooked carrots (foods that are easily speared and are likely to stay on the fork tines).
   - **Spreading with a knife:** soft butter on tortillas, sturdy crackers, or thick toast; soft peanut butter on toast (foods that spread easily or foods that do not crumble or break easily during spreading).
   - **Cutting with a knife:** fish fillets, tender boneless chicken, omelet (foods that cut easily).

4. Enlist peers without disabilities to serve as peer buddy tutors during snacks and mealtimes. Peers should be taught to model target skills, prompt their partners in the correct use of skills, interact with their partners socially (see Chapter 7), and reinforce the correct use of skills. Teachers should also reinforce their students with autism for imitating their partner's eating habits ("You're eating just like Cameron! Good for you!").

5. As discussed in Chapter 6, use milieu teaching to teach relevant vocabulary such as favorite foods, labels for eating utensils, napkins, place mats and so forth, appropriate verbs (e.g., eat, cut, drink), functional adjectives (e.g., hot, cold, slimy, wet, spicy, salty, sweet), and how to appropriately ask for or refuse more food.

6. Use picture or video prompts to cue students to engage in target behaviors, such as using utensils and napkins.

7. If students display inappropriate mealtime behaviors that interfere with correct eating (e.g., leaving the table during mealtime, self-stimulatory behaviors that involve the hands) or that will make them undesirable mealtime partners (e.g., self-stimulatory behaviors or idiosyncratic eating habits such as smelling each bite before eating or regurgitating food), plan to reduce these behaviors using techniques covered in Chapter 3.

8. Mealtimes should be completed within a reasonable time. Correct pacing of meal consumption may need to be addressed. One student we know typically takes a minimum of 90 minutes to finish his lunch! On the other hand, students should not be allowed to gulp their food so they are finished in a few minutes. For slow eaters, finishing meals within a specific time (use a timer) should be differentially reinforced, perhaps with a favorite dessert (otherwise no dessert). Students who eat too fast might be taught to put their fork down after every bite or after a preset prompt (Anglesea et al., 2008) or are reinforced if they take longer than a specified time to finish a meal.

9. For students who may prefer only a few foods, food colors, or food textures, thus running the risk of malnutrition and other medical issues, thoughtful intervention planning is required (Ledford & Gast, 2006; Marshall, Hill, et al., 2014). For example, one student we know insists on eating only white foods. Verify that increasing the variety of foods a student will eat is a goal agreed on by teachers and parents. If so, utilize ABA-based strategies found to be effective for this purpose (e.g., Marshall, Ware, et al., 2014). We wish to point out that we do not necessarily think the goal of getting students to eat a greater variety of foods is important *unless* the student's diet is severely deficient in certain food groups or the student is not getting sufficient nutrients. Like peers without disabilities, children with autism should be allowed their preferences within reason.

10. Finally, most school contexts do not present naturally occurring opportunities to practice some skills such as eating meals family style (passing bowls, serving self, etc.). Therefore, teachers will need to create opportunities if these skills are instructional targets. Cafeteria workers in most schools are eager to help students with special needs. The authors used to have "class lunch" one day each week. On these days, cafeteria staff cheerfully served our students' lunches in bowls and on platters to allow students opportunities to practice serving themselves, passing dishes, and asking for desired items. Each lunch, three or four special guests were invited, including peers without disabilities, other teachers, school staff, and administrators. In addition to providing good opportunities for eating skills instruction, these lunches also served as venues for socialization. Not only did the students with autism benefit, but also other people in the school came to know the students with autism on a personal level. This resulted in spontaneous social initiations outside of the classroom such as greetings in the hall, initiations on the playground, and reciprocal invitations to other classes' activities.

8-2d Dressing Skills

Children with autism and ID tend to acquire daily living skills at a slower rate than those without ID (Bal, Kim, Cheong, & Lord, 2015). This includes dressing skills such as tying shoes, putting on a coat, removing a pullover sweater, putting on socks, or any of the many other dressing skills required for current and future independence. Thus, school personnel should work collaboratively with parents to target age- and skill-appropriate goals in this

TABLE 8.6 ● **Dressing and Dressing-Related Skills**

Young children (preschool, primary) typically are able to:

- Put on all basic clothing items (socks, shoes, pullover shirt, button-down shirt, pants, underwear).
- Remove all basic clothing items.
- Identify own clothing.
- Pick out clothing they like and wish to wear; clothing may not be coordinated or appropriate for weather or occasion.
- Fasten most closures—large (front) zippers, buttons, snaps, hooks.

Primary to intermediate-age children typically are able to:

- Put on all clothing items.
- Remain clothed until time to change clothes.
- Remove all clothing items.
- Choose own clothing for play and school.
- Fasten all closures (including belts, shoelaces).
- Tell someone when clothing does not fit comfortably.
- Fold clothing simply (match socks, fold underwear, fold shirts and pants in half).
- Place items of clothing on hangers (button-front shirts, coats).
- Polish or clean shoes.

Adolescents typically are able to:

- Care for own clothing (wash and dry, iron, fold or place on hangers).
- Make some clothing repairs (sew on missing button, sew small seam rips).
- Select own clothing for purchase.
- Create a personal style with clothing.

---

area. Further, as with specific food preferences, students with autism may have distinct preferences for clothing items, usually based on texture (APA, 2013). Students may refuse to wear new clothes and may disrobe in public if clothing becomes irritating. It will be important to use preferred clothing to teach dressing skills and may require additional instruction to teach about appropriate dress for various situations.

Like the other self-help areas discussed so far, dressing skills also include related skills, such as changing clothing regularly, choosing clothing items that match and are appropriate for the weather, and recognizing when clothing needs to be laundered, does not fit properly, or is in need of repair, and so forth. As you will see from the list of dressing skills given in Table 8.6, many of these skills are typically acquired in late childhood and adolescence.

Teaching Dressing Skills

The general guidelines previously discussed for teaching self-help skills also apply to teaching dressing skills. These include the following.

- Use effective ABA-based teaching techniques (task analysis, chaining, reinforcement, various types of prompts, and progress monitoring).
- Teach skills in context as much as possible. This may be difficult because children without disabilities typically do not work on dressing skills at school unless they are very young students. However, opportunities for such instruction do exist (e.g., arriving at and leaving school, changing clothes for PE).
- Teach skills with regard to students' privacy (e.g., putting on blouses or undergarments).
- Teach appropriate vocabulary, preferably with DTT and MT (see Chapter 6) as dressing takes place.
- Modify clothing and fasteners to make the dressing task easier. Examples of such modification for dressing tasks were previously described in this chapter.
- Reinforce specific dressing tasks and an appropriate pace of dressing (not too slow or fast).
- Reinforce students who tend to inappropriately disrobe for remaining clothed for a specified period of time (see differential reinforcement of other behavior in Chapter 3).

- Use actual clothing to teach dressing skills. Commercial materials such as dressing boards, dressing vests, or shoe-tying boards will do little to enhance generalization of dressing skills because these materials are different than what the child must actually button, zip, tie, snap, and so forth. Plus, fastening buttons on a button board in front of you requires a different orientation than fastening buttons on your shirt. Skill generalization is always a priority and is much more likely to occur when instructional materials are the real thing, not a clever-looking commercial imitation.

8-2e Personal Grooming and Hygiene Skills

The last self-help area to consider for students with autism is personal grooming and hygiene (PGH). Having some degree of proficiency in these skills is important to health, independence, dignity, and social acceptance (e.g., Hendricks, 2010). PGH skills include dental hygiene, feminine hygiene, physical cleanliness, and grooming activities. Table 8.7 provides a partial list of PGH skills that students with autism might not learn without explicit instruction.

Teaching Grooming and Hygiene Skills

One of the goals in teaching these skills is for students not only to do PGH tasks without assistance but also to do them without reminders. Few adolescents without disabilities need to be reminded to brush their teeth at least once a day, wash, blow their nose, comb their hair, and so forth. Therefore, teaching PGH skills should include attention to *when* to perform the grooming tasks. Of course, many of the PGH tasks listed in Table 8.7 are normally done at home in the morning or before bed. PGH skills can best be taught with task analysis, chaining, shaping, various prompting techniques, and reinforcement. Picture or written schedules are often used to prompt students through activity task steps (e.g., toothbrushing, hair brushing, bathing). The pictures can be stored in notebooks available to each individual or taped to bathroom walls or mirrors. Video modeling and cueing have also been found to be effective in teaching hygiene skills to individuals with autism both to

TABLE 8.7 ● **Grooming and Personal Hygiene Skills**

Young children (preschool, primary) typically are able to:

- Wash and dry hands and face.
- Bathe or shower with supervision.
- Brush teeth.
- Comb hair.
- Use tissue to blow nose.

Primary to intermediate-age children typically are able to:

- Bathe or shower independently.
- Wash and dry own hair.
- Request certain hairstyles.
- Trim nails.
- Polish nails.
- Cover mouth to cough or sneeze.

Adolescents typically are able to:

- Bathe or shower daily without reminders.
- Take care of feminine hygiene
- Tell barber or stylist how they want their hair cut or styled.
- Comb their hair into a variety of styles (if appropriate for hair length).
- Curl own hair with rollers or curling iron.
- Take care of fingernails, toenails, and cuticles.
- Apply makeup.
- Shave.
- Apply deodorant daily.

cue appropriate times to engage in the behavior and to provide prompted steps for performing the behavior chains (Cardon, 2012; Cardon & Wilcox, 2011). Both types of prompts can be made available, perhaps on handheld devices, in school and at home, where hygiene would best be taught.

However, because students may need daily practice in these skills, teachers should schedule PGH tasks at appropriate times during the day. For example, "morning tasks" such as washing face, brushing teeth, combing hair, and shaving could be done first thing in the morning. Washing and styling hair and applying makeup could be done after PE or swimming, for example.

As mentioned previously, one aspect of teaching students when to engage in PGH skills involves teaching them to recognize when those tasks are needed. For example, a student should be taught to examine his or her hair to see if it needs combing. Rather than just telling a student "You need to blow your nose," students should be taught to pay attention to the sensation that means they need to blow their nose. For example, the teacher might say "A.J., do you feel something on your nose? What do you need to do?" (e.g., see the MT mand-model strategy described in Chapter 6).

Perhaps as important as teaching students when it is appropriate to engage in PGH tasks is teaching them when it is *inappropriate* to do so. Students should be taught that many PGH tasks should be done in the privacy of one's home, bedroom, or bathroom. Even some tasks that some people do in public (e.g., comb hair, clean nails) should not be done in certain situations (restaurants, at the table, in formal situations such as church or class).

Teachers and parents should work collaboratively to plan instruction in PGH tasks. Parents may wish for teachers to take the lead in teaching certain skills such as shaving. If so, parents could tell their son before he leaves, "You need a shave! Good thing you'll do that at school." Also, parents and teachers should discuss vocabulary, basic steps, and materials to be taught in PGH tasks. For example, does a student use both shampoo and a separate conditioner? Does the student need to learn to blow-dry hair? Should the student have access to a curling iron? These types of potential skills should be identified through ecological assessment. In regard to skills typically performed at home, regular communication with parents about what is to be taught and how it will be taught will facilitate acquisition and generalization of target skills.

8-3 Play, Leisure, and Recreation Skills

Independent participation in leisure and play activities benefit all children, including individuals with autism. These benefits include the opportunity to make friends, enhanced quality of life, improved emotional, cognitive, and physical well-being, and social acceptance (Bada, Orgaz, Verdugo, Ullan, & Martinez, 2013; Dodd, Zabriskie, Widmer, & Eggett, 2009; Jordan, 2003). Unfortunately, students with autism, particularly adolescents, typically have limited participation in social and community activities (Shattuck, Orsmond, Wagner, & Cooper, 2011). Thus, attention to developing age-appropriate and socially acceptable play, leisure, and recreation skills is another important instructional area for students with autism.

Most of us do not require formal instruction to participate in play and recreational activities, pursue leisure time interests, and develop specific skills and talents. However, this is not the case for individuals with autism. Without systematic instruction in play, leisure, and recreational skills, it is unlikely that they will learn them on their own. Cognitive delays may affect the rate of learning, and social and communication deficits and restricted and repetitive interests often preclude motivation to learn these skills or participate in these types of activities (APA, 2013; Eversole et al., 2016; Jung & Sainato, 2013). For example, students with autism who do acquire leisure and play skills typically choose solitary, often sedentary, activities (e.g., listening to music with headphones, playing video games, watching a movie, swinging), and may be less likely to engage in formal and physical activities (e.g., organized sports) (Eversole et al., 2016). These researchers also found an inverse relationship between cognition and leisure activity enjoyment, meaning that students with ASD and ID were less likely to display enjoyment in leisure activities than students without ID.

In addition, as you learned in Chapter 7, decreases in maladaptive social behavior have been associated with increases in appropriate play and leisure skills (Machalicek et al., 2009). For individuals with autism, this suggests that in addition to the benefits of leisure and recreation activities already described, developing these skills and participating in related activities may help mitigate socially unacceptable behaviors.

8-3a General Considerations for Teaching Play, Leisure, and Recreation Skills

One of the more challenging aspects of teaching (and parenting) children with autism is that these children show distinct differences in leisure and play engagement during unstructured time. Although many children with autism choose to engage in solitary, sedentary, and sometimes inappropriate activities, children without disabilities are more likely to interact with one another and play social games (Jordan, 2003). During unstructured time, adolescents without disabilities would undoubtedly talk to one another or the teacher, sleep, write notes, or work on homework. Without specific instruction and prompting, an adolescent with autism might do none of these but would instead sit alone, possibly engage in self-stimulation, or pace at the back of the room. These differences may adversely affect potential friendships, social integration, and social and physical development in general. Following are curricular and instructional recommendations for teaching play, leisure, and recreational skills.

Curriculum

An important consideration for play, leisure, and recreation instruction is skill selection. Like every other curricular area, skill selection must be individualized and based on ecological assessment. This assessment should also include a preference survey because play and leisure activities should reflect what an individual finds enjoyable (Eversole et al., 2016). Another important component of the curriculum-selection process is determining what types of activities age peers in the school and community engage in and what students' families do in the way of leisure activities so the curriculum can match available leisure and play opportunities.

One unique aspect of this life skills area for the general population is the wide range of activities that are characterized as "play, leisure, and recreation activities." Just in your own circle of friends, you may know people who prefer reading as a relaxation activity, while others find relaxation by preparing for and participating in triathlons. Some acquaintances may like playing cards, while others love golf, fishing, or watching baseball. Some people prefer solitary leisure activities; others seek group pursuits. Some individuals like spectator sports, whereas others want to engage in the sport themselves. The point here is that, given such a wide array of possibilities, teachers and parents should be able to find activities that each student enjoys and that reflect varying skill levels. Parent surveys and direct observation can offer information about individual preferences. Remember, however, that preference alone should not dictate this curriculum. Also, keep in mind the possible social integration benefits and the physical and cognitive benefits of various activities.

One option for selecting leisure activities is to choose activities that incorporate a student's restricted interests or obsessive preferences (e.g., Baker, 2000). We discussed this in Chapter 3 with regard to finding appropriate alternatives for these behaviors. This concept can be expanded to target potential leisure skills as well. For example, a child who engages in proprioceptive self-stimulation would probably be a good candidate for activities that result in considerable sensation in the muscles and joints such as lifting weights, gymnastics, yoga, Tae Bo, ballet, swimming, or aerobics. A student who likes to touch different textures may do well with finger painting, clay or ceramics, creating fabric collages, making bread or dough for pizza crusts, or making cookies that require forming the dough into small balls. A student who sniffs as a self-stimulatory behavior could make potpourri mixtures (and sell them perhaps) or experiment with combining fragrances and essential oils to create new fragrances. A student who obsessively lines up objects might be a natural at setting up domino paths in intricate patterns. Like many other aspects of teaching students with autism, determining leisure activities requires collaboration with parents and significant creativity.

Remember that it is important to target age-appropriate skills for instruction. However, in leisure and recreation areas, perhaps a little more leeway is seen with regard to this caveat. For one thing, many leisure and recreation activities are age appropriate for all ages, including swimming, reading, watching movies, running, playing badminton, bowling, cycling, watching TV, cooking, and art projects. Social media, video games, and playing on the Wii are age appropriate for children, adolescents, and adults. Sometimes, adolescents and adults engage in "youthful" leisure activities: swinging on a park swing, building sand castles, collecting dolls or baseball cards, or building model cars or airplanes. Therefore, we urge teachers and parents not to be overly stringent in the "age-appropriate" rule when it comes to leisure and recreation activities. There are two general rules of thumb. First, if the activity preferred by the student is clearly age inappropriate (e.g., a 10-year-old student loves playing with an infant's busy box), try to find a more age-appropriate version of the activity or more age-appropriate material for the preferred activity. Second, good leisure instruction means teaching a variety of skills: solitary activities, group activities, passive as well as active participation, and related social communication skills.

Because of a typical preference for working on computers, it is often thought that individuals with ASD would readily engage in screen-based leisure activities (e.g., television, computer games, video games, social media). Although individuals with ASD reported a preference for watching TV and playing solitary video games, Mazurek and Wenstrup (2012) found that they did not spend much time socially interacting through screen-based activities such as e-mail, text messaging, visiting social network sites. Solitary leisure engagement will do little to promote friendships and social skills, so teachers should be sure to also target activities requiring social interaction. Basically, we recommend developing a leisure or play curriculum by targeting skills necessary for both low-energy and high-energy activities as well as solitary activities, partner activities, and group activities, remembering to embed student preferences and interests. Keep in mind the importance of teaching skills and activities that will enhance friendships, social skills, and motor development. Table 8.8 lists sample activities by age group in each of these areas.

Instruction

In addition to *what* skills are taught, *where* and *how* skills are taught are also important. In this section, we describe preferred strategies for teaching leisure and play activities.

Explicit instruction with embedded interests has been found effective for teaching both solitary and interactive play and leisure skills (Jung & Sainato, 2013). Specific leisure and

TABLE 8.8 ● **Sample Leisure and Recreation Activities**

PRESCHOOL TO PRIMARY
SOLITARY OR PARTNER ACTIVITIES

- Look at books.
- Play with toys.
- Ride riding toys.
- Watch TV or videos.
- Fingerpaint, play with clay, draw pictures, color.
- Play imagination games.
- Card games (e.g., Old Maid, Go Fish).
- Board games (e.g., Candyland, Mouse Trap).
- Play hopscotch.

GROUP ACTIVITIES

- Hide-and-Seek.
- Duck, Duck, Goose.
- Various forms of Tag.
- Four square.
- Play jump rope.

(continued)

TABLE 8.8 ● Sample Leisure and Recreation Activities (*Continued*)

INTERMEDIATE

SOLITARY OR PARTNER ACTIVITIES

- Collect and organize items (e.g., baseball cards, Matchbox cars, glass figurines).
- Playing games on Wii.
- Read books, magazines, comics.
- Ride bike.
- Play video games and computer games.
- Horseback riding.
- Practice sports (e.g., dribbling and shooting baskets, hockey, kicking soccer ball, playing catch).
- Practice dance, instruments, singing, and so on.
- In-line skating.
- Fishing.
- Swimming.
- Rock climbing.
- Board games (e.g., Monopoly, Sorry, Life, Risk).
- Camping.
- Taking care of pets.
- Listening to music.

GROUP ACTIVITIES

- Organized sports.
- Lessons (e.g., dance, karate, art).
- Roller skating, roller blading.
- Organizing and performing skits, puppet shows, and so on.

ADOLESCENT

SOLITARY OR PARTNER ACTIVITIES

- Engage in social media (texting, e-mail, Snapchat, Instagram, etc.).
- Read.
- Watch TV.
- Play video games or computer games.
- Play games on Wii.
- Write letters.
- Talk on the telephone.
- Listen to music with earbuds or headphones.
- Shop.
- Attend sporting events, music shows, plays, and so on.
- Physical fitness activities (e.g., aerobics, lifting weights, Tae Bo).
- Play tennis, golf, racquetball, bowling, swimming.
- Play a musical instrument.
- Dating.
- Going to movies.
- Horseback riding.
- Finding and watching YouTube videos.

GROUP ACTIVITIES

- Group sports.
- Giving and attending parties.
- Line dancing.
- Clubs and service organizations.
- Theater, band, dance group, cheerleading.
- Hanging out and talking.
- Playing partner or group video or electronic games (e.g., Minecraft, Pokémon Go).

play activities should first be task analyzed and then taught using activity schedules, chaining techniques, reinforcement, and various prompting procedures such as those found in DTT and MT (Brockett, 1998; Carlile, Reeve, Reeve, & DeBar, 2013; Jung & Sainato, 2013; Rettig, 1994). For example, after task analyzing the activity of assembling a puzzle, a logical instructional choice might be backward chaining. To teach the skill, the teacher would assemble all pieces of the puzzle (except for the last piece) followed by the S^D "Martin, put your puzzle together." When Martin responds, he is reinforced, and the trial is repeated with either the same puzzle (but a different final piece) or a different puzzle. Eventually the student will complete the puzzle by inserting the last two pieces, then the last three pieces, then the last four, and so forth until he is able to do the puzzle independently. Once skills are acquired, generalization should be addressed by then providing opportunities during the school day for the student to engage in target activities or use leisure or play materials in social interactive contexts (e.g., working on a puzzle with a partner).

Brockett (1998) recommends a procedure for teaching solitary play and leisure activities using instructional and organizational strategies described in Chapter 5. The steps in this procedure are as follow.

1. Choose a target activity using ecological, survey, and observational assessment methods described earlier in this chapter.
2. Determine a system to guide the student through solitary free-time activities. The system should include a signal to the student that he has finished the activity. For example:
   - **Left to right with finish box.** In this system, individual activities are placed in separate boxes and arranged from left to right. The student completes the activity in each consecutive box and selects the finish box, which contains a reinforcer. According to Brockett, this is the easiest system for students to use. For example, during leisure time, the student would complete each activity in order (e.g., a puzzle, a Lego activity in which the student designs a Lego structure to match a pattern provided), subsequently obtaining the reinforcer from the finish box.
   - **Matching.** This system requires the student to select activities by matching activity cards labeled with a number, letter, or color to the appropriate activity boxes. Once all cards have been used (e.g., activities completed), he chooses the reinforcer box.
   - **Written.** The child's play or leisure activities are written on a card. He uses the card to guide selection of materials or activities, perhaps crossing off each item as he finishes it.
3. Determine what type of visual cueing system will help the student complete activities independently such as activity schedules or other stimulus prompts. For example, Carlile and colleagues (2013) taught students with autism to engage in independent leisure activities using activity schedules on an iPod Touch.
4. Devise an organizational structure to store the activities. This might be cardboard shoeboxes, clear plastic shoeboxes, manila envelopes, expanding file folders, dress boxes, and so forth. For example, an activity box for making a bead necklace would include the string, beads (in a small packet with a small bowl to put the beads in), and perhaps pattern cards. An activity box for listening to music might include an iPod, charging cord, earphones, and the picture sequence card to direct the student how to turn the iPod on, select the music, and listen with earphones. A large tub for finished activities should be part of the routine so that when the student finishes the activity (e.g., completes the necklace patterns, the timer indicates time is finished, or finishes the puzzle), he places the completed product (or used materials) in the finish tub.
5. Teach the activity, prompting system, and organizational system using DTT or MT or both.
6. After students have learned the activity, have them use the activity boxes in context (e.g., during play or free time). Prompt as needed—but remember that prompts must ultimately be faded before the skill can be considered mastered.
7. Begin by having the student complete one activity box. When he is able to do this independently, add a second box to the routine (using the left-to-right system, matching system, etc.), then a third, and so forth, as appropriate for the student's age, developmental level, and classroom time constraints.

Once students learn this system, parents could implement the same system at home. This would address parents' frequent requests that teachers help their son or daughter learn how to "entertain himself (or herself)." Remember to teach relevant vocabulary and use parents' input when planning play and leisure activities. It is important to teach activities, vocabulary, and materials that the student will be able to access at home.

In addition to solitary activities, most leisure pursuits take place with other people, often in public places. Therefore, at some point, skill instruction should occur in natural contexts where target activities typically occur, or in multiple situations to facilitate generalization, and with other individuals, including peers without disabilities. So, croquet may be taught in the park, at the school, and in a student's backyard, with a group of young people consisting of some students with autism and some peers without disabilities. Swimming might include peers and water games. Cycling might be taught along bike pathways in the park. Board games or card games (e.g., checkers, chess, Monopoly™, Uno™, Spades) could involve peers without disabilities, who prompt correct responding and could be taught in any classroom, the cafeteria, or the student lounge.

Much like socialization interventions (see Chapter 7), both peer-mediated and adult-mediated approaches have been used to teach play and leisure activities to children and adolescents with autism. In peer-mediated programs, students without disabilities are taught to initiate, model, prompt, and reinforce interactive activities with their peers with autism (e.g., Zercher, Hunt, Schuler, & Webster, 2001). Adult-mediated interventions include video and live modeling, systematic prompting, use of activity schedules, pivotal response training (see Chapter 6), integrated play groups, and script training (Jung & Sainato, 2013). For example, researchers used a video showing adults playing with tea party toys and modeling shopping and baking. After watching the video, their young student with autism was able to imitate the models using the toys appropriately with no further prompting or reinforcement (D'Ateno, Mangiapanello, & Taylor, 2003). Sherrow and colleagues (2016) used video models to teach adolescents with autism to play games on Wii.

To some people, teaching play and leisure activities may not seem an important task for teachers, but engaging in appropriate play and leisure activities encourages the critical goals of increased social and communicative interactions and appropriate behavior while discouraging inappropriate behavior (Jung & Sainato, 2013; Machalicek et al., 2009; McConnell, 2002). For further resources in this area, OTs and adaptive physical education teachers may be able to assist with skill selection and obtaining materials, and they may offer advice about the instruction of leisure and play skills and activities. If your school district does not employ OTs or adaptive physical education teachers, then you might consult the PE or therapeutic recreation departments of a local university. General education PE teachers may also be helpful sources for teaching advice, materials, or information about developmental skill sequences.

8-4 Vocational Skills

Work is a central part of most adults' lives. Being employed means being independent, contributing to society, being part of a social network, making choices and decisions, and being seen as contributing to the common good (Roux et al., 2013). Unfortunately, the employment outlook for students with ASD is not encouraging. Bouck and Joshi (2014) found that a majority of high school graduates with ASD were neither working nor attending postsecondary vocational training options two years out of high school. Holwerda, van der Klink, Groothoff, and Brouwer (2012) found as few as 25% of adults with ASD were employed, and Taylor and Selzer (2011) followed 66 adults with ASD for 10 years finding only 6% were competitively employed after that time. Behavioral and cognitive challenges associated with ASD may somewhat account for low employment rates, as do intellectual disabilities often associated with ASD (Walsh, Lydon, & Healy, 2014). For these reasons, it is extremely important to establish long-term work goals for students with autism and attempt to mitigate negative contributors to unemployment.

Preparation for employment can start with very young children, teaching skills that are necessary prerequisites for any type of job. For example, preschoolers with and without disabilities typically learn to clean up their work and play areas, put away their toys, and follow directions (Westling & Fox, 2008). Elementary school students learn to do classroom and home chores, be on time for classes, ask for help when needed, work and play with peers, and possibly travel around the community independently. By middle school, teachers may conduct various types of vocational assessments for their students with disabilities to determine aptitudes and interests and to identify potential employment possibilities in the community. Intense and focused vocational training for students with disabilities often occurs in high school, with students spending the majority of their day in some type of prevocational or vocational preparation, including on-the-job training.

As you learned in Chapter 4 (see Box 4.1), long-term vocational planning is required by law as part of the **individualized transition plan (ITP)**. IDEA 2004 requires school personnel to begin planning for a student's transition to independent living and employment by age 16 and earlier, at age 14, where appropriate. State vocational rehabilitation counselors are to be part of these planning meetings because they will assume responsibility for the young adult with disabilities after high school graduation under the Rehabilitation Act of 1973. Thus, the IEP or ITP committee for adolescents with autism should include school personnel who work with the student, vocational rehabilitation personnel, the student's family, and the student when appropriate. The ITP must include:

1. appropriate measurable postsecondary goals based upon age-appropriate transition assessments related to training, education, employment, and, where appropriate, independent living skills; and
2. the transition services (including courses of study) needed to assist the student with a disability in reaching those goals (U.S. Department of Education, 2017, p. 1).

Transition services, as required, could include any of the following: assistive technology, travel training (e.g., riding the bus or light rail), vocational assessment, work experiences with coaching, direct instruction of work skills, self-determination or self-advocacy, management of home and personal finances, and self-help and social skill training. The IEP team may use the following process steps to develop the ITP:

- Set long-term goals in the areas of employment, independent living, recreation, and community participation.
- Identify community and family resources to help achieve and maintain those goals; this includes delineation of services by adult service agencies (e.g., rehabilitation agencies, employment agencies, mental health agencies, agencies serving individuals with ID, health agencies, private nonprofit and for-profit agencies).
- Task analyze each long-term goal into annual goals and short-term objectives.
- Provide for regular monitoring of progress toward those long-term outcomes.
- Plan to reevaluate the ITP on an annual basis.

8-4a General Considerations for Teaching Vocational Skills

Employment is one of the most desirable achievements for every individual when entering adulthood, even those with autism (Roux et al., 2013). If successful, it increases an individual's social status and financial independence (Fleming, Fairweather, & Leahy, 2013). Thus, preparing students for the world of work should be a thoughtful and critical process. The long-term goal of vocational training is successful employment in the community (Westling & Fox, 2008). All instruction should be designed with this goal in mind. Following are some curriculum and instruction guidelines pertaining to vocational training.

Curriculum

Several general rules apply to development of a vocational curriculum. First, as you learned in Chapter 4, vocational tasks should be age appropriate and functional. It is important to conduct an ecological assessment to determine possible adult employment placements so that high school curriculum can be matched to the skills and knowledge necessary to be successful in that type of employment. This list, along with general vocational skills (e.g., asking for assistance, problem solving), becomes the curriculum. Remember it is best to teach functional skills in natural contexts when possible and use materials and methods well matched to the ultimate goal of successful employment in the student's community. In this way, the materials and instructional strategies will be age appropriate and functional.

Second, vocational training should reflect the types of jobs that parents and other members of the IEP committee feel are appropriate and available in the community for a given student rather than designing vocational instruction around general published curricula. For example, it is of little benefit to teach assembly tasks if only a few jobs in the community require assembly skills. On the other hand, if a large number of office worker positions are available, IEP team members may decide that employment, as an office aide is an appropriate goal for a student. In this case, this student's vocational instruction should consist of learning to operate different types of office machines such as photocopiers, fax machines, and shredders. Walsh et al. (2014) conducted a literature review of studies targeting employment skills of adults with autism and found that individuals were trained in skills related to clerical work, operating photocopiers, T-shirt folding, delivering newspapers, preparing products for shipping, cover letter writing, cleaning, recycling, stocking inventory, sorting mail, and self-employment. Four individuals were trained to be customer entertainers or store promoters in costume. One was also trained to use a washing machine and make noodles as corresponding life skills, and some were trained in interview and asking for assistance skills.

Third, vocational goals and instruction should reflect the interests and aptitudes of individual students. It may also require recognizing autism not as a handicap toward employment but as a competitive advantage for employers. Many individuals with autism may display exceptional persistency, attention to detail, and the tendency to thrive on routine, all possible employment benefits (Sonne, 2009). Individuals with autism may also possess the ability to be highly focused in certain situations and display excellent visual perception abilities (Kellems & Morningstar, 2012). When designing a vocational curriculum consider such abilities and characteristics. For example, a student who is highly active may do better in a job that allows for movement (e.g., working outside, cleaning, delivery) than a job that is more sedate (e.g., sitting at a desk or work center). Or an individual who is persistent and thrives on routine may become a great lettuce shredder at a fast-food restaurant.

It might also be helpful to consider a student's restricted interests in designing vocational curriculum. For example, one teacher we know had a student who shredded paper as a form of self-stimulation. The teacher channeled this "interest" into a job for the student: hand shredding confidential documents from the school counselor's office. The student's highest on-task time was during work time. A student who insists on lining up items may do well straightening canned and boxed items on shelves in a grocery store or replacing and straightening books on a library shelf. Creativity is an asset when it comes to developing vocational goals and designing vocational instruction for students with autism.

Fourth, it is also necessary to attend to possible barriers to employment and challenges to maintaining employment such as social and communication skill deficits and behavioral excesses. Communication problems might include an inability to read between the lines or read facial expressions, using an inappropriate tone of voice, asking too many questions, and communicating in an inappropriate manner (Hurlbutt & Chalmers, 2002, 2004). Social barriers might include inappropriate hygiene and grooming skills, difficulty following social rules, an inability to understand affect, insistence on working alone, and acting inappropriately toward individuals of the opposite gender (Koning & Magill-Evans, 2001). Behavioral challenges may include tantrums, self-injury, aggression, property destruction, and ritualistic behaviors (Burt, Fuller, & Lewis, 1991; Hendricks, 2010; Kobayashi & Murata, 1992). It is important to use ABA-based strategies discussed in this book to decrease challenging behaviors and teach appropriate communication, social, and life skills to ensure vocational success.

Finally, it is important to consider teaching adolescents with autism **self-determination** skills (i.e., the ability to exert personal control over one's life and make choices). Self-determination skills might include listing personal strengths and abilities, listing areas for improvement, problem solving, making choices, asking for assistance when needed, discussing one's disability, participating in IEP meetings, helping out at home and in the community, setting own goals and celebrating when those are accomplished, sharing dreams for the future, and listing personal resources (Wisconsin Department of Public Instruction, 2013). Self-determination has been associated with improved outcomes in vocational participation after high school for individuals with autism (Chiang, Cheung, Hickson, Xiang, & Tsai, 2012). Research has also shown that for students with disabilities in general, acquisition of skills necessary for self-determination has been associated with higher academic productivity, better employment outcomes, and better problem-solving skills (Konrad, Fowler, Walker, Test, & Wood, 2007). Wehmeyer and colleagues (2006) recommend particular self-determination skills that can be included in the curriculum-development process. Wehman, Smith, and Schall (2009) provide additional recommendations for transition and vocational considerations specific to individuals with autism.

Instruction

All of the instructional methods described in Chapter 5 will be needed for vocational instruction. In a review of vocational training studies targeting specific vocational skills for young adults with autism, it was found that skill training included direct instruction, reinforcement-based strategies, modeling, simulation-based training, video modeling (individual watches a video of adult models completing a task), audio cueing (recorded and verbal prompts), visual supports including written schedules, both antecedent and response prompts, performance feedback (also given through headphones from afar), and self-monitoring (Walsh et al., 2014).

Task analysis of target jobs is also an important step to teaching vocational skills. Steps can be taught using forward or backward chaining or total task presentation. Teaching target skills using direct instruction or DTT allows educators to closely monitor the student's progress toward task independence and to make data-based decisions about task or instructional modifications. Multiple types of prompts will undoubtedly be necessary in the acquisition stages of instruction but should be faded in a timely manner to facilitate fluency and generalization. If tasks are initially taught at school, prompts may again be needed temporarily to facilitate generalization in target contexts outside of the school.

Once again, we recommend teaching vocational tasks in settings as close to the target employment environment as possible (Wehman et al., 2014). For example, if the goal is for a student to bus tables at a local restaurant, then the initial skills might be taught in the school cafeteria (e.g., removing leftover trash, wiping the table thoroughly, sweeping), but as soon as the student is able to perform these tasks with or without verbal prompts, he should begin learning to do the job at the restaurant. Begin on-site instruction at times when the restaurant is less busy, gradually moving toward working during peak times. Likewise, if the vocational goal for a particular student is to stock shelves at a grocery store, instruction should take place in the grocery store as soon as the student masters basic skills related to the job.

Material and task modifications might also be needed for students with autism to learn complex skills. For example, some tasks may lend themselves to the use of a within-stimulus prompt. Other modifications might include placing a bright green stick-on dot on the "print" button of the photocopier and covering other buttons not frequently used, drawing outlines on storage shelves to delineate where products should be placed, and highlighting the last names of staff persons on mailboxes.

In addition, many of the visual guidance strategies described in Chapter 5 can be applied to increase success in vocational tasks. A picture activity schedule could be used to prompt a student whose job is to prepare utensil bundles (a knife, fork, and spoon wrapped in a napkin). A student whose tasks vary from day to day could pick up a visual activity schedule (video, picture, or written) of the day's tasks when he checks in at work. This schedule might be a file folder with pictures attached with Velcro or a video on a handheld device. For example, a student who works at a grocery store might have a folder that contains several lines of pictures representing the day's assigned tasks. The first line might show cartons of cake mixes in the storage room, then a picture of the student placing boxes of cake mix on the shelf, then the student flattening the carton, and placing the carton in the recycling bin. The student can be taught that after he completes a pictured task (or portion of a task), he removes the picture and places it in the "Finished" folder or even in the pocket of a carpenter-type apron to be worn while on the job. Or he could simply check off that item on his schedule.

Hart and colleagues (2010) and Datson and colleagues (2012) recommended the following to better prepare students with ASD for vocational success:

- Instructing students in natural environments as often as possible.
- Conducting person-centered ecological assessments.
- Developing cross-agency coordinating teams.
- Providing regular behavioral consultation at the job site from a BCBA.
- Providing structured to unstructured job rotations while in school.
- Providing behavioral definition to the student of workplace expectations, social skills, and vocabulary.
- Providing job coaching and supports on the job.
- Enhancing social and communication skills.
- Using visual supports for instruction and on-the-job prompts.
- Providing self-monitoring reinforcement programs in which the individual reinforces himself for a job well done.
- Enhancing self-determination and self-advocacy skills.
- Providing continuous progress monitoring.

8-4b Employment Options

The ultimate vocational goal is for the student to obtain and maintain paid competitive employment with little need for external supports to maintain that employment. However, many students may not be able to achieve that level of independence. This does not mean these students are destined for unemployment; it simply means we have to explore and develop supports to help individuals with disabilities obtain and maintain a job of some type. This is called **supported employment**.

Supported employment is an umbrella term that refers to several different models. According to the Rehabilitation Act Amendments of 1992 (P.L. 102-569), supported employment is:

> competitive work in integrated work settings for (a) individuals with severe [disabilities] for whom competitive employment has not traditionally occurred; or (b) individuals for whom competitive employment has been interrupted or intermittent as a result of severe [disabilities], and who, because of their [disability], need ongoing support services to perform such work. (Title I, Sec. 103, i)

All of the supported-employment models involve a **job coach** who provides training and supervision for individuals with disabilities on the job until they are able to do the job independently, at which point the job coach provides intermittent ongoing support (Westling & Fox, 2008). The following are the most common supported-employment models (Agran, Test, & Martin, 1994; Westling & Fox, 2008):

1. **Individual placement model.** Individuals with disabilities are placed in regular job settings and trained and supervised by a job coach. Although this model offers the greatest integration with workers without disabilities, it is not available to all who could benefit from it because of cost and a shortage of job coaches (e.g., Hendricks, 2010).
2. **Enclaves.** Small groups of individuals with disabilities work together in a job setting and are trained and supervised by either a job coach or an employee of the business. A hotel we stayed in recently used an enclave arrangement: Rooms were cleaned by a group of individuals with disabilities.
3. **Work crews.** This arrangement is similar to enclaves, except that the workers with disabilities travel from job site to job site. For example, a work crew might provide lawn maintenance services or janitorial services. Both enclave and work crew models have been criticized because they usually pay less than minimum wage (Westling & Fox, 2008) and tend to keep workers with disabilities isolated from workers without disabilities and the public (e.g., Rusch, Johnson, & Hughes, 1990).

4. **Group placements.** This model offers the benefits of the individual placement model with the efficient aspects of enclaves and work crews. A group of individuals with disabilities is placed at the same work site, but individuals are assigned separate jobs throughout the work setting rather than working in proximity (such as in an enclave model). For example, rather than the individuals with disabilities working together as a group to clean rooms, some of those individuals might be paired with employees without disabilities to clean rooms, and others might be assigned to work in the restaurant or on grounds maintenance.

5. **Entrepreneurial model.** This model is represented by, for example, a small business that employs both individuals with and without disabilities. The business provides specific products or services (e.g., a bakery, a cleaning service, a workshop that sells handmade furniture, a commercial laundry). We know of several secondary special education programs for students with autism and other developmental disabilities that have created and maintained successful entrepreneurial programs at the school such as selling nachos or popcorn in the main hallway one day each week; taking custom salad orders from staff, making the salads, and delivering the finished product and collecting payments; and planting and selling pots of flowers, vegetables, herbs, and so on.

Educators and parents need to determine what types of supported services are available in their community because preparation may take a different slant for the various models. In her research review, Hendricks (2010) recommended grouping vocational supports into five major themes: (a) job placement (e.g., based on well-defined abilities and interests), (b) supervisors and coworkers (e.g., flexible, tolerant, supported), (c) on-the-job provisions (e.g., task training, behavioral interventions), (d) workplace modifications (e.g., visual schedules, reduced noise, crowding, interruptions, lights), and (e) long-term support (e.g., job coach transfers support to on-site supervisor or coworker).

Job Development

Finding jobs for students with autism may pose an interesting challenge for teachers and parents. We say "interesting" because employment opportunities, particularly for students with more severe disabilities, may not be immediately obvious. Teachers and parents may need to be creative in designing, creating, or modifying jobs for students with autism. In addition, the teacher (or other professional) or parent may have to convince the employer that hiring an individual with autism may benefit his or her business (Walsh et al., 2014) and quell fears or concerns about the challenges the individual may present. Some examples of jobs that teachers or parents we know created for their children with autism and other severe disabilities follow.

- Return books to correct place on shelf and straighten books in library.
- Wipe off tables in grocery store cafe.
- Deliver intrabuilding mail at the state capitol building.
- Wipe off menus at a local restaurant.
- Bus tables at a restaurant.
- Assemble picnic packages for local food store.
- Collate hard-copy packets in an office.
- Operate photocopier in an office.
- Fold T-shirts in a retail clothing store.
- Sales assistant in a costume shop.
- Shelf stocker in a bookshop.
- Cleaning assistant at a local hospital.
- Cleaning assistant at local YMCA.

One important component of job development for students with autism is to find employers who are flexible and tolerant of behavioral differences. The job itself may need to match sensory differences of each student. For example, a student may need a job in a quiet location with low lights. Another may need to be able to work with visual schedules rather than verbal demands. Job placement may involve training employers or supervisors in specific strategies (cueing, prompting, redirecting, reinforcement) and might include consultation with someone skilled in ABA-based behavior reduction strategies. The important aspect of job development is to match the job to the individual's needs, abilities, and interests while not demanding too much compromise from possible employers.

Vocational Preparation

As previously mentioned, vocational preparation would best begin in early childhood and continue through adulthood with instructional emphasis gradually becoming more focused on training for specific job tasks. Vocational training includes teaching not only specific job skills but also general interpersonal, problem solving, communication, and work-related skills (Walsh et al., 2014). For example, many of the communication and socialization tasks described in Chapters 6 and 7 and the behavior reduction strategies described in Chapter 3 are important for successful long-term employment. In addition, Table 8.9 lists skills that, although not actual job tasks, may be important for obtaining and maintaining employment.

If you are unsure as to the exact job a student may eventually obtain (e.g., the student is too young to determine a potential job, the student is moving to another community on completion of school), it would be best to teach generic tasks that have widespread application. Although the details of these tasks may vary with contexts, they are similar enough to justify as targets for instruction. Table 8.10 lists vocational skills that may be applicable in a variety of employment situations.

TABLE 8.9 ● Skills Related to Vocational Success

- Follows directions, rules, and routines.
- Works independently on assigned tasks.
- Produces satisfactory quality of work.
- Works at appropriate speed.
- Works cooperatively with other employees.
- Interacts appropriately with customers.
- Behaves appropriately both on the job and during breaks (e.g., no self-stimulatory behavior, inappropriate hygiene behaviors, inappropriate language).
- Accepts negative or constructive feedback.
- Accepts interruptions in routine.
- Accepts new tasks, routines, or procedures.
- Solves problems independently or asks for help.
- Tells time or has time-awareness skills (e.g., gets to work on time, takes breaks of appropriate length).

TABLE 8.10 ● Vocational Tasks with Wide Applicability

- Answering phones
- Filing
- Photocopying
- Shredding
- Collating, stapling
- Folding letters, stuffing envelopes, applying address labels
- Distributing mail
- Intrabuilding or intraoffice delivery (e.g., supplies, messages, documents)
- Caring for plants (watering, trimming, dusting)
- Tidying offices, lobbies, public areas
- Cleaning bathrooms, break rooms
- Vacuuming
- Sweeping exterior areas of buildings
- Making coffee, setting out coffee supplies
- Loading, unloading commercial dishwashers
- Filling napkin holders, resupplying condiment bins and plastic utensil bins
- Emptying trash
- Straightening and ordering items on shelves
- Gathering shopping carts from parking lot
- Washing cars, trucks

Summary

Teaching students with autism basic life skills is critical to their future success because they characteristically do not learn these skills on their own and will need them to achieve independent functioning as adults. Without ongoing, systematic instruction, many individuals with autism will require long-term assistance with basic self-care tasks, may miss out on the many benefits of play, leisure, and recreational engagement, and may not be able to participate in one of the most basic of life activities—work. Failure to acquire functional life skills, including social, communication, and self-determination skills also means individuals with autism may likely be relegated to more restrictive living and work environments. Teachers should work to avert such failure and take care to view functional adult goals as a guide for every teaching decision in their classrooms.

Key Points

1. Youth with autism often do not learn life skills without formal instruction.
2. Life skills curricula should be developed through an ecological assessment of target environments, direct observation, and information from developmental and adaptive inventories, interviews, and checklists. Long-term goals compared with a student's current level of functioning in each life skill area provide necessary information for formulating the individualized education plan.
3. Life skills must be systematically taught using ABA-based strategies such as DTT, MT, various prompting procedures, antecedent modifications, reinforcement procedures, and progress monitoring.
4. Teachers should include social and communication skills with all life skills instruction.
5. Developmental appropriateness should be a prime consideration when selecting life skills for instruction.
6. An important component of life skills instruction is assessing how target skills can be modified or have prompts added to facilitate acquisition. This means modifying materials, adjusting how the skill is performed, or adding visual, including video, prompts to remind students of what to do.
7. Teaching in the natural context is especially important for life skills. These skills are useless unless the student is able to use them in a variety of environments under a variety of conditions. On-site instruction of leisure and vocational skills is particularly important for enhancing generalization.
8. Employment should be a goal for adolescents and adults with autism. Creativity in job development in a variety of employment arrangements will increase the likelihood that students will be and remain employed as adults.

References

Agran, M., Test, D., & Martin, J. E. (1994). Employment preparation of students with severe disabilities. In E. Cipani & F. Spooner (Eds.), *Curricular and instructional approaches for students with severe disabilities* (pp. 184–212). Needham Heights, MA: Allyn & Bacon.

Alper, S., McMullen, V., McMullen, R. D., & Miller, P. J. (1996). Application to special education curricular areas with no general education parallels. In D. L. Ryndak & S. Alper (Eds.), *Curriculum content for students with moderate and severe disabilities in inclusive settings* (pp. 215–226). Needham Heights, MA: Allyn & Bacon.

Alwell, M., & Cobb, B. (2009). Functional life skills curricula intervention for youth with disability: A systematic review. *Career Development for Exceptional Individuals, 32*, 82–93.

American Psychiatric Association (APA). (2013). *Diagnostic and statistical manual of mental disorders*, 5th ed. (DSM-5). Washington, DC: American Psychiatric Association.

Anglesea, M. M., Hoch, H., & Taylor, B. A. (2008). Reducing rapid eating in teenagers with autism: Use of a pager prompt. *Journal of Applied Behavior Analysis, 41*, 107–111.

Ardiç, A., & Cavkaytar, A. (2014). Effectiveness of the Modified Intensive Toilet Training Method on teaching toilet skills to children with autism. *Education and Training in Autism and Developmental Disabilities, 49*, 263–276.

Ayres, K. M., Lowery, K. A., Douglas, K. H., & Sievers, C. (2011). I can identify Saturn but I can't brush my teeth: What happens when the curricular focus for students with severe disabilities shifts. *Education and Training in Autism and Developmental Disabilities, 46*, 11–21.

Ayres, K. M., Lowery, K. A., Douglas, K. H., & Sievers, C. (2012). The question still remains: What happens when the curricular focus for students with severe disabilities shifts? A Reply to Courtade, Spooner, Browder, and Jimenez (2012). *Education and Training in Autism and Developmental Disabilities, 47*, 14–22.

Azrin, N. H., & Foxx, R. M. (1971). A rapid method of toilet training the institutionalized retarded. *Journal of Applied Behavior Analysis, 2*, 89–99.

Bada, M., Orgaz, M. B., Verdugo, M. A., Ullan, A. M., & Martinez, M. (2013). Relationships between leisure participation and quality of life of people with developmental disabilities. *Journal of Applied Research in Intellectual Disabilities, 26*, 533–545.

Baker, M. J. (2000). Incorporating the thematic ritualistic behaviors of children with autism into games: Increasing social play interactions with siblings. *Journal of Positive Behavior Interventions, 2*, 66–84.

Bal, V. H., Kim, S., Cheong, D., & Lord, C. (2015). Daily living skills in individuals with autism spectrum disorder from 2 to 21 years of age. *Autism, 19*(7), 774–784.

Bennett, K. D., & Dukes, C. (2014). A systematic review of teaching daily living skills to adolescents and adults with autism spectrum disorder. *Review Journal of Autism and Developmental Disabilities, 1*, 2–10.

Bouck, E. C., & Joshi, A. S. (2014). Does curriculum matter for secondary students with Autism Spectrum Disorders: Analyzing the NLTS2. *Journal of Autism Developmental Disorders, 45,* 1204–1212.

Brockett, S. (1998, November–December). Developing successful play activities for individuals with autism. *Advocate, 31*(6), 15–17.

Browder, D. M., & Spooner, F. (Eds.). (2006). *Teaching language arts, math & science to students with significant cognitive disabilities.* Baltimore: Paul H. Brookes.

Browder, D. M., & Spooner, F. (Eds.) (2014). *More language arts, math, and science for students with severe disabilities.* Baltimore: Paul H. Brookes.

Burt, D. B., Fuller, S. P., & Lewis, K. R. (1991). Competitive employment of adults with autism. *Journal of Autism and Developmental Disorders, 21*(2), 237–242.

Cardon, T. A. (2012). Teaching caregivers to implement video modeling imitation training via iPad for their children with autism. *Research in Autism Spectrum Disorders, 6*(4), 1389–1400.

Cardon, T. A., & Wilcox, M. J. (2011). Promoting imitation in young children with autism: A comparison of reciprocal imitation training and video modeling. *Journal of Autism and Developmental Disorders, 41*(5), 654–666.

Carlile, K. A., Reeve, S. A., Reeve, K. F., & DeBar, R. (2013). Using activity schedules on the iPod touch to teach leisure skills to children with autism. *Education and Treatment of Children, 36*(2), 33–57.

Chiang, H. M., Cheung, Y. K., Hickson, L., Xiang, R., & Tsai, L. Y. (2012). Predictive factors in participation in post secondary education for high school leavers with autism. *Journal of Autism and Developmental Disorders, 42,* 685–696.

Cicero, F. R., & Pfadt, A. (2002). Investigation of a reinforcement-based toilet training procedure for children with autism. *Research in Developmental Disabilities, 23,* 319–331.

Coie, J. D., Rabiner, D. L., & Lochman, J. F. (1992). Promoting peer relations in a school setting. In L. A. Bond, B. E. Compas, & C. Swift (Eds.), *Prevention in the schools.* Newbury Park, CA: Sage.

Courtade, G., Spooner, F., Browder, D., & Jimenez, B. (2012). Seven reasons to promote standards-based instruction for students with severe disabilities: A reply to Ayres, Lowery, Douglas, & Sievers (2011). *Education and Training in Autism and Developmental Disabilities, 47,* 3–13.

D'Ateno, P., Mangiapanello, K., & Taylor, B. A. (2003). Using video modeling to teach complex play sequences to a preschooler with autism. *Journal of Positive Behavior Interventions, 5,* 5–11.

Datson, M., Riehle, J. E., & Rutkowski, S. (2012). *High school transition that works: Lessons learned from Project Search.* Baltimore: Paul H. Brookes.

Dodd, D., Zabriskie, R., Widmer, M., & Eggett, D. (2009). Contributions of family leisure to family functioning among families that include children with developmental disabilities. *Journal of Leisure Research, 41,* 261–286.

Eversole, M., Collins, D. M., Karmarkar, A., Colton, L., Quinn, J. P., Karsbaek, R., Johnson, J. R., Callier, N. P., & Hilton, C. L. (2016). Leisure activity enjoyment of children with autism spectrum disorders. *Journal of Autism and Developmental Disorders, 46,* 10–20.

Fleming, A. R., Fairweather, J. S., & Leahy, M. J. (2013). Quality of life as a potential rehabilitation service outcome: the relationship between employment, quality of life, and other life areas. *Rehabilitation Counseling Bulletin, 57*(1), 9–22.

Fleury, V. P., Hedges, S., Hume, K., Browder, D. K., Thompson, J. L., Fallin, K., El Zein, F., Reutebuch, C. K., & Vaughn, S. (2014). Addressing the academic needs of adolescents with autism spectrum disorders in secondary education. *Remedial and Special Education, 35*(2), 68–79.

Hart, D., Grigal, M., & Weir, C. (2010). Expanding the paradigm: Postsecondary education options for individuals with autism spectrum disorder and intellectual disabilities. *Focus on Autism and Other Developmental Disabilities, 25,* 134–150.

Hendricks, D. (2010). Employment and adults with autism spectrum disorders: Challenges and strategies for success. *Journal of Vocational Rehabilitation, 32,* 125–134.

Hendricks, D. R., & Wehman, P. (2009). Transition from school to adulthood for youth with autism spectrum disorders: Review and recommendations. *Focus on Autism and Other Developmental Disabilities, 24,* 77–88.

Holwerda, A., van der Klink, J. J. L., Groothoff, J. W., & Brouwer, S. (2012). Predictors for work participation in individuals with an autism spectrum disorder: A systematic review. *Journal of Occupational Rehabilitation, 22,* 333–352.

Hurlbutt, K., & Chalmers, L. (2002). Adults with autism speak out: Perceptions of their life experiences. *Focus on Autism and Other Developmental Disabilities, 17*(2), 103–111.

Hurlbutt, K., & Chalmers, L. (2004). Employment and adults with Asperger syndrome. *Focus on Autism and Other Developmental Disabilities, 19*(4), 215–222.

Jordan, R. (2003). Social play and autistic spectrum disorders: A perspective on theory, implications and educational approaches. *Autism, 7,* 347–360.

Jung, S., & Sainato, D. M. (2013). Teaching play skills to young children with autism. *Journal of Intellectual and Developmental Disability, 38,* 74–90.

Keen, D. V. (2008). Childhood autism, feeding problems and failure to thrive in early infancy: Seven case studies. *European Child and Adolescent Psychiatry, 17,* 209–216.

Kellems, R. O., & Morningstar, M. E. (2012). Using video modeling delivered through iPods to each vocational tasks to young adults with autism spectrum disorders. *Career Development and Transition for Exceptional Individuals, 35,* 155–167.

Kobayashi, R., & Murata, T. (1992). Behavioral characteristics of 187 young adults with autism. *Psychiatry Clinical Neuroscience 52,* 383–390.

Koning, C., & Magill-Evans, J. (2001). Social and language skills in adolescent boys with Asperger syndrome, *Autism 5*(1), 23–36.

Konrad, M., Fowler, C. H., Walker, A. R., Test, D. W., & Wood, W. M. (2007). Effects of self-determination interventions on the academic skills of students with learning disabilities. *Learning Disabilities Quarterly, 30,* 89–113.

Ledford, J. R., & Gast, D. L. (2006). Feeding problems in children with autism spectrum disorders: a review. *Focus on Autism and Other Developmental Disabilities, 21,* 153–166.

Machalicek, W., Shogren, K., Lang, R., Rispoli, M., O'Reilly, M. F., Franco, J. H., & Sigafoos, J. (2009). Increasing play and decreasing the challenging behavior of children with autism during recess with activity schedules and task correspondence training. *Research in Autism Spectrum Disorders, 3,* 547–555.

Marshall, J., Hill, R. J., Ziviani, J., & Dodrill, P. (2014). Features of feeding difficulty in children with Autism Spectrum Disorder. *International Journal of Speech Language Pathology, 16,* 151–158.

Marshall, J., Ware, R., Ziviani, J., Hill, R. J., & Dodrill, P. (2014). Efficacy of interventions to improve feeding difficulties in children with autism spectrum disorders: A systematic review and meta-analysis. *Child: Care, Health and Development, 41,* 2, 278–302.

Matson, J. L., Hattier, M. A., & Belva, B. (2012). Treating adaptive living skills in persons with autism using applied behavior analysis: A review. *Research in Autism Spectrum Disorders, 6,* 271–276.

Mazurek, M. O., & Wenstrup, C. (2012). Television, video game and social media use among children with ASD and typically developing siblings. *Journal of Autism and Developmental Disorders, 43,* 1258–1271.

McConnell, S. R. (2002). Interventions to facilitate social interaction for young children with autism: Review of available research and recommendations for educational intervention and future research. *Journal of Autism and Developmental Disorders, 32,* 351–372.

McLay, L., Carnett, A., van der Meer, L., & Lang, R. (2015). Using a video modeling-based intervention package to toilet train two children with autism. *Journal of Physical and Developmental Disabilities, 27,* 431–451.

McManus, M., Derby, K. M., & McLaughlin, T. F. (2003). An evaluation of an in-school and home based toilet training program for a child with fragile X syndrome. *International Journal of Special Education, 18,* 73–79.

Ninci, J., Neely, L. C., Hong, E. R., Boles, M. B., Gilliland, W. D., Ganz, J. B., Davis, J. L., & Vannest, K. J. (2015). Meta-analysis on single-case research on teaching functional living skills to individuals with ASD. *Review Journal of Autism and Developmental Disorders, 2,* 194–198.

Palmen, A., Didden, R., & Lang, R. (2012). A systematic review of behavioral intervention research on adaptive skill building in high-functioning young adults with autism spectrum disorder. *Research in Autism Spectrum Disorder, 6,* 602–617.

Rehabilitation Act Amendments of 1992, 29 U.S.C. § 701 et seq. P.L. 102–569.

Rettig, M. A. (1994). Play behaviors of young children with autism: Characteristics and interventions. *Focus on Autistic Behavior, 9*(5), 1–6.

Roux, A. M., Shattuck, P. T., Cooper, B. P., Anderson, K. A., Wagner, M., & Narendorf, S. C. (2013). Postsecondary employment experiences among young adults with an autism spectrum disorder. *Journal of the American Academy of Child & Adolescent Psychiatry, 52*(9), 931–939.

Rusch, F. R., Johnson, J. R., & Hughes, C. (1990). Analysis of co-worker involvement in relation to level of disability versus placement approach among supported employees. *Journal of the Association for Persons with Severe Handicaps, 15,* 32–39.

Sharp, W., Jaquess, D., Morton, J., & Herzinger, C. (2010). Pediatric feeding disorders: A quantitative synthesis of treatment outcomes. *Clinical Child and Family Psychology Review, 13,* 348–365.

Shattuck, P. T., Orsmond, G. I., Wagner, M., & Cooper, B. P. (2011). Participation in social activities among adolescents with an autism spectrum disorder. *PLoS ONE, 6*(11), e27176.

Shattuck, P. T., Wagner, M., Narendorf, S., Sterzing, P., & Hensley, M. (2011). Post high school service use among young adults with autism. *Archives of Pediatrics and Adolescent Medicine, 165,* 141–146.

Sherrow, L. A., Spriggs, A. D., & Knight, V. F. (2016). Using video models to teach students with disabilities to play the Wii. *Focus on Autism and Other Developmental Disabilities, 31*(4), 312–320.

Snell, M. E. (1993). *Instruction of students with severe disabilities* (4th ed.). New York: Merrill.

Snell, M. E., & Farlow, L. J. (1993). Self-care skills. In M. Snell (Ed.), *Instruction of students with severe disabilities* (4th ed.). Upper Saddle River, NJ: Pearson.

Sonne, T. (2009). *Ashoka Ireland World Leaders in Social Innovation.* Retrieved from http://www.ashoka.ie/work/

Spencer, V. G., Evmenova, A. S., Boon, R. T., & Hayes-Harris, L. (2014). Review of research-based interventions for students with Autism Spectrum Disorders in content area instruction: Implications and considerations for classroom practice. *Education and Training in Autism and Developmental Disabilities, 49*(3), 331–353.

Stokes, J. V., Cameron, M. J., Dorsey, M. F., & Fleming, E. (2004). Task analysis, correspondence training, and general case instruction for teaching personal hygiene skills. *Behavioral Interventions, 19,* 121–135.

Szyndler, J. (1996). Toileting problems in a group of children with autism. *Child and Adolescent Mental Health, 1,* 19–25.

Taylor, J. L., & Seltzer, M. M. (2011). Employment and post-secondary educational activities for young adults with autism spectrum disorders during the transition to adulthood. *Journal of Autism and Developmental Disorders, 41*(5), 566–574.

Volkmar, F. R., & Wiesner, L. A. (2009). *A practical guide to autism: What every parent, family member, and teacher needs to know.* Somerset, NJ: John Wiley & Sons.

Walsh, L., Lydon, S., & Healy, O. (2014). Employment and vocational skills among individuals with autism spectrum disorders: Predictors, impact, and interventions. *Review Journal of Autism and Developmental Disorders, 1,* 266–275.

Wehman, P., Schall, C., Carr, S., Targett, P., West, M., & Cifu, G. (2014). Transition from school to adulthood for youth with autism spectrum disorder: What we know and what we need to know. *Journal of Disability Policy Studies, 25*(1), 30–40.

Wehman, P., Smith, M., & Schall, C. (2009). *Autism and the transition to adulthood: Success beyond the classroom.* Baltimore: Brookes.

Wehmeyer, M. L., Gragouda, S., & Shogren, S. A. (2006). Self-determination, student involvement, and leadership development. In P. Wehman (Ed.), *Life beyond the classroom: Transition strategies for young people with disabilities* (4th ed., pp. 41–69). Baltimore: Brookes.

Westling, D. L., & Fox, L. (2008). *Teaching students with severe disabilities* (4th Ed.). Upper Saddle River, NJ: Prentice Hall.

Wisconsin Department of Public Instruction (2013). *Opening doors to self-determination skills: Planning for life after high school.* Retrieved from http://www.witc.edu/stusvcscontent/docs/accommodations/Opening-Doors-self-determination.pdf

U.S. Department of Education (2017). *A transition guide to post-secondary education and employment for students and youth with disabilities.* Office of Special Education and Rehabilitation Services.

Zercher, C., Hunt, P., Schuler, A., & Webster, J. (2001). Increasing joint attention, play and language through peer supported play. *Autism, 5,* 374–398.

9

Evidence-Based Practices for Students with Autism

LEARNING OBJECTIVES

After reading this chapter, you will be able to:

9-1 Discuss common components of evidence-based practices (EBPs).

9-2 Describe strategies for determining evidence-based practices.

9-3 Discuss various guidelines for evaluating educational strategies and programs.

9-4 Describe reasons why education programs for students with autism may fail.

© Lang

Never before have so many treatment and intervention programs been promoted for use with individuals with autism, and the number of options continues to grow. For example, Green and colleagues (2006) surveyed 552 parents of children with autism worldwide and identified 108 different therapies, medications, treatments, and intervention approaches that parents reported their children had received. The explosion in the number of programs is partly the result of the increased awareness of and interest in autism, desperate attempts by parents to find a cure for the disorder or strategies to alleviate the unique symptoms and partly the result of efforts by entrepreneurs who see ripe opportunities for profit.

Furthermore, lack of understanding of the exact cause or causes of autism contributes to the confusion surrounding the efficacy of program options, particularly medical treatments, which are dependent on such understanding (Offit, 2008). As a matter of fact, the lack of a definitive medical etiology for the disorder makes educational strategies and programs the default treatment of choice for students with autism. This puts more pressure on teachers and schools to become critical consumers of the various programs that are promoted.

Unfortunately, popular press books, television news and daytime talk shows, newspapers and other media outlets, social media, and Internet websites continue to spread the false notion that autism can be cured or, at the very least, the symptoms alleviated to allow an individual with autism to lead a "normal" life. This proliferation of unsubstantiated autism "treatments" is often intuitively appealing; because many are easy to administer, family members often rush to try them. However, numerous of these "treatments" are costly and potentially dangerous in many cases (Travers, Tincani, & Lang, 2014). A more important point is that the vast majority of these treatments have no scientific evidence to support their claims. In their review of approximately 400 autism treatments found through Internet searches, Romanczyk and Gillis (2008) reported that less than 2% have strong research support for their purported outcomes. For their National Standards Project, a team of experts at the National Autism Center (NAC) reviewed 775 studies that evaluated autism interventions; of those, only 11 were identified as likely to be effective for individuals with autism (National Autism Center, 2009, 2015).

Evidence-based practices are important because potential problems develop when ineffective strategies and programs are promoted directly to families and schools before being vetted by the scientific process or after they have failed to show beneficial outcomes during rigorous intervention research. For example, using close physical "hugging" to help the individual develop attachment to another person (Tinbergen & Tinbergen, 1983) is not an evidence-based practice and is quite different from using applied behavior analysis (ABA) strategies, which we know to be effective for targeting behaviors to be decreased (e.g., self-injurious behavior or aggression) or increased (e.g., communication skills, interpersonal skills). Unfortunately, in many instances, parents and educators embrace different ideas and feelings about what constitutes effective educational practices for a student with autism. These disagreements about basic special education services can lead to individualized educational program (IEP) meetings that last for many hours across multiple days and end with one party or the other requesting a due process hearing and not with an agreed-on IEP. Nor is it uncommon for both sides to involve advocates or lawyers to discuss appropriate programming, resulting in the development of programs that favor the side that presents the most compelling legal argument and not necessarily the one with the strongest evidence that best matches the needs of the student involved.

Families and educators of children with autism are no doubt exposed to countless exciting, hopeful stories of strategies and programs that have vastly improved the lives of individuals with autism. Regrettably, many of those stories promote approaches that are backed only by emotional appeals to fears, concerns, and feelings of hopelessness that caregivers and educators share and not by scientific evidence (Offit, 2008; Travers, Ayers, Simpson, & Crutchfield, 2016). Fortunately, since the 1960s, there has been increasing focus on using rigorous and scientific methods for identifying the most effective interventions for individuals with autism (Wong et al., 2013). Education, in general, has also seen a shift toward EBPs for all students, including students with disabilities. Three federal education laws mandate the use of evidence-based practices: The No Child Left Behind Act of 2001 (NCLB, 2006), Individuals with Disabilities Act (IDEA, 2004), and the Every Student Succeeds Act (ESSA, 2015). The U.S. Department of Education provides guidance regarding EBPs, instructing state and local education agencies to use "evidence-based activities, strategies, and interventions" (U.S. Department of Education, 2016, 2).

A separate but related development further highlights the importance of relying on EBPs for teaching students with disabilities—specifically, autism. IDEA was originally crafted to ensure that students with disabilities receive a free appropriate public education. Over the years, litigation between families of individuals with disabilities and public school districts has attempted to define criteria for an

- Americans spend billions of dollars each year on unproven medical treatments and products, some of which are actually dangerous (U.S. Federal Trade Commission, November 2011)?
- Between 50 percent and 75 percent of children with autism are receiving some sort of alternative (and unproven) treatment for autism (Singer & Ravi, 2015)?
- Increase in autism prevalence has resulted in a proliferation of fad cures or "treatments" that are often promoted by popular media (Foxx & Mulick, 2016)?
- Problems can arise when stakeholders (parents and educators, teachers and administrators, etc.) disagree on or ignore what constitutes effective strategies and programs?
- Relying on reputable sources of information can help practitioners choose strategies and programs that are most likely to produce desired outcomes?

"appropriate" education. The most recent—and high profile—effort to establish that standard occurred in January 2017 with the U.S. Supreme Court decision in *Endrew F. v. Douglas County School District RE-1*. In that case, Endrew (Drew) was a student with autism and attention-deficit hyperactivity disorder. Drew exhibited behaviors that interfered with his learning and made little progress in elementary school. Alleging that the school had not effectively addressed his behavioral needs, Drew's parents withdrew him and enrolled him in a private school, where he made significant academic and behavioral progress. The Supreme Court unanimously ruled that an appropriate education means that a child's educational program *must provide more than minimal benefit*. Students with disabilities who participate in the general education academic curriculum should be expected to make progress commensurate with their peers. Students whose placement is other than the general education classroom must be offered an educational program that is "appropriately ambitious in light of his circumstances," and the student should have the opportunity to achieve "challenging objectives" (*Endrew F. v. Douglas County School District RE-1*, 2017, 3). This decision does not directly address the issue of reliance on evidence-based practices. However, given this expectation that students should make progress toward "challenging objectives," it seems clear that use of evidence-based practices is essential to help ensure steady and substantial progress, especially for students with the most severe disabilities.

The field of autism in particular has endeavored to quantify EBPs targeted for children and youth with autism through professional policies and major EBP reports. For example, in 1989, the membership of the Association for Behavior Analysis International approved a position statement on the right to effective behavioral treatment. This position statement provides guiding principles that inform assessment and treatment procedures and is intended to protect individuals with autism from harm as a result of inappropriate services (Van Houten et al., 1988).

Further, in an effort to identify the most effective approaches for individuals with autism, the NAC conducted two comprehensive reviews of strategies and programs that target educational and behavioral needs of individuals with autism. Phase 1 of its National Standards Project (2009) focused on interventions for children and adolescents. In the phase 1 report, 11 treatments were classified as established (e.g., clear evidence of efficacy), 22 were classified as emerging (e.g., limited, but promising, evidence of efficacy), and 5 were unestablished (e.g., no acceptable evidence of efficacy, and possibility that the treatment could be harmful) (National Autism Center, 2009). The phase 2 report (National Autism Center, 2015) updated the original review, expanded the target age range to adults, and adopted the term "intervention" in place of "treatment." Phase 2 results were 14 established interventions, 18 emerging interventions, and 13 unestablished interventions.

Similarly, the National Professional Development Center on ASD (NPDC) reviewed autism intervention research published from 1997 to 2007. Using published guidelines for evaluating research, they identified 175 studies for review. After evaluations, they recognized 24 unique interventions as evidence based. The NPDC released a 2014 update to its original report, evaluating autism intervention research published between 1990 and 2011 (Wong et al., 2013). The review by Wong and colleagues resulted in 27 interventions that met their established criteria for evidence-based practices. Later in this chapter, we summarize the practices identified in both the NAC and the NPDC reports and the number of studies identified in each report that support the interventions listed.

Because it is so important for teachers to use EBPs, we will provide information for recognizing these strategies and programs, discuss sources for identifying EBPs, and list criteria for evaluating strategies and programs. In addition, we will discuss popular, but unsupported, interventions that educators of students with autism may encounter, and we will summarize why those interventions should not be considered EBPs.

9-1 Definition of Evidence-Based Practices

There is no single, accepted definition for what constitutes an evidence-based practice (Reichow, Volkmar, & Cicchetti, 2008). As awareness of the importance of EBPs has grown over the past several decades, many education-related groups, organizations, and agencies have developed various working definitions of EBPs, typically targeted to their population of concern, organization, or agency. For example, a quick Internet search for "evidence-based practices definition' produces results from the fields of medicine, nursing, mental health, speech and hearing, education, autism, and others. Even a search for evidence-based practices in special education produces results targeted to specific populations (e.g., early childhood, autism) or practices (e.g., assessment, behavior management). However, most definitions of EBPs share common criteria for determining an EBP, including the following.

- Multiple studies have evaluated a particular intervention or combination of interventions to be effective with the target population.
- These studies utilize high-quality research designs that increase assurances that results are, in fact, the result of the intervention provided and not extraneous, intervening variables.
- The interventions studied produce consistent beneficial outcomes.
- The intervention studies have been replicated across participant age groups, settings, and other variables (Agran, Spooner, & Singer, 2017; Spooner, McKissick, & Knight, 2017).

9-2 How to Determine EBPs

Determining what is and is not an EBP clearly can be a complicated undertaking. Thus, we encourage readers to rely on reliable, reputable sources for information and updates on EBPs. Albeit still somewhat difficult, it has never been easier to stay abreast of EBPs in the field of autism. Government agencies, professional organizations, university autism clinics and research centers, and advocacy organizations are usually good sources for information regarding EBPs, and each source may make reports available free of charge (or nominal charge only) on Internet websites. In Table 9.1, we provide a partial list of recommended sources for identifying EBPs to guide educational practices for students with autism. Read the reports with the intent of identifying how EBPs were determined and compare these criteria to the preceding bulleted list. Any report listing EBPs should be able to provide a list or discussion of such criteria. Avoid websites that appear to have a vested interest in a particular intervention and do not provide detailed criteria for determining that a strategy is an EBP.

9-2a Effective Practices as Identified by the NAC and NPDC

As examples of sources for EBP's and autism, we have described the work undertaken by the NAC and the NPDC to identify effective intervention practices. Basically, each group identified interventions in one or more of two broad categories: (a) comprehensive treatment models (CTMs) consisting of a broad set of practices designed to affect core symptoms of autism (e.g., the Lovaas Institute, the Denver model, Division TEACCH) and (b) focused interventions

TABLE 9.1 ● Reliable Sources for Identifying EBPs

GOVERNMENT AGENCIES

- The What Works Clearinghouse division of the Institute of Education Sciences https://ies.ed.gov/ncee/wwc/FWW

  The WWC reviews and summarizes scholarly research on specific practices, curricula, programs, and other intervention resources. The website does not provide reports specific to autism, but it does provide reports by populations (e.g., students with disabilities and English Language Learners [ELLs]), areas of concern (e.g., behavior, literacy), or age (e.g., early childhood, K–12). Additional filters can be applied to narrow results for type of intervention (grade, class or school type, delivery method, outcomes, etc.) or to focus on specific populations (race, gender, ethnicity, etc.).

- The National Professional Development Center on Autism Spectrum Disorder (NPDC) http://autismpdc.fpg.unc.edu/

  The NPCD was funded by the U.S. Department of Education from 2007 to 2014 with the goal of identifying and promoting the use of EBPs for children and youth with autism. Implementation guidance is available on the website for each of the 27 practices originally identified as EBPs.

- The IRIS Center of Peabody College, Vanderbilt University (funded by the U.S. Department of Education) https://iris.peabody.vanderbilt.edu/

  The IRIS Center provides a comprehensive website designed not only to identify EBPs but also to guide implementation of those practices. Multimedia modules are available on a variety of topics of concern to educators, including accommodations, diversity, behavior and classroom management, and transition. In 2017, two modules specific to autism were added: (1) an Overview for Educators and (2) Evidence-Based Practices.

- The Technical Assistance Center on Positive Behavioral Interventions and Supports (PBIS) http://www.pbis.org/ (funded by the U.S. Department of Education)

  This site provides comprehensive information about research support for and implementation of a multitiered framework associated with positive behavior interventions and supports. The site provides a wealth of implementation examples, assessment tools, presentations, research, and other resources related to universal, targeted, and tertiary tiers of PBIS organized around home, school, and community issues and practices.

PROFESSIONAL, RESEARCH, AND ADVOCACY ORGANIZATIONS

- The Council for Exceptional Children (CEC) https://www.cec.sped.org

  CEC is the professional and advocacy organization for school-aged students with disabilities, educators, and families. In 2014, CEC published a report on quality indicators to help consumers read and interpret special education research. Also available on its website is CEC's Ethical Principles and Practice Standards for Special Educators, which include a standard that educators rely on evidence and research for making educational decisions.

- National Autism Center's National Standards Project http://www.nationalautismcenter.org/

  The NAC's website provides information about autism, services, research, and resources. Both phase 1 and phase 2 reports are available for download.

- The Association for Science in Autism Treatment (ASAT) http://www.asatonline.org/

  ASAT's stated goal is to disseminate scientifically sound information to guide treatment decisions. Its website provides summaries of educational, psychological, therapeutic, and biomedical treatments that are classified as treatments that work, need more research, do not work, or are untested. The site also provides resources to guide consumers in making sound treatment decisions.

(e.g., reinforcement, prompting, peer-mediated interventions, discrete trial training) that can be applied to increase, decrease, or maintain specific skills (Odom, Boyd, Hall, & Hume, 2010). Odom and colleagues identified 30 CTMs and evaluated each model across multiple variables. They found that CTMs were strongest in terms of organization and operationalization of their models, which means that they had clearly described implementation procedures and materials. However, CTMs did not fare as well on indicators of efficacy compared to published efficacy studies of focused interventions. In this book, we have emphasized focused interventions (strategies and methods) and described research support for those interventions.

Table 9.2 lists evidence-based practices (those found to be established) identified by the NAC's National Standards Projects, phase 1 (National Autism Center, 2009) and phase 2 (National Autism Center, 2015), and by the NPDC (Wong et al., 2013), along with the number of studies reviewed for each. Note that the NAC and the NPDC used slightly different approaches to categorize treatments. For example, the NAC grouped behavioral interventions, whereas the NPDC presented specific behavioral strategies separately. Also note that the interventions listed are only those that were classified by the groups as established or evidence based. The NAC's National Standards Project reports also list emerging treatments that are not included on this table.

TABLE 9.2 ● **Established Evidence-Based Practices Identified by NAC and NPDC**

ESTABLISHED INTERVENTIONS (CTMS AND FOCUSED)	EXAMPLES OF TECHNIQUES INCLUDED IN EACH CATEGORY	NUMBER OF STUDIES REVIEWED		
		NAC – NSP 1	NAC – NSP 2	NPDC
Antecedent-Based Interventions	Contriving motivational operations Prompting and prompt fading Modification of task demands Errorless learning Time delay	99		32
Behavioral Interventions	Function-based interventions Chaining Prompting Modeling Reinforcement	231	155	
Cognitive Behavioral Interventions	Visual scales to help students identify emotions Homework to practice specific skills related to emotional regulation	3	10	4
Comprehensive Behavioral Treatment for Young Children	Intensive ABA services provided for young children (ages 0–9), including DTT, shaping, modeling, reinforcement, and language development interventions	22	20	22
Differential Reinforcement of Incompatible, Alternative, or Other Behavior				26
Discrete Trial Teaching				13
Exercise				6
Extinction				11
Functional Behavior Assessment				10
Functional Communication Training				12
Joint Attention Intervention		6		
Language Training	Modeling Prompting Reinforcement	10	2	
Modeling, Video Modeling	Video modeling	50	28	Modeling = 5; VM = 31
Naturalistic Teaching Strategies (e.g., Milieu Teaching)		32	3	10
Parent Training Package	Training parents in strategies for developing imitation, joint attention, play	37	11	20
Peer-Mediated Interventions		33	3	15
Picture Exchange Communication System				6
Pivotal Response Treatment®		14	6	8
Prompting				33
Reinforcement				43

(continued)

ESTABLISHED INTERVENTIONS (CTMS AND FOCUSED)	EXAMPLES OF TECHNIQUES INCLUDED IN EACH CATEGORY	NUMBER OF STUDIES REVIEWED		
		NAC – NSP 1	NAC – NSP 2	NPDC
Schedules, Visual Supports		12	2	18
Scripting		6	5	9
Self-management		21	10	10
Social Skills Training		14	21	15
Story-Based Interventions or Social Narratives		21	15	17
Structured Play Groups				4
Task Analysis				8
Technology-Aided Instruction and Intervention				20
Time Delay				12

9-3 Developing and Evaluating Effective Educational Programs

As part of educational planning for students with autism, IEP teams may have to consider multiple programs or intervention options (Reichow et al., 2008). We propose that teams consider the four essential areas described in the following sections to evaluate those intervention options. The information presented in each area is not meant to be comprehensive but to serve as initial criteria for evaluating interventions with regard to individual student needs. Once the educational program has been agreed on, the final step in IEP development should be to determine how program effectiveness will be evaluated. In the following sections, we explain the four essential areas to consider in choosing interventions and considerations for program evaluation. These essential areas of consideration are encompassed in a list of questions for education planning teams to consider before adopting any strategy or program and are presented in Table 9.3.

9-3a Intervention Outcomes

The IEP team should consider whether the outcomes promised by the intervention match the student's IEP goals. This simply means that each child's individual needs as addressed in IEP goals must drive decision making about interventions. If the IEP team determines that the purported outcomes of the intervention match the student's IEP goals, the team should next consider the likelihood that implementation of the program with a particular student will likely result in those outcomes. This can be done by comparing descriptions of students who have benefited from the program to characteristics of the student for whom the program is being considered. Students who do not fit these descriptions may not demonstrate the same outcomes.

In some cases, there may be little to no intervention research involving participants with characteristics and goals similar to that of your student. For example, there is little research on improving reading comprehension for high school students with autism that are English Language Learners (ELLs). In such cases, the best course may be to select from options that have been effective in improving reading comprehension for high school ELLs without autism and then adapting those strategies to be more suitable for your student (e.g., embedding the child's perseverative interests into the reading) (e.g., El Zein, Solis, Lang, & Kim, 2016). As with all educational programs, ongoing data collection and progress monitoring should be conducted, and revisions to the program should be made based on that process.

TABLE 9.3 ● **Guidelines for Discussing Intervention Options**

1. To guide consideration of the appropriateness of an intervention option for supporting a student's IEP goals, the team may ask:
   a. Have meaningful goals been written for the student?
   b. Do the goals promote independence and self-determination?
   c. Do the outcomes promoted by the option match the goals written for the student?
   d. Is the student similar to other individuals who have benefited from the program?

2. To guide consideration of the appropriateness of an intervention option based on the presence of potential risk, the team may ask:
   a. Are there any immediate or eventual health or behavioral risks for the student?
   b. Are there immediate risks for family members or school personnel?
   c. Will the option negatively impact the quality of life for the student, family, or school personnel?
   d. If the option fails, will the financial, time, and energy resources have been justified?

3. To guide consideration about how best to evaluate the effectiveness of an intervention option, a team may ask:
   a. What criteria will be used to objectively determine if an option is effective?
   b. Who will be responsible for conducting all necessary components of evaluation?
   c. How will bias in evaluation be controlled?
   d. How frequently will evaluation be conducted?
   e. What criteria will be used to decide if an option is to be continued or discontinued?

4. To guide consideration of determining the effectiveness of an intervention option, a team may ask:
   a. Are there a number of studies to support the effectiveness of the option?
   b. Are the studies of high quality?
   c. Is there empirical validation for the option or is all the support in the form of personal testimonials or case studies?
   d. Does the option promise the same benefits for all who participate?

5. To guide consideration of the potential value of an intervention option based on what other options would be excluded, a team may ask:
   a. Does this option require exclusive use or imply exclusivity based on intensity?
   b. What will be eliminated because of the excluded options or opportunities?
   c. Are less restrictive or less intensive alternatives available that may be just as effective?
   d. Are other options better researched than the one being considered?
   e. Does this option support the attainment of the functional needs of the student?

9-3b Potential Intervention Risk

After the IEP team has ensured that the student's goals and likely intervention outcomes are aligned and appropriate, the team should consider the potential for any negative outcomes; that is, the team should consider whether or not there are any inherent risks in the intervention. The team needs to consider potential risk not only for the student but also for family members and school personnel. Risk may be related to physical health, behavior, or quality of life. Using one approach to the exclusion of other options might diminish the quality of life for a student and his family (Donnelly, 1996).

In addition to considering the potential negative effects for the student, family members, and school personnel, the team should also determine what would be lost if the strategy or program fails. Teams may commit substantial time, energy, and financial resources to implementing an option, but if the option fails to produce the desired result, then what will the team have lost (Green, 1999)? High-cost options that fail can strain school system budgets, empty savings, and exhaust insurance coverage. Teams will want to consider less costly options that have the potential to produce the same or similar results. "Cost" should be considered not only in terms of financial resources needed but also in terms of ethics. Consider the case of a student for whom 2 years in one-on-one programming does not produce meaningful benefit. Now the student is 2 years older and has lost many opportunities to socialize and develop relationships. Or consider the student who spends a majority of the school day receiving computerized instruction. The student enjoys working on the computer and demonstrates gains on targeted skills but makes no progress in developing pleasurable relationships with others. Or consider a student for whom the exclusive focus of intervention is developing social relationships and, as a result, he never learns basic functional skills. Intervention failure has implications not only for resources expended but also for opportunities lost.

9-3c Evidence

One of the most contentious issues that the IEP team should address is the availability of proof to substantiate the effectiveness of a treatment or intervention option. As mentioned previously, school systems are held accountable for their decisions and are required to use empirical evidence to make (and defend) their choices (Simpson & Myles, 1995).

In this chapter, we have discussed resources and criteria for identifying EBPs. Unfortunately, families may desperately seek improvements in their children's learning and relief for themselves (Lehr & Lehr, 1997) and therefore may be willing to try even unsubstantiated approaches (Boynton, 2012). This willingness can result in hope being replaced by despair and personal and financial resources being drained (Christopher & Christopher, 1989; Todd, 2012). Educators should listen carefully to parents' goals for their child and frustrations with previous educational programs, and they should use that information to choose EBPs that are most compatible with the student's educational needs and the parents' wishes while still adhering to a standard of evidence (Fox & Mulick, 2016).

Currently, most proof supports the use of a structured educational program that has been individually tailored to the student's developmental abilities, educational and behavioral needs, and long-term goals. The program should use systematic, ABA-based instructional practices and should be provided in an intensive manner with specific programming for generalization. Parents should be involved in educational planning, which should emphasize social and communication training (Maurice, Green, & Foxx, 2001). The strategies described in this book meet these criteria.

9-3d Considering Alternatives

Finally, a team considering intervention options should discuss how the selection of particular options might affect the use of other approaches. Some program options require the exclusion of others. For example, imagine a situation in which a family insisted that a child's teachers use only facilitated communication, not an EBP, for communication purposes. No other form of communication was allowed. In this case, the intervention being insisted on—facilitated communication—is likely the most notorious of dangerous and ineffective interventions, and the risk clearly out weights the possibility of any benefit (Boynton, 2012; Todd, 2012; Tostanoski, Lang, Raulston, Carnett, & Davis, 2014). Further, this type of exclusionary practice is not only unnatural (e.g., most individuals, even children with autism, use multiple forms of communication) but also has potential for negative outcomes for the student if the exclusive practice does not produce desired outcomes. As discussed previously, such a situation may present a potentially unacceptable form of risk.

Although few options specifically exclude the use of other programs, some can become exclusionary because of the amount of time required for implementation. For example, to decide to require many hours (e.g., 40 hours per week) of any approach means there is little time available for anything else. This becomes particularly critical when the 40 hours must be provided in an isolated setting, denying the student access to peer interactions and eliminating the opportunity to benefit from other strategy or program options. Any treatment, with specific or coincidental exclusions of other options, must be carefully considered.

9-3e Program Evaluation

If an intervention supports a student's IEP goals, presents manageable risk, has objective empirical evidence of effectiveness, and may be used in conjunction with other interventions, then the team may recommend its implementation as a part of the student's IEP. Before implementing the option, the team should decide how to measure the effectiveness of the strategy or program, usually with student progress data, although other types of program evaluation may also be used (e.g., parent or student satisfaction or both). Direct observation of target behaviors is recommended as the preferred objective evaluation method for monitoring student progress. Chapters 2 and 5 describe the process of selecting appropriate progress monitoring techniques for evaluation purposes.

Another component of program evaluation may include data collection to show how well the specific strategy or program is being implemented; this is known as **fidelity of implementation** (see Chapter 5). For example, discrete trial training (DTT) is implemented in a systematic fashion that adheres to specific criteria. The person providing DTT should be observed to ensure that she or he is using the technique accurately. This is particularly important when paraprofessionals are given the responsibility of implementing significant portions of a child's education plan in general education settings (Rispoli, Neely, Lang, & Ganz, 2011). Fidelity of implementation can be monitored using simple checklists that provide a task analysis of the procedure being observed and some sort of rating system to evaluate each step (e.g., implemented correctly, partially correct, or incorrectly). It can also include a teacher self-evaluation such as the one provided in Chapter 5.

In addition to considering how to evaluate strategies or programs, the IEP team should determine who will be responsible for program evaluations. Several members of the team may be given responsibility for portions of program evaluation, or consideration may be given to asking individuals who are not on the team (outside evaluators) to conduct evaluations. Persons qualified to evaluate interventions must have knowledge of the student and the program components and should follow a fidelity checklist for consistency across evaluators and across evaluation times.

Once the team has determined how to evaluate an intervention and has decided who will be responsible for conducting evaluations, the members should discuss how often to evaluate. Infrequent evaluations hinder the ability of the team to make timely modifications, whereas too frequent evaluations may unnecessarily drain time and other resources. The team should delineate clear outcome criteria before program implementation and use lack of progress toward those criteria to decide when to discontinue the strategy or program (Nickel, 1996). In addition, the team may agree that the strategy or program will be discontinued if only minimal progress is made within a 2-month period or immediately if the student or family suffers negative side effects. Further, a strategy or program might be abandoned if improvements are temporary and disappear within a short period of time. Implementation of an educational strategy or program should not become an end unto itself but rather a means to achieve desirable outcomes for a student (Hanft & Feinberg, 1997).

Because autism constitutes a lifelong disability, individual needs will change over time. The team must be sensitive to those changes and modify strategies and programs accordingly using agreed-on guidelines to facilitate ongoing discussions. The next section delineates reasons why programs may fail to benefit students. To enhance the likelihood that students will make progress toward IEP goals, teams should discuss strategies to circumvent these possible programming weaknesses.

9-4 Why Education Programs for Students with Autism Can Fail

The process of giving careful consideration to a variety of educational options will likely result in individually tailored and effective programs. As you have learned, the best programming for students with autism often consists of a structured educational program that is appropriately matched to the student's behavioral, communicative, and educational needs and long-range expectations. The use of guidelines for discussing the multitude of available options can facilitate agreement among IEP team members as to what constitutes an appropriate program. In the case of disagreement, the result is all too often due process proceedings and hearing officers, which may not be helpful but may be extremely time consuming.

In cases of disagreement, judges are increasingly being asked to make programming decisions based on the most compelling legal arguments for a particular program. These decisions often adhere to the letter of the law (lack of adherence is called a "procedural violation") and not evidence of an appropriate program. For example, it is not uncommon for a hearing officer or judge to tell the school district that it must provide whatever programming a parent requests because the district failed to give adequate notice of a meeting. It is less common but still possible for a hearing officer or judge to find that programming provided by the school district might be adequate and find against the parents because the parents never placed the student in the district's program. Analysis of hearing decisions and litigation outcomes reveals five issues that influenced due process decisions. These issues can affect arguments presented by parents as well as school districts. To construct a carefully crafted program, advocates must guard against the following mistakes.

9-4a Lack of a Clearly Articulated Program

Since the signing of PL 94-142 in 1975 (the original Education for All Handicapped Children Act, now the IDEA), decisions about how a student will be instructed have been generally left to the discretion of the schools (Boomer & Garrison-Harrell, 1995; Yell, 2011). The decisions of how best to facilitate goal attainment are primarily decisions regarding instructional methodology. Unfortunately, methodology controversies have been and continue to be the basis of many disagreements among IEP team members when determining an appropriate education for students with autism.

A clearly defined program consists of *carefully conceived and well-described elements* designed to address specific educational goals, with the understanding that these elements have been used successfully with other children with similar characteristics. We encourage IEP team members not to describe their programs or program components as "pilot" or "new," which communicates that a tested model is not yet available. Should a disagreement arise in these situations, due process decisions are likely to favor the party who has proposed programs and practices with documented benefits (*Delaware Co. IU #25 v. Martin K.*, 1993). Documented benefits are positive outcomes that are attributable to the program being provided. In pilot programs, the benefit is yet to be demonstrated.

Program intensity also influences outcomes. Programs may be found inadequate if they are not implemented with *appropriate intensity* (*Delaware Co. IU #25 v. Martin K.*, 1993). However, there is no magic number of hours of programming. The intensity of the programming provided must be balanced against the needs of the student. For example, a 40-hour-a-week program provided across school and home may be inappropriate or even impossible for some families. For example, Osborne and colleagues (2008) found that high levels of family and parenting stress may reduce the effectiveness of early teaching interventions for children with autism who require too many hours of intervention services. To create a clearly defined program, the team should specify appropriate intensity that will likely enable the student to make progress toward IEP goals without detracting from the child and family's quality of life (Cohen, 1998).

Finally, a clearly defined program will *emphasize meaningful outcomes* for the student. The program developed by the IEP team should support student progress toward all goals. A program with an exclusive emphasis on teaching reading, for example, will fail to promote progress toward attainment of other and maybe more functional skills (e.g., communication, toileting, play). A program with a singular emphasis on socialization may ignore other priority needs (e.g., vocational training), perhaps resulting in inappropriate programming (*Mark Hartmann v. Loudoun County Board of Education*, 1997). A well-defined program is one that links methodologies to student progress toward meaningful outcomes. Lack of a well-defined program may be insufficient to support goal attainment and may be indefensible if due process is requested.

9-4b Choosing Popular Rather than Appropriate Options

A program for a student with autism runs a risk of failing if the IEP team incorporates options that are popular at the time rather than those that have been demonstrated to have beneficial outcomes as defined by the criteria described in the previous sections. Nowhere is this more apparent than in the area of placement decisions. Although IDEA 2004 specifies that a full continuum of placement options be available and that placement decisions be individualized, the presumption of the least restrictive environment requires IEP teams to consider not only the student's educational needs but also the settings closest to general education where those needs can be effectively met. Thus, it is incumbent on IEP teams to make placement decisions based on individual needs rather than on popular philosophy (e.g., full inclusion) or even the availability of resources (e.g., the special education teacher is only available in the afternoon).

Implementing a popular option such as full-time placement in general education without considering the student's unique needs may lead to program failure. The same is true of implementing the latest "cures" presented in the media. To avoid program failure, IEP teams should evaluate options based not on their popularity but on their merits as revealed through careful analysis using the guidelines recommended in the preceding section. Implementing educational strategies and programs with demonstrated benefit, rather than popular acceptance, can best guarantee success.

9-4c Teaching Dependency

Throughout this text, we have emphasized the goal of increasing students' independence. Unfortunately, programs often unwittingly promote the opposite when students are routinely given personal assistants or "shadows," as discussed in Chapter 7. For example, a teaching assistant may be assigned to help a student respond to teacher directions or peer initiations. However, what the student may learn is not to line up when the teacher gives the direction or to say "Hi" when a peer gives a greeting but to line up or say "Hi" only when the assistant provides a prompt. Further, teaching assistants working in these assignments should be taught to prompt the student *where* to obtain the necessary information, as opposed to prompting the student only on what to do. For example, it is better to prompt by saying "look and listen to the teacher," right before the teacher gives the instruction to line up, or to point to the line of students at the door and ask "What should you do when you see others lining up?" than it is to simply prompt the student to "go line up." The later prompt is more likely to make the student dependent on the support, and the former options are more likely to result in the student learning what to attend to when in the classroom.

Unfortunately, the decision to provide a teaching assistant does not always include discussion of how the assistant's presence will be faded. Instead of the assistant being part of a planned strategy to provide appropriate prompts for promoting participation and independence (as described previously), and gradually fading those prompts and the assistant's physical presence, the one-on-one assistant may become a permanent feature. Ultimate program success will most likely be enhanced through systematic instruction in skills that promote independence without the need of one-on-one monitoring and prompting.

9-4d One-Size-Fits-All Mentality

Programs may also fail when they apply identical services to all students with autism. By creating a uniform and inflexible "autism program," a school district is suggesting that all students with autism will need the same type of services. In designing a single program to meet the needs of a heterogeneous group of students, school districts may be opening themselves up to allegations of taking a "cookie cutter approach" (Board of Education of the Ann Arbor Public Schools, 1996; Independent School District No. 318, 1996), a position that is indefensible in due process proceedings. In other words, intervention should be individualized; although autism programs can certainly be put in place that serve groups of children, those programs must be designed in such a way that individualization is possible and encouraged.

Often the one-size-fits-all mentality is evident in the number of hours that programming is offered to students. For example, some districts offer young children a half-day program and older children a full-day program. These standard options may be inappropriate for students with autism. A young child with autism may benefit from a full-day program, whereas an older student may benefit from a half-day program in academics and a half-day program in community-based instruction. Furthermore, the length of the standard school year may not meet the needs of individual students. Students with autism may need a longer school year and even need services during long holiday breaks. For other students with autism, breaks from school programming may not inhibit progress toward IEP goals and may offer important opportunities for other types of educational experiences (e.g., family trips). Thus, all programming must incorporate aspects that can be tailored to meet individual students' needs.

9-4e Lack of Documentation

Programs may fail when school personnel are unable to demonstrate a relationship between program components and student outcomes. To support a program's effectiveness, data must be collected demonstrating that the implemented program, not other factors, resulted in progress toward IEP goals. Typically, school personnel conduct pretesting and posttesting of special education students at the beginning and end of the school year in an effort to demonstrate such a relationship. However, it is difficult to conclusively correlate strategies and program components to developmental or skill gains when evaluations occur 9 months apart. Fortunately, ABA relies heavily on frequently collected data for decision-making purposes. Teachers who use ABA-based instruction such as DTT and who rely on ABA data-collection techniques are well prepared to document student progress and successes with direct, objective data. Failure to incorporate ongoing data collection and analysis may result in program failure.

In summary, the likelihood that a program will be successful depends on carefully defined meaningful outcomes, efficacious methodologies that promote the outcomes, and appropriate program intensity. Educational methodologies should be chosen based on their effectiveness as demonstrated in research, not by their popularity as might be evidenced in movies, magazine articles, and celebrity diatribes. Remember, too, that the use of one-on-one teaching assistants can result in increased dependency. Alternate strategies should be considered so that students progress toward independence and self-management. Schools should avoid creating an "autism program" that might deny students' unique needs. Instead, programming must be individually tailored for each student in terms of length of school day, length of school year, and individual learning characteristics. Finally, frequent and ongoing data collection must be used to support claims that the chosen strategies and programs are responsible for promoting the attainment of IEP goals.

Summary

There is overwhelming evidence that educators, parents, and other caregivers and advocates who are involved in the lives of children and youth with autism have the potential to make enormous positive changes. Indeed, implementation of appropriate strategies and programs at appropriate times in a child's life can result in the amelioration of many undesirable overt characteristics associated with autism, along with significant improvement in the quality of life for these individuals and their families. However, strident debate and disagreement remain regarding which educational strategies and programs hold the most promise and are the most efficacious. This problem of methodology and program choice and judgment is exacerbated by an ever-increasing number of available options, many of which seductively offer undocumented claims of extraordinary benefit (e.g., Tostanoski et al., 2014).

Related to these controversies, this chapter provided information and guidelines that may form the foundation for a solution. Guidelines for evaluating the efficacy, utility, and appropriateness of various strategies and programs were given, along with a list of options judged to meet evidence-based standards for applications with students with autism. We also provided a discussion of legal precedents aimed at addressing some of the issues related to developing appropriate and efficacious programs for students with autism.

Key Points

1. A lack of agreement exists regarding which strategies and programs are best for students with autism and related disorders, and this results in confusion and conflict among educators, parents, and advocates.

2. In general, ABA-based approaches provide the strongest evidence of effectiveness.

3. Before choosing interventions or programs, IEP teams should evaluate options on four critical areas: outcomes, risk, evidence, and alternatives.

4. Before implementing any intervention or program, IEP teams should develop a plan for monitoring strategies or programs in terms of fidelity and effectiveness.

5. Educational programs fail for many reasons, including lack of defined components, choosing popular rather than evidence-based options, teaching dependency, using a one-size-fits-all approach, and lack of documentation about student progress.

References

Agran, M., Spooner, F., & Singer, G. H. S. (2017). Evidence-based practices: The complexities of implementation. *Research and Practice for Persons with Severe Disabilities, 42*(1), 3–7.

Board of Education of the Ann Arbor Public Schools. (1996). 24 IDELR 621.

Boomer, L. W., & Garrison-Harrell, L. (1995). Legal issues concerning children with autism and pervasive developmental disabilities. *Behavioral Disorders, 21,* 53–61.

Boynton, J. (2012). Facilitated communication—what harm it can do: Confessions of a former facilitator. *Evidence-Based Communication Assessment and Intervention, 6,* 3–13.

Christopher, W., & Christopher, B. (1989). *Mixed blessings.* Nashville: Abingdon Press.

Cohen, S. (1998). *Targeting autism: What we know, don't know, and can do to help young children with autism and related disorders.* Berkeley: University of California Press.

Delaware Co. IU #25 v. Martin K., 831 F. Supp. 1206, 1211 (E.D. Pa. 1993).Donnelly, J. A. (1996, July–September). The pros and cons of discrete trial training: Is the "Lovaas" behavior modification method appropriate for my student? *Autism Update,* 20.

El Zein, F., Solis, M., Lang, R., & Kim, M. K. (2016). Embedding perseverative interest of a child with autism in text may result in improved reading comprehension: A pilot study. *Developmental Neurorehabilitation, 112,* 141–145.

Endrew F. v. Douglas County School Dist. RE–1, No. 15–827, 580 U.S. ____ (2017), slip. op. at 11.

Foxx, R. M., & Mulick, J. A. (2016). *Controversial therapies for autism and intellectual disabilities: Fad, fashion, and pseudoscience in professional practice.* New York: Routledge.

Green, G. (1999). Science, pseudoscience and antiscience: What's this got to do with my kid? *Science in Autism Treatment, 1*(1), 5–7.

Green, V. A., Pituch, K. A., Itchon, J., Choi, A., O'Reilly, M., & Sigafoos, J. (2006). Internet survey of treatments used by parents of children with autism. *Research in Developmental Disabilities, 27,* 70–84.

Hanft, B. E., & Feinberg, E. (1997). Toward the development of a framework for determining the frequency and intensity of early intervention services. *Infants and Young Children, 10,* 27–37.

Independent School District No. 318 (1996), 24 IDELR 1096.

Lehr, S., & Lehr, B. (1997, November). *Scientists and parents of children with autism: What do we know? How do we judge what is right?* Draft paper distributed at the Autism National Committee and Greater Georgia ASA Conference, Decatur, GA.

Mark Hartmann v. Loudoun County Board of Education (1997). [Online]. Available: http://lw.bna.com/lw/19970722/962809.html

Maurice, C., Green, G., & Foxx, R. M. (Eds.). (2001). *Making a difference: Behavioral intervention for autism.* Austin: Pro-Ed.

National Autism Center (2009). *National Standards Project: Findings and Conclusions.* Randolph, MA: Author.

National Autism Center (2015). *National Standards Project: Findings and Conclusions, Phase 2.* Randolph, MA: Author.

Nickel, R. E. (1996). Controversial therapies for young children with developmental disabilities. *Infants and Young Children, 8*(4), 29–40.

Odom, S. L., Boyd, B. A., Hall, L. J., & Hume, E. K. (2010). Evaluation of comprehensive treatment models for individuals with Autism Spectrum Disorders. *Journal of Autism and Developmental Disorders, 40,* 425–436.

Offit, P. A. (2008). *Autism's False Prophets: Bad Science, Risky Medicine, and the Search for a Cure.* New York: Columbia University Press.

Osborne, L. A., McHugh, L., Sounders, J., & Reed, P. (2008). Parenting stress reduces the effectiveness of early teaching interventions for autistic spectrum disorders. *Journal of Autism and Developmental Disorders, 24,* 247–257.

Reichow, B., Volkmar, F. R., & Cicchetti, D. V. (2008). Development of the evaluative method for evaluating and determining evidence-based practices in autism. *Journal of Autism and Developmental Disorders, 38,* 1311–1319.

Rispoli, M., Neely, L., Lang, R., & Ganz, J. (2011). Training paraprofessionals to implement interventions for people autism spectrum disorders: A systematic review. *Developmental Neurorehabilitation, 14,* 378–388.

Romanczyk, R. G., & Gillis, J. M. (2008). Practice guidelines for autism education and intervention: Historical perspective and recent developments. In J. Luiselli, D. C. Russo, & W. P. Christian (Eds.), *Effective practices for children with autism: Educational and behavior support interventions that work.* New York: Oxford University Press.

Simpson, R. L., & Myles, B. S. (1995). Effectiveness of facilitated communication with children and youth with autism. *Journal of Special Education, 28,* 424–439.

Singer, A., & Ravi, R. (2015). Complementary and alternative treatments for autism Part 2: Identifying and avoiding non-evidence based treatments. *AMA Journal of Ethics, 17,* 375–380.

Spooner, F., McKissick, B. R., & Knight, V. F. (2017). Establishing the state of affairs for evidence-based practices in students with severe disabilities. *Research and Practice for Persons with Severe Disabilities, 42*(1), 8–18.

Tinbergen, N., & Tinbergen, E. A. (1983). *"Autistic" children: New hope for a cure*. London: Allen and Unwin.

Todd, J. T. (2012). The moral obligation to be empirical: Comments on Boynton's "Facilitated Communication—what harm it can do: Confessions of a former facilitator. *Evidence-based Communication Assessment and Intervention, 6*, 36–57.

Tostanoski, A., Lang, R., Raulston, T., Carnett, A., & Davis, T. (2014). Voices from the past: Comparing the rapid prompting method and facilitated communication. *Developmental Neurorehabilitation, 17*, 219–223.

Travers, J., Ayers, K., Simpson, R. L., & Crutchfield, S. (2016). Fad, pseudoscientific, and controversial interventions. In R. Lang, T. Hancock, & N. N. Singh (Eds.), *Evidenced-based practice in early intervention for children with autism*. New York: Springer.

Travers, J., Tincani, M., & Lang, R. (2014). Facilitated communication denies people with disabilities their voice. *Research and Practice for Persons with Severe Disabilities, 39*, 195–202.

U.S. Department of Education. (2016). *Non-regulatory guidance: Using evidence to strengthen education investments*. Washington, DC: Author.

U.S. Federal Trade Commission (November 2011). Miracle health claims. Retrieved from https://www.consumer.ftc.gov/articles/0167-miracle-health-claims

Van Houten, R., Axelrod, S., Bailey, J. S., Favell, J. E., Foxx, R. M., Iwata, B. A., & Lovaas, O. I. (1988). The right to effective behavioral treatment. *Journal of Applied Behavior Analysis, 21*, 381–384.

Wong, C., Odom, S. L., Hume, K. Cox, A. W., Fettig, A., Kucharczyk, S., . . . Schultz, T. R. (2013). *Evidence-based practices for children, youth, and young adults with Autism Spectrum Disorder*. Chapel Hill: University of North Carolina, Frank Porter Graham Child Development Institute, Autism Evidence-Based Practice Review Group.

Yell, M. (2011). *The law and special education* (3rd ed.). Upper Saddle River, NJ: Merrill/Prentice Hall.

Glossary

acquisition The first competency level of learning wherein a student has learned to perform a target skill but has not yet become fluent (efficient) and may not have generalized the ability to perform the skill in novel contexts (generalization).

activity reinforcer Contingent access to engagement in preferred activity that results in an increase in a target behavior; computer access or extra recess time are potential examples of activity reinforcers.

aggression A form of challenging behavior that includes any topography with the potential to cause injury to other people; sometimes includes threatening physical harm via verbal or gestural behaviors and property damage.

aided systems Augmentative and alternative communication systems that require external equipment and/or support to produce messages (e.g., speech-generating devices).

alternative and augmentative communication (AAC) Topographies of communication other than typical vocal speech such as sign language, speech-generating devices, and visual communication systems. AAC may be aided or unaided.

antecedent The first element in the three-term contingency—that is, antecedent, behavior, and consequence—that refers to the condition of the environment; emphasis is placed on changes in the environment that occur immediately before a target behavior.

antecedent prompting Instructional technique in which an adult remains in proximity to the student in natural settings and uses words, gestures, pictures, or touch to encourage the student to engage in a particular behavior.

applied behavior analysis (ABA) The applied branch of behavior analysis concerned with the application of behavioral technology to improve socially meaningful human behavior; assumes that learning (defined as a relatively permanent change in behavior) can be achieved through an analysis of behavioral deficits and excesses, the manner in which people respond to those behaviors (reinforcing or punishing), and direct training focused on observable and measurable skills.

assistive devices Support or scaffold for students to prevent errors in completing complex tasks; often designed to reflect the demands of a particular task or the needs of individual students who must complete that task (e.g., adapted eating utensils to improve grip).

auditory prompts Additional spoken directions or examples giving more information about responding.

autism spectrum disorder (ASD) An umbrella term for a wide range of symptoms that include "persistent deficits in social communication and social interaction across multiple contexts" and restricted, repetitive patterns of behavior such as the presence of stereotyped behavior, interests, and activities (APA, 2013).

autistic leading A term used to describe a behavior of some children with autism in which the child pulls on another person's hand or clothing to direct the person to an object the child desires.

automatic reinforcement A contingent consequence involving sensory stimulation that increases the likelihood of a behavior occurring again but does not usually involve interaction with another person.

backup reinforcer Stimuli within a token economy system that are delivered contingent on the exchange of token reinforcers; often available in a school store.

backward chaining Teaching a task in order from the last step to the first step.

baseline A period of time before intervention is implemented when target behavior is measured; baseline is compared to intervention to determine if target behavior is increasing or decreasing.

baseline data Data that constitute the baseline phase; reflects the level of performance before an intervention.

behavioral deficits A behavior that occurs too infrequently or is entirely absent and, as a result of this shortcoming, an individual is disadvantaged and in need of intervention to increase the occurrence of the behavior.

behavioral excesses A behavior that occurs to often and, as a result of the over-occurrence, the individual is disadvantaged and in need of intervention to decrease the occurrence of the behavior; behavioral excess are often dangerous or disturbing behaviors that are not commonly displayed by others of the same age.

behavioral momentum A procedure involving the delivery of multiple high-probability requests immediately before the provision of a low-probability request; behavioral momentum is used to increase the likelihood of compliance to the low-probability request.

behavioral objectives Short-term targets that communicate the goal and intent of instruction.

behavioral theory Posits that most human behavior is a function of learning and environmental influences.

behavior intervention plan (BIP) A formal plan that specifies interventions for challenging behaviors.

behaviors The second element in three-term contingency—that is, antecedent, behavior, consequence—referring to actions that influence the environment; sometimes referred to as *responses*, include challenging behavior, verbal behavior, academic behavior, and all other movements of living organisms.

behavior-specific praise Affirmative feedback that includes a description of the reason why praise is being delivered; for example, "great job sitting in your chair quietly!"

Board Certified Behavior Analyst (BCBA) Personnel who have met educational and testing requirements delineated by the Behavior Analysis Certification Board (BACB).

chaining A method for combining several response steps into a complex behavior.

challenging behaviors Actions that are harmful or dangerous, that interfere with a child's learning, or that interfere with desired social and developmental goals; includes aggression, self-injury, property destruction, and other similar undesirable responses.

communication A behavior with a socially mediated function; any behavior that is intended to influence another person's behavior; includes speech, hand gestures, picture-card exchange, and use of a speech-generating device; may be referred to as *verbal behavior*.

communicative intent Refers to behaviors that occur for the purpose of sending a message to another person.

community-based instruction Instructing students in the natural environments where targeted activities and skills would typically occur (e.g., in the student's home, in a restaurant, or at a place of employment).

compliance training A systematic teaching procedure used to improve the ability to follow directions wherein multiple opportunities to comply with task demands are contrived and compliance is reinforced; noncompliance results in prompted compliance.

concomitant improvements Collateral changes in nontargeted behaviors.

concurrent grouping An instructional grouping in which students in a group are required to listen and respond in unison to a teacher S^D.

conditioning See pairing.

consequences The third element in the three-term contingency—that is, antecedent, behavior, and consequence—referring to the environment's response to a behavior that may influence the future probability of a behavior via reinforcement or punishment.

contingent Refers to a dependency between at least two variables wherein a specific change in one variable results in a specific change in another variable and this change in the second variable would not have occurred otherwise; for example, reinforcement can be made contingent on the occurrence of a target behavior.

continuous reinforcement (CRF) The densest possible reinforcement schedule wherein every occurrence of the target behavior is reinforced.

criterion of the immediate environment Goals for functioning under current conditions.

criterion of the next environment Reflects target goals for a student's school placements or living placements within the next 3 to 5 years.

criterion of ultimate functioning An ever-changing, expanding, localized, and personalized cluster of factors that each person must possess to function as productively and independently as possible in socially, vocationally, and domestically integrated adult community environments.

curriculum What you teach (i.e., skills, activities, strategies, concepts, content) arranged as a course of study (organized, sequenced); usually written as goals and objectives.

curriculum-based assessment (CBA) Assessment matched directly to a specific curriculum to ascertain which particular aspects of the curriculum need to be taught.

data point Entry on a behavior graph. Each data point reflects performance during one collection period.

data probe Data gathered during a subset of a student's day or some days but not others.

delayed echolalia Repeating what someone else has said wherein the latency between the first utterance and the repeated echoed utterance is more than a few minutes; the repetition typically duplicates the intonation, pitch, and articulation patterns of the speaker and may be repeated several times.

descriptive sentences Used in social stories to provide information about the social context (setting, people, activities, etc.) targeted in the story.

developmental theory Explanation that holds that individuals naturally move through various stages to acquire cognitive, language, social, motor, and physical maturity.

differential reinforcement A behavior change procedure designed to reduce a challenging behavior through a combination of reinforcement and extinction.

differential reinforcement of alternative behavior A behavior change procedure used to reduce a challenging behavior through a combination of extinction and contingent reinforcement of a target replacement behavior.

differential reinforcement of incompatible behavior A behavior change procedure used to reduce a challenging behavior through a combination of extinction and contingent reinforcement of a target replacement behavior wherein the replacement behavior cannot physically occur at the same time as the challenging behavior.

differential reinforcement of lower levels of behavior A behavior change procedure used to reduce a target behavior by delivering reinforcement contingent on the target behavior occurring less often than some predetermined criteria.

differential reinforcement of other behavior A behavior change procedure used to reduce a challenging behavior through a combination of extinction and contingent reinforcement for the absence of challenging behavior for some period of time; also referred to as differential reinforcement of zero rates of behavior.

direct assessment The primary essential component of a functional behavioral assessment that involves the observation of the behavior by the person conducting the assessment.

directive sentences Used in social stories to instruct the student what to do in a particular social situation.

discrete trial training (DTT) A highly structured teaching method based on the three-term contingency—that is, antecedent, behavior, and consequence—with five steps, delivered as multiple trials.

discrimination training Providing a clear, discrete antecedent stimulus and reinforcing correct responses to that stimulus while *not* reinforcing incorrect responses so students eventually learn to perform appropriate responses under natural conditions (bringing responses under stimulus control).

discriminative stimulus (S^D) A feature of the antecedent condition that indicates reinforcement may be available; when the S^D is present, a specific behavior (or class of behavior) is more likely to occur.

duration recording A measurement technique that involves identifying the amount of time a behavior (or some other phenomenon) occurs.

echoing Repeating what someone else has said; may also be referred to as *echoing*.

echolalia Repeating what someone else has said; may be immediate, delayed or mitigated; the repetition typically duplicates the intonation, pitch, and articulation patterns of the speaker and may be repeated several times; may also be referred to as *echoing*.

ecological assessment A process of delineating current and long-term environments in which an individual must or will function for the purpose of listing activities and skills necessary to do so successfully. This list becomes the individual's curriculum.

ecological inventory The process of systematic identification of all of the functions critical for success in the collection of settings that one individual currently encounters and can be expected to encounter in the future.

enclave A supported employment model in which a small group of individuals with disabilities work together in a job setting and are trained and supervised by either a job coach or an employee of the business.

enhanced milieu teaching (EMT) A form of naturalistic intervention that focuses on connecting, supporting, the development of early language skills, blends developmental and behavioral intervention strategies. .

entrepreneurial model A supported employment model in which students with disabilities operate a business that provides products or services (e.g., a bakery, a cleaning service, a workshop that sells handmade furniture, a commercial laundry).

environment Refers to the location (e.g., home, school) and features within that setting (other people, objects, noises, etc.) immediately surrounding a person.

errorless learning An approach to teaching that aims to prevent students from making mistakes by providing clear expectations, frequent and supportive prompts, and appropriate curricular goals.

ESSA Every Student Succeeds Act (2015). Reauthorization of the Elementary and Secondary Education Act.

event recording A measurement technique that involves counting occurrences of target behavior; indicates the number of instances of a behavior; used to measure behaviors that have a clearly observable onset and end. May be referred to as *frequency recording*.

evidence-based practices (EBPs) In general, those practices (interventions, programs, etc.) that have been evaluated through multiple high-quality research studies, replicated across age groups and settings that have documented beneficial outcomes.

exclusionary time-out An ill-advised form of punishment that involves removing a person from the environment altogether; not a recommended practice; in many cases, it cannot be implemented because of legal or ethical concerns; also called *seclusion*.

executive functions (EFs) Distinct cognitive skills that are thought to be essential for self-management.

expansion Method of facilitating language development by expanding a student's language through repeating a child's utterance or gesture and adding one word or sign for more complex grammar.

explicit instruction Systematic, direct, engaging, and success-oriented instructional format(s).

expressive language The ability to produce a communicative message that can be accurately received by another person.

extinction A behavior change procedure that reduces the future probability of a behavior by ensuring the absence of contingent reinforcement of a target behavior.

extinction burst A phenomenon occasionally observed when extinction is first applied that results in an immediate increase in the behavior targeted for reduction before the behavior reduction is observed.

fading (fade) To gradually increase the ratio of behaviors to reinforcers such that more target behavior must occur for reinforcement to be delivered over time; also refers to the process of gradually reducing the helpfulness of prompts such that the student's ability to perform a skill independently increases over time.

fidelity of implementation Consistency of teaching procedures.

fluency The level of skill development after the acquisition level of learning wherein the student performs the skill more efficiently and without atypical supports or prompting.

forward chaining A process for teaching a multistep task that involves dividing the task (behavior chain) into components and then teaching each component in order from step 1 to the last step.

frequency count A method of data collection that involves counting the number of times a discrete behavior is emitted within a set period of time.

frequency recording *See* event recording.

full prompts A prompt procedure that provides enough assistance that student does not have to complete any of the behavior without complete support.

function Refers to the purpose a behavior serves in terms of the contingent consequences maintaining the behavior, such as obtaining or avoiding people, tasks, tangibles and internal states.

functional activity or task Any task or activity that someone else would have to perform for a student if the student himself could not do it (e.g., feeding self).

functional assessment The multistep process used to identify the antecedents, consequences, and other contextual variables associated with the occurrence of an operant behavior; also called a *functional behavioral assessment* (FBA). Primarily used to identify the function of challenging behaviors in an effort to create a function-matched intervention to reduce challenging behavior.

functional behavioral assessment (FBA) Procedure used to identify function of challenging behavior (e.g., the reasons the challenging behavior is exhibited).

functional communication Communicative responses that act as replacement behaviors for excessive or challenging behavior based on functional behavioral assessment findings.

functional communication training (FCT) A form of differential reinforcement that reduces challenging behavior through a combination of extinction and contingent reinforcement of a replacement behavior that serves the same communicative function as the challenging behavior.

functional skills Abilities that an individual must perform to avoid dependence on others.

function-matched intervention A type of treatment intended to reduce challenging behavior that is aligned with the function of a challenging behavior; typically designed based on the results of a functional behavioral assessment.

general case programming Programming used to facilitate generalization by varying the components of instructional lessons.

generalization Expansion of an individual's capabilities beyond acquisition and fluency of a skill. Stimulus generalization requires the individual to display the behavior under various conditions. Response generalization requires the individual to vary the acquired behavior.

generalization training Methods used to teach students to apply skills under a variety of conditions and to maintain skills over time.

group placements A supported employment model in which a group of individuals with disabilities is placed at the same work site, but the individuals are assigned separate jobs throughout the work setting rather than working in proximity to one another.

high-functioning autism A colloquial description of less severe forms of autism in which the individual typically has functional language, and typical levels of intellectual functioning.

holophrase A one- or two-word utterance used in a variety of contexts for multiple purposes; typically names of favorite objects and people.

IEP Individual Education Program; mandated in IDEA 2004.

immediate echolalia Repeating what someone else has said wherein the latency between the first utterance and the repeated echoed utterance is very brief; the repetition typically duplicates the intonation, pitch, and articulation patterns of the speaker and may be repeated several times.

indirect assessment A component of a functional behavioral assessment that involves data obtained through means other than direct observation; typically refers to questionnaires and checklists completed by people who have directly observed the behavior in the past.

individual activity schedule A sequence of pictures or print directions for students to use each day that communicates which activities should be completed, at what time, and in what order.

individual placement model A supported employment model in which an individual with disabilities is placed in regular job settings and trained and supervised by a job coach.

individual transition plan (ITP) A plan that is part of the individualized educational program (IEP) for students who are 16 and older that provides a structure for preparing an individual to live, work, and play in the community as fully and independently as possible.

instructional approach to behavior management ABA-based technique that assumes instruction in alternate replacement behaviors is required to reduce problem behavior.

intermittent reinforcement A reinforcement schedule wherein some (but not all) occurrences of the target behavior are reinforced.

intertrial interval Pause before the next trial in discrete trial training.

intraverbal A verbal behavior that occurs in response to another person's verbal behavior.

jigs Materials that are adapted to prevent mistakes in completing complex tasks (e.g., a series of boxes and outlined shapes to facilitate collating and stapling).

job coach Individual who provides training and supervision for individuals with disabilities on the job until they are able to do the job independently.

joint attention A foundational social and communication ability that involves two people simultaneously attending to the same stimulus; often initiated by one person with the second person following the direction of the initiator's eye gaze to focus on the stimulus and then shifting gaze back to make eye contact.

language There are many competing definitions of language. This book uses Lefrancois's definition "the use of arbitrary symbols, with accepted referents, that can be arranged in different sequences to convey different meanings" (1995, p. 228).

least restrictive environment (LRE) The environment closest to general education where the needs of a student with disability can most appropriately be met.

low-functioning autism A colloquial description of autism in which the diagnostic symptoms of autism are more severe and are accompanied by intellectual disability.

maintenance The third stage of learning following acquisition and fluency in which the individual is able to perform a target behavior at an acceptable rate days, weeks, or months after initially acquiring the behavior and in the absence of the intervention.

mand A verbal behavior motivated by the desire to obtain or avoid something; requests maintained by socially mediated reinforcement (i.e., another person honoring the request).

milieu teaching (MT) Set of procedures using naturally occurring antecedents (S^Ds) and prescribed prompting techniques to obtain social and communication responses followed by reinforcement, usually obtaining or avoiding the original natural S^D.

mitigated echolalia Repeating what someone else has said; unlike other forms of echolalia, the repetition may differ slightly in terms of word choice or order, intonation, pitch, and articulation patterns.

modeling Demonstration of the correct response(s).

morphemes A combination of phonemes that has a referent for which it clearly stands; a unit of meaning often within a word; for example, "baseballs" is a single word with three morphemes—"base-ball-s."

morphology Refers to the components forming words (e.g., root, prefixes and suffixes) and relations between words.

motivating operation (MO) An environmental variable or internal state (e.g., hunger and illness) that affects a stimuli's reinforcing power and thereby increases or decreases the likelihood that behaviors that function to obtain or avoid that stimuli will occur.

mute A condition wherein an individual does not produce speech.

naturally occurring reinforcers Stimuli that are contingent on behavior in applied real-world environments that result in an increase in the future probability of the behavior.

NCLB No Child Left Behind Act (2001). Reauthorization of the Elementary and Secondary Education Act.

negative punishment A type of consequence that involves removing a reinforcer (e.g., sent to time-out) that results in a decrease in the likelihood that the preceding behavior will occur in the future.

negative reinforcement A behavioral contingency that involves avoiding a tangible, attention, environment or activity (e.g., work and task demands) that results in an increase in the future probability of a behavior.

noncompliance A form of challenging behavior that includes any topography that involves failure to comply with task demands, follow instructions or meet expectations.

noncontingent reinforcement (NCR) A behavior change procedure that involves the provision of a stimuli that normally functions as a reinforcer regardless of behavior.

nonexclusionary time-out A form of time-out that involves removing a person from an activity but not from the same general environment (classroom) as other people participating in that activity.

nonverbal communication Topographies of communication including bodily contact, proximity, physical orientation, appearance, posture, head nods, facial expressions, gestures, and eye contact; does not include spoken language; conveys interpersonal attitudes and assists in establishing relationships.

observational learning A behavior change mechanism that occurs when the learner observes a model perform a target behavior and then imitates the model.

operational definition A description of behavior that focuses on observable features and movements; should be unambiguous and free of references to intentions or the observer's opinion; enables multiple people to reach agreement on the occurrence or nonoccurrence of the defined behavior; facilitates accurate and reliable data collection.

operationalizing When target behaviors are precisely described using observable, measurable terms to accurately measure progress.

overgeneralized When a behavior is performed under conditions where it should not be performed.

pairing A process that establishes a stimulus as a secondary reinforcer by presenting a reinforcer in close temporal proximity to a nonreinforcer; also called *conditioning*. Often used to teach students to value stimuli that are commonly contingent on target behavior; for example, praise and good grades are stimuli that may need to be paired with existing reinforcers to be useful in the education and treatment of children with autism.

palilalia A form of oral imitation like echolalia, but the original speech being imitated ("echoed") may be from hours or even weeks before the imitation (e.g., repeating lines from a movie a week later); also called *delayed echolalia*.

paraprofessional A teaching assistant who may not require professional or state certification. Typically works under the supervision of a certified teacher.

partial prompts Provide some assistance by requiring the student to do some of the behavior alone.

peer confederates Peers who are trained to assist with socialization interventions by initiating or maintaining social interactions with students with autism.

peer-mediated interventions Socialization interventions that rely on socially competent peers to initiate and maintain social interactions with students with autism.

perceptual and cognitive theory Posits that brain malfunction can lead to specific differences in the thinking abilities of individuals with autism.

perseveration When an individual repeats the same words or phrases over and over or insists on discussing only one specific topic.

perspective sentences Sentences used in social stories to describe feelings of individuals involved in particular social situations.

phase line A dashed vertical line on a behavior data graph that indicates a change from baseline to intervention or denotes modifications or withdrawals of the intervention.

phonemes Individual speech sounds used within a language; English has approximately 40 phonemes.

phonology Study of the relation within and between phonemes (sounds) that constitute spoken language.

physical prompts Involves physically guiding a correct movement; also called *tactile prompts*.

picture-exchange communication system (PECS) Method that teaches a child to communicate by handing another person a picture (or set of pictures) that symbolizes the individual's intended message.

pivotal behaviors Responses that are central to many areas of functioning such that when a pivotal behavior is acquired, collateral improvements in behaviors not directly targeted by intervention; for example targeting the pivotal behaviors of social interaction, joint attention, and play may lead to concomitant improvements in social skills, communication and stereotypy.

positive punishment A type of consequence that involves delivering an aversive stimulus (e.g., harsh reprimand) that results in a decrease in the likelihood that the preceding behavior will occur in the future.

positive reinforcement A type of consequence that involves obtaining a tangible (e.g., toy), attention, or access to an environment or activity and that results in an increase in the future probability of a behavior.

positive reinforcer *See* reinforcer.

pragmatics Context of language including speaker–listener interaction; includes who says what to whom, how they say it, why and when they say it.

preference assessment A systematic procedure used to identify potential reinforcers for use in instruction; the child's choice or approach to a specific stimulus used in the assessment is considered an indication of their preference for that option over other available options.

primary reinforcers Stimuli that are reinforcing because of biological necessity (e.g., food, drink, sleep and physical needs); may be paired with other stimuli to establish secondary reinforcers; may be referred to as *unconditioned reinforcers*.

probes *See* data probe.

program common stimuli A technique to facilitate generalization by making the training situation as much like a real-life situation as possible.

progress monitoring Collecting data on a regular basis to substantiate whether a student learned what was intended to be taught.

prompt Optional stimuli such as instructions, gestures, demonstrations, touches, or other things that we arrange or do to increase the likelihood that children will make correct responses.

prompt fading procedures Strategies for removing prompts as the S^D and bringing behavior under the control of the intended or natural S^D; *see also* fading.

pronoun reversal Using the pronoun *you* when referring to *I*, and vice versa.

prosody Refers to the tone, inflection, cadence, rhythm, and pitch of speech.

punishment A behavioral contingency that decreases the future probability of a behavior (e.g., response cost and time-out).

receptive language The ability to understand language and receive a communicative message.

reinforcement The process of providing a consequence contingent on a target behavior that results in an increase in the future probability of the target behavior occurring again in similar circumstances.

reinforcement schedule The ratio of behavior to reinforcement ranging from 1-to-1 wherein every occurrence of the target behavior is reinforcer to extinction wherein the target behavior is not reinforced; may also include time requirements such that target behaviors must also occur within a specific period of time to contact reinforcement.

reinforcer The specific stimulus involved in reinforcement; for example, praise, tangibles, and breaks from tasks may be reinforcers used in positive or negative reinforcement procedures. *See also* activity reinforcer, backup reinforcer.

reinforcer power or reinforcer value Refers to the degree of influence a specific reinforcer has on the future probability of a behavior and influences the amount of effort (energy expenditure) required of an individual.

replacement behavior The more desirable behavior targeted for increase within behavior intervention plans designed to reduce challenging behavior; typically serves the same function as the challenging behavior.

response class A group of behaviors that serve the same function; may include challenging behavior and appropriate behavior.

response cost A form of punishment that reduces a challenging behavior through the contingent removal of a reinforcer; typically used within token economy systems by subtracting previously earned tokens contingent challenging behavior.

response generalization The occurrence of a topography of behavior that was not directly prompted but serves the same function as a different topography of behavior that was taught (e.g., a child taught to say "Hello" now also says "Hi" even though "Hi" was not directly taught during intervention).

S-delta The signal that a behavior will not be reinforced.

seclusion *See* exclusionary time-out.

secondary reinforcers Stimuli that function as reinforcers as a result of having been paired with primary reinforcers; may be referred to as *conditioned* or *learned reinforcers*.

self-determination The ability to exert personal control over one's life and make choices.

self-injurious behavior (SIB) A form of challenging behavior that includes any topography that involves self-directed aggression with the potential to inflict physical injury to one's own body.

self-mediated interventions Socialization interventions in which the student with autism does something to facilitate the use of target skills, such as self-monitoring or video self-modeling.

self-monitoring A self-mediated socialization intervention in which a student is taught to systematically record each time a target behavior is performed.

self-stimulatory behaviors A topography of behavior maintained by automatic reinforcement; often used to describe stereotypic behavior; may also be referred to as *stereotypy, stereotypic behavior*, or *restrictive and repetitive patterns of behavior*.

semantics The general meaning of language, including discrete words and contextual connotations.

sequential grouping When students in a small group are instructed one at a time and participate in independent activities while waiting their turn.

shaping A reinforcement strategy for gradually achieving a desired response by strengthening approximations of that response.

sign language A form of communication that involves making symbols and gestures with the hands to send a message.

social competence How other people perceived the social performance of an individual.

socially valid skills Social skills that are valued by peers and teachers. Use of socially valid skills helps lead to social competence.

social reinforcers A social response (e.g., praise, high five, and hug) delivered contingent on a target that results in an increase in the future probability of the target behavior; may be referred to as a *socially mediated reinforcer*.

social skills Discrete social behaviors that are typically exhibited by socially competent individuals such as maintaining eye contact, asking relevant questions, greeting others, taking turns in conversations and other interactions, joining peers in play, and standing an appropriate distance from others.

Social Stories™ A commercial story-based socialization intervention in which brief situation- or behavior-specific stories are read to the student immediately before certain activities.

social validity The concept of acceptability of a program by its consumer.

speech-generating device (SGD) A computer or device (e.g., iPod, iPad, or tablet) with software and speakers that produce a spoken message (prerecorded or digital) when activated; used by children with autism as an alternative and augmentative communication device.

splinter skills A specific ability that does not match the overall cognitive profile of an individual.

spontaneous recovery The return to previous levels of a behavior that was reduced temporarily by extinction.

stereotypic behavior Restrictive or repetitive patterns of behavior that may include body movements, vocalizations, and perseveration on specific stimuli; one of the diagnostic features of autism spectrum disorder; often maintained by automatic reinforcement.

stereotypy *See* stereotypic behavior.

stimulus control Describes the contingent relationship between a discriminative stimulus (S^D) and a behavior wherein the behavior reliably occurs in the presence of the S^D but is not likely to occur in the absence of the S^D; for example, stepping on the gas pedal (behavior) should be under the stimulus control of a traffic light turning green (S^D), and a child responding "four" (behavior) should be under the stimulus control of the teacher asking "what is 2 plus 2?" (S^D).

stimulus generalization Even if antecedents like instructional cues, materials, people, time of day, and settings change, a student can still perform a specific behavior at the same acceptable rate.

stimulus overselectivity Only attending to unimportant environmental cues.

story-based interventions A socialization intervention in which a brief, individualized story is read to a student immediately before a situation where challenging behavior is expected to occur. The purpose of the story is to remind the student of expected behavior(s) to use in that situation.

supported employment An umbrella term that refers to several different models for helping individuals with disabilities succeed in employment.

syntax Grammar rules governing sentence structure, use of articles, and other comparable language conventions.

tact A verbal behavior that involves labeling or identifying a stimulus in response to a S^D that does not involve the verbal behavior of another person.

tactile prompt A teacher behavior that involves physically touching the student in an effort to help them produce the correct response (e.g., guiding the student's hand while teaching how to tie shoes); typically considered the most intrusive form of prompting..

tandem grouping An instructional grouping model that begins with one-to-one instruction and systematically expands to include more students.

tangible reinforcers Physical objects (e.g., stickers, toys, pencils, and other items that have mass) that when delivered contingent on the occurrence of a target behavior result in an increased probability of the target behavior occurring in the future.

target behavior A specific response (behavior) that is the focus of an intervention, treatment, or educational program designed to increase or decrease that behavior's occurrence; the desirable behavior a teacher intends to teach or a challenging behavior

that is to be reduced; may also be referred to as a *target response* or *target skill*.

target skill *See* target behavior.

task analysis An instructional technique that involves breaking complex target skills into subskills or simplifying content into subcontent so that the steps of learning are more accessible to the learner.

teacher-mediated interventions Socialization interventions that are directed by the teacher. Include direct instruction of social skills, story-based interventions, and antecedent prompting.

teaching strategies Everything a teacher does to facilitate learning.

telegraphic speech Short phrases that leave out unnecessary words; for example, it includes word combinations such as "Give juice?"

theory of mind (ToM) The ability to understand another person's point of view; assigning other's perspectives to one's own perspective.

three-term contingency The relationship between antecedent, behavior, and consequence wherein the consequence is contingent on the behavior and the behavior is contingent on the antecedent; the basic conceptual unit in applied behavior analysis used to illustrate the interaction and influence of the environment on behavior and behavior on the environment.

time-out A form of punishment that reduces a challenging behavior by removing an individual from a reinforcing environment or activity; *see also* exclusionary time-out, nonexclusionary time-out.

token reinforcers The stimuli delivered contingent on target behavior within a token economy system; pictures, points, stars, stickers, and poker chips are often used as token reinforcers; tokens are exchanged for backup reinforcers sometimes available in a school store.

topography The appearance or form of a behavior; includes only the physical movements, body position, or vocalizations that can be directly observed.

total communication An approach to communication that includes more than one topography to send messages; often refers to the combination of manual sign and speech; may be referred to as simultaneous communication.

total task presentation Teaching a task in its entirety rather than in steps. The entire task is taught each time (e.g., eating breakfast).

transition The phase from high school to postschool activities, specifically educational, employment, and living options; also called *transition service*.

transition curriculum Curriculum designed to teach skills students need to prepare them for future environments.

transition plan A formal plan, required by IDEA for some students, that delineates services to be provided to help the student move from school to post-school activities.

trial The totality of presentation of the five steps in discrete trial training; has a clear onset and offset.

unaided language system A type of alternative and augmentative communication that does not involve physical support or equipment (e.g., sign language).

verbal behavior A behavior with a socially mediated function; any behavior that is intended to influence another person's behavior; includes speech, hand gestures, picture card exchange, and use of a speech-generating device; may be referred to as *communication*.

video modeling (VM) An intervention in which the student with autism views a brief video of a model (another child or an adult) demonstrating a target skill.

video self-modeling An intervention in which the student with autism views a brief video of himself engaging in a target behavior in an effort to increase the frequency of the that behavior; sometimes involves editing the recording to remove prompts such that the student appears to be more independent when performing the target skill.

visual communication system Form of aided augmentative and alternative communication that relies on objects, pictures, symbols, or printed words (e.g., the picture-exchange communication system).

visual prompts Include gestures such as touching, tapping, or pointing to the correct response. Also includes modeling.

whole-class schedules Schedule developed to delineate what each member of the teaching team will be doing with which students for each time period during the day. These usually do not vary much from day to day.

within-stimulus prompt Situation in which an S^D, usually a material, is altered in certain ways (size, color, position, texture, or some other dimension) to make it more likely that the child will respond correctly.

work crew A vocational arrangement similar to an enclave, except that the workers with disabilities travel from job site to job site.

workstations Self-explanatory tasks, designed to be completed independently, often requiring matching, assembly, job, or discrimination skills.

Index